College Football

John Sayle Watterson

College

THE JOHNS HOPKINS UNIVERSITY PRESS

BALTIMORE AND LONDON

H I S T O R Y

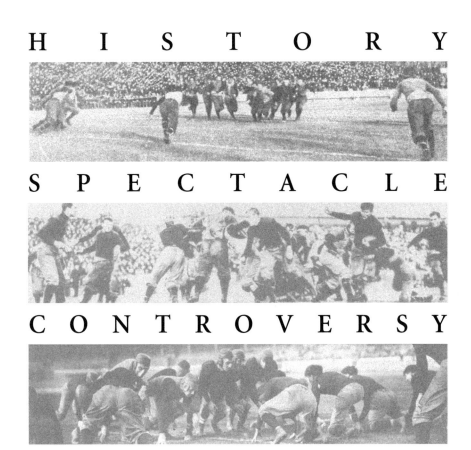

S P E C T A C L E

C O N T R O V E R S Y

Football

The Johns Hopkins University Press
2715 North Charles Street
Baltimore, Maryland 21218-4363
www.press.jhu.edu

Library of Congress Cataloging-in-Publication Data will be found
at the end of this book.

A catalog record for this book is available from the British Library.

ISBN 0-8018-6428-3

To Yvonne

Contents

Illustrations appear following pages 98, 176, and 286.

In 1995 Wesleyan University played Williams College in football at Middletown, Connecticut. One of the early college teams in the United States, Wesleyan played big-time football in the 1880s and 1890s, scheduling teams such as Harvard and Yale. But a hundred years later they played a small-college schedule and belonged to the Little Three, which also included Amherst and Williams. Though Wesleyan and Williams played Division III football, Williams in 1995 was a powerhouse, with the longest winning streak among small colleges.

This game stood in stark contrast to big-time college football. Even on a cold and windy November day, the crowd of about five hundred spectators proved to be surprisingly small, made up mainly of students, parents, alumni, and townspeople. Before the game a student glee club performed a "whiff 'n' poof" medley of college fight songs, and athletes in other sports operated a small-time football concession. None of this infused spirit into the spectators in the Wesleyan bleachers. The noisiest group turned out to be a group of Williams's rooters on the far side of the field. Only one crimson-bedecked Wesleyan alumnus, looking as if he had descended upon the football field through a time warp, wore his school's colors, from feathers in his fedora to the cuffs of his trousers. He reigned in solitary splendor.

This lack of enthusiasm at Wesleyan was surprising because its football field sits squarely in the midst of its campus. The academic buildings still border Andrus Field, and above the south end zone looms the library, which has the equivalent of the view from luxury boxes. Along the east side of the field stretches Brownstone Row, including the old gym, the ivy-covered chapel, and the classroom buildings, which date from the turn of the century. Faculty and students walked to and fro across the campus within several hundred yards of the field. But, in spite of their proximity, few cared enough to watch the best small college team in the country or, for that matter, their own team.

The scale and location of the field were sadly compromised by an absence of interest. "The problem at Wesleyan," wrote columnist Josh Stedman in the Wesleyan *Argus*, "is that too many people don't go to games." And the paucity of fans in the stands resulted, he confirmed, from an absence of interest on campus. "Half the people in our stands," Stedman wrote, "are alumni and family from out of town." That was exactly how it looked to a visitor from Virginia.

It was not always this way. My own father played for a small-college team, Western Reserve University (WRU) of Cleveland, in the 1920s, when schools like Wesleyan and WRU still created almost as much interest and excitement as big-time schools. Though only 5′ 7″ and 160 pounds (some of the Wesleyan and Williams players weighed in at 290 pounds or more), John S. Watterson Jr. played at quarterback and at end for two years until a broken collarbone ended his career. He always regretted the play in the big game with across-the-street rival, Case Institute of Technology, in which a pass bulleted through his hands after he had broken into the open. The game ended in a 0-0 tie, but he always believed that he could have scored the winning touchdown. In his era pictures of small college games not only at Western Reserve but also at Wesleyan show enthusiastic crowds of spectators, some of them pulled to the side of the field in their automobiles. Even these lesser-known institutions in or near urban areas had the capacity to generate interest.

Much has changed at small colleges since my father played football, and the Wesleyan game provided a base line for measuring some of the changes that have occurred in college life. That game in 1995 illustrated a difference between Division III and the elite institutions in college football. Big-time football generates far more interest and monumentally larger revenues than smaller college and university teams. Major college teams play for gate receipts, TV revenue, and glory, and as a result they virtually pay their players to play; small college teams play because football is part of college life, and the games at some colleges—like Wesleyan's opponent, Williams—still create interest. Only slightly more than one hundred four-year colleges or universities have big-time football teams, and the top twenty-five of them monopolize most of the interest and harvest the major revenue. If major college football began as a sport, it has definitely turned into big business.

When I first happened upon grainy photos of 1890s games, I initially experienced a vague longing for a golden age of football. I assumed that this world wholly different than the big-time football that Virginia and Northwestern, two schools that I attended, had attempted to play. After I learned that schools such as Wesleyan had lost 136-0 to Yale in the 1880s, my sense of nostalgia turned into curiosity. I was especially curious about the football upheaval that began in the 1890s and reached a climax in the early 1900s, a crisis in which Wesleyan played a role. My sources indicated that President Theodore Roosevelt had intervened, that some colleges had abolished or threatened to abolish football, and that the rules had undergone a major overhaul. Colleges and conferences reformed the practices and culture of football. As a historian, I was astounded at the similarities between the crusade to reform football and other changes that took place in the United

States during the Progressive Era, before World War I. Football reform seemed to fit into the pattern of flight from disorder and disorganization which resulted in the modern version of twentieth-century American life.

As a result, I intended to pursue my research in this book only up to World War I. But the story simply failed to end. The evils and excesses that reformers addressed in the early 1900s only grew in size and sophistication in the period between the two wars. From 1919 on, big-time football moved inexorably toward highly profitable, subsidized athletics. The changes represented nothing new except in scale, but a big-time, non-amateur gridiron system rumbled beneath the surface erupting into view from time to time. Some schools, like Wesleyan, no longer played big-time teams such as Harvard and Yale after World War I, but other smaller institutions in urban areas tried to capitalize on football mania. My father's alma mater, Western Reserve University, moved briefly into big-time football, scheduling major teams, instituting jobs and tuition for athletes, and even leasing Cleveland's giant Municipal Stadium for its annual big game with Case Tech.

As it turned out, I could not stop my story at the second major upheaval in the 1950s or, for that matter, in the 1960s, 1970s, or 1980s. Many of the same problems remained, and the reforms that survived the piecemeal repeals either favored big-time football or did not impede its progress. I reached the end of the twentieth century, but the story still did not seem complete.

Looking back as a historian at a century of football crises, I am astounded at football's ability to survive and grow. Each of its three major upheavals has been a prelude to a growth spurt or came in the midst of a boom on the college gridiron. While baseball and basketball entered into the story, football had written the script for big-time college athletics and, at the end of the twentieth century, continues to play a leading role. But its role exacts a price. Almost from the beginning the colleges (or universities) have inevitably faced the fact that football never fit the academic definition of a college activity; at best it was almost a slightly squared peg jammed into a round hole. Perhaps that is why so few people at Wesleyan bothered to walk over to Andrus Field to watch the game. At a highly intellectual institution like Wesleyan, football simply did not connect with the interests of most students or faculty.

That said, the fact remains that football between two major teams in a large stadium has no equal. My mother attended games at the University of Virginia until she was eighty-one and then watched them on television when her health did not permit her to go in person. I know a number of hard-core Virginia alumni and boosters who drive the interstates from near and far to attend the semiprofessional events in Charlottesville. Though it is not necessarily so for the most academically inclined, football provides a link to the institution which is far more exciting than anything that most universities can provide. Yet for the institutions it also remains a drain on resources; a huge edifice sits empty all but five or six Saturdays during the fall, and huge amounts are spent to stage eleven games each year. For this reason, I believe, football has created a chronic problem of resources, dishonesty, and injury to players, to college personnel, and even to the student body.

In my own research I found that some of the changes in college football have mirrored those in the larger society. Inevitably, this book had to deal with the problem of race, notably the slow influx of African-American players into football at major state institutions. As a result, I have not tracked the history of African Americans in football at predominantly black institutions, a story that needs to be told. Instead, I have attempted to show how black players, once a beleaguered handful at white institutions, have become a real presence and how they have become an enduring influence on the game. Put simply, African-American players have proved themselves indispensable to intercollegiate football's prosperity. The story of these players has proved tragic, heroic, dramatic, and often disturbing.

On the other hand, the role of women in college football has been far more elusive, in what has remained an almost exclusively "*his*tory." Nevertheless, one finds fascinating glimpses of gender relations in football history, such as the segregation of women in separate cheering sections in the early 1900s and the emergence of female cheerleaders at southern schools in the 1920s and 1930s. The starkly male character of football players, their coaches, and boosters, however, has played a role in the recent crises of college football. Promoting equality between men and women's sports, as required by Title IX of the Education Amendments of 1972, has not only increased athletic costs at institutions of higher learning but has also isolated football as the last bastion of exclusively male-dominated sports.

In that sense I, too, am an outsider. This book originated solely from my interest in the history of spectator sports and in the history of college life rather than from my experience on the gridiron. Perhaps I would have written a more personal, game-oriented book if I had played college football. Actually, I came to this study without strong views about big-time college sports; they developed as I did research and wrote. On the other hand, I have had a lifetime of experience as a student and teacher, but even as a member of the faculty I have never served in an official athletic capacity. While I don't mean to downplay the usefulness of athletics, I believe that I have learned more of interest and lasting value by getting to know college presidents, at least in their athletic capacity, through my research in their official papers.

Let me add that my own association with football research has had a profound influence on my life. I have traveled to colleges in almost every part of the country, places that I would never otherwise have visited. I have developed a sports history course that originated from my football interests. I have made friends with a small but thriving group of sports historians. Where I have lived since the 1970s, when I first discovered football research, has been influenced by my research. The research itself led to some unexpected personal experiences. I can still vividly remember my interview with Harvard All-America of 1909, Hamilton Fish, who served for twenty-four years in the U.S. Congress; I also recall the lunch and tour of the Indiana University campus given to me by an archivist who thought it was more important for me to talk with her and to see her institution than to immerse myself in musty records. I also interviewed Janet Camp Troxell (Walter Camp's daughter) and Amos Alonzo Stagg Jr. (son of the legendary coach), and I chatted briefly by telephone with Alice Roosevelt Longworth (Theodore Roosevelt's daughter). I also had the good fortune to interview two nieces of Archer Christian who gave me insights into and enabled me to write two articles on his tragic but significant death in 1909. And I even got to know a maverick professor who led a successful campaign to halt the revival of big-time football at a well-known liberal arts college.

The people who have helped me on this project are too numerous and far-flung to cite by name. The archives and libraries at Virginia, Northwestern, Harvard, Yale, Princeton, Brown, Chicago, Case Western Reserve, Georgia Tech, Kansas, Oregon, Swarthmore, Wesleyan, and William and Mary were especially helpful in finding materials for research. A number of archivists, sports publicists, college officials, and librarians at various institutions have helped me by mail, telephone, or by Internet. In the 1980s, when I had no institution to support me, Marjorie Carpenter of Interlibrary Loan at Northwestern University generously obtained materials that I needed, expressing her confidence that I would complete my as yet unstarted book. A few individuals at Southern Methodist University have enabled me to understand a little better what was for them a painful and difficult experience. In addition, I have derived insights and knowledge into sports history and college football by belonging to the North American Society of Sport History, attending their annual conventions, where I heard or presented papers, and got to know the handful of historians who are working in the same field. Specifically, I owe a special debt to Ronald Smith of Pennsylvania State University, Bill Baker of the University of Maine–Orono, and Robin Lester, a former headmaster of Trinity School in New York and biographer of Amos Alonzo Stagg, for reading the first draft of my manuscript and making helpful comments—and to Ronald Smith for sharing both materials and insights. Robert O'Neill, Alan Williams, and Larry Gerlach have helped me by discussing their own bird's-eye impressions and insights, not to mention several sports historians who gave me helpful direction with my research. Frederick O. Mueller of the University of North Carolina–Chapel Hill generously provided me with materials pertaining to deaths and serious injuries in college football. Martha Williams, Elizabeth Gratch, and JoDee Dyreson helped immeasurably.

Among those who have significantly advanced this work, I owe a lasting debt to David L. Holmes of the Department of Religion at the College of William and Mary, who read the manuscript and made numerous stylistic changes—and shared with me the remarkable story of his father, Coach David L. Holmes of Wayne State University, who remained a staunch believer in amateur, ethical athletics. I also owe a debt to my special editor, Lara Bergen of New York, who alternately infuriated and enlightened me by her rigorous editing—and to my editor at the Johns Hopkins University Press, Bob Brugger.

Looking back at my career as a historian and teacher, I can also see how important the mentoring and friendship of a few people in academic life has been. I acknowledge a debt to the historians at Western Reserve University in 1964–66, to my advisor at Northwestern University, Clarence Ver Steeg, and to the remarkable group of faculty in that institution's Department of History in the late 1960s; to my late friends and colleagues at the University of South Dakota, Cedric Cummins and Stephen Ward; and to the chairmen of the history departments at Virginia Commonwealth University and James Madison University, George Munro and Michael Galgano, who enabled me to teach sports history, thereby advancing this work.

I especially owe more than I can ever repay to my wife, Yvonne Guy Watterson, who helped me to put this project on fast-forward and devote the incredible amounts of time that it demanded, and to my small canine companion, Annie, for stationing herself loyally at my side.

College Football

Introduction

In the 1890s college football had already created strong emotions of love and hate. Big-time eastern football had demonstrated that it could draw large crowds, create alumni support, and build an identity that would attract new students. The fact that it had little to do with classical education bothered only the traditionalists on campus and a handful of crotchety purists elsewhere who wrote critically of football in magazines, newspaper articles, and official college reports.

Outward appearances may have changed, but the gridiron problems in that era appear remarkably similar to the present. In the 1890s big-time recruiters and alumni contacts scoured the eastern prep schools for talented juniors and seniors ready to entice them to Harvard, Yale, or Princeton. Occasionally, unscrupulous alumni convinced students to quit high school before they graduated in order to enroll at an institution with a big-time team. Boosters funneled tuition money to poor but athletically talented boys from the coal fields of Pennsylvania and the industrial towns of the Northeast to preparatory schools in order to prepare them for big-time college athletics. Some of these young men were in their mid-twenties when they finally entered college. Other athletes went from school to school selling their services, phantom players who had no academic ties with the institution.

Big-time alumni football entrepreneurs—the counterpart of today's athletic directors—arranged a schedule of games which began with weak teams and worked up to big money games held in New York, Boston, and Philadelphia. Gridiron profits supported stadium building, sumptuous living quarters and training tables for players, as well as Pullman cars for retinues of trainers, massagers, alumni coaches, and other hangers-on who followed the team to the big games. What was left over went to support an array of lesser sports that big-time football had eclipsed.

At the major football schools critics complained that football players became the campus elite, admired by their fellow students and regarded skeptically by many faculty. In the absence of professional football, players basked in the attention of the media, and the names of the gridiron stars appeared regularly in the sports pages of big city newspapers. Even college faculty and presidents had to be properly worshipful of football and its elite because they knew that football advertised their schools and helped to retain the loyalty of alumni. As a result, they often ignored or remained blissfully unaware of scams to admit unqualified students, play athletes who never enrolled, or resort to stratagems to keep weak players eligible.

Though booster organizations did not exist outside of alumni groups, booster alumni and townspeople, student managers, and even faculty engaged in unethical acts. A Princeton alumnus named Patterson entertained football players and made every effort to entice them to his alma mater. Authorities at Swarthmore lured the huge lineman, Bob ("Tiny") Maxwell, from the University of Chicago and arranged for the president of the college to pass his bills to a prominent alumnus. Professor Woodrow Wilson, a fanatic Princeton enthusiast, shamelessly used football when he spoke to alumni organizations and vigorously opposed football reform in the 1890s and early 1900s. In contrast, Theodore Roosevelt, a Harvard graduate, who gloried in the strenuous life and strongly supported Harvard football, turned against football brutality in 1905 and initiated the first efforts in his capacity as president to reform the spirit in which big-time football teams competed.

We know that the prototype for athletic organization began at eastern institutions in the 1880s and 1890s. Yale's Walter Camp, "the father of American football," became the model for the coach and athletic director. While pursuing a business career, he also acted as Yale's de facto vice president for athletic operations, who dominated the rules committees and ceaselessly publicized the game. From the profits of big games in Boston and New York, Camp created an ample reserve fund that supported lesser sports, afforded lush treatment for athletes, and provided the money that eventually went toward building Yale Bowl, the first of the modern football stadiums. By making Yale into an athletic powerhouse, Camp built the school's reputation, making it second only to Harvard. Because he succeeded so well, Camp became the first big-name foe of sweeping football reforms—and an especially hard-core opponent of the forward pass.

By the turn of century the deaths of players in football led state legislators to introduce laws banning the gridiron game. Players for big-time teams, critics charged, were coached to injure their opponents or "put them out of business." The nature of the game, with its mass formations and momentum plays, made football less an athletic contest than a collegiate version of warlike combat. Eventually the violence in football led to attempts to reduce its brutality through reforms. New rules put a strong emphasis on better officiating and on less dangerous formations, but they did not necessarily improve the athletic environment.

The deaths and brutality presented an excellent opportunity to root out the worst excesses of the runaway football culture. In the 1890s and early 1900s, responding to public opinion, professors and presidents spent a great deal of time talking about the overemphasis of intercollegiate athletics—and, in some cases, passing rules at the conference and institutional level to regulate college sports. Why, then, did college presidents and faculty, who had far more authority over their students than their modern counterparts, fail to control the gridiron beast? Put differently, why did the presidents and faculty often themselves become part of the athletic problem?

One problem might be that faculty members played major roles in introducing early football. In addition to Woodrow Wilson, who served as a part-time coach at Wesleyan, an English instructor at Oklahoma who had recently come from Harvard, Vernon Parrington, taught the fundamentals of football on the windswept practice field in Oklahoma. At Miami University of Ohio the president called upon all able-bodied members of the faculty to go out for football. In a game between North Carolina and Virginia a member of the North Carolina faculty scored the winning touchdown. Often the faculty proved helpful to the budding football programs in other ways such as giving athletes passing grades or writing articles arguing that football built intellect. Only a handful, like Wisconsin's Frederick Jackson Turner, made a determined effort to root out the abuses in the culture of college football such as the intense media attention given to the sport and its tendency to cushion star athletes from academic requirements.

That was more than a century ago. When we turn to the 1980s and 1990s, what do we encounter? Outward appearances of football may have changed, but the problems appear hauntingly similar. Big-time football teams induce players to attend their institution with offers of cars and money as well as running booster operations to funnel cash to blue-chip players. Players who obtain special admission or enter the institution fraudulently do so only to play football and often leave without graduating. Schools manage to keep their players eligible by manufacturing credits or by easing them into simple courses in which they are assured of receiving passing grades. Some coaches engage in violence toward players in practice and even try to drive them out of school so that they can use their scholarship slot.

Athletic departments and institutional officials have become obsessed with the potential for profits from televised big games or bowl games. Big-time teams in the NCAA try to manipulate the organization so that they will be able to have more coaches, scholarships, and only minimal academic requirements. Players commit acts of violence and brutality, then manage to avoid the consequences. College presidents whose salaries and prominence fall far short of the head football coaches dutifully show up at football games and related alumni events, treading cautiously around the mire of big-time college athletics.

All of this has added up to major athletic scandals, most of them involving big-time football. Scandals such as the pay-for-play violations at Southern Methodist and Auburn from the late 1970s to the early 1990s managed to create internal disruptions and negative publicity at numbers of big-name institutions. Yet, in spite of the obvious flaws in college football, it continues to enlarge its grip on the major universities. The athletic foundations persist in enlarging their massive gridiron complexes, selling the rights to buy tickets for upscale luxury boxes and suites, and then collecting additional revenues for the sale of high-priced tickets. The major teams have created indoor facilities out of donations that might have gone to deserving but impoverished nonathletes for scholarships. While quasi-professional student-athletes play the game, ordinary students have little to do with the sport. In an atmosphere of highly specialized career coaches, publicists, trainers, and tutors, college football reflects more than ever the professionalism that reformers long ago set out to de-emphasize.

No one would deny that football constitutes one of the most entertaining and enjoyable spectator sports. In the early days some faculty believed that the student enthusiasm for football would enable the institutions to alleviate the pervasive antisocial behavior of undergraduates. Being aware of its appeal, most athletic critics and reformers attempted to change football rather than to abolish it. The few colleges that dropped football did so it because the school had no choice or, occasionally, because a college president happened to wield unusual power at a critical moment in football's history. Far and away the largest group of thoughtful gridiron critics have attempted to reform football and to reshape it in such a way that it fit more reasonably and appropriately into the spirit and life of the university. Why have they not succeeded?

Beginning in the 1890s and continuing into the 1990s, reformers have spent tens of thousands of hours attending meetings and conferences, devising new rules to solve the latest problems that have cropped up, and generally trying to work out better systems for their own institutions; in the early 1900s moderate reformers founded the NCAA to deal with deaths and brutality and to put football securely under the thumb of the faculty and college presidents. Again in the early 1950s, in a groundswell of outrage against cheating, gambling, and subsidies for athletes, college presidents and faculty members tried to create stricter standards to reduce the greed and professionalism in football rather than to drop it altogether. In the 1980s and early 1990s an outbreak of scandal in big-time football resulted the same response of temporary uneasiness and halting reforms which had become by then a pattern in the history of college football.

The outbreak in the 1980s once again clearly emphasized the failure of reform to bring about real change. In three major periods of gridiron upheaval the colleges have been unable or unwilling to eliminate the causes of chronic cheating. While political reforms by Congress and the states have achieved some enduring success, football and big-time athletics generally have had to face the same issues again and again—much like Sisyphus repeatedly pushing the stone uphill. Why does big-time football manage to be almost constantly in a state of crisis? Is there some quality about football, or college sports generally, or a flaw in higher education which causes this turmoil? If the Greek ideal of education stands for the training of body, spirit, and mind, why have the colleges failed so abysmally at their mission?

PART ONE

Injuries

CHAPTER ONE

The Origins of Big-Time Football, 1876 to 1894

On Saturday, November 24, 1894, Yale and Harvard converged at Springfield, Massachusetts, for their annual gridiron contest. The two schools had the oldest athletic rivalry in the country, beginning with a dual rowing match held in 1852. The contests had grown to embrace football, an American version of rugby introduced by Harvard in 1875 when it defeated Yale in New Haven. Since then Harvard had only won once against Yale. In contrast, the powerful Yale teams had reeled off a streak of thirty-six consecutive victories between 1891 and 1893. Harvard entered the 1894 contest without having scored against Yale in three years.[1]

Trainloads of partisans had left Boston and New Haven early that morning. A special train had pulled onto a track in Cambridge near Harvard, and hundreds of boisterous Harvard students clambered aboard. Many of them wore crimson feathers in their hats, and they cheered and sang as the train jerked into motion. Whenever the color blue, Yale's colors, came into the sight, they began to hoot and yell derisively. At the Boston and Maine station a contingent of sixty Radcliffe girls appeared wearing bright, red chrysanthemums and singing Harvard songs. Wealthy patrons chartered lavishly catered parlor cars carrying parties of sixty or more. By 7:30 A.M. so many people had crowded the Boston and Albany station that arriving passengers could barely push their way through the crowd. Trains were pulling out of the station as rapidly as they could be filled up.[2]

One of the most startling events had taken place an hour earlier when a contingent of one hundred Boston policemen marched two abreast from the street through the station and onto the train. Their job was to keep order among the thousands of football fans and often unruly students who were about to pile into the small city of Springfield. One newspaper reporter had written of Springfield, "Tonight the town is budding, tomorrow it will bloom, and Sunday it will die." Already speculators appeared on the streets hawking fifty-cent tickets for fifty or sixty dollars. In New York, Boston, and Springfield loyal partisans placed bets at odds of 2-1 or 3-1 in favor of Yale or to wager that Harvard would not score or score a touchdown. Newspapers reported that only a few Harvard men had wagered this year on the Crimson because so many had bet on Harvard in 1893 when the two teams had seemed more evenly matched.[3]

The two teams had left for Springfield early on Friday afternoon so that they would have time to hold light workouts. When the Yale players left the university, hundreds of students were on hand to cheer them. They gave cheers for each of the eleven players, a separate cheer for Captain Frank Hinkey, and one for good old Yale. Most of the Yale team had played together on the starting eleven for three or four years. Already they had played and won all fourteen games of the season, and after this game they would have one big game remaining with Princeton in New York.[4]

The Bloody Battle of Hampden Field

At 1:30 P.M. the Yale players arrived at Hampden Field, followed soon after by the Harvard players. In cities larger than Springfield the teams led a grand procession through streets bedecked with banners, followed by large, horse-drawn coaches known as tallyhos, carrying groups of cheering students. Springfield's size did not permit a full-dress parade, but the crowds outside the gates cheered the players as they appeared. Already a crowd estimated at five thousand had gathered around the gates of Hampden Field. Vendors selling frankfurters circulated among the crowd yelling, "All hot, all hot," and "fakirs" hawked banners and badges. Already the red and blue of the Harvard and Yale partisans gave a festive look to the throng waiting to pay their fifty cents to be admitted.[5]

The big game had become big business for both of the schools. In 1893 Harvard spent $18,754 on football, including $3,226 for transportation, $1,887 on summer practice, and $3,469 for the training table. Their custom-tailored leather uniforms cost $125 apiece. In turn, Harvard's total receipts reached a record $32,092, $15,409 of it from the Yale game alone. In addition to the profits from the Princeton game in New York, Yale could gross as much as $20,000. No wonder that in 1893 Yale could charter a four-car train to carry the team, coaches, team advisors, trainers, rubbers, and camp followers as well as their considerable baggage from New Haven to Springfield. The enthusiastic crowd at the stadium gates made it possible for the players to travel in style.[6]

When those gates swung open, the Yale and Harvard supporters surged through the portals kicking over baskets of frankfurters placed too near the entrance. "Repent and be saved," a Salvation Army preacher exhorted fruitlessly as the spectators streamed past. Eventually, the crowd in the stadium would swell to twenty-five thousand cheering and whooping fans. A reporter for the *New York Tribune* described the scene: "The two college colors were worn in many ways. Sometimes they were rich, sometimes gaudy, and often they were expressed in fancy." He described some of the young women as looking "positively Mephistophelian in their crimson gowns, cloaks, and hats." As for the Yale side, it looked as if "it rained blue ribbons, flowers and flags over there." And Harvard matched them plume for plume.

"Equally lavish," the reporter declared, "was the display of bright crimson in the opposite tier."[7]

Some of the students had hardly sat down before they began to sing and cheer, a cacophony of sound rising from the east and west stands.

> Yale Men fight and Yale men play
> We don't care what Yale men say
> Yale is far too fresh and gay
> And Harvard is going to win today.[8]

And Yale constantly repeated its nonsensical cheer after every song and chant.

> I can nock en no
> I can nock en oko
> I can nock en no
> Y-a-l-e![9]

At two o'clock a Harvard man at the north end let out a shout, and the Crimson supporters leaped to their feet as twenty players came tumbling out onto the field. Soon after, the Yale team emerged, and the stadium erupted into bedlam. The members of the undefeated Yale team, arguably the best in the country, bore little resemblance to the gargantuan size and weight of later championship teams. Their weight averaged out at 181, and only two players topped 200 pounds. Though a half-dozen stood over 6′ and two were 6′3″, the swift and aggressive left end, Frank Hinkey, measured only 5′9″ and weighed only 157 pounds; his taller brother, Louis Hinkey, the right end, was even scrawnier.[10]

The Harvard players appeared soon afterward led by their crippled captain, Robert Emmons, who would be replaced by Bob Wrenn at quarterback. Just how badly were men like Emmons hurt? Remarkably few serious injuries took place in the big games between the best teams. Still, football (or "foot ball," as it was written at the time) posed dangers to players, who suffered from broken limbs, bruised faces, and sprains. In the 1890s sporting goods manufacturers had developed masks and padding to protect vulnerable parts of the body. One of the most bizarre and foreboding was the nose mask, which like a modern face mask provided some protection to the nose and teeth. Shaped like a shoehorn with three small breathing holes in the snout, the mask gave a porcine profile to the figure in the ad. Sporting goods firms also offered various belts and pads and guards, wrist supporters, and "the Walter Camp foot ball shoe," made from kangaroo hide and featuring screw plates and leather spikes. Bowing to Victorian decorum, Spalding had less to say about the athletic supporter, except that it was worn by "Cranston, the great centre rush of Harvard's Eleven." Only the skulls remained exposed, because players did not yet wear helmets or head harnesses. Instead, football men made a fetish of wearing long hair to mat their skulls.[11]

As the teams went through their exercises, the Harvard eleven suddenly stood up, trooped to the center of the field, and abruptly gave a Harvard cheer for the Yale eleven. Though it impressed the newspaper reporters, this act of good sportsmanship went all but unnoticed by Yale. All business, Yale players continued with their warmups, until the referee blew his whistle for the game to begin.

Captains Frank Hinkey of Yale and Bob Wrenn of Harvard met at the center of the field for the coin toss. Harvard won, and Yale's Hinkey—"the silent youth from Tonawanda [New York]"—took the ball to midfield for the kickoff. The sky was gray and the temperature in the low forties, a slight breeze furling the banners. Players would appreciate this weather because the playing field in late-season games could often turn into a cold, soggy quagmire or, worse yet, into a frozen board that posed a hazard to uncovered heads and necks. One story circulated in the 1880s that a Harvard player complained of a Yale player trying to drown him on a particularly rain-soaked field.

The game that Yale and Harvard played at Springfield on November 24, 1894, differed radically from the version that would emerge in the next twenty years. Because of football's rugby origins, players in the 1890s could not throw a forward pass but instead had to pass the ball backward. Rather than four downs to make 10 yards, the rules required players to make 5 yards in three downs. The field was 110 yards long, and end zones did not yet exist, only the goal and uprights above it. Touchdowns counted for four points and the kick after for two; goals from the field were worth five points if they sailed through the uprights. The game lasted two hours and twenty minutes, seventy minutes per half, measured from the opening to the final whistle. The teams had a mere ten minutes between halves, and the halves were not yet subdivided into quarters.

The players on the line often sparred with one another, shoved, or even slugged one another before the snap of the ball. Guards and tackles could take up positions in the backfield because the rules did not specify that linemen had to be at the scrimmage line. Teams normally consisted of eleven iron men, who played both offense and defense for the entire game, and an equal number of reserves in case of injuries. Once a player has left the game, he could not return. Hence, injured players often staggered around the field until they collapsed or asked to be taken out of the contest.[12]

One of the Harvard team advisors who arrived in Springfield held a special place in pre-game speculation. Lorin Deland, an advertising consultant from Boston, had neither played football nor attended Harvard. Two years before, working with the team on a voluntary basis, he had devised a play for Harvard to begin the half, the notorious "flying wedge" that contributed to a growing chorus of criticism about the dangers and brutality in football.

The flying wedge in its brief life span functioned as a sort of gridiron kamikaze weapon forged of human bodies. Napoleonic tactics, a passion of Deland, involved a concentration of maximum force at a given point on the battle line, and Deland found an intriguing way to combine military theory with football. Under the old rugby rules, teams could either tap the ball with the foot at the start of the half or after a score—or use a kickoff to put the ball in play. If he chose the symbolic kickoff, the man with the ball touched it to the ground beginning the play and then handed off to a teammate, enabling his team to retain possession and move the ball forward. Why not use this bogus kickoff, Deland had decided, to begin a massive wedge that would shield the ball carrier and deliver a colossal blow to the players on the first line of defense?

According to Deland's plan for the Yale game in 1892, one group of five heavier players would start in motion just before a formation of four lighter players. Both groups of players would head at angles toward the team captain, who would tap the ball and then hand-off to the halfback. The prospective ball carrier would wait alongside the "kicker" for the two groups to converge. Then, as the two groups met at midfield, the ball would be touched down and handed to the ball carrier, who then followed the wedge downfield toward the goal.

After a scoreless first half, Harvard sprung this surprise strategy. The *New York Tribune* commented that "the most striking and successful [play] was the one with which the Harvard team began the second half of the game. Harvard had the ball and ten of the eleven formed a giant wedge." While it caught Yale by surprise, the "giant wedge" gained only twenty yards, and Harvard failed to score. In the end Yale won the game 6-0, but the flying wedge had created a sensation and was widely imitated the following season.

"What a grand play!" the *New York Times* declared, "a half ton of bone and muscle coming into collision with a man [player] weighing 160 or 170 pounds." A grand play for the football enthusiast but unacceptable to the growing band of critics. The flying wedge ignited criticism because it seemed to pose more danger than any other play. While no one was killed by one of Deland's juggernauts, the flying wedge presented critics with a bludgeon to hammer at the intercollegiate game.[13]

From the flying wedge Yale had developed a power V-wedge to use from plays at the line of scrimmage. All of the linemen except for the center and the guards lined up in the backfield, fifteen yards behind the point at which the ball would go in play. "As this wedge started before the ball was put in play, and as the latter was not snapped until the wedge was about to strike its objective point," wrote Parke Davis, an early player, coach, and historian of the game, "it is needless to say that the impact was such that the objective point usually remembered it for years."[14]

There had been so much controversy, in fact, that the spectators who crowded Hampden Field in 1894 would not see the notorious flying wedge or Yale's power wedges. Earlier in the year the members of the rules committee, controlled by Yale's football advisor, Walter Camp, had outlawed the flying wedge by ruling that only two men could go in motion before the start of the play. They had also decreed that teams should no longer use the men in motion or pushing and pulling, a provision that was designed more to reassure the public than to reform the spirit of college football. Both Harvard and Yale would use mass plays, because the rules had not specifically banned teams from pushing and pulling their ball carriers. Though the new rules had doomed most of the wedge plays from scrimmage, the newspapers on November 24 wondered what blockbuster play Deland had prepared for this game.[15]

Instead of using the flying wedge, Hinkey launched a booming kick that forced Harvard nearly back to its goal line. In the sequence of downs Harvard advanced the ball only to its twenty before it was forced to punt on third down. Experts had expected the game to become a seesaw battle, but the play that shaped the game happened in the first minute. As Edgar Wrightington of Harvard tried to kick, Yale's McCrea broke through and blocked the punt, which rolled across the goal, where McCrea fell on it for four points. After the touchdown the player who had scored punted out from the goal to his teammate near the twenty-five-yard line kicked the goal for two extra points. In less than a minute Yale had unexpectedly scored from what later generations would call its special teams, which amounted merely to an aggressive pass rush.

Harvard then kicked a squib kick, a sort of 1890s version of the modern onside kick, and recovered the ball. The ball changed sides several times before Harvard finally mounted a drive, moving the ball to Yale's twenty-five-yard line, where the team lined up for a five-point field goal. Again Harvard failed to execute properly in a critical situation. Fairchild of Harvard kicked the ball straight enough, but it failed to carry through the uprights hitting the crossbar and dropping to the ground. Yale had the ball at Harvard's one-foot line, but Harvard failed to force a safety. Soon afterward Harvard again got in position for another field goal, but Yale blocked the kick. At about this point Harvard's Charlie Brewer suffered an ankle injury that virtually immobilized him. Writhing on the ground, Brewer had to leave the game, the first of many such injuries.[16]

Hayes of Harvard, who replaced Brewer, was unable to move the ball, and it rested inside Yale's five-yard line. Twice Harvard tried to advance the ball and failed to gain. Almost when it seemed that Harvard would never score, Hayes was pushed by his teammates across the goal line. The Harvard supporters erupted in elation at the score, the first time that the Crimson had breached Yale's goal in four years.

Yet Harvard's ineptness in critical situations persisted with the try for the two extra points. The spot on the goal where Hayes had crossed the line turned out to be a bad angle for punting out, and the kicker, Bob Wrenn, called for the usual fair catch before making the try for the points after, but he fumbled the ball, and Yale fell on it. After three years of frustration Harvard had finally scored, only to have the chance to tie Yale snatched from its fingertips.

Some commentators later observed that Harvard's frustration might have set off the chain of violence that would mar the rest of the game. The first act of violence occurred when Waters of Harvard jammed his finger into the eye of Yale's tackle, Frank Butterworth. According to the *New York Herald,* blood gushed from the eye, obscuring Butterworth's eyesight and disorienting the Yale attack. As his eye grew worse, a newspaper reporter described him as "staggering around the ball, weak and useless."[17]

The game had grown noticeably rougher, and Yale's Frank Hinkey, who was notorious for his rough and brutal play, would soon escalate the violence. After failing to move the ball, Yale dropped back to punt, and Thorne of Yale boomed a punt to Edgar Wrightington of Harvard, who caught the ball and fell to the ground. Abruptly Frank Hinkey leaped on Wrightington's shoulder and neck, breaking the Harvard player's collarbone with his knee. "Look at that man's knee, Mr. Referee," shouted Emmons from the sideline, "he fell on that man's neck with his knee." Wrightington had to leave the field in pain, his season ended. Yale suffered a penalty, but the umpire, Alex Moffat of Princeton, allowed Hinkey to remain in the game, when he should have ejected the Yale captain. It was possibly the most notorious act of wanton violence in the 1890s. Stretched thin by Emmon's absence and Brewer's injury, Harvard only had eight of its regulars on the field.[18]

Yale's next score came on what seemed like a break for the Crimson, a failed Eli field goal. After Yale's kick fell short, Harvard took over in the shadow of its goal post but failed to move the ball and faced a punting situation. Hayes of Harvard kicked the ball off the side of his foot, and it went out of bounds one yard from the scrimmage line on the Yale four. Yale failed to gain anything on first down, but Harvard suffered an offsides penalty that moved the ball half the distance to the goal line. Then Yale plunged across the goal line for its second touchdown and kicked the goal after, to lead 12-4.

The frustration had begun to mount for Harvard, and soon a rash of injured and exhausted players caused numerous delays in the game. Yale now concentrated on keeping Harvard from scoring before the end of the half. Harvard had possession and made a few gains, but the referees called the end of the half at ten minutes after three. The players retired to the sidelines for ten minutes of rest.

In the second half violence and injuries replaced the big plays. Upset by Yale's rough play and its own failure to score more than four points, Harvard began to deviate from its game plan. "They soon were confronted by so much viciousness," wrote Dr. W. A. Brooks, a Harvard team advisor, "that if they wished to be in the game they must give as well as to take." After Yale's tackle Murphy poked a finger in Mott Hallowell's eye in the first half, Harvard had been out to get the big Yale tackle. Murphy had already suffered a hard blow to the head which left him disoriented. According to the *Boston Globe,* he had to be told after each play the direction of his own goal. Murphy revived during halftime but was hit again in the second half, collapsed to the turf, and had to be removed on a stretcher. Seeing him temporarily lying along the Harvard sideline, a newspaper reporter described the moribund Yale player's "mud splashed and corpselike face turned to the skies and his battleworn hands lying at his side."[19]

The umpire, Alex Moffat, tried to maintain his tenuous hold on the game. Soon afterward he ejected Armstrong of Harvard and Hayes of Yale for slugging. Though both players later denied throwing punches, they were ready to erupt. The account of the game in the newspapers the next day read like a caricature of 1890s football: "Thorne kicked. Fairchild caught the ball, and was promptly tackled by Beard in the center of the field. Adee was hurt. Gonterman [the substitute for Hayes] gained five yards around right end, but the play was called back and the ball was given to Yale for holding. Thorne got past Arthur Brewer [brother of the injured Charlie Brewer], and in the scrimmage that ensued Hallowell was hurt having his nose broken, and Wheeler went on in his place."[20]

Harvard fought valiantly with "never say die" spirit, but Yale succeeded in its cautious second-half strategy of protecting its lead. The teams seesawed back and forth without scoring. Each team had opportunities to score, but the other side played superbly when it had to. Harvard had moved to Yale's fifteen, but the Eli's held, and the Crimson lost possession. Of the three attempted Yale field goals, Harvard blocked two, while the third failed to carry the uprights.

In the final five minutes Harvard mounted a desperate drive from its own thirty-five-yard line and moved to Yale's twelve-yard line. Stymied by Yale's defense, the Crimson had no choice but to try a field goal. Just as the ball was snapped, the referee's whistle sounded. Fairchild of Harvard launched a perfect kick that split the uprights. It would not have won the game but might have allowed Harvard some satisfaction. In fact, the clocks showed that sixty-six minutes had elapsed, and in theory the Crimson should have scored five points and followed it with a kickoff. Since the ball was already in play, the referee should have allowed the five points.

An angry crowd of Harvard supporters circled the referee waiting for his explanation, which, if he gave it at all, was never divulged. Referees had broad powers to halt the game when they felt that it was growing dark or that time was about to run out. Nevertheless, the failed field goal left a sour taste in the mouths of the already frustrated Harvard spectators, who felt that the umpire, Alex Moffat, should have ruled Frank Hinkey off the field in the first half after his violence against Edgar Wrightington.[21]

This game had resulted in more injuries and violence than anyone could remember. Nine substitutes had replaced injured or ejected players who normally played both halves of the game. Six players had been seriously injured, and one of them, Wrightington, was definitely out for the final game against Pennsylvania. Murphy of Yale, who had suffered a concussion, was taken to a hospital, where he remained in a coma until 7 P.M. Rumors circulated after the game that he had died from his injuries, which proved untrue.[22]

Harvard fans talked about Yale luck in blocking a punt for a touchdown and in getting the ball on the abortive punt at Harvard's five-yard line just after Yale's kicker had missed a field goal. In spite of Harvard's spirited performance, Yale again proved that it was the better, more consistent team, a conclusion that the Harvard football experts grudgingly acknowledged.

In spite of the absence of Yale's football advisor, Walter Camp, who had gone to the West Coast to coach Stanford in its big game against California, the blue machine of Yale had functioned almost flawlessly. It was a tribute to Camp that Yale had won its fourth consecutive game against Harvard and its sixteenth victory in eighteen contests since Harvard had introduced rugby football in the autumn of 1875.

Injuries and controversies would not interfere with the financial windfall for the gridiron promoters of the two schools that had staged the flawed spectacle. The profits from the overflow crowd amounted to almost $11,000 for each of the two teams. In addition, the railroads reaped a harvest of $75,000 from the fifteen thousand spectators who arrived at Springfield by train. The *New York Times* calculated the revenues from the game at $119,000, close to $2 million in late-twentieth-century dollars.[23]

The spectacle at Hampden Field proved damaging, however, to football's reputation. It was the bloodiest and most appalling display of out-and-out violence yet witnessed in a big game. Dr. Brooks of Harvard, one of the graduate advisors who frequently officiated at big games, changed his mind about officiating at the Yale-Princeton game in New York the following Saturday. "So deeply have I been impressed by today's exhibition, and so prejudiced do I feel toward Harvard's opponents," he declared, "I consider it absolutely impossible for me to act as referee in the Yale-Princeton contest."[24]

At Yale, where the faculty rarely questioned athletics, rumors surfaced that the faculty might intervene to keep Yale from traveling to New York for the Princeton game the following week. President Theodore Dwight of Yale and Professor Henry Wright, an athletic advisor, denied it, however. Wright said that he knew no reason why the game should not be played. An article in the *New York Times* reported that the faculty would consider whether football was a game fit for students to play but would make its decision after the Princeton game.[25]

Murphy was taken to a hospital in New York, where a physician who visited him declared that his injuries had not been serious, even though the Yale player had spent four hours in a coma on Saturday at Springfield. Half-humorously, the doctor told the newspaper reporters that he had prescribed beefsteak, training table fare, for his patient. The doctor said that Murphy had suffered his injury because of exhaustion. On Tuesday Murphy returned to New Haven and prepared to play on Saturday against Princeton. In fact, the entire team except for Murphy, Butterworth, and Jerrens, who was recuperating at New Haven, practiced on Monday. Butterworth had gone to New York to have his eye treated.[26]

As expected, the clergy from its pulpits denounced the game for its brutality. In addition, Superintendent Byrnes of the New York Police Department announced that police would patrol the sidelines at the Yale-Princeton game at Manhattan Field on Saturday. He ordered his men to stop the game "if it proved to be anything else than a purely scientific game between two college teams." He was determined, he declared, that the game would not assume the character of a prizefight.[27]

On Thanksgiving, November 29, a depleted Harvard team lost to undefeated Pennsylvania, 18-4. In contrast, Yale easily defeated Princeton, 24-0, to finish with a 16-0 record. The newspaper reports remarked on the lack of rough play in the game.[28]

The chief casualty of the "bloodbath of Hampden Field" turned out to be the annual Harvard-Yale game. In the week that followed, angry remarks filled the newspapers, which built up to a crisis between the two schools. After Yale refused a demand for an apology, Harvard broke relations, ending for two years the profitable but volatile relationship. The two teams would not resume their annual rivalry until 1897.[29]

"The Father of American Football"

The spectacle witnessed on November 24, 1894, had developed from quite modest beginnings in the 1870s. Students had competed in intercollegiate matches in crew and baseball for more than twenty years. Though Rutgers and Princeton had played the first intercollegiate kicking game in 1869, that game more resembled soccer more than American college football.[30]

Then, in 1874, McGill University of Montreal challenged Harvard to a game at Cambridge. McGill played a British variation of football called rugby, using an odd-shaped, slightly oblong ball. Rugby differed from the existing "Association" football (named for the association of eastern colleges that played it) in that each of its players were allowed to run with the ball. The teams agreed to play the first game under Harvard rules and then to compete in a game of rugby. The second game played under the McGill rules marked a turning point in college athletics. Players and spectators discovered a much more exciting and zestful game, even though the outcome was scoreless. At the champagne party celebrating the match both teams agreed that rugby was superior.[31]

After a return match in Montreal and a game at nearby Tufts, Harvard insisted on introducing the game to Yale at New Haven. Yale lost that first rugby game four goals and four touchdowns to nothing but, like Harvard, agreed that rugby was superior to the Association kicking game. And it was rugby that Yale freshman Walter Camp played when he took the field in 1876.[32]

When eighteen-year-old Walter Camp joined the Eli team, beating Harvard at any cost was the primary goal. The players practiced in the morning for an hour and after classes in the afternoon. Before bedtime they ran for three miles. Tall and sinewy, Walter Camp proved to be an agile runner and an outstanding kicker. As a junior, he became captain of the team, a position he held again in his senior year. Under Camp the Yale strategy became, and would remain, "method, not men." Twice, Camp resigned on the eve of big games when players refused to accept his strategy or failed to observe his curfew rules. Team members pleaded with him to remain and did what he wanted. Though Camp rejoined his teammates and agreed to play, his belief in the team's need for blind obedience reflected an even stronger desire to win—and a conviction that his leadership was essential to winning.[33]

But the mythic proportions of Camp's reputation ultimately resulted from his role as a rules maker and diplomat. At the association's annual preseason rules convention in 1878 Camp made his first proposal that the number of players on the field be reduced from fifteen, as it was in the 1870s, to a more manageable eleven. Fewer players would mean fewer difficulties gaining faculty permission to travel; it would also leave more possibilities for open field strategy. For two successive years, however, Camp's eleven-man proposal was rejected. Finally in 1880, after Camp had graduated and entered medical school, he persuaded the convention not only to adopt the eleven-player rule but also a more significant innovation. The team with the ball could retain possession by simply putting the ball to the ground.[34]

This rule marked the great gridiron divide that led American football down the opposite slope from British rugby. In rugby the referee tossed the ball into an interlocked gaggle of players, who "heeled" the ball out to their teammates. Now football became less open to chance and slightly more controllable. The new rule opened the game up to a series of changes championed by Camp, who continued to coach, advise, and legislate throughout graduate school and during his professional life. Eventually, Camp's success at Yale and his role in reshaping the rules earned him the title the "Father of American Football."

Initially, however, Camp's changes brought about confusion rather than order. Once the eastern schools adopted the possession rule, they found that other rules were necessary, such as those concerning yards and downs. As Yale and Princeton squared off in the 1881 championship game, each team believed that a tie would guarantee the title for its school, since each regarded itself as champion from the previous year. Princeton's strategy was to hold the ball—which it did for the entire first half. It accomplished this by moving the ball backward to what was called the touch-in-goal, diagonal to the playing field and next to the area just beyond the goal line, which later became the end zone—after which it was brought out to the twenty-five-yard line. "This happened many times," a Yale player recalled. With a strong wind in their face, the Yale players decided to repeat the same strategy in the second half, and the scoreless tie enabled each team to proclaim itself champion.[35]

To avoid a repeat of such a fiasco in the future, Camp persuaded the rules convention in the following years to adopt a system used in Canada whereby a team would have three opportunities to move the ball five yards forward or ten yards backward. "If on three consecutive fairs or downs," the rules read, "a team shall not have advanced the ball five yards or lost ten, they must give up the ball to the other side where the first down was made." White lines were also added, at Camp's suggestion, at five-yard intervals, which one delegate said disparagingly would convert the field into a "gridiron" and thereby wreck the game. The sobriquet stuck, though the fears of chaos proved exaggerated. To the contrary, football became more systematic, less like the spontaneous game that had appeared in the 1870s and more tied to discipline and organization.[36]

In 1882 Camp dropped out of medical school and went to work for a clock company in New York. In the business world he learned organizational skills and how to manage money, and he soon returned with his skills to Yale and a job with the New Haven Clock Company, where he would eventually become president.

Although Camp was never head coach of Yale football in the modern sense, he resembled the athletic chairman of the board. Once back in New Haven, he was free to attend practice after work and confer with team leaders in the evenings. Sometimes at practice he removed his coat to demonstrate a play, and often in strategy sessions he sketched or explained the plays that the team might use.

Gradually, Camp assumed the role of perpetual graduate advisor at Yale—a departure from the tradition of the previous year's captain as coach and advisor. Unlike a modern coach, Camp did not devote his time exclusively to football or to athletics. Though he often visited the practice field, Camp dispensed much of his football wisdom in evening meetings with the team leaders. Unlike modern coaches, he did not sit on the bench and did not coach from the sidelines. For several years, because he traveled to California to coach Stanford for its big game, he missed the big games with Harvard and Princeton.

In 1888 Camp began his annual ritual of choosing an All-America team. At first all of the players whom Camp and sportswriter Caspar Whitney chose for their teams played for eastern colleges. When Camp added "western" players, he missed Yale games to travel to the Midwest to watch teams and players in order to make his All-America selections. In short, he was the personification of the gentleman amateur who coached because of his interest in the game and competitive instincts rather than for professional reasons or monetary gain. His invention of the graduate advisor who helped to teach technique and plot strategy proved to be a halfway house between the old student player coach and the later paid professional.

Under Camp's tutelage Yale seldom lost—only fourteen losses from 1876 to 1909. And success on the field gave Camp a vested interest in the rules that he pushed through the early rules conventions. After the changes brought about by the possession and yards and downs rules, Camp played a part in later innovations such as numerical scoring, which in 1882 replaced the highly imprecise system of determining the winner by comparing the various scores made by each team. Later he was responsible for two changes in 1888: a rule that allowed blocking in front of the ball carrier and a rule that permitted tackling below the waist. What were once formations that spread the width of the field now contracted to bunches of players lined up more compactly around the ball. Such configurations, in turn, led to further changes; players on offense began engaging in pushing and pulling the ball carrier through the defensive line and increased their momentum by going in motion before the ball was snapped. Mass and momentum football replaced the rugby-style, open-field running and kicking that had characterized the early stages of American football. Knees now came into contact with heads when players made tackles below the waist, a lethal combination. As a result, football started to appear—and, in fact, became— far more violent and dangerous than it had ever been before.[37]

In 1888 Camp married Alice Sumner, the younger sister of Yale professor (and Social Darwinist) William Graham Sumner. Allie Sumner had no interest in football when she married Walter Camp, but she proved an apt student. When team leaders gathered at the Camp house for their nightly meetings, she listened and absorbed. She often attended practice and reported to Camp in the evening if he had not been present. In 1888 "Mrs. Walter," as she was called, even substituted for her husband when business obligations made him unavailable. Yale's All-America end, Amos Alonzo

Stagg, later coach at the University of Chicago, recalled that Mrs. Walter was "more coach than he. She was out every afternoon for practice and made a detailed report from notes at night to her husband." That season Yale was undefeated. At the team's twenty-fifth anniversary dinner the menus featured photos of the two Camps with the title "Head Coaches, 1888."[38]

And during the 1880s Camp and his counterparts at other eastern schools reduced the role of the student athletes. Already big games played in New York provided growing revenues, enabling the teams to cover most of their own modest expenses. In a nutshell the football alumni converted football into a more professional, systematic, businesslike enterprise, establishing a system for meeting and regulating the games. Like the student coaches, the student manager lost out to the alumni such as Camp who had more expertise in organizing the team and who had the experience to supervise the finances as well.

As treasurer of the Yale Athletic Association, Walter Camp controlled the finances of the entire athletic system at Yale, including a secret fund built from football revenues. Camp may have begun this fund to provide for emergencies, but it grew by the early 1900s to a sum that exceeded $100,000. When the fund became public in 1905, it created a minor scandal because Camp operated the fund as if it were his own and tapped it only to provide money for the football team. Though he had played tennis and participated in track at Yale, Camp had little use for lesser sports such as swimming and often refused to use football revenues to fund them. In 1899, when Arthur Hadley became president of Yale, he formalized Camp's status as his advisor on athletics, an early version of the athletic director. Eventually, Camp organized the other graduate advisors at eastern institutions into a Graduate Advisors Committee, which met to make and revise the rules, another sign that the players' rules conventions had receded into the past. Not surprisingly, Camp dominated the committee, though he was unfailingly diplomatic, letting others have their say, waiting until someone asked, "What do you think, Walter?" Then he forged ahead with his opinion. Occasionally, his colleagues attempted to rebel against Camp's dictatorial methods, such as one time when he was late and they prepared to overthrow him. But invariably these attempts were thwarted. After all, the "father of American Football" knew more about "his" game, served as its spokesman, and possessed more guile than his colleagues. "Dear Oligarch," wrote one friend half in jest. He was right on the mark.[39]

Camp's "czar system" may have carried the seeds of its own destruction, but it worked well while football was expanding and someone was needed to steady the helm. While serving as secretary of the football committee, Camp edited the rules books and interpreted the rules. Despite disputes between schools, Camp remained the most influential figure in the football establishment.

Neither Camp nor his colleagues had much sympathy for academic concerns, especially faculty interests or complaints. In their view students came to college for four years of social and educational immersion, but for Camp and his friends the struggle for supremacy on athletic fields defined the college's identity.

Faculty Intervention in the 1880s

In contrast to Yale, Harvard stood out both as the most highly respected academic institution and as a reforming influence in athletics. Being the largest university in the country, it had an illustrious faculty and a well-known president, Charles Eliot, who distrusted big-time college sports. Unlike professors at other schools, the Harvard faculty tried far more seriously than others to limit or abolish football, and, just as the intellectual reforms at Harvard percolated down to other schools, the reform tendencies of the skeptical faculty and president showed up at other colleges a decade or more later.

Even at Harvard, however, undergraduates and alumni were often conventional in their tastes, preferring athletics to intellectual pursuits and spending as much time at the practice fields as in Harvard's voluminous library. Most of the undergraduates and many of the alumni cared as much about football as if they had matriculated at Yale or Princeton. Therefore, Harvard faculty were engaged in a constant struggle against the excesses at their own institution. Between 1884 and 1906 the faculty frequently attempted to abolish football, succeeding only for brief periods on two occasions. For all of its considerable influence, Harvard was an institution divided against itself.

In 1885, dissatisfied by the failure of the eastern football teams in their pre-season rules conventions to stem the brutality, the Harvard faculty athletic committee tried a radical reform. They persuaded the general faculty to suspend football, though only for a single year. As so often happened, Yale and Princeton refused to go along with Harvard's strict measures to cleanse football. And, as long as Yale and Princeton competed for the championship, they served as a counterweight to reform attempts at Harvard. Facing pressure from students and alumni, the athletic committee reconsidered. It decided that the brutality that it had condemned only a year before had abated. Acting on the committee's recommendation, Harvard reinstated the game the following year.[40]

Walter Camp did not trust faculty to make decisions on athletics, perhaps because he knew of their long-standing objection to football, especially at Harvard. In the early 1880s, long before other faculties recognized its dangers, the recently formed Harvard athletic committee, made up of faculty, took its first critical look at football. Football as it was played in 1883 was deemed too violent. The committee already objected to the "three slugs and you're out" rule that allowed players to slug their opponents three times before being ejected. And there were complaints about players who were ineligible to compete because they were not regular students in good standing. The committee also criticized the prizefight atmosphere in New York, where Harvard initially played its big games, and the city's corrupting effects on callow undergraduates. When the faculty committee failed in its efforts to have Harvard abolish football, the committee decided to send three of its members to attend games played between various schools the next year and report back to the general faculty.

What the three members saw utterly appalled them—violence, above all. In each of the contests that they observed, violence and unsportsmanlike conduct dominated the game. The two referees proved inadequate or unwilling to control the unruly players. Fistfights often had to be broken up by bystanders or by the police. In the Harvard-Princeton and Yale-Princeton games players knocked down their opponents with blows to the face. In the Wesleyan-Pennsylvania game the committee encountered an even worse act of brutality. According to the report, one player threw an opponent out of bounds. As the downed player was getting up, the same player who first hit him did it again and then seized the football. He strutted back to his teammates, while the referees stood aside.[41]

The committee also found football demoralizing, not only to the players but also to the spectators. The crowd seemed incapable of recognizing or reacting to unfair play, and their reaction discouraged sportsmanlike conduct. Committee members were shocked to hear cries of "kill him," "break his neck," "hit him," "knock him down," much as they might hear at a prizefight. The three faculty members concluded that football was dangerous and unfit for gentlemen. If a team played like gentlemen, it stood no chance of winning. The subcommittee recommended that Harvard discontinue football until the rules were changed.[42]

Not surprisingly, the violence persisted. In 1889 the *New York Herald* commented that a player in the Harvard lineup had come to the team after advertising himself as a football slugger to the highest bidder. In the Harvard-Yale game, the newspaper reported, he distinguished himself by kicking a Yale man in the face. "It is astonishing that Harvard employs him," the reporter commented.[43]

From the beginning football encouraged its participants to demonstrate their machismo. In 1879 the beefy Yale player and future artist Frederick Remington claimed that he went to a local slaughterhouse and dipped his uniform in blood to make it "more businesslike," as much an indication of his dramatic flair as his penchant for violence. Andrew White, president of Cornell, noted in his diary: "Great football on our grounds—Yale vs. Cornell—Our boys scoring not one point. Great crowd, game brutal as usual, two men hurt." White had earlier refused to allow his team to travel to Cleveland for a game with Michigan and in the process came up with one of the finest sports quotes of all time: "I will not permit 30 men to travel four hundred miles merely to agitate a bag of wind."[44]

Reports of slugging and other violent practices were so widespread that few who had seen a game or who had played college football could deny its roughness. "In all my playing days I was never hurt," wrote Amos Alonzo Stagg, "but I escaped narrowly in 1886." One of the guards left the game, he wrote, requiring eight stitches to close a cut over the eye, and the eyes and lips of one right tackle "were mangled and hideously swollen." The only personal injuries that Stagg recalled were a "perpetually skinned nose, due to the sandpaperlike surface of Smock's canvas jacket [the football uniform then in use], bruised knees and sore arms."[45]

A former Princeton player charged that his teammate Knowton "Snake" Ames, the Red Grange of the 1880s, may have intentionally used his knee to disable Albert Holden, a Harvard player. A teammate recalled that he and Ames took turns kneeing the Harvard star until the player was unable to get up. The Princeton team then gave the necessary permission for Holden to be taken out of the game. On the following issue of *Harper's Illustrated*, however, Snake Ames fired off a response denying the charge. "Also I submit," Ames added, "that it would be quite a difficult task to hit such a brilliant and fast player as Mr. Holden in the chest while running with the ball and that such an act no one would plan to carry out in advance." Did Ames's memory betray him, or were he—and his teammate—genuinely innocent?[46]

The public gradually became aware of football because of the big games in New York and because of the violence that became football's hallmark. By the late 1880s the big game had become not only a public spectacle but also a means for teams to earn the profits that would make up for their early season losses. Because of former players like Walter Camp and enthusiastic alumni, the football spectacle grew up without official scrutiny or, in Yale's case, without the sanction of the institution. In an age of runaway problems football would become one of the topics of concern in the early 1890s, an increasingly profitable enterprise that seemed to resemble highly commercialized ventures in the private sector rather than physical training designed to teach character and morals.

CHAPTER TWO

The First Football Controversy, 1893 to 1897

On February 14, 1894, nine months before the Harvard-Yale game at Hampden Field in Springfield, Massachusetts, an audience of men and women gathered for a meeting of the Contemporary Club in New York. Professors Woodrow Wilson of Princeton and Burt Wilder of Cornell had agreed to debate a highly controversial topic, "Ought the Game of Foot Ball to Be Encouraged?"

Woodrow Wilson was no stranger to football. As an undergraduate at Princeton, he had shown an intense interest in major college sports. While the future president never played football or baseball, he became obsessed with the two sports. He wrote editorials for the *Daily Princetonian* urging support for athletic teams. Of the seventy-two editorials he wrote as a student, twenty-two had to do with athletics. As Bruce Leslie has pointed out, "Wilson glorified victory, lambasted those who failed to support athletics, criticized teams' failure, and carped about victorious rivals."[1]

As a professor at Wesleyan and at Princeton, Wilson followed the fortunes of his teams with an intensity that bordered on fanaticism. At Wesleyan he helped to coach the team and, according to some stories, leaped from the stands during games to lead cheers. When he returned to Princeton in 1890 as a government professor, football became even more important to him. According to his wife, Ellen, Wilson was palpably distressed when Pennsylvania upset Princeton in 1892. "Really I think that Woodrow would have had some kind of collapse," Ellen Wilson wrote prophetically, "if we had lost in politics too" (Grover Cleveland, a Democrat, had won the presidency the previous week).[2]

Burt Wilder of Cornell, who shared the podium with Wilson on February 14, had begun teaching long before the emergence of the sports craze of the 1880s and 1890s. Wilder, who claimed to have played football forty years before, believed that colleges should stop playing intercollegiate sports. While Wilson had claimed that football provided moral training, Wilder disagreed. If football built moral character, he asked, why did teams have to hire an "umpire to keep the young men in order"? He wondered why Wilson had not suggested ways to improve the game and declared that he would only support football if the game could be improved.

Taking the affirmative side, Wilson argued that football developed moral and intellectual qualities—he listed precision, decision, presence of mind, and endurance. He believed that the colleges that opposed football had failed to organize their teams effectively. "They have not succeeded [not] because they did not have manly men," Wilson declared, "but because they did not have the sort of organization to produce a good plan which wins in foot ball."

In his debate with Wilder, Wilson had used Harvard to illustrate his point on lack of organization. "Why is it that Harvard don't win in foot ball?" Wilson asked. "President Eliot says they don't play well because of the elective system of studies, and I think he is practically right." The elective system did not encourage discipline, and football by its nature required discipline and organization. Harvard almost always lost to Yale and frequently to Princeton.[3]

Charles Eliot: Football's First Big-Time Critic

There was a more important reason why Wilson mentioned Harvard and its president, Charles Eliot. That same week Eliot had released his report for the previous academic year in which he roundly criticized college sports, especially football. Only a week before, the delegate from Cambridge in the Massachusetts House of Representatives had introduced a bill to punish anyone who played football in the presence of paid spectators or who as a student "beats, strikes or intentionally wounds or bruises another person engaged in playing such a game." While the bill never became law, it reflected a growing mistrust of football which had become a public debate in 1892 and 1893, after the flying wedge and other wedge plays were introduced.

Charles Eliot had emerged, in fact, as football's most widely known critic, the first well-known college president to launch an assault on bigtime college sports. From 1875 to 1909 Eliot presided over the largest educational institutions in the United States—until Columbia topped Harvard's enrollment in the early 1900s. As an unapologetic elitist, Charles Eliot believed that colleges existed to bring culture and a commitment to service to diligent students. In almost twenty-five years as Harvard's president Eliot had compiled a remarkable number of academic achievements. He had introduced the lecture system to Harvard, strengthened and expanded the faculty, established professional schools, and created a controversial elective system—to which Wilson had referred—which gave students virtual autonomy in the choice of courses. Under Eliot the number of students and courses increased dramatically, though college building was still gathering steam in the 1890s. Though "cold as an icicle," in the words of one of his students, Eliot possessed an ability to convey his views not only to his classes and his faculty but also to the larger public.[4]

As he worked to transform Harvard into a modern institution, Eliot ran headlong into the growing enthusiasm for college athletics. In the 1880s he had come to believe, along with many of his faculty, that intercollegiate athletics detracted from Harvard's reputation. By the 1891–92 academic year he was ready to speak out. Eliot felt that there was something "exquisitely inappropriate in the extravagant expenditure on athletic sports at such institutions at Harvard and Yale . . . painfully built up by the self-denial, frugality, and public spirit of generations that certainly did not lack physical and moral courage, endurance, and toughness." In other words, football made a mockery of Harvard's long and distinguished tradition.[5]

In his 1894 report for the previous school year Eliot let loose his first cannonade against college sports, namely baseball, crew, and especially football. Like his Puritan forebears, Eliot preached a gospel of simple and unadorned truth. He rejected the competitive and deceptive spirit in college athletics, criticizing, for instance, the curve ball in baseball because it was designed to deceive the batter. He also showed extreme distaste for the win-at-any-cost commercial spirit of college athletics—what he called "an unwholesome desire of victory by whatever means." He deplored the way in which intercollegiate athletics put colleges in the business of entertaining the noncollegiate public. Eliot also criticized the amount of time that competitive athletics took from a student's daily life and the false image of university life which college sports projected, a point to which he frequently returned.[6]

Above all, Eliot despised football because it perverted rather than built character. If baseball deceived with the curve ball, football players practiced deception on a much grander scale. Football was filled with "tricks, surprises and habitual violations of the rules" which became a means of winning. He also expressed views shared by others in the early 1890s: that the risks of injury and death in football were not only "inordinate and excessive" but were also increasing. Youthful coaches, he believed, contributed to the problem by overtraining and overtaxing the players. Those students who were not injured physically were impaired intellectually. Eliot believed that football rendered students unfit for intellectual activity.[7]

The outspoken Harvard president proposed a number of changes, many of them later adopted by Harvard and other colleges. Neither freshmen nor professional students should be allowed to play, colleges should stage their games on their own grounds rather than in New York or Boston, and athletes should be limited to one sport. Eliot proposed less rather than more football. He believed that intercollegiate sports should be played in alternate years, thereby allowing a student to resume his normal academic life. Furthermore, "no football should be played," he wrote, "until the rules are so amended as to diminish the number and violence of the collisions between the players and to provide for the enforcement of the rules."[8]

This and other criticisms not only angered football enthusiasts at Harvard but also worried supporters at other schools, where the contagion of

Eliot's antagonism might spread. Eliot's words were opinions only, but there was always a fear that he might actually make good on his rhetoric. Because his criticisms received publicity in the eastern press, they lent support to those who shared his views and helped to fuel a debate over football. More important in the long run, Eliot continued to criticize football for the next decade, thereby imprinting his rhetoric on a small body of influential football haters. When football faced its first great crisis in 1905 and 1906, other college presidents, like James Angell of Michigan, used the same arguments to indict football.

Eliot never denied the value of college athletics in moderation. Recalling his own experience, he believed that college sports could play a wholesome role in students' lives. When an undergraduate at Harvard, Eliot engaged in rowing. In one race against the "Irish" and other crews, Eliot reveled in his victory and the acclaim of the crowd, especially the cheers of Harvard faculty in attendance. Still, writing to his fiancée before the race, he voiced the theme that would typify his attitude toward athletics: "I had rather win than not," he wrote, "but this is a mighty little matter whether we beat or are beaten—rowing is not my profession, neither is it my love—it is only recreation, fun, and health."[9]

At Harvard in the 1890s, however, intercollegiate athletics proved a distraction to academic life. Surrounded with opportunities for learning, Harvard students seemed to care more about their failure to defeat Yale in football than in the vast possibilities of absorbing the abundance of academic delicacies offered to them by the elective system. For all their freedom Harvard undergraduates would resemble their counterparts at other schools. They engaged in occasional pranks, devoted their time to extracurricular activities, and traveled to the great cities for big games. William James, the father of American psychology and a member of the Harvard faculty, despaired, too, of their lack of responsibility. James wondered if undergraduates should be treated as men or boys and saw their absence of moral courage as the Achilles' heel of the Harvard character. He once observed that he felt as if he spent his time in a nonconducting medium; his own vibrations died away "like the sound of a bell in an air-pump."[10]

College Football and Student Violence

On February 21, 1894, Cornell University, the institution where the outspoken foe of football Burt Wilder taught, made headlines of a different kind. In an age of student violence disguised as class rivalries, tensions ran especially high between the freshmen and sophomores. Much of the rivalry consisted of athletic or pseudo-athletic activities such as driving the sophomores off the traditional fence at Yale. At Cornell the class of '97 had defeated the sophomores in all interclass games and were to hold a victory banquet. But first they had to make their way through a wall of sore-losing sophomores. Marching eight abreast, the freshmen had to literally fight their way into the banquet hall. "Friends and foes," the *Boston Globe* reported, "slugged each other and bruised faces and torn clothes were the order rather than the exception." Called in to keep order, the beleaguered police had to swing their clubs just to fend off the crowd. The sophomores stopped their pursuit at the doors of the hall only because the juniors, the interclass allies of the freshmen, waited upstairs armed with baseball bats.[11]

Then, around midnight, twenty panicky freshmen emerged from the building. Coughing and choking, they rushed to a nearby drugstore in a frenzied search for an antidote to chloride. A cook, described as "an elderly colored woman," staggered out beside a younger woman, who was screaming. Ten minutes later the elderly woman was dead. Someone, it later appeared, had placed a jug of chlorine gas near the kitchen. The woman had died from gas inhalation. The students all recovered, but the episode made national headlines. Newspapers reported that the entire sophomore class was to be suspended until an investigation could take place, though this report proved unfounded.[12]

The editor of the *New York Evening Post,* E. L. Godkin, a reformer and dyspeptic critic of football, thought he saw a connection between it and the event. The episode at Cornell, Godkin believed, fit into a larger scheme. "It is more than a chance coincidence," he wrote, "that this recent revival of brutality accompanies the over development of college athletics and the football craze." According to Godkin, President Eliot had identified this phenomenon. In his recent Harvard alumni report, he declared, Eliot had commented on the violent collisions of heavy men, often in groups, racing at full speed. Injured players, he observed, often had to be carried from the field. Yet the game went on with substitutes, and scarcely anyone noticed the absence of the injured players. "The sensibilities both of the players and of habitual spectators are blunted by such sights," Eliot was quoted as saying. "To become brutal and brutalizing *is the natural tendency of all sports which involves violent personal collision between the players, and the game of football is a nonexception to this rule.*"[13]

Did a connection exist, or was Godkin simply indulging his distaste for football? Had the Cornell incident truly occurred because football games blunted the students' sensibilities? Or did the poisoning occur as a part of college hazing and class rivalries that predated college athletics? Obviously, Godkin believed that football games were somehow responsible. Ironically, charges of poisoning occasionally occurred in college football. After Princeton lost to Pennsylvania in 1894, rumors abounded that the losers had suffered from an undisclosed form of poisoning, since none of the team members displayed any spirit or ferocity.[14]

On the other side of the fence, many advocates of intercollegiate sports insisted that baseball and football had diminished the number of student pranks and acts of violence. One of the first to make this claim was Eugene Richards, a former football player turned professor of mathematics at Yale. In an article written a decade earlier he had argued, like Wilson, that sports improved student behavior and student character. He pointed to high spirits, or animal instincts, of young men and insisted that football was responsible for channeling those tendencies in a constructive direction. This argument persisted for the next quarter-century, until the controversies over football began to wane. Faculty and presidents who had been students or had taught in the Civil War era recalled the student riots, vandalism, and profligacy. Charles Eliot, himself, it should be noted, believed that athletics supplied "a new and effective motive for resisting all sins which weaken or corrupt the body"—a commonly used, slightly veiled reference to sex and drinking.[15]

In spite of apparent contradictions, many college presidents and faculty in the 1880s and 1890s believed that student behavior on campus in the 1880s and 1890s had grown less ungovernable. They frequently credited this welcome change to sports, especially to big-time sports like baseball and football. Richards wrote glowingly of a "republic of students" brought to life by the athletic revolution. And in 1894 many of the responses to a questionnaire sent by Walter Camp to former players and school officials, and published as *Football Facts and Figures,* would echo the same theme.[16]

Ironically, a later episode at his own university would dramatically illustrate the workings, and limits, of Richards's "republic." In September 1895 a Yale student had his off-campus room invaded in the dark of night. The students who broke into his room had suspected him of stealing money from them and, as they expected, found ten dollars in his shoe. The thirty vigilantes had signed a pledge to stand by one another. If one of them were expelled, the rest would resign. Together they gagged the student and dragged him onto the campus. After extracting a confession, they coated him with tar and feathers. Then they released him. The student returned to his bedroom, where he spent the night crying. In the morning the university president had him cleaned off and then promptly expelled him. As for the vigilantes, they avoided censure—as the *Yale Daily News* called it, an "encouraging sign." At the time, no mention was made, one way or the other, of college football. Yet, like the episode at Cornell, one could argue, the incident of midnight justice was the result of either the positive or harmful effects of college athletics. What is certain is that each violent incident had the capacity to play into the debate beginning to rage in the 1890s over the value of football.[17]

Among the graduate football advisors and their allies, the attack on football became a matter of concern. Walter Camp worked with fellow supporters of football to stave off critics and to create a climate of opinion fa-

vorable to the college game. While Camp was never adverse to some changes
—his changes—he also believed that football had reached a desirable point,
where it was interesting to the spectator, beneficial to Yale, and capable of
unlimited growth. He may have perceived that football's violence was not
a small contributor to its popularity.

It was undoubtedly a result of the changes made by Camp's Graduate
Advisory Committee in 1888 that football had become far more violent. Allowing players to be in front of the ball carrier, blocking, and tackling below
the waist changed the nature of the game. Put simply, tackling below the
waist put heads in the way of knees. Power plays across the middle or mass
plays meant pushing, shoving, or even catapulting the ball carrier, resulting
in jarring collisions. But it was truly the accompanying formations known
as momentum plays which threatened the worst injuries. Momentum plays
were wedge plays wherein offensive players clustered together, much as they
did in screen plays decades later. The rule that gave the wedge play its power
and savagery was one that permitted the players to go into motion before
the "center-rush" snapped the ball. As the players jostled at the line, the five
or six (or sometimes more) men back of the center or in the backfield began
to move toward the ball carrier. The play began in earnest when the center
gave the ball to the quarterback, who then handed off the ball to one of the
men in motion.

Once the most dramatic and potent of plays, the flying wedge fell victim, after barely two seasons, to sensational publicity. The newspapers covering the big games with small armies of reporters played up violence like
the flying wedge with gusto. For at least five years the reporters had either
reveled in the violence of the big games or had professed shock or indignation at what they took for violence or at least found humor in the extravagant reports of injuries. In its account of Yale-Princeton game in 1892
the *New York Times* commented that the most popular way to disable an opponent was to step on his feet, kick his shins, give him a dainty upper cut,
or gouge his face while making a tackle.[18]

The simple fact that rules had to be put on the books against hacking
(kicking), throbbing (shutting off a man's wind), and butting (running into
a player with the shoulder lowered) was the clearest indication that football
was growing more dangerous. As if to confirm football's unsavory reputation, President Grover Cleveland called off the annual Army-Navy game for
1893 following a report detailing the number of injuries and lost days suffered by players at the academies as a result of football.[19]

College Football in the Early 1890s: Image and Reality

In the early 1890s the reputation of football also suffered from lack of
unity. The earlier solidarity of schools participating in rules conventions had

become fragmented. Beginning in 1889, the eastern schools engaged in five years of gridiron disputes, mainly regarding eligibility, leading to the breakup of the existing association, the Intercollegiate Football Association (IFA). Though fragments of the IFA remained and Camp's guidebooks continued to appear, college football lacked direction in the early 1890s. Occasionally, faculties or presidents either called for the suspension of football or even temporarily succeeded. Worse yet for defenders of football, gridiron critics had made a convincing case that football had become brutal and dangerous.

In 1894 Walter Camp published *Football Facts and Figures,* a collection of responses to questionnaires that he had sent to players, former players, and school authorities. In addition to the assembled responses, the book contained several introductory essays, including one by Camp himself, which described football in glowing terms. Camp concluded that his survey represented a vote of confidence for football and proved that it posed scant danger.

In all of the introductory pieces the writers marshaled facts and figures in support of football, making incisive points to defend the sport. Sportswriter Caspar Whitney lashed out at E. L. Godkin of the *New York Evening Post,* criticizing his "misstatements and ignorance." Camp also staunchly defended the game in his introduction. While not yet two pages into the book, Camp referred to the tragic episode of five Harvard students who had drowned recently while sailing, an accident that came across as more deadly by far than anything that had happened or was likely to happen in football.[20]

The opportunity to compile a defense of football resulted from a decision by the Harvard Board of Overseers to conduct a study of the problems of college to establish the "facts" about the dangers of football. Composed of some alumni who supported football, the board lacked the strong opposition to football which marked Charles Eliot and the Harvard faculty. That the study was probably intended to establish a less hostile image of football is suggested by the Overseers' decidedly partial act of inviting Camp to conduct the study. Camp devised a simple questionnaire for present and former college players which would, he believed, ascertain the severity of injuries and the value of football. He then expanded the scope of his inquiries to encompass heads of private schools and some members of the faculty who were advising football or athletics. Camp asked them to comment on the influence of football on their own or their students' academic work and on the injuries suffered in the gridiron game. He further asked them to assess the role of football on college discipline and on the well-being of the students, players, and the college or school.

At least one scholar has argued that Walter Camp withheld about 20 percent of the responses. And, in one sense, Camp did cleverly convert what might have been a potpourri of opinions and recollections into a resoundingly pro-football polemic. Rather than discuss the results of his survey,

Camp began the book with a barrage of football propaganda. The pieces that greeted the reader consisted of comments by Professor Eugene Richards of Yale, sportswriter Caspar Whitney, the superintendent of West Point, and, of course, Walter Camp.[21]

For the most part, the responses to the questionnaire strongly supported football and reported few and sometimes no injuries. The respondents claimed high scholarship and better health for football players, even for players who suffered minor injuries. Typical of the more colorful replies, one former player recalled that his grades were always higher during the fall term. "But besides the 'humanities' which were dinged into me in the classroom," he observed, "I value what I would be pleased to call the 'inhumanities' dinged into me on the football field."[22]

According to other replies, the gridiron game promoted manliness and checked moral vices (sex and drinking). A game like football, one former player wrote, "flushes the ducts and avenues of his being, prevents deceit, morbidness; makes him manlier, freer, franker, and healthier." Some players credited football with developing self-reliance and coolness in difficult situations. Others went so far as to praise football for nurturing their intellect. Many agreed that football taught qualities not acquired in the classroom—"a broken bone is a small thing compared with the coolness, the self-control, and the manly spirit which football more than another sport gives the player."[23]

Several former players recalled that they had entered secondary school as spindly, weak boys and that football had built their bodies and their self-confidence. A doctor from Swarthmore College testified that football had endowed him with muscular strength, from which he derived endurance, "vitality," and quickness. "It has allowed me to live to this day," he asserted, "for I was so delicate as a boy as to be predicted a corpse before I was sixteen." Former Yale tackle and All-American, W. W. "Pudge" Heffelfinger, perhaps the greatest player of his time and anchor of the undefeated 1888 Yale team, claimed that his academic standing remained as good, if not better, during football season than when he was not playing. He had not suffered a single injury, nor had he seen anyone who was seriously injured. And besides developing his muscles, he added, he had learned to control a terrible temper.[24]

The irrepressible western artist Frederick Remington, whose sense of humor ran to the irreverent and who had done sketches for an article on Yale football in *Harper's Weekly,* bluntly inquired who was creating the furor over football. He hoped that state laws would not be passed against football. In short, Remington did not believe in all this "namby-pamby talk, and hope[d] that the game will not be emasculated and robbed of its heroic qualities, which is its charm and its distinctive character." He advised those who disliked football to try whist.[25]

Despite the testimonials to football, a number of criticisms were also sandwiched between the otherwise laudatory views, sometimes even in the same response. One writer from Atlanta, who said he had never suffered injuries from football, also insisted that "the battering-ram idea is all wrong." Another respondent objected to the recently legalized practice of "interference [blocking], which is nothing more than 'off side' play—call it as you will." Still another condemned the wedges. "As for the mass plays (relics of the Theban phalanx!)," he commented, "if they be not positively dangerous, they seem to be so."[26]

Yet, overwhelmingly, most agreed with one former player, who wrote that all "this talk of terrible roughness and brutality in the championship games seems to me to be absolutely untrue." Several held the press responsible for inventing or exaggerating the problem. One respondent from Idaho concluded by blaming the uproar on the faculty and college presidents—he probably meant Charles Eliot and the Harvard faculty, since his letter was dated just after the release of Eliot's report in 1894. Few responses were consistently hostile to football.[27]

Anyone who read Camp's book, especially the introductory excerpts, might come away wondering what all the critical fuss was about. According to the "facts and figures" so authoritatively interpreted, no one suffered permanent injuries, and all but a cranky handful agreed that football's virtues outweighed its shortcomings. If some critics saw brutality, the authoritative excerpts seemed to indicate that they simply did not understand what was happening on the field.

The publication of *Football Facts and Figures* was a temporary victory for Camp as well as for those at Harvard who wanted to stave off Charles Eliot and other opponents of football. Yet Camp's success turned out to be temporary. It would not take long for the evidence from the football field itself to support criticism, and, while defenders managed to avoid significant changes in the mid-1890s, they would face a palace revolt just over a decade in the future.

Taken in tandem, *Football Facts and Figures* and Eliot's annual report helped to focus the debate on the need for reform, a controversy that would last for years to come. As football continued to grow, Camp and his fellow founding fathers sought to protect the game that they had created and nourished. On the other side, Charles Eliot and a handful of critics showed equal determination to condemn football whenever they had the chance. In 1894 the newly reconstituted rules committee tried to resolve the controversy by outlawing the flying wedge and decreeing that "no mass-momentum plays shall be allowed." According to the committee, no more than three men could move before the ball was put in play. The flying wedge disappeared, but three men in motion proved enough to allow momentum plays to continue. Fertile minds soon found new ways to pull linemen into the backfield and to aim plays at vulnerable points.

In the meantime Charles Eliot again denounced college athletics in his report for 1893–94, which was released in 1895. "The evils of the intercollegiate sports, as described in the President's report of last year," he wrote, "continue without real redress or diminution. *In particular, the game of football grows worse and worse as regards foul and violent play, and the number and gravity of injuries which the players suffer.*" Eliot added that the game had become "unfit for college use," that the present rules caused so many injuries, including broken bones, sprains, and wrenched body parts, they had to be changed. Even when teams played the game fairly, he declared, the number of injuries reached what he regarded as dangerous levels as a result of rules that encouraged the players to engage in "reckless violence" and "shrewd violations" to maximize their team's advantage. This growing distaste for football fit well with Eliot's opposition to war and his belief in arbitration to settle international disputes. Though he despised football in all facets, Eliot came to believe that the rules shaped many of its undesirable features. Without some way to control the brutality, Eliot and other critics believed that football had the chaotic and violent character of a military conflict and perhaps some of the same results.[28]

Eliot probably had in mind a fatality in a big game inconceivable only a few years before, an event that had taken place since his first report and seemed to confirm his earlier predictions of danger. In November 1894 Georgetown played a Thanksgiving game in the District of Columbia against the semiprofessional Columbia Athletic Club. As was the case in such games, college students in their late teens or early twenties were pitted against well-developed, mature, and experienced players. The semiprofessionals were not only more physically developed, but they also had no reason to refrain from violent play. They did not have to answer to college faculties, presidents of opposing colleges, coaches, or conferences. They just had to win. In Washington the Columbia Athletic Club turned the big event into a violent and tragic affair. Targeted by Columbia, the Georgetown quarterback George "Shorty" Bahen suffered a paralyzing broken vertebrae. Though he lingered into January, Bahen died of his injuries; even before he died, the Georgetown faculty abolished football.[29]

An even more highly publicized fatality would occur three years later in a game between the Universities of Georgia and Virginia in Atlanta, when a Georgia player, Richard "Von" Gammon, was killed in a line-bucking, or pushing and pulling, play. This tragic event led to movements both in Georgia and Virginia to ban football. Shocked by the event, the Georgia legislature went so far as to pass a bill to prohibit football in the state and presented it to the governor for his signature. In a turnabout that would periodically occur, a relative, in this case Gammon's mother, intervened and persuaded the governor not to sign the bill. In Richmond a petition campaign among women soon fizzled as well, though the effort itself showed that fatalities could cause shock waves beyond the locale of the injury. As for the tendency to exonerate football and look upon a fatality as an act of God or an unlucky combination of circumstances, such attitudes may have typified a period when cholera and typhoid still took the lives of college students or when high rates of infant and child mortality remained common.[30]

The most notorious act of football violence, Hinkey's violent late hit against Wrightington in the Harvard-Yale game in 1894, did not result in a fatality, but it might as well have. It is hard to say whether Hinkey's act or the number of injured players received more coverage, but the notoriety of the game and Hinkey's violent assault reinjured football's image. The reaction to this game also illustrated how northeastern football cut a wide swath in sports pages across the country and how a broken collarbone at the Yale-Harvard game could elicit more extensive comment than the death of a player in Washington or Georgia. A similar incident occurred the same year when a Michigan player wantonly jumped on and seriously injured a Kansas player after he had crossed the goal and scored a touchdown, an act that the officials failed to see or ignored. The incident in Kansas also received far less publicity. Nevertheless, as long as the possibility of death or paralysis stalked the gridiron, presidents and graduate advisors had to recognize its gravity. One college president frankly confessed: "Formerly when I saw a man get laid out in a game, I felt sorry but I was rather anxious to have the game started again. Now my first thought is how can I square it with his mother"—indicating that deaths and serious injuries had begun to alarm college presidents.[31]

Thus, by the mid-1890s the battle lines were drawn, and debate over football would soon become part of the general debate between reformers and defenders of the status quo. Football had become one of the many persistent problems of the late nineteenth century, along with the tariff, corruption, immigration, and, according to one observer, the "servant problem." As with other problems of the age, there was not only political debate but also a search for solutions. Yet the image of football varied according to the traditions of the particular college, the religious affiliation of the institution, the aggressiveness of the alumni, the success of the team, and the degree of violence reported in the media. On the campuses presidents and faculty began to face up to the need for tighter controls. Whereas football might cause public disapproval when deaths or injuries occurred, college personnel had to deal with the problems of football from week to week and season to season. In the accounts of the big games newspapers nearly always reported acts of violence or, conversely, informed the readers that the game had been free of injuries.

The mild reforms such as abolishing the flying wedge gave the game a reprieve that lasted for just about a decade. During that time the awareness of gridiron evils failed to ignite an upheaval but merely caused controversies in the press and local crises when a player like Georgia's Richard Gammon died playing football. The hesitancy in reforming intercollegiate sports paralleled tepid attempts to deal with trusts and political corruption which resulted in mild and ineffectual measures such as the Interstate Commerce Act and the Sherman Antitrust Act. As in those other realms, football enjoyed an uneasy relationship with public opinion which occasionally flared up and then faded after the season or disturbance was forgotten.

Despite its first bout of controversy, college football continued to spread and grow in popularity. Walter Camp's advocacy of football had overwhelmed the criticisms of Charles Eliot and Burt Wilder. Colleges in distant venues cared more about fielding a successful team than in guarding against player injuries and threats to academic integrity. But, as football gained a stronger hold, the protests that had troubled football in the East took place with more frequency elsewhere. The snags and reefs in the turbulent waters of college football would eventually create a crisis of national proportions.

CHAPTER THREE

Spreading Scandal: Football in the 1890s

In 1892 Walter Camp received a request to send a coach to assist Stanford in its second game against California. In March Stanford and California had played the first college football game on the Pacific Coast in San Francisco. The city of San Francisco engaged in a slavish imitation of the big city game in the East. The pregame activities included a noisy parade down streets bedecked with school colors. Tickets sold so fast that the Stanford student manager, future president Herbert Hoover, and his California counterpart, could not keep count of the gold and silver coins. When they finally totaled up the proceeds, they found that the revenues amounted to $30,000—a fair haul for a game that had to be temporarily postponed because no one had thought to bring a ball! The proceeds were also equivalent to what one might have expected from a big game in the East.[1]

Because of his reputation as a football coach and rules maker, Camp received numerous requests from schools that needed a coach to begin a team or simply to receive instruction on the finer points of the game. Normally, he sent a recent graduate to do the job. In 1892 he received a request from James H. Kilvan, an instructor at Notre Dame University in Indiana, who asked Camp to "kindly furnish me with some points on the best way to develop a good Foot Ball team." Originally from New Haven, Kilvan had seen "good many Yale games," and he realized that Camp was an "authority" on the game. He signed the letter, "Your sincere Admirer," and obviously meant to convey more than a mere formality. Kilvan's letter differed from other requests only in that he did not ask Camp to send a coach or to come himself.[2]

When he received the letter from Stanford, Camp decided to break from his normal procedure of sending a former Yale player and to do the coaching himself. He and his wife, Alice, set off for the West Coast and spent several weeks at Stanford. For the Camps the trip west was a vacation. In contrast, Stanford regarded the game as the most important of its season, a crucial step in promoting its image. Despite his expertise, Camp could only manage a tie with California.

Later that year a contributor to Camp's book, *Football Facts and Figures,* proclaimed that "ten thousand people saw the game between the Leland Stanford University and California on Thanksgiving day, and there is no longer any doubt about the popularity of football out here on the Pacific

Coast, and among our most cultured people." This pattern of rapid growth proved typical. Yale's version of college football spread rapidly in the 1890s through attempts on the part of schools new to football to imitate the big games in the East and to draw eastern players for a year or two of coaching the team. The excesses of big-time football at these institutions reflected attempts to recreate Yale's successful athletic program at smaller, less-developed institutions. And many of Camp's disciples made up the first generation of professional football coaches, sowing the seeds of big-time football in other parts of the country. To give an example, it was Camp's former player Lee "Bum" McClung who coached the California team that opposed Camp in his first stint at coaching Stanford.[3]

Football's Diaspora

In 1892 one of the most influential of those disciples, Amos Alonzo Stagg, carried the Yale system to the Midwest, or "West," as it was then called. Distilled from Camp's procedures at Yale, the Stagg approach to coaching and athletic administration at the University of Chicago became the prototype of college football administration. Stagg came to Chicago as the result of its president, a former Yale divinity professor, William Harper, who persuaded oil billionaire John D. Rockefeller to donate a huge sum to jumpstart his university. Harper then recruited well-known faculty members and embraced novel ideas such as extension courses and institutionalized athletics. He not only planned to incorporate physical education into his curriculum but also hoped to use football to create the best-known university in the Midwest.[4]

Influenced by Yale's history of athletic success, Harper wanted to build a winning football team to instill the school tradition that his new institution would inevitably lack. In his classes at Yale and at Chautauqua Institute in western New York, where he ran the summer program, he had worked with a remarkable athlete, a dedicated Christian like himself who now coached at the International YMCA school at Springfield, Massachusetts. Harper made up his mind that his former student, Amos Alonzo Stagg, would head up the Department of Physical Culture and Athletics at Chicago and serve as football and baseball coach.

As a poor boy of working-class origins, Stagg had early on exhibited outstanding athletic ability and driving ambition. He dreamed not just of attending college but of matriculating at Yale, and in 1882, after two years of preparing at Philips Exeter Academy, he entered Yale, at the age of twenty-two. For the next six years he played baseball and football and in 1888 won a spot on Camp's first All-America team. He could easily have gone on to play professional baseball, but, instead, the pious Stagg planned to become a minister.

When his six years at Yale ended, Stagg began to waver on his long-held clerical ambitions. Claiming that he could not speak in public (though he later excelled at it), Stagg enrolled at the YMCA school at Springfield, Massachusetts, an institution that trained its students to become athletic instructors for the YMCA spreading evangelical Christianity by means of athletics. As the school's football coach, Stagg had compiled an outstanding record against small and large college competition. And, though the school had a total of only forty-two students, the "Christians" under Stagg nearly defeated Yale, his alma mater.[5]

Approached by Harper in 1892, Stagg was promised not only an ample salary but also support for the athletic program at the University of Chicago. In keeping with his belief in institutional athletics, Harper made Stagg a tenured faculty member, placed him at the head of the athletic department, and encouraged him to build a prominent football team. "I want to develop teams that we can send around the country and knock out all the colleges," Stagg later recalled Harper proclaiming. "We will give them a palace car and a vacation." In other words, he wanted to send the team on the road to advertise the school.[6]

Harper had undoubtedly observed Walter Camp's dictatorial control at Yale—his czar system. By making Stagg a department head and a tenured faculty member, Harper may have tried to avoid Camp's undefined power as de facto head of Yale athletics. Camp operated behind a student athletic association that served as a cover for alumni control—his own control. By placing athletics under institutional control, Harper's system was designed to avoid the problems caused by high-handed alumni. Harper gave Stagg the power to run athletics at Chicago, but he also created a board of control to keep an eye on athletic policies and finances. He hoped that his plan of athletic checks and balances would keep baseball and football from causing problems for the president and faculty. But, if Harper thought that he was avoiding a Walter Camp, he underestimated his new physical director. Authoritarian and grasping, Stagg would create headaches for the president and the faculty.[7]

Nevertheless, Stagg did accomplish Harper's goal of building a strong and prominent team. Lacking a full complement of players, Stagg himself played quarterback during the first season, since, without conference eligibility rules, he could play on both the football and baseball teams. Stagg also persuaded students to construct a fence around the field so that he could collect admissions. In his third year he defeated the redoubtable University of Michigan, and, at the end of the season, he took his team on a remarkable trip by rail to the Pacific Coast, where Chicago played Stanford in a precursor to the Rose Bowl. After a hair-raising trip across the frigid, snow-covered Rockies, Stagg's Chicago team defeated Stanford by a 24-4 margin. Only three thousand spectators saw the game, which resulted in returns of a mere $1,099.35. In order to finance the trip home, the team played a second game against Stanford in Los Angeles, which they lost 12-0, and games against semiprofessional athletic clubs in San Francisco and Salt Lake City.[8]

By the mid-1890s Stagg's teams had overtaken Northwestern as the premiere sports attraction in Chicago. And the annual Thanksgiving game with Michigan which he started became not only a source of revenue but also of local prestige and publicity. In 1896 the game held in the friendly confines of the Chicago coliseum yielded gross revenues of $10, 812, a record for games in the Midwest. More important, the big game became a late-autumn society event that attracted the wealthy and prominent acquaintances of William Harper, potential friends and patrons of the fledgling university.[9]

As Harper watched his vision of a powerful football team rapidly mature, his commitment to football became as unshakable as if he presided over Yale or Princeton. Like a captain of industry, he defended football from those who saw it as a source of injury and death. "If the world can afford to sacrifice lives for commercial gain," he wrote, "it can more easily afford to make similar sacrifices on the altar of vigorous and unsullied manhood." In other words, deaths and disabling injuries could be brushed off as easily as those in the industrial sector, where there had been so few attempts to regulate working conditions.[10]

Unfortunately, Harper's great contribution—his attempt to take Walter Camp's informal athletic system and encase it in a department of intercollegiate athletics—only partially succeeded. His coach Amos Alonzo ("Lonnie") Stagg, a professional version of Walter Camp, ended up frustrating his plans at the same time he fulfilled them, an omen of what could happen when other colleges placed athletics under institutional control. In theory the department of physical culture should have been subject to the controls of other departments that had to answer to the faculty and the president. Stagg stubbornly refused to allow the athletic board to exercise control, and, when it asked to examine the eligibility of players or showed any sign of asserting its authority, he complained vigorously to Harper. While Stagg created a winning football program, he frequently quarreled with other institutions and stretched the rules on awarding assistance to athletes to their limits. Through football Stagg put Chicago in the limelight but often seemed more interested in his own reputation than in the institution that employed him. Beginning as an evangelical Christian who worked with athletes, Stagg matured into a big-time football coach who refused to allow any interference by university authorities in his bloated athletic domain and often appealed to President Harper for special treatment. By 1906 his large salary as coach and physical director made him one of the highest-paid members of the Chicago college community.[11]

In the early 1890s football was spreading across the country like a late-twentieth-century computer virus. For the most part there was no master plan, though the inevitable progression toward eastern-style organization was always on the agenda. Not only did most of the early coaches come from eastern schools, but the rules they had to rely on came from Walter Camp's annual guide. Yale graduates, however, did not stand alone in supplying gridiron mentors. In 1893 some students from Washington University in St. Louis who wanted to begin a football team approached A. L. McCrae, who had spent a year at Harvard and was teaching physics at the University of Missouri. Agreeing to their request for a game, McCrae found enough students at Missouri and practiced with them once for a Thanksgiving game in St. Louis. Similarly, Parke Davis, a Princeton graduate who had "entered college undersized, underdeveloped, and in very poor health from all study and no play," played college football at his alma mater and then migrated to Wisconsin, where he served as coach and athletic director. He was followed by Princeton's All-America, Phil King, who had helped Princeton to upset Yale in 1893 and who continued to coach Wisconsin into the early 1900s.[12]

Similarly, Vernon Louis Parrington, a former scrub quarterback from Harvard who was teaching English at the University of Oklahoma, organized a team in the 1890s, in the former Indian territory. Parrington, who later became a major figure in English literature and won the Pulitzer Prize, taught the Harvard system of wedges and tackle-back formations and organized cheering. Dressed in a gray cap and tweeds, he trotted up and down the field behind the team critiquing their play. Speaking with perfect diction, he demonstrated cross-blocking on the windswept field and rolled brown paper cigarettes when he finished his instruction. Faculty like Parrington who helped out in football's early stages did so out of conviction. In those first few years there was no struggle for the soul of most western universities because football itself struggled in its infancy to survive. Alumni and boosters in outlying areas had not yet taken control from the students and faculty, though they soon would become a factor.[13]

Before the 1860s and even for some time after, the tedium of college life often seemed to bring out the worst in students. Acts of vandalism and personal violence were not uncommon, and students delighted in pranks at the expense of the president and administration. Students fouled the daily chapel with smoke, tore up fences and boardwalks, rang the college bell in the middle of the night, and smashed windows in college buildings. In the South they occasionally killed or seriously maimed members of the college community, as when a faculty member was shot to death by a student at Virginia in the 1830s. Nevertheless, some college presidents and faculty tolerated or encouraged football because they believed, like Eugene Richards, that it channeled the often antisocial tendencies of students and built loyalty among alumni.

As athletics gained a following, students directed their energies toward sports both as players and spectators. When they arrived on campus, they embraced the athletic teams with near-hysterical enthusiasm. One instructor at Beloit College in Wisconsin reported that football had welded the students into a "compact whole, and given them a unity of feeling and purpose such as rarely seen here." He added that the role of football in developing college loyalty was enough to justify its presence on campus. An eastern college president, Joseph Tucker of Dartmouth, observed that the athletic frontier was where the inner university and outer world met. "It was as easy," he wrote, "to cross this line from without as from within." Like his western colleagues, Tucker perceived that football and baseball brought together the conflicting interests of students, alumni, and townspeople, sometimes even making believers of presidents and faculty.[14]

Eventually, "big men" on campus became football and baseball players, not scholars, to the extent that one alumni magazine would ask, lamenting, where were the bonfires and cheering when student published an article or returned with honors after studying in Paris or Berlin?[15]

Athletic enthusiasm spilled over into other extracurricular activities such as journalism. Formerly literary magazines that contained shreds of outdated campus news, college newspapers in the 1890s began to take their cue from the city dailies and filled at least one page and sometimes more with football and baseball articles. If a big game was to be played, the editors plastered the front page with enticing news and predictions. Editorials encouraged the students to show more enthusiasm and to cheer more vigorously. When the teams won, the newspapers waxed euphoric, as the headlines at Ohio State indicated after a victory over Kenyon College:

What's the Score
Why Twenty to Four
Kenyon College on the Floor
OSU for evermore.[16]

At Wisconsin Professor Joseph Pyre, who had played football himself at Wisconsin, remarked upon the profound change in campus life since the 1880s. Just a decade before, Pyre recalled, male students lived in austere rooms and rarely possessed expensive clothes such as suits. "Now there are plaid suits," he wrote, " pink collars and green neckties, and vests." Coeds came to dances bedecked in resplendent and expensive gowns. Male students converted their rooms into dens, spent money on elaborate carriage rides, and went to balls and to the theater. Whereas they used to retire to literary societies to read or debate, students no longer talked of profundities or engaged in intellectual discussion. Instead, "month after month [students discuss] no questions of politics, of books, of life, art, ethics, but thrash over the same touchdowns week after week."[17]

But no professor could deny that a winning football team built enrollment. While exaggerating its school's academic credentials, the Kansas student newspaper correctly saw winning football as a potent recruiting tool. Despite faculty and course offerings equal to eastern schools, the reporter declared, the truth was that "a crack foot-ball eleven or a winning baseball nine" had a powerful effect in attracting students. After a 7-0-1 season, the Kansas newspaper argued that the "influence and result of our football victories can hardly be estimated . . . It has advertised the University more than an outlay of a thousand dollars could have done in any other way."[18]

In addition, the enthusiasm over football victories created paroxysms of excitement and newfound popularity for university heads. After a heroic victory by the University of Kansas, featuring a run by the Kansas halfback the entire length of the field, Chancellor Francis Snow delivered a rousing speech and basked in the winning limelight. When Tulane went undefeated and unscored upon in 1901, President Edwin Alderman, who had gone all out to promote the team, happily took credit for the outstanding season. Presidents who remained wary of the new fad taking the West and South by storm were careful not to reveal their misgivings—and, more often than not, displayed unbridled enthusiasm. Alderman declared that he would rather see a "boy of mine on the rush line fighting for his team than on sideline smoking a cigarette." The president of Miami of Ohio even urged all young and active faculty to go out for the football team, while the president of a southern school, Florida Agricultural College (later the University of Florida), scrimmaged with his own football team.[19]

Without fully realizing it, inexperienced faculty and presidents were setting themselves up to be held hostage by alumni and boosters. Many college football teams in their early days operated on a shoestring and were forced to appeal for outside help. The athletic association at Indiana University regularly went bankrupt and had to pass the hat before the first game or in mid-season, and Indiana was not alone. Unlike at Harvard, where expensive leather suits replaced lace jackets or smocks, football uniforms at lesser schools like Indiana consisted of quilted pants and light, unpadded jerseys. Players often had to play in their own clothing and devise ingenious forms of footwear by using an old pair of boots or shoes with cleats nailed to the soles. While shin and nose guards were available in the early 1890s, players outside the East could not afford this protection. Eventually, they turned to alumni and boosters as proven sources of support, selling subscriptions before the start of the season or arranging for wealthy patrons to pay the expenses of indigent players.

Given the initial precariousness of athletic revenues, new teams quickly followed the examples of Harvard, Yale, and Princeton by relying on big Thanksgiving Day games in cities like Richmond or Kansas City to supplement their meager budgets. And for colleges that treated football as a "science," schools soon found they could reap immediate dividends much as Stanford and California had done in their first big game. Those profits, however, required a winning team— and, increasingly, the schools would find, creating a winning team meant importing players who had no formal connection with the college, attended no classes, and left the school as soon as the season ended.

Like other college sports, football posed as an amateur sport. Gentlemen sportsmen like Walter Camp and his counterparts in the East rejected the notion of engaging in football or baseball for pay. Despite a brief foray as a college student into summer baseball, Amos Alonzo Stagg had spurned the tawdry atmosphere of a life in professional baseball to prepare for the ministry and then to coach at a YMCA school. The conflict between amateur and professional had created rifts in American sports almost from the beginning. In baseball and later in football the original teams played as amateurs but were supplanted by semiprofessional tramp, or vagabond, athletes, who rode the rails during the depression of the 1890s and played baseball or football for room, board, and expenses, comfortably accommodated at the college or in a local hotel.

Not surprisingly after its troubled history in the East, the more rapidly football spread, the more often reports of abuses surfaced. Taking their inspiration from semiprofessional summer baseball, players mysteriously began appearing on college football teams, sometimes enrolled but often having no formal connection, and then departing after the big game on Thanksgiving or at least by the end of the semester. At the University of Michigan in 1894 seven out of the eleven members of the starting lineup neither enrolled in school nor attended any classes. Occasionally, the tramp athletes jumped from one team to others during a single season, probably as the result of being offered higher sums to play by alumni or boosters. Historian Frederick Rudolph relates that the Oregon team was startled to see a single player on three different teams in three successive games.[20]

While he was a law student at West Virginia in the mid-1890s, the future "point-a-minute" Michigan coach, Fielding Yost, moved temporarily from West Virginia to compete for Lafayette in its big game against Pennsylvania, then returning to play and get a law degree from West Virginia. By the time Yost began coaching, he knew firsthand about the ineligible players known as tramp athletes. When he coached at Kansas, Yost did what came naturally. He produced an unknown player to help crush the University of Missouri in their Thanksgiving game. When the team returned to Lawrence, the hero had unaccountably vanished.[21]

Some of the tramps were a threat to ordinary players because they were not only older but also more physically mature, not unlike modern professional athletes. In Georgia Tech's game with Georgia in 1893, a powerful guard named Wood dominated the game for Tech. Like an oversized army mule, Wood pushed and pulled through the Georgia defense for three touchdowns. Irate and rowdy spectators yelled insults at the referee and hurled rocks from a nearby plowed field at Tech players. When a large stone opened a three-inch gash in his head, Wood wiped the blood off on an opponent. With Wood in its lineup, Georgia Tech won easily.

As Patrick Miller has shown, the thirty-three-year-old Captain Leonard Wood was an army surgeon recently returned from the Indian wars against Geronimo's Apaches in the Southwest. According to a later campaign biography, the future general and presidential contender went to a local hotel after the game and sewed up his wound. Like other vagabonds, he was not enrolled at the institution he represented.[22]

Yet the public, which got its information from newspaper accounts of the big games, became far more aware of injuries to players on the field of play. Except to faculty and a few presidents like Charles Eliot, violence seemed a far more compelling argument against football than the perversion of college values. Thus, the recurring public criticisms of the 1890s stemmed from controversies over violent and unsportsmanlike play or from injuries. The worst moments of crisis appeared like sudden storms such as when the unlucky college student, Richard "Von" Gammen of Georgia, lost his life playing football in a game against Virginia in 1897.

Violence in 1890s football games or as a result of college, class, or racial rivalries was also notorious and not confined to a single region. Students often found ways to injure one another without ever taking the field. At the University of Wisconsin in 1898 an undergraduate student shot a fellow student in the foot because he had not supported the team. Pitched battles at or after the games sometimes took place among armed and violent southerners. The first game between two African-American colleges in Tennessee degenerated into a race riot provoked by drunken whites and resulting in the death of one black spectator.[23]

At about the same time, Vanderbilt engaged in a near bloody riot when it played the University of Nashville. Having recently begun a medical department, Vanderbilt recruited the medical students to play against Nashville, which also had medical students on its roster. A Vanderbilt player took out his frustration on Nashville by slugging a fellow medical student in full view of the crowd. As the contest became more violent, spectators spilled onto the field and engaged in their own battles, forcing the officials to suspend the game. When the game resumed, students brandishing knives and canes threatened to create a still more violent scene. Reports of the game found their way into eastern newspapers and resulted in an investigation by college authorities.[24]

A worse, and potentially lethal, encounter occurred a few years later in South Carolina. The annual college rivalry between Clemson and the University of South Carolina spun dangerously out of control when Clemson cadets became resentful at South Carolina's insults after losing to their in-state rivals. At issue was a transparency paraded through the college town of Columbia showing a South Carolina Gamecock crowing over a Clemson Tiger. Armed with bayonets and swords, Clemson cadets marched to the campus, where thirty South Carolina students waited behind a low wall with clubs and cocked pistols. By pleading with the students, the South Carolina coach gained a few valuable minutes, allowing faculty and police to reach the scene. At length the authorities helped to negotiate a truce. As if it were just a game, the two sides then ended up cheering for each other, evidently oblivious to the bloodshed that had nearly occurred.[25]

When these battles royal occurred, the impetus was usually a heated rivalry or a big game played off campus. A group of rowdies wielding stones and bricks attacked the Oberlin team as they were leaving the field after a game in Cleveland. Students frequently engaged in drunken brawls such as the uproar in the New York theater district after the Yale-Princeton game in 1893, when students disrupted a musical revue and others fought on the street, leading to a number of arrests. So unsavory were the on-field encounters such as at the Harvard-Yale game at Springfield in 1894 that police began to patrol the sidelines. Faculty who attended a conference at Brown University in 1898 called on colleges to play athletic contests on or near their campuses. Not long afterward, in 1903, Harvard completed Soldiers Field within walking distance of the main campus, a forerunner of the Yale Bowl and the massive arenas of the 1920s.[26]

Caging the Gridiron Beast: Attempts to Reform Football

The most extreme solution to the problems on and off the field was to abolish football altogether as an intercollegiate sport. Schools in the 1890s, such as Trinity (later Duke), Alabama, Georgetown, and Columbia, each abolished football for varying lengths of time because the sport appeared to interfere with academic work and collegiate values. In the 1890s some faculties still possessed enough power or the boards of trustees were skeptical enough to nip football in the bud. However, few presidents in the 1890s (and in later years, as we will see) were so willing to court the unpopularity that almost always accompanied abolition.

In 1894, soon after Charles Eliot had unleashed his first anti-football barrage, President Henry Rogers of Northwestern, a Methodist clergyman who was president of a Methodist institution, broached the possibility of abolition. Before acting, he decided to consult with the presidents of major colleges. To get a cross-section of opinion, Rogers sent out inquiries to presidents at major football-playing colleges in the East and Midwest, including Charles Eliot of Harvard, William Harper of Chicago, and James Smart of Purdue, asking them to comment on abolishing football. Possibly as a means of stimulating discussion on abolition or as a prelude to abolishing football at Northwestern, Rogers asked the presidents for their opinions on whether an institution acting alone could reasonably expect to abolish football.

The presidents who responded to Rogers were decidedly skeptical about the possibility of a single school abolishing football. James Smart of Purdue replied that athletics had become so entrenched that a college president would have difficulty rooting them out. In keeping with his thinking in the fall of 1894, Smart strongly supported reform of athletics but hinted that football might be abolished if there were no reforms. Charles Eliot doubted that any school could by itself abolish football—his belief no doubt resulting from failed attempts at Harvard. Of the presidents that Rogers queried, only William Harper of Chicago unequivocally rejected the idea. He assured Rogers that Chicago would continue to play as long as two or three institutions remained to compete against. As a result, Rogers backed off from the idea of abolishing football at Northwestern in the 1890s. Instead, Northwestern would attempt to strengthen its football in the late 1890s and early 1900s, thereby profiting by its city rivalry with Chicago.[27]

Rather than attempting to abolish football, most presidents who fretted about gridiron excesses would attempt to regulate football by acting through athletic conferences. By the 1880s colleges in Ohio and Indiana had already established conferences similar to those in the East, loose alliances of institutions which attempted to regulate the worst abuses in baseball and football. In Ohio and Indiana college presidents passed rules against violence and unsportsmanlike conduct such as slugging and swearing and also took steps to prevent tramp athletes by passing stricter eligibility rules. In Indiana the college presidents in 1894 insisted on a number of sweeping changes to control violence and eligibility. These reforms included rules confining contests to college grounds and banning semiprofessional players who either played under assumed names, had played as professionals, paid for pay, or were ineligible because of poor academic standing.

In the same year President James Smart of Purdue went a step further. To go beyond the state conferences President Smart proposed an interstate conference made up chiefly of public institutions. Smart may have been inspired by laws passed by Congress prohibiting corrupt practices of railroads and corporate monopolies in interstate commerce. It is also important to note that his proposal would lift the best-known institutions in the region, including Purdue, out of purely state athletic conferences and link them in a regional athletic alliance.

At first glance Smart appeared to be attacking the problem of tramp athletes and semiprofessional teams. Examined more carefully, his plan also would have protected Purdue football revenues. Though the Indiana colleges had limited ordinary games to college campuses, the best teams were scheduled to play a championship game in Indianapolis at Thanksgiving—in this particular year, DePauw and Purdue. To President Smart's dismay a militia unit, an artillery company with a semiprofessional team, threatened to stage a competing game in Indianapolis, which, unlike New York, could barely accommodate one game on Thanksgiving. Smart learned that the artillery company would seek out Butler University of Indianapolis to play, and, if Butler refused to participate, the University of Illinois would be next on its list. Immediately, Smart dashed off a letter to President Theodore Draper of Illinois.[28]

In his letter to Draper, Smart insisted that the abuses in athletics extended beyond state boundaries just as Congress had legislated on business in the Interstate Commerce Act restricting railroad abuses five years before. Smart made the novel proposal—at least for college football—that representatives from major public and private schools meet in Chicago early in 1895.

After writing President Draper, Smart also wrote more specific letters to presidents of institutions in Wisconsin and Illinois, and his proposals brought enthusiastic responses, and in January six schools—Purdue, Illinois, Wisconsin, Chicago, Northwestern, and Lake Forest—met in Chicago. (The next year Michigan would replace Lake Forest, and three other schools would later join to complete what became known as the "Big Nine," or "Western Conference".) Calling themselves the Intercollegiate Conference of Faculty Representatives, the schools agreed on the principle of faculty control of athletics. Following the model of the Indiana Athletic Conference, they restricted games to college campuses and forbade players to accept pay or gifts. Not surprisingly, the conference also attempted to rid the Midwest of tramp athletes by drawing up a definition of eligibility. In theory, if not in practice, Smart's conference isolated college football from the taint of professional groups such as the Indianapolis artillery company. The conference also protected an essential source of revenue from professional encroachment and attempted to elevate football to a strictly college and amateur game.[29]

The Intercollegiate, or Western, Conference (known informally as the Big Six, Big Nine, and later the Big Ten) served as a blueprint for athletic reform. At the same time, however, it left the door ajar for the exciting contests between major football teams which would lift the new alliance above the state conferences. By bringing together the largely public institutions from adjoining states, the founders of the conference enhanced the moneymaking possibilities of interstate rivalries, especially when the games were played in Chicago. It is doubtful, however, that the college presidents of the fledgling conference had a clear vision of how lucrative football in the Western Conference in and near Chicago would become.

In the East football had become more entrenched and impervious to change. Because Yale dominated eastern football, their competitors found it difficult to cooperate because any changes that did not include Yale would place their teams at a disadvantage. Walter Camp, who dominated Yale athletics, distrusted faculty control and refused to address their grievances about the exaggerated role of football in college life. Yale possessed an advantage in her system of training and control which Camp did not want to surrender. In fact, her competitors had to respect Yale because games with such a successful rival attracted large crowds and generated much revenue. By the same token the gridiron alumni of Harvard and Princeton hungered each year to defeat the near invincible Yale eleven.

In the 1880s and early 1890s it was common for schools to have faculty athletic committees, but gradually many of those committees were enlarged or restructured to include alumni and students. Even at Harvard the non-faculty members outvoted the academic members, and the Board of Overseers had to authorize any changes, such as the abolition or reform of football. The change in the composition of the athletic committees represented a loss of control by faculties, who had once disciplined or controlled their students. In an era in which faculty loyalty still rested with the colleges that employed them rather than with their professions, the faculty sought to win back a measure of that control.

As controversy surrounding college football escalated, so did the faculties' opposition. Objections to students who spent too much of their time following football and too little on their studies became commonplace. Most of the opponents also disliked the methods of training in football which had little in common with education and bore more resemblance to the commercial practices of semiprofessional athletic clubs or professional baseball. In the 1890s many athletic clubs, such as the Columbia Athletic Club in Washington, fielded teams made up of tough and mature athletes whose behavior on and off the field made a mockery of the amateur ideal. These groups differed little from professional baseball teams that enjoyed an unsavory reputation in the 1890s because of the gambling, drinking, violence, and rowdyism that often took place at their games.

On February 18, 1898, faculty, alumni, and undergraduates from seven eastern schools, later to form the Ivy League, met at Brown University to discuss the state of athletics and to attempt to fashion reforms. The most influential participants, members of a committee that composed its final report, consisted of faculty headed by Brown's Wilfred Munro, who hosted the conference. Possibly influenced by similar meetings of midwestern schools, the faculty attempted to influence the course of athletic, largely football, policy. Only mighty Yale, still under the sway of Walter Camp, who clung to his view that faculty control "runs amok on the question of rules, regulations, and statistics," refused to attend. The initial report of the day's meeting strongly condemned the effect that college athletics had on academic life and the evasions of the amateur ideal. Affirming the principle of faculty control, the delegates made about twenty recommendations.[30]

Professor Munro of Brown and other faculty members were not breaking new ground. Earlier efforts by Harvard and Columbia to deal with athletic problems had failed to get off the ground, but the persistent complaints against college football and baseball finally convinced the faculties that they had no alternative. The unruly behavior of players and spectators at a game in New York four months earlier between Brown and the Carlisle Indians may have jolted Munro and his colleagues into action. Spilling out on the field in the midst of the players, the crowd blocked two fine runs. Then, near the end of the game, unruly Brown players began slugging their opponents, while irate spectators threatened to take the field and set off a full-scale riot.[31]

As at the conference in Chicago, the delegates at Brown specified control of athletics by faculty-controlled committees. After all, the faculty had a direct mandate from the Boards of Trustees to operate their colleges and considered themselves best able to make athletic policy and to carry out crucial decisions. In the opinion of the delegates the alumni were the enemy—they blamed the alumni for much of the acrimony between the colleges. As for the students, the faculty held them only responsible for mismanagement of athletics.

Among the Brown conference's recommendations was the establishment of faculty-dominated committees to approve any and all football retainers, from coaches to managers, captains, and trainers. The faculty should also have the right, the committee held, to examine team schedules and to approve any students who participated in more than one sport. Yet the delegates to the Brown conference made it clear that they preferred to avoid the headaches of athletic administration. They allowed the alumni and managers to retain these functions.

The delegates at the Brown conference were strongly committed to amateur athletics—no athlete should receive pay or gifts. And in a further attempt to close the loopholes on tramp athletes the conference specified a one-year probationary period before a student could play and forbade sleight-of-the-hand transfers from one part of the university to another. Potential college athletes would also have to pass entrance requirements.[32]

The Brown conference also made some proposals designed to downsize the bloated, commercialized football programs: the attendees wanted to make more tickets available to students; called for all contests to take place on college grounds; opposed out-of-season practice, such as sessions in the summer or in September, before school began; and insisted on banning training tables, which they put in the same category as pay-for-play.

Unlike the meeting in Chicago, which was sponsored by college presidents, the Brown conference faced a minefield of opposition from eastern presidents and alumni. Before adjourning, the conference appointed a special committee to tone down the original draft in hopes of making it more palatable to the boards of directors. The second draft, however, did not win the approval of a single institution, all of which evidently distrusted faculty control. Of course, if a majority of the colleges had given the thumbs up, the conference recommendations still would have proven difficult to enforce. Yale's absence placed the first and last nails in their coffin.[33]

Unrealistic as its goals were, the Brown, or the Munro, conference, as it has also been called, demonstrated many faculty members' profound discontent with big-time college athletics. The delegates were clear-headed men who saw big-time athletics honeycombed with evils. And, while it failed to persuade the presidents or boards, the Brown conference in February 1898 injected a powerful note of discontent into the dialogue over eastern college football—which would only grow more shrill in the early 1900s.

Schools for Scandal, 1898 to 1905

Though the Brown conference failed to enact reforms, some of the seven institutions eventually succeeded in putting the rules into effect. In the case of Columbia University it required a gridiron scandal before the faculty and administrators woke up to the problems of football corruption. Columbia University had abolished football in 1891 but decided to resume the sport in 1899. Since the faculty—as opposed to the institution—had subscribed to the Brown reforms, Columbia might have been expected to adopt a carefully supervised, faculty-controlled, low-profile program. Instead, the athletic association hired a former Yale standout, George Foster Sanford, at a remarkably high starting salary of thirty-five hundred dollars, a sum that was probably subscribed by alumni and supporters and which would later be raised.

Except in the earliest games, big-time college sports in the 1890s were never entirely free of what contemporaries loosely referred to as "professionalism." This term encompassed semiprofessional players who competed for athletic clubs, college players who received money or perks to play, or simply the large number of spectators who paid high ticket prices to watch the big games. In some sports such as crew, colleges hired professional coaches as early as the 1870s, and by the early 1890s recent eastern college graduates often served as paid seasonal football coaches for one or two years. William Harper of Chicago set a new precedent by paying a generous salary to a talented and ambitious football coach, Amos Alonzo Stagg, conferring legitimacy on him by appointing him to the faculty and making him physical director, the late-nineteenth-century version of the modern athletic director.

In an age that prized "gentlemen-amateurs" like Walter Camp, Columbia coach Foster Sanford represented a wholly alien concept, the highly paid, single-sport coach who was hired solely to create a big-time football program. The coaching job at Columbia in 1899 eventually carried a hefty salary of five thousand dollars. In many respects Sanford was a perfect candidate for the job, a remarkable athlete who knew a great deal about football and especially about Yale's vaunted system. Sanford played football for only a single season at Yale, in 1891. Nevertheless, he became well-known as a player and assistant coach. Playing next to the great W. W. "Pudge" Heffelfinger, Sanford invented the "roving center," who did not simply snap the ball but also defended the ball carrier and pursued the ball on defense. A superb athlete, Sanford could place drygoods boxes on the shelf and break them with his elbows. For a big man he had exceptional speed and could sprint "like a deer." He specialized in foot races and supported himself for a summer in England out of prize money from running in local races. After receiving a law degree from Yale in 1897, Sanford served in the Spanish-American War. Following the war he took a job in New York, and Columbia hired him after hours to coach its team, much as Walter Camp left his job early to coach the Yale team. No doubt Sanford was hired not only for his coaching ability but also because he knew the Yale system.[34]

Before Sanford arrived at Columbia, in 1899, the undergraduate manager assembled the ingredients of a powerful team. The arrival of big-time players at Columbia, an urban school without a team or a gridiron tradition, suggested either a miracle or blatant disregard of the rules, and the latter proved to be the case. The student manager, William Mitchell, had lured several top-notch players by paying their tuition, board, and incidental expenses, all of the amounts stated as loans to the players. He had managed to recruit other players working in the New York area who had no interest in registering as full-time or even as part-time students. To do this, he kept two sets of financial books, one that showed that he had underpaid visiting teams the share of the profits guaranteed them by Columbia. He misrepresented the amounts that backers had subscribed to the team so that he could use the monies to help with his system of subsidies. Put simply, Mitchell had operated the first recorded slush fund, or secret payment system, which would become common in later years. Though Mitchell may have had help in setting up this system, the faculty athletic committee held him responsible and relieved him as student manager. In addition, Columbia expelled him in the spring of 1900.[35]

Not surprisingly, the team achieved remarkable success in its first year. Fortified by a paid coach and top talent, Columbia scheduled major eastern teams such as Yale and Princeton. Sanford took the team to summer practice at his father's farm in upstate New York, an act that directly violated the letter and spirit of the Brown agenda, and the manager scheduled some of the top eastern teams. In Sanford's first year at Columbia his team shut out Yale, 6-0. Yale charged that Columbia watered down the field, neutralizing the speed of Yale's offense, but newspaper reports indicated that Sanford's team played a strong game. According to one report, Yale was "outrushed, outtackled, outkicked, outgeneraled and outplayed at every point." In his second year Columbia lost to Yale but defeated Princeton, 6-5, an amazing feat for a team in its second year. In Sanford's third and final year Columbia knocked off Pennsylvania, as it turned out a weak Penn team, and otherwise had a mediocre season.[36]

The revelations that erupted in the spring of 1900 cost Sanford his reputation—and, ultimately, probably his job. Sportswriter Caspar Whitney reported that Columbia was playing at least four "ringers," who were being given tuition and expenses. The faculty athletic committee later dismissed two players who, they declared, failed to meet amateur standards. Two other players, a special student in political science and a second-year law student, were removed from the team. The administration of President Seth Low and the faculty had appeared blissfully ignorant of how its freshly minted football program mounted a winning team in 1899. The faculty athletic committee wrote to Low that it "has been demonstrated that college authorities can no longer afford to ignore the existence of athletics."[37]

Instead of conveniently disappearing, two of the players admitted to being ineligible, or, more precisely, defended their integrity. The two indignantly wrote to the newspapers to "emphatically deny the current rumors that we received any pecuniary or educational benefit from playing football with Columbia last season." They did not attend lectures, they declared, and never had any intention of formally enrolling. "We played as a favor to Columbia," they wrote angrily, "and at great sacrifice to our business." One of those ringers was Sanford's first All-American, William Morley, who in 1905 coached at Columbia. In spite of the Columbia faculty's assent to the Brown principles, they had allowed the very evils that their representatives had earlier condemned to take place under their noses.[38]

Barely a month later a financial crisis and internal dissension overtook Columbia athletics. The football program was four hundred dollars in debt, and no money was available. According to newspaper reports, lesser sports had sopped up all the surplus from football's profits. Graduate or alumni coaches in other sports complained that Sanford's exorbitant salary had drained the athletic treasury. Sanford managed to avoid the blame or at least the penalties for hiring ineligible players. Yet the faculty and graduate advisors at Columbia and other schools assumed that Sanford knew that he was playing "professionals." When Nicholas Murray Butler, a foe of football, became president in 1901, Columbia rid itself of its big-time coach and reclaimed his exorbitant salary by dismissing him at the end of the season.[39]

Sanford appeared to personify the eastern version of the professional coach, a figure that gentlemen-amateurs of the football world held in low esteem. Bill Reid, who coached in 1901 and 1905 to 1906 at Harvard and became a key figure in the football reform movement of 1905, doubted that the professional coach was capable of setting a decent moral example. "The man who coaches as a regular thing," Reid wrote, "is likely to be a man of trifling ambition and small ideals, very often not a college graduate, and often lacking in the finer instincts." Among those "evils" proselytizing or recruiting, tripping, slugging, filthy talk, and coaching from the sidelines particularly stood out. The worst class of coach, Reid believed, differed little from professional baseball players or boxers whom the upper-class athletic elite regarded with disdain. Actually, youthful college coaches sometimes could not control their players or, for that matter, their own behavior. At the University of Kansas one coach was fired for swearing at his players and another for fornicating with a freshman coed.[40]

While Sanford never engaged in crass or immoral behavior, he acquired the reputation as a "mucker coach" who would resort to unethical practices in order to win. Sanford paid dearly for his stint at Columbia, becoming the bad boy of eastern football and earning the undying enmity of the Yale football elite. "That is why I am so bitterly and unilaterally opposed to professional football coaching," he later declared. "I was eager for the law. I took to it strongly, and I believe I had a future in it. But that easy $5,000 for a short season's work, that and the virus of the game killed my aspiration and nearly ruined my whole career."[41]

Sanford not only paid dearly, but he also learned from his experience; he never again coached for pay, and when he later coached at Rutgers from 1913 to 1923 he became a highly respected figure on campus. Yet Foster Sanford's problems as a youthful coach and his disastrous stint at Columbia illustrated an inconsistency in the system. While football programs professed amateur ideals, they also placed an enormous premium on winning. Athletic revenues and the school's reputation seemed to depend on it. The team could not be sure that amateur talent would keep the edge necessary for victory, and amateur standards constantly warred with the market-style approach needed to produce football stars.

Among the eastern preparatory schools Andover and Exeter were football "feeders" for Yale, Harvard, and Princeton. The preparatory school alumni learned of poor boys with exceptional athletic skills and used their graduates to recruit them. Talented baseball and football players such as Amos Alonzo Stagg worked their way through these elite secondary schools while waiting on tables or cleaning classrooms. Each of the Big Three schools had recruiting ties to the major prep schools, which sometimes used former stars to help out with their coaching. Occasionally, the prep school athletes were more than simply callow schoolboys. James J. Hogan, for example, later captain of the Yale team, entered Exeter at twenty-three. "He was certainly old enough to know his own mind," the journalist Henry Beach Needham observed, "for he matriculated [at Yale] at the age of twenty-seven."[42]

Though from a poor family, Hogan lived in the finest dormitory. He also took a free trip to Cuba with the Yale trainer, Mike Murphy, and was given the lucrative franchise of representing the American Tobacco Company on campus. According to an official of the company, the player talked up the cigarettes to his friends. "They appreciate and like him; they realize that he is a poor fellow, working his way through college and they want to help him," a company official declared. "So they buy our cigarettes, knowing that Hogan gets a commission on every box sold in New Haven." Asked if other Yale students had this opportunity, the official responded that they did not—Hogan's job was simply an experiment.

The same articles described the Princeton booster Charles Patterson, a self-styled recruiter notorious for his sojourns at Exeter and Andover, a foreshadowing of later fanatic football booster. Patterson, a zealous Princeton alumnus, made it his business to seek out top football material at the two prep schools. As an undergraduate in the 1880s, he had left Princeton without graduating but later returned and was known as the "oldest living undergraduate," and in 1901 received a Master's degree, perhaps to ease him off campus. Patterson's first snare was a lineman named James L. Cooney, the son of a Pennsylvania coal miner, who entered Exeter at twenty-one. Cooney had passed his entrance exams for Harvard and was poised to enroll, but Patterson continued to try to sell him on Princeton, "pestering" him with offers of scholarships and opportunities to earn money.[43]

After having told friends he was going to attend Harvard, Cooney abruptly enrolled at Princeton, where he became manager of an eating club and received exclusive rights to sell scorecards at baseball games. Contrary to Princeton's story that it simply needed a tackle to fill a vacant spot, the article insisted that Patterson had convinced Cooney to attend Princeton because he was a coveted, blue-chip player. "Mention recruiting to the officials of Princeton, and they are the first to speak Patterson's name," the reporter Henry Beach Needham added wryly. "Then they bitterly decry his bald methods, declaring that he has done Princeton incalculable injury."[44]

Next, Patterson descended on Andover, determined to recruit any student who had football potential, no matter what his class status. He set out to convince students who were one or two years from college to go ahead and take the entrance exams. When the Princeton exams were held in 1902, thirty-one students showed up for the exam, many of them football players and some of them sophomores and juniors. The assistant professor sent from Princeton to monitor the exam excluded only four of those whose class standing should have excluded them from the exam. Later the headmaster asked one of the younger students why he had taken the exam. "You are a long way from college," he remarked to the student. "Well, Professor," the boy replied. "At the top of my paper I wrote my weight—205 pounds. I guess I'll pass all right. Patterson said I would."[45]

The student passed the exam but wound up playing football for Yale. Even "the oldest living undergraduate" could not counter the Yale mystique. In the meantime the student left secondary school academically unprepared for college. While the articles in *McClure's Magazine* deplored Patterson's practices, the writer also found the system at fault. Hogan and Cooney were "victims of a vicious system, subsidized through no fault of theirs, stand before preparatory school boys as successful college men." The writer further asserted that Hogan and Cooney, as subsidized athletes corrupted by commercialism, "have no proper place on college teams." What the author left unsaid was the role of the major eastern colleges in tolerating these practices.[46]

Deaths, Injuries, and Violence

Less than a week before the Brown conference met in February 1898, the battleship *Maine* exploded in Havana harbor, and within two months the United States declared war. Many of the expansionists of the 1890s who clamored for war with Spain, men such as Theodore Roosevelt, Oliver Wendell Holmes, and Charles Francis Adams, staunchly upheld football because they believed that football built tough bodies and manly character. Roosevelt went off to Cuba with a regiment of Rough Riders composed of cowboys and college athletes, and by year's end the United States had gained possession of several Spanish colonies, acquiring a "splendid little empire," to paraphrase the words of Secretary of State John Hay.

In the aftermath of war the debate over college football grew more intense. Between 1898 and 1904 the public became more concerned with the brutality and violence. Ironically, the success of the Spanish-American War did not translate into a vote of confidence for college football. To the contrary, a tidal wave of Progressive reform in the early 1900s propelled the football controversy that had persisted for the past decade into a national gridiron crisis. The partial rules reforms of the early 1890s seemed to demonstrate that the rules committee had merely swept the problem under the rug by abolishing mass and momentum plays but not spelling out the illegal actions or specifying that guards and tackles had to line up at scrimmage.

While the flying wedge plays had been legislated out of existence in 1894, the remnants of momentum plays remained in formations in which linemen such as guards and tackles lined up in the backfield. Once the ball was snapped, they pushed and pulled the ball carrier, often a tackle or a guard, through the defensive line. More popular in the East than the Midwest, these mass formations, known as tackle back and guards back plays, proved effective in moving the ball. Increasingly, critics of football, especially of eastern football, held the grinding line play responsible for fouls, brutality, and injuries. Probably mass play was more responsible for slugging at scrimmage because the officials had difficulty seeing the violations. Undoubtedly, acts of brutality occurred in the tangled mass of bodies that lined up at scrimmage, often engaging in combat near the point where the ball was put in play. By the same token the absence of a clear definition of when the ball was actually dead led to downed ball carriers trying to crawl to eke out a final yard and opponents jumping on them to prevent their progress.

Whether football was becoming more deadly remains questionable. According to a professor at the University of Illinois in the early 1900s, Edwin Dexter, whose findings were based on responses to questionnaires sent to fifty-eight colleges, only one in thirty-five students who played football suffered injuries serious enough to keep them out of the classroom. Of the 22,766 engaged in football over a ten-year span, from 1893 to 1902, Dexter reported that only 2 percent had been seriously injured—and, of those, only three had died as a direct result of injuries suffered on the field. Unfortunately Dexter, who had a clear pro-football bias, failed to show the causes of deaths or the names of the victims; he also failed to document the injuries that he cited. While Dexter's study had numerous defects, he was correct in his conclusion that few players died in college football. With the growing interest in football and larger numbers playing, more fatalities would have occurred if it were as murderous and brutal as critics portrayed it. Mass plays may have been controversial or even boring, but the injury and fatality rates in college football (as opposed to high school and sandlot) probably remained stable or actually declined. Players on the top eastern teams who specialized in mass play may have suffered from light concussions or broken limbs, but none died from their injuries in the 1890s or early 1900s.[47]

While Edwin Dexter may have correctly diagnosed the injury problem, he failed to appreciate the public's growing concern about any fatalities in football. Increasingly, the public refused to tolerate even the relatively low death rate that Dexter suggested, much less the larger number of deaths and serious injuries that were thought to occur. Measured against higher standards of public health and safety, college football appeared to be growing more dangerous. If Dexter's findings had any validity, other factors must have been at work.

What factors could have caused the public perception of football as an increasingly brutal and murderous sport? To start with, newspapers rarely tried to tally the numbers of deaths, and, when they finally did, the figures that met the reader's eye tended to be deaths at all levels of play. Dexter later referred to this phenomenon as "newspaper hysteria," a term that standpatters readily embraced and critics of the game dismissed as hypocritical. Newspaper reports still failed to define, and in some cases actually distorted, the causes of serious injuries and fatalities. In a letter to a New York sportswriter, Chancellor Francis Snow of the University of Kansas tried, in 1896, to correct the report that a Nebraska player died in a mass play. Not so, according to Snow. In reality the doomed player, who weighed only 150 pounds, was making a run-around end for a touchdown. He was crossing the goal line, when a Doane College player threw him to the ground. According to Snow, the real cause of the player's death "was his being out of condition," since a head injury in the previous week's game with Kansas had knocked him unconscious. Snow made a strong case that the first injury, possibly a concussion, left the Nebraska player more susceptible to a second fatal head injury. If Snow was correct—and he probably saw the earlier Kansas game—the newspaper account gave readers the misleading view that a player had died from mass play.[48]

In theory the use of protective equipment, grudgingly accepted by players in the 1890s, should have cushioned the players against certain injuries. A. G. Spalding, the former baseball player who had created a mammoth sports supply combine and who subsidized Walter Camp's guides to football rules, advertised nose masks and shin guards. Football rules prohibited any hard substance such as metal which might place opponents in danger, but the softer padding undoubtedly was an improvement over unprotected flesh and limbs. Since the American public would demand increasingly higher standards of safety, one might expect that the use of equipment would become more prevalent and would safeguard players against the most serious injuries.[49]

Nevertheless, this equipment—and especially the football helmets—suffered from numerous drawbacks. The "head harness," as it was called, did not come into general use until the early 1900s, and even then many of the players refused to wear "helmets," complaining that they added weight and interfered with their hearing. Some traditionalists objected to equipment made of harder sole leather because they believed that it both introduced an element of danger and interfered with playing the game. Writing to Walter Camp in 1906, a former player objected to shin guards, heavy shoes, leather shoulder pads, nose guards, and, of course, leather head harnesses. He despised these accessories as dangerous and criticized the playing of "cripples" who required the loathsome padding.[50]

It is even possible that protective equipment reinforced the negative image of football. The grotesque, foreboding look of football players with helmets and nose guards, frequently appearing in cartoons and drawings, probably created exaggerated notions of football violence. By the late 1890s critics of football referred to players as "gladiators," and the word *gladiatorial* appeared in the first version of the Brown conference report. Occasionally, critics coupled their criticisms with references to "gladiatorial" equipment. When the list of casualties mounted in 1905, cartoonists pictured players going to their deaths in the modern gridiron version of the Roman Coliseum. Ironically, the gladiatorial image of football players clothed in protective equipment may have contributed in an unintended way to reform of the rules by reinforcing the negative views of football.

And what part did the rules committee play? Critics would later skewer the Intercollegiate Football Rules Committee for its unwillingness to reform the rules by redirecting play away from the line and into the open field. Sponsored by the New York Athletic Club and made up of representatives of the major eastern schools, the self-perpetuating committee of football rules experts rested on a weak foundation. It was not so much that the committee did not attempt to make changes but, rather, that the numerous football-playing institutions had no input. Eventually, this closed system of eastern rules makers from the older, big-time schools caused festering resentment and vehement criticism. Initially, the system resulted in threats by the Big Nine to create its own rules committee, which it started to do in 1897. Though the rules framed by the midwestern schools varied only slightly, the threat of a fragmented system may have been enough to push the reluctant committee into action.[51]

Inspired by Walter Camp, the rules committee responded to the midwestern malcontents by inviting Amos Alonzo Stagg to join the committee in 1898. Stagg turned down the invitation, pleading a heavy load of obligations. Yet the attempt to recruit him proved to be a shrewd move on Camp's part because the Chicago coach had led the move to revise the rules in 1897 and was critical of eastern rules making. The invitation to the influential Stagg may have helped to pacify the increasingly restive westerners, and eventually, in 1904, Stagg did agree to join the committee.

Because the rules makers had helped to shape the existing game, they saw American football from the standpoint of a successful, finished product and proceeded slowly in making changes. As a result of increasing pressures, however, in 1903 the committee made some moves toward creating an open game. One significant change, a harbinger of the revolution of 1905–12, required seven players to be on the line of scrimmage between the twenty-five-yard lines. Moreover, the quarterback, who previously took the snap, could now carry the ball into enemy territory (a line of scrimmage did not yet exist) as long as he was five yards from either side of the spot where the ball was put in play. By allowing him to cross scrimmage, the committee was departing from the long-standing rule that the quarterback had to hand off the ball or lateral it after receiving the snap from the center. Similarly, other players, such as backs, guards, and tackles, who first took the ball had to veer five yards to the side before crossing the imaginary line. These rules forced the ball carriers to the outside while they were in the midfield area. When the offensive team reached the twenty-five-yard line, the rules reverted to the old-style, bone-crushing line play. In the final analysis the committee members wanted to make sure that teams reaching the "red zone" would have to score under the old rules.[52]

This simultaneous experiment with two sets of rules reflected the cautious nature of the committee—and especially of its consummate diplomat, Walter Camp. The participants seemed to be saying: "Yes, we have attempted to look at the problem scientifically; we have set aside half of the playing field for new styles of play." Curiously, the committee's new rules required vertical as well as horizontal lines—to determine where the quarterback crossed the line of scrimmage—so that a portion of the playing field now became a checkerboard rather than a gridiron. Typical of the committee's tinkering mentality, the delegates then altered the seven-man rule that applied in midfield. In 1904 only six players had to be on the line, but the seventh lineman, if he became the fifth man in the backfield, had to play outside the final player on the line. Presumably, this lonesome back position would prevent the fifth back from leading interference on mass plays. Of course, the play still reverted to the old rules when the ball reached scoring territory, allowing five men at any point in the backfield. To be sure, some of these experiments gained full acceptance after the crisis in 1905. Indeed, the new rules reflected tepid experiments marking the debut of an era that would eventually bring revolutionary changes.

In addition, persistent complaints about unsportsmanlike play such as slugging and kneeing had tainted the image of football since the 1880s. The committee paid some attention to this problem from 1898 to 1904 but, as it turned out, not nearly enough. In 1898 the rules decreed that teams committing fouls would have to forfeit the ball and would be further penalized ten yards. The committee also gave officials more latitude in penalizing personal fouls. Nevertheless, the effectiveness of the rules depended on the competence and impartiality of the officials, a lesson that would prove costly to the national committee in 1905, when failures in officiating contributed to the hue and cry against football.

In spite of these changes, public opinion was rapidly outpacing the cautious experiments of the rules committee. Prophetically, a letter to the *New York Times* in 1904 remarked that the agitation against football would *not* die a natural death, unlike the outcry against football in the 1890s. An editorial in a Sioux Falls, South Dakota, newspaper declared that the current football season was "about as productive of casualties as was the recent Spanish war." The homicidal and brutal elements of football, all to gain possession of an inflated piece of leather, must be controlled.[53]

In early 1905 the South Dakota House of Representatives passed a bill to disqualify players who committed injuries, an act that was deemed freakish by the *Daily Maroon,* the student newspaper at the University of Chicago. Within a year, however, the faculty senate at the reporter's own school would itself try to ban football altogether. Along with several other Big Nine universities, faculties would force a showdown on football that would go much farther than the South Dakota bill. The student reporter was not the only gridiron enthusiast who failed to see that football was living on borrowed time. From Walter Camp at Yale to Theodore Roosevelt in the White House, friends of the game would soon face the most serious crisis that had yet confronted college football in its brief but tumultuous history.[54]

CHAPTER FOUR

Football's Longest Season: The Fall of 1905

During October 1905 President Theodore Roosevelt, having just intervened in a national coal strike and the Russo-Japanese War, turned his formidable attention to another kind of struggle. The president, a gridiron enthusiast who avidly followed the fortunes of his alma mater, Harvard, summoned representatives of the eastern football establishment—Harvard, Yale, and Princeton—to the White House. He wanted to discuss brutality and the lack of sportsmanship in college play.

Theodore Roosevelt believed strongly that football built character, and he believed just as strongly that roughness was a necessary, even desirable, feature of the game. In 1894, while a civil service commissioner, Roosevelt received a gift of *Football Facts and Figures* from Walter Camp. In his note thanking Camp, Roosevelt deplored the anti-football outlook of Harvard's Charles Eliot as well as Eliot's attempts to drop football. Being an intensely loyal Harvard fan, Roosevelt worried that Eliot might do the "baby act," as he once described it, and abolish football. He valued football, Roosevelt declared, above all sports. "I would rather see my boys play it," he said, "than see them play any other." And injury, he expressed, was neither detrimental to football nor exclusive to it.[1]

In his own life Roosevelt reveled in the rough sports in which he had taken part and even relished the injuries that he had received. "Since I left college, I have worked hard in a good many ways, and sports has always been a mere accessory to my other business," he declared, "yet I managed to ride across the country a good deal, to play polo, and to shoot, and the like. I was knocked senseless at polo once, and it was a couple of hours until I came to. I broke an arm once riding to the hounds, and I broke my nose another time, and out on the roundup I once broke a rib and at another time the point of my shoulder."[2]

After reading Camp's *Football Facts and Figures,* Roosevelt concluded that risks to college boys were minimal. He declared that more fatalities had taken place in college boxing than in football. He also commented that the "double runner sled is about twenty times as dangerous as the gridiron field." As a result, he displayed contempt for milk-toast reformers such as Charles Eliot and E. L. Godkin. In his letter to Camp he quoted his new friend and future president William Howard Taft, a Yale graduate, who said he preferred reformers "who ate roast beef and were able to make their blows felt in the world."[3]

Roosevelt and Football: Changing Attitudes

Roosevelt's infatuation with rugged sports dovetailed with the crisis of modern society which alarmed him and other hardy aristocrats. The trend toward leisure and luxury, they insisted, had sapped the spirit of a once sturdy frontier people. Like his fellow advocates of a tough, manly character, he worried that Americans would fail to develop the physical and mental strength to stand up to predatory powers or third-world hordes. "We were tending steadily in America," he wrote, "to produce in our leisure and sedentary classes a type of man not much above the Bengalee baboo." To Roosevelt football served to revitalize an effete population physically and mentally unprepared to defend themselves or take their place on the world stage.[4]

What did worry him about football was the brutal and unsportsmanlike way in which it was played. To Roosevelt brutality meant extreme and intentional violence that went beyond merely a hard tackle or an aggressive line play. No doubt he heard the complaints of Harvard alumni about Hinkey's brutality against Wrightington in the Harvard-Yale game in 1894. In this same letter to Camp, Roosevelt deplored the game's needless roughness and speculated on ways to prevent it. In spite of Roosevelt's distaste for brutality, he still feared the results of reform, especially if they should happen to emasculate football. He would even go so far as to tolerate brutality and lack of sportsmanship, he insisted, rather than to see football abolished, a back of the hand to President Eliot and other squeamish reformers.

Between 1895 and 1905, as he rose to the pinnacles of power, Roosevelt's life changed drastically. Not only did he become president, but he also raised a family indoctrinated with his views of the rugged life. In 1905, because his sons played the game, he paid far more attention to eastern football and concluded that the game was growing too violent. Roosevelt still believed that football built character, but he worried that brutality and lack of sportsmanship destroyed the good effects of football. As he had done in deadlocks between management and labor, he was prepared to intervene to bring about a more wholesome spirit of competition.

A persistent myth holds that Roosevelt saved football in 1905 by threatening to abolish it if the colleges did not enact reforms. At the beginning of the 1905 season, after seeing a newspaper photo of Swarthmore lineman Bob Maxwell's bloodied face, so the story goes, Roosevelt threatened to end football if it were not reformed. Unfortunately for a good story, President Roosevelt had already taken steps to hold a football conference at the White

House before Maxwell's injury. Nothing about the player or the game seems to have been said publicly or in private to the gridiron experts whom he summoned to the White House on October 9, two days after the first Saturday of the 1905 football season.[5]

Roosevelt could not have ordered an end to gridiron violence or football even if he had wished to do so. With the exception of the service academies, he had no authority to issue edicts binding the colleges or altering their athletic policies. As Roosevelt clearly indicated, he had no desire to abolish a sport that he regarded so essential for building toughness and character. In contrast to wielding the big stick, Roosevelt's approach to reform in this case, rather, was to "speak softly" to members of the football establishment. Yet he hoped that football would be shorn of its most violent and dangerous aspects.

In June and July 1905 the journalist Henry Beach Needham, a friend of Theodore Roosevelt, published two sensational articles in *McClure's Magazine* in which the journalist delved into the scandalous world of eastern college athletics. Needham joined a select group of *McClure's* muckrakers which included Ida Tarbell, who had documented the abuses of John D. Rockefeller, and Lincoln Steffens, who had revealed the corruption of big city political bosses. Noted for their careful research and documentation, these journalists exposed moral and practical problems that threatened the well-being of American society. Roosevelt publicly criticized them, bestowing the name *muckraker* in a fit of pique. Deplore as he might their penchant for describing the dark side of American society, Roosevelt depended on these journalists to supply him with the sordid facts to dramatize his crusades. Roosevelt met with Needham in the summer of 1905 when the *McClure's* articles first appeared, and he soon shared Needham's outrage with the deterioration of eastern college athletics.[6]

Even before they appeared, Needham's articles caused concern among the eastern schools. The secretary of the Yale corporation, Anson Phelps Stokes, wrote to *McClure's*, asking the magazine to suspend the article "until allied facts on which it is based be carefully scrutinized." Samuel McClure might well have laughed at the gentlemanly request to put Needham's articles on hold. No less than big business, corruption in college athletics sold magazines. Like Steffens and Tarbell, Needham had compiled a ripe store of sensational revelations.[7]

The implications for football at the major eastern collegiate institutions were evident as soon as the first segment appeared. Needham chronicled the activities of Princeton's Patterson and the rise of Cooney and Hogan from their humble beginnings. He also portrayed the Foster Sanford era at Columbia in its worst possible light. Though Needham described the evils of summer baseball, abuses in football accounted for most of the first article. Needham argued that football had become the big business of college athletics; he described cutthroat competition existing between the schools which resembled widely condemned corporate excesses—he even calculated the revenues that college received from athletic events, mainly from football. Throughout the two articles Needham seldom strayed from his contention that systematic violations of the amateur ideal contributed to the tawdry big-time athletics. Colleges professed one set of ideals but lived by a quite different set of practices.[8]

Needham spiced the first article with some choice examples of tramp athletes who had played with two or three colleges in a single season. One athlete who began the season playing for Pennsylvania State College (now Penn State) played so well against the big-time University of Pennsylvania that he jumped teams overnight. On the Monday following the game he practiced with Penn, and, though ineligible under the Big Three agreements, he still played three games for his new team. Needham also described other instances of Penn players pirated from various schools. The left end for the Quakers played five years for Middlebury College before joining Penn, and another player had competed for both Colorado College and Lafayette before appearing in Philadelphia. Needham alleged that Penn virtually "kidnaped" a promising schoolboy from a nearby prep school to replace a departing All-American guard. After he arrived, Pennsylvania authorities shifted him among the professional schools, beginning with the dental school, where no entrance exams were required, and then moving him to the Wharton School of Finance and Commerce.[9]

Other muckrakers set standards of morality against which to measure the lack of performance of city politicians, manufacturers, and financiers. Needham's agenda was to reveal the practices of college teams and the actions of behind-the-scenes manipulators, who, like the cunning and rapacious corporations and political bosses, were undermining college athletics and through the same sort of underhanded practices. Nowhere did Needham attempt to condemn big-time athletics or call for their abolition. Rather, he insisted that honesty in college athletics meant strict adherence to the amateur athletic code. No wonder Roosevelt liked Needham's approach. Strict amateurism and a spirit of fair play fit Teddy Roosevelt's own code of muscular morality.

Needham did not dwell on brutality, but he did cite one memorable example in which the star for Dartmouth's football team, an African American, suffered a broken collarbone early in a game against Princeton. Afterward an Andover teammate of the Princeton quarterback who had inflicted the injury, himself also African American, confronted the offender. Aware of the large southern contingent at Princeton, the former teammate, who was now playing at Harvard, accused the quarterback of acting out of racism.[10]

Needham reconstructed the conversation:

"At Andover," the Harvard player challenged him, "You used to say that race or color does not count: it is the stuff in the man."

"I stand by that now," his former teammate coolly replied.

"No, you don't, Princeton doesn't believe it," the Harvard player retorted, "'and I'm afraid you have absorbed Princeton ideas ... You put him out because he is a black man.'"

"We didn't put him out because he is a black man," the Princeton player said indignantly. "We're coached to pick out the most dangerous man on the opposing side and put him out in the first five minutes of the game."[11]

Theodore Roosevelt: Football Reformer

Soon after *McClure's* published the first article, Roosevelt had a chance to bring up athletics in a commencement speech at Harvard, where he conveniently coupled deplorable conduct in football with blatant disregard of principles in industry. When he stepped to the podium on June 28, Roosevelt spared neither business nor athletics. Speaking before a capacity crowd of twenty-five hundred, he made a plea not only for Harvard graduates to apply college ideals to their future business careers and strive to become more than "glorified pawn brokers." In like manner, he called upon them to take up arms against sensationalism and professionalism in college athletics. Just as the "malefactors of great wealth" (as he later termed them) violated the spirit of the law, the lords of the diamond and the gridiron were violating the sacred code of sportsmanship. Both were to be deplored.[12]

Back in the 1890s Roosevelt had criticized lack of sportsmanship but dismissed the demands for football reform. Convinced now that athletic problems cried out for change, the president was ready to act. And two months later, in September 1905, he received a plea from Endicott Peabody, his son Kermit's headmaster at Groton, writing on behalf of the heads of eastern private schools, asking for something to be done to combat the evils in eastern collegiate football.

Peabody proposed a meeting of the Big Three, and Roosevelt immediately consented. Though presidential intervention in athletics had no precedent, Roosevelt had accustomed the public to the unexpected. Before he became president in 1901, American presidents seldom acted in domestic or foreign matters without the advice and consent of Congress. Roosevelt pioneered a new presidential style. He used the presidency not only as a "bully pulpit" but also as a behind-the-scenes power center to break up political logjams. Since becoming president, he had intervened to bring about a settlement in the 1902–3 coal strike and had mediated a peace treaty that ended the Russo-Japanese War, a conflict that threatened American interests in the Far East. The end of the war between Russia and Japan occurred just before the president became involved with college football; it perhaps made him think that he could motivate pigskin potentates in the same way that he had done with the Russian and Japanese governments.[13]

Roosevelt also had a keen personal interest that season in the problems of eastern football. His eldest son Ted, he realized, might possibly be playing for the Harvard freshmen, and young Kermit competed for Groton. As a lineman, Ted was small, at 5'7" and less than 150 pounds, for the rugged line play of eastern college football; Roosevelt realized that Ted would compete only as a freshman because his relatively small size would keep him from making the varsity. Though he approved of Ted's gridiron ambitions, Roosevelt had some fatherly concerns about his vulnerability. Later in the season the president admitted to his son that the First Lady, Edith Roosevelt, worried about her son's safety and hinted that he shared her anxieties. "Still, though I would not have had you fail to play, and think it was a mighty good thing for you," he wrote to Ted, "I sympathize with mother in being glad that after next Saturday your playing will be through."[14]

Even if partially moved by family concerns, Roosevelt still acted in a power broker style that he normally reserved for matters of state. He invited six football insiders from Harvard, Yale, and Princeton—the head of the alumni committee and the football coach from each institution. The six representatives included Walter Camp and John Owsley of Yale, Bill Reid and Edward Nichols of Harvard, and John Fine and Arthur Hilldebrand of Princeton. On October 9 the six powerful gridiron figures—plus one "outsider" invited by Roosevelt, Secretary of State Elihu Root, a Yale graduate—sat with the president around the dining room table at the White House.

Roosevelt opened the meeting by citing some examples of unsportsmanlike conduct by each of the colleges. These included linemen being coached to break the rules and a player who was said to have faked an injury to mislead the opposing team into attacking him rather than another player who actually had been injured. According to Bill Reid's account of the meeting, "[Walter] Camp made some considerable talk but was very slippery and did not allow himself to be pinned down to anything." The Princeton and Yale men denied knowing anything about the episodes described by the president.[15]

After lunch the group retired to the porch and continued to talk, while the president took care of national business. When he returned, Roosevelt asked the three senior representatives to draft an agreement on their train trip home. And, indeed, the three dutifully drafted a statement in which they agreed to carry out "in letter and spirit the rules of play." They pledged they would follow what was already in the rule books and would honor the spirit of the rules. There is no evidence that Roosevelt threatened to abolish football. To comply with the president's request, Walter Camp, the best known of the six, released the preliminary draft of their agreement to the press.[16]

On October 10 an editorial in the *New York Times* expressed a favorable view of Roosevelt's intervention: "Having ended the war in the Far East, grappled with the railroad rate question . . . prepared for his tour of the South and settled the attitude of his administration toward Senator Foraker, President Roosevelt to-day took up another question of vital interest to the American people. He started a campaign for reform in football." Roosevelt later remarked that he found his attempts to resolve the conflicts in football more complicated than settling the Russo-Japanese War. Certainly, those attempts proved less successful.[17]

Unfortunately for the president, football did not lend itself to mediation as readily as diplomacy or politics. By singling out football, Roosevelt's intervention had an unintended effect. As if by publicly acknowledging that serious defects existed, Roosevelt gave legitimacy to past and future criticism and spotlighted a debate on football injuries which had been ongoing for a decade but had never received so much attention in so many parts of the country.

Of course, this criticism probably would not have swelled to such a tidal wave without the events that accompanied the 1905 season. Just before the White House meeting, a riot occurred between the Columbia and Wesleyan teams in the first game of the season, when a Wesleyan player kicked a downed Columbia ball carrier in the stomach. Players charged onto the field, and Coach William Morley, who had starred in the Foster Sanford era, became entangled in the fracas (possibly he helped to curb the violence, but there are indications that he may also have thrown a punch). The game resumed only after police restored order. Later in the season, when Harvard played Pennsylvania in a particularly rough game in Philadelphia, the Harvard center, provoked by a Penn player who kneed him persistently, slugged his antagonist in the face. The referee ejected him but seemed to take little notice of the fact that the Quakers had soaked the field so they could take advantage of their longer cleats, a practice sometimes used by the host team to give it a home court advantage. Pennsylvania won the game 12-6.[18]

As for the results of Roosevelt's intervention, the memorandum drawn up and signed by the Big Three after the White House Conference became virtually a dead letter in the final month of the season. If Roosevelt expected it to have an effect, he gave no sign and never publicly rebuked the Big Three. Like his intervention, it had no force in law, nor did it embrace the other institutions that played Harvard, Yale, and Princeton. Roosevelt was trying to alter a pattern of behavior which had existed since the 1880s in college football, and the pledge of the Big Three simply proved inadequate to bring about change. The events in the final four weeks of the season would amply demonstrate that players and coaches bent on victory needed more than good intentions to break the skein of brutality.

As the season progressed, the incidents between Pennsylvania and Harvard proved to be a prelude to more grave episodes. In the Harvard-Yale game the Harvard freshman Francis Burr was fielding a punt. After Burr called for a fair catch, two Yale defenders ran into him; one of them, Yale's Jim Quill, "struck him square in the face" with his hand, breaking his nose, while another player probably delivered a body blow with his feet which knocked Burr "senseless" for a moment. The official who should have called a foul, Paul Dashiell, happened to teach at the Naval Academy and also chaired the Intercollegiate Football Rules Committee, the same committee that Camp so skillfully manipulated as secretary and editor of the annual rules guide. But, although Burr's nose was gushing blood, Dashiell refused to call a penalty. Notoriously partial to Yale, Dashiell claimed that the referees had detected no intentional blow to the punter's face.[19]

Harvard coaches and football fans seated near the field reacted angrily. A storm of hissing suddenly erupted. The venerable Thomas Wentworth Higginson of Harvard's Board of Overseers passed a note to Bill Reid demanding that he withdraw the Harvard team from the field, but the Harvard coach ignored Higginson's demand, and the game continued. Reid later complained that the Yale players were even rougher in the second half, using their fists indiscriminately and rarely receiving a penalty. And, when Walter Camp congratulated Reid after the game, the Harvard coach barely managed a handshake with Camp, whom he blamed for the unsportsmanlike play. But the angry storm of criticism among Harvard alumni and officials gathered about the official, Paul Dashiell. Even Charles Eliot in a letter to Roosevelt in December caustically remarked that "Mr. Dashiell is one of the things that has to be reformed." It was a sad conclusion to the lofty rhetoric of the Big Three memorandum drawn up at the president's request in October.[20]

Roosevelt carefully weighed the recent displays of brutality in eastern football. A week before the Burr-Quill episode Ted had suffered a broken nose in the Harvard-Yale freshman game. The Yale offense repeatedly aimed its plays at Ted's position, probably because he was the lightest player on the line. When he heard of the mishap, the president showed immense pride in Ted's gritty play, but, since he was not at the game, he did not know at first the seriousness of Ted's injury. Both father and son scornfully denied the inevitable reports that Yale players had been gunning for the president's son (first lady Edith Roosevelt vehemently disagreed). Yet the series of well-publicized injuries—Ted's injury required surgery—may have convinced the president that he should monitor the efforts to clean up football rather than intervene directly.[21]

In the next month Roosevelt tried to find out who was responsible for the unpunished act of violence against Burr at the Harvard-Yale game. The president tried to keep an open mind. He called Bill Reid to the White House and corresponded with the indignant Charles Eliot. Ironically, Paul

Dashiell, the official who had failed to make the call, was chairman of the national rules committee, the same group closely identified with its long-time secretary Walter Camp. The president listened patiently to Dashiell's explanations but ended up agreeing with Reid and, for once, with Harvard President Charles Eliot, who condemned Yale's behavior. Roosevelt concluded that Dashiell should have called a penalty. If Dashiell had called the foul, Roosevelt pointed out, Burr could have tried to make a free kick for a field goal. By making the late hit, the president had come to agree, the Yale tacklers were trying to put Harvard's kicker out of the game.[22]

Despite Roosevelt's concern about brutality and unsportsmanlike play, he came to believe that the growing public clamor against football had gone too far. He had always favored a middle-of-the-road approach, and football proved no exception. Dismissing the outcry against football as "hysteria," he refused to play a further public role. But by the end of the football season the game of football was itself being brutalized by a host of critics. Whether he liked it or not, the intense criticism of football had gone beyond Roosevelt's attempts to influence good behavior by talking out football problems with football experts.[23]

On November 25, the same day as the fractious Harvard-Yale game, a far more serious and tragic event took place in New York which proved to be a turning point in the campaign to reform college football. In a game between Union College and New York University (NYU) the end for Union, Harold Moore, received a fatal injury in a game that NYU won 11-0. NYU had the ball and was moving it steadily toward Union's goal, using mass plays and variations on tandem plays in which linemen were drawn into the backfield. Moore was playing on the side of the line in which NYU ran the ball and tackled the ball carrier around the shoulders. Just as he wrestled the ball carrier to the ground, another Union player jumped into the play, and his knee probably struck Moore's head. When Moore fell to the ground unconscious, several doctors and coaches from both teams rushed out on the field. One of the doctors ordered an ambulance, but an alumnus with a car offered to take Moore to Fordham Hospital. Though he reached the hospital in ten minutes, the doctors could do nothing to help the stricken player. He died four hours later of a cerebral hemorrhage.[24]

Chancellor Henry MacCracken of NYU, who had already expressed misgivings about college football, telegraphed the senior president of the eastern institutions, Charles Eliot of Harvard, urging him to summon a conference to reform the rules. Eliot refused because he no longer believed that reforms could ameliorate football, especially reforms in the rules of play. "Deaths and injuries are not the strongest argument against football," he responded. "That cheating and brutality are profitable is the main evil." Whereas MacCracken believed that the crisis stemmed from the rules of play, Eliot believed that football itself was the problem—and could not be solved by a change in the rules committee.[25]

Eliot thrust the problem of football back onto MacCracken's shoulders. MacCracken confessed to the faculty and students of NYU that he had "waited for some of the larger and older universities to take the lead to favor either the abolition or the complete reform of football." In his opinion football, the version that had killed Harold Moore, should be abolished.[26]

Since he could not get Eliot to act, MacCracken, joined by his faculty, asked the NYU administrative council to act independently. NYU then sent invitations to all the schools that it had played since 1895. Of the nineteen invited to attend, thirteen agreed to send two representatives (one administrator and one faculty member). In the end twenty-four delegates from twelve colleges showed up. In typical standoffishness President Woodrow Wilson of Princeton declined to attend or send a delegate; he explained that Princeton had its own proposal (no blocking in front of the ball carrier) which could not be compromised by joint action. Harvard received no formal invitation other than the initial plea to Eliot from MacCracken. Yale had never played NYU, and Walter Camp distrusted faculty reformers. As a result, none of the Big Three attended the first of two New York conferences.[27]

To give some structure to the meeting, the faculty at NYU framed questions for the delegates. The first question was whether the colleges believed that the "present game ought to be played," and, if it were not abolished, what steps should be taken to reform it. This issue had already come up before they met on December 8. Columbia University, the largest institution in the country and a participant in the conference, abolished football while the students were on their Thanksgiving break. President Nicholas Murray Butler of Columbia, a friend of Theodore Roosevelt, who considered football "an academic nuisance," used the injury crisis as well as the disruptive effect of football to justify Columbia's action. Butler instructed the Columbia representatives attending the conference to vote against retaining football.[28]

The clamor that occurred in the fall of 1905 and led to the New York conference raises the question of whether college football truly faced a threat to its existence—or whether the number of serious injuries in college football had become serious enough to create a crisis. Historians have sometimes concluded that the controversy, so filled with sound and fury, signified nothing about the survival of college football; if anything, they argue, the gridiron game was so strongly entrenched that nothing could have uprooted it.

Yet in this crisis and the one that followed four years later the participants did not share this conviction, nor did the journalists who helped to fan the flames. The abolition of football by Columbia as well as by Union

College showed that the possibility had become a reality. Even if the delegates to the New York conference did not abolish football, they would have to decide whether to substitute another game or to reform it so thoroughly as to eliminate deaths and serious injuries. The problem of reforming football was rapidly moving beyond the scope of the rules committee's power to control its outcome.

The New York Conferences, December 1905

Meeting on December 8, the first MacCracken, or New York, conference immediately voted on the first NYU resolution of whether to abandon the existing game. This vote would be the most important of any because it had the potential to determine the future of football among the colleges that played in the New York area. Opponents of football included NYU, Columbia, and Union College. Major Palmer Pierce of West Point, future president of the National Collegiate Athletic Association (NCAA), rallied the majority—Army, Fordham, Haverford, Rochester, Rutgers, Swarthmore, Syracuse, and Wesleyan—who wanted to retain and reform the existing game.

By a narrow margin the colleges supported an amended motion to reform rather than abolish football at their twelve schools; they made "football as now played," instead of abolition, their focus. The wording meant that the existing game of football could no longer be played under rules that caused serious injuries. Sensing that the twelve colleges lacked a broad enough mandate to reform the rules, the majority called for a general meeting of all football-playing institutions. Their purpose was to create a new committee to bypass the existing committee dominated by the Big Four—Yale, Harvard, Princeton, and Pennsylvania. In their call for the second meeting the delegates took one radical step; they sought to exclude from it anyone who directly profited from athletics, including coaches, alumni, and hangers-on who had dominated football in the past.[29]

The Intercollegiate Football Rules Committee, as the older committee chaired by Paul Dashiell was called, held a scheduled meeting a few days later. Drawn almost entirely from big-time eastern schools, the committee included Walter Camp (Yale), John Bell (Pennsylvania), J. B. Fine (Princeton), L. M. Dennis (Cornell), Bill Reid (Harvard), and Amos Alonzo Stagg (Chicago), the sole western member. In an effort to respond to the cascade of criticism, the members came up with a variety of proposals. Still secretary of the committee, Walter Camp once again proposed the ten-yard rule by which teams would have to gain ten yards in three downs. He also suggested a ban on tackling below the waist and called for a central board of officials to improve refereeing. Among those present John Bell of Pennsylvania caused the most attention by calling for a forward pass. Bell also wanted to place four of the six backs behind the line and the remaining two with the end men on the line. Only Bill Reid of Harvard refused to support these changes; he was waiting for the proposals from an alumni committee at Harvard which he had set in motion in October.[30]

The members of the rules committee had not met during the season. Hamstrung by Harvard's obstinacy and by radically different viewpoints, they were unable to agree on a program of reform to head off the MacCracken reformers. The rules committee had always acted deliberately, and outwardly it showed no sign of alarm. Its inaction only strengthened the hand of the McCracken conference reformers, however, by giving the impression that they were wedded to the status quo. Even Walter Camp, in a letter to President Hadley of Yale, criticized his fellow members for their failure to act—he doubted that they would approve his ten-yard rule. Yet Camp was so completely wedded to this one proposal that he would have had difficulty sponsoring a full slate of committee proposals. When members of the committee tried to hold a second meeting, Bill Reid of Harvard refused to participate, and the committee decided not to meet.[31]

Faced with the threats to eastern football, the unwillingness of Harvard to cooperate posed a serious problem for the old committee. Gridiron unrest at Harvard appeared in early November 1905, a month after the White House conference had focused attention on football. Bill Reid became alarmed that the Harvard authorities, prodded by President Charles Eliot, might decide to abolish football and that the faculty would strongly support the decision. "The same feeling is to a certain degree prevalent among other college faculties," Reid also noted in his diary. As a member of the football rules committee—what would soon become the "old committee"— Reid wrote that Walter Camp, who had visited Canada to observe the ten-yard rule, which was Camp's panacea for football reform and for heading off more radical measures. Requiring teams to make ten yards rather than five in three downs might open up the game slightly, but the objectionable aspects such as the grinding line play would remain.[32]

To block Camp's initiative, Reid wrote a carefully worded letter calling upon Harvard's graduate athletic association to examine the possibility of reforms. "By getting this letter printed now, and particularly before the Penn game has been played [November 11]," he had noted in his diary, "Harvard will be in the front seat of the band wagon and some of Yale's fire will be stolen." The deliberate alumni appointed a committee to draw up proposals, a group that included Reid, two former coaches, and the highly respected Dean LeBaron Briggs. The committee pondered Reid's design for the remainder of the season. No doubt coached by Reid, they refused to work for reform within the old rules committee but waited to see how the situation would unfold. Still not ready to make their recommendations, they ordered Reid in December to refuse to support any attempt by the intercollegiate rules committee—the old committee—to make premature reforms. When the committee finally met on December 29, Reid scrupulously followed the instructions to withhold his vote.[33]

Even if the members of the old rules committee had managed to agree, it is doubtful that they could have recaptured their influence. No matter what reforms the committee or individual members made, the second Mac-Cracken conference still would have taken place in late December. The first New York meeting on December 8 had stolen the mantle of legitimacy from the discredited old guard. In a speech to NYU alumni on December 11 Mac-Cracken likened the old rules makers to the troglodyte "Grand Dukes of Russia." President Roosevelt, he declared, enjoyed less success with the grid-iron old guard than the czar had with the reactionaries in Russia, and he was prepared, if necessary, to have football, as it existed, abolished.[34]

By the week after the first MacCracken conference college football was under siege. Despite student and alumni protest, the embattled Columbia University president, Nicholas Butler, held fast to his abolition of the game. Students held a mass meeting on December 21 in which they chanted, "To hell with Butler" and "Damn the faculty." On the following day Butler was hissed at by the students when he appeared before another meeting but managed to secure an uneasy truce by promising that he would not permanently abolish any sport without consulting the students.[35]

At Harvard a student, not an administrator, was making news. Harvard tackle Karl Brill announced that he was quitting the game. "I believe that the human body was not made to withstand the *enormous* strain that football demands," Brill declared, and further condemned the game on moral grounds. "It is a mere gladiatorial contest," he insisted.[36]

In the same month as the reform conferences, December 1905, the *Harvard Graduates' Magazine* published an article so highly critical of Yale that it shook the fragile relations between the two institutions. Although it was intended to expose the dichotomy between Harvard and Yale, the article could have applied to the tension between athletics and education within any college or university. Published at the height of the football controversy, the article seemed designed to fan the flames of Yale-Harvard rivalry.[37]

"Will the historian of American education when he comes to write the history of the years from 1870 to 1905," the anonymous author scoffed, "be able to point to any important contribution made by Yale to either educational or administrative progress?" According to the author, Harvard had pioneered the elective system, the case system, and graduate education. Yale would receive credit, he ironically stated, only for "the most remarkable athletic system ever seen in American or English universities and for the 'modern game of football,' developed by Walter Camp." The author ridiculed the comparison of Harvard and Yale to Oxford and Cambridge. Yale had contributed nothing, he declared, to science or to educational method, only to the science of football.[38]

The article further condemned Yale for refusing to cooperate with Harvard in reforming football. Football was not only the tail that wagged the bulldog at Yale but also the dog itself. The author recalled the episode that had occurred in 1894 when Hinkey landed on Wrightington, injuring the Harvard ball carrier and causing a break in football relations. Yale's president, Theodore Dwight, he claimed, did nothing to rebuke Hinkey. In fact, Dwight had applauded him at the next athletic banquet. The author's conclusion: Yale had no commitment to the "world's progress and the spiritual and intellectual uplift of mankind." To the contrary, Yale authorities from presidents to the faculty "have cringed before the athletocracy."[39]

Quoted almost in its entirety in the Boston newspapers, the article distressed Harvard alumni who identified with the success of Yale athletics. Conveniently the author ignored completely the big-time football sentiment that resided at Harvard. Try as it might to clothe itself with virtue, Harvard shared the tainted glory of Walter Camp's invention. While it had not shaped big-time college football, Harvard had enthusiastically collaborated. In seeking to defeat Yale, Harvard or at least its pro-football element would now propose new rules less favorable to Yale. Those changes might prove to be the gridiron equivalent of Charles Eliot's renowned elective system— and, contrary to the article in *Harvard Graduates' Magazine,* later historians of education might consider Harvard's role in the reinvention of college football as significant as Yale's earlier contributions to the American intercollegiate game.

During the last week of the year, on December 28, 1905, slightly more than sixty schools convened at the Murray Hill Hotel. The majority of schools may have wanted reform, but few of the big-name football institutions were among them. None of the eastern football giants such as Harvard, Yale, Princeton, or Pennsylvania appeared at the conference and for good reason. With representatives on the rules committee, they had little to gain from participating. Of the teams that competed against the eastern powers, only Army attended and played a leading role. The major powers of midwestern football also boycotted the meeting. Only the University of Minnesota and its coach, Dr. Henry Williams, had made the trek to New York. None of the schools from the Pacific Coast had sent delegates. What might have struck the observer as a national conference was largely a gathering of smaller eastern and midwestern colleges whose status as football powers counted for little. Only their numbers made them appear formidable.[40]

Most delegates hailed from smaller colleges in New England, New York, Pennsylvania, and Ohio; faculty and a few presidents and chancellors made up the bulk of the representatives. As the distance from New York increased, attendance thinned, but delegates nevertheless appeared from the University of Texas and Colorado College. Max Farrand, a historian and political scientist, had planned to represent far-distant Stanford. At the last moment, however, President David Starr Jordan canceled Farrand's trip, after deciding to turn his back on the rules system altogether and substitute rugby for American football. Perhaps the most unusual delegate was Alexander Pell, a mathematics professor from the University of South Dakota, who began as a Russian Revolutionary and then served as an agent for the czarist secret police. Wanted for murder in Russia and pursued by revolutionary groups, he had changed his name and migrated to South Dakota.[41]

The conference required only nine hours to accomplish the agenda set forth by the earlier meeting. The majority of delegates lacked the authority or, for that matter, the intent to abolish football. Instead of a daylong discussion on whether to keep football, the delegates debated whether to create a new rules committee—and what powers to give it. Though the concept met with approval, the delegates had trouble agreeing on whether they should work with the old committee or strike out on their own.[42]

In the end, led by the moderate Palmer Pierce of the U. S. Military Academy, the conference passed a series of "West Point" resolutions calling for combining the old with a new committee. The delegates set the guidelines for the new committee, which should consist of seven "practical men" chosen to represent various regions of the country, presumably from the assembled delegates. If the old committee refused to cooperate, the new committee would have the right to create an "open game," or, in other words, to create its own rules.[43]

Yet it was hoped that the threat of an entirely new rules committee would persuade the old committee to support drastic changes in the rules. The net result of joining the two committees would be a power-sharing arrangement that would enable the reformers to employ the old committee's expertise. The reformers were correct in believing that they shared common goals with the intercollegiate football rules committee. In words reminiscent of Walter Camp and the old committee, the conference insisted not only on new rules but also on rigorous enforcement by a permanent body of more capable and better-trained officials who would act decisively against brutal acts such as the Burr-Quill episode in the Harvard-Yale game.

Equally important, the new organization—referred to as the Inter Collegiate Athletic Association, or ICAA—pledged to help root out professionalism. At the first New York conference the delegates had opposed "offering inducements to players to enter universities because of their athletic ability" and supporting those athletes while in school. They also condemned proselytizing (or what would come to be known as "recruiting"), as exemplified by Princeton's "oldest living undergraduate." Like the Brown conference, the second New York conference called for an end to the unethical methods of manipulating the system that allowed academic washouts and unregistered players to compete. Recalling perhaps the president's objections, the delegates also mentioned the problem of intentional injuries, such as the episodes in the Harvard-Yale and Swarthmore-Pennsylvania games which had stirred criticism during the 1905 season. Though the conference did not call for faculty control, it was clear that coaches and athletic committees should answer to college authorities for any infraction of the rules. Unfortunately, these proposals never took root, since in its first constitution the members of the ICAA, drawn from numerous athletic conferences, decided to rely on persuasion rather than coercion to promote their principles.

Finally, in an ambitious move the delegates appointed a permanent set of officers, naming Palmer Pierce of West Point as president, and scheduled a second meeting for the following December. Unlike the Brown conference in 1898, the ICAA would perpetuate itself and five years later would change its name to the National Collegiate Athletic Association, or NCAA. Major Pierce, who would serve as president for two decades, later described how the outcry against football had brought his organization into being. "The game of football was under a special fire of criticism," he recalled. "The rules of play were severely handled by the public press. The Football Rules Committee was charged with being a self-constituted, self-perpetuating and irresponsible body, which had degraded a once noble sport to the plane of a gladiatorial contest."[44]

In 1905 the place of football in college life faced a storm of criticism and a series of assaults as had never before occurred. Though it dated from the early 1890s, protest against big-time college athletics would lead in 1906 to the first effective campaign to reform the entire landscape of college football. Issues that had attracted only brief spurts of attention in the 1890s now coalesced into demands for all sorts of reforms. While these protests would change the way in which football was played, the groundswell of criticism also challenged the emphasis placed on football and the absence of athletic standards. Simmering for a decade, the Camp-Eliot polarities had finally crystallized; now focused, the controversy stood ready for a full-dress debate. If the 1890s represented football's first crisis of confidence, the early 1900s were to produce a number of rapid-fire crises in nearly every part of the country.

CHAPTER FIVE

Football in Crisis, 1905 to 1906

In the East the big games had tarnished football's image, but in the prestigious Big Nine (the future Big Ten) the "big game" for the championship had none of the violence of the Harvard-Yale game; the game between Chicago and Michigan was dramatic, cleanly played, and injury free. And Amos Alonzo Stagg won the biggest victory in his career against Fielding Yost's Michigan team, which had gone undefeated for three years.

Only ten days before the first MacCracken conference, the two midwestern powerhouses met at Marshall Field in Chicago. Since he became coach at Michigan in 1901, Yost's teams had won fifty-eight consecutive games. Much like the Yale teams in the 1880s and 1890s, Yost's first team at Michigan totally dominated its opponents, scoring 550 points and holding the opposition scoreless. In 1905 Michigan racked up 495 points and once again was unscored upon. Unlike the previous four years, Chicago also entered this contest undefeated, having yielded a mere 5 points.

Across the street from Chicago's Marshall Field the university's forty-seven-year-old founder and president, William Rainey Harper, lay dying of cancer. Harper had grown so weak that he could not leave his house to go to his son's dormitory room to watch the game. Yet from his bed Harper had planned many of the details such as ticket selling, seating, and ushering. During the game his son telephoned reports to his father's bedside. At halftime he sent his attendant, language professor Elizabeth Wallace, to deliver a message to the team. Stagg made sure that his players understood that it was Harper's last game.

In addition, Walter Camp had traveled to Chicago for the game, perhaps to observe his future All-American selection, quarterback Walter Eckersall. Weighing only 145 pounds, Eckersall held the key to the Chicago offense and defense, and his presence quickly became a factor. Contrary to expectation, neither team was able to threaten the opponent's goal. Eckersall, booming punts from deep in Chicago territory, kept Michigan from working the ball to Chicago's goal line. With the ball at his own three-yard line in the second half, Eckersall dropped back to his own end zone to punt but, instead, faked a kick and dashed around the left end, gaining twenty yards before being forced out of bounds. On a similar play Michigan also faked a kick and sent the ball carrier down the sidelines—only a game-saving tackle by "Eckie" prevented a score.

Eventually, one of Eckersall's punts paid off. From past midfield the Chicago quarterback lofted the ball from his own forty-five-yard line across the Michigan goal. The Michigan punt receiver tried to do what Eckersall had done. With Chicago tacklers bearing down on him, he took the ball behind the goal and started to run with it. He slipped through one tackler, and, just as he was about to cross the goal line, a second tackler hit him and hurled him back. The crowd, which had begun to cheer, hesitated, and then the referee held up two fingers for a two-point safety. That small lead, 2-0, became the margin of victory.[1]

In a nearly flawless game Chicago had managed to hold to its narrow margin in what turned out to be the end of the traditional big game; the opposition of reformers would make this the last Thanksgiving championship in the Western Conference and the final big game between two major football rivals, at least for several years. In the fall and winter months reform would begin to sweep the old rules and rules bodies out of gridiron history. Ironically, a game without injuries or brutality had no impact on a rules controversy that grew out of the public's perception of serious injuries.

Nevertheless, the Midwest would experience its own football crisis, which would result in its own brand of controversy. In spite of its intensity, the midwestern upheaval would have been merely a blip on the screen if eastern brutality and injuries had not served as the catalyst for reform. Many of the reformers in the Midwest and other parts of the country would be glancing anxiously at the events in the East to see if football could survive the struggle to reform the rules and whether they should take the entire reform process into their own hands.

Harvard Seizes Control of the Rules

When the second MacCracken conference adjourned in New York on December 28, 1905, college football had sunk into a state of chaos more severe than the outburst a month before. By founding the ICAA and creating a second rules committee, the football reformers had torn a hole in the seamless fabric of gridiron rules making. The divisions in college football had the potential for changing the game radically and for forming an ICAA game separate from the existing one. At the worst the ICAA rebels could use the possibility of a new set of rules to force the members of the old committee to agree to meaningful reforms.

The outcome depended on the leaders, and the members of the ICAA rules reform group chose the cantankerous Dr. Henry Williams of Minnesota to head their group and to negotiate with the old committee. Being a staunch defender of the game, the former Yale player wasted no time in making contact with the old group and working out procedures for merging the two committees. Reeling from the rapidity of events, Camp, Dashiell, and their colleagues on the old rules committee insisted on consulting with their various institutions, a way of buying time to work out their own response to the reformers. By January 12 the two committees prepared to hold separate meetings in New York at nearly the same hour in nearby hotels. The members of both committees seemed prepared to merge. Bowing to the inevitable, even Walter Camp and President Arthur Hadley of Yale were reported to support "coalition."[2]

In addition to the two rules bodies, the special committee of the Harvard Graduate Athletic Association and Coach Bill Reid of Harvard were also prepared to play a role in the politics of reform. Because they were still drawing up their reform proposals, the Harvard committee had ordered Reid to block the second meeting of the old rules committee scheduled for mid-December. On January 8, 1906, the Harvard reformers announced a list of sweeping proposals, including the ten-yard rule, the forward pass, and the neutral zone between the two teams. The alumni committee also called for sterner measures against brutality, roughness, and "insulting talk to opponents or officials." Any players found guilty of foul play more than once would have to sit out the season. In addition, the committee called for a second umpire and a linesman who would be strategically placed so that they would have a clear view of the play.[3]

The Harvard alumni further instructed Reid to withdraw from the old "Camp" rules committee and to meet with the ICAA committee. This did not mean that Harvard was joining the ICAA, because an official decision of this magnitude would require the sanction of the Harvard Board of Overseers. The alumni committee wanted Reid to present their reform agenda, an initiative that the old committee would normally have opposed in whole or in part. Since the ICAA reformers had no slate of proposals, the Harvard agenda would fill the vacuum. In many respects the plan of Reid meeting with the ICAA committee was filled with many "ifs." It presumed that the reformers would welcome a representative of an institution that had not attended the second New York conference in December and which was a member of the old committee. On top of this, Dr. Henry Williams, the chairman of the committee, had played football at Yale under Walter Camp, and the Harvard proposals challenged the old system of football created by Camp.

On the evening of January 12 Reid appeared at the Murray Hill Hotel, where the new committee was meeting, and asked to be admitted. While Reid waited in the lobby, the committee discussed his extraordinary request and then invited him to come upstairs. It is likely that Reid had already contacted some members of the new committee, because once he was admitted events moved swiftly. James Babbitt of Haverford, the secretary of the reform group, telephoned his counterpart, Walter Camp, who was meeting with the old committee just around the corner. After he asked that the two committees meet together, the old committee agreed to join Babbitt, Reid, and the other reformers. As soon as they met, however, the two committees began to jockey for position, and after several hours of preliminaries they managed to work out an agreement. The Cornell representative from the old committee, L. M. Dennis, would become chairman; James Babbitt would take over as secretary in place of "the father of American football," Walter Camp.[4]

Or so the old committee thought. Reid and Babbitt had worked out a different scenario. Once the two committees joined, James Babbitt startled the old committee by resigning as secretary and designating Bill Reid to take his place. In less time than it took to play one half of a football game, Harvard had unveiled the flying wedge of football politics. "We treated Harvard virtuously in the December meetings, and they have taken advantage of it," Yale's president Hadley pouted in a letter to Camp soon afterward. "This ought to be a lesson for the future."[5]

The special committee of the Harvard Graduate Athletic Association had achieved a remarkable victory by Reid's maneuver. Because of Reid's position and Harvard's prestige, Walter Camp would have little opportunity to block the changes recommended by the Harvard alumni. On January 15 the Harvard Board of Overseers further reinforced the reform proposals set forth by the alumni committee by abolishing football and making its resumption subject to the enactment of Harvard's program. Since the special committee included both Reid and Dean Briggs, the Board of Overseers would undoubtedly take their advice when it decided whether to reinstate football. It was now up to the joint committee to pass a satisfactory version of the Harvard proposals if it wanted Harvard, the most prestigious university in the country, to resume football.

When he set up the committee in November, Reid had feared the influence of Harvard's president, Charles Eliot. Lacking the power to abolish football, Eliot could only try to influence the Board of Overseers or to use his prestige to persuade the Harvard faculty, which in late February voted to call off football for the following season, subject to approval by the Harvard authorities. By rebuffing MacCracken's overtures, Eliot had handed over the future of football to friendly reformers, including the big-time football faction at Harvard which had seized control of rules reform and converted it into a national agenda. No wonder he grumpily remarked that "there are too many of the old committee on the new" and added that he would never support the resumption of football until players had tested the new rules on the field of play—even if they were Harvard's rules.[6]

Despite his failed campaigns against athletics, Eliot's barbed criticisms had not entirely fallen on barren ground. Indeed, the seeds of his opinions on football sown in the 1890s would spring to life in the Midwest and echo in the calls for reform of the Big Nine. After lying dormant for a decade,

Eliot's radical approach to college athletics would become the basis for faculty reform of football in the winter of 1906.

The Struggle for the Souls of the Midwestern Universities

One reason that the big games in the Midwest, like the Chicago-Michigan game, lacked the shocking injuries and brutality grew out of the different gridiron styles employed by eastern and midwestern coaches. Midwestern teams played a more open style of football featuring end runs and booming punts. Needham's article in *McClure's Magazine* dealt exclusively with eastern colleges, and Roosevelt had summoned officials from the Big Three to discuss abuses on the eastern gridiron. Midwestern faculty and athletic officials often boasted that they lived in a less brutal football environment marked by more interesting and safer play and undergirded by a closer regard for the rules. As the crisis worked its way west, however, these attitudes rapidly changed. The big-time culture that pervaded Big Nine football, the pigskin critics proclaimed, hardly differed from eastern practices. As a result, the public outcry for gridiron reform also swept the Midwest in the fall of 1909.

On November 11 an article in *Collier's Weekly* dealt football in the Midwest a serious blow. The author of the article, Edward Jordan, had graduated from Wisconsin six months before. His dramatic muckraking debut, "Buying Football Victories," may have created more controversy than Henry Beach Needham's articles on eastern football. Put bluntly, Jordan charged that Wisconsin's conference rivals—Illinois, Northwestern, and Chicago—were engaged in unsavory recruiting. Though much of the article consisted of hearsay, Jordan interviewed athletic directors Amos Alonzo Stagg of Chicago and George Huff of Illinois. While he was properly respectful of the highly regarded Chicago coach, Jordan reserved his criticism for the institution's alumni, whom he accused of mounting a "win-at-any-cost" recruiting campaign in 1901.[7]

In spite of Stagg's flair for public relations, the accounts of recruiting dealt a setback to the football program's image. Leo DeTray, the Chicago halfback who had suffered a partial loss of eyesight in the recent Northwestern game, served as an example of the recruit with his hand extended. Before DeTray enrolled at Chicago, Jordan alleged, the player's father demanded board, tuition, books, and the cost of traveling back and forth from the Big Nine schools that he contacted. DeTray, a Chicago native, had not required funds for transportation, since he lived near Hyde Park. Still, the reader was left with the impression that he had received other favors.[8]

Chicago's quarterback and the hero of the big game with Michigan, Walter Eckersall, also fit neatly into Jordan's rogue's gallery of players who subsisted as wards of the university. Eckersall rarely attended class, Jordan declared, and took a small number of carefully managed courses from the faculty, who always gave him passing grades. Jordan reported that the university paid Eckersall's tuition from a "legitimate" fund of eighty thousand dollars set up to pay the expenses of needy students. He also was deeply in debt to fellow students, a fact that would come to light after the end of his college football career, in 1906.[9]

Even Northwestern, one of the least successful Big Nine schools, had engaged in "bidding wars" for promising high school athletes, or so the author claimed. Walter Steffen, the future jurist and football coach who became heir to Eckersall's "All-America" mantle at Chicago, was said to have told a Northwestern recruiter: "You fellows can't get me at Northwestern, and they can't get me at Wisconsin. You haven't got the money."[10]

Jordan's scattershot approach caused immediate tremors of outrage at Big Nine schools. At Northwestern Professor Amos Patton told students that the conference authorities should investigate charges and expel the offenders. In contrast, Stagg and Northwestern's athletic director denied the charges, but such revelations in a big-name publication were not so easily dismissed. Because football was already under attack, the article received more attention than it might have six months before. And a second article published a week later spread the author's charges to other Big Nine institutions.[11]

Jordan's revelations did not stop with the Illinois teams. In his second article, which appeared a week before the Chicago-Michigan game, he singled out his alma mater, the University of Wisconsin, alleging that an absence of resources, poor management, and athletic hangers-on had led to cheating at Wisconsin. Although short on details, Jordan as a recent graduate certainly had ample contacts and was familiar with the athletic scuttlebutt. Put simply, he charged several players with being "kept" or paid outright stipends. Others had easy jobs such as serving as cheering or heckling sections for speakers at political rallies in Madison, the state capital, where the university was located. In addition, Jordan claimed that Wisconsin had played two ineligible, or "tramp," athletes on its team. The faculty representatives and director of athletics failed to monitor the athletic program and encouraged student managers to put aside ethics in the quest for victory, Jordan charged, and incompetent management had caused the athletic department to fall ten thousand dollars into debt; attempts to liquidate the debts meant that the authorities kept alive the vicious circle by going more deeply in debt.[12]

As a result of Jordan's exposés, Frederick Jackson Turner, the eminent American frontier historian who taught at Wisconsin, joined the growing number of Big Nine faculty who fumed at the shocking revelations. As a graduate of Wisconsin whose career was identified with the institution, Turner was disgusted by the allegations of cheating. He deplored the weak stand of President Charles Van Hise, who, he firmly believed, countenanced the athletic evils. In a state and a city that prided itself on good government, and which had produced a leading Progressive figure in Governor Robert La Follette, Jordan's charges cried out for immediate action.

When the Big Nine representatives held their regular meeting of faculty representatives on December 1, 1905, they failed to enact reform measures. Instead, they went on record as deploring the high cost of admission, which was said to "magnify unduly the athletic side of student life," but did nothing to curtail it. Equally important to extreme critics like Turner, they failed to consider the possibility of suspending football or altering the game. Soon afterward, the athletic director at Wisconsin, Thomas Adams, who had attended the meeting and shared Turner's disgust at the delegates' inaction, proposed a special committee to examine the role of athletics within the University of Wisconsin and recommend changes. When the committee took shape, Turner emerged as its most prominent and outspoken member. As a result of its recommendations, the general faculty at Wisconsin proposed a two-year suspension of football. Such a breathing spell, they declared, would help to redress the balance between athletics and academics.[13]

In December Turner also fired off letters to friends at other Big Nine institutions asking for their opinions. Already local newspapers reported the rising tide of opinion against football in the East, an unsettling influence among faculty and administrators. Although the rules controversy in the East fanned the flames, Turner was more interested in the exaggerated role of football at midwestern colleges. All of the replies condemned existing practices laid out by Jordan—though many pro-football officials and faculty believed that football should be reformed rather than suspended. As Turner's biographer Ray Allen Billington points out, Turner prevailed upon the Wisconsin president to lobby for a special Big Nine meeting on athletics. After seeking advice from friends at other schools, the beleaguered Van Hise wrote President James Angell of Michigan requesting him to call a reform conference on football, and Angell acquiesced. Delegates to this conference would possess the authority to agree to reforms subject only to the approval of their faculty senates.[14]

In fact, the discontent at Wisconsin existed among faculty at other Big Nine institutions as well, especially at the University of Chicago. The faculty at Chicago had met on December 2, while the bonfires still burned celebrating Chicago's victory over Michigan and only one day after the conference representatives had held their meeting. Instead of merely criticizing, the faculty took a tough stand against college football. The first motion, made by an eminent classicist, William G. Hale, demanded the abolition of the game of football identified with mass play and tackling, or, in other words, the existing game. In response, sociologist Albion Small, one of Turner's contacts at Chicago and friendlier to football than Turner, pro-

posed a severe but less restrictive motion that left the door open to reforming football. In the end the university's faculty senate resolved that
football, "if not all intercollegiate contests, be discontinued for a term of
years."[15]

The midwestern opposition to football rose to a crescendo in December. Early in the month the presidents of sixteen Presbyterian colleges met,
seeking to bring about reform in the rules of football or possibly to abolish the game. The *Chicago Tribune* ran a feature in which presidents of
major colleges gave their largely critical opinions of the game. On December 27 the *Tribune* prominently quoted the statement of Shailer Matthews,
a professor of divinity at the University of Chicago, released two years earlier to the *New York Times,* condemning football as "a social obsession—this
boy-killing, man-mutilating, education-prostituting, gladiatorial sport."[16]

The movement to suspend football would reappear at the special Big
Nine conference, or Angell, conference scheduled for January 23, though the
conference did not take place on schedule. As if to express his displeasure,
William Rainey Harper died on January 10, putting the conference temporarily on hold and delaying it for a week. On February 2, however, the delegates gathered at the Chicago Beach Hotel on the wintry shores of Lake
Michigan. President Angell did not attend, but his keynote letter, read to the
conference, set the agenda. A recent convert to football activism, Angell had
presided over the most successful football program in the "West"—and had
heretofore shown little concern about abuses at his institution. Faced with
the task of striking a properly critical note, Angell apparently consulted
Charles Eliot's highly indignant 1894 report or had access to it through
Turner and others. Like Eliot, Angell deplored the roughness and brutality
of football, a theme that was so pervasive in 1905–6 that it hardly required
elaboration. He further condemned the perverted image of colleges and
universities conveyed by football (Eliot had criticized the dispensing of entertainment for noncollege audiences, which, he declared, distorted the role
of academic institutions in the public mind). Angell also mentioned the
huge expenditures that football entailed; he might have also mentioned the
profits that could amount to between $40,000 and $50,000 for a season at
Chicago.[17]

Angell also repeated familiar criticisms of football which the academic
public had become accustomed to hearing. He attacked the perversion of
college life caused by the attention to star football players, the spread of big-
time practices with their overtones of commercial and professional sports,
and the distorted role model that exalted "men of brawn rather than men
of brains." The newspapers filled their pages with the lacunae of injuries and
condition of team members whose slight ailments, Angell declared with a
flourish, "are chronicled with as much promptness as are those of a King
in his Court gazette." But Angell complained chiefly about the obsessive be-

havior, or "excitement," bred by football, a variation of what Nicholas Murray Butler had termed "an academic nuisance" when he banished football at Columbia. It was the same theme, in fact, to which faculty and reform-minded presidents would return again and again.[18]

In the Midwest, as in the Northeast, the emphasis on profit making and publicity had all but wiped out the favorable impression that gridiron game had created among faculty and presidents in its formative years. Football had grown fat and unresponsive from a steady diet of privilege, power, and media attention. The faculty in the Intercollegiate Conference of Faculty Representatives, or Big Nine, strived to accomplish what had eluded the Brown conference in 1898 by riding the crest tide of the injury crisis and using the public concern with the rules of play to enact its own reforms.

The discussion held by the delegates in Chicago beginning on Friday morning, January 19, 1906, ranged across a variety of these issues and complaints. Many practices, such as high ticket prices, the lengthy season, eligibility of players, professional coaches, and the intense rivalries, came up in discussions. The most vociferous critic, Frederick Jackson Turner, who regarded football as more brutal in the East than in the Midwest, aimed his criticisms at academic excesses. Football stifled intellectual activity, he declared, and it even played havoc with high school preparatory programs. After listening to Turner and others discuss what they thought was wrong with football, the delegates turned to the proposals for reform. As they labored into the evening, the members put their proposals into a tentative report. The report concluded that the "evils" of football fell into two categories: (1) physical danger and brutality; (2) the "moral evils attendant upon the gradual raising of the game into a thing of absorbing and sometimes hysterical public and collegiate interest." The latter would occupy most of the highly controversial report.[19]

When the conference reconvened on Saturday, Frederick Jackson Turner offered a motion to suspend football for two years. Turner was expressing not only his own distaste for football but also the strong anti-football sentiment among the faculty at Wisconsin. But, as it turned out, only Turner, his colleague Thomas Adams at Wisconsin, and Albion Small of Chicago supported this far-reaching motion. Instead, the majority adopted a resolution to abolish football "as played at present," code words for reforming the evils of the existing game and, as such, a far more moderate approach.[20]

The sensationalist Chicago newspapers declared that the conference had pronounced a death penalty on football. But these headlines were merely newspaper hyperbole. If readers digested the contents of the reforms, they learned that this was not the case at all. The conference had only condemned the high-profile, big-time features of the midwestern gridiron. In one of its most controversial proposals the conference insisted that coaches must be members of the faculty, potentially disqualifying Michigan's Fielding Yost. The delegates also called for a shorter season, five games each season rather than nine or ten. Moreover, the season would have to end before Thanksgiving, thereby bringing an end to the excitement of the big game such as the recent Chicago-Michigan contest (the Big Nine would later strengthen this measure by banning traditional rivalries). They also called for the end to training tables and preseason practice. Like the Brown conference in 1898, the delegates at the first Angell conference demanded faculty control not only of finances but also of athletics in general. Indeed, the faculty who gathered at the Chicago Beach Hotel had disinterred the Brown reforms buried for eight years under an avalanche of alumni, student, and administration opposition and apathy.[21]

How were the decisions of the Angell conference influenced by the nearly concurrent meetings of the joint rules committee? Of athletic officials in the Big Nine institutions, only Amos Alonzo Stagg and Henry Williams represented the conference on the rules committee. Both had attended the second New York conference, and Williams as chairman of the ICAA rules committee had set up the joint meeting between the two committees in January. Because of the distance and conflicting schedules, the two midwestern delegates did not attend further committee meetings, which meant that the two reform groups had no direct contact. While the reformers at the Angell conference expressed their dismay with injuries, they displayed more concern with the exaggerated role of football in college life. For the most part they acted as if the joint rules committee would enact reforms and that football would be played in 1906. Yet they also decreed that, if the national rules committee failed to reform the rules of play, the reformers in the Big Nine would take matters into their own hands.

Even though the faculty senates still had to ratify these decisions, the sweeping proposals alarmed students and alumni. While alumni generally took a more practical, less reactive position, students in fraternities and dormitories seethed with hostility. At both Chicago and Wisconsin, where faculty had staked out a clearly anti-football position, students feared for the worst. Because the conference reformers threatened to reject the new rules, they worried that the conference would call off football for the 1906 season. At Chicago students planned a mass meeting to organize the opposition; at Wisconsin moderate student leaders persuaded the rank and file to wear crepe armbands instead of carrying out their original plan to burn Frederick Jackson Turner in effigy.[22]

While the reforms ignited general opposition, student and alumni anger at Michigan focused on the proposal to prohibit seasonal coaches, specifically Fielding Yost of Michigan, who spent only the fall in Ann Arbor and pursued his business interests in Tennessee for the remainder of the year. Yost received a full-time professor's salary of thirty-five hundred dollars for his brief stint and was demanding a raise to six thousand dollars. Alarmed officials at Michigan lobbied frantically to alter the coaching resolution and to stave off the danger to their nearly invincible coach. Rivalries normally reserved for football rose to a fever pitch as Michigan accused Chicago of instigating a plot against Yost. Even Michigan delegate to the Angell conference, Albert Pattengill, who had failed to stop the Yost resolution tried to place the blame on Michigan's rivals such as Chicago and Wisconsin for proposing the idea. Because Amos Alonzo Stagg was a member of the faculty, he escaped the designation as a seasonal coach.[23]

The unsettled issues such as the fate of Fielding Yost prompted a second conference to resolve the disputes and give final approval to the measures voted on at the first meeting. On March 12 the second Angell conference assembled at the same hotel near Lake Michigan. In theory the delegates could rescind their measures and pass more radical motions, but the second meeting had as its purpose the final refinement and ratifying of their initial agreements. Some faculties such as Chicago's had instructed their delegates to agree to the reforms, though they remained on record as opposing football. The entire package might still be negotiable, but the crucial issue boiled down to whether the delegates could agree to their original measures de-emphasizing and redefining football.

In order to get Michigan's approval, the conference watered down the controversial measure on seasonal coaches. Largely in recognition of Michigan's important role in calling the conference, the rule outlawing such positions would be grandfathered so that it did not apply to existing coaches. The thirty-four-year-old Fielding Yost could pursue his seasonal career as long as he wished, which turned out be twenty-two more years as a full coach and eleven thereafter as Michigan's athletic director. While this concession paved the way for a general agreement, it would not remove the hostility generated by the controversy or the alumni's distaste for the reforms which would lead to Michigan's exit from the Big Nine in 1908.[24]

While the conference backed down on its coaching proposal, it held firm on the other reforms. In fact, the delegates answered the complaints against football in the life of the university as effectively as any such group in the history of college football. Of all the reforms passed by the Angell conferences, the attempts to de-emphasize football stand out as most ambitious. In spite of the revenues that they would lose, the delegates decreed that their teams would play only five games, an action that cost the major teams well over $100,000 in gross revenues, as measured by the big games in 1905. Moreover, they ruled that the season had to end before Thanksgiving, thereby eliminating the profitable and highly publicized Thanksgiving Day games. The reformers further went on record as opposing the traditional rivalries that caused so much excitement on campus and diverted the students from their academic work. In addition, they declared that ticket prices would henceforth be set at fifty cents, another decision that would prove costly to the athletic departments. All of these reforms sought to reverse the trend toward a highly commercialized, semiprofessional college spectacle that had more to do with making money than training students. By shrinking football, the delegates hoped to deflate its exaggerated role in student life.[25]

The delegates at the second Angell conference did not stop with the highly commercialized and professional nature of college football. Equally important were the measures having to do with the eligibility of athletes, their primary obligations as students, and the separate status of college sports. To remove pressure from freshmen, the conference required a year's residence before a student could participate in intercollegiate games—another effort to downplay the imperial role of football in college life. Playing for freshmen or scrub teams, the student athletes could no longer compete against other schools, and, for that matter, the varsity teams could no longer play against high school squads. The purpose of such rules was to seal off freshmen from big-time varsity athletics and to protect high schools from contagion by the colleges. Indeed, varsity players now had only three years of eligibility. While the conference grandfathered players who were already enrolled, athletes who entered in the fall of 1906 could no longer hang onto eligibility four years as marginal students. Now they would have to take the required courses, and their institutions would be required to certify that they were full-time students in good standing making "normal progress" toward a degree. The era of playing fast and loose with a academic standards and credits, a variation on the theme of the tramp athlete, had apparently ended.[26]

The reformers also tried to create a setting in which athletes would not occupy a privileged position. Like the 1898 Brown conference, they swept away preseason training and training tables. By banning freshmen from varsity teams, they sought to prevent the tendency of incoming students to acquire the athletic virus. They even anticipated that the fifty-cent limit on the cost of tickets would enable students to view the contests on the same footing as the general public. Tickets that cost two and three dollars, they believed, worked a hardship on students, who had less resources than outsiders. Similarly, pricing tickets at fifty cents would send a message to students that athletics should not become the most important facet of college life.[27]

The Angell conferences had answered two decades of faculty criticism. The reformers sought to reduce privilege and introduce democratic values. Instead of favoring wealthy football outsiders, the Big Nine reformers strongly endorsed equality in ticket prices. This equality extended to the position of athletes and nonathletes on campus as well as to the stature of teams' schedules within the conference. In an era when teams did not play a full conference schedule, the reforms would compel high-profile teams such as Chicago to play less prominent, less profitable games with teams like Illinois and Purdue. Athletes like Walter Eckersall would no longer lead a coddled, nonacademic career, and Eckersall himself would be dropped by Chicago after the 1906 football season. Under the Big Nine reforms he would never have become eligible to play football for the University of Chicago.

For a time Big Nine football would be radically changed and students removed from the commercialized big-time football. Nevertheless, the fate of football in the Midwest remained unsettled. Though the Big Nine itself stepped back from abolition, the universities had not yet all decided on the future of football. In March Northwestern, a private Methodist institution, where football languished in the early 1900s, took the action that students and alumni feared. Pleading insolvency of their athletic programs, the school's administration was able to suspend football and do so with a minimum of student protest.[28]

At Wisconsin, however, the opposition to football produced a highly combustible mix. The results of the second Angell conference only increased fears that the Wisconsin faculty might suspend football, made no less intense when, upon his return, Frederick Jackson Turner gave a speech denouncing the game. Since football anchored the athletic system, athletics in general began to show signs of disarray. A standout fullback who announced that he planned to transfer was followed by the captain of the baseball team, who dropped out of school. In a show of solidarity the track team announced that they would not compete until football was clearly out of danger. When students learned in late March that Northwestern faculty had suspended football, the news had a catalytic effect. The anti-football stance of the Wisconsin faculty suggested a domino effect. With President Van Hise temporarily out of town, the athletic cauldron of teams, students, and alumni threatened to boil over.[29]

Students regarded Frederick Jackson Turner as their chief adversary, an opinion that he had done nothing to discourage. Now they prepared to go after him, using violence if necessary. On the night of March 27 students gathered on campus armed with rifles and revolvers and began to march toward faculty residences shouting "death to the faculty." When the arch foe of football appeared on his front porch, voices cried out, "When can we have football?" to which Turner quickly replied, "When you can have a clean game." Unwilling to back down, Turner shouted above the din, "It's been so rotten for the last ten years that it is impossible to purge it." His words were then lost in the hisses and calls of "Put him in the lake." Luckily for Turner, the students lost interest and moved on to other houses before disbanding. Still, his was one of three faculty members' effigies burned before the morning.[30]

The Far West Adopts Rugby

In November 1905 the football controversies spread to the major football-playing institutions on the West Coast, the University of California at Berkeley and Stanford. The opposition of the two presidents, Benjamin Ide Wheeler of Berkeley and David Starr Jordan of Stanford, as well as of their faculties led to a major athletic change, the most revolutionary of any collective decision in the 1905–6 upheaval. Unlike the East and Midwest, the West Coast had few institutions of higher education and few teams that played big-time football. At a time when most schools had given up playing semiprofessional athletic clubs, the two West Coast institutions had to depend on games with these noncollegiate competitors. In order to play a normal schedule of college games, the two teams had to include Nevada and Southern California or occasionally host contests with universities in far-off Oregon and Washington. With a dearth of rivals, the big-game between Stanford and California assumed an imperial status. And it was this rivalry that had provoked the most complaints by Jordan, Wheeler, and their two faculties.[31]

Football on the West Coast had grown up in the image of northeastern football. In 1892, when Stanford and California had played each other in their first football game, they had done so against the backdrop of banners, parades, and cheering students, a carbon copy of big games in the East. The teams had imported eastern coaches to prepare them for their annual contest, not the least being Walter Camp, who had coached Stanford in its big games with California. Along with the trappings of football rivalries came the evils of tramp athletes and athletic loafers. By the late 1890s the extravagance of the big game had turned it into a profitable semiprofessional spectacle. The Stanford and Berkeley teams were sequestered in San Francisco hotels a week before the contest to build morale and isolate them from distractions such as studies. The governor of California held a special audience to congratulate the winning team. As a result of the big game, the team reaped profits of sixteen thousand dollars for the season.[32]

Alarmed by these decidedly nonacademic practices, the schools in the late 1890s enacted athletic regulations such as one requiring the big games to be played on campus rather than in San Francisco. As David Starr Jordan, president of Stanford, pointed out, their schools had banished the "athletic loafer, the professional and the bruiser [the brutal player]." Wheeler and Jordan, presidents of California and Stanford, both taught in the East before migrating to the West Coast. Jordan had served as president of the University of Indiana, while Wheeler had attended the Brown conference while teaching at Cornell. Wheeler kept up an unlikely correspondence with Walter Camp, unlikely because Wheeler advocated far more sweeping reforms of football than Camp and periodically condemned the eastern rules cartel.[33]

Like eastern presidents, Wheeler and Jordan both deplored the excitement that accompanied the big game between their two schools. Though the teams played on campus, the intensity of the rivalry had not diminished, and the prospect of the big game kept the students in feverish excitement for weeks before the contest. The game still contained all the ingredients of a Harvard-Yale or Chicago-Michigan clash, including the wildly cheering students, waving banners, gatherings of rejuvenated alumni, fight songs, and pregame and postgame celebrations. So intently did the students prepare for the big game that a controversy erupted at California in 1904 when student cheerleaders tried to ban peanut vendors from the cheer practice sessions because they might break the students' concentration. "It was considered proved," a student reporter solemnly declared, "that eating peanuts and yelling could not be carried on at the same time."[34]

Wheeler and his faculty believed that the excitement of the big game was detrimental to academic life, and for this they blamed the East. While Jordan at Stanford proved less militant, both presidents condemned the eastern rules cartel because they felt that it had not done enough to address the problem of injuries or professionalism. Wheeler declared that, if Jordan thought that the football situation could be improved by better officiating, he was nurturing "an ancient and unfulfilled hope." The California president admitted that he himself had nurtured this illusion for many years while he discussed college football with the redoubtable Burt Wheeler at Cornell. Though Wheeler corresponded with the architect of that cartel, he bitterly condemned the chairman of the committee, Paul Dashiell, rather than Camp, possibly because it allowed him to continue his friendship—and correspondence—with the "father of American football."[35]

Neither president thought that the evils of football on the West Coast had become as serious as in the East. Nevertheless, they believed that American football still had far more evils than their institutions could tolerate and that it contributed to the overblown Stanford-California rivalry. Isolated from the eastern game, the two big-time schools controlled the college sports scene in California enough to determine the type of reforms that seemed appropriate. As it turned out, they decided that their two schools should cease their connections with eastern football and make their own rules. This meant that they could substitute a game such as soccer or rugby which would preserve the rivalry but would create, they hoped, far less hysteria. Wheeler believed that the students would prefer rugby because it was closer to football and was, in fact, the game from which American football had evolved.[36]

As football in the East deteriorated in November, the western institutions decided to sever their ties with American football. In early December Wheeler wrote to Columbia president Nicholas Murray Butler that "we shall make our game, probably Rugby, with 'socker' [*sic*] as a substitute." Wheeler was referring to a special meeting between the presidents and faculty of Stanford and California at which the two presidents had recommended adopting rugby for a year. As if to ratify their decision, Stanford canceled the trip East by delegate Max Farrand to the second MacCracken conference. Of their decision Wheeler wrote, "We shall go our own way."[37]

Indeed, the two schools went a far different way than the eastern institutions. The joint decision of Stanford and California to drop American football had little to do with the orgy of concern over deaths and injuries which led to rules changes in the East. To be sure, the two presidents believed that rugby would result in fewer injuries because the game in the early 1900s was faster than American football and less dominated by collisions of beefy players. Like the faculty members of the Big Nine, however, the presidents and faculties of the two schools insisted that football spectacles sent the wrong signals to the students, overshadowing the academic business of the universities. Taking advantage of the injury hysteria, they made an effort to end the intrusion of big-time athletics into the tranquil academic life of the university. Though the decisions of the two schools fit neatly into the academic rebellion that accompanied the injury crisis, they led to a more unique outcome.[38]

Surprisingly, the presidents contended that rugby would prove a safer game than the grinding, mass contact sport of American football. British rugby and soccer teams played a far less brutal and less injurious form of football. The presidents may have correctly gauged the often brutal and injurious brand of football as played in the Northeast, but the game itself was only part of the problem. While they debated soccer versus rugby, the presidents seemed blissfully unaware that the games could result in the same degree of roughness as American football. Neither president appeared certain which game to adopt; not until the two colleges watched a rugby exhibition between New Zealand and Australian teams were they convinced to go with rugby.

In opting for a British version of football, Wheeler and Jordan might have paused to consider the opinions expressed by the intractable Charles Eliot, a friend and correspondent of Jordan (who later came to agree with Eliot on this point). Interviewed after the Harvard-Yale game in 1905, President Eliot was asked if he had seen a "'soccer [*sic*] football'" exhibition between English and American teams at Soldiers Field at Harvard. "Yes, I saw the socker [*sic*] game," he said, "and it is very pretty as they played it, but our American college boys would spoil it in five minutes."

"What do you mean by that?" the reporter asked.

"Oh, there is plenty of opportunity for brutality in the socker [*sic*]," he replied.[39]

Bill Reid of Harvard, himself a native of California, where his father had been president of the University of California, echoed Charles Eliot's prediction that American college boys would pervert rugby, making it into a brutal and unsportsmanlike game, thanks to the American temperament. In the words of a witticism popular in the 1890s, "in England, the boy kicked the ball; in Ireland, the boy kicked the boy; and in America, the boy kicked the boy and the ball."

In February 1906 the two schools made their decision to substitute rugby, and the presidents found a number of reasons other than brutality and injuries to justify their decision. The British game promised a number of reforms that eastern reformers had tried unsuccessfully to legislate. Rugby enthusiasts believed that their game would prove neither commercial nor professional. In an open-field game smaller, athletic men could stand out as players much as they had in the early "rugby" days of American football. As a thoroughly amateur sport, rugby would require less time for practice and would shed the trappings of big-time football, such as big-name coaches and the spectacle of parades, organized cheering, celebrity players, and excessive publicity. Because of its international roots, the college teams could also engage visiting Canadian, Australian, and British teams.[40]

As a result, the Stanford coach, James F. Lanagan, spent part of the spring in British Columbia studying the finer points of rugby. Despite grumbling by alumni and students, the switch to rugby was greeted with enthusiasm by the presidents and faculty. The students tolerated it because they wanted to preserve their football rivalries, and rugby had turned into the only game in town. Because Wheeler and Jordan lobbied hard for rugby, writing letters to school officials, a number of teams in Oregon, Nevada, and southern California (and the high schools in California) switched to rugby. In the Bay area St. Mary's College of Oakland and Santa Clara College, the two prime Catholic rivals, adopted rugby soon after California and Stanford announced their decision. Later colleges to the South including Pomona and Southern California took up rugby, as did several athletic clubs in the North. Beginning with the schools located near rugby-playing colleges, the vast majority of high schools in California embraced rugby.[41]

Undoubtedly, the West Coast experiment stands out as one of the most unheralded episodes of the reform era. It was as if the West had seceded from the United States and declared itself a western republic, and the rules committee had no way to force the two schools back into the fold. Because of their remoteness, the two California universities faced less pressure to conform. Unlike big-time institutions in the East, Wheeler and Jordan only had to deal with fractious alumni and students who complained but failed to alter the decisions of the two presidents and their faculties. Because the opponents had no place to turn for American football and the two institutions had acted in concert, neither alumni or students were able to muster the support necessary to change their policies. In short, the conditions proved to be nearly as perfect as could be expected for dropping a big-time sport and conducting an academic experiment. By manipulating the rules crisis to their advantage, the two institutions converted their isolation from the rest of the country into a temporary advantage, a sort of athletic and academic petri dish.

The flip side of this experiment and why it caused so little uproar was that it took place in an extremely distant and unpopulated setting. While some sportswriters in the East ridiculed the experiment, most football enthusiasts hardly cared. Of the seventy-six million Americans counted in the 1900 census, only four million lived in the tier of states running from Wyoming, Montana, and Colorado to the West Coast. By far the largest of those states was California, which had a mere million and a half in population. Compared to the Northeast with twenty-one million and the Midwest with twenty-six million, the Pacific Coast was barely a footnote to the body politic.

For ten years rugby football continued to be played as the fall game in California but not with much enthusiasm. Though relieved that the Stanford-California rivalry survived, the students at the two schools never warmed to the new sport. As it turned out, the Great Experiment would not last much longer than the ten-year abolition of football at Columbia, testifying to the power of American football and the success of the reformed rules. In 1915 the student-controlled athletic association at California broke the pact with Stanford because it ostensibly wanted to play freshmen, who had been ineligible. In fact, California used the break as a means to return to American football. In 1916 it played its big game against the University of Washington, which had never dropped the gridiron game. Following World War I Stanford students and alumni agitated successfully for a return to American football, a pastime that was now deemed safer and more governable than the old 1890s game.[42]

A decade earlier Wheeler and Jordan had been able control the future of college football on the West Coast because the reports from the East caused alarm among their faculty and members of the general public, disarming the normally influential students and alumni. Throughout most of the country in 1906 the new rules for American football rapidly defused the injury crisis and led to a more optimistic view of football's future. In February 1906 the public had its first glimpse of the major reforms passed by the rules committee, including the forward pass and the ten-yard rule. A friend of Walter Camp would write that he heard that "forward passes and other dream-like things have been brought into the realm of possibilities, even probabilities." Indeed, they had been.

In spite of Camp's skepticism, the rules committee was introducing the most revolutionary changes in college football since Camp's possession rule in 1880. Big-time football had survived the crisis of confidence and put the pieces of the rules process back together again. The faculty reformers had made a determined assault on football's redoubtable defenses. While the radicals had achieved some of their objectives, the friends of football such Bill Reid who attempted to preserve football by making it more acceptable to the public would enjoy far greater success.

The assaults on football and the reforms did not stand alone in the early 1900s, as Theodore Roosevelt had shown in his 1905 Harvard commencement speech linking unethical business practices with foul play on the football field. The Progressive era of the early 1900s witnessed more reforms or attempts at reform than any other period of modern American history. Most of these efforts had the effect of preserving existing institutions by either introducing major changes or by creating the illusion of significant change.

Football proved no exception. The attempt to bring about a renewal of democratic values in academic life, one lofty goal of reformers, clearly fit the spirit of gridiron reform in the crisis of 1905–6. Like reformers on other fields, those of the pigskin brigade attempted to reshape football so that it fit their ideal of a safe, thoroughly amateur sport. The attempt to find new solutions would lead to a second crisis in the reshaping of modern football. As a result, the thoroughly reformed rules of play would prove to be one of the most enduring legacies of the Progressive era.

The notorious flying wedge captured in early sports photography—above, from ground level (Harvard with the ball, playing in 1892) and below in a bird's-eye view (as Princeton set up the play in its 1893 game against Yale). Manhattan Field in uptown New York City—later the Polo Grounds— provided the setting for the 1893 Yale-Princeton classic, with thousands watching from the high ground above the stands. Thanksgiving Day games in New York attracted as many as thirty-five thousand paying fanatics, or "fans," and earned enough money to return a comfortable profit for the big-time teams. COURTESY OF YALE UNIVERSITY ATHLETIC ARCHIVES.

Though few casualties were reported, football in the 1890s drew increasing attention as a dangerous and brutal sport. This drawing appeared in *Harper's Weekly*, Aug. 31, 1891. COURTESY OF YALE UNIVERSITY ATHLETIC ARCHIVES.

The University of Pennsylvania devised a guards-back formation during the 1890s, bringing a guard, John Outland, into the five-man backfield to carry the ball. *Above*, a Chicago newspaper article diagramed the formation; *below*, the University of Washington practices a variation of it. COURTESY OF SPECIAL COLLECTIONS, UNIVERSITY OF CHICAGO LIBRARIES; UNIVERSITY OF WASHINGTON SPECIAL COLLECTIONS.

Yale's team of 1893, *above*, demonstrating the linked-arms method linemen used to protect, push, and pull the ball carrier in "mass play." The University of Oregon team at about the the turn of the century, *below*, with linemen placed on the line of scrimmage but arms still at the ready. COURTESY OF YALE UNIVERSITY ATHLETIC ARCHIVES; UNIVERSITY OF OREGON ARCHIVES.

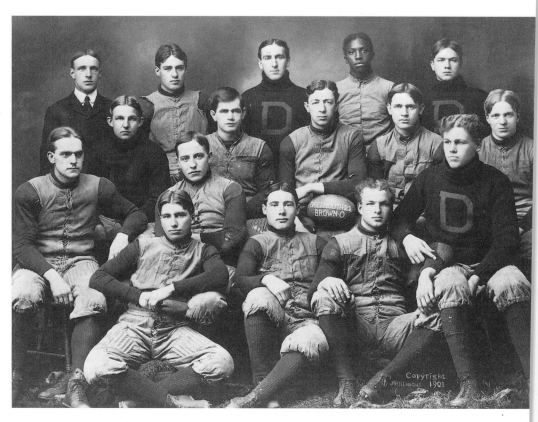

The Dartmouth Eleven—every one appearing a perfect gentleman—pose after defeating Brown 22-0 in November 1901. One of the few African-American players in the country at the time, Matthew Bullock, would have his collarbone broken in a game with Princeton. Coaches often told players to single out the best opposing man and "put him out of business" early in the game. COURTESY OF LIBRARY OF CONGRESS.

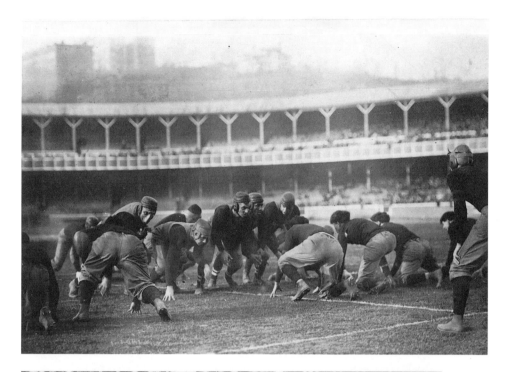

Collegiate action at about the turn of the century. Players wore any protective devices available to them, including makeshift noseguards, *above,* or nothing at all, *below.* Many early athletes flaunted their toughness by avoiding head-gear. COURTESY OF YALE UNIVERSITY LIBRARY, DEPARTMENT OF ARCHIVES AND HISTORY.

Punting from their own twenty-yard line. A rule change of 1903 placed lines on the field perpendicular to the yard markers, converting it from a gridiron to a checkerboard design. On the offensive side, whoever took the ball from the center could only cross into the opposing team's territory after having moved five yards right or left of the point of the snap, and the quarterback could not throw directly across what later the rules referred to as the line of scrimmage—the idea being to spread play over the field. COURTESY OF YALE UNIVERSITY LIBRARY, DEPARTMENT OF ARCHIVES AND HISTORY.

Pushing, pulling, and mauling of the sort had led to serious injuries and deaths in the early game. COURTESY OF YALE UNIVERSITY LIBRARY, DEPARTMENT OF ARCHIVES AND HISTORY.

This program cover for the Harvard-Yale game of 1905 managed to capture the frenzied emotions long associated with the rivalry. COURTESY OF YALE UNIVERSITY ATHLETIC ARCHIVES.

In September 1905 President Theodore Roosevelt called a White House conference to discuss football brutality. A month later his son Ted, a guard on the Harvard freshman team, suffered a broken nose against Yale and had to be helped off the field, *above*. As if he had seen this photo, John McCutcheon of the *Chicago Tribune* produced a cartoon later that same season showing a young man being carried off the field in the same manner, while cheering in the stands continued for the University of Chicago, *below*. McCutcheon entitled the scene "The Educational Influence of College Football." COURTESY OF THEODORE ROOSEVELT COLLECTION, WIDENER LIBRARY, HARVARD UNIVERSITY, AND SPECIAL COLLECTIONS, UNIVERSITY OF CHICAGO LIBRARY.

In 1905 Bob "Tiny" Maxwell, *above,* a 240-pound guard, anchored one of the largest and heaviest lines in the country at tiny Swarthmore College. In a game against Penn in 1905, Maxwell was battered by double- and triple-teaming Quakers, leading to the legend that his injuries inspired the reforms of 1905–6.

COURTESY OF FRIENDS HISTORICAL LIBRARY OF SWARTHMORE COLLEGE.

"The Grim Reaper Smiles on the Goal Posts." Fanning anti-football sentiment, the Cincinnati *Commercial Tribune*, in December 1905, claimed that 25 players had died that season at all levels of play (the correct number in college football proved to have been a mere 3), and 168 suffered serious injury. Harold Moore's death in the Union-NYU game on November 25 led to reform meetings in New York, new rules, and the group that became the NCAA. COURTESY OF LIBRARY OF CONGRESS.

"Just Out of College." In January 1906 the Big Nine (forerunner of the Big Ten) held a special conference of college faculty to consider the evils of college football. The conference voted to suspend football "as played at present," leading Chicago newspapers to give the impression that the Chicago faculty had abolished the game. COURTESY OF SPECIAL COLLECTIONS, UNIVERSITY OF CHICAGO LIBRARY.

In 1906, after a round of reforms, a "celebrity" actress posed for what as easily could have been a vaudeville or college football promotional photo. Football and sexuality had already developed a lasting relationship. COURTESY OF LIBRARY OF CONGRESS.

In mid-November 1909 fullback Kemp Yancey of Virgina, absent a helmet, races around the end in a game against Georgetown at Hilltop Field, Washington, DC. Fellow running back Archer Christian, a freshman, received a fatal concussion during the game—another casualty that led to controversy over the rules and reform. UNIVERSITY OF VIRGINIA YEARBOOK, *CORKS AND CURLS*, 1910. COURTESY OF UNIVERSITY OF VIRGINIA ARCHIVES.

Amos Alonzo Stagg asked Coach Hugo Bezdek of Arkansas to experiment with the new formations in the early spring of 1910 as the rules committee struggled over reform proposals. Walter Eckersall, *left front, hands in back pockets,* a former Chicago All-America and *Chicago Tribune* sportswriter traveled to Arkansas to observe the experiments. Stagg favored retaining the forward pass and eliminating the pushing and pulling of mass play. COURTESY OF SPECIAL COLLECTIONS, UNIVERSITY OF CHICAGO LIBRARY.

Students demonstrate their enthusiasm for football by holding a pep rally and performing a snake dance at the University of Washington in 1911. COURTESY OF UNIVERSITY OF WASHINGTON ARCHIVES.

A football game at Wesleyan College in 1913. After the reforms of 1910 football gained in popularity among students, faculty, and college presidents alike. At Wesleyan automobiles were permitted to pull up to the field next to Brown-stone row, near the center of the campus. Intense interest in football after World War I, even at smaller colleges, would lead to soaring attendance figures and intense competition for talented players. COURTESY OF WESLEYAN UNIVERSITY ARCHIVES.

Paul Robeson, the future singer, actor, and critic of racial injustice played at tackle and end for Rutgers from 1915 to 1918, winning All-America honors. Known as the "Giant Negro," Robeson, one of the few African-American players at predominantly white institutions in this era, made Foster Sanford's Rutgers team into one of the top teams in 1918. COURTESY OF RUTGERS UNIVERSITY SPECIAL COLLECTIONS AND UNIVERSITY ARCHIVES.

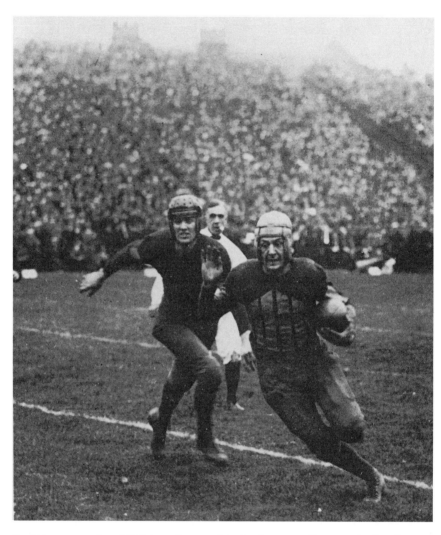

Red Grange against Michigan in 1925, his final year at Illinois. The "Galloping Ghost" created controversy at the end of the season by quitting college and signing a contract with the professional Chicago Bears. COURTESY OF LIBRARY OF CONGRESS.

CHAPTER SIX

The Game in Flux, 1906 to 1909

In the early days of the game women played a highly visible role in big-time football. Whether they truly relished the violence, women embraced the spectacle with visible enthusiasm and showed a grasp of the game which occasionally astounded reporters. Beautifully attired for the big games and sometimes mingling with male students at afternoon practices, women briefly in the 1890s formed part of the colorful backdrop for college football. Though they worshiped at the shrine of male dominance, women achieved a minor yet identifiable niche in the early history of college football. Very occasionally, women who were married to coaches or presidents helped to influence football policy and practice, such as Alice Sumner Camp, when she subbed for her husband as coach in 1888, and Edith Roosevelt, whose concern for her sons may have influenced her husband in calling the White House Football Conference and working behind the scenes for a less brutal game.

In the early 1900s male college students injected a much more serious, even puritanical, approach into gridiron relations between the sexes. During the Progressive era a dread of women's influence, or "feminizing" of society, swept across America. Words such as *manliness* and *baby act* filled the vocabulary of Theodore Roosevelt when he worried about a generation of "mama's boys" who would one day lead the country. College presidents and trustees worried that coed institutions with a large proportion of women, such as Northwestern and Swarthmore, would become known as women's institutions. Wesleyan University in Middletown, Connecticut, even tried to shed its image as a feminized institution by banishing women from the campus and becoming an exclusively male institution. A strong football team, in the case of Swarthmore College, proved to be a way that it could avoid the label of a coed school predominantly for women. More than any other feature of a college, football served the function of attracting males, whose careers in business and professions would place the school in the center of national life and eventually result in generous gifts by its alumni.[1]

During the Progressive era the male gridiron culture made its most determined effort to put women in their gridiron place, resulting in a segregation of the sexes. As cheering and singing at games became more organized, women were seen as a distraction. No longer were coeds or off-campus female admirers encouraged to attend cheer practice. Student leaders believed that male cheering sections served a vital "twelfth man" role and argued that women could only detract from concentrated cheering. Football fanatics among male students wanted to isolate women in their own seating sections at the games. In 1903 the University of Washington decreed that women had to sit in their own cheering section. Males at Chicago and Northwestern sought to expel women as well. In 1905 even progressive Harvard refused to allow women in its cheering sections. As late as 1939, California had its women rooters enter the stadium by a separate tunnel, and Syracuse did not disband its separate cheering sections until after World War II.[2]

Viewed broadly, this form of gender separation fit with the attempts to defeminize society. Since football played a vital part in the male sense of self, the presence of women simply seemed to contradict it. Just as males performed the vital jobs of banking and brokering in society, they also formed an athletic monopoly on the gridiron. Ladies' men or dandified gents who devoted their attention to women hardly met the criteria of a manly "hit-the-line-hard" society. The literary critic Bernard DeVoto, who had come of age in this era, later expressed a variation of this attitude when he mocked the twenty thousand women attending a Northwestern game, insisting that only forty of them really understood or appreciated football. They went to the game because the men who sat with them in the stands lacked true manliness. "All the men they have ever known," he wrote, "are unheroic, timorous and commonplace men who wear rubbers, who tread quietly when a [wager] is abroad."[3]

The Revolution in the Rules, 1906 to 1909

In football the changes had just begun. At the beginning of 1906 the wider football public, which included women as well as men, had fresh hope that the rules committee would devise a new, safe, sportsmanlike, and orderly game to replace the thoroughly discredited spectacle of the 1890s. While faculty reformers grappled with academic reforms, the dominant movement for change that engaged the public's attention had to do with the rules of play. Since the two rules committees had agreed to meet together in January, the near certainty of major rules changes posited more drama than the dry reforms of the Angell conferences or the abrupt turns on the far-off West Coast.

Propelled by the proposals of the Harvard alumni, the joint rules committees stood ready to throw open the gates to change. The prevailing wisdom—Harold Moore's death seemed to prove the point—held that football injuries and fatalities resulted from the collision of heads and bodies near the point at which the ball was snapped. Old grads who had played in the 1870s and 1880s looked back nostalgically to a period before the bunching of players near the center, a golden age of kicking and broken field runs, when serious injuries seldom occurred. The reformers wanted to redirect play so that running, throwing, and kicking would become more common, a game in which teams would take advantage of the open field. They hoped to rewrite the rules so that grinding line play would be less profitable and that penalties would discourage foul play.

In mid-February 1906 the joint rules committees completed much of their work, making the initial results public. Facilitated in great part by Harvard's agenda, a remarkable number of those alumni proposals were either adopted or expanded. Among the changes were Walter Camp's—or, more accurately, the Canadian—rule for gaining ten yards in three attempts.

Though Camp only served as editor of the rules book, he attended the 1906 meetings and contributed to the refining of the new rules. While he chose not to obstruct the reforms, Camp used his expertise to help shape the nature of the committee's experiments. His general concern with refereeing, for instance, resulted in a central board of referees, an innovation that would prove more useful, at least in the short term, than any of the other attempts to improve the game. Also, Walter Camp was one of three members of a subcommittee that helped to define and limit the scope of the forward pass, a fact that helps to explain the cautious rules governing the new strategic weapon.[4]

One of the most widely discussed proposals, the ten-yard rule, received the assent of the joint rules committee in its first meeting, though some members wanted to limit it to the midsection of the field, between the twenty-five-yard lines. The proposal for extending the yards necessary for a first down from five to ten originated with Walter Camp, who, in turn, observed it when visiting Canada and lobbied hard for it in 1904 and 1905—and used it to exclude other measures that might, he believed, alter the nature of the game. In spite of their antipathy for Camp, the Harvard alumni committee included it in its reform agenda. Camp believed that the challenge of gaining ten yards would force teams to try more innovative plays, especially plays run to the outside of the field.[5]

One rule that survived almost precisely as the Harvard committee proposed in January required the two teams to line up across a neutral zone measured by the length of the ball, or what became known as the line of scrimmage. Previously, the teams had lined up so close to each other that officials could not see the pushing, holding, and slugging that occurred before the play. By defining a neutral zone, the officials could spot infractions, especially the sparring that occurred between linemen before the snap. To ensure that there were enough eyes to cover the line play, the committee provided for a fourth official. To prevent the fatigue that caused injuries, the rules makers reduced the length of the game from seventy to sixty minutes, which would consist of thirty-minute halves with a ten-minute break. They also prohibited hurdling, which could often result from several players tossing the ball carrier across the line, a maneuver that could easily lead to head or neck injuries.[6]

The committee also spelled out more precisely the nature of unnecessary roughness. By the new rules' definition, unnecessary roughness would include tripping, tackling out of bounds, piling up, and hurdling an opponent at scrimmage who was still on his feet. Similarly, the committee moved to penalize unsportsmanlike conduct, including abusive and insulting language to opponents and officials, with fifteen yards and expulsion from the game. Likewise, with blows to Harvard's punter Francis Burr in the 1905 Harvard-Yale game fresh in their minds, the committee defined personal fouls as "striking with the fist or elbow, kneeing, kicking, meeting with the knee, and striking with locked hands by linemen breaking through [the line of scrimmage]." The guilty team would suffer a penalty of fifteen yards, and the offender would be banished from the game.[7]

In an effort to eliminate the old momentum plays—the remnants of the once potent flying wedge and flying interference—the committee specified that only five players could line up in the backfield. This change was a far cry from the 1890s, when teams could put half the team far behind the line of scrimmage. Like the old flying wedge, the backfield had once been allowed to start in motion before the play began, seven men moving pell-mell toward the line before the center snapped the ball. In 1894 the rules committee had ruled that only two backfield men could go in motion and five players had to be lined up at scrimmage, but this meant that two linemen could still take up positions in the backfield.

These changes merely redirected the heavy artillery of gridiron warfare. After 1894 the guards back tackle back plays had enabled teams to station burly linemen in the backfield who were allowed to start moving before the snap of the ball, either to carry the ball themselves or to push and pull the ball carriers. Motivated by public outcries, the old committee experimented with partial reforms. In 1903 it required seven men on the line but then decreed that this rule applied only to the area between the twenty-five-yard lines, or, in other words, the midfield area, where hard-nosed line play in front of the goal line did not take place.[8]

The new rules placed limits on the tackles and guards in the backfield—even as the team neared the goal line. Instead of acting as a fullback or blocking back, the often beefy linemen had to line up outside the last player on the line and no more than five yards behind the new scrimmage line. The committee also ruled that teams had to place at least six men on the line of scrimmage, bringing football closer to the soon-to-be-legislated seven-man line. The seventh man could still line up in the backfield if the team desired, but no longer could he act as a ball carrier crashing full tilt into the line.

Since he had to station himself outside the last man, he could not easily act as a blocking back, except on plays that went to the outside.

In addition, linemen could not exchange position with players in the backfield unless they remained as backs. Again, this rule was an attempt to eliminate the tackle back and guards back formations, the remnants of the wedge plays of the 1890s. Once again, the committee sought to limit the dangerous collisions at the line of scrimmage which were thought to cause deaths and serious injuries, another example of the attempts to modify line play and encourage open field plays. Since the 1890s critics of the rules had singled out the growing tendency for beefy players to push, pull, and catapult the ball carriers through the defense. The media and the public identified the fatalities in football with the growing tendency toward "line bucking," or sending the ball carrier across the middle of the scrimmage line. As a result, reform became synonymous with measures to discourage pushing and pulling (mass play) and putting men in motion toward the line before the snap of the ball (momentum plays).[9]

Most of the reforms extended rules changes that previous committees had set in motion, but the forward pass stands as an exception. Like the invention of the airplane, the forward pass turned out to be the most revolutionary gridiron change of the early 1900s. Earlier proposed by, among others, Georgia Tech coach John Heisman and championed by John Bell of Pennsylvania (the father of future National Football League commissioner, Bert Bell), the forward pass managed to win the committee's approval because of its potential to open up the game and redirect the grinding line play. In fact, the committee enlarged the Harvard proposal that would have otherwise limited the forward pass between the twenty-five-yard lines to encompass the entire field.[10]

Still, in establishing the rules for the forward pass, the subcommittee moved cautiously with this untested weapon. Far from seeing it as a means to score touchdowns, the founders designed the forward pass as a device to promote open-field plays. Hesitant to give it full rein, the members of subcommittee, which included Walter Camp, an opponent of the pass, hedged it with penalties and restrictions. The ball had to cross the line of scrimmage five yards outside where the ball was received from center; only players lined up at the end of the line could catch the ball; and the team that tried to throw the ball near or directly across center would automatically lose possession. Likewise, the forward pass could not cross the goal line. If it did, officials would treat the infraction as a touchback and award the ball to the other side.

In addition, the committee awarded all incomplete passes to the other team; in this way the forward pass would not dominate play, or so they imagined. If any of the nine ineligible receivers happened to touch the ball, the opponents would get possession. If the ball did not cross the line five yards on either side of center, the opponents got the ball. Most risky were passes missing the pass receiver altogether; passes that hit the ground without being touched would go over to the opponents where the ball touched the ground. If the ball went out of bounds, any player could pursue and recover it, leading to, as former rules maker and coach David Nelson has written, "many a cinder burn when players scrambled for the ball on the running tracks surrounding the fields." As a result, the rules on incompletions seemed to make the pass, if used too often or too recklessly, a foolhardy play.[11]

Nonetheless, the forward pass proved to be a brilliant addition that provided coaches with more weapons in their offensive arsenal. Spectators also found the forward pass a breathtaking innovation that transcended its purpose of creating open-field play. It is questionable, however, whether the forward pass succeeded in preventing or reducing injuries. While catching or running with passes, receivers could suffer injuries nearly as severe as those that occurred at the line of scrimmage. Teams also began throwing passes into groups of players, who would bat the ball forward and fall on it—and one another—to gain a few extra yards. They also used it as a decoy to set up the line plunges that they were designed to prevent, a maneuver that posed dangers to the linemen in the path of the play.[12]

Many football insiders felt that, rather than the forward pass, which one West Pointer insisted would require too much accuracy and result in too many uncertainties, the onside kick would best open up play and speed up the offenses. The committee in 1906 had passed a new version of the onside kick, whereby a punt hitting the ground ten yards beyond scrimmage could be recovered by any of the twenty-two players on the field. This punting version of the modern "onside" kick, however, held out much more promise than it actually delivered. Even compared to the risky forward pass, coaches and players found this "trick play" almost impossible to control.[13]

Despite their spotlight on safety, the committee still hesitated to prohibit mass plays in which blockers pushed and pulled the ball carrier across the line of scrimmage, a lapse that proved harmful to the 1906 reforms. Mass plays often resulted in the battering of the ball carrier as well as those who stood in his way. Instead of making pushing and pulling illegal, the committee chose to approach the problem by encouraging open-field play. The ban on hurdling and the rule requiring six men on the line of scrimmage marked the limits of efforts to legislate mass formations out of existence. The committee evidently believed that the forward pass and the ten-yard rule would discourage this practice by making it more profitable to direct plays to the outside. As a result, this final relic of the older, cruder game had a temporary stay of execution, though it would prove to be the weakest link in the new rules.

By their sixth meeting, on April 14, the committee put the new rules in print and had only to draw up the preamble. In spite of their lack of limits on pushing and pulling, members of the rules committee had made more changes than at any time since the 1880s—including far-reaching changes that would affect the flow of the game for many years to come. Only in their failure to address the broader problems of ineligible athletes and the spirit of college football did the committee ignore the mandate of the second MacCracken meeting.

Why did the rules committee fail to extend its scope to ethical problems affecting the rule of play? Initially, one subcommittee on brutality consisting of John Bell of Pennsylvania, Paul Dashiell of Navy, James Babbitt of Haverford, and F. H. Curtiss of Texas did attempt to frame elaborate rules on eligibility. One section stated that the "most demoralizing form of professionalism results from the purchase of players directly or in disguise by athletic associations, alumni, or other friends of the college." It recommended that each institution appoint a committee, including the president, to examine the list of the players to ascertain whether they represented the school. They also attempted to define what constituted ineligibility. This effort to legislate a solution to the problem of tramp athletes and "athletic loafers," however, never got beyond the subcommittee stage. In all probability the difficulties of getting the big-time schools from the old committee to agree on definitions of eligibility and the much narrower focus of most delegates with rules of play doomed this well-intentioned effort.[14]

In the months before the 1906 season began, coaches and captains tried to figure out how the rules of the new football rules would work. In September more than a hundred colleges—just about sixty had attended the second New York meeting—gathered in New York for a crash course on interpreting the rules. This conference gave skeptics and worriers a chance to voice their misgivings in public. Somewhat correctly, the pessimists feared that neither team would be able to gain ten yards and that the games would degenerate into punting contests. Others worried that teams would move their heavy linemen into the backfield (as the permissible fifth man) and use them as blocking backs as teams had done with the old guards or tackle back plays. According to the *New York Times*, the Harvard coach, Bill Reid, tried to persuade his fellow coaches and football advisors that there was little alternative. The faculties, he warned, would not stand for evasion. If teams started to backslide into the old "grinding" game, the Harvard faculty, for one, would have football "rooted out."[15]

Of all the changes, the forward pass put the biggest question mark on the smooth operation and credibility of the new rules. Put simply, the challenge of throwing the pass—underhanded like a long lateral or overhanded with a slight spinning arc—had yet to be worked out. The rounded ball itself made passing far more difficult than after the ball became more elongated in 1912. Since the use of the pass under the 1906 rules was risky business, teams had to decide when to throw it and how far it should go. The ball would have to be thrown to an end (the rules committee had decreed that only players on the end of the line were permitted to receive the pass), who would catch the ball and then, if possible, move the ball forward.

Sportswriters and historians have tried to pinpoint the exact moment when the forward pass first flew across the line of scrimmage, an exercise like determining the origins of football itself. Technically, the first passes may have been thrown in a game between Washburn and Fairmont in Kansas in December 1905, but forward passing was merely experimental, and the rules committee had not yet legalized it. Many teams attempted passes in preseason games and in the earliest games of the season in both the East and Midwest. One could describe a number of firsts. Coach Eddie Cochems took his St. Louis team to Lake Beulah, Wisconsin, in July, and he recalled that his halfback heaved the ball great distances in practice shortly after he demonstrated the technique. In early September Bradbury Robinson of St. Louis threw the first legal forward pass against Carroll College in what others have described as a practice game.

On September 29 Princeton completed a pass from a halfback to an end in a game against Villanova in a regular season game; it went for a substantial gain. In the week that followed, Yale, Wesleyan, and Williams also completed passes. In the Midwest newspapers reported a number of games in which teams successfully managed to execute the new offense. In the Illinois-Wabash games both quarterbacks hurled passes frequently but fruitlessly in a 0-0 tie. In deciding which teams threw the first passes, much depends on when school terms began and when college teams officially went into action, a date that varied according to college and region.

All in all, Midwestern teams, which already played a more open game, used the pass more frequently than the big-name eastern schools. An outmanned Purdue team out of desperation took to the air against Chicago in early October. Having fallen behind early, Purdue resorted to a flurry of passes but failed to score and then had a pass caught by Chicago (*intercepted* was a word not yet invented) and returned for a touchdown. Later in the season Stagg used passes in his fifth and final game to smother Illinois, 63-0.[16]

The most adept innovator, Coach Eddie Cochems of St. Louis University, and his halfback Bradbury Robinson ended up using passes that ranged from thirty to more than forty yards with devastating efficiency. Forced to pass with the rounded football of that era, Cochems beat the best teams in the Midwest. Playing an Iowa team that had defeated St. Louis 31-10 the year before, St. Louis won 39-0, completing eight of ten passes averaging twenty yards. On the final play, as the timekeeper was about to end the game, St. Louis threw a ball for twenty-five yards which was caught on the run and carried across the goal line for a touchdown. Later in the season against Kansas, Cochems's team threw passes of forty-five and forty-eight yards. In another game the left end for St. Louis hurled a sixty-seven-yard pass, truly a breathtaking achievement.[17]

In the East, where teams used the pass sparingly, Army, which had championed rules reform, used the pass against Yale to set up a touchdown and later intercepted a Yale pass but ended up losing, 10-6. Princeton defeated Army on a thirty-yard pass, and a few weeks later Navy employed the pass to beat the hapless cadets. In the Harvard-Yale match on November 24, the big game on which Harvard's Bill Reid rested his coaching future, the two teams threw only three passes, but one of these set up Yale's only score in its 6-0 victory. Defeated and demoralized, Bill Reid of Harvard, who had initiated the rules reform in the fall of 1905, quit coaching at Harvard, where he had been the highest-paid coach in the country, for a career in business.[18]

The public quickly warmed to the pass for the simple reason that it added zest to the game. One reporter in the *New York Times* who assessed the new features of the game believed that, though the pass had too many restrictions, it could become an exciting play with many variations. "When forward passes have worked successfully they have been exceptionally pretty plays," he declared. "The element of surprise which is necessary to their success, the clean handling of the ball, the sudden shift from one point of the field to another, the resultant open field play, and the bringing to the earth of the runner by a clean tackle are all inspiring." The writer believed that, with practice, teams would perfect the art of passing and that players would learn how to use passes in a greater variety of situations. Yet until the rules were changed, he believed, teams would rely on passes that guaranteed short, reliable gains. When they were deep in their own territory, they would hesitate to pass at all because a ball hitting the ground without being touched by either side would go over to the opponents.[19]

Yet a number of football authorities disliked the forward pass. Soon after the season ended, a writer in the *Times* acknowledged that the passing game often proved spectacular and thrilled the onlookers, but he insisted that the forward pass, as well as the ten-yard rule, made it difficult for teams to sustain their offenses. Weaker teams played better than they might otherwise have, he declared, and mistakes often decided the game. Fumbles and interceptions inevitably played an exaggerated role, and even the weather could influence the outcome when a team had a strong wind at its back. As a result, he argued, weakened offenses often resulted in scoreless ties. To demonstrate this point, he cited the Yale-Princeton game; between failed passes and fumbled punts, the two teams barely penetrated the twenty-five-yard line of their opponents. Even an onside kick by Yale netted only fifteen yards. The best Yale could manage was to move to Princeton's fifteen-yard line just as time was called.[20]

Still, the football spectators and gridiron critics regarded the new rules as a qualified success. The rules committee had designed its handiwork to encourage the open-field game and to discourage the dangerous running plays across scrimmage, and the pass did a large part of the job. While end runs proved difficult to execute, the pass had the ability to move the ball downfield quickly. As a result, spectator interest in college football proved brisk, and, best of all, the public seemed to have forgotten about serious injuries and deaths.

If one perused the headlines and opening paragraphs, deaths seemed to have declined. That decline had far more to do, however, with the news media's treatment of serious injuries than with the actual dangers on the gridiron. Throughout the 1905 season the newspapers had stoked the fires of public outrage by combining both college, high school, and sandlot deaths and failing to distinguish direct deaths incurred from accidents on fields of play from indirect deaths such as heatstrokes and heart conditions. When the newspaper headlines proclaimed a total of eighteen deaths in 1905, that figure encompassed all levels of play—college, high school, and sandlot. Buried in the stories were the statistics for college football, in which only three players had died. Simply put, it would have been difficult for the new rules to have reduced what was already an extremely low number of casualties.

In 1906 the *New York Times* listed 11 football players killed out of all those engaged in the sport at all levels—down from 18 (and some reports had given even higher figures) the year before—and the 104 players who were seriously injured under the new rules marked a reduction of nearly 35 percent from the previous year. Quite remarkably, however, the casualties for college football in 1906 remained the same as in 1905: three college players died, precisely the same number who had been killed under the old rules. More to the point, none of the three deaths in 1906 occurred in the East, where newspapers reached large numbers of readers and gridiron injuries had the potential of triggering cries for reform. The three gridders who died in college football played at small, relatively unknown institutions. And of the eight deaths in high school or sandlot play, none aroused unusual attention. Summing up, there were no high-profile deaths such as Harold Moore's in 1905 which would lend themselves to sensational stories in big-city newspapers nor acts of brutality such as the Burr-Quill episode in the Harvard-Yale game the previous year.[21]

The relatively low numbers of casualties under both sets of rules raise serious doubts about whether deaths and injuries were the underlying cause of the crisis in the fall of 1905. To be sure, no one would question that football had faced the gravest moment in its history. Harold Moore's death in the Union-NYU game, the Burr-Quill incident in the Harvard-Yale game, and even the White House meeting bathed football in negative publicity, and the media exploited these events for all they were worth. Because of the flurry of criticism, the controversy in 1905–6 presented a golden opportunity for opponents such as Frederick Jackson Turner, Nicholas Murray Butler, and Harold MacCracken to launch attacks on the game or to call for the reform of big-time athletics. Ironically, the reformers who did the most to bring about changes in the rules of play got at most a marginally safer game. What the gridiron gods had dealt them were clearer and more innovative rules that curtailed the most visible brutalities while providing far more interesting strategies, a game that could be followed more easily by the average spectator.

From 1906 to 1908 football enjoyed a brief vacation from controversy. With the apparent decline of deaths and serious injuries, the public and media suspended their criticism of football. The reforms enacted by conferences and colleges had quieted the uproar from faculty and college presidents. Except at Columbia, Northwestern, and the West Coast schools, nearly all of the major colleges continued to play football. Yet the controversies of 1905–6 had been so serious and the emotions so roiled that undercurrents of discontent still flowed. People who recalled the brutality of football in 1905 or the corrupt practices of coaches and alumni did not necessarily drop their opposition to football simply because the rules had been changed. The debate over football still stirred just below the surface and required only a catastrophic event to bring it to the surface.

In spite of changes, football injuries remained an only slightly less newsworthy topic. After each season newspapers printed summaries of deaths and serious injuries, comparing that season with ones immediately before. While these brief reports held less interest than in 1905, they indicated that the press and the public still regarded gridiron casualties as worthy of an article on the sports pages. This preoccupation with the health and safety of college and high school students playing a rough sport had much to do with the temper of the times. Whereas the public tolerated the inevitability of serious injuries in 1890s or occasionally applauded the manly, rugged character of football, the balance of opinion shifted visibly in the early 1900s. The injury controversy of 1905 was one of the first indications that college presidents and politicians cared enough to make the spirit and rules of football into a national issue.

It is worth further noting that one reason that injuries caught the attention of the college presidents and politicians had to do with the public's impatience with safety hazards. Between 1905 and 1909 muckrakers and political reformers helped to make the general public less tolerant of risk in everyday life. Prompted by a muckraking novel by Upton Sinclair, *The Jungle,* Congress passed the Pure Food and Drug and Meat Inspection Acts in 1906, landmark laws that symbolized a turning point in the public's attitude toward death and serious injuries where negligence and greed contributed to the problem. The media also responded to the new sense of outrage by bringing tragic and dangerous situations to the reading public's attention. To give just one example, an explosion at Cherry Hill, Illinois, in November 1909 shared the front page of the *New York Times* with the fatal injury of a player in a football game between Georgetown and the University of Virginia. Though the two were hardly similar in magnitude, both were sensational events that occurred as a result of imperfect rules and negligent practices.[22]

The Upheaval of 1909

Having undergone its share of trauma in 1905 and then apparently solved its problems, college football now began to descend into another abyss of deaths and serious injuries. After two years of relatively safe play in 1906 and 1907, the football proconsuls were so obsessed with fine-tuning the rules that they barely noticed the rise in deaths at all levels in 1908. Yet the absence of scoring that typified the big games probably had a connection with the rise in casualties. As teams resorted to new strategies to move the ball, deaths in college football jumped from two to six in 1908. While the number of deaths in high schools actually dropped to a record low of four, the number of serious injuries to high school gridders leaped from twenty-four to fifty-one. Even allowing for the wild inaccuracies in reporting injuries, the number of college deaths and high school injuries under the new rules suggest that serious problems existed in 1908—and that the number and severity of injuries would mushroom in 1909.

The rise in 1908 and 1909 seemed to contradict the apparent success of football rules makers in making the game safer. Believing that an injury crisis occurred in 1905, historians have erroneously concluded that reforms greatly alleviated the "murderous" character of football, ignoring the fact that the number of deaths hardly varied from 1904 to 1906. More accurately, the deaths and injuries in 1909 not only rose dramatically but almost certainly resulted from the new rules.

If the 1906 "reforms" brought a delayed upturn in injuries, what exactly went wrong? What virus infected the new rules after such an auspicious beginning? That the rules committee neglected to outlaw the pushing and pulling of the ball carrier created a serious flaw that resulted in a larger number of concussions and created a new round of damaging publicity. Dangers to the tackles isolated by fake passes proved more serious because the rules committee had not prohibited mass play, or, in other words, the pushing and pulling of ball carriers. Simply put, the juggernaut of players blasting through the line posed a danger to the vulnerable linemen. While the deaths did not rise in 1906 and 1907, the players and coaches soon found ways to pervert the rules or to defend against the new open-field plays with greater effectiveness.

The new football in 1908 began to look like the old grinding, pushing and pulling game again—especially in the East, where coaches preferred running plays to the forward pass. Rather than use the forward pass to gain yardage, many eastern teams used it, instead, to decoy their opponents. The team with the ball would fake throwing the forward pass or throw a short decoy pass to trick the defense into playing farther off the line. Then the ball carrier would come smashing across the weakened tackle position, often ac- companied by men on all sides to push and pull him through the defense. Whereas this trend received scant notice in 1908, it had probably caused a number of serious injuries, and by 1909 the alarming number of casualties brought it into sharp focus.

In short, the crisis of college football returned with a vengeance. Fol- lowing the upward trend in the previous year the number of casualties in college football rose dramatically in 1909, resulting in eleven deaths in col- lege play and an overall total at all levels which reportedly rose to twenty- six. Notably, several of the collegiate deaths occurred in games between the best-known college teams. This second injury crisis, often overlooked by historians, proved to be far more serious from a medical standpoint than the one that preceded it. It was as if the new rules had created a wider array of dangers than had existed before the 1906 reforms.[23]

The series of well-publicized injuries began early in the season. On Oc- tober 16, 1909, quarterback Edwin Wilson of Navy was seriously injured in a game with Villanova as a result of a tackle that occurred in the open field; paralyzed from his injuries, he hovered near death for nearly six months. Two weeks later, when Harvard played at West Point, the powerful Crimson team relied on line plunges to move the ball, often targeting Army's left tackle, Eugene Byrne. The umpire Edward K. Hall later recalled that Byrne was virtually dead on his feet. "The plays had been steadily directed at Byrne, and he was all tired out," Hall wrote. "Al Sharp who was refereeing the game sent word to the Army coach to take him out."[24]

The Army coach kept him in the game. On a short forward pass to Har- vard's All-American tackle Hamilton Fish, Byrne sustained a slight injury. Next, Harvard ran a play across Byrne's position, throwing him to the ground. Byrne did not get up. Unconscious, he was taken to the hospital, where he finally regained consciousness at 11 P.M. but still had to be given oxygen and artificial respiration. Later that night Byrne slipped back into a coma, and at about 6 A.M. he was pronounced dead. According to the au- topsy, a dislocation of his vertebrae had caused lesions in the nerve centers affecting his breathing. Following his death, the U.S. Military Academy called off the rest of its schedule. Because the episode was reported in detail by the New York newspapers, Byrne's death resulted in a reawakening of the concern with the dangers of football.[25]

On November 13, two weeks after the fatality at West Point, the University of Virginia traveled to Washington to play Georgetown. The game at Hilltop Field was pitifully one-sided, and the Virginia backs had little trouble pushing the ball down the field for two touchdowns in the first half. Running "cross bucks" or "skin tackle" plays across the tackle position, Virginia freshman halfback Archer Christian was enjoying the best game of his young career. Christian was known for his backward "broad jump," or swan dive, in which he launched himself backward across the defense just as he was about to be tackled, a dangerous maneuver that might net a few extra yards. By the second half the versatile young halfback had kicked a field goal and then scored the team's third touchdown, to put the Orange and Blue ahead 21-0.[26]

On Virginia's next possession Christian took off across Georgetown's left tackle. Escorted by blockers, or "pushers," on either side and one man to block in front, Christian again broke through the Georgetown left side for perhaps eight yards, but then the gap quickly closed. Christian abruptly toppled back across a Georgetown player as others fell on top of him. When the players got to their feet, the Virginia halfback remained prostrate. Carried to the sidelines, he appeared barely conscious. "Oh, I'm suffering Pop," he said to the trainer. "Please do something for me." He then slipped into a coma.[27]

Because of a premonition, or so it was said, Christian's mother, though in Washington, had stayed in her hotel room rather than attend the game that day. But, when she learned of the injury, she rushed to Georgetown Hospital. She then summoned the renowned surgeon Harvey Cushing from Baltimore, who had just the month before attended to Midshipman Edwin Wilson of Navy. Unfortunately, neither Cushing nor the University of Virginia doctor who worked alongside him in the three hours of surgery could save Archer Christian; he died early next morning of a hemorrhaging in his brain.

Coming so soon after Cadet Byrne's fatal injury, the death of Archer Christian amplified the criticism of football rules which had begun in the week after Byrne's death. The tragedy made the front page of the *New York Times* Sunday edition, which also ran an editorial pleading with college presidents and faculties to stop football until the pushing and pulling of mass play were ended. By not suspending football, the *Times* declared, the universities were being "strangely blind to the greater propriety of canceling all games before the next boy is killed."[28]

The newspaper accounts differed in the way that they portrayed Christian's death—and the style of play that had caused it. According to the *New York Times,* his accident had resulted from mass play: first, Christian's teammates had dragged him across the line, then he had stumbled. After that, the *Times* reported, just as he was getting to his feet, several Georgetown players converged on him and knocked him on his back. While the *Times* account sounded firsthand, the newspaper had to depend on news agencies or stringers for the details rather than its own reporters.

In contrast, the Virginia student newspaper disputed these accounts. "Contrary to what has been printed in several papers," *College Topics* reported, "the death-dealing play was not one of the dangerous mass formation manoeuvres, and twenty-one players did not heedlessly pile on the injured player." While the student reporter did not say exactly how Christian was killed, he implied that the Virginia halfback had simply died in an unlucky accident. A story in the *Baltimore Sun*, however, indicated that Christian might have attempted one of his patented backward dives, a maneuver that had little to do with mass play.[29]

Even the Virginia coach described the play as a straightforward run through the line which did not depend on pushing and pulling and occurred well beyond the line of scrimmage. The school's president, Edwin Alderman, wrote to the Virginia coach after the accident asking him to describe the play in which Christian was killed. Coach John Neff replied that there was nothing unusual or brutal about the play. He insisted that Christian had headed into the line led by a single blocker; newspapers had reported that he had a teammate on either side. Like Eugene Byrne, Christian sustained his injury in a play run across tackle, but Neff suggested that he had broken into the open. Even if it was not a conventional mass play, the persistent runs across tackle had led to the Georgetown players rapidly converging on him once he crossed the line of scrimmage.[30]

Putting these accounts together, it is likely that Archer Christian got through the line fairly quickly, which would indicate that pushing and pulling played little part in the initial part of the play. When he encountered the Georgetown defensive tacklers, he may have fallen and attempted to get up. It is also possible that he tried a final leap for extra yards when he saw that he was going to be tackled, perhaps a backward dive in which he did not have time to launch himself. While he probably was not a direct victim of a mass play, the fact that he took off across tackle and abruptly ran into a number of tacklers made it appear that a mass play had sent him to his grave.

Almost immediately, Father Joseph Himmel, president of Georgetown, announced that his institution would suspend football for the rest of the season. President Edwin Alderman of Virginia quickly followed, as did North Carolina, which would have played Virginia in its final contest of the season. On November 17 the Georgetown faculty went a step further and abolished football indefinitely. This was only the beginning of a Jesuit campaign against football. In December Father Himmel would gather with the presidents and faculty of other Jesuit colleges to discuss the possibility of

eliminating football and to pass a series of reform measures designed to reduce the exaggerated role of college football.[31]

Edwin Alderman and the Rules Crusade

Even before Georgetown's action, the president of the University of Virginia, Edwin Alderman, found himself in an excruciatingly difficult situation. Though he had not attended the game, he needed to show that he not
only mourned Christian but also had a plan to prevent such a tragedy from
happening again. Unlike other presidents, Alderman would not be content
simply to deplore the defects in the rules. As a friend of the game, he realized that, unless he took a firm position, critics of football might attempt to
call for abolishing it at Virginia or for changes that would cripple the gridiron sport.

By a remarkable coincidence Harvard's Charles Eliot had been in Charlottesville just one week before Archer Christian's fatal injury. Recently retired, he was speaking at the University of Virginia at the invitation of his
friend President Alderman. Following his speech he had traveled to Washington, where he was staying at the British embassy on Saturday, November
13. Immediately, when he heard of Christian's death, Eliot wrote Alderman,
offering both sympathy and a few carefully chosen words of advice. "The
grave event," he subtly reflected, "may oblige you to say something about
the risks of the American game."[32]

Eliot deplored the time-honored defense offered by supporters of football. "Men are killed and wounded," Eliot conceded, "in hunting, rowing,
riding, horseback on a road or in steeple chase, sailing boats, canoeing, and
climbing mountains," but what distinguished football from other dangerous sports, he insisted, was that dangers in football resulted from "risks of
the game, *deliberately planned and deliberately maintained.*" The threat of
death and injury on the football field resulted not from random accidents
but from playing the game according to the rules.[33]

Alderman replied immediately. In the aftermath of Christian's death Alderman was going "through a shocking experience," he told Eliot, "which I
have never yet had to undergo." As a college president in the early twentieth
century, he had a moral and educational responsibility. He knew that simply calling off the final game of the football season would not provide an
adequate response. But he also believed, as he tried to explain to Eliot, that
football was essential to the students' morale in the small and limited world
of Charlottesville, Virginia.[34]

When he had served as president of North Carolina and Tulane, before
coming to Virginia, Alderman enthusiastically promoted football and, despite the recent gridiron tragedy, still felt that football had its role to play
in college life. While the Virginia president lamented Christian's death, he

managed to find ways to defend football in a public statement published only three days after the accident. "A boy cannot play football successfully," he declared, "without the use of self-denial, self-restraint, of resoluteness, of patience, of well-ordered attention, of loyalty to a cause, of a distinct form of unselfishness." By banishing football, colleges would suffer a calamity, if for no other reason than the lack of diversion in small towns like Charlottesville—many of the same arguments used to defend football in the 1880s and 1890s.[35]

Alderman embraced Eliot's suggestions in the statement that he prepared for the press at the beginning of the week. Feeling the need to devise a formula for reform, Alderman leaned heavily on Eliot's reasoning, using his logic to build an argument. He even employed the former Harvard president's words verbatim, though quite openly, because he sent a copy of the statement of his reply to Eliot. The resulting proposal, however, would prove far different than Eliot's anti-football stance. Published on November 17, Alderman's statement turned Eliot's words into a proposal for reform. What distinguished football from other sports, he wrote, was that "*inordinate risks and danger to life existed in the rules of the game deliberately planned and deliberately maintained,*" precisely the words used by Eliot. But, whereas Eliot opposed big-time football and distrusted the rules committee, Alderman both supported football and believed that the rules committee members, which included Virginia's Dr. William Lambeth, worked for the best interests of the colleges. Hence, he portrayed the rules makers as men of good intentions who had somehow failed to create a game that would prevent fatal accidents. They must devote all of their expertise, he declared, to finding a solution.[36]

Eager to play a part in football reform, Alderman made plans to attend the ICAA annual convention in late December. He hoped to lead a full delegation of southern college presidents, but his colleagues had neither the time, interest, or funds to travel to New York and regarded Alderman's chances of influencing football reform with skepticism. Instead, the Virginia president sponsored a conference of Virginia schools to Charlottesville to lend support to his call for rules reform. While this conference could not materially affect the course of national deliberations, Alderman would convey its results to the leaders of the ICAA as additional support for changes in the rules. It stood as another example of Alderman's efforts to remain in the vanguard of educational reform.

Supported by Virginia educators and his own school's Board of Visitors, Alderman's mission to save football had only one acerbic critic, former Civil War guerilla leader, John Mosby. Now seventy-five and a lawyer in Washington, the irascible Mosby had been expelled from Virginia and sent to jail in 1851 for shooting another student in the neck, after the much larger boy threatened the diminutive, acid-tongued Mosby. Since Mosby did not serve on the Virginia Board of Visitors, his virulent and widely publicized letter written from his home in Washington to a friend in Charlottesville failed to derail Alderman's New York-bound express. The Virginia president tactfully dismissed Mosby's objections to football as a violent pastime unsuited to higher education. Alderman was determined to travel to New York for the ICAA convention, where he planned to deliver a ringing ultimatum to the members of the joint rules committee.[37]

The ICAA that Alderman appealed to had sixty-seven members in 1909, a bare majority of the football-playing institutions. It still had not enrolled big-name football institutions except for Harvard, which joined in December. The gridiron powers other than Harvard held back from joining the ICAA partly because the organization represented a large number of smaller and less-known institutions. Since the major eastern schools had members on the joint rules committee, they had little to gain from joining a group whose principal power lay in its rules committee. By sponsoring the reform football rules committees in 1906, however, ICAA members enjoyed some influence with big-time eastern institutions and their veteran rules makers like Walter Camp and Paul Dashiell. They had the right, if they chose, to withdraw their members from the committee and simply make their own rules as they had contemplated doing in 1905–6.

At its meeting on December 27 the executive committee of the organization met to determine the policy of the ICAA toward football and to review the results of a survey taken among the members. The members of the association had voted by mail to determine whether they wanted to see the game retained. Almost unanimously, the colleges replied yes. When asked to decide whether the rules would be continued or revised, a vast majority agreed to recommend a change in the rules.[38]

Before Alderman spoke on December 28, Henry Williams of Minnesota, the chairman of the rules committee, acknowledged that football's rules had again become a center of controversy. Several tragic accidents, he believed, had been used to whip up concern among college faculties and the general public. Of all the deaths at all levels of play attributed by the newspapers to football—and he mentioned an unusually high figure of thirty-two—he declared that only four could be chalked up to college football. Though he believed in reforming the rules to safeguard against injuries, he cautioned that rules changes could never wipe out all serious injuries and fatalities.[39]

In the chaos following Williams's report delegates called for all kinds of changes, including the abolition of the forward pass and the return to a rugby-style game. When Dartmouth's Edward K. Hall moved to refer the problem to the rules committee, Edwin Alderman then rose to make a plea for rules reform. He cautioned the delegates that the breakdown in the rules had not resulted, as Williams suggested, from newspaper hysteria. He described to the delegates the anguish that he had felt when one of his students had perished. He even accused Williams of trying to defend football rather than seeking to make it safer. Alderman's call for reform made an impression on the delegates. The proceedings of the 1909 convention recorded that Edwin Alderman "made an eloquent address, telling of the sad experience of his institution this year in the death of one of their promising students, and stating in his judgment football as an American college sport was doomed unless radical reforms were made."[40]

In this speech and a second one delivered before a vote was taken by the convention, the Virginia president avoided making specific recommendations because he knew so little of the technical side of the game. Instead, he directed his admonitions to the rules committee. He bluntly told Dr. Williams and the other four rules makers in the audience that he would inform the Virginia assembly that the committee was prepared to make radical changes. Otherwise, he was certain that the legislators would try to abolish the game. Professor Short of Delaware followed up Alderman's remarks by warning that, if the rules were not changed, the legislatures would surely make it a crime to play football.[41]

Alderman and the other speakers could only hope that the committee would heed their admonitions. Because the Virginia president was not an expert on football, he made no effort to speculate on the causes of the crisis or to advise the rules makers on what they might do. Nevertheless, he was a vigorous advocate for the college presidents and athletic officials, who believed that football was in danger and hoped to save the game.

Following Alderman's speech Professor Henry A. Peck of Syracuse stood up to call for changes in the rules committee itself. Unlike Alderman, Peck distrusted the members of the old committee who formed half of the joint rules committee because most had not joined the ICAA. The major eastern schools still played a major role in rules making, though except for Harvard they held themselves above the 1905 reform group. "Let us appoint our own committee to revise and modify the rules," Peck declared, "and if the other colleges don't like it let them play among themselves." The delegate from Harvard, W. F. Garcelon, replied that the ICAA by itself lacked the authority to make the rules. James Babbitt of Haverford, a member who had served on the joint committee since 1906, felt that it would not be fair to the members of the old committee, an indication of how closely knit the two committees had become. "Give our associates on the rules committee a fair and equal chance to bring about a proper revision in this serious crisis for football," he pleaded. "If we fail, call a new convention and begin all over again."[42]

The criticism of the old committee reflected the lingering animosities from the rules controversy of 1905–6—or, more precisely, the distrust of Walter Camp and Yale. Many of the members still regarded the old committee as responsible for the failure of the rules in the fall of 1909. They not only condemned the big-time football schools for refusing to join the ICAA but also blamed them for the failure to eliminate mass play. Following Peck's criticism the delegates overrode E. K. Hall's resolution to refer the rules controversy to the committee, insisting that the members of the old committee formally join the ICAA committee and threatening to delegate the rules making exclusively to its own committee.[43]

It should be recalled that the changes in the rules from 1906 to 1909 had resulted from a series of reforms cobbled together by the Harvard alumni. For all the care that the Harvard alumni took in drawing up their proposals, they had two overriding goals in mind. The first was to prevent Charles Eliot and the various college faculties from abolishing football and the second to head off Walter Camp's attempt to seize control of the reform process. The Harvard alumni committee had done its best to achieve these goals while responding to the public's concern with safety. Needless to say, Harvard's political agenda and the rules committee's urgent need to draw up its preliminary reforms kept the rules makers from a thorough study of the rules changes and how they might affect the safety of football. In their haste to reform the rules they had failed to eliminate pushing and pulling, the most criticized practices in college football.

Inevitably, the rules committee destroyed the balance achieved by playing under the same basic rules for almost twenty years. Some of the changes such as the forward pass actually created dangerous tradeoffs, such as the perilous plays across tackle. By 1909 some of these unforeseen dangers resulted in a game that became at least as dangerous as the discredited old game played before 1906—and possibly more so. In short, the rules committee was faced with an imbalance between offense and defense which they had inadvertently created.

In a larger sense the injury controversy of 1909–10 had resulted from football itself. The obsession with winning had meant that coaches and players would always try to subvert the rules in ways that would enable them to achieve victory. In a game whose byword was *violence,* the attempts to blast holes in the line by isolating the tackle would naturally result in some serious injuries and deaths. Given the number of exposed heads and spinal columns, big-time football already had the capacity to kill and maim, and nothing that the rules committees could do in 1910 would change that fact. As long as college students wanted to play college football and as long as rivals put the highest premium on winning, football would continue to be a battlefield in which the combatants injured and sometimes murdered one another.

Still, the rules committee had a unique opportunity to complete the work that it had begun four years earlier. In 1909–10 the committee did not face the earlier blitz of negative publicity about the culture of football from college faculty, presidents, and journalists; the reforms in 1906 had given at least the illusion that teams and players were less out of control. As for the committee, it still could operate nearly as independently as it had in the years of Walter Camp's hegemony, and in 1910 the most thoughtful and progressive rules makers were determined to make essential reforms. To restore the good standing of football, the rules committee had to fix the game that it had changed radically four years before. Unfortunately, some of those earlier reforms would prove near-fatal obstacles to change.

CHAPTER SEVEN

The Invention of Modern Football, 1910 to 1917

When the ICAA adjourned late on the day on December 29, 1909, the delegates to the conference had made it clear that injuries threatened football and that the rules committee should make sweeping changes. Not easily alarmed, Amos Alonzo Stagg, a member of the rules committee since 1904, betrayed a note of desperation when he wrote to his mentor Walter Camp, "We have certainly got to do something Walter, for the season has been a mighty bad one for a number of individuals as well as for the game."[1]

Stagg reflected the alarm felt by the friends of football as they faced the stormy response to deaths and disabling injuries—and the discord displayed by football's critics and friends at the ICAA convention in December 1909. The two rules groups from the crisis of 1905–6 had not yet merged and now threatened to go their separate ways. Just as it had done in 1906, the ICAA convention had passed a resolution calling upon the old committee to amalgamate, and, if the veteran rules makers refused, the new committee was to "formulate rules under which football shall be played in 1910." The ICAA delegates ignored these instructions, however, and met with the old committee as if they were a single committee, without demanding that the other seven institutions represented by the old members join the ICAA.

Opposition to Mass Play and the Struggle to Save the Pass

Even before the joint rules committee met, Harvard, Yale, and Princeton had attempted to create their own rules committee that would prevent the national rules makers from passing hasty or radical rules changes. Initiated by Yale's conservative president, Arthur Hadley, in December 1909, the attempt to devise a Big Three version of the rules proved to be not only a failure but also a prelude to the disagreements among the members of joint rules committee.

Walter Camp and Arthur Hadley harbored a profound distaste for rules making by faculty groups, a compelling reason for Yale not to join the ICAA. Camp had never liked the forward pass and worried about radical reforms that might result from the public clamor. Yale had just enjoyed an undefeated season in which the team had employed the old weapon of mass play. Fearing the possibility of rash changes, Hadley contacted Harvard's new president A. Lawrence Lowell, who had succeeded Charles Eliot when he retired in October 1909. Soon after the end of the season the two presidents met to discuss the possibility of forming a common policy on football reform. To Hadley's relief Lowell was far more pragmatic toward football than Eliot, and he seemed to care more about the image of his institution than gridiron casualties. "Personally, I have never been so frightened at the risk [of injuries or deaths]," he declared, "as by the fact that they might take place in the presence of vast masses of spectators which has in my mind a demoralizing effect." Hadley and Lowell agreed to appoint an in-house committee of their coaches and football experts to investigate injuries and suggest solutions to the joint rules committee.[2]

When Hadley and Lowell sought to include Woodrow Wilson of Princeton, however, they encountered a discordant note. Wilson said that he found Hadley's approach to investigating injuries "technical and microscopic." The future president, who had played only a minor part in the earlier movements for reform, wanted to bring about the end of "mass play" and to create a game that was "more attractive." Neither Hadley or Lowell entertained such a visionary approach, and Wilson proved to be a fly in their gridiron ointment.

While the three presidents managed to agree on the need for a committee, the alumni coaches and football experts at Harvard and Princeton distrusted Yale's Walter Camp, who, they believed, had brainwashed Hadley with his own private views. The coach and athletic advisor at Princeton, Bill Roper, insisted that Camp was merely interested in safeguarding Yale's interests. "Mr. Camp is violently opposed to the new rules [the early version of the 1910 rules changes]," he wrote, "because Yale's style of play is practically destroyed, there being no further pushing and pulling of the runner allowed."[3]

Even though the Big Three presidents set up their committee, they could not prevent disagreements among their football experts. On top of that, the same experts—Camp, Haughton, and Roper—who could not agree in the Big Three sessions all participated in meetings of the joint rules committee of the ICAA, and they carried their disagreements from the Harvard-Yale-Princeton deliberations into the larger committee.

Much the same could be said of the entire committee. Of the fourteen delegates who gathered in New York on February 5, 1910, the seven members of the old committee, and their seven institutions, adhered to strong and often contradictory views regarding the 1906 changes. To be certain, they also possessed more experience in making rules than did the rules makers drawn from the ICAA. Indeed, a surprising number of those who had come from Camp's old committee had served at least five years on the joint rules committee. Five of the seven members—all except Crawford Blagden of Harvard, who had replaced Bill Reid, and Parke Davis, the former coach and football historian, who represented Princeton—had participated in the historic proceedings in the winter of 1906. The familiar names of Walter Camp, Amos Alonzo Stagg, L. M. Dennis, John C. Bell, and Paul Dashiell (represented at this meeting by an "alternate," or substitute) all remained on the roster of the joint committee.[4]

In contrast, the seven members drawn from the reform committee appointed by the ICAA in 1905 had changed considerably; all except James Babbitt of Haverford, Dr. Henry Williams of Minnesota, and William Dudley of Vanderbilt had joined the committee since its first year. These newer members hailed from both eastern and noneastern institutions as well as large and small colleges. Besides Babbitt, Dudley, and Williams, the ICAA group included H. B. Hackett of West Point, C. W. Savage of Oberlin, Dr. William Lambeth of Virginia, and Edward K. Hall of Dartmouth. As a former player and coach turned business executive, Hall served as secretary of the rules committee in 1910 and, alone among the newer members, vigorously opposed the forward pass, as had his predecessor in that position, Walter Camp.[5]

When the joint committee first met in February 1910, a poll was taken to decide on the causes of injuries and how to remedy them. The fourteen rules makers approached the problems from remarkably different viewpoints. Some members objected to 1906 reforms such as the forward pass and the onside kick. Others disliked the flying, or diving, tackle whereby players threw themselves at runners in the open field. One member perversely insisted that the greatest risk occurred when a ball carrier was *not* pushed or pulled by his teammates. Another singled out the neutral zone created in 1906 as the principal source of danger. Based on this initial sampling of opinion, the rules experts appeared to be as far apart as the delegates who had tried to discuss the rules at the ICAA convention in December.[6]

From February until May this diverse group spent much of its time discussing proposals, combinations of proposals, and amendments to proposals. After assessing the causes of danger, the committee voted to put an end to mass play, the most notorious of the existing rules. To be more precise, a motion was made to require seven men on the line of scrimmage and that there should be no pushing or pulling of the ball carrier. Surprisingly, some delegates continued to resist more precisely worded measures to eliminate pushing and pulling, even though this omission in 1905 had led to bitter controversy four years later. Throughout the debates language calling for "seven men on the line of scrimmage" appeared in virtually all plans but often failed to specify pushing and pulling. Unfortunately, experience suggested that merely requiring seven men on the line would not prevent players from doing whatever was necessary to get the ball carrier across the line. None of the delegates wanted to tarnish their reputations by out-and-out support of mass play. Yet some of the diehards straddled the fence by requiring seven men on the line without declaring mass play itself unlawful.[7]

After attempting to pass individual rules, the delegates turned to packages of proposals reflecting their own visions of the game. On February 6 Amos Alonzo Stagg, a member of the old committee, unveiled the first plan; it called for an end to the pushing and pulling of the ball carrier, required seven players on the line of scrimmage, retained the forward pass allowing it to cross any part of the scrimmage line, limited open-field tackling, and abolished the onside kick. Stagg's bundle of proposals proved to be the first of several plans proposed at the February meeting. Initially a member of Camp's "old guard," Stagg, who had played a minor role in the rules making four years earlier, turned into an energetic champion of the forward pass, an offensive tool that had worked so well for him at Chicago.[8]

From the start, the plans to reform the rules contained attempts to modify the forward pass, a controversial approach that would polarize the group and prolong its deliberations. Despite his disrepute in New Haven, Foster Sanford represented his alma mater as an alternate or substitute for Camp, probably because the former Columbia coach, who lived in New York, hewed to the Yale position on the forward pass. Sanford first introduced the controversial measure to limit the pass behind the line of scrimmage. Once the receiver snared the ball in the backfield, Sanford proposed, he would be allowed to run anywhere. In all likelihood this plan would have severely limited the use of the pass, converting it into a forward lateral with limited offensive potential. In its other features Sanford's plan incorporated some of Stagg's ideas, such as calling for seven men on the line of scrimmage and prohibiting the flying tackle. Unlike Stagg's package, it would not outlaw pushing and pulling of the ball carrier, nor would it have eliminated the onside kick. By comparison, it was much more conservative and controversial than Stagg's scheme and served a rallying point for those who wanted to retain as much as possible of the old football.[9]

Before the March meetings Amos Alonzo Stagg had experimented with the forward pass in Fayetteville, Arkansas, where he had a former Chicago player, Hugo Bezdek, now a coach at Arkansas (and later a well-known coach at Penn State), conduct field trials. Through Bezdek, Stagg stripped the pass of its limitations, such as the rule restricting who could catch the ball. As a result of these trials, Stagg argued for keeping the rule that only players on the end of the line should be eligible to catch the ball, or the offense, he reasoned, would enjoy too many advantages.[10]

Likewise, in April Walter Camp held his own field trials. Camp limited one team to passes behind the line, and a second group was allowed to throw fairly wide-open passes. He also experimented with a defense that could be spread no further than the offensive line. In his field trials at Yale,

Camp tried to limit the diving or flying tackles so that two feet remained on the ground while the tackle was made. The results failed to support the arguments for limiting the flying tackle. As Camp suspected, more chest and stomach injuries occurred because defensive players relied on their weight and strength rather than on a well-timed leap to bring down the ball carrier. Ironically, at the same time, in Baltimore, Edwin Wilson of Navy, whose severe injury in an open-field tackle had sparked the debate, died of his injuries, almost ensuring that the committee would have to limit the diving, or flying, tackle.[11]

Walter Camp conducted his experiments because at the March meetings he and H. B. Hackett of Army planned to introduce another set of proposals that would have limited the pass to the area behind the line of scrimmage. At each meeting the delegates who represented one side or the other tried to present a plan that would win the final approval of their colleagues. To make their proposals more attractive Camp and Hackett would have prohibited pushing and pulling and outlawed the diving tackle. Yale had always produced hard-nosed tacklers who pursued the ball carrier with tenacity and tackled ferociously.[12]

Camp had a reason to protect the style of play that worked so well for Yale. It was true that Camp's Yale team of 1909, his last great team, had gone undefeated. Yet it is also well to remember that Camp had a vested interest in football which transcended his remarkable record at Yale. In a letter written while he was still the team's graduate adviser, Camp admitted that Yale alumni had become overconfident, willing to sanction any game that Camp approved, because they were certain that he could always win. Clearly Camp felt pressure to retain the status quo because his game had succeeded so brilliantly at his alma mater.

Camp further confessed that he had a "very distinct desire, apart from anything that Yale might do, to see the game which I have worked so hard keep its general characteristics." He dreaded what committee members might try to do if they were given the chance. "When legislators commence to suggest that we should fool with the defense and station men at different points on the defense and keep them there," he once declared, "it makes me feel like throwing up my hands at the hopeless entanglement that will ensue both with officials and players."[13]

These entanglements took several months to work out. If the committee had met continuously, it might have wrapped up its work in a week or two. Instead, it spent one weekend each month in formal meetings held in either New York or Philadelphia. Spread across the East, South, and Midwest, most of the members could ill afford the travel time to and from the proceedings, let alone spending two days each month at the lengthy sessions. When the committee met in Philadelphia on April 29 and 30, four delegates failed to appear, including Walter Camp and Amos Alonzo Stagg. In spite of Camp's being absent once again, the fierce struggle between Harvard and Yale over rules reform which had begun way back in the fall of 1905 would once again emerge.[14]

On the first day of the meeting, Crawford Blagden of Harvard proposed a number of reform measures including a less strict version of the forward pass. Because they became the points of departure for the invention of modern football, the proposals in the Blagden Report are worth noting: (1) four twenty-minute periods instead of the thirty-minute halves; (2) seven men on the line of scrimmage instead of six; (3) eight yards to be gained in three downs instead of ten; (4) the ball receiver could cross the line at any point, including directly over center (before this the ball carrier had to cross the line five yards beyond the point at which the ball was placed down as if he were running a modern option play); (5) no pushing or pulling of the ball carrier, which reiterated the motion passed at the first meeting; (6) onside kick or punt had to go at least sixteen yards beyond the line of scrimmage instead of twenty yards; (5) the tackler had to have at least one foot on the ground when making the tackle.

The liberalized proposals governing the forward pass deserve even more attention because they became so hotly contested that they prolonged the deliberations and drove a wedge between the members. Blagden's version of the forward pass consisted of four radical changes: (1) the pass could cross the line at any point, not just five yards to either side, but the receiver could not be more than sixteen yards from scrimmage; (2) the men in the backfield instead of only the ends could catch the pass; (3) potential receivers could not be checked or obstructed once they had crossed the line of scrimmage; (4) on incomplete passes the ball would be returned to the point where the pass was made instead of counting it as a fumble if touched.[15]

This list of proposals stood out as the most far-reaching set of reforms yet introduced, removing many of the restrictions that had hampered the forward pass. Unlike other sets of proposals, the Blagden plan did not divide the field into two sectors, whereas the old Camp approach had permitted a more open style of play in the middle of the field then let teams return to the old style when they approached the goal line. Instead, the rules provided for the whole field to be seamless, opening up the possibility of a single, unified style of reformed football.[16]

For the remainder of the two-day session the members kicked around the details of the Blagden plan. Much of the session was taken up debating the use of the hands to block and push a potential pass or kick receiver. And, although the meeting made slow but steady progress on a series of complicated motions, the committee reached the end of its session and still had not yet devised satisfactory means to protect pass receivers. One can only imagine the fatigue and frustration of the delegates as they voted that "the rules as adopted were so intricate and complex, as to make it practically certain that there would be an almost interminable tangle in undertaking to either play or officiate the game." In a nutshell the delegates considered the day's rules making as wholly unproductive.[17]

After hours of motions and amendments, the secretary, Edward K. Hall, abruptly recorded the following resolution: "VOTED: To rescind all legislation of the present session, and to adopt the following as a basis for the game." As if a storm had swept through the room blinding their vision, the weary delegates passed an eight-point set of proposals that confined the forward pass behind the line of scrimmage and merely required seven men on the line without outlawing pushing and pulling. The conservatives had evidently waited until the end of the day, when they could more easily secure a majority, either because delegates had left for home or because fatigue and frustration clouded their judgment. The Yale forces had bided their time waiting for the opportunity to torpedo the forward pass. Even though Camp was not present, he may have orchestrated a strategy to combine a less rigorous approach toward mass play with emasculating the forward pass.

It was not a comfortable solution, and the details of the new plan remained incomplete. The members therefore set up a subcommittee of three, including Crawford Blagden of Harvard, Carl Williams of Pennsylvania, and the chairman, E. K. Hall of Dartmouth, "to work out the details of the game under the foregoing vote." The subcommittee would then reassemble on May 13 and 14 in New York to complete the final draft.[18]

When the session reconvened, the subcommittee presented its report. Blagden, Williams, and Hall agreed that the eight points adopted at the end of the day on April 25 created neither an attractive game nor one that provided much opportunity for ground gaining. Either the offense had to be strengthened, they declared, or the defense weakened. Two out of the three—Blagden and Williams—favored the forward pass. Given the larger committee's mandate for a pass behind the line, however, the full-fledged forward pass no longer served as an option for their final proposal.

Faced with a virtually impossible task, it is not surprising that the plan that the three-man group came up with was one that would have produced a wildly disjointed game. To keep the pass behind the line, the subcommittee proposed an unlimited number of passes, all back of the line of scrimmage. The players behind the line would be able to go in motion in any direction but forward; players on the center of the line could interchange positions with those in the backfield. To encourage the multiple passes behind the line, the plan declared that all of these tosses would be dead once they struck the ground, thereby eliminating the possibility of a fumbled lateral or muffed pass. In addition, the offense would have five downs to gain fifteen yards, the equivalent of three yards per down adopted in 1906, allowing the team more opportunities to spring a big play. "The foregoing 15 items [the components of the plan] produce a game which as already stated," the members concluded, "is the best and most feasible one which your committee can develop under our instructions, and a game which your committee (with the reservations already stated) recommend."[19]

On the morning of May 13, as soon as the report was delivered, Harvard's coach, Percy Haughton, launched a blistering attack on the rules allowing passes behind the line and men going in motion before the snap of the ball. He argued that these plays would prove both impractical and unsafe. The sheer number of players running around the backfield before and after the play would make the job of the officials nightmarish. Moreover, a return to the momentum style of football might revive the flying formations of the early 1890s, resulting in even more injuries. He doubted that it would strengthen the offense because a player breaking through the line could easily intercept one of these passes and take it for a touchdown. According to the minutes of the meeting, Haughton believed that "the possibility of the forward pass back of the line was theoretical rather than practical; that the possibility of two forward passes tended to complicate the game."[20]

Haughton's response may not have come as a surprise to at least two members of the subcommittee, Blagden and Williams. While there is no way to know exactly what happened between the April and May meetings, the advocates of the forward pass—Blagden and Percy Haughton of Harvard, Howard Henry and Bill Roper of Princeton, as well as Carl Williams of Pennsylvania—seem to have plotted a careful and concerted assault on the idea of multiple passes and, more conspicuously, against the forward pass behind the line. Possibly Blagden and Williams led Hall into the trap of devising the multiple passes as a means of demonstrating the folly of abolishing the forward pass. Of the three members only Hall, who opposed the pass, did not participate in the attack on the mini-pass that the committee had concocted.

Rather than stop with their multiple-pass ambush, the five advocates of the forward pass worked out a hybrid alternative, known as the Blagden Report, or, for the purpose of this work, referred to as the second Blagden Report. This plan resembled Blagden's first report but modified some of the rules to make them conform to the existing game: (1) four fifteen-minute quarters instead of twenty-minute quarters; (2) seven men on the line of scrimmage; (3) ten yards to be gained in three downs instead of eight yards; (4) the first man running with the ball to cross the line at any point; (5) no pushing or pulling or interlocked interference, thereby eliminating any possibility of mass play; (6) the onside kick to go twenty yards instead of sixteen; (7) the forward pass crossing the line at any point but with the passer five yards back of the line and the pass receiver twenty yards from the line of scrimmage; (8) the ends and the men in the backfield to be eligible to catch the pass, the same as in the first Blagden report; (9) no interference with the pass receiver after he had crossed the line of scrimmage; (10) on the first and second downs incomplete passes to be brought back to the spot where the pass was thrown and on third down the opponents to get the ball at the point at which passer had thrown the ball; (11) players to have at least one foot on the ground when tackling, thereby eliminating the diving tackle.[21]

After the committee had recessed for lunch, the delegates returned to vote on reinstating the forward pass. By the narrow vote of eight to six the forward pass wriggled back into the rules. In its final form the second Blagden report altered and strengthened the rough outlines of the first report. Above all, it included the motion passed on the first day which eliminated mass play by requiring seven men on the line of scrimmage—and by outlawing pushing and pulling. Had mass play remained, even the least possibility of it, this survival of 1890s football might have produced still another round of criticism. Nearly all of the previous plans had called for seven men on the line of scrimmage, but not all explicitly banned pushing and pulling. If the committee had not acted decisively, linemen and backs would probably have found ways to engage in the old practices, just as they had done after the 1906 rules had been passed.[22]

In later amendments the committee prohibited crawling by the ball carrier after he was down, allowed officials to call for the removal of players who were no longer in condition to continue in the game, and liberalized the rule on substitutions. It also allowed one player in the backfield to go in motion either laterally or toward his own goal (the same rule remains today). As for the onside kick, or bogus punt, which had shown itself far less useful than the forward pass, it managed to survive for two more years.

Only one member of the rules committee, Walter Camp, refused to affix his signature to the 1910 rules. Uncharacteristically, Camp had missed both the April and May meetings when the crucial debates on the forward pass had taken place. It is true that Camp, as president of the New Haven Clock Company and as a member of many boards, had his share of business and philanthropic obligations. From time to time he had to miss committee meetings, and the frequent meetings in 1910 made far greater demands on his time and patience. Nevertheless, Camp's long tenure on the rules committee and his strong convictions about the nature of the game suggest a more complex explanation.

Evidently, Camp became fed up with the rules committee. His work had begun far back in December when he assisted President Hadley in setting up the in-house Harvard-Yale-Princeton committee to explore the causes of injuries. The other members of that ill-matched committee, Percy Haughton of Harvard and Howard Henry of Princeton, had exacted a pledge from Camp that he would not stand in the way of rules changes, an action that undoubtedly tried his patience. In Camp's struggles to limit the forward pass, his adversaries included Houghton and Coach Bill Roper of Princeton, who had criticized him bitterly as caring only for Yale's interests. According to Richard Borkowski, Camp felt insulted as editor of the rules book because the committee omitted him from the committee to codify the rules. Subsequently, Camp complained of the codifiers' delay in sending him the rules and apparently washed his hands of the rules reformers who had failed to employ his talents.[23]

The End of Rules Reform, 1912 to 1917

It had taken nearly fifteen years and a number of high-profile fatalities to achieve, but the rules reform of 1910 marked the beginning of a new era. As if following Woodrow Wilson's injunction to eliminate mass play and to make football more "attractive," the committee finally scrapped what remained of the crude "old game" of the 1890s. Without mass play ball carriers had to use their blockers far more adeptly than when their teammates pushed, pulled, and catapulted them. No longer depending so much on weight and bodies piled on top of one another, the new football put a higher premium on speed and deception. Though players still formed wedges on kickoffs or later with screen passes, they could not endanger opponents by getting a flying start. Quarterbacks or other ball carriers who took the ball from scrimmage now had the option of running across center rather than crossing five yards to either side. In place of the old game the rules committee had retooled its new offensive weapon, the forward pass, which would turn out to be the most fascinating and potent innovation since the yards and downs rule of the 1880s.

The new rules would breathe new life into the gridiron game. On November 10, 1910, in a brief talk to the Princeton team Woodrow Wilson, now the governor-elect of New Jersey, declared that the "new rules are doing much to bring football to a high level as a sport, for its brutal features are being done away with and better elements retained." All of this reflected a rebirth of American ideals, he proclaimed, and a rejection of pure material success. The political reformer thereby placed his seal of approval on changes to a game that he had followed so long and so intensely.[24]

Whether the rules changes in 1910 reflected a rebirth of American ideals, they indisputably proved a turning point for college football. In contrast to the hurried and incomplete rules changes of 1906, the four-month process of reworking the rules involved a careful and thorough reexamination of American football's underlying principles. The opposition to the forward pass, which now appears as self-centered and remarkably short-sighted, enabled the rules makers to engage in a thorough examination of how the pass should work, a process that would lead to a more wide-open passing game. Above all, the rules changes marked the watershed between the old rugby-style version of football and the new, streamlined version that had less to do with the feet than with the legs and hands as well as the space above the field where forward passes would soar.

And, indeed, the reforms seemed to solve the problem of deaths in college football, which fell from eleven to four, with serious injuries declining from thirty-eight to seventeen in the fall of 1910. In reality the reduction in deaths meant a return to a figure that had been typical of seasons before 1908 and 1909. More important, the casualty figure that most people saw in the headlines—deaths at all levels—dropped from twenty-six, as reported in the late fall of 1909, to a more reasonable figure of fourteen. This reduction in deaths no doubt struck newspaper readers as more normal than the soaring numbers in the previous year. By the same token the plunge in the serious injuries appeared encouraging, though injury figures would unaccountably return to previous levels in 1911. As a result of the drop in fatalities, no one cried out for the reform of the rules, and, despite the dearth of scoring, the experts did not demand further drastic reforms.

Did the rules changes, then, close the book on opposition to the forward pass? Possibly they did, but one story told twenty years later by rules maker and football historian Parke Davis of Princeton suggests that the old guard made a final, and nearly successful, assault on the forward pass in 1911. After Edward Kimball Hall's death in 1933, Davis wrote that Hall, a virulent foe of the forward pass, had actually saved the pass and possibly the joint rules committee itself. Davis recalled that anti-pass members of the committee had voted to abolish, or limit, the forward pass in what he described as an extremely close vote—probably a razor-thin majority, like the vote of the committee in restoring the pass in 1910. Davis, himself a member of the committee, wrote that Hall, as the joint rules committee chairman, faced a rebellion of the southern and western members, who threatened to walk out of the session and vote for their own rules. Hall then reconvened the committee, changed his vote, and put the pass back in the rules book.[25]

If Davis had his facts straight, this final blitz against the pass probably resulted from a revolt by the former ICAA members, who, except for Hall of Dartmouth, represented schools in the South and Midwest. Following the brouhaha at the ICAA meeting in 1910, the delegates to the convention directed the seven reform members on the joint committee to withdraw and make their own rules, an order that the reform group had fortunately ignored. If the revolt of 1911 had occurred as Davis remembered, the abolition of the pass may have been another attempt to limit the pass behind the line rather than to abolish it outright. This heroic effort to preserve the 1905 merger of the two committees would have been in keeping with the character of Edward Hall, a former coach turned business executive, who put a high premium on corporate solidarity. Possibly as a result of this episode, the old committee and the reform committee would finally decide to amalgamate in February 1912. By this time the Intercollegiate Athletic Association had renamed itself the National Collegiate Athletic Association (NCAA), a sign of its growing numbers and perhaps a recognition of its role in making the rules for college football.

These rules committee sessions marked still another turning point. According to the 1912 minutes, the former diehard opponent of the pass, Walter Camp, no longer advising the Yale team, gave up his opposition to the forward pass. Because of the scoring drought, Camp wanted to do away with the restriction of twenty yards on the forward pass, which would greatly expand its scope. "Don't throw away the present rules [presumably the forward pass and the rules against mass play]," the notation next to Camp's name read, a tribute either to the pragmatism of Camp or to the persistence of his opponents.[26]

Having retired as Yale's football advisor, Camp had less reason to defend Yale's style of play, a role that had caused bitter complaints from Princeton's coach, Bill Roper, in 1910. Camp may also have recognized that Harvard's success under Percy Haughton meant that Yale had to adapt to the new style of play. Above all, Camp had an emotional commitment to the game which he had virtually created in the 1880s. Always the pragmatist, he and other last-ditch opponents of the pass may have recognized that they could no longer oppose the 1906 innovations without badly damaging football's corporate identity. If Edward Hall voted to retain football in 1911, it made no sense for Camp to oppose the chairman and a majority of the committee.

Despite the popularity and apparent success of the 1910 rules, a number of delegates including Camp felt that the scoring had become too difficult and a simplified approach to the forward pass could strengthen the offense. As a result, the rules committee in 1912 voted unanimously to accept a number of changes that would open up the pass and make scoring easier. The rules would now permit the ball to be thrown across the goal line with impunity. To accommodate touchdown passes, the committee reduced the field of play from 110 to 100 yards so that teams could add "end zones" of 10 yards without forcing Harvard or other big-time schools to redesign their stadiums. At Camp's suggestion it voted the twenty-yard limit on the pass out of existence. And it added a fourth down to gain ten yards. The long-undervalued touchdown went from five to six points, and the extra point turned into just that—a single point. Only the 1906 version of the onside kick, which had survived the 1910 rules changes, met with opposition. It proved to be the only one of the major reforms retired to the museum of football oddities.

Rather than simply retain the pass, the committee took active steps to encourage it. In a move that would improve passing length and accuracy, the committee made its first reduction in the size of the football. The 1912 rules provided: "It shall be tightly inflated . . . Circumference, long axis, from 28 inches to 28½ inches; short axis 22½ inches to 23 inches. Weight, from 14 to 15 ounces." In short the ball's elongated dimensions became more friendly to the newly liberated pass.[27]

One of the apparent paradoxes of the 1909–12 rules controversies was the absence of concern over the emphasis and excesses of football in college life. Most of the articles and correspondence relating to college football pertained to the serious injuries and fatalities. The clamor for rules changes was not accompanied by nearly as many complaints about the abuses of college life and the perversion of the academic mission. In fairness to the earlier reformers, the schools in the Midwest and on the West Coast believed that they had already reformed football. Many colleges and smaller conferences had already acted to curb the worst problems, such as ineligible players or athletic loafers who failed to make progress toward degrees. On the other hand, a hotbed of opposition emerged in the state universities in the Plains states of the Middle West, where Progressive political reform had recently taken root. In contrast to the East and Midwest the faculty, presidents, and boards of trustees of these institutions had not raised a ruckus in the earlier 1905–6 upheaval. Only some smaller Methodist colleges that already were suspicious of this violent and unredeeming pastime had threatened to abolish football.

In April 1910 the leading group of colleges in the Plains states, the Big Six Conference, meeting in Kansas City, voted on whether to suspend football. The opposition to football was led by the small-town newspaperman William Allen White, a regent at the University of Kansas and editor of the *Emporia Gazette,* who was also an influential figure in the Progressive wing of the Republican Party. "One aspect of life at Kansas University which infuriated White was college football," William Johnson has written. "If he could have smashed it as a sport, he would have been elated." White, who had attended Kansas before football caught hold, despised football because he was convinced that it made university life too materialistic. His fellow regent, Willis Gleed, opposed football because he believed that it celebrated force and brute strength rather than the humane values. As if awaking from a long sleep, the two regents led a determined assault on football which resembled the activism of Frederick Jackson Turner four years earlier.[28]

Why had White and the Kansas regents stood aside during the 1905–6 turmoil only to spring to life in 1910? Actually, William Allen White had left Kansas temporarily in 1905 to go east. White, who had only recently joined the board of regents, spent much of his time in New York attempting to organize a new muckraking magazine modeled on *McClure's,* a publication to which he had contributed extensively. While he was not available to campaign against football in Kansas, White undoubtedly learned a great deal by observing the turmoil on the eastern gridiron, reading the muckraking articles of Henry Beach Needham, and following the movement for suspending or reforming football in the Big Nine. As a friend of Theodore Roosevelt since 1896, White may also have been inspired by the president's brief foray into football reform.[29]

In truth the authorities at Kansas had not been totally unresponsive in 1906. The athletic board at Kansas had incorporated some reforms in its contract for resuming football relations with Nebraska, a series that had been dropped several years before. The board provided for "an arbiter of the Chicago [Angell] Conference" to decide all disputes between the two schools and had decreed that all questions between the two schools would be governed by the rules of the Angell conference. But the militant opposition that had accompanied Frederick Jackson Turner's campaign against football had been lacking until White made his attempt in 1910 to convert the injury crisis into a movement to suspend football.[30]

The attack on football by the Kansas regents triggered smoldering disputes evocative of the Big Nine controversies four years before. When the students at Kansas heard of the proposal to suspend football, they immediately rose up in arms. Though not as violent as the Wisconsin vigilantes of 1906, they held rallies protesting the threat to the game. In the end, when the vote was taken, only five of the thirteen delegates favored dropping football. Nevertheless, they passed a number of conference reforms that showed the imprint of the Angell conference. The Big Six decreed that, from then on, teams must play their games on college grounds rather than in the big cities like Kansas City and Omaha. Moreover, the conference made plans to establish higher standards for eligibility, scheduling, and rules of play. Reformers also insisted that the conference examine the amount of time devoted by students to athletics.[31]

White, who closely followed state and national politics, knew that the Kansas alumni strongly opposed his position on football. "I realize that there is a certain danger," he wrote to Chancellor Frank Strong of Kansas, "in going further than we can carry University sentiment with us, and yet I feel, naturally, I desire to gain every inch we can and do not wish to stop until we have reached the end of the rope." Evidently, they had nearly reached the end of the rope, for White proposed to Strong that they reserve the right to stop football if accidents and deaths persisted in the early part of the season. Because the rash of accidents did not occur, football survived White's personal crusade.[32]

The reform movement in Kansas was the last car on the reform train that had begun its ascent up the mountain of big-time football during the 1890s. Not always successfully, the colleges and athletic conferences had dealt with the football's worst evils stemming from the breaches of ethics and perversion of education. The rules committee had resolved the most severe in-

jury problems in 1910 and smoothed the rough edges from the new rules
in 1912. By the time that these amended rules emerged, the enthusiasm or
need for further reforms had virtually disappeared.

At the 1912 NCAA convention George Ehler, athletic director at Wisconsin, who chaired the committee on fatalities, could find no college players who had died in the past season. The newspapers listed one college fatality, which Ehler had perhaps overlooked; even if this single death
occurred, it was a vast improvement over the eleven casualties that made
the headlines in 1909. The *Chicago Tribune* listed the deaths at all levels as
ten, all but one of those occurring in high school, sandlot, or semiprofessional play, a tolerable level for readers who had seen reports of thirty or
more only three years before.[33]

As hoped, the reforms for a time helped to equalize the size and strength
of big-time football schools and their early season opponents. For twenty
years after the reforms in 1910, a remarkable number of lightly regarded,
smaller colleges pulled off major ambushes or fielded highly successful
teams. Swarthmore defeated mighty Pennsylvania in 1912 and 1916, and
Stagg's mighty "Monsters of the Midway" lost their first game in 1916 to unheralded Carleton College. No wonder Coach Henry Williams observed
after Minnesota's 1910 upset by the University of South Dakota that "the
small college under the present rules has come into its own." No longer did
an early-season game mean an effortless trampling of a smaller college but,
rather, "a contest of skill and brains between a light contestant and a heavier, more slowly developing and less perfected rival, oftentimes to the great
discomfiture of the latter."[34]

One opportunistic smaller college proved to be Notre Dame, which defeated a good but not great Army team in 1913 by exploiting the reformed
rules on forward passes. By dint of an upset of Michigan in 1909, Notre
Dame had established a reputation in the Midwest. Unlike nearby small colleges like Wabash and Beloit, however, Notre Dame had difficulty scheduling games with big-name opponents in the nearby Big Nine. Though anti-Catholicism undoubtedly played a part, the Big Nine institutions also
regarded Notre Dame's eligibility requirements as far less rigorous than
their own. Thwarted in his attempts to play big games near home, Notre
Dame coach Jesse Harper contacted Army, or "West Point," in 1913; having
played Notre Dame in baseball a few months earlier, Army readily agreed to
schedule a football game that fall. The Military Academy had used the pass
since 1906 and had faced eastern teams that regularly threw passes. But for
them, as well as for most teams, the forward pass served to set up running
plays or spread the defensive secondary. In contrast, Notre Dame's coach
Harper, who had played under the innovative Amos Alonzo Stagg, saw the
pass as an equalizer for his lighter and faster team.[35]

On November 1, 1913, Notre Dame used the pass with the length and sophistication that few eastern teams had thought possible. The Notre Dame quarterback, Gus Dorais, and his favorite end, Knute Rockne, had practiced the pass while working at a resort, Cedar Point, near Toledo that past summer. Facing a heavier team, Notre Dame initially employed the forward pass as a means of survival. After two incomplete passes by Notre Dame, the visitors moved the ball to Army's thirty on running plays. Then Dorais ran right, stopped, and fired a pass diagonally across the field to Rockne, who caught it over his shoulder and went for a forty-yard gain. Army countered with its own forward passes, which set up two touchdowns, giving the academy a 13-7 lead. Notre Dame scored before halftime, making the score at halftime 14-13.[36]

After halftime Army seized the advantage, taking the ball to Notre Dame's two-yard line before being thrown back—and then having a forward pass intercepted in the end zone. By a combination of runs and passes, Notre Dame pulled away in the second half. After throwing the pass so effectively in the first half, Notre Dame surprised Army by using its running game to batter Army's defenses. The success of the running game in the third quarter wore down Army's heavier line, which had less help from the defensive secondary so preoccupied with guarding Notre Dame pass receivers. In the final quarter Notre Dame pulled away from the dispirited cadets, scoring on plays set up by passes and winning 35-13. All told, Dorais had completed thirteen of seventeen passes for a total of 243 yards; his longest pass, a thirty-five-yard completion, caused ripples of applause among West Point spectators, though only one of the thirteen passes crossed the goal line for a touchdown.[37]

The headline in the New York Times read, "Notre Dame's Open Play Amazes Army." The lead paragraph reported that "the Westerners flashed the most sensational football that has been seen in the East this year, baffling the cadets with a style of open play and a perfectly developed forward pass, which carried the victors down the field thirty yards at a clip." After the game one official, former Princeton coach Bill Roper, observed that he had always felt that the pass might be used in this way but had never seen it brought to this level of perfection. With the recent changes in the size of the ball, the moment was ripe for exploiting longer, more accurate passes.[38]

Who would have guessed that the outburst of concern over gridiron casualties in 1905 and 1909 would lead to an aerial circus at West Point in 1913, a dazzling display of athletic symmetry that would make a gridiron version of a silk purse out of a sow's ear?

Injuries to Reform

When Notre Dame beat Army in 1913, the controversies that had enveloped football for almost twenty years had already waned. Seldom in its history did football attract less notoriety than in the years immediately preceding World War I. Lists of deaths and injuries and, in truth, any discussion of gridiron hazards virtually disappeared from the newspapers. College faculties and presidents seemed to have lost interest in the problems caused by big-time athletics in college settings. The meetings of the NCAA proved to be islands of optimism and self-congratulation. Yet some skeptics remained who did not see football through the patina of the sports pages.

One of the few criticisms of football after the rules changes of 1910 came from the commandant of West Point, Colonel Clarence Townley. In his annual report of November 1913 Townley declared that "football served no useful purpose in the physical development or training of the Corps." To the contrary, football tended to make cadets unfit for military duty. Though no deaths occurred, Townley classified as "serious" eleven out of sixty-one gridiron injuries suffered by West Point players in 1912. According to Commandant Townley, the number of days spent by football players in the hospital—as a percentage of all days to hospital stays—ranged from 60 percent in 1910 to 75 percent in 1913. Sounding reminiscent of Charles Eliot, the West Point superintendent insisted that football did little more for West Point than entertain the corps.[39]

In spite of Townley's reservations, most football experts kept no statistics on lost classroom days, nor did they look at football from the standpoint of the rank-and-file student's physical development but, instead, measured success by the reduction of casualties. In 1914, two years after the final round of rules changes, the chairman of the committee on football fatalities, George Ehler, declared in his report to the NCAA that he no longer saw a point in having an annual report on injuries and deaths. Cautioning that football was strenuous, Ehler called for every player to receive a physical exam. At that point he closed the book on the era of injuries and deaths. "The cause for an outcry against football as a brutal and degrading sport cannot be maintained," he insisted, "and the sensationalism that has attached to it heretofore should cease to exist." And in 1915 the NCAA took Ehler's advice and abolished the committee on casualties.[40]

Created in the wake of the first injury crisis, the NCAA seems to have become indifferent, ironically, to the very problem that brought it into being. It took little interest in the precise causes of death and injury. Even the statistical distribution of deaths—the place, age, and type of injury—did not seem worth recording. In spite of reports of deaths and injuries in the 1920s, Edward K. Hall, who remained as chairman of the rules committee, believed that the new football had reached its pinnacle of safety and spectator interest. In the wake of football's growing popularity Hall and his colleagues persisted in this self-satisfied frame of mind until a disturbing upturn in fatalities in the Depression years made the football public take notice again.[41]

In one way Ehler correctly diagnosed the problem of deaths and serious injuries in college football. Except in 1908 and 1909, college football casualties had seldom risen above five deaths. Since football was regarded as a rough game, the public expected that a few college players would die each year, and some pigskin potentates and college presidents still felt that the benefits of gridiron dangers outweighed the costs. Certainly, they were right in believing that football players stood a better chance of survival than students who took joyrides in sailboats or automobiles. College players who were more physically mature and better conditioned probably had a better chance of surviving serious injuries than callow high school students. Nevertheless, the experts might have saved lives at all levels if they had chosen to piece together profiles of injury-creating situations or injury-prone players, but unfortunately that would not happen until the 1930s.

The NCAA, regional athletic conferences, and the coaches and trainers could also have saved lives if they had paid more attention to protective gear. Before World War I the use of helmets was not yet mandatory (and would not become so until 1939), and a number of players simply refused to use them. In photos of games in 1909 three to five players on each team were not wearing helmets, with ball carriers being the worst offenders. Because helmets were not only heavy and uncomfortable but also made signals harder to hear, running backs regarded these devices as a hindrance. Archer Christian, the Virginia halfback who died in the game against Georgetown in 1909, was probably not wearing a helmet, nor was his fullback Kemp Yancey, who did not die. In a 1912 book on football Coach Glenn Warner of Carlisle wrote that he did not encourage their use but would not interfere with a player who chose to wear one. "I have never seen an accident to the head which was serious," Warner insisted, "but I have many times seen cases when hard bumps on the head so dazed the players receiving them that they lost their memory for a time and had to be taken out of the game."[42]

Warner went on to say that ball carriers might wear "light head protectors to guard against such accidents." Probably Warner witnessed light concussions that luckily did not result in serious internal bleeding. A statistic on causes of death for 1913, which did not distinguish between college and other casualties, showed five players out of fourteen at all levels dying of concussions and four from spinal injuries.[43]

Gridiron fatalities would persist under the new rules, but the lack of statistics after 1915 makes it impossible to know precisely how many died or suffered catastrophic injuries. One can speculate that head injuries—most of them nonfatal—were still a problem after the last round of rules reforms. In 1917 a Harvard professor of physical education, Edgar Fauvier, sent questionnaires to 376 former players who had competed at Amherst, Dartmouth, Harvard, Princeton, and Yale. The results of Fauvier's investigation as published in *American Collegiate Athletics* in 1929 unfortunately did not reveal the years that the participants played. Yet, among the players who responded, 134, or more than a third, reported at least one or two concussions, and 21 said that they had suffered three. It is safe to assume that a number of these players and possibly all of them played in the early 1900s, when medical authorities began to discuss the problem of head injuries—and some probably played after the reforms in 1910 and 1912.[44]

As for football's corruption of the colleges, that concern had always played second fiddle to the supercharged belief that growing numbers of college boys were going to their deaths on the gridiron. Yet by 1912, with the worst evils apparently in check, the complaints about commercialism, distortion of the football's role in college life, and various player and alumni abuses had shrunk from sight. Many faculty and college presidents seemed confident that they had purged football of its worst evils, or at least that they had accomplished all that one could reasonably expect. Yet a few solitary critics still professed to glimpse a lawless underside of football which remained impervious to change. A faculty representative from Northwestern attending a Big Nine meeting in 1912 protested violations of the 1906 reforms but got no response from the others in the room. Most of the delegates at the NCAA meetings in the years from 1912 to 1917 rarely brought up the dark side of football.[45]

One member of the rules committee, Charles Savage of Oberlin, regarded the recent changes as merely cosmetic. In 1914 he prophetically used still another gardening metaphor to observe that "we are industriously pruning and trimming the athletic tree, plucking a leaf here and a diseased blossom there, but we hesitate to lay ax to the root." Sadly, Progressive reform had not succeeded in altering football's highly professional and commercialized system. "The coaches and managers in our great colleges leave no stone unturned [so] that victories may result," Savage insisted. "Money is poured out like water." In spite of faculty control, eligibility rules such as those passed by the Big Nine, and agreements between coaches to engage in fair play, the Oberlin athletic director observed, schools still hired players who misrepresented their status and played far beyond the normal three years.[46]

Even where the changes were not cosmetic, intercollegiate football regained a foothold where it had earlier lost ground. Columbia University's return to football marked the most dramatic turnabout, a decision that represented a triumph for frustrated students and persistent alumni. Under the autocratic hand of President Nicholas Murray Butler, Columbia had not only become the first major school to abolish football in 1905 but also held the line for ten years. In 1915 the school finally capitulated and reinstated football but began by only playing a small-college schedule. Within another decade, however, Columbia succumbed to big-time football fever and hired former Harvard coach Percy Haughton. After Haughton died prematurely, in his second season, Columbia tried, and nearly succeeded, in recruiting Knute Rockne from Notre Dame. Being a major power under Coach Lou Little in the 1930s, Columbia went to the Rose Bowl in 1934, the final appearance of any future Ivy League team in a postseason game.[47]

In 1915, when Columbia resumed football, the war in Europe had altered the way in which Americans regarded death and serious injuries on the gridiron. In contrast to what was happening overseas, how could college football be anything but benign? With fighting raging on the Western front, once-critical newspapers like the *New York Times* saw college football as a sea of tranquillity compared to the turmoil in Europe. In fact, the *Times,* which had lavished criticism on football in the early 1900s, now saw the game from a different, pro-American perspective, "an exhibition of friendly rivalry within a big-hearted neutral country," compared to European nations "smashing each other with instruments of warfare real and awful." One *Times* editorial, built around comments in the *Yale Alumni Weekly,* suggested that Europe lacked the foundation for competitive sports. In contrast, stadiums around the United States reflected the spirit of friendly competition.[48]

The friendly stadiums would all but close, however, in the fall of 1917, when the United States entered World War I, and college football dwindled to a few remaining players and teams. Schools had to play skeletal schedules to preserve fuel and manpower, or they sacrificed football altogether to the war effort. West Virginia had only fourteen players available when normally they would have had substitutes for each position and scrubs who practiced with the team. Because it had so few opponents, Yale canceled its varsity schedule, while Harvard closed Soldiers Field and began its season in late October.[49]

The Great War was hardly the beginning of the end for the gridiron game. On the contrary, as the U.S. girded for battle, football graduated from colleges into a much larger arena. At no time had such a golden opportunity existed to teach athletics to young Americans as in World War I, and football provided the vehicle. In a single afternoon a visitor to a military camp reported observing forty-seven different games of football. For morale as well as exercise, each camp fielded a varsity team, much as if it were a college gearing up for the fall season. In addition to big-time players, the military authorities conjured up college rituals such as organized cheering and lusty college tunes delivered by military bands at halftime.[50]

Military authorities also worked the gridiron game into their training, hiring experts such as Walter Camp to help map out strategy. At Camp Upton in upstate New York a drill called "Over the Top" closely resembled line play. Two platoons of men lined up with hands behind their backs. A line similar to the goal line loomed fifteen yards behind the first platoon, and the two platoons faced each other a few feet apart. When the training sergeant fired his pistol, Platoon A tried to break through Platoon B, which meant as many participants as possible crossing the line. The brawl went on for five minutes, and a five-minute half time ensued. Then the platoons reversed their positions, and Platoon B went on the offensive.[51]

The model of big-time football emerged live and well in the military camps, bringing tens of thousands of recruits into contact with a sophisticated game heretofore known chiefly to students at colleges or the better-known secondary schools. As a result, the war created an insatiable demand for football in the postwar era which even colleges could not satisfy. And the football that the military taught and that the recruits learned proved to be the sleek, fast-moving version that the rules committees had brought to near perfection in 1910 and 1912. World War I provided the new football with a timely and powerful weapon to drive it into the hearts and minds of the American public.

Just as the political reform impulse of the Progressive era ended with World War I, so also did the passion for reforming big-time college football. The concerted efforts to de-emphasize football which began with the Brown conference of 1898 and lasted until the injury controversy of 1909–10 hardly stood a chance of revival. No longer would it be possible for a single faculty member like Frederick Jackson Turner to threaten football at his own school or for an entire section of the country like the West Coast to banish football and convert it to rugby. Ironically, the war to make the world safe for democracy would also make the college gridiron more vulnerable than ever to greed, power, and unsavory practices of big-time football.

PART TWO

Subsidies

CHAPTER EIGHT

Playing and Coaching for Pay in the 1920s

In the 1920s big-time football experienced an explosive growth that few insiders would have predicted in the years of crisis during the early 1900s. President Calvin Coolidge's statement that the "business of America is business" might well have been applied to football in the 1920s and, for that matter, to sports generally. Football became so popular that colleges hastily constructed mammoth stadiums, while the twilight world of semiprofessional football emerged as the National Football League. Not surprisingly, the abuses of amateurism known as "professionalism," or coaching and playing for pay, acquired a new life in the 1920s.

In the 1920s the attractive game that reformers revitalized in the early 1900s brought far more spectators to college games, resulting in a jump of two million in a single year and more than ten million in annual attendance by the end of the decade. After World War I veterans who had played in the army helped to pump vigor into previously mediocre teams, and smaller teams seasoned with vets continued to upset their big-name competitors. Newspapers with eye-catching photojournalism and colorful writers such as Grantland Rice, Heywood Broun, and Paul Gallico converted accounts of gridiron games into more than simply a collection of sports articles. By the end of the decade the number of inches devoted to sports in some metropolitan dailies had quadrupled since the beginning of the decade.[1]

After shrinking to dwarf institutions in World War I, colleges experienced a boom in enrollments from 1919 to 1925. To be sure, some of the increase reflected the influx of veterans who had had their college careers interrupted or who had never set foot on campus. But the trend toward higher enrollments persisted as prosperity made it possible for larger numbers of young people to attend college, while the job market increasingly looked to college-educated workers. In the early 1920s more than sixteen thousand students strolled the campus of Columbia, and eleven thousand were in residence at the University of California at Berkeley. Most Big Ten institutions reported student populations of between six and eight thousand.[2]

As the size of colleges burgeoned, so did their gridiron ambitions. As they had before the war, some small private colleges, such as Washington and Jefferson, had remarkably successful teams; in 1922 the Presidents of W&J went to the Rose Bowl. But the small private colleges such as W&J had reached their heyday in the early 1920s. By the middle of the decade state schools and ambitious private schools in urban settings began to surpass the small liberal arts colleges and to attract far more fans. With its star running back, future movie star Johnny Mack Brown, the University of Alabama went to the Rose Bowl after the 1925 and 1926 seasons. Georgia fielded teams that defeated once mighty Yale in 1927 and 1930. A gridiron upstart, Southern California, which had itself gone to the Rose Bowl in 1922, began a profitable and high-profile intersectional series with Notre Dame in 1926, providing grist for its perennial reputation as a "football school." Other strategically located institutions tapped into the football bonanza. Inspired by Notre Dame's success in scheduling big games against Army in New York, a host of urban schools, including Boston College, Carnegie, Marquette, Fordham, New York University, Columbia, and the University of Detroit (coached by former Notre Dame quarterback Gus Dorais) began to win big games and draw big crowds.[3]

Prosperity and the New Professional

Since so many schools competed for football talent, strictly amateur athletics became an endangered species. Beginning in the 1920s, a new era of subsidized football appeared. Undoubtedly, this new highly subsidized football had its roots in the 1890s, when the major eastern teams played big games in the hippodromes of New York and Chicago—and when alumni and boosters hired tramp athletes or raided the secondary schools for the cream of the football talent. Subsidies given to players in the 1920s resembled the profitable sidelines enjoyed by players like Hogan at Yale and Coogan at Princeton in the early 1900s or the large salary that Columbia paid its youthful coach, Foster Sanford, from 1899 to 1901. In the 1920s, however, the practice of subsidizing football coaches and players became far more systematic and surreptitious. The scale and extent of subsidies in big-time football dwarfed the small-time perks given to a few players in the 1890s and early 1900s or the big money that several coaches earned. No longer was college football—or, for that matter, coaching—the preserve of the "gentleman amateur." It had matured overnight into a well-paid profession.

In the 1920s the old traditions in coaching were rapidly disappearing. Big-time colleges now had coaches who were full-time physical educators, and a few, such as Amos Alonzo Stagg and Bob Zuppke of Illinois, were members of the faculty or coached track in the spring enabling them to look for speedy and talented halfbacks. Probably a majority of smaller colleges still hired younger coaches for two or three years, but a host of major teams had big-name coaches whose careers were associated with a single school. In truth many of these men were seasonal coaches who held jobs in law or business and coached on the side, such as Walter Steffen, the former Chicago All-America, who was a judge in Chicago and commuted on weekends to Pittsburgh to coach at Carnegie Tech. In the next decade the number of these weekend warriors would rapidly dwindle.[4]

One throwback to the earlier era of coaching was Foster Sanford, who began in 1913 as a part-time coach at Rutgers and ended up coaching there for eleven years. Ironically, Sanford had helped to pioneer paid coaching at Columbia in 1899 and 1900, when he was first paid thirty-five hundred dollars (later raised to five thousand) to assemble a powerful team that could challenge the Big Three. Sanford had never entirely lived down his reputation as a "mucker coach," and he had never achieved his ambition of returning to Yale on a full-time basis. He had spent single years coaching at Virginia, Northwestern, and St. Marks, an eastern preparatory school, and even occasionally spot coached at Yale. He had gravitated to selling railroad insurance in New York when, in 1913, one of his clients, a member of the board, asked him to help coach at Rutgers. Sanford took up the challenge, and, when his co-coach had to step down, the former bad boy of eastern football became the sole coach, commuting from New York to New Brunswick during the football season.[5]

In his career at Rutgers, Sanford became a respected and popular figure on campus. In his first three years "Sandy" converted a small-time college team with a losing record into a solid team that won consistently. From 1916 to 1918 Rutgers had the good fortune to recruit the talented athlete, and student, Paul Robeson, who played tackle and end on the football team (and won letters in four sports and was chosen as his class valedictorian). Robeson, known as the "giant Negro," won a position on Walter Camp's All-America team in 1918. The future singer and actor starred as a pass receiver and as the World War I version of linebacker. Sanford, who was able to fend off some of the racism directed at Robeson, had one of the best teams in the country in 1918, a year when the few remaining college teams played largely military competition. For all his success at Rutgers, Sanford never accepted pay for his coaching and asked his players to take a pledge never to coach for pay. Ironically, the coach who had stood in the forefront of coaching for pay became one of the best-known gentleman amateurs, a throwback to his former coach and mentor, Walter Camp.[6]

At Rutgers, Sanford, who achieved a reputation for sportsmanship and fair play, evolved into the model of the gentleman amateur. In 1923, when he retired, football coaching practices that critics regarded as "mucker football" had become far more common and far more like the no-holds-barred football practiced at Columbia twenty years before, in the "Sanford era." In the period before World War I the rules banned sideline coaching, and coaches were supposed to sit in the stands or remain mutely on the bench. By the 1920s sideline coaching had not only become common but coaches had also devised ingenious ways to signal their players who were prohibited from using frequent substitutes to convey plays. One team had two Hawaiian brothers, one playing and the other on the sidelines, who shouted plays to each other in their native language.[7]

Scouting was another practice that had become increasingly common. Scouting, or "spying," had a long history dating back to Walter Camp's days at Yale, when he once missed a game so that he could watch an upcoming opponent, Amherst College. In the 1880s and 1890s teams persistently traded accusations of spying, or stealing the plays practiced in secret. While formal scouting was still frowned upon, teams would use knowledgeable alumni or boosters to report on what they had observed at an opponent's games. Knute Rockne, for example, had a network of well-trained alumni and former players (some of them coaches) who continued to serve their mentor by scouting Notre Dame's opponents. Sometimes Rockne went himself, as he did in 1927, to watch the Army-Navy game; he paid a steep price when Carnegie Tech upset the undefeated Notre Dame coached by a Rockne assistant. A veteran coach like Glenn Warner of Carlisle, Pittsburgh, and Stanford did not consider scouting unethical but simply one facet of preparing for the game. In the Darwinian struggle for victory the coach who did not use every trick at his disposal would go the way of the wooly mammoth.[8]

Knute Rockne stood out as the best-known and most successful coach of the 1920s, extending sports buccaneering beyond its old boundaries, cashing in on lucrative speaking engagements and endorsements. He lent his name to Wilson Sporting Goods to put on its footballs as well as its helmets. Most rewarding was his contract with South Bend-based Studebaker Motors, which used him to make motivational speeches to the automaker's employees and lend his name to company enterprises. According to Murray Sperber, Rockne earned at his zenith an annual retainer of seventy-five thousand dollars from Studebaker, more than the company president's salary. Using a ghostwriter, the Notre Dame coach also published a syndicated football column in which he discussed the teams and predicted the outcomes of the next week's games. In addition, he published books on playing and coaching football and sponsored schools for high school and college coaches, an endeavor that netted him twenty-two thousand dollars in 1927.[9]

Because Rockne coached at a school known almost entirely for its football and attained a celebrity status, he was able to sidestep criticism at a time when controversy caught up with some big-time football programs and their coaches. When a college coach commanded a salary four times as high as a senior professor, the faculty understandably felt that the system was out of kilter. At big-time schools professional coaches with high salaries and unchecked abuses created deep resentment among faculty and officials. Yet the abuses of professional coaching were less well-known than other features of 1920s life, such as the bootleg crime syndicates and the new moral-ity of "flaming youth." Chiefly, it was the faculty who resented the empire building by football coaches like Rockne, especially their carte blanche in scheduling games and their growing tendency to install athlete-friendly courses or painless physical education majors for their players.

Prewar reformers had pressed for rules to enable coaches to travel tenure paths hoping to subject big-time athletics to academic control. That Progressive mode of thought gained some adherents in the 1920s, but it had built-in flaws. Tenure-track football coaches owed their appointments to presidents, trustees, and only occasionally to the faculty. Indeed, this was a change from the 1890s and early 1900s, when alumni or student athletic as-sociations picked the college coach. The outcome, however, proved to be the same. Where boards of trustees appointed the coaches, pro-football alumni who served as trustees frequently influenced the decisions to hire or fire. Presidents who had control over appointments seldom opposed a coach who was recommended by an athletic board or group of trustees.[10]

One youthful coach who challenged the boundaries between the ath-letic and academic sectors was Alvin Neale "Bo" McMillin, one of the best-known players and successful small-college coaches in the 1920s. McMillin's career began as a player in the unlikely setting of Centre College in Danville, Kentucky. Eager to improve its football team and enhance its image, the small and obscure institution admitted the twenty-two-year-old McMillin in 1919, despite the fact that he had not collected enough credits to gradu-ate from high school. For the next five years the talented pool hall hustler and quarterback brought glory to the Praying Colonels, never quite finding the time to attend classes.[11]

With the guidance of Coach Charlie Moran, who had himself played professionally and coached at Texas A&M, McMillin developed into a su-perb quarterback and inspiring team leader. Soon the scores against smaller teams, once Centre's equals, grew lopsided. In 1919 the "predatory Colonels" feasted on Georgetown of Kentucky 95-0 and Howard of Kentucky 120-0 and in 1920 handily defeated Indiana, Virginia, West Virginia, and Kentucky, after which Moran began to scout for bigger games. In 1920 Centre lost only two games, one to an undefeated Harvard team and the other to Georgia Tech.[12]

In 1921 the twenty-seven-year-old Bo McMillin led his team to Cam-bridge for a rematch against Harvard. Academically, McMillin should have been ruled ineligible; he lacked 35 credits out of the 120 necessary to grad-uate and had failed one out of his three courses the previous semester. While McMillin and praying cohorts vowed to beat Harvard, after having impaled Transylvania 95-0 the week before, the Crimson seemed unimpressed by their backwoods opponents—that is, until McMillin made a remarkable stutter-step, thirty-one-yard run for the only score in the second half. For the first time since 1916 Harvard lost a regular season game, vaulting Centre into what would later be known as the Top Ten, with a good chance of becoming national champions, until they were finally upset by Texas A&M in a forerunner to the Cotton Bowl. A year later McMillin ended his five-year college career without a diploma when Centenary College of Shreveport, Louisiana, hired Bo as coach to breathe life into its football program.[13]

A pocket-sized school consisting of forty-three students and seven faculty, Centenary was perilously close to being sucked into an academic black hole. The president of the college, William Ganfield, calculated that the reputation of the South's, if not the nation's, best-known player would attract notice and revive the college. And so, with the proviso that he could play professional football if Centre traveled north, the budding gridiron entrepreneur asked for and got close to eleven thousand dollars, a salary that dwarfed the annual pay of the senior faculty and nearly equaled the president.[14]

Within a year, just as Ganfield had hoped, McMillin's reputation as a player, dedication to football, and lengthy apprenticeship in Kentucky paid dividends. Immediately, Centenary's enrollment shot up as McMillin produced a winning team that lost only once to Tennessee. The "Gentlemen" of Centenary featured a two hundred–pound line, including the future pro-football and baseball-umpiring immortal, Cal Hubbard.

In 1923 Bo McMillin once again journeyed to Boston to battle another emerging power, Boston College, and managed to slip in a professional game on this as on other northern trips. In his years as a player and coach McMillin demonstrated that an enterprising and successful young coach could leap into the higher echelons of pay. As a player and coach, McMillin had brought fame to Centre and Centenary and boosted enrollments. Academically, however, he had damaged the reputation of the two schools and put them at loggerheads with the regional Southern Association of Colleges and Secondary Schools. Because of suspicions about McMillin's academic status, Centre had failed to gain admission to the Southern Association, and, though already certified, Centenary faced expulsion by the Southern because of its lax athletic policies. The team's star lineman, Cal Hubbard, imitated his coach McMillin by accumulating a mere thirty-two credits in two years. Threatened by loss of accreditation, Centenary decided to jettison McMillin.[15]

After Moran resigned at Centenary, the perfect marriage presented itself to Centre's trustees. If McMillin, or "Colonel Bo," were now available, why should he not return to his alma mater? For Bo to come home would cost Centre nine thousand dollars, more than the annual salary of the school's president, the salary McMillin demanded to remain in residence full-time. If the college paid McMillin a higher salary than the president, the college would be clearly placing athletics over academics. Because it distrusted small schools with high-flying athletic programs, the Southern Association would most likely withhold accreditation.

From McMillin's point of view the return to Centre would prove costly. If he received a mere seventy-five hundred dollars, the salary of the president, he would lose almost a fourth of his new salary. The trustees tried to restructure their offer, so that Bo would receive seventy-five hundred dollars in salary and fifteen hundred dollars for field activities such as recruiting. With some logic McMillin replied that the Southern Association would view this split salary as a subterfuge. McMillin clearly would have to receive a big-time salary to come home, and, just as clearly, the financial commitment would doom the institution to academic purgatory.[16]

Centre's new president, R. Ames Montgomery, courageously faced up to the question. If Centre College were to prosper, Montgomery believed, the institution needed a stronger academic base—not an inflated football department. Moreover, the Southern Association had called the athletic system at Centre "rotten." By withholding its imprimatur, the accrediting agency could make it difficult for Centre to hire faculty and lure qualified students. Montgomery realized that high-cost, high-profit football ran counter to faculty sentiment in the upper South and in other parts of the country. "In America," he wrote in his 1922 report to the trustees, "a general conviction has taken possession of us that the highest paid man is the important man." If a full professor made two thousand dollars, how could the school justify a salary of nine thousand dollars for the football coach? "No athletic department," he declared, "can maintain itself without an academic foundation, and it is not fair to start the athletic department off on a money making career while the academic is condemned to poverty." Montgomery strongly urged the trustees to reject McMillin, and the board reluctantly complied. As a result, the football program quickly withered on the vine.[17]

After 1923 McMillin went to Geneva College in Pennsylvania and then to Kansas State and Indiana and finally to a professional coaching career with the Detroit Lions. His progress as a college coach reflected a career track in which the old concept of "gentleman amateur" had no place. The amateur code had nothing to say about coaches because it had been framed in an earlier era, when coaching as a profession barely existed. Without enforcement powers, the NCAA could hardly control the excesses of paid coaching, though its charter stated that "directly or indirectly receiving pay or financial benefits" violated the amateur code. Indeed, the NCAA constitution had nothing to say about athletes who had graduated or those who advised or coached the team. Even the NCAA's lofty constitutional rhetoric on playing for pay outside the institution reflected the older concerns with athletes who played summer baseball under assumed names.[18]

In the 1920s coaching became big business, and ambitious teams competed for coaches almost as fiercely as they did for victories. In 1925 Columbia University negotiated a contract with Knute Rockne which would have paid him twenty-five thousand dollars per year, more than any football coach in the country received and more than the salaries of most college presidents. Rockne frequently expressed interest in openings for coaches in large part because he could use them as bargaining chips in his negotiations with Notre Dame. Fed up with the picky Notre Dame faculty committee, Rockne was as eager to embrace the offer at Columbia as the New York school was to bring him to Morningside Heights. When Columbia prematurely released the news, Rockne, who faced intense pressure from Notre Dame alumni to stay in South Bend, had to renege on the offer. In the meantime Notre Dame's president, Matthew Walsh, told a faculty member of the governing board to document Rockne's chronic disputes with the faculty board. As Murray Sperber has observed, Notre Dame's president and faculty understood that the empire building of the football coach, his touchiness, and outright greed could undermine their academic edifice.[19]

Gridiron Demonology: College Boys Turning Professional

If coaching could become a profession, why not football itself? The possibility had begun to alarm the coaching profession in the early 1920s and had led to the formation in 1921 of the American Football Coaches Association. The coaches strongly opposed not only pay for amateur play but also professional football itself. In their founding resolution they declared that American football was an "academic" game. They regarded the professional game as "detrimental to the best interests of American football and American youth" and called upon their members to fight a holy war against the professional game.[20]

In previous decades "professionalism" normally referred to paid coaches or under-the-table payments to college players, not to the players themselves. In truth the term *professional* normally referred to baseball players who played for money. Almost immediately after World War I, coaches and college authorities began to rail against the football professional. The old meaning remained, but *professionalism* became inextricably linked with players profitably plying their football talents, a pejorative term heretofore applied to a few fortunate players and coaches as well as the commercial practices of big-time teams like Yale, Harvard, and Princeton.

Professional football itself had emerged as a shadowy Sunday afternoon town sport in the decade before World War I. Though its roots lay in Pennsylvania and Ohio, the sport spread throughout the larger towns of the industrial Midwest after World War I. Some of the best players, like George Halas of the Decatur (Illinois) Staleys, were former college players who had continued their careers with military teams during the war. In pro football's early days players normally received salaries of $50 a week, and those who made a living from football, like Halas, received $2,323, as a player, coach, and manager of the team.[21]

Before World War I college athletes who played for pay created frequent scandals but rarely in football. Only a few college players who competed on Sunday afternoons or during school breaks attracted attention, probably because summer baseball players vastly outnumbered them. In the early years of college football disputes over eligibility almost always had to do with enterprising gridders who also played summer baseball. The bulk of the summer players such as Amos Alonzo Stagg and future president Dwight David Eisenhower were never caught, but highly visible athletes were far more likely to face challenges by rival colleges or by associations such as the ever-vigilant Amateur Athletic Union (AAU). In the most celebrated case Carlisle star Jim Thorpe lost both his Olympic medals and his amateur status because he briefly played summer ball for pay. Whether Thorpe was, as many people say, a victim of racism or merely a casualty of a petty interpretation of the rules, he was not alone. In 1915 players at Pennsylvania, Wisconsin, and Minnesota lost their eligibility when rivals challenged their amateur status.[22]

When towns began to field football teams before World War I, the numbers of college players who played with them increased. If a town needed extra players, its team might turn to a nearby college, and players sometimes picked up a little extra cash by traveling to a city at a distance from their own institutions. One Sunday in 1912 an acquaintance met Knute Rockne on a train to Canton, Ohio, traveling to play in a semipro game. While an undergraduate, Rockne also coached occasionally for pay. And college players were not alone. The future African-American star and All-America at Brown, Fritz Pollard, played football for a team in Evanston, Illinois, even before beginning his college career.[23]

Following World War I college players who competed for professional teams were like ticking bombs waiting to explode. A major controversy might well have occurred in Canton, Toledo, or in the coal mining towns of western Pennsylvania; instead, what some newspapers at the time called the worst scandal in college football history occurred in an unlikely venue: a farming community in rural Illinois. In an era when most town rivalries did not yet center around high school athletics, the story began normally enough. The town of Carlinville, south of Chicago, decided to pick the pockets of its rival, Taylorville, by scheduling a football game between the two towns and rigging the outcome so that Carlinville would win—and win big money. The bankers and businessmen of Carlinville put fifty thousand dollars in the pot, and to reassure their backers and protect their bets the promoters hired eight Notre Dame players to create what appeared to be an unbeatable team. The players were to receive two hundred dollars, high-stakes pay for an important game.[24]

With so many bettors involved, the "confidential" plans found their way to Taylorville, where local promoters reacted with alarm. To counter the Notre Dame juggernaut, the Taylorville promoters recruited nine players from the University of Illinois. The Carlinville boosters hired a train to travel to Taylorville, the site of the game, much as college alumni and students might do for their big game. By this time the stakes had risen to $100,000, as the story had circulated and professional gamblers had put money into the pot.

Unfortunately for Carlinville, the Notre Dame players did not bring a quarterback, and, instead, an end had to take charge of the offense. In the first half of the game Taylorville mounted a 7-0 lead using strictly local talent against the team anchored by the Notre Dame players. After halftime the nine Illinois players entered the game to protect the lead, and Taylorville won handily, 16-0. An owner of the Carlinville grocery store concluded, "We got beat at our own game," or, in other words, Taylorville "outringed" the ringers. Though each town had a population of six thousand, the game's attendance reached ten thousand, outstripping many college and most professional games. With such a large turnout, so many college players from big-name schools, and big money on the line, the efforts to keep the story quiet for more than a few weeks stood barely a ghost of a chance. That more than a month elapsed before the story broke in the big city newspapers indicates that sportswriters knew the implications of the scandal and shied away from divulging the details. When the story became public, the colleges had to declare the players ineligible.[25]

Few would deny that professional college coaches like Stagg and Yost dispensed strong doses of hypocrisy. While they reaped the benefits from college sports, the idea of former college players making money from football professed to shock them. In fact, the illicit money earned by college players demonstrated that big-name players were eager to profit from what had become their college major. If celebrity athletes in other sports or football coaches like Rockne could earn big money, why not the players? In his boxing match against Jacques Carpentier in 1921, Jack Dempsey was guaranteed $300,000, which he probably had to split with his manager. Far distant as pro football was from this bonanza, its spurt in popularity suggested that opportunities lay beyond the colleges. Given the national rage for football, the sport would sooner or later produce a Babe Ruth or Jack Dempsey, a player who could combine athletic ability with celebrity and whose moneymaking potential would mock the cant of the coaching fraternity.

Interestingly, the University of Illinois, where the players for Taylorville were recruited in 1921, cradled Harold "Red" Grange, the first big-time celebrity football player. After strengthening his muscles by delivering ice in the steamy midwestern summers, the quiet redhead from Wheaton, Illinois, piled up 1,260 yards in 1923, his first year on the varsity, and led Illinois to a tie for the Big Ten championship. One sportswriter in the *Saturday Evening Post* described his remarkable running style. "With infinite care," the writer observed, "he picks his way through the line." Normally, Grange ran like an ordinary halfback, but he also had the ability to spring and maneuver "like a fiddler crab." As tacklers came for him, he twisted his body like a "contortionist," straight-armed his opponents, and headed like a race car for the goal line.[26]

On a single afternoon during his junior year Grange became a national celebrity. On October 18, 1924, Illinois was dedicating its new stadium in a game against Michigan, and Coach Bob Zuppke had been pumping up his players' morale for almost a year. Because of Grange, Zuppke's planning paid off handsomely. In the first twelve minutes of play Grange scored four touchdowns of 95, 67, 56, and 44 yards, including a return of the opening kickoff. In the third quarter he scored his fifth touchdown then passed for a sixth in the final quarter. In the end Grange ran for a total of 402 yards and passed for 64 more. This game represented a watershed for Grange and college football. Still hefting ice to help with his college expenses, Grange enjoyed the public acclaim of 1920s pro sports celebrities, as epitomized by the name "Galloping Ghost" bestowed on him by sportswriter Grantland Rice.

Near the end of his final season speculation about Grange's plans led to frenzied anticipation. Before his last game with Ohio State some newspapers reported that Grange had signed a gridiron contract with the pros. Other stories had Grange going to Florida to sell real estate or heading west to begin a movie career. One source even claimed that he planned to run for Congress, though he was four years under age. Michigan coach Fielding Yost said that he would "be glad to see Grange do anything but play professional football"; he would rather see the clean-living Grange "go into the movies, or write, rather than turn professional."[27]

As his final game approached, the pressure on Grange became almost unbearable. Suffering from media fatigue, the galloping ghost went home to Wheaton to talk with his father, a deputy sheriff. "We are not rolling in wealth," his father remarked, "and I think that the public would approve of anything that Harold does." Grange later declared that neither his father, his coach, Bob Zuppke, or the athletic director, George Huff, tried to talk him out of his decision to turn pro.[28]

Arriving at the station in Columbus, Ohio, to play Ohio State, Grange had to use all of his player's ability to weave through the crowd of curiosity seekers. Arriving at the hotel by taxi, he followed his beefy fullback, Earl Britten, as he sprinted through the crowd and into the lobby. Grange was supposed to ride on a float in a pregame parade, but, to spare him the stress, Zuppke arranged for another player in uniform to impersonate him.[29]

Against Ohio State, Grange carried the ball twenty-one times for 113 yards, caught nine passes, and made two interceptions. Illinois managed to win 14-9. Immediately after the game, Grange announced that he and his agent, C. C. Pyle, had negotiated a pro contract with the Chicago Bears. He planned to jump immediately from college ball to the pros, leaving school and joining the Bears for a Thanksgiving Day game, finishing the season with the professional team. "The only thing I regret," his coach, Bob Zuppke, declared, "is that he will no more graduate from Illinois than will the Kaiser return to power in Germany," referring to the exiled German emperor. And Zuppke was right.[30]

The college coaches vented a chorus of outrage and dismay at Grange's defection to the professional ranks. Although he had not broken any rules and the public generally supported him, critics insisted that an avaricious and crafty agent had manipulated the naive hero, though Grange insisted that he had signed for another reason. "I'm out to get the money," he said, "and I don't care who knows it." Grange's agent, C. C. Pyle, who owned movie theaters in the Champaign-Urbana area, emerged as an innovative sports entrepreneur who in 1926 would try to set up the first professional tennis league. Grange would later write that the media had unfairly berated Pyle as a "notorious and money-hungry promoter who used me to further his own ambitions." According to Grange, Pyle had treated him "more than fairly" and was one of the finest people he had ever known.[31]

In his first game at Wrigley Field, Grange split his half of the gate with Pyle, which earned them each twelve thousand dollars. Actually, the game proved disappointing, as the teams battled to a scoreless tie and Grange's longest carry was for six yards. After two games during the next week Grange arrived in New York to play against the New York Giants, attracting a crowd of sixty-five thousand, not to mention the twenty thousand disappointed fans who had to be turned away. The Bears won 19-7 in what Grange called "one of the most bruising battles I had ever been in." Nevertheless, he ran, passed, and made a key interception against the Giants, who were clearly tougher and better trained than the teams that he had played against at the college level.[32]

While he was in New York, Grange signed several lucrative contracts, endorsing "Red Grange chocolates," a soft drink, a cap, a sweater, and a Red Grange football doll. He also signed a movie deal, which led him to Hollywood in 1927, a year when he was recuperating from a serious knee injury. Later, after an unsuccessful attempt by Pyle to start a new team and a new league, Grange returned to the Bears, where he played until 1934, never again able to execute his brilliant runs but developing into an adept defensive player.

Crowds, Stadiums, and Criticism

Grange's revolutionary step demonstrated that big-time, play-for-pay football had returned to the Midwest in a new guise. Twenty years after the Chicago conferences Red Grange had achieved his reputation in a sport that supposedly had been de-emphasized by the Angell reforms. He had signed a profitable deal with the Bears and made a small fortune endorsing products. Yet Red Grange also brought fans to the Illinois games and made profits for teams in the Western Conference. The *New York Times* reported that 371,000 spectators had seen him play in his final year, and in the Ohio State game he attracted the largest football crowd of the year, 85,500. In seven games Grange had not only created publicity and profits for college football but also achieved a cult following. His popularity created a much larger problem that the college coaches only dimly grasped. If Grange could become a celebrity, so could others, and celebrity players could convert professional football into a respectable vocation. The budding NFL posed a threat to the colleges and to college football in ways that few people outside athletics appreciated. In December the athletic directors of Big Ten schools issued a call to arms against the pros.[33]

At the annual 1925 NCAA convention the association took the unusual step of coupling two conflicting topics, the overemphasis of football and the effects of the growth of professional football on college football. To place these discussions in context it is important to keep in mind that the NCAA delegates in the 1920s normally listened to useful, normally upbeat speeches and reports on trends in athletics. These sessions were interspersed with stirring speeches from NCAA President Palmer Pierce and, in previous years, from Walter Camp, who had died earlier that year. Though the speakers identified needs and problems, they rarely had deep or lasting insights into the vast changes taking place in college athletics. In his report from the eastern region, however, Professor Charles Kennedy of Princeton (a future president of both Princeton and of the NCAA) looked at the effects of professionalism from a broader perspective. Displaying a keen but critical understanding, Kennedy disputed the athletic personnel who dismissed pro football as "a flash in the pan." Unlike major league baseball, professional football could only get its material from the colleges. Large numbers of football enthusiasts, Kennedy declared, who could not get seats for the major college games would gravitate to professional games. In an era before televised sports Kennedy grasped that teams such as the Bears and Giants provided the only opportunity for many noncollegians to experience big-name football. "Such a close contact between a college sport and that same sport organized upon a commercial basis," Kennedy declared, "should certainly be viewed with concern."[34]

In spite of Kennedy's concern, the success of college football would rapidly drown out the warnings of the oracles who viewed professional football as a threat to the colleges. The sheer number of spectators at collegiate contests had swelled dramatically as a result of a surge in stadium building. As in the past, Yale had led the way, building Yale Bowl in 1914 on land that Walter Camp had earlier purchased out of his secret "sinking" fund. The construction of Yale Bowl proved a benchmark gridiron event because its simple and original plan met the needs of big-time football. Architects had the builders scoop out a large hole and then used the dirt to build up an oval mound around the side. What Yale Bowl lacked in majesty, it made up in comfort and practicality. The structure had thirty entry ways, all of them at ground level. Half of the seats were above and half below; seats had back rests contoured to the shape of the spectator. Its capacity of seventy-eight thousand, as one social historian has noted, "would have more than sufficed for every member of the University and all living alumni."[35]

In the 1920s the need for greater seating capacity—or, in some cases, the demands of alumni and local businesses—led to an orgy of stadium building. Dirt flew while trucks and train cars filled with concrete and steel arrived at stadium sites often located away from the campus. Colleges resorted to creative financing, since the stadiums could cost as much as $1,700,000, as did the site of Red Grange's heroics at Illinois. At most institutions, such as Illinois and Stanford, a stadium authority issued bonds, which were eagerly snapped up by investors and gridiron boosters. Kicking off a new financial gambit, Yale sold seating to boosters to bolster the financing of Yale Bowl, a practice followed by many other schools. Not every institution built, or needed, a brand new edifice. Where stadiums already existed, school authorities might decide to upgrade the seating capacity, as at the University of Chicago, where the stadium remained where it was. Almost every big-time school with football aspirations, however, built or rebuilt a stadium to hold from thirty-five thousand to eighty thousand fans. Critics complained that big-time football facilities preempted space and money that might otherwise have gone for intramural facilities or, for that matter, for classrooms. That stadium construction became almost a subspecies of architecture was a sign that big-time football had drowned out all hopes for more modest athletic programs and delayed the plans for building academic structures such as libraries and classroom buildings. Critics saw the massive stadiums used for four or five games each year as a warning that football had become so highly commercialized that it endangered the concept of amateur athletics.[36]

In April 1926 the American Association of University Professors (AAUP) delivered a scorching attack on college football, a sign that academic reformers had returned to the scene. A lobbying group for faculty and higher education generally, the AAUP in a journal article revived many of the criticisms that Charles Eliot and James Angell had earlier leveled at big-time football. Football created "hysteria," or overexcitement, among students, the report declared, diverting them from their studies. Though the hysteria might last only for the season and peak in the final games, "the distortion of values lasts throughout the college course [the students' years in college], if not through life." The AAUP disparaged the vast amounts spent on football and the adulation heaped on successful players who then turned professional, creating a false sense of values among their fellow students. The article had harsh words for the stadium mania. "The sheer physical size of the stadium," the authors insisted, "dwarfs the significance of the library, laboratory, and lecture hall." The report also touched on the problem of illegal subsidies, which it called "the crudest form of dishonesty" and charged that the college authorities connived with the alumni to propagate this evil.[37]

The criticism of football by the "professors" caused enough concern that a number of colleges felt compelled to rebut the charges or, at least, to deny that their institutions were guilty of overemphasis. While he brushed aside these problems at Columbia, Dean Herbert Hawkes admitted that they existed at many other colleges and universities. Dean Christian Gauss of Princeton spoke for many institutions when he described the game as healthy and wholesome. Few of those who issued statements for specific institutions agreed with the AAUP that football was a "menace" to higher education.[38]

The AAUP report might well have passed without further public comment except for the announcement that the Carnegie Foundation for Teaching would embark on a two-year study of the relationship between college athletics and college curriculums. Actually, this report proved to be misleading. Howard Savage, the head of the project, had already gone to England to study British college and public school athletics. Prodded by the NCAA, the foundation would soon plunge into an investigation of college athletics in all its facets. The result would be the most thorough effort in athletic history to document the frequency and modus operandi of subsidized athletics and a document that provided a clear picture of the transition taking place from the era of tramp athletes and athletic loafers to the modern age of the highly subsidized "scholar-athlete."

CHAPTER NINE

The Growth of Subsidized Football, 1920 to 1929

In the early 1900s, as we have seen, male football enthusiasts virtually banned female students and guests from the all-male precincts of the cheering sections. At the brink of World War I the sun was setting on this era—the early 1900s "Dink Stover" (of the popular "Stover at Yale" series) masculine pipe and bulldog sweater era of college life. After the 1913 Virginia-Georgetown game in Washington, newspapers described the postgame revelries in which boys and girls engaged in a riotous drinking bout at a local hotel. Bottles, glasses, and trays were smashed on the floor, and the crowd fought for places at the tables. "And young girls, some of them surely not over eighteen," reported the *Washington Star*, "were in that crowd of fighters, adding their soprano laughter to the vile curses of the men." Rumors filtered to the Vatican, and the president of Georgetown added his voice to the official protest.[1]

Fifteen years later men and women casually engaged in such behavior at many colleges with only a few raised eyebrows. Coed drinking at games and school dances became commonplace. In Percy Mark's novel *The Plastic Age,* set at a small New England college, the author describes the erotic atmosphere at a prom, where "the syncopated passion screaming with lust, the drums, horribly primitive, the drunken embraces." In an article entitled "Graceless Gals" the *Daily Northwestern* related a story of a clergyman who went into a smoking lounge and was shocked to find himself sitting next to coeds discussing petting techniques. Yet football still preoccupied the students at the Samson College in *The Plastic Age,* and in the fall months few male students discussed anything but the college's gridiron prospects. "Even religion and sex, the favorite topics of bull sessions," wrote the author, who had graduated from the University of California before coming east and was teaching at Dartmouth when the book was published, "could not compete with football especially when someone mentioned Raleigh College [Samson's rival]." In its season football had a priority over sex, at least in male dormitory rooms, and it continued to stand in the way of serious academic endeavor, a problem that caught the attention of educational reformers.[2]

The Carnegie Foundation: The Origins of Its Probe

This indifference to learning did not sit well with purists, who believed that college football and its trappings merely debased the coinage of higher education. As a result, the major agency in the reform of higher education, the Carnegie Foundation for the Advancement of Learning, contemplated a preemptive strike against college athletics. Henry Prichett, president of the foundation, advocated the probe of athletics as a step toward his goal of elevating higher education. Drawn from a scientific and Progressive tradition, Pritchett believed strongly in the need for efficiency as applied to human resources. Because of the resources that the Carnegie Foundation commanded, Pritchett had become one of the country's most influential academic reformers.

While serving as president of MIT in the early 1900s, Pritchett got to know Andrew Carnegie just as the steel king was starting his career as a philanthropist. Though he channeled his gifts in several directions, Carnegie as a self-educated and self-made man made his largest gifts to education and especially to higher education. In 1905 he called upon Pritchett to help him set up an endowed corporation for providing pensions to college faculty. Accordingly, the Carnegie Foundation spawned a pension system that eventually became Teachers Insurance and Annual Annuities, or TIAA. Under Pritchett's bold leadership it also began to conduct studies of professional educational agencies, beginning with a landmark study of medical schools conducted by Abraham Flexner in 1910, a project that became a model for a number of studies by the foundation, including the study of college sports.[3]

If one word characterized Henry Pritchett's view of progress, it would have been *standards*. As president of the Carnegie Foundation, he strongly championed a number of methods for creating higher and more uniform standards in academic life, such as establishing the Educational Testing Service, which would rely on the Scholastic Aptitude Test for college admissions, and the use of Carnegie units to signify legitimate courses on high school transcripts. Following Flexner's report on medical education, the Carnegie Foundation had conducted studies on legal education, engineering schools, and public school education. Pritchett was not, strictly speaking, a crusader against big-time college sports and never belonged to the army of noisy football critics. Only because big-time college athletics violated his notions of elite, no-nonsense education did he regard them as worthy of investigation and reform.[4]

Pritchett believed that colleges struggled for students much as railroads fought for passengers. While railroads filled their Pullman cars by reducing fares, the colleges filled their classrooms by cutting admission requirements. College athletics provided one of the nonacademic methods for attracting students, or, as Pritchett put it, "the attractions of athletic distinction were added to other reasons for choosing a particular college." Being an unapologetic elitist, Pritchett had become obsessed with the legions of applicants to colleges which had spiraled in the early 1920s and which, he believed, diluted the intellectual integrity of academic life. He contended that college athletics played a part in the drift that had reduced the caliber of the major colleges. Moreover, Pritchett even produced a list of evils in college athletics: the paid coach, gate receipts, training tables, special railroad cars, demoralizing publicity, the unconscionable amount of time devoted to training, and the diluting of standards. Athletes lacked time and energy for "any serious intellectual effort." The compromises in getting students through school "give an air of insincerity to the whole university-college regime." In a nutshell Pritchett echoed the criticism of Charles Eliot, except that Eliot's moral indignation became Pritchett's paradigm of efficiency, his conviction that athletics contributed to the overall problem of inefficient institutions glutted with poor students.[5]

Beginning in 1921, Pritchett had placed his athletic concerns before the Carnegie board, but the board generally put off his proposals. One exception proved to be a thousand-dollar grant to the Southern Association for the study of college sports in the South, a gesture of protest against the athletic excesses that had threatened colleges like Centre and Centenary. After the association got this grant, reformers and critics in academia flocked to the foundation with similar requests, which the board was reluctant to fund. In 1925, however, the foundation sent a young researcher, Howard Savage, to investigate college athletics at English public schools and universities. As an alumnus of Tufts and Harvard, Savage had taught English at Bryn Mawr from 1915 to 1923 before joining the Carnegie staff. His study of British athletics displayed the close attention to detail which later characterized the Carnegie Report, but it accomplished little else. "Whatever may be said for its interest," Savage wrote of the British investigation, "it had little utility or effect beyond demonstrating a method of inquiry by visit and interview."[6]

After spending the seed money for Savage's British project and a pilot study of athletics at twenty American institutions, the association responded favorably to a request from the NCAA for a larger study and voted on January 8, 1926, to embark upon the grand project. After an unsuccessful attempt to gather data via questionnaires, Savage and three other investigators took on the monumental project of visiting 130 colleges and universities in the United States and Canada. Mistaking the academic demeanor of Savage's team, some of the coaches and athletic directors seemed to believe that the investigators would not single out their institution by name or, for that matter, that their schools had passed the investigator's scrutiny. They may not have read the prepublication results that the investigators had sent to the president of each institution, which minced no words about what they had found.[7]

The year 1925 provided some jarring notes on the direction and practices in college athletics. In the late fall and into December the sports pages were filled with stories on Red Grange's departure to the NFL and the highlights of his early pro games. With mammoth stadiums, soaring attendance figures, and inflated coaching salaries, college football had reached the point at which educators could no longer ignore it. Rumors of lavish and systematic cheating had begun to trigger a flurry of criticism which would, in time, coalesce into a new movement for athletic reform. These trends confirmed suspicions that the older tramp athlete and academic ward of the university had not disappeared but had been updated into a new, more widespread system of play-for-pay.

In 1925, just before the start of the football season, a lurid feature entitled "The Story of a Graduate Manager" appeared in a number of newspapers. The "story" claimed to give an inside glimpse of a corrupt football program in action. The anonymous graduate or alumni manager who wrote the piece described the network that existed to recruit and support college athletes. Like a shadow cabinet in politics, the network extended from a graduate or alumni manager—who might make as much as $18,000 (more than $100,000 at the end of the twentieth century)—to a host of student lackeys who provided for the needs of college football players and watched out in myriad ways for the money invested by alumni in the football program.[8]

The lavish return of that shadowy alumnus known as the graduate manager roughly equaled the cost, which the author estimated at twenty-five thousand dollars, of conditioning, equipping, and training players for a single game. The manager supervised tutoring, provided for the material needs of the player, and coordinated the activities of his student helpers. To describe the undergraduates who worked under the graduate manager, the authors unveiled a whole new vocabulary. "Widows" made certain that athletes found their way to the right classes, while "rats" trailed the laggards to report on their class attendance and hours of study. A recruiter known as a "uhlan" was a student with a car who fraternized with high school players and pitched his institution to promising high school athletes. Above all, the graduate manager served as an expert on procuring subsidies for the players. He found cushy jobs for the players near campus or set up scholarships tailored to athletes. He arranged for the payment of laundry bills so that the team could project an engaging, neat appearance. He even tucked away promising freshmen at remote summer camps until the beginning of fall training; otherwise, they might be snatched away by competing schools.[9]

Though the graduate manager of this exposé claimed to ply his trade at an eastern institution, the members of the Big Ten and their spokesmen were the first schools to defend their reputations. Former All-America Walter Eckersall turned sportswriter for the *Chicago Tribune* insisted that football subsidies existed in eastern football but not on the midwestern gridiron. He contended that "Western Conference or Big Ten is as pure an organization as there is in the country." Though his university had coddled and pampered Eckersall in his football-playing days, the former Chicago star chose to ignore similar methods developed by the schools in the Big Ten to build and support their own big-time football programs.[10]

In truth the hub of big-time football had gravitated to the Midwest, a change demonstrated by the caliber of its teams and the numbers of spectators. In a conference as highly competitive as the Big Ten, a college needed the tacit cooperation of the administration, an alumni system for recruiting and supplying the athlete with the 1920s equivalent of an athletic scholarship, and a willingness to bend the rules on eligibility. Athletes who had to worry about academic requirements were unable to devote their energies to big-time sports. In order to create a football program an institution needed a president and alumni who were willing to work behind the scenes to create the proper environment for athletics. A strong president who built up other facets of the university normally used football as a method of publicizing his institution, much as schools had done at the turn of the century.

One midwestern school that built a stronger, higher-profile university through football in the 1920s proved to be straitlaced Northwestern University. Like so many Methodist schools, Northwestern had toyed with the idea of abolishing football in the 1890s, and in the reform year of 1905–6 the faculty had actually suspended football for two years, the only school in the Big Nine to do so. From 1908 until World War I, Northwestern had only one good season, 1916, when it nearly won the conference title. In every other year Northwestern had a losing record, and its football grew so uncompetitive that Wisconsin proposed dropping the Purple from the conference. Following World War I Northwestern football once again fell into the doldrums. After the team failed to win a game in 1921, Northwestern appointed a committee to recommend what could be done to improve its intercollegiate athletics. Proposing that the alumni, students, and faculty initiate a program to promote college athletics, the committee especially appealed to Northwestern alumni, who would become the center of an intense campaign to recruit high school football players and bring them to Evanston.[11]

Walter Dill Scott, the recently installed president, strongly supported athletics since, as an undergraduate at Northwestern in the 1890s, he had played guard on the football team. In a distinguished career as a psychologist Scott had pioneered the field of business psychology, serving as president of the American Psychological Association. In his first ten years as president of Northwestern, Scott enjoyed remarkable success in raising money to enlarge the endowment and to improve faculty salaries. As a result of Scott's efforts, Northwestern strengthened its professional schools, began the Medill School of Journalism, and opened an evening division. By the 1930s he had transformed Northwestern from a small, underfunded religious institution into the North Shore competitor to the University of Chicago.[12]

Scott's efforts to improve the football team began to bear fruit in 1925, when Northwestern tied for the Western Conference, or Big Ten, title. But the campaign to improve the team was tied to a larger effort to change what was thought to be Northwestern's effete reputation. By building on its grid-iron prowess, Scott sought to draw more male applicants and shed its image as, according to the instructor and critic Bernard DeVoto put it, "a school for young women to which young men are also invited." In an era of stadium building Scott helped to raise money for a new football stadium that would open in 1926 and put Northwestern in the front ranks of Big Ten football institutions.

To bring players to the school, athletic director Kenneth "Tug" Wilson and Glenn Thistlwaite, a talented former high school coach in Oak Park, encouraged the alumni to go after promising recruits. Fifty alumni scouts watched for blue-chip athletes, who were given "loans" to cover freshmen tuition payments. In 1925 the former "Fighting Methodists" shared the Big Ten championship with Michigan, after Northwestern eked out a 3-2 victory over the Wolverines in hopelessly muddy conditions in downtown Chicago's Soldier Field, a newly built public arena that held more than 100,000 spectators. As a result, Northwestern football enjoyed unprecedented press coverage in a city where Amos Alonzo Stagg had virtually monopolized the Chicago sports pages before the mid-1920s.[13]

In 1926 Scott made his most controversial foray into football rebuilding at Northwestern. Leland "Tiny" Lewis, a top running back but an indifferent student, made a pact with the faculty that he would sit out a year until his grades improved. At the outset of the 1926 season, with a powerful team in the making, Scott learned that Lewis had earned fifteen credits, nine in the spring and six in the summer, which would restore his eligibility. Though Lewis had agreed not to play in 1926, Scott chose to go over the heads of the faculty. In a letter to Lewis he reviewed the arguments pro and con and concluded that "no faculty has ever refused to allow a student participate in an intercollegiate contest if he was eligible to participate." Despite Tiny's pact with the faculty, Scott declared him eligible. Northwestern went on to an outstanding season, tying Michigan for the championship but without the stigma that had accompanied the mud-stained victory over the Wolverines in 1925.[14]

Some rivals chafed at Northwestern's ascendancy. Amos Alonzo Stagg, the dominant athletic figure in Chicago football for thirty years, doubted that the "Wildcats," so handily banished in earlier years, followed conference rules against subsidizing. Stagg charged that Northwestern had legions of alumni scouring the territory, "his" territory, for prospects, much as Chicago alumni had done in the early 1900s and Michigan alumni had resumed doing after World War I. After the players were enrolled, they received loans and other forms of assistance, or so Stagg contended. Probably

Stagg was correct, but few schools in the Big Ten lacked for dirty linen in their closets, and the conference seldom cracked down on offenders unless the cheating became so notorious that it had no choice. In 1929 the Big Ten expelled Iowa from the conference for a highly publicized slush fund or illegal payments scandal. That expulsion only lasted a year because Iowa was said to have enough dirt on the other conference schools to embarrass and discredit them.[15]

No doubt Stagg had grown irritable about the turn of events that placed his team near the bottom of the Big Ten. After a close victory over the Wildcats in 1925, he agreed to play Northwestern in Evanston at the dedication of its stadium the next year, only to be pummeled, 38-7. Immediately after this humiliating loss, Stagg announced that he planned to substitute Indiana for Northwestern (Big Ten institutions would not play a full conference schedule until the 1940s). Writing to Fielding Yost after the loss to Northwestern, Stagg vented his frustrations and suspicions. "I am satisfied that Northwestern at the present is loaded with athletes who have been induced to go there by the offer of free tuition and in certain cases something additional." In his six years remaining at Chicago, he never again played Northwestern, though he would bring his team to Dyche Stadium in 1946, while coaching at the College of the Pacific, for a final flogging.[16]

Northwestern made all of the necessary moves to achieve success in bigtime football. Unlike Chicago and Michigan, it scheduled Notre Dame at a time when the Rockne teams had a tremendous following in the Windy City and earned the nickname, the Wildcats, by their scrappy performances against superior Rockne teams played before overflow crowds at Soldier Field. Like the eastern institution in "The Story of a Graduate Manager," Northwestern developed a system for locating, recruiting, and supporting its athletes. At a time when Chicago was developing stricter academic standards, Northwestern accepted athletes who had little to offer academically— and kept them eligible. It also supported its athletes, skillfully skirting the conference rules against subsidization. In short Northwestern epitomized the evils that Henry Pritchett had in mind when he pushed for the investigation of intercollegiate athletics.

The Carnegie Foundation and the Great Football Scam

From 1926 to 1929 Howard Savage and his associates visited an exhaustive number of colleges and universities, observing and asking probing questions wherever they went. In their visits to college campuses they sought a wide view of athletic practices, including intramurals, medical and training procedures, public relations, and scholarships, to name a few. Though their goal was to examine athletics generally, they inevitably kept bumping up against football because of its popularity and because of the shady gridiron practices that they uncovered. Their investigation ended up documenting football more fully than they admitted.

Not surprisingly, when the Carnegie Report appeared in 1929, the chapters on recruiting and subsidizing caused the most comment and the most outspoken denials by presidents, conference heads, and athletic directors, indicating that they hit raw nerves. According to Savage, the Carnegie investigators visited some of the 130 colleges and universities as many as three times. Rather than relying on elusive paper trails, they interviewed college officials, athletic personnel, students, and alumni, and the results of these investigations conveyed to the presidents often led to protests. The foundation published these protests as footnotes to the text of what was initially prosaically titled *Bulletin Number Twenty-Three*. Because of the exhaustive investigation, the researchers used only a "fraction," as Savage put it, "of the material gathered." Looking back at the study almost a quarter of a century later, Savage called it "encyclopedic in scope, thorough in method, and unprejudiced in method." He added, "Its chief faults were its length and its detail and yet without sufficient preponderance of evidence it would have failed of its purpose altogether."[17]

Few institutions received a clean bill of health from the Carnegie Report. Of the 130 institutions visited, the investigators named only 28 that did not subsidize their athletes. A mere 8 of these schools played big-time football—Chicago, Cornell, Illinois, Marquette, Tulane, Virginia, West Point, and Yale. Of these only Cornell and Yale had reasonably strong football programs in 1929. One scholar has suggested that Amos Alonzo Stagg, who engaged in many of the practices regarded as nonamateur by the Carnegie Report, managed to mislead the investigators. A remarkable number of the schools visited and listed in the book were located either in Pennsylvania or nearby, such as Carnegie Institute, Pennsylvania, Rutgers, Washington and Jefferson, Western Maryland, Lehigh, and Lafayette. The practices of the Pennsylvania colleges seemed to mirror the popularity of football in the towns of Pennsylvania in the early 1900s, which gave rise to early semiprofessional teams and for many years provided a unique pool of football talent for both college and professional teams.[18]

The bulk of the "clean" schools were relatively small, obscure, and unknown for athletics such as Dalhousie, Laval, MIT, Queen, Reed, Saskatchewan, Tufts, and Wooster. In this sense the report was a blanket indictment of big-time college athletics and especially the crafty and deceitful practices of college football programs.[19]

Many of the topics caused little or no controversy, such as those on hygiene, British athletics, or intramural athletics. The revelations that caused most of the most debate were contained in the chapter "The Recruiting and Subsidizing of Athletics," which dealt largely with practices in big-time football. This chapter was particularly effective because it named colleges (and some preparatory schools) which engaged in controversial practices. The authors deftly pinpointed the schools that engaged in athletic sleight of hand and recited the names of the institutions as if they were so many actors on a playbill.

Without scolding or berating the schools, Savage and his colleagues noted facets of recruiting or subsiding and examples of schools that practiced them. "Funds for subsidizing according to need or demand may come," the report declared in one typical paragraph, "singly or in combination, from alumni or friends of the college, from the athletic association or organization, or from the institution (Allegheny, Carnegie Institute of Technology, Centre, Dickinson, Grove City, Lafayette, Lebanon Valley, University of Pennsylvania, Western Maryland)." The report even singled out two Pennsylvania prep schools, Bellefonte and Kiskiminetas, for disguising athletic subsidies as "advertising expenses."[20]

For the first time a study documented the various forms of largely surreptitious actions involved in supporting athletes. Some of these methods reached back to the 1890s, such as using loans as subsidies and finding employment for athletes either on the campus or with football boosters. Savage and his cohorts made it clear that many of these jobs involved negligible duties. They observed that "an organized attempt, directed perhaps by a paid official, to provide and assign work away from the campus, approaches more nearly the nature of subsidizing (Denver, Drake, Southern California)." Sometimes the schools allowed athletes to get paid for nominal work, or they were "subsidized" under the guise of working as salesmen of insurance and bonds (Columbia, Wisconsin), clerks in clothing stores (California, Drake, Ohio State), agents for business (Chicago, Colgate, Iowa, SMU, Wyoming), sporting good sales (Dartmouth, Drake, Texas, Washington, Wyoming), ad sales reps (Michigan, Missouri, Northwestern, Penn), and other less common jobs such as employees at movie studios, children's companions, and writers. *Guise* indicated the skeptical attitude of the authors, who believed that these make-work jobs simply served as a means of funneling money to players who were patently unqualified to sell bonds or act as agents for businesses. Frequently, employers were boosters who felt sympathetic toward the players and loyal to their institutions, while others were said to be merely interested in athletics. Occasionally, boosters simply made private loans that were little more than payments to "needy" athletes.[21]

The study identified for the first time the athletic scholarship, a means of support that was classified with other forms of nonamateur subsidies. Athletes already received a number of scholarships disguised as awards for leadership and all-around performance or based on committee or personal recommendations. "We now turn to those forms of aid," the authors declared, "which are frankly and unequivocally termed as athletic scholarships." These grants usually came in the form of tuition waivers or waivers on room and board. Again, the researchers carefully documented examples of the schools, the numbers of scholarships, and the variations in each form of assistance. "The amounts or numbers of such awards available and the bases of the award at the time of each field visit varied considerably," they wrote and then proceeded to give the numbers: "(Blue Ridge, twelve; Colgate, twenty-five; Geneva, thirty-five; Georgetown, unspecified; Pennsylvania State College [Penn State], seventy five; Syracuse, $14,000; West Virginia Wesleyan, twenty; Ursinus, sixteen)."[22]

Unlike the modern era of athletics, observers in the interwar period regarded athletic scholarships as a new form of subsidy; even though these awards were open and above board, purists regard them as a manifest violations of amateur standards. The most insidious and secretive form of subsidy, however, was the slush fund, or black box fund, accumulated by boosters or coaches and dispensed in the form of payments and subsidies. In many respects these awards resembled the modern athletic scholarship because they provided for a player's cost of living and, if given by the coach, they could be revoked if the player failed to make good. The numbers of players paid in this way varied considerably, ranging from thirty-five at Lafayette and sixteen at Northwestern to six at Western Maryland. Far from uniform, the amount of the grant depended on negotiations between the players and their coaches, who took into account the food and lodging provided by fraternities or jobs available to the athletes.[23]

Of course, many other factors came into play. Most institutions required students to maintain a minimum academic standing in order to keep their scholarships. As "The Story of a Graduate Manager" indicated, a number of schools used tutors, or "special instruction," to keep their athletes eligible. The investigators also regarded the training table as a form of subsidy through which athletes could eat for free, and fraternities often provided food or lodging for their athletic brothers. Many athletes, then as now, received complimentary tickets that they could sell at a profit.[24]

One of the most interesting sections had to do with athletic subsidies at Roman Catholic colleges and universities. A member of the investigating team, Terry McGovern, had visited these colleges, possibly because he was the only Catholic among the investigators. The authors made it clear that these institutions cooperated fully with the inquiry. Contrary to the expediency that motivated other colleges, the Catholic institutions had a set of principles that governed their support of athletes. "These principles," the authors wrote, "begin with a conviction that every young man who desires an education is expected to prove himself worthy by honoring in some way his college or university." Just as he might play the organ if talented in music, he would participate in athletics if blessed with athletic skills. Priests, alumni, and parochial school coaches understood that their duty was to direct athletically talented youth to Catholic institutions. "To the loyal alumnus, the devoted priest, the enthusiastic undergraduate, the professional coach," the report declared, "athletic ability readily becomes the most important of these qualifications, and the other qualities of character, if outstanding, tend to be taken for granted." Naturally, these athletes received various forms of subsidies in return for their athletic participation.[25]

Other institutions engaged in recruiting just as aggressively and relentlessly as the Catholic institutions. If the researchers were correct, the athletes at non-Catholic schools felt less devotion to principle and more to getting what they could from the college. In attempting to single out the evils in recruiting, the researchers made a rather ambiguous distinction between "professional" and "nonprofessional" in describing how recruiters sold their school. An institution like Northwestern, which assigned its alumni "counselors" to seek out the best athletic talent, would fit into the professional category; at other schools with "professional" programs coaches, the alumni secretary, and even members of the academic staff might participate. Nonprofessional recruiting tended to be low-keyed and unsystematic. If a family member or an alumnus wanted a talented player to attend his alma mater, they might approach the youth without attempting to exert pressure or offer inducements. "Frequently it is difficult to determine the exact moment," the authors candidly admitted, "at which innocent enquiries end and recruiting begins."[26]

It was not uncommon for the "schoolboy athletes" themselves to initiate the correspondence with athletic departments. The researchers concluded that the high school or private school students proved to be remarkably adept at marketing themselves, going so far as to send out press clippings highlighting their performances. These letters normally proved to be the first phase in negotiating for subsidies. A typical letter began, the authors declared, "what can you do to attract a promising but needy athlete?" Normally, the athletic department acted as the clearinghouse for these inquiries.[27]

When the Carnegie team visited athletic departments, the coaches and athletic directors at big-name institutions were all too glad to hand over the hundreds of letters they received. They could also show off the letters that they wrote in return, which were often carefully worded and noncommital. Sooner or later the head coach got to examine these letters and usually had an assistant or college official respond. Some of the schools that the study regarded as high-minded (Bates, Bowdoin, Brigham Young, Chicago, Cornell, Lehigh, Stanford, Tulane, and Virginia) would typically reply: "The only inducement we offer to any student is that of a good education. This is all the right kind of athlete expects of us."[28]

As they scoured the athletic terrain of higher education, the Carnegie team found remarkably few high-minded recruiting programs. The majority of institutions had aggressive, systematic recruiting campaigns run by the coach, alumni, or fraternities or organized around track meets in the spring. Already a number of schools had assigned an assistant coach or a coach who was less busy in off-season or a trusted agent such as an alumni secretary to scout and visit high school athletes.

Sometimes a team of recruiters combined in a campaign to snare a sought-after prospect. The researchers cited a number of offenders, including smaller college such as Bucknell, Ohio Wesleyan, Western Maryland, Oglethorpe; future Ivy League schools such as Brown and Columbia; Big Ten institutions such as Michigan, Ohio State, Northwestern, Purdue, and Wisconsin; state schools in the South such as Georgia, Georgia Tech, and Tennessee; and Oregon Agricultural (Oregon State) and Southern California on the West Coast. Not surprisingly, well-known presidents such as Walter Dill Scott of Northwestern lodged protests or caveats that appeared in footnotes below the researchers' allegations: "I am not aware of such solicitation being 'officially' done," Scott declared. "The Assistant Alumni Secretary is not authorized to subsidize athletes. He may inform prospective students that there are a number of scholarships." The recently hired athletic director at Harvard, Bill Bingham, who would play a large role in the de-emphasis of football at Harvard, replied that he planned to do away with such compromising practices.[29]

Frequently, the colleges or their athletic departments played a subtle part in recruiting by offering to find the athlete employment or by acting as an employment agency within the athletic department. Usually the athletic staff could offer a job to the athlete, but sometimes the jobs went through the college appointments office. Typically, the athletic department paid from thirty to seventy-five cents an hour for a variety of jobs from dispensing towels to serving as lifeguards and janitors for gymnasiums. The most common, and satisfactory, job identified by the authors was waiting on training tables, not onerous labor and done in the belly of the beast. All told, the number of schools where athletic departments offered employment extended from Dartmouth to Washington State. It included members of the Big Three such as Harvard and Yale but also small colleges such as Middlebury and urban institutions once identified with reform such as New York University. In short it embraced institutions in every part of the country. And, since working one's way through college was hardly unknown, the authors could confidently infer that offers of jobs to athletes had become a common recruiting tool.[30]

If jobs had been the only issue, the discussion of recruiting would have stirred only modest criticism. The authors implied, however, that these programs not only singled out athletes for favored treatment but also demanded very little work. Often athletes received higher pay than nonathletes and occasionally were members of "bogus brigades" who were paid for nonexistent services. To be precise, big-time athletes at small and large colleges survived or even thrived on subsidies; similarly, college and athletic officials used jobs often mixed with outright subsidies to draw recruits and provide for their needs upon their arrival. And all of these institutions supposedly lived by the creed of amateur athletics.[31]

The Carnegie Report and Its Critics, 1929

Though the Carnegie Report made news because of its chapter on subsidies and recruiting, the value of the research itself transcended the controversy it generated. Less publicized chapters were filled with valuable information, including facts on the hiring and pay of coaches and coverage given to college sports by the newspapers as well as to the athletic relations between colleges, all of which rounded out the picture of college athletics in the 1920s. Savage provided updated material on many of the evils descried by reformers in the early 1900s, such as problems involving lack of faculty control and ineligible players as well as the persistent difficulties involving summer baseball. He also provided information on athletic organizations, conferences, the NCAA, and international athletic events, all of which proved more informative than sensational. He even upbraided the newspapers for increasing the size of their sports sections by increasing their coverage of college sports.

One of the most useful and neglected chapters of the book, "The Hygiene of Athletic Training," delved into the care of college athletes. The investigators were appalled by the trainers whom they met or heard about. According to the authors, the training of athletes and the care of their bodies had fallen far behind the methods of recruiting and subsidizing. When an injury occurred on the gridiron and the team doctor was unavailable, it was usually the trainer's jobs to administer first aid. Yet the trainer, more often than not, had not even the most basic medical training. "As a not infrequent result," the report observed, "tradition, superstition, and prejudice have usurped the place that should be filled by scientific reason and knowledge." According to Savage and his colleagues, the trainer's locker contained a melange of old-fashioned quackery, "overflowing with proprietary ointments, liniments, and washes" and little more. Similarly, the training room, rather than being a place to treat injuries, was little more than "a museum of old and new appliances for applying heat, water, light, massage, and electricity." The authors also heard of instances in which coaches had plaster casts removed from players' ankles, allowing them to play before the injury had time to heal.[32]

What little shock value contained in this section had to do with drugs used to stimulate the players. To revive fatigued athletes, the investigators found that coaches and trainers turned to caffeine or to strychnine tablets, or they allowed their athletes to play when injured or fatigued. On the other hand, the coach at one college gave his players "bread pills" to calm their nerves, a nostrum that presumably would have the same effect as a carbohydrate-laden meal. More notorious and less alien to modern experience proved to be the use of cocaine to allow injured players to reenter the game. The authors charged that coaches "chose deliberately to sacrifice the actual or potential physical welfare of a player or players to the putative exigencies of victory."[33]

The Carnegie Report also called into question the popular assumption that football, as it had been reinvented prior to World War I, was a safer game. While the report cited no figures on fatalities, it did suggest that serious injuries such as concussions had, in fact, risen. Since no records were kept of fatalities and severe injuries in college football, the investigators had little except their own data on which to base their conclusions. They incorporated figures that compared the injuries in football "among 43,923 participants in Intercollegiate and Intramural Athletics at twenty-two Representative Colleges." Because it was a small sample, they did not divulge the sources of their statistics nor the names of the colleges, but they did not hesitate to make judgments, especially on football. Played by eleven of the twenty-two schools in their mini-sample, intercollegiate football had by far the highest percentage of accidents and injuries, more than twice the number of any other sport. By serious injuries the authors meant for the most part fractures, dislocations, and chronic sprains as well as concussions that disabled players for more than three weeks. "From the point of view of physical injury," the authors declared, "it appears that football is the most hazardous of college sports."[34]

Though recruiting and subsidizing stole the report's headlines, the potential for football injuries should have attracted more attention. Buried in a less controversial (except for the use of drugs) middle chapters, the topic received little fanfare. Perhaps if the researchers had included the names of the colleges and the years surveyed, the problem of injuries might have spurred the newspapers and football coaches to examine more closely the number of deaths and injuries in football during the 1920s. Unfortunately, the Carnegie Report did not cite injury figures for the 1920s or refer to reports of deaths or serious injuries, which proved to be a glaring inconsistency.

If readers had searched the sports pages in the 1920s, they would have found periodic reports of casualties on the gridiron. In 1923 the *New York Times* ran an article reporting that eighteen players had died, the same number that had precipitated the campaign against football in 1905, followed by reports of twenty in 1925, seventeen in 1927, and eighteen in 1928. Most of these short articles on casualty figures came at the end of the season, and few of the deaths had occurred in college football. The only injury that received front-page coverage came in 1929, when a grandmother in Helena,

Montana, fractured her leg playing football with her grandchildren, a story that fit well with what the popular historian Frederick Lewis Allen called "the age of ballyhoo," when the goal of sports journalists, like their front-page counterparts, was to entertain rather than inform.

The contents of the Carnegie Report reached the public in the last ten days of October 1929. History decreed that the study would play second fiddle to the grand finale of that lavish era. Though coming in the middle of the football season, its release coincided almost precisely with the stock market crash. As a result, the report had to compete with stories of huge sell-offs and plummeting stock prices. Yet it received more attention than any other Carnegie Foundation publication, with the possible exception of the earlier study by Abraham Flexner on medical education. "The book of twelve chapters and 347 pages," Howard Savage wrote, "had a rousing reception in thousands of newspaper columns, speeches in support and in denial, and special articles."[35]

College presidents attempted to protect their schools' reputations while demonstrating their belief in pure athletics. The study was correct in principle, the presidents acknowledged, but they denied that it applied to their schools or athletic conferences. The president of Stanford insisted that his institution would never tolerate subsidized athletics, even though its coach, Glenn Warner, had a reputation both at Carlisle Indian School in the early 1900s and later at Pittsburgh of cutting corners and using his own position for personal profit. At Vanderbilt the chancellor cheerfully declared that, if any cheating took place, "I do not know it in my official capacity." The president of the new southern power, the University of Alabama, explained that "many students are employed in part-time work and not for athletic prowess."[36]

In contrast, the president of Lafayette College praised the report because it brought into the open "back-stairs gossip." Among those schools that still gave scholarships, the president of Lebanon Valley (Pennsylvania) College, G. D. Gossard, gave one of the few candid responses admitting that his school awarded athletic scholarships. The president of Blue Ridge College in New Windsor, Maryland, E. G. Bixler, revealed that his institution had quit football because the competition with other schools had made the cost of their scholarships prohibitive. "We had to drop football," Bixler admitted, "because we had to get in too many extra players for the size of the school."[37]

John Griffiths, the Big Ten commissioner, roundly denied that eight of the conference schools engaged in major violations of amateur athletics. Most of the eight schools cited in the report—Michigan, Northwestern, and Wisconsin—appeared frequently. Commissioner Griffiths used the recent suspension of Iowa for operating a slush fund as evidence that the Big Ten insisted on strictly amateur athletics, but the report hardly mentioned Iowa.

Instead, Iowa cited the report to argue that other Big Ten institutions engaged in more widespread cheating and the Hawkeyes had been only guilty of minor infractions. As a result, Iowa officials were said to be jubilant when they heard that the conference would reinstate them, as it, in fact, did in 1930.[38]

Many of the coaches, athletic directors, and alumni managers not only displayed hostility toward the investigators but also questioned the report's premises. Bert Bell, athletic director at Pennsylvania, pronounced his school as clean as any in the world. But he prophetically added, "There is no reason why a boy who happens to be an athlete and a student should not be helped as much as the student who receives a scholarship for his high standing scholastically." Lou Little, football coach and athletic director at Georgetown, was angry at the treatment that he had received from the investigator. "I well remember the visit of John T. McGovern of the Carnegie Committee in the fall of 1927," Little declared, "and have in my possession a letter from McGovern assuring me that athletics at Georgetown were in a healthy state and we had nothing to fear in this report." Misrepresentation was a common complaint. At Bucknell the alumni manager accused the Carnegie Foundation of "broken faith" because the investigator assured him that names would not be mentioned. Frequently mentioned in the report, Southern California referred to a similar act of betrayal.[39]

Among the student newspapers the *Daily Northwestern* wanted to know why the report created big waves—everyone knew that athletics were not "simon-pure" and never had been. Though pleased with its institution's A rating, the *Yale Daily News* criticized the report for including Harvard and Princeton among the malefactors and insisted that it was hardly fair to the two institutions, which had almost entirely cleaned up their programs. The *Columbia Spectator* took the report to task for "generalities and innuendoes" and charged it with "cheap sensationalism." In truth the Carnegie Report had identified four future Ivy League members—Brown, Columbia, Dartmouth, and Pennsylvania—with subsidization and recruiting that differed little from big-time programs in the Midwest.[40]

Few faculty spoke out either in support or criticism of the report unless they were deans or headed administrative committees. "There is no slush fund at Northwestern for the benefit of four athletes, and any charge of that nature is ridiculous," declared Professor Delton Howard, chairman of the Northwestern committee that administered loans and scholarships. One reason for faculty indifference might have been that the authors had little to say about the faculty role in athletics or how faculty might be able restore integrity to college athletics. Ironically, Savage's panacea was to return to a much earlier, primitive and vaguely remembered era when the students had briefly run intercollegiate athletics. As John Thelin has pointed out, many of the worst abuses had occurred when students in league with alumni ran the athletic associations. Nowhere did the report call for the toothless NCAA either to set standards or to assume a stronger role in enforcement of rules, which might logically have flowed from their indictment of athletic practices and from the role of the NCAA in requesting the study.[41]

Nevertheless, the Carnegie Report proved hard to refute. In the face of denials, indignation, and indifference, Savage stood behind the findings of the Carnegie Report. Some evidence exists in the footnotes that a few schools had hurriedly cleaned up their athletics after the team visited their institution and delivered the results of their findings to the college presidents. The president of Penn State College, R. D. Hetzel, wrote that faculty and students had opposed giving further scholarships, and the head of West Virginia Wesleyan, Homer E. Wark, claimed that the school had stopped giving scholarships to athletes.[42]

Occasionally, the report did bring about changes. The reaction of the authorities at Brown University proved so negative that an observer might have wondered if the school had something to hide. A spokesman called the references to football at Brown so misleading that he did not see how the Carnegie Foundation was willing to attach its name to it. Nevertheless, when Brown conducted an internal probe, it found that the practices of subsidizing athletes were every bit as bad as the foundation had alleged. "There was praise and blame enough for all," Savage later concluded about the report, "yet not one of the myriad details of the volume was ever successfully refuted."[43]

The volume contained one embarrassing discrepancy. In his preface Henry Pritchett blamed the professional coach for the objectionable practices described by the Carnegie Report. Yet Savage singled out the coach as only one factor in the problem. It is hardly surprising that Pritchett's short-sighted view distressed the authors of the report. "Their [the authors'] view was that the paid coach was only one manifestation," Savage explained, "and that he was a result rather than the inclusive source of the defect." Instead, Savage placed the responsibility squarely on the shoulders of the college president. "Such are the position and the powers of the American college president," he declared, "that once having informed himself of the facts," and if he had the moral fortitude, he would eliminate the problem. Yet the responses to the study while in progress indicated that the presidents, such as Walter Dill Scott of Northwestern, preferred not to know the facts or allowed themselves to be blinded to the contradictions in college sports.[44]

In addition to its embarrassing discrepancy, the Carnegie Report had a far more fundamental flaw. Pritchett and Savage predicated the study on the ideal of amateur athletics. Yet Savage and his team produced so much evidence of aggressive recruiting and surreptitious subsidies that it hardly seemed possible that colleges could return to an era of strictly amateur athletics. Savage recognized that the practices that he identified could probably never be entirely extirpated. What the authors failed to do with their vast materials was to propose a realistic system that would standardize the existing practices in an acceptable way. Ironically, the report's findings probably contributed to the changes in the 1950s which led to far more standardized methods for recruiting and subsidizing athletes, a bastardized version of the high academic standards that Pritchett had long espoused.

Undoubtedly, the results of the report proved disappointing to the investigators. Savage later acknowledged that it had come out at an unfortunate time. Not only did it compete with the stock market crash for front-page headlines, but the report also failed to get the backing that might have enabled reformers to follow up. The best known of the other Carnegie reports, the Flexner Report on medical education in 1910, had set the standard for subsequent investigations—and created expectations for determined follow-ups. Though the medical profession had already begun to weed out the weakest and least solvent schools before the report appeared, the Flexner Report had assisted with both publicity and support. Unlike Flexner's study, which was forward looking, Savage's report not only measured itself by the failed reforms of an earlier era but also failed to reach for a new and realistic standard to which college athletic programs could adhere. Possibly as a result, the Carnegie Corporation of New York, the funding arm of the Carnegie philanthropies, which normally made follow-up grants, never helped out in the reform of college athletics. Just as likely, the lack of support may have resulted from the worsening economic problems after 1929 which forced the colleges to downscale their athletic programs and the Carnegie to husband its resources. "For a short time," Savage acknowledged, "a view was current that 'Carnegie money' would be used to improve college athletics; none was forthcoming, however, for this purpose; the study had uncovered both defects and merits in the system which was left—as it belonged—to the institutions themselves: presidents, trustees, faculties, undergraduates, and alumni." Given the data in Savage's report, it is hard to imagine all of these groups arriving at a satisfactory conclusion without some assistance or pressure from the outside. Multiplied many times over, reform in big-time athletics would have required a higher degree of coordination than would have been possible in the early 1930s.[45]

Unlike the reaction to the controversies of the early 1900s, the public and the academic institutions displayed only fleeting concern. One of few national columns devoted to the report, and one of the most interesting came from the vitriolic pen of Westbrook Pegler, whose invective often disguised his commonsense observations. In two pieces on the Carnegie Report, Pegler best articulated the lack of public interest in athletic problems. "There is no essential immorality in subsidizing a college player to the extent of one thousand dollars a year, which would be about five times as much as the average per capita subsidy," he declared. "It is only the pretense and concealment couched in resolutions and agreements of the most elaborate athletic piety, that is immoral." Pegler added that this hypocrisy permeated so many facets of American life that these controversies had lost their ability to shock the public. In other words, Pegler, speaking for and to the public, regarded Savage's professorial commitment to amateurism as sheer hypocrisy.[46]

Seen from a broader perspective, the practices documented by the Carnegie Report were not abuses at all. Buoyed by its popularity and competing for blue-chip players, college football was gravitating toward a new system of support. The subsidies and methods of recruiting which appeared so boldly innovative and blatantly dishonest were merely refinements of a system that had existed in the 1890s, albeit on a smaller scale. What Savage and his colleagues had so carefully documented proved to be experiments with athletic scholarships and aggressive recruiting methods. So strong was the tradition of strict amateurism that few schools, or their alumni, could openly admit to tempting athletes with offers of assistance or providing them with aid when they arrived. What persisted from the 1890s, however, would be the chronic system of lies and deceptions which college football partisans not only employed in the 1920s but also continued to use long after their methods had become legitimate.

Though it failed to alter athletic policies, the Carnegie Report led an underground existence in the 1930s and afterward. It proved to be by far the most comprehensive effort to document specific athletic practices and to present a complete picture of college athletics. As a result, reformers frequently cited the Carnegie Report or called for a new investigation to update its findings or even used its format for muckraking articles. If it accomplished anything, the report offered support for a small group of diverse critics who had appeared in the late 1920s and who would step up their efforts to reform the highly commercial and flagrantly deceptive practices in college athletics.

Notre Dame's backfield, which sportswriter Grantland Rice dubbed the "Four Horsemen of the Apocalypse," pose after Notre Dame defeated Army, 13-7, in October 1925. Inspired by a Rudolph Valentino film, Rice immortalized a good but not great backfield as "Death, Pestilence, Famine, and War." An innovative student publicist at Notre Dame came up with the idea of photographing the four players on horseback when they returned to South Bend. In the 1920s prosperity, film, and radio coverage helped to produce truly national sports heroes such as the Horsemen, Jack Dempsey, and Babe Ruth. COURTESY OF LIBRARY OF CONGRESS.

Blocking practice at Princeton, 1930s. Along with rules changes and improved equipment, refined technique had some effect in silencing critics of the game. Even so, the "chop block" remained legal until 1980. COURTESY OF SEELY G. MUDD MANUSCRIPT LIBRARY, PRINCETON UNIVERSITY.

In the early 1900s student leaders at the University of Oregon banished women from undergraduate seating on the grounds that women detracted from effective cheering. As late as the 1930s, women still sat in their own section, male cheerleaders whooping it up in front of them. COURTESY OF UNIVERSITY OF OREGON ARCHIVES.

Cheerful members of the University of Nebraska Pep Squad in the late 1920s or early 1930s. The squad assisted in a role that remained largely in a the hands of males until after World War II. COURTESY OF LIBRARY OF CONGRESS.

Cheerleaders at Alabama in 1936, Paul "Bear" Bryant's senior year as a player at "'Bama." The first female cheerleaders in college football appeared in the South in the 1920s. UNIVERSITY OF ALABAMA YEARBOOK, *COROLLA*, 1937. COURTESY OF SPECIAL COLLECTIONS, UNIVERSITY OF ALABAMA.

Spectacle sells. In a move that greatly enhanced the popular appeal of college football, the University of Illinois organized one of the first marching bands in the country in 1910. Its music and drill formations filled the time between halves of the game, as in this formation in 1932. COURTESY OF UNIVERSITY ARCHIVES, UNIVERSITY OF ILLINOIS AT CHAMPAIGN–URBANA.

Big-time football swept across the South in the 1920s and 1930s. Marian Wolcott, a photographer for the Farm Security Administration, a New Deal agency, captured this photo of bandleader Kay Kyser, a Duke alumnus, leading cheers at the Duke–North Carolina game on November 18, 1939. A crowd of 50,800 in Durham saw the Blue Devils win against the undefeated Tar Heels, 13-3, a record for a southern football game. COURTESY OF THE LIBRARY OF CONGRESS.

Nearing the end of his career at the University of Chicago, the legendary Amos Alonzo Stagg began his thirty-ninth season assembling his team for spring practice in 1930. Two years later the Robert Hutchins administration forced Stagg to retire. He went to the College of the Pacific, where he coached for fourteen more years, winning Coach of the Year honors for his team's remarkable performance in 1943. COURTESY OF LIBRARY OF CONGRESS.

A slayer of the dragon, Hutchins playfully dons football attire for the Quadrangle Club Revels in 1949. Undercutting their support, the University of Chicago Maroons had suffered through their worst season ever in 1939, losing to Michigan 85-0 and taking a 61-0 thumping at the hands of both Harvard and Ohio State. COURTESY OF SPECIAL COLLECTIONS, UNIVERSITY OF CHICAGO LIBRARY.

A photo from inside the University of Illinois huddle during a practice session shows further improvements in helmets, which in 1939 the NCAA football rules committee required all players to wear throughout the game. A more protective leather helmet with improved suspension would be followed by durable plastic headgear. COURTESY OF LIBRARY OF CONGRESS.

CHAPTER TEN

Overcoming Hard Times: Gridiron Strategies in the 1930s

In the early 1930s the nation plunged into the greatest economic cataclysm in its history, and college football felt the loss of jobs and disposable income. Football attendance, which had skyrocketed in the 1920s, now fell by 25 percent between 1929 and 1933. Colleges had gone into debt to build great stadiums and now found it hard to pay the interest on their stadium obligations. Athletic departments awash in athletic revenues only a few years before suddenly found themselves in debt. At Cornell the surplus in the athletic treasury in 1929 amounted to $416,369. By 1934 that figure had dwindled to $23,237, forcing the cancellation of spring practice. At Ohio State and Iowa deficits in the football revenue forced the universities to cut back on their minor sports; members of football coaching staffs whose salaries and numbers were normally untouchable now found themselves among the unemployed.[1]

In the gloom of the Depression big-time football for a time reduced its lavish subsidies, and students and alumni, who had to cut back on expenses, attended fewer games. In his follow-up to the Carnegie Report in 1931, Howard Savage insisted that the college undergraduates as well as the general public had tired of big-time college sports. Using slivers of evidence, Savage argued that "the person whose interests are most important is not the alumnus, the faculty member, the coach, the newspaper writer, or the townsman, but the undergraduate." Savage stuck out his neck even further. "Almost every current indication," he wrote, "is to the effect that the undergraduate is tiring of 'big-time' athletics."[2]

Because they sought to justify the 1929 study and their distaste for big-time football, Savage and other gridiron critics missed the point of the change in the early 1930s. The recruiting and subsidies of big-time football managed to survive the hard times, and, once the economy had stabilized, the much maligned practices of recruiting and subsidies singled out by the Carnegie Report returned to their pre-1929 levels. Though the flurry of reforms in the early New Deal had no counterpart in college football of the 1930s, the persistent efforts to pay football players would lead to a crisis of confidence in the ability of colleges and conferences to police themselves. The flouting of amateur standards would create a dialogue over college athletics which would lead to a change in the laissez-faire approach to enforcement by the end of the decade.

Causes for Alarm: Real and Imagined

One cause for alarm in the early 1930s growing out of the hard times proved to be an outbreak of deaths and serious injuries. At the NCAA convention in 1931 the chairman of the rules committee, Edward K. Hall, reported on a large number of injuries that had occurred in the 1931 season, which some newspapers reported to be as high as forty-nine. Though the deaths in college play numbered no more than eight, the publicity led to calls for changes in the rules to reduce the hazards. In the early 1930s the high schools still played by the same rules as the colleges, so that the casualties served as a wake-up call for rules reformers of the last crisis such as Hall, who believed that the revolution in the rules which he had helped to bring about in the pre–World War I era had solved the problem once and forever.[3]

Like much of what happened in the early 1930s, the spurt of deaths and serious injuries in the early 1930s resulted more from the Great Depression than from defects in the rules. Authorities believed that the school districts that were hit even harder than the colleges by the effects of the Depression allotted less money for coaches and equipment. Because of better supervision, training, and equipment, football at the college level proved far less prone to the most common causes of death such as concussions, spinal injuries, and heat stroke. Though the rules committee made changes in 1931, the public concern with football injuries played second fiddle to a society plagued by the desperate problems of unemployment and bankruptcy.[4]

Of the few college casualties, the death of an Army player in the Yale-Army game reawakened painful memories of Cadet Eugene Byrne's fatal injury in 1909, a game that Edward Hall had refereed. In October 1931 Cadet Richard Brinsley Sheridan of Army suffered neck injuries during a play in which Yale scored on a eighty-eight-yard touchdown. No one saw Sheridan's injury, but he was probably hit with a hard block. Rushed to the New Haven Hospital, he was attended by the ubiquitous Harvey Cushing, who had worked on Eugene Byrne and Archer Christian in 1909. Using an artificial respirator, the physicians kept Sheridan alive a little longer than Byrne and Christian, but he died two days after the accident.

Though the newspapers carried detailed accounts of Sheridan's injury and his final hours, the accident did not create the public clamor for reform which had occurred in 1905 and 1909. Edward Hall's committee revised the rules, and the number of deaths in 1932 temporarily fell to more acceptable levels. Injuries and deaths plagued high school football through the 1930s, but the high levels fell short of creating a general crisis. Colleges, which had to deal with declining enrollments and reduced appropriations, did not use the injury problems, as they had in the early 1900s, to mount an attack on the evils of college football.[5]

Nevertheless, the early years of the Depression did bring some attempts to reform the culture of college football. Possibly because they believed, like Howard Savage, that big-time football was on the wane, a panel of college officials in 1932 attempted to draw up a program of reforms. Chaired by President Thomas Gates of Pennsylvania, whose school's recruiting practices had long caused controversy, the five presidents on the Gates Commission attempted to set forth a plan for restoring amateurism to college athletics. In the tradition of Charles Eliot the report declared that "we must place athletics in their proper relationship to all that we are attempting to do in fitting young men and women for the many-sided responsibilities, opportunities, and pleasures of life."[6]

The report set forth standards for amateur athletics. It condemned spring practice, "training houses" or athletic dormitories, and subsidies such as special loans, jobs, or allowances for college athletes, perks for college athletes that persisted in spite of the Depression. It further backed a series of practices designed to downsize college football, including intramural sports, contests with "natural rivals," shorter seasons, and making coaches members of the faculty. The report also called upon colleges to educate their alumni or, in other words, to persuade them to observe the rules against tampering with athletes.

Coming three years after the Carnegie Report, the Gates Report might have become a footnote to a footnote. Yet the report would provide a connective with the issues of reform dating from Charles Eliot's criticism and, of course, from the Carnegie Foundation reports. Some of the language and concepts, such as "natural rivals," came into general use among reformers. The proposal to eliminate out-of-season training, while not new, acquired new life.

One reason for the influence of the Gates Committee had to do with its members, such as Acting President John Newcomb of the University of Virginia, who would soon afterward help to draw up the puritanical Graham Plan adopted by the Southern Conference. Newcomb represented a link with Virginia's outgoing president, Edwin Alderman, whose career and brief attempts at reform went back to the early years of football in the South and to the crisis of 1909. Another member, Ernest Wilkins of Oberlin, headed the institution that supplied the athletic director, who played a pivotal role in the abolition of football at the University of Chicago.

Actually, the presidents who drew up the Gates Report underestimated the tenacity of big-time practices, or what they would have called "commercialism" and "professionalism" at major institutions. For the most part the wrongdoing—activities of alumni, the subsidies to athletes, and the hotly contested recruiting for big-time athletes—seldom came to the surface. If the details became public, they surfaced in bits and pieces that failed to describe fully the systematic evasion of the NCAA's amateur code which took place just barely out of sight.

One institution, however, opened up a remarkably clear window to the way in which big-time athletic departments operated during the 1920s and 1930s. Otherwise undistinguished, the University of Pittsburgh had become a football power when Glenn "Pop" Warner arrived from Carlisle in 1914. Warner, who had coached top teams that included Jim Thorpe, had lost his job at Carlisle, a government "vocational" school for Native Americans, when as a member of the board of a canning company he negotiated a contract that supplied food to the institution.

Under Warner the University of Pittsburgh gained a reputation for producing some of the best teams in the country. One of Warner's best-known stars was All-America John "Jock" Sutherland, who, after his college career, coached at Lafayette and served as a professor in the dental school at Pittsburgh. Being a keen student of the "old buccaneer," Sutherland twice held Pittsburgh scoreless in his first coaching job at Lafayette. When Warner left for Stanford in 1924, the charismatic Sutherland took over the job.

Sutherland fielded great teams because he knew what it took to keep his cattle in clover. The amount of Pitt's subsidies in the 1920s and 1930s varied according to the political struggles between coaches and administrators as well as the state of the national economy. Muckraking journalist Francis Wallace, who wrote a two-part series of the turmoil at Pitt in the 1930s, described the amounts between 1924 and 1936 as varying through three phases: (1) 1924–27-players received cash payments, the amounts based upon their abilities and bargaining power. While some players got as much as one hundred dollars a month plus tuition and books, the average figure was fifty-five dollars a month, out of which players paid their room, board, and expenses; the average industrial worker in Pennsylvania in the same years received almost one hundred dollars per week, but laborers also had to work as many as sixty or seventy hours; (2) in 1933 the salaries, which appeared high by Depression standards, were cut to forty dollars a month, and the players were expected to pay for their room, board, and tuition; (3) in 1934-36 players now got forty-eight dollars each month for ten months, a figure that allowed slightly more for out-of-pocket expenses. Wallace speculated that some of the players, especially in the 1920s, received additional amounts from alumni and boosters, which would have provided them with a healthy income. By contrast, a worker in a blast furnace around Pittsburgh would have received slightly more than one hundred dollars each week at the low point of the Depression but would have toiled between fifty and sixty hours each week in backbreaking labor.[7]

Two years before Sutherland arrived, John Bowman became chancellor of the institution in downtown Pittsburgh. A former president of Iowa and director of the American College of Surgeons, Bowman encountered a college plagued by poverty of mind and body, an institution that had only its football team to engender a sense of pride. "The school was facing foreclosure on an indebtedness of two million dollars, which was fifty per cent more than it was worth," he declared. "I found one of the poorest faculties I have ever seen." Bowman envisioned a grand Cathedral of Learning, a high-rise education center that would house the classrooms, laboratories, and offices and, in Bowman's words, "lift the eyes of drab Pittsburgh from earth to heaven." But the first thing on the minds of the alumni and fund-raisers was a football stadium that would enable the Panthers to keep up with the Big Ten schools, which were building their own capacious football facilities.[8]

While Bowman labored to solve the financial and teaching problems, football partisans began a campaign for a new stadium, a project that generated more passion than did academic fund-raising. Though Bowman was deeply committed to his cathedral project, he went along with the stadium campaign. Completed in 1925, the stadium cost $2,100,000, locally financed through stadium bonds, but arrived far over budget. After the stadium was completed, Bowman began his own fund-raising drive for the forty-two-story high-rise academic building, which eventually reached completion in 1937.

Despite Bowman's plans for the soaring cathedral, the University of Pittsburgh became far better known for gridiron rather than academic excellence. In 1934, when Pitt lost only one game, word got out after the season that a majority of the starters were married. In a later era a "married man's team" would have hardly been worth a headline, but in the hard times of the 1930s most young people lacked the money to go to college and, for lack of resources, had to postpone getting married. Even in good times middle-class boys and girls traditionally began their adult lives by getting an education, a life trajectory that would lead to jobs and then marriage; rarely did students attend college if married, and many schools frowned on married undergraduates or banned them altogether. Both the high subsidies and the married players stigmatized Pitt as a school that gave highly favorable treatment to its athletes. Some opponents used this as a reason not to schedule the formidable Panthers. In turn, the school's administration, which had been looking for a reason to curtail the football program, had a rationale for regulating subsidies, since Pitt now sported a reputation as a semiprofessional, "married man's" team, whose players received a worker's wage.[9]

By the mid-1930s, about the time Pitt revised its subsidies, college football began to revive. In 1933, after college football hit rock bottom in attendance, it began to reverse itself as the economy stabilized. As in basketball, college football teams had played round-robin contests in the early 1930s to raise money to aid the unemployed. While these contests seldom made money for the schools, the reasonably priced contests did attract college football fans. In 1935 college athletic officials heaved a sigh of relief when ninety thousand fans saw Stanford defeat California in a showdown for the

Rose Bowl. By mid-decade attendance at college football games approached pre-Depression levels, and between 1935 and 1941 many college football teams thrived, and a few others tried to take advantage of growing gridiron attendance by launching higher-profile programs. Because of the competition for scarce entertainment dollars, college athletic programs had more reason to make their recruiting and subsidies more efficient and even to extend their recruiting activities.[10]

One small but helpful source of income came from the sale of radio broadcasts. In the mid-1930s colleges began to consider the possibility of contracts for commercial broadcasts of their games. In the previous decade radio stations broadcast some big games, such as the Illinois-Michigan game in which Red Grange ran wild, but rarely did they carry the team's entire schedule. Faced with a new source of gridiron dollars, purists worried that sponsors would further taint the game, and profit-minded athletic directors tried to decide whether radio would erode attendance. In 1936 Yale took the plunge by agreeing to let Atlantic Refining broadcast its games for twenty thousand dollars. Michigan and Stanford insisted that, if they did not broadcast their games, other less scrupulous entrepreneurs would receive the credit—and the revenues. For Iowa and Illinois, which cleared less than four thousand dollars per season, the profits barely justified commercial radio. Nevertheless, the profit motive triumphed in most cases over arguments for preserving amateur athletics. By 1940 Harvard and Princeton, which had tried to hold the line, decided to broadcast their annual contests. In spite of the trend toward radio, live attendance would remain the means by which the schools met their athletic costs, paid their stadium debt, and helped to finance jobs and subsidies for their athletes. "It is generally accepted that radio has popularized the sports," H. Jamison Swarts, athletic director at Pennsylvania, would declare in 1947, "and that is reflected in greater attendance."[11]

During the 1930s a number of cities in the South and Southwest such as Dallas, Miami, New Orleans, and Phoenix attempted to revive their economies by creating Rose Bowl replicas. Struggling in the shadow of Depression and the prestigious Rose Bowl, the larger bowl games such as the Orange, Cotton, and Sugar Bowls managed to carve out a niche for themselves, as did the East-West and North-South All-Star Games. By the late 1930s bowls with the names like the Celery, Dixie, Eastern, Flower, Fruit, Glass, Grape, Orchid, Pineapple, Salad, Silver, and Steel dotted the landscape. Football reformers in the late 1930s who deplored the commercialism embodied in these postseason contests made the intersectional game into a mantra for opposition to big-time football. While some of these festivals sprouted outside the South, the bowl contests and the North-South all-star game all seemed to flow from the entrepreneurial energy of a New South that strained at the boundaries of traditional football practices.

Origins of a New Reform Movement

Unlike the colleges in the Midwest, Northeast, and upper South, the schools in the deep South made little effort to disguise widespread support for football players. In 1935 the members of the five-year-old Southeastern Conference (SEC) voted to allow scholarships for their athletes. To athletic officials and college presidents in other regions, it was as if the South had opened fire on Fort Sumpter again; the simple admission that the Southeastern Conference intended openly to flout amateur ideals shook the football establishment as well as academic authorities.

While subsidies and work programs flourished in the East and Midwest, southern athletic departments had opted for a different approach. In 1929 the *Washington Post* commented that "the South today seems inclined to adopt a 'ho, hum,' and 'well, what of it?'" attitude toward subsidizing athletes. Schools in the South had become less inclined to give athletes jobs or provide partial support through loans and under-the-table payments.[12]

Already located in a chronically depressed part of the country, many colleges in small southern towns simply could not find jobs for their athletes or wealthy alumni to support the players. In addition, many southerners adhered to a casual approach toward aiding athletes, reflecting attitudes that dated back to the era of tramp athletes, a practice that had aroused far less concern below the Mason-Dixon line than in other parts of the country. The states of the deep South, where these customs were most deeply rooted, refused to play by the rules imposed on them by the eastern and midwestern colleges, where athletic officials insisted on their own prickly versions of amateur athletics—systems that did not work well in the largely rural South.

Above all, aggressive policies of athletic subsidies reflected the white South's way of restoring its pride so badly damaged by the Civil War, Reconstruction, and the chronic hard times that dogged much of the South well into the twentieth century. Alabama's defeat of Washington in the Rose Bowl in 1926 and Georgia's conquest of Yale at New Haven in 1927 helped to raise regional morale and show that southerners could indeed defeat the North on gridiron battlefields.[13]

Football also became a convenient way for the South's booster governors to promote their states. The most flamboyant approach to building a reputation through football occurred at Louisiana State University, where Governor Huey Long made football his pet project. To be sure, Governor Long took an interest in other parts of the university, pumping money into faculty salaries, professional schools, medical facilities, and classroom buildings. Viewed from that perspective, football remained a sideshow to LSU's overall growth but one that demonstrated the open approach to subsidizing and recruiting in southern athletics.

Huey Long kicked off his involvement by arriving at the practice field one afternoon in November 1930 with LSU's new president. After introducing the president, the governor watched the team practice and even tried unsuccessfully to boot an extra point. For the next four years Governor Long made the football team his personal project. Like a freshly minted, backwoods Knute Rockne, he insisted on giving locker room speeches at halftime and lent his win-at-any-cost perspective to team councils. After learning that Tulane had a talented quarterback, he suggested that LSU purchase the player's services by giving his father a state job. To the LSU coach's irritation, Long frequently interfered with the team, even introducing plays he had designed. To promote the team, the university, the state, and his political career, he planned to take the team and three thousand students on a rambling train ride across the Midwest to play Army at West Point. Shedding these grandiose plans, which were perhaps conjured up for their effect on future voters, he announced to the students that he would have to stay at home and would send only the band and the team—luckily, it turned out, because Army vanquished LSU, 25-0. Despite his four-year love affair with college football, the Tigers did not emerge as a gridiron power until after Long was assassinated in 1935.[14]

One might attribute all of this quaint boosterism to vintage Huey Long had it had not reflected trends in southern and, to a lesser extent, in northern athletics. Outdone only by some schools in Pennsylvania, college teams in the deep South went after football talent far more openly than most northern institutions. An article in the *Chicago Post* in 1929 had proclaimed that "'proselyte openly' is a Dixie word." In 1936 a former Mississippi coach informed his mentor, Bob Zuppke of Illinois, that "Zup" should borrow a page from southern practices to revitalize his own sagging programs: "The Southern schools are getting it down to a science," the coach declared, "greeting and hand shaking, seeing that they have a place to eat, a place to sleep, often they pay the traveling expenses for the better boys, they try them out just to see [how fast they could run and how well they withstood physical contact]." The southern colleges, he explained, even sponsored free coaching schools for high school coaches. Aware of alumni criticism of Zuppke, the former players offered to help the beleaguered coach introduce more aggressive, "southern" recruiting techniques.[15]

In the upper South, East, and Midwest athletic officials reacted with alarm in 1935 when the Southeastern Conference decided to give outright football scholarships. Following this declaration John Griffiths, commissioner of the Big Ten, wrote to Amos Alonzo Stagg, now in California, that the deep South was letting down the bars. He wondered if there should be "white lists" of teams that were ethically eligible to play. Griffiths rejoiced when the National Collegiate Athletic Association in December 1935 passed seven resolutions that condemned recruiting and subsidizing. Still, the moribund organization had no way to enforce their code. Instead, it appointed a committee to study the problems of enforcement, an action that proved to be the first small step toward regulating the behavior of its members and ultimately making the NCAA a great deal more than a forum for ideas and discussion. For the next few years, however, the NCAA majority merely expressed veiled disapproval of the SEC.[16]

One might question why Stagg and Griffiths reacted so violently to the Southeastern Conference's declaration, when many Big Ten schools engaged in their own stealthy modes of subsidization. One might explain that inconsistency by noting that many college officials and faculty still believed strongly in amateur athletics, an ideal incorporated in the bylaws of the NCAA. Increasingly, opponents of semiprofessionalism tried to define the scope of amateur athletics and the point at which amateurs became professionals. Not surprisingly, the advocates of strict amateurism rejected assistance to athletes not open to nonathletes. While they disliked the practice of paid coaches, they believed that coaches should become members of the faculty so that their salaries would not exceed those of senior faculty and practices. They also rejected the notion of spring practice and of postseason games. They criticized institutions like Pittsburgh, where football excluded other sports and where the notion of intramural sports played a secondary role to big-time athletics.

Football subsidies enjoyed less support among college presidents in the upper South. The decision by the Southeastern Conference to give scholarships in 1935 proved alarming enough that Southern Conference presidents met to consider a thoroughly amateur policy. By a slim one-vote majority the college presidents voted to adopt what was called the "Graham Plan." Named after the highly respected president of North Carolina, Frank Graham, the puritanical code outlawed both athletic subsidies and assistance from alumni, a plan that was drawn from principles drawn up by Graham and President John Newcomb of Virginia, who had served on the Gates Commission.[17]

From the beginning the Graham Plan faced insurmountable odds. Ironically, the same school to which the Graham Plan owed its name was one of the region's worst subsidy offenders. The *Daily Tar Heel* at North Carolina published a manifesto by a student group called the Campus Cabinet opposing the plan. "Recognized or Not," as the manifesto was called, summoned up a litany of arguments against purely amateur athletics. Players "don't come to Carolina to play football," the authors wrote, "they play football to come to North Carolina." While the Campus Cabinet absolved the Graham administration, it felt certain that "alumni can never be stopped from helping good athletes through school; we simply question whether they should be stopped." The cabinet called for an end to the hypocrisy inherent in the Graham Plan, which required athletes to renounce subsidies at institutions where they were already receiving generous under-the-table assistance. The idea of amateurs in a world of semiprofessionals, the cabinet argued, resulted in "murder," either disabling injuries to the players or lopsided scores against the team. "We can't afford to become simon pure and lose out like Virginia," they observed in reference to Virginia's awful teams. Commended by the Carnegie Report for running a clean program, Virginia had also suffered through the 1930s with consistently losing seasons. In 1935, the year of the Graham plan, Virginia struggled to eke out four scoreless ties against Davidson, Hampton-Sydney, William and Mary, and Virginia Military Institute. In its final game Virginia again scored no points, while Frank Graham's university smothered its simon-pure neighbors to the north, 61-0.[18]

The Graham Plan lasted for barely a year, since it was clearly unworkable. "The Graham Plan is a farce," one Virginia alumnus wrote, "since every school in the conference is violating the very principles of it." In 1936 Virginia withdrew from the Southern Conference because of these discrepancies and set up alumni scholarships that were more readily available to athletes. As a result, Virginia teams began to improve. Shortly after, the presidents of the Southern Conference emasculated the Graham Plan, relieving the members of any scruples they may have felt about covert subsidies. Nevertheless, Virginia refused to reaffiliate with the Southern Conference, which soon afterward itself began to make scholarships more available to athletes.[19]

In the Big Ten, still the citadel of the amateur supporters, other schools threatened to follow the Southeastern Conference's example. Rumors circulated in 1936 that Wisconsin was prepared to offer athletic scholarships, but it did not happen. In truth the Big Ten schools had no need to give athletic scholarships and might actually have found them expensive and unnecessary, since Big Ten players already had access to easy jobs. One All-America lineman for Northwestern later recounted that he had worked as a night watchman at Northwestern's Dyche Stadium, a job that he described as more boring than taxing. He related that he had received payments to help him with his expenses, though he never knew who provided this assistance. These jobs and payments were not precisely athletic scholarships because they did not constitute a "full ride." While many athletes at big-time schools got a combination of aid in the form of school jobs, summer employment from alumni, tuition "loans," and some money under the table, athletic officials still believed that they stayed within their definition of amateur athletics. To round out this aid, fraternities often provided not only jobs but also free room and board for big-time athletes.[20]

Obviously, subsidies did not stop with campus jobs. At Ohio State the athletic department managed to get jobs for the leading athletes, such as the sprinter Jesse Owens, at the nearby state capitol; Owens ran an elevator, and others served as pages for the legislators. Governor Martin Davey of Ohio in a press conference tried to deflect questions about the employment by joking about how athletes fit into state hiring practices. In a shaky conclusion the conference commissioner, John Griffith, like later masters of "spin," insisted that the players received the same rate of pay and had the same chance for employment as nonathletes.[21]

Simon-pure or strictly amateur athletics seldom existed at big-time schools, and the definition of amateur athletics changed drastically over the course of the twentieth century. In the 1920s and 1930s athletic officials in the North made it their task to define amateur athletics, which were, strictly speaking, no longer amateur. These institutions permitted aid to athletes as long as it did not amount to a full scholarship—and they called their players "amateurs" in much the same way that the NCAA would later call its big-time scholarship players "scholar-athletes." While athletic officials may have known that their opponents paid their players, a gentleman's agreement kept them from informing on one another. Only when schools like Pittsburgh exceeded the tacit limit on aid to athletes or outright scandals like Iowa's slush fund in 1929 came to light did the officials or the faculty representatives either refuse to play or expel the offender.

To attract and retain players, coaches had to turn to alumni or boosters, who donated money, jobs, or other forms of aid. One method that gained popularity in the 1920s was to organize booster groups that would surreptitiously aid the athletes. On the West Coast, where fierce regional rivalries had sprung up, booster clubs thrived in the 1930s. At UCLA, then a rising football power, the Young Men's Club of Westwood (the section of Los Angeles where UCLA was located) used its fifty dollars annual dues to fund under-the-table payments to team members. "We aided the players substantially," recalled Blanche and Robert Campbell, who ran a bookshop near the campus, "and gave the boys what the other schools were giving." The existence of those payments would become more obvious in the slush fund scandals that would hit the West Coast schools in 1939.[22]

According to amateur precepts, colleges were not supposed to approach a high school player or to make offers that would induce him to attend the institution. Though Knute Rockne held coaching clinics for college coaches, he used them primarily for moneymaking and self-promotion rather than overtly for recruiting. The midwestern schools of the Big Ten used their alumni to recruit and carefully hid their subsidies from public view. Given a clean bill of health in the Carnegie Report, Coach Bob Zuppke of Illinois did not actively recruit but relied on the reputation of his team and its success in the Red Grange era. Unfortunately, the results were losing teams and angry alumni, who in the late 1930s campaigned to force Zuppke's resignation. Recruiting and subsidies were so intertwined that successful teams devised strategies to offer the schoolboys what amounted to sub rosa athletic scholarships. The difference between semiprofessionals who received assistance for playing football and amateurs who merely received school loans or legitimate academic scholarships often varied within conferences or among team members. What are known today as "walk-ons," players who initially receives no athletic assistance, were still fairly common at big-name institutions. Though they might receive some free meals at their fraternities or work at jobs provided by the schools, their status did not appreciably differ from that of ordinary students.

In contrast to these athletes, the competition for blue-chip recruits could turn into nasty battles, and the alumni and friends of the institution often did the dirty work. Throughout the Big Ten recruitment battles raged in the mid-1930s. One of these recruiting contests swirled around Tommy Harmon, the blue-chip high school star from Gary, Indiana. Eighteen schools sought after Harmon in 1936, until the choice narrowed to Purdue and Michigan. A local sportswriter recounted that Harmon was sequestered on Saturday and part of Sunday at the house of a physician in South Bend. "Early the following morning a caravan rolled toward Ann Arbor [Michigan] with Harmon in one of them," he recalled. "Purdue scouts spent the week looking for Harmon, but never found him." Harmon won the Heisman Trophy for Michigan in 1940.[23]

At Pittsburgh, which did not have the protection of an athletic conference, the effort to end outright athletic subsidies proved nearly as costly as the subsidies themselves. Beginning in 1935, not only did the school prohibit married football players, but it also enacted a code that required players to hold down jobs in exchange for tuition and board. Prodded by President Bowman and his allies, the athletic department reduced the subsidies to three hundred dollars, more in line with other schools, and included a provision for two hours of work each day. A far tougher code would be drawn up for players entering in 1939, who would have to work from three to five hours a day to pay back the three hundred dollars. Known as the Code Bowman, it restricted spring practice, put college athletics under faculty control, and required that athletes make normal progress toward their degrees. President Bowman hoped that a return to amateur athletics would enable Pittsburgh to take advantage of Chicago's recent football misfortunes and to replace the Maroons if they left the Big Ten.[24]

In the spring of 1939, sensing the impending decline in football fortunes, Coach Jock Sutherland resigned. Already in 1938 Pittsburgh had begun to suffer from an uncharacteristic lack of depth. As an outspoken advocate of football subsidies, Sutherland had become an embarrassment to the school. In the struggle against encroachment by Bowman's forces, Sutherland had gradually lost his influence in the athletic department and understood that if he stayed others would make the decisions. As a player and coach who had rarely lost, Sutherland wanted no part of the losing seasons that he undoubtedly would have had.

Just before the 1939 season the Pitt freshmen players went on strike, protesting the reduction in subsidies which put them at a lower salary scale than the players who had entered in previous years. Inspired by the wave of sit-down strikes sweeping through the steel and automobile industries, they were able to shame the administration into restoring the reductions. The publicity proved harmful to the institution and its football program, leading to a series of articles by Francis Wallace about Pittsburgh football conflicts in the *Saturday Evening Post*. By 1940 the Panthers had suffered their first losing season since Glenn Warner had arrived in 1914.[25]

In the 1940s Pitt would pay the price for a de-emphasized football program. Despite its amateur approach to athletics, it failed in its efforts to join the Big Ten, and its de-emphasis resulted chiefly in empty seats. Bowman's attempt to find a solution for Pittsburgh athletics had much in common with the efforts by the NCAA to enforce strictly amateur standards. While Bowman struggled to scale back football subsidies, the story of Pittsburgh's big-time football would ironically prove a catalyst for those who thrived on examples of big-time athletic scandals and even for reformers like Robert Hutchins who wanted to eliminate football altogether.

Pitt's problems reached the public through articles written for the *Saturday Evening Post* by Francis Wallace. As a graduate of Notre Dame, who had begun as a college publicist for Knute Rockne, Wallace had worked as a screenwriter in Hollywood, even creating a character who resembled Coach John "Jock" Sutherland for *Touchdown* in 1931. Besides his contacts at Notre Dame, Wallace had a reporter's instinct for scandal and the ability to ferret out and recount a good story and to create in his readers a sense of what was known as "gee whiz." In the fall of 1939, as the Pitt scandal reached its climax, Wallace wrote a "tell-all" two-part series for the *Post,* which made Pitt a symbol of football excess and strengthened "the voice of reason," among them officials at smaller colleges who were trying to de-emphasize football, faculty representatives in the Big Ten and the Pacific Coast Conference who had an idealistic view of college sports, and reformers who had formed their view of football in the Progressive era.

Wallace also joined a small group of sports journalists whose interests ran to stories of football evils and excesses; in the 1930s and 1940s he and others cranked out a series of anti-football features. Besides his article on Pitt for the *Post,* Wallace published an exposé of football recruiting, "I Was a Football Fixer," in which he posed as a savvy recruiter who could deliver star halfbacks. He mentioned the wealthy boosters, not necessarily alumni, who would adopt a top player and "give him all the advantages which accrue to the son of a rich man." Wallace reported that there were "fabulous

tales of spending accounts, automobiles, vacation trips and wardrobes."
While Wallace did not regard these as commonplace, he also declared that
they were "not unusual." Telling the story in a fictional first-person voice,
Wallace blamed the colleges for this sorry state of affairs.[26]

Wallace insisted that the colleges engaged in bidding wars for high
school athletes' services. "They pay these boys and masquerade the payment," he declared. "They train this talent using expert coaches and modern scientific equipment." According to Wallace, the colleges merely wanted
to exploit the athletes as cheap labor. "They present the athletes in great out-
door stadia and charge all that the traffic will bear," he observed. "Because
they pay low prices for raw material and services, and charge high for the
finished product, they make profit."[27]

An even more relentless critic of football's moral transgressions and
pretentiousness was Harvard graduate John Tunis, an Episcopal minister's
son who became a sportswriter and an author of juvenile fiction. Tunis
wrote a series of articles, at first predicting football's decline and by the mid-
1930s calling attention to growing subsidies in big-time football. First in 1936
and then in 1939, Tunis published articles modeled on the chapters on recruiting and subsidization in the Carnegie Report. Modeling his indict-
ments on Savage's listing of purely amateur programs, Tunis divided the
football-playing schools into four groups: (1) amateur insofar as no scholarships were given, such as Brown, Chicago, Johns Hopkins, Wayne, and
more than forty small colleges in the East; (2) slightly tainted by small
amounts of aid, such as six of the eight future Ivy League schools plus Indiana, Kansas, Nebraska Minnesota, and Stanford; (3) highly subsidized,
such as Michigan, Northwestern Ohio State, Pittsburgh, California, UCLA,
Southern California, and Washington; (4) and, finally, those such as the
members of the Southeastern Conference, Southwest, and Southern which
gave outright scholarships.[28]

Like Howard Savage, Tunis also described the techniques of subsidizing, such as the use of preparatory schools, where football recruits could
spend extra years learning algebra and English composition. Like his muckraking predecessors, Tunis objected to the way in which big-time football
morally undermined not only higher education but also American society.
He updated his traditional moral perspective to reflect the realities of the
post–World War I sports world, though his amatuer standards differed little from earlier critics like Charles Eliot and Harold MacCracken. Unlike
Wallace, he did not attribute the evils of big-time football to a lust for profits. In Tunis's world each of the colleges were like bands of unsupervised
young males trying to demonstrate their macho qualities by stretching and
breaking the rules; he predicted that this perverse way of competing would
eventually destroy the wholesome quality of a game that he greatly admired.
As it turned out, Tunis and Wallace would play a part in the best-known

football reform of the era, Robert Hutchins's preemptive strike at the University of Chicago.

The End of an Era: Chicago, 1939 to 1940

When Tunis began his crusade in the late 1920s, only an oracle would have predicted the demise of football at Chicago. Hardly perceived as a small college, the University of Chicago, through its legendary coach Amos Alonzo Stagg, had long embodied the ideals of amateur virtue. Somewhat mistakenly, the public perceived Coach Stagg as a Galahad in gridiron armor who played strictly by the rules and still fielded winning teams. His reputation remained intact when Chicago inveigled its way onto the "A" list of schools singled out as "amateur" by the Carnegie Report and into the strictly amateur group compiled by John Tunis.[29]

Over the years, however, winning teams at Chicago had become a dying breed, as the proximity of Notre Dame and Northwestern eclipsed the Maroons as Chicago's top football attraction. Though Stagg and his alumni struggled to attract promising players, the caliber of his recruits deteriorated. After winning the Big Ten championship in 1924, he suffered four seasons without a winning record before eking out a 7-3 mark in 1929. In Stagg's last decent year three of his victories came against small colleges and only one against a Big Ten rival. Games at Stagg Field drew at best mediocre attendance and, after the onset of the Depression, pathetically small crowds. Spectators now attended games at South Bend, Soldier Field, or Dyche Stadium, where spectators could watch Notre Dame and Northwestern.

If William Harper's university had survived as its founder intended, Stagg might have continued to recruit and retain talented players. In the 1930s, however, Harper's institution became President Robert Hutchins's university, and the tougher academic requirements discouraged athletes from signing up for Chicago's football team. In his early years at Chicago Hutchins devoted his energies to implementing the academic reorganization begun in the 1920s. While he did not at first oppose big-time athletics, Hutchins clearly lacked the interest and enthusiasm of William Harper. When Hutchins emerged as a foe of big-time football, the team had become so embarrassing to the university that football fell into his hands like a sour apple ready to be tossed in the gridiron garbage. When Hutchins embraced football reform, he did so on his own terms and on his own turf.[30]

A decade-long study, concluded before Hutchins arrived in 1929, had led to sweeping proposals in the structure of the Chicago curriculum. In the same year that the youthful prodigy became president, the faculty adopted an ambitious and rigorous undergraduate format. Formally introduced in 1931, the "New Plan had much more in common with a graduate program than the normal undergraduate curriculum." In much the same way that

Harvard had revolutionized its curriculum with Eliot's elective system, the University of Chicago abolished required courses for freshmen and sophomores and made class attendance voluntary. In their first two years students would take a "college curriculum" followed by a qualifying exam. In the final two years they would pursue specialized studies in divisions of the university. For the garden-variety athlete, no longer able to be channeled by the athletic department into easy majors or "crip" courses, the torturous road to a college degree proved daunting. In addition, the college dropped physical education courses, which had enabled many an athlete to build up his average.[31]

At the end of the 1932–33 school year Stagg, who had already been stripped of his powerful post as athletic director, reached the mandatory retirement age of seventy and reluctantly had to step down. Committed to physical education, the new director of physical culture and athletics, T. Nelson Metcalf, imported from Oberlin by President Hutchins, showed only mild enthusiasm for big-time athletics. The presence of a close ally as athletic director allowed Huchins far more flexibility in the late 1930s than if Stagg had stayed on as athletic director or, for that matter, continued as coach at Chicago.[32]

In 1933, after retiring the "Old Man," Metcalf hired a young football coach, Clark Shaughnessy, who had a reputation as a brainy tactician, to replace the legendary Stagg. In fairness to Shaughnessy, he did his best with the thin material available at Hutchins's university and relied on either word of mouth or informal alumni contacts to recruit players. Remarkably, in the twilight of Chicago football the team was blessed with the greatest halfback in the school's history, Jay Berwanger, who came to Chicago because a neighbor in Dubuque, Iowa, an alumnus, made an informal sales pitch. Known as the "man in the iron mask" (his nose had been broken so many times that he had to wear a modern-style face mask), Berwanger led the Maroons to three respectable seasons from 1933 to 1935 and several remarkable victories. In 1934 Berwanger scored two touchdowns, leading his team to a 27-0 upset of Michigan. Though Chicago never did better than break even, its rugged halfback carried on his broad shoulders a mediocre team that might otherwise have declined far more rapidly. While Chicago won only four games in 1935, the last "Monster of the Midway" won the first Heisman Trophy.[33]

After Berwanger graduated, football at Chicago descended rapidly into the stygian depths. Unlike many of its Big Ten opponents, Chicago had no system of subsidies or job programs specifically for athletes. Over the next three years after Berwanger graduated, the Maroons recorded only one "Big Ten" victory (against Wisconsin in 1936). To rub their noses in the turf, Stagg, who now coached at the College of the Pacific in Stockton, California, returned to Stagg Field in 1938. After being showered with honors, including forty-one drumbeats for each of his years at Chicago, Stagg crushed the feeble Maroons, 32-0.

In the early 1900s students had enthusiastically supported football, and few critics dared to stick up their heads. As Robin Lester has observed, "football and fraternities were closely intertwined, and the combination accounted for much of campus social life; at the same time, many students were more politically active and some never attended the game." In the 1930s students such as William McNeill, editor of the *Daily Maroon,* and Edward Rosenheim, editor of the *Pulse,* dared to criticize football. The faculty, which had at times avidly followed Chicago football and in 1906 led a movement for reform of Big Nine football, chiefly displayed indifference. Only the alumni who remembered the glory years of football at Chicago strongly supported the team or cared enough to criticize the coaching. And, among the vast majority of pro-football students and alumni, the support for losing football would prove surprisingly brittle and short-lived.[34]

In 1939 the team suffered a near total collapse. Beginning with a defeat by unheralded Beloit, the Maroons were able to manage only two victories over small college teams, Wabash and Oberlin. In their other games the Maroons suffered crushing defeats, losing by 46-0 to Illinois and 47-0 to Virginia and by 61-0 to Harvard and Ohio State. In their fourth game, on October 21, Chicago suffered its most humiliating defeat, 85-0, to Michigan. Against big-time teams, some of them only mediocre, Shaughnessy's gridders showed neither offense nor defense. Horribly outmanned, the players sometimes looked as if they had stumbled into one of Chicago's legendary gang wars.[35]

By the end of disastrous 1939 season Hutchins and certain trustees believed that Chicago must abolish football, both to protect the battered and outmatched players as well as to safeguard the hallowed reputation of the school. Somewhat inconsistently, Hutchins, who opposed big-time football, could not bear to drop into the ranks of the second or third tier of competition, where the team might have competed successfully.[36]

Hutchins had already donned the mantle of a football foe when, in 1938, he published "Gate Receipts and Glory," an article that appeared in the *Saturday Evening Post.* Criticizing big-time football practices, Hutchins insisted that institutions should place academics above athletics. "Since the primary task of colleges and universities is the development of the mind," Hutchins declared, "young people who are more interested in their bodies than their minds, should not go to college." And, above all, he might have added, they should not consider the University of Chicago.[37]

When he applied these arguments to football at Chicago, Hutchins would point out that the institution faced no danger of losing students or potential donors. In fifteen years of mediocre and terrible football the level of giving had not suffered, and the lower enrollment could be chalked up to the demanding curriculum. If Chicago abolished football, Hutchins told the trustees, the university would "confirm the pioneering reputation of the university and in one stroke do more to make clear what a university should be than we could do in any way." In his campaign against football Hutchins would use "Gate Receipts and Glory" as well as the recent articles by Francis Wallace on the scandals at Pittsburgh and John Tunis's piece "What Price Football?"[38]

In December 1939 Hutchins became the best-known enemy of football since Charles Eliot. Unlike Charles Eliot, who often stood above the fray, Hutchins played an active part in caging the weakened gridiron tiger. In November and December he rolled up his sleeves and lobbied effectively to persuade members of the board. Hutchins realized that he had to mount a lightning assault because football-minded alumni, Chicago businessmen known as the "LaSalle Street Coaching Staff," were trying to launch an eleventh-hour campaign to attract local high school talent. A former president of the alumni club, John William Chapman, had sponsored a tour of the school for 125 high school seniors, who were treated to an evening of Chicago gridiron nostalgia at the annual football banquet. Hutchins had also to complete his campaign before alumni fund-raising went into high gear in mid-January.[39]

Hutchins succeeded in convincing an influential alumnus and fund-raiser, John Nuveen, that Chicago's football team posed a threat to the school's reputation. As a trustee who had closely followed the team's ups and downs, Nuveen lost his appetite for Chicago football in the fall of 1939. Prodded by Hutchins, he shed his allegiance to big-time football and to football at Chicago. Intercollegiate football at Chicago, he conceded, had to go. Once converted by Hutchins, Nuveen worked hard to convey his belief that no football would be better for Chicago than the disasters that had befallen the team in 1939. "Present situation of overwhelming defeats does affect alumni," Nuveen telegraphed an influential alumnus. "They [the board] feel we should either play better football or discontinue playing."[40]

Together Nuveen and Hutchins proved indefatigable in persuading the alumni, beginning with board chairman, Harold Swift, head of the meat-packing giant Swift & Company. Swift was not only a longtime supporter of Chicago football but also performed tasks such as recruiting, scheduling, pricing tickets, and conducting press relations. Perhaps because of his long and intimate association with Chicago football (he once had his company supply the team with beef on a road trip), Swift refused to lend his support to the abolitionist movement, but he stood aside and did nothing to oppose Hutchins's campaign, enabling Hutchins and Nuveen to proceed as if the board was unanimous when it really was not.[41]

On December 21, 1939, the board of trustees voted to eliminate football, but at the same time Hutchins and the board members decided to stay in the Big Ten. With reasonable strength in basketball and other sports in the late 1930s, university officials felt that their teams could still compete, a hope that proved unfounded. Once the largest school in the Big Ten, Chicago, with less than a thousand male undergraduates, resembled its smaller competitors like Beloit and Oberlin. In contrast, Indiana, which had low enrollments for a state school, enrolled three to four times as many undergraduates as Chicago, while Michigan, Minnesota, and Ohio State boasted male undergraduate populations of more than ten thousand. Even Northwestern, the only other private institution in the Big Ten, had at least five times as many males at the undergraduate level as Chicago and greater flexibility in its ability to admit and retain athletes than did Hutchins's university.[42]

Needing a scapegoat, armchair experts blamed the hapless coach, Clark Shaughnessy. "I'm tired of all this pussyfooting and statistics," one disgruntled alumnus wrote in December. "There is not a football man here but thinks the coaching at Chicago was bad—bad, lousy, rotten—and that Chicago could get enough men and get them on the level to have a good winning team if it had a new coach." Another alumnus who blamed Hutchins tried to condemn him as a football-hating curmudgeon by quoting the statement often attributed to Hutchins (but coined much earlier by Thorstein Veblen) that football bore the same relation to education that bullfighting did to agriculture.[43]

Football partisans who opposed Hutchins held a belated meeting in January. Some alumni believed that the freshman class contained the best football material since Berwanger, though it is highly unlikely that the team could have achieved a turnabout. When a straw vote was finally held, the *Chicago Tribune* reported that 246 members stood up in opposition to the board's decision, but a surprising 236 supported it.[44]

On January 12 Hutchins held a meeting to explain the decision to the students. Initially, students had opposed the decision to drop football. Once the board and Hutchins acted, surveys indicated that the balance had shifted. By a slim majority students favored the decision. The future historian William McNeill, editor of the *Daily Maroon,* lauded the school's action. "If this school's football has been dead for years," McNeill wrote, "we can only breathe a sigh of relief now that it has its burial."[45]

Other Chicago sportswriters and hard-core alumni who regarded football as essential to college life lashed out at the policies of the board and President Hutchins, berating Chicago for taking a cowardly and unnecessary course. One alumnus wrote that he would not send his son to Chicago but to Northwestern. "For the time I have felt an overstressing of academic life on campus," he lamented. "Red-blooded young men and women demand a well-balanced environment for study . . . Football has it[s] place in college athletics. In the eyes of the collegiate world Chicago has quit."[46]

Arch Ward, the well-known sports columnist for the *Chicago Tribune* and a stout defender of big-time college football, skewered Hutchins for his decision and questioned why Chicago had played the toughest teams in the conference. Did Chicago have a fetish with losing, or did the team simply insist on playing teams that the great Stagg had once conquered? Why did Hutchins, he asked, insist on quitting football altogether instead of playing an easier schedule?[47]

To say that Hutchins abolished football simply because Chicago's teams lost does him a disservice. Hutchins clearly felt that big-time football had no place in his plan for a high-powered undergraduate and graduate institution. Still, he made no effort to interfere with football from 1932 to 1938, leaving athletic policy to his director of athletics, T. Nelson Metcalf. More precisely, he displayed little interest in football until 1938, when the *Saturday Evening Post* published his article "Gate Receipts and Glory," a time when Chicago football had gone into free fall. That he emerged as a gridiron reformer only after the team stopped winning suggests that his strong stand in 1938 merely served as a preamble to the drama of abolishing football at Chicago. And, in some respects, the highly persuasive president manufactured dramatic and nostalgic elements to adorn his whirlwind crusade. The sacred memory of the supposedly incorruptible Amos Alonzo Stagg served as a handy piece of confection which could be used to distinguish the evils of highly subsidized, big-time football from the highly idealized, blurred portrait of the past. When the disastrous 1939 season unfolded, Hutchins had both his own reputation as a foe of football and the tradition of the Chicago gridiron to lend credibility to his assault against the already moribund football program.

Strictly speaking, Robert Hutchins hardly qualifies as a major reformer, since he abolished football only at Chicago and, unlike Henry MacCracken, showed no interest in spearheading a movement for broader athletic reform. After December 1939 he displayed more concern about the possible return of football at Chicago than about its insidious presence at other institutions. Yet the abolition of football at Chicago became, and remained, so widely known that purists perceived it as a major landmark on the highway of gridiron reform. Hutchins had pretty much said that, if his school could not play honest football, it should not play at all.

If he achieved any larger point, Hutchins vindicated the belief of reformers that college presidents, by acting decisively and forthrightly, could prevent the evils of subsidies and aggressive recruiting or even bring about major reform, a conviction that has underpinned the arguments of reformers from the early 1900s to the present. Unlike other presidents, however, Hutchins enjoyed great advantages because of the team's pitiful performance. While presidents have occasionally reformed athletics, they have rarely found themselves in a situation like Robert Hutchins in which the football gods so clearly favored change.

In December 1939, just after the board of trustees abolished football at Chicago, the NCAA adopted a tougher code at its convention in Chicago. This get-tough policy had grown out of challenges to amateur athletics since 1935 posed by the Southeastern Conference's scholarship policies, the Pittsburgh scandal, Hutchins's assault on college football at Chicago, and the school of journalists such as Francis Wallace and John Tunis who held gridiron practices up to public scrutiny. It is possible that the NCAA also sought to head off more wrenching changes like the abolition of football at Chicago by blunting the criticism of football's foes. A stricter policy might also have been seen as a means of preventing a costly bidding war between the colleges that gave traditional subsidies and the upstart southern institutions that offered full scholarships.[48]

Nevertheless, the resolutions to arm the NCAA with enforcement powers marked a sharp turn in the association's history. In 1906, when it framed its first bylaws, the ICAA had toyed with the possibility of becoming an enforcement body but hastily rejected this idea. In that age of laissez-faire politics the members would have balked at interference with their institutional autonomy. This policy of local autonomy held true for trade and professional organizations generally. Except for the American Medical Association, most national groups in the early 1900s provided ethical guidance and professional expertise. In the 1930s all of that changed when the federal government proposed a series of recovery and reform measures that greatly expanded the role of government. Almost by reflex, the professional groups such as the American Bar Association took steps to convert themselves into quasi-regulatory bodies. As a result of the "Black Sox" scandal in 1919, professional baseball already had its own commissioner, Judge Kenesaw Mountain Landis, who reigned as baseball's "czar." Other groups would attempt to avoid federal intervention by reprimanding and punishing their own members.[49]

The NCAA in 1939 expanded its bylaws to include a definition of *amateur sportsman* and demanded that its members follow specific rules. Scholarships should be based on need, and control of athletics had to go through the institutions. Athletes could not receive aid from athletic departments except for legitimate employment. And, finally, the most important change involved enforcement. The new bylaws authorized the NCAA to examine the practices of prospective members and, by a vote of two-thirds of the membership, expel offenders.[50]

In spite of its tough stand, the NCAA in 1939 was far from prepared to convert itself into a self-policing body. Its president, William Owen of Stanford, reported to the business meeting that he had found "little, if any, sentiment on the committee [for constitutional revision] in favor of a change which would seek to establish the Association as a governing body." The committee for constitutional revision had decided, Owen hinted, that the

NCAA would have to expel members who did not live up to the organization's standards, though the NCAA still hesitated to assert its authority to investigate and discipline offenders. "The major problems which confront us today call for aggressive, determined action," Owen declared. "Isolated action by individual institutions or conferences will not adequately meet the problems." Such a statement might have emanated from the office of a New Deal administrator only a few years earlier, in the depths of the Depression.[51]

After determining to root out athletic evils, the NCAA faced the sober truth that its modest revenues would not permit an enlarged role. In later decades, when television revenues filled its coffers, the NCAA's lavish resources enabled it to hire a team of skilled investigators, who kept the worst offenders on the run. In stark contrast to more recent eras, the barely solvent NCAA would have required a grant, presumably from the Carnegie Foundation, to set up a system to investigate and punish offenders. As the NCAA president L. K. Neidlinger jokingly put it, the NCAA had less money available than the Western Conference or Big Ten. In 1940 the principal source of income, a profit of $10,000, came from the NCAA basketball playoff. Other NCAA tournaments such as track and boxing ran deficits that had to be covered by institutions that ended up playing host. Since the NCAA had no executive director or permanent staff, its expenses were modest and its labor largely voluntary; clerical costs only ran $325, and its largest item, printing costs for its rules books, ran slightly less than $1,000. To cover these various costs, the NCAA's dues of $25 per institution returned only $5,945, a small cash flow even for the 1930s. And the cash on hand, a mere $10,346.61, virtually precluded the association from launching a major assault on cheating. For all its ambitious rhetoric the NCAA would have needed a generous grant from the Carnegie Foundation to enforce its bylaws, and this plan never came to fruition.[52]

As it turned out, the threat of war created still another obstacle. A year later, in December 1940, the Nazi conquest of western Europe had transformed public opinion; like most Americans, the NCAA delegates spent much of their time discussing their role in achieving military preparedness. Though the preparations for war created the most stir, the NCAA in 1940 took another step toward implementing its 1939 bylaws. It passed resolutions enabling the body to translate the bylaws adopted in the previous year into practical policy, a task for which the NCAA was admittedly unprepared. At the business meeting President Neidlinger not only asked for the authority to investigate violations of the amateur code but also called for the association to obtain a grant to enlarge its investigations and to implement its new rules.

Neidlinger downplayed the need to go after colleges that violated the code. Instead, he insisted that colleges would want to be investigated to put rumors of wrongdoing to rest. Suppose that a sportswriter reported that "our star fullback is being paid a hundred dollars a month," he asked. "I think it would be to our interest to ask the NCAA to investigate the circumstances of that athlete's connection to our institution." By establishing the facts, the NCAA investigation would "protect the institution from the damage which is now being done by wild and unfounded rumors and will enable the NCAA to interpret the code through its application to specific cases."[53]

Put simply, this far-fetched scenario was merely a clever argument to soft-pedal the need for tougher policies. The code of the "amateur sportsman" posed a difficult problem for those who believed in pure athletics. At many of the larger institutions football had outgrown its amateur roots, and the quest for "gate receipts and glory" had made liars out of coaches and college presidents. There were still many dedicated members of the NCAA, however, who took amateur athletics seriously and believed that the job of the organization was to protect their students and institutions from corrupt alumni, designing boosters, and win-at-all cost professional coaches. In 1940 much of the sentiment for the new code came from this rapidly dying breed.

Did the football players actually need the NCAA to protect their strictly amateur athletic status? Critics of the system such as sportswriter Paul Gallico were correct to call college football "one of the last strongholds of genuine old-fashioned hypocrisy . . . the leader (among sports) in the field of double-dealing, deception, sham, cant, humbug, and organized hypocrisy." The players at big-time institutions played under two sets of standards, one that enabled the teams to get football talent and the other sculpted for a public that insisted that the players came to their school first as students and only then as athletes. While it may have been true at smaller institutions, most big-time institutions managed to find means of support for needy athletes, enabling them to play football and eventually to obtain a degree. The institutions thereby involved many of their players in the hypocrisy that Gallico referred to, a double standard would persist in later years, when they became alumni or, for that matter, began their own coaching careers.[54]

Returning to strict amateurism, in all likelihood, would have made the double standard even worse, though few critics of illicit subsidies could see that danger. Fortunately for the NCAA, the changes in college life during World War II would postpone the showdown between the amateur traditions and the hard realities of big-time athletics. In the meantime it was business as usual. Because the NCAA was not able to implement its initiatives until after the war, the conferences and institutions still had wide latitude in how they interpreted and enforced their rules.

Viewed broadly, the NCAA's revolution of 1939 and 1940 represented a major change in policy which demanded precise standards and measures for the association to enforce its code and bylaws. At the grass roots the NCAA leadership had issued a warning to its members that they should obey the creed of amateur athletics on which the group was founded or leave the organization. Big-time football had already become so pervaded with dishonesty, however, that the new bylaws merely invited conflicts among the NCAA's member institutions and conferences.

Nevertheless, the change to measures for enforcement from mere hand-wringing would bring about a far different NCAA, and football would provide the key to this change. Only by taming football, the sport that produced gate receipts and glory, could the NCAA return to the ideal of the amateur sportsman. The NCAA's revolution of 1939 would test the determination of the member schools to reform the game that had made these revolutionary changes necessary.

CHAPTER ELEVEN

Saints and Sinners, 1941 to 1950

When the Japanese bombers attacked Pearl Harbor on December 7, 1941, the colleges had barely completed the football season, and the bowl games had yet to be played. On the West Coast the fear of Japanese invasion proved so intense that the Rose Bowl Committee hesitated to play the game in Pasadena. Since Duke was playing Oregon State, the Rose Bowl committee decided to play the game in Durham, North Carolina, where Oregon State won 20-16 before a crowd of fifty thousand on January 1, 1942.

The shift of the Rose Bowl symbolized the flexible state of college football during World War II. Because of shortages of cars, tires, fuel, and students, attendance at college sports events fell sharply during the war, but some schools still played only a slightly smaller version of prewar football. As in World War I, football still played its part in the campaign to win the war, and the military again embraced college football. While many colleges suspended football from 1942 and 1945, others fielded highly competitive teams staffed by military trainees. In an unpredictable turnabout, athletes who might have been condemned as professionals before the war now played football on Uncle Sam's "amateur" teams.

Women's role in football, though marginal, grew during World War II. At a few southern schools in the 1920s and 1930s female cheerleaders had caught on, but they had been largely confined to the South. As Mary Ellen Hanson has noted, Trinity of San Antonio had a pep squad in 1923 which included fifteen women, and soon afterward there were more women on the squad than men. In 1925, when Northwestern played Tulane, the team and sportswriters were astounded to see women leading cheers for Tulane. In the mid- to late 1930s major state institutions, notably Alabama and Tennessee, added coeds to the previously all-male squads of women cheerleaders. Though a few northern schools such as Nebraska had pep squads made up of women, few coed cheerleaders challenged the traditional male voices or gymnastic routines.

During World War II, with the absence of males on campus, the use of women to lead cheers spread to institutions outside the South. By the postwar era coed cheerleaders who engaged in choreographed routines had become a staple of big teams in various regions. It was still another sign that big-time college football really had evolved into highly orchestrated athletic entertainment; the show biz routines of Hollywood musicals could embrace a contest that had begun as two teams of college boys trying to force a ball across a goal. By the time that college football graduated to color television, big-time college football had matured into a highly entertaining marketable spectacle formed around the collision of male bodies but also an extravaganza in which women played a supporting, nonviolent role.[1]

War Subsidies to College Football Players

As in World War I, military planners utilized college football as both a training exercise and as a means of boosting morale. Military leaders believed that football built leadership qualities, inculcated discipline, sharpened aggressive instincts, and taught its officers to react quickly under pressure. In particular, the Navy stationed officer candidates on campuses where they played intramural and varsity competition. Former Navy coach Tom Hamilton helped to plan the Navy preflight training, or V-5, which emphasized body contact and thinking "offensively." Each unit of trainees engaged in scrimmages and intramurals, and the best players played against other colleges or against military bases that also had their varsity teams. The V-5 units produced well-known postwar coaches such as Ohio State's Woody Hayes and Oklahoma's Bud Wilkinson who also served aboard naval craft and stateside coaches Paul "Bear" Bryant and Jim Tatum, who worked with trainees. West Point's Colonel Earl "Red" Blaik, using Army's elite military trainees, fielded powerful teams from 1943 to 1946 which dominated college competition.[2]

Many of the Navy's preflight trainees joined the few remaining nonmilitary players at major training centers such as Iowa, North Carolina, Georgia, and St. Mary's, which enjoyed a form of subsidization unthinkable a few years before. Other navy and army trainees were farmed out to smaller, less known institutions. With the aid of naval trainees, the octogenarian Amos Alonzo Stagg of Pacific, who would be voted the nation's coach of year in 1943, fielded together one of the best teams on the West Coast. Playing perennial powerhouse Southern California before seventy thousand spectators for the Pacific Coast Conference championship, Stagg's gridders barely lost 6-0, frustrated by two touchdowns called back by the officials. Though these government-subsidized elevens looked like prewar gridiron powers, navy brass and football coaches could pass off their stars merely as military trainees who happened to be assigned to college campuses.[3]

During the war Congress passed the GI Bill of Rights, by which Uncle Sam agreed to pay veterans fifty dollars a month for school expenses. While students on the GI Bill could not receive other forms of aid, the law did not prohibit them from playing football. From 1945 to 1948 teams would have the best of both worlds by using both the GI Bill veterans and the college-age athletes who received job subsidies, loans, or alumni support. Two-platoon football, introduced by Coach Fritz Crisler of Michigan against Army in 1945 and rapidly adopted by big-time teams, would be facilitated by the government subsidies, which would enable teams to field squads for offense and defense.

At the 1943 NCAA convention George Rider of Miami University reported that the war had temporarily done much to clean up big-time athletics; the draft of young men into the military had reduced the prewar bidding for football talent. Reform-minded college presidents looking into their crystal balls saw potential for postwar reform. At the NCAA convention of 1946 held in St. Louis, President Arthur Compton of nearby Washington University praised the "Ivy League," a name that did not yet officially exist, for agreeing to eliminate the worst abuses.[4]

Compton referred to a recent meeting between presidents of the eight future Ivy League institutions who in November 1945 met together for the first time and drew up a voluntary code to scale down their big-time football practices. Though students, faculty, and athletic directors had called for an Ivy League since the 1930s, the presidents of Harvard, Yale, and Princeton had kept the other "Ivies" at arm's length. Following World War II, however, President James Conant of Harvard had agreed to extend the Big Three's policies to its five lesser rivals, though he refused to establish a de facto Ivy League. The eight presidents affixed their signatures to an agreement that called for an end to athletic subsidies, postseason games, and long absences for players on intersectional trips. They also agreed to tighter restrictions on eligibility; students could play only after their freshmen years and then only if they were undergraduates in good academic standing. More important, the presidents agreed to appoint committees that would meet periodically to draft new rules and clarify existing ones. The agreements of the Ivy presidents in 1945 did not establish a conference round-robin, nor did they, strictly speaking, bind the institutions. They did indicate that some of the eight institutions wanted to avoid big-time football practices without abandoning intercollegiate football.[5]

Soon after he returned from this historic conference, President James Conant of Harvard received a letter from Chancellor Arthur Compton of Washington University in St. Louis concerning football. Having once been a small college power, Washington, a private institution, was engaged in a reappraisal of its athletics. Compton, who agreed with the principles of the Ivy Group Agreement, hoped to organize a similar grouping in the Midwest to include schools "for whom football is an avocation rather than a vocation." To extend the eastern reforms to the Midwest, Compton proposed to Conant—and the other seven Ivy presidents as well—that Washington and other amateur-minded institutions become affiliated with the Ivy League. Such a relationship would require an exchange of delegates to ensure common policy. He even suggested contests, possibly one game each year between schools in the East and Midwest. In addition, he invited Ivy representatives to send observers to a meeting in St. Louis which he planned to hold immediately after the NCAA convention in January.[6]

Though Conant was acquainted with Compton, the Harvard president passed the letter to his athletic director, Bill Bingham, who then drafted a suspicious and slightly insulting reply, quite in keeping with the often supercilious attitude of the Big Three. The irascible Harvard athletic director declared that there was no true Ivy League and that each school could schedule whomsoever it pleased. Bingham appeared to believe, like other insular Ivy presidents, that Compton merely wanted to schedule contests with their prestigious institutions.[7]

Yet Bingham not only strongly favored the Ivy League concept but, as Harvard's fortunes declined, had also come to oppose big-time football. When he attended the annual NCAA meeting in St. Louis, Bingham ended up staying for an extra day to attend Compton's conference. As Bingham soon learned, President Compton had assembled delegates from a diverse group of largely private institutions—Washington, Western Reserve, Case, Cincinnati, Oberlin, Vanderbilt, and the state-supported Miami of Ohio— to explore the possibility of forming a new athletic conference. Surprisingly upbeat, the blustery Bingham did all he could to assist Compton in support of strictly amateur athletics, lending the prestige and credibility of his position as Harvard athletic director. One academic dean at Washington, W. G. Bowling, praised Bingham for his strong support. "At times during the meeting," Bowling observed, "the discussion seemed almost to indicate that this was a combined Harvard and Washington University proposal."[8]

In this diverse assemblage the presence of a delegate from Harvard merely emphasized the conflicting athletic approaches—and the absence of a consensus such as existed at the Ivy League meeting. The smaller and larger private colleges appeared to be headed in wholly different directions. While Harvard already belonged to a budding conference, schools such as Western Reserve of Cleveland and Cincinnati planned their own mid-level conference, which became the Mid-American Conference. Others, like Case Tech of Cleveland and Oberlin College, played largely small-college rivals in Ohio, Pennsylvania, Michigan, or Indiana, and Vanderbilt played a big-time schedule in the Southeastern Conference (SEC). Unlike the Ivy eight, most of these schools hardly fit into the neat mold of traditional rivals who had enough in common to play round-robin competitions. In the next decade some of these institutions would go in the direction that Compton advocated, but in 1946 they were not ready to give up their own rivalries or their postwar gridiron plans.

Still, the Ivy presidents might have benefited by working out an understanding with Compton. Looking back at athletics in the postwar era, what strikes the observer is the shortsighted attitude that kept the Ivies from seriously exploring an intersectional reform alliance. Instead of forming a conference, Washington withdrew from the Missouri Valley Conference and de-emphasized its athletics. Though Washington played occasional contests with teams like Western Reserve and Oberlin, Compton's vision never got off the ground.

To believe, as Compton may have, that smaller private colleges like Washington could influence big-time powers like Ohio State or Missouri would have been highly misleading, for big-time football was simply too entrenched. While the once competitive private schools had compelling financial or ideological reasons to alter their own athletics, most postwar reformers showed little interest in evangelizing the nearby state institutions, and the eastern Big Three merely wanted to escape the contagion of major college athletics. The idea of home rule by individual schools and conferences still held sway.

Increasingly, the football played by the big-time conferences generated far more money and headlines than smaller colleges like Carnegie or Centre. Big-time football had once again created both attendance records and sordid headlines. By 1946 and 1947 football attendance picked up where it had left off in the pre–World War II era and enjoyed another spurt of growth. Whereas the attendance for major teams in 1939 and 1940 hovered around 23,000, that figure leaped to 26,731 for 1946 and 27,690 in 1947. The total attendance for all football games stood at 11,715,370 in 1947, a 5 percent increase over 1946. In the Midwest crowds at major football games averaged 34,229 in 1947, and the Michigan Wolverines, who won their conference title, drew more than 76,000 spectators per game. The ticket takers could barely accommodate the crush of 104,953 fans who turned out for the Notre Dame–Southern California game at the Los Angeles Coliseum.[9]

At the NCAA convention in 1945 Dean A. W. Hobbs of North Carolina predicted fierce competition for talented veterans once football had returned to postwar normalcy. "Recruiting, subsidization, athletic scholarships, and the like are sure to be just as prevalent as ever, if not more so," he declared. "There are hundreds of good athletes in the armed forces who were not in the colleges before the war, but who will be sought after with great vigor when it is over." In 1946, just as Hobbs had warned, a series of news stories chronicled the cutthroat bidding for football talent and the payments to athletes which had violated the spirit of the prewar NCAA bylaws.[10]

In "Football's Black Market" Francis Wallace collected a number of these stories, such as a report that Illinois' African-American football star, Buddy Young, had received twenty-five offers while still in the Navy before deciding to return to Illinois, where he was rumored to be receiving an annual paycheck of twenty-five hundred to five thousand dollars. According to the coach at Oklahoma A&M (later Oklahoma State), Jim Lockabaugh, eight of the players for Tulsa's 1945 Orange Bowl team, had been lured to nearby Oklahoma. Being one of the few coaches to admit that his school subsidized its team, Lockabaugh reported that his players received fifteen dollars a month plus room and board but insisted that his "subsistence payments" were no different than the payments made in the Southwest and Southeastern Conferences. He charged that the Big Ten teams used the same system of subsidies paid by alumni to keep the coaches from soiling their reputations. Lockabaugh darkly alluded to larger incentives such as cars and mortgage payments furnished by rogue institutions: "Some of the players who will oppose us this fall will be drawing as high as $10,000 a year." Since that figure would have been the 1990s equivalent of well over $100,000 per year, Lockabaugh may have inflated his figures in order to lessen the impact of his team's much more modest payments.[11]

At American University in Washington, DC, where the president and board faced alumni pressure to resume football, President Paul Douglas called football players "slaves" caught up in the biggest black market operation ever related to educational institutions." Douglas observed that the players had enslaved themselves to football because the GI Bill had raised their pay to unprecedented levels. In addition to their government benefits, Douglas charged, the players received money for all their needs plus additional sums ranging up to two hundred dollars a month, enabling them to live at a level far beyond the lifestyle of most recent college graduates.[12]

The scramble for gate receipts and glory also embraced the most prestigious and powerful football school of the World War II era, the United States Military Academy at West Point, which had so aggressively pursued football talent during the war. In an unseemly controversy with Mississippi State, Thomas "Shorty" McWilliams (who actually stood over six feet) tried to transfer to West Point from Mississippi State, where he had won third-team All-America honors as a freshman in 1944 (because of manpower shortages, the NCAA during the war had suspended the rule against freshman participating on varsity teams). After competing a year for Army, the talented back, who played behind the nation's best backfield duo, Doc Blanchard and Glenn Davis, announced in the summer of 1946 that he was returning to his old institution. When West Point pointed out that he had to serve out his military obligation, his former coach at Mississippi State, Ayleen McKeen, charged that Army would not allow him to quit because he was a football player. In "Football's Black Market" Francis Wallace reported that McWilliams had received an offer of fifteen thousand dollars in cash, plus a car, three hundred dollars a month in cash, and a job offer for the same amount, all of it from a free-spending football Mississippi State alumnus.[13]

During the war the U.S. Military Academy had engaged in a recruiting racket that enabled its students who signed a contract with the military to become exempt from the draft. If a player went to West Point, he could play for four years, and, if he attended classes, he could graduate with a commission. By the time he graduated the war might well have ended, and he could serve out his time as a commissioned officer. While this scenario made sense in wartime, it lost some of its luster after VJ Day in August 1945. Nevertheless, the commandant of West Point, General Maxwell Taylor, reacted vehemently to Williams's case. Taylor, the future chief of staff and ambassador to South Vietnam, denied that the Army had refused to let McWilliams resign simply because he played football. Taylor reviewed examples of players who had flunked out because of academic deficiencies and had to serve out their military obligation as enlisted soldiers. He pointed out that West Point enabled its students to complete their courses in three years rather than four, thereby losing their services of many talented athletes, though he did not cite any examples. Then, going on the attack, he charged that McWilliams had "received a particularly lucrative financial offer from a certain quarter." Without mentioning the "quarter," he left no doubt that it was Mississippi State, a member of the Southeastern Conference.[14]

The commissioner of the Southeastern Conference reacted as if bigtime athletes were as spotless as lambs; athletes at SEC schools, he contended, could only profit by getting a chance to obtain an education. More realistically, the commissioner fired back at Taylor by calling it a case of "the pot calling the kettle black," an allusion to West Point's wartime practice of raiding colleges for football talent. Even coaches in the East, Midwest, and Southwest felt compelled to reply, and Coach Lynn "Pappy" Waldorf of Northwestern contemptuously dismissed the charges as "not worth comment." Only the venerable Coach Jess Neely of Tennessee, another SEC institution, upheld Taylor's charges. "We haven't had any trouble along that line," he commented, "and we haven't hung any money bags in front of the players— but from some of the stories I've heard the general might be right."[15]

In September the War Department decided to wash its hands of McWilliams and allowed him to return to Mississippi State. After being flown back to Jackson by a wealthy businessman, the athlete announced that he would not take the booster's offer but would settle for a simple football scholarship. In the three years that followed Shorty won All-SEC honors, and after graduation he played for the Los Angeles Dons and the Pittsburgh Steelers. When the Korean War broke out in 1950, he was activated with his air national guard unit and served for the duration of the war.[16]

In 1945 players like McWilliams struck the military authorities as turncoats and draft evaders. As more and more players resigned from West Point and Annapolis, President Harry Truman ordered draft officials to induct the renegade players, presumably because they no longer were eligible for the draft and preferred to opt out of a military career. When Truman's military aide, General Harry Vaughan, criticized the players as draft dodgers, he found himself confronted by an irate Illinois congressman, Edward Kelly, whose football-playing son had quit Navy to enroll at Notre Dame; the son had enlisted in the navy at seventeen and served twenty-two months as an enlisted man. General Harry Vaughan's apology only served to demonstrate the complexity of the transition from wartime to peacetime gridiron relations, which proved to be anything but peaceful.[17]

The NCAA found itself obliged to respond to this difficult postwar transition. Just before Pearl Harbor the organization's leaders had mailed out a letter to its members asking if the NCAA should become a legislative body. The association had already taken several steps in that direction by amending its bylaws so that it could expel members who failed to honor the definition of amateur athletics. The results of the poll were: yes, forty-four; no, thirty-nine; doubtful, twenty-four. Since the vote came on the brink of war, the NCAA had a reason to hold off on enforcing its new code. The survey had shown that major differences in opinion and practice warranted further study by the NCAA Executive Council in order to draw up a code that would satisfy its diverse constituency.[18]

More precisely, the vote sent a mixed message signifying that a "majority" wanted to duck the responsibility of enforcing the new standards or might themselves be part of the problem. Presidents of the Southern Conference, for example, wanted to wait until they held their annual meeting. "Most of the reservations," former president Neidlinger reported, "were due to the fact that in various conferences there are some regulations which are rather more liberal than was suggested by the N.C.A.A. code." Though most college presidents declared their policies in line with the code, the tentative response of southerners raised a red flag. As a result, the NCAA leadership decided to move more cautiously. The results of the vote indicated that a significant number persisted in their belief in "home rule," another way of describing the institutional autonomy that had been traditionally withheld from the NCAA.[19]

In 1946 the violations of the amateur code had become more difficult to define because the war had introduced so many exceptions. The battle-toughened veterans who played football in the postwar era made the "amateur sportsman" into a relic of college sports history. Aside from support from alumni and boosters, the confusing array of subsidies in the postwar era provided a strong argument for an across-the-board NCAA code. While some players received benefits from the GI Bill, nonveterans received various subsidies and jobs. The Southeastern Conference awarded athletic scholarships simply on the basis of athletic ability. Some smaller institutions such as Western Reserve University in Cleveland provided loans and jobs for football players. The University of Virginia had developed a system of alumni scholarships that were channeled through the institution. In stark contrast to southern schools that gave full rides, the Big Ten still favored work-related assistance for needy athletes, who held jobs on campus or worked for alumni and boosters during summers and part-time during the school year. On top of the "legitimate" above-board jobs, loans, and tuition subsidies, a stream of largely unseen and unreported aid flowed into the pockets of prized recruits at big-name schools in every section of the country. Given the sensational stories such as Shorty McWilliams's defection from West Point, the members of the NCAA had compelling reasons to design a specific code that could be enforced by the threat of expulsion from the association.

Football's New Deal: The Sanity Code, 1946 to 1949

In July 1946 the NCAA and the regional athletic conferences, led by Kenneth "Tug" Wilson, the NCAA treasurer and Big Ten commissioner, sponsored a meeting in Chicago to draw up a new code and to plan a strategy for winning its approval. After framing a series of resolutions on subsidies and recruiting, they decided to send questionnaires to four hundred institutions to get their institutions' opinion and to use the results to modify their resolutions. The influential big midwestern and West Coast schools wanted to return to a system of need-based subsidies, which could be supplemented by aid that flowed from unseen sources. Above all, the NCAA resolutions had a particular appeal in 1946 because they would simplify the rules on subsidies and would permit a small amount of purely athletic assistance. Small schools could interpret the code as a return to largely amateur athletics, and large state schools might well have seen it as a green light for athletic subsidies.[20]

Expecting an expanded role, the association in 1946 finally increased its dues, quadrupling them to $100 for big-time institutions and doubling or tripling them for smaller schools. Adding the dues increase to the NCAA's basketball tournament and sale of rules books, the NCAA's cash on hand increased to $52,335.06 and showed every sign of continuing to grow. The leaders of the movement for new bylaws did not allude to seeking a grant in order to enforce the association's decrees, as they had contemplated doing in 1940.[21]

The new bylaws largely reflected the same prewar emphasis on academics and amateur athletics. Placed before the members in January 1947 and enacted into law a year later, it allowed athletes (1) to receive no more than the cost of tuition and incidental fees plus a single meal per day in the season during which they competed; (2) to be awarded aid only on the basis of need; (3) to be given assistance only through the institution itself rather than directly from alumni or booster groups; and (4) to be paid for jobs "commensurate with the services rendered." If the recipient stood in the top 25 percent of his high school class and maintained a B average, however, he could receive additional athletic aid. Of course, brainy students who were also athletes could be awarded academic scholarships, but they were not allowed to feed at both troughs.[22]

Given the unsavory postwar pursuit of athletes, the NCAA officials felt compelled to tackle the knotty problem of recruiting. Reports from the high schools portrayed legions of coaches and alumni invading the campuses and home turf of the youthful athletes. These collegiate nuisances made frequent visits to high schools to talk to principals about the athletes or to talk to athletes themselves. While the less promising athletes might have few visits, if any, the most sought-after players received visits from as many as seventy-five colleges. Some of the visits by college coaches came during school hours, and occasionally the college recruiter persuaded the athlete to quit high school so that he could work out with the college team in spring practice. Many principals objected to the pressure that alumni placed on high school students, some of them near the bottom of their class, to attend their alma maters. Describing one experience, a principal wrote that "the alumni would sit at his [the high school athlete's] house late at night in an attempt to persuade him. Finally he told them he would attend their university just to get them to leave his house." A few months after entering college, the student quit school to join the army.

In 1947 the NCAA passed recruiting regulations that would have prevented the coaches or athletic personnel from making contact off campus. This section created much opposition from southern institutions. "I think that this is a policy that has originated out on the Pacific Coast," William Alexander of Georgia Tech declared, "and has been adopted by the Big Nine [Chicago had withdrawn from the Big Ten], and I don't believe anybody else in the country gives a hoot about it." As a result of such complaints, the council liberalized the rules on recruiting in 1948. In spite of the complaints about recruiting practices, the code simply decreed that no athletic official on or off the campus could offer aid to induce players to attend the institutions, even though he would be allowed to visit recruits off campus. The NCAA did not try to resolve the larger problem of alumni recruiting, which was left to the conferences and institutions.[23]

Though the new "Purity" Code left it unsaid, the bottom line would turn out to be article 4, section 6, adopted in 1939, which allowed the members to expel an institution that failed to maintain scholastic and athletic standards required of the members. This "get-tough" provision had lain dormant for seven years largely because of the war and uncertainty about how and where to apply it. It is also likely that the members of the NCAA hesitated to invoke the measure because it flew in the face of the traditional policy of institutional autonomy. Not that the accused would be summarily drummed out of the organization. In a worst-case scenario, when the NCAA found that an institution was not complying, the leadership had to give four months notice before it could bring an offender to the bar, and the members would then vote whether to expel the member at the annual meeting in early January.

Known first as the Purity and, later, the Sanity Code, the new academically oriented bylaws sailed through the 1948 convention without opposition. Given the fact that many schools were not in compliance, its acceptance remains something of a mystery. To understand why the majority blithely endorsed the new code, one must first keep in mind the angst felt by academic authorities at many schools in 1935 when the Southeastern Conference began to give outright athletic scholarships; add to this the postwar scramble for athletic talent, and one senses an uneasiness with the changing athletic mores. The majority of big-time institutions that believed in the NCAA's postwar definition of *amateurism* without living up to its standards may have believed that they could live within its framework. The most cynical and corrupt among them may have doubted that the clubby NCAA membership would pursue its threat to terminate membership. Without a permanent staff to investigate offenders, the NCAA leaders would have difficulty building a case against a group of schools that failed to comply. In the South, where many schools were not in compliance, the presidents probably decided to wait until they could see the direction in which the northern leadership was proceeding and then decide if they wanted to remain in the association. For the time being, no institution or conference wanted to cast a vote that would brand itself or its members as athletic wrongdoers.

Viewed from a lengthier perspective, the true believers who proposed and defended the largely amateur Sanity Code acted as if the beleaguered amateur code loomed as the rubicon of college sports. If they abandoned this time-honored set of principles, they might have no standards to fall back on. Some of the older presidents and athletic personnel undoubtedly had skeletons in their closets, but they hewed to the concept of amateur college athletics as a necessary part of higher education. While they opposed placing athletes in a separate category, they believed that the traditional jobs system of aid to athletes would allow needy players to supplement the meager aid sanctioned by the Sanity Code.

As it turned out, the new rules represented a largely unrecognized change in the NCAA's attitude toward subsidized athletics. Heretofore, the NCAA had not permitted any form of subsidies for football players or other athletes. In contrast, the Sanity Code permitted the schools to pay for an athlete's tuition, incidental fees, and a meal per day in season. For the first time the NCAA treated athletes as a separate group, and, by so doing, it created the precedent for larger subsidies, eventually culminating in the "free ride." In short, the code was a critical step toward officially subsidized athletics.

In terms of money in their pockets, the Sanity Code promised little to the players who already received various forms of subsidies. They would find it difficult to pursue their studies if they had both to work and play football. The problem of converting outright pay to jobs had caused the football strikes at Pittsburgh when subsidies were phased out. But the issue was neither acknowledged by athletic officials or by college presidents in 1947 and 1948. As a result, the NCAA created an impossible situation at many big-time football schools, where the officials would be almost obliged to cheat or to defy the code openly.

Nevertheless, the NCAA thought it had a way of disciplining offenders by expelling those institutions not in compliance by a two-thirds vote. In 1948 a compliance committee was established, but it was hamstrung by the lack of an executive staff. Rather than hiring an investigative staff, it had to depend on questionnaires sent out to member institutions. In order to indict the institution, the NCAA would have to secure a voluntary admission of guilt or to use other institutions as informers. At the annual NCAA meeting in January 1949 the incoming president, Karl Lieb of Iowa, announced that the association was making good on its commitment to root out wrongdoing. Perhaps to strike fear into the sizable number of schools that were not in compliance, he issued a warning at the convention: "We have sent private detectives into the field to investigate institutions not complying." Being aware that most schools had simply received questionnaires, he warned that the NCAA was prepared to put "teeth in the code." Violators, he declared, would be expelled.[24]

Within a year the Sanity Code seemed to have transformed the NCAA into a super-conference that had at last set a single standard to which all members would adhere. Actually, tremors of opposition rumbled just beneath the surface. At the annual NCAA meeting in January 1949 the head of the American Football Coaches Association, Harvey Harman of Rutgers, ostensibly speaking for the coaches who had elected him, depicted the code as a noble but unworkable experiment like the failed prohibition amendment in the 1920s. He did not object to the goals of the code, Harman insisted, only to the methods and administration, or, in other words, to the threat of expulsion to keep the colleges in line.

More to the point, his statements suggested that he not only disliked the methods but also the code itself. Harman berated the faculty, who still made up a large number of the NCAA delegations and, along with the college presidents, had helped to shape the Sanity Code. "Coaches have never been able to understand," he declared, "why regulatory bodies sometimes composed of members who have never known the blood and sweat of a football field—or any kind of competition—should be established for the good of the game." Harman argued that coaches should never try to set rules for teaching Romance languages or investigate glee clubs for "making sour melodies." If football did not interfere with specific courses, the academic faculty should steer clear of athletics.[25]

And the football coaches were not the only malcontents. Institutions in the Southern, Southeastern, and Southwest Conferences chafed at the restrictive, job-oriented, need-based Sanity Code. Simply put, the three conferences would now face the unenviable task of reshaping their existing athletic scholarships to fit the criteria of the NCAA regulations. In addition, in poorer states like Alabama and Mississippi, abundant jobs did not exist on or off the campus. The beneficiaries of the Sanity Code were well-established football programs in the East, Midwest, and West Coast, not to mention the smaller institutions that could not afford the cost of subsidized football.

Therefore, it is hardly surprising that athletic and college authorities in the South resented the Sanity Code as another attempt at control by the big-time schools in the East and Midwest. That control would hobble southern efforts in recruiting and supporting players. Need-based scholarship worked best in the Northeast and in the Midwest, where affluent alumni could help out the players with jobs or money. Ultimately, the top teams would harvest the largest gate receipts, garner the most publicity, and attract blue-chip recruits. In the 1940s big-time football had a huge following in the Midwest, and in 1946 the Big Ten had signed a contract with the Rose Bowl to supply the eastern team that would play in that most prestigious of bowls. In the 1920s and 1930s a number of southern teams, beginning with Alabama in 1926, had played in Pasadena on New Year's Day. In 1940 Tennessee had earned $130,000 playing Southern California in the Rose Bowl, a sum that it could never have duplicated in one of the numerous southern bowl games. The fact that the president of the NCAA and the permanent secretary-treasurer were both from the Big Ten and that the NCAA itself was based in Chicago further fueled authorities' resentment.[26]

In May 1949 representatives of the Southern, Southeastern, and Southwest Conferences met in Atlanta to discuss changes in the Sanity Code and proposed changes in the nature and extent of aid. Whereas the Sanity Code was academically oriented, the changes proposed by the southern schools would have tilted it to the athletic side. The delegates wanted to expand the code to embrace: (1) a training table during season and practice periods; (2) extra assistance to athletes who met the individual institution's scholarship criteria, not merely those with a B average; (3) help with living and school expenses such as room, board, and books as well as for laundry, cleaning, and pressing. The conference also discussed the problem of southern schools that had not yet set up methods for compliance and would be declared in violation of the Sanity Code, which led to a debate on whether the three conferences should withdraw from the NCAA and go it alone. While no consensus was reached, it appeared that the South might once again secede if the NCAA did not change its code—and a few months later the first state did.[27]

The Sinful Seven Challenge the Sanity Code, 1949 to 1950

In July 1949 the University of Virginia announced that it could not comply with the Sanity Code, thereby inviting the NCAA to expel it at the annual meeting in January. Its president, Colgate Darden, argued that "there is no way whereby a student at Virginia can play football, earn enough by working and at the same time keep up his studies." Initially, Virginia was one of twenty-eight schools not in compliance with the NCAA regulations; that number had dropped to seven by September 1949, as the others certified that they had met the NCAA's requirements. Besides Virginia, those schools that stood outside the association's bylaws included the University of Maryland, Virginia Polytechnic Institute (VPI), Virginia Military Institute (VMI), and the Citadel as well as Villanova and Boston College. Of these schools VMI, VPI, the Citadel, and Maryland competed among the many teams that still remained in the Southern Conference. Of the "Seven Sinners," or "Sinful Seven," only Maryland had a powerful football team fueled by more than eighty football scholarships. The rest played mediocre to poor football, with Boston College, the Citadel, VMI, and VPI fielding losing teams in 1949; besides Maryland, only Virginia and Villanova would have winning records. Not surprisingly, Maryland and its president, H. C. "Curley" Byrd, managed the campaign against the Sanity Code, though Virginia's Colgate Darden became identified with the opposition because of his apparent candor.[28]

To be sure, some of the recalcitrants had compelling reasons not to comply. VMI and the Citadel were military colleges whose afternoon drill and other training exercises meant that its players did not have time to work at jobs; VPI also had a large cadet training corps, which for many students made it a military school. Boston College and Villanova apparently did not comply soon enough to meet the NCAA's deadline of September 1, 1949, but Boston College would be virtually in compliance by the time of the convention in January 1950. Only Maryland had a large-scale scholarship program, but that too would have been difficult to convert into jobs. Though Virginia could have created campus-based jobs for its players, Darden had made it clear in July that he preferred to withdraw from the NCAA rather than force the students to give up their study time.

Virginia's announcement caught the athletic world by surprise, particularly because, as the *Washington Star* put it, "Virginia is not one of the football factories in the South." It was a bit like a teetotaler announcing that he was about to open a liquor store, or at least that was the public image of Virginia's refusal to comply. Twenty years earlier the Carnegie Report had singled out Virginia as one of the few schools that pursued strictly amateur policies. "I admire Virginia's stand," observed the athletic director at Georgetown in the summer of 1949. "They've got the guts enough to say that can't live up to it, and, consequently, want no part of the code." The author might have added that the university's founder, Thomas Jefferson, once wrote that a little rebellion now and then was a good thing.[29]

While Virginia had a history of rebellion, it usually had a strong, underlying motive, and its stand against the Sanity Code proved to be no exception. Since its withdrawal from the Southern Conference in 1936, Virginia had maintained its status as an independent by playing a mix of state schools such as VMI and VPI, Richmond, and Washington and Lee; an Ivy institution like Harvard, Penn, or Princeton; and a major institution in an adjacent state such as West Virginia or North Carolina. Except for the Ivy schools, most of its state and regional competitors still belonged to the Southern Conference.

In 1936, when Virginia left the Southern Conference in reaction to the Graham Plan, it moved to introduce quasi-athletic scholarships funded by the alumni. Based on moral as well as physical and academic criteria, the scholarships helped to revive its moribund football team. A year after they were introduced, the scholarships were merged into an alumni fund to be administered by an employee of the athletic fund instead of by alumni chapters. This jack of all gridiron trades would also be assigned to raise money and scout the secondary schools for football talent. As a result, Virginia's football improved, and in 1942 the school produced its first All-America running back, Bill Dudley.[30]

By the late 1940s Virginia had made the transition from largely amateur football to a major football program with a system of scholarships set aside chiefly for the support of needy football players. One indication of Virginia's change to big-time athletics came in the form a plaintive letter from Kemp Yancey, who had played in the same backfield as the ill-fated Archer Christian in 1909. "Let's get rid of all professional taint in our athletics," wrote the former fullback to President Darden, "and offer equal opportunities to compete to the entire student body." But it was too late. At the time it challenged the NCAA, Virginia was giving between thirty and forty scholarships to football players, some of them on the freshman team, subsidies that amounted to about twenty-six thousand dollars; it also had a staff of four full-time varsity and two freshman football coaches. The head coach, Art Gueppe, received a salary of eight thousand dollars, which matched the highest figure that a full professor could earn.[31]

In 1947 and 1948 Virginia compiled winning records largely against instate rivals plus George Washington and North Carolina State. Except for Harvard, which it routed 47-0 in 1947, the team failed to win victories

against strong, out-of-state rivals like Penn, Princeton, Tulane, and North
Carolina. Virginia's football did not generate the revenues of northern teams
because its stadium held slightly more than thirty thousand, and the revenues had to carry the expenditures of the athletic department. If gate receipts and glory were the measure of a truly big-time football team, Virginia
had precious little of either when it became one of the seven sinners in the
summer of 1949.

In 1949 Virginia surprised its strongest supporters by pulling off its most
celebrated upset since its defeat of Yale in 1915 when it humbled a highly
regarded Penn team at Franklin Field by a score of 26-14. Ironically, the Cav-
aliers had never defeated Penn in fourteen attempts dating back to the 1890s
and had lost 40-0 to the Quakers the year before. In an article on the upset
in the *Saturday Evening Post* Virginia's coach, Art Gueppe, made a point of
emphasizing that his team had won without resorting to subterfuges. Only
twenty-four players at the time of the game, Gueppe declared, got any form
of aid; only a mere handful got a full ride, and the team captain received
no aid at all. Gueppe may have slightly exaggerated, however, when he attributed Virginia's upset solely to careful preparation against a single-wing
team in an era when most teams had gone to the T-formation.[32]

To be precise, Virginia had graduated to subsidized football but at a level
that did not come close to the most successful of the Seven Sinners, the University of Maryland. Whereas Colgate Darden had no personal interest in
football, the president of Maryland, H. C. "Curley" Byrd, was a former
Maryland football coach. Lacking an institution with the mystique of Jefferson's Virginia or the longevity of nearby Georgetown, Maryland's President Byrd personally transformed Maryland from a sleepy agricultural
school to a state university that could boast of its buildings, enrollment, and
football. While Curley Byrd preferred to negotiate rather than to defy, he
had more at stake than Virginia. If Maryland were expelled, the school
would find recruiting more difficult, and, given its more than eighty scholarships, it might become known for its football and nothing else. In athletic
terms Byrd needed to defeat the Sanity Code because it threatened Maryland's revenues, its ability to recruit, and the institutions's reputation. As a
result, Byrd played an active role in forming a coalition against the code.[33]

Byrd's efforts continued in the fall of 1949 and in the days before the
meeting of the NCAA's full membership. In September he drafted a letter
to Clarence Houston, president of the NCAA, in which he charged that the
northern schools were engaging in strictly illegal recruiting practices.
"Frankly, we would rather withdraw from the National Collegiate Athletic
Association," he declared, "than to engage in the kind of hypocrisy [*sic*]
which I know that some of these universities are employing." He proposed
amendments to the NCAA which would transform the Sanity Code into the
system favored by the southern institutions when they met in Atlanta. He

corresponded with southern college presidents about the Sanity Code and planned a meeting with athletic directors from the Southern, Southeastern, and Southwest Conferences before the convention formally convened.[34]

The annual convention of the NCAA, which reflected a clash of values and of institutions, began quietly enough on January 10, 1950. "Delegates exchanged pleasantries and gossip in the lobby and the corridors," reported the *New York Times,* "and then disappeared from sight to clinics, executive and registration sessions, luncheons, dinners, and symposia." But underneath the normal rhythms of an academic convention the NCAA's grand inquisitors were preparing for the vote by the full membership on whether to expel the Sinful Seven. The Citadel announced that it would resign from the NCAA no matter what happened on the floor of the convention. In the meantime the Compliance Committee interviewed the offenders. Colgate Darden reported that his interview lasted about one minute. When asked whether Virginia would or would not comply, Darden replied: "I told them, of course, that we were not complying."[35]

On Saturday, January 12, at its business meeting, the council of the NCAA recommended expulsion of the Sinful Seven. A motion to vote individually on the schools failed, and three hours of discussion ensued. The indefatigable and enterprising Curley Byrd, who had lobbied aggressively before and during the convention to line up votes, acted as floor manager for the defense of the Seven Sinners. "Does Ohio State want to vote for expulsion of Virginia," Byrd asked, "when Ohio State has facilities to take care of four or five as many athletes as Virginia?" Byrd continued to jab at the Big Ten colossus. "Ohio State has some rather unusual jobs," he remarked, trying to disparage the practice of the numerous OSU athletes working for the state. In contrast, a spokesman from the Pacific Coast Conference asked the delegates, "Are we going to stand or retreat and if we retreat when will we come back?"[36]

The Executive Committee needed 136 votes to carry the motion to expel. When the votes were tallied, 111 delegates had supported expulsion, and 93 had opposed it. Apparently confused, NCAA president Karl Lieb announced that the motion had carried. Some delegates called out, "No, no, two-thirds is necessary." Flustered, Lieb paused and then smiled. "You're right," he admitted, as if caught in a sleight of hand. "The motion was not carried." The Sanity Code had been desanitized.[37]

Who had voted against expulsion? As former NCAA executive director Walter Byers, a witness to the vote, has pointed out, many of the schools were located in the South but by no means all of them. Eastern schools in competition with the Ivy League institutions, Byers believes, may have helped to defeat the resolution. On his way home Byers recalled that Hugh Willett of Southern California, the NCAA's incoming president, commented that "it wasn't just the southern schools that did it to us, look at the northern votes." While there is no evidence that Virginia had colluded with the schools in the three southern conferences, it effectively acted as a stalking horse for those institutions that wanted to topple the Sanity Code.[38]

After the Seven avoided the NCAA's retribution, other colleges waiting in the wings for the outcome, such as Richmond and Florida State, announced open subsidization, or, in the new terminology, grants-in-aid. The bulwarks of code support, the Big Ten and the Pacific Coast Conference, did not abandon their get-tough policy, but clearly the code was doomed. In September two more southern schools, North Carolina and North Carolina State, announced that they would no longer comply, timing their announcement so that the NCAA could not take action against them for sixteen months.

In January 1951, after a year in which the NCAA continued to threaten Virginia and other gridiron recusants with expulsion, a coalition of eastern, southern, and border state schools abandoned the limits on subsidies by a two-thirds vote, thereby draining the marrow of the Sanity Code. Potential sanctions still hanging over the offenders, like the perpetual sword of Damocles, were dropped. The southern schools had not only won their struggle, but their growing support from institutions in other regions of the country also appeared to cripple the NCAA's role as an arbiter of athletic conduct.[39]

The defeat of the Sanity Code returned the problem of subsidies to the schools and conferences, marking an end to strictly amateur athletics and a beginning of sanctioned grants-in-aid by schools in every part of the country. This first major upheaval in college football and athletics since the early 1900s would force the leaders of the NCAA to search for policies that would satisfy a wide and divided membership. It served as a red flag that said, "Proceed with caution." Some of the large minority of fellow sinners that had voted with the Sinful Seven had compelling reasons to keep the NCAA at arm's length.

CHAPTER TWELVE

Crisis and Reform, 1951 to 1952

In the same year that Virginia was wrestling with the problems of the Sanity Code, another Old Dominion institution was starting a tortured journey of its own which would cast a shadow over its long and distinguished reputation. Though the College of William and Mary would not be the only offender, the scandal at the nation's second oldest institution would prove instrumental in prompting college faculty, presidents, and educational agencies to embark on a national campaign to cleanse college athletics.

The events of 1951, which included a basketball point-shaving scandal involving thirty-three players and forty-nine fixed games, a cheating scandal at West Point, and the William and Mary scandal, would lead to the "big bang" in college athletics, shocking revelations that resounded more loudly than any athletic controversy since the early 1900s. These episodes would result in a major debate on the reform of college athletics, highlighted by attempts to de-emphasize football and to reinvoke the mantra of amateur athletics. The alarm caused by the William and Mary scandal had an impact that far outweighed the size and scope of the school, largely because it occurred at a moment when faculty, college presidents, and academic organizations regarded big-time college athletics as spiraling out of control.

On August 13, 1951, the *Norfolk Virginian-Pilot* announced that the two major athletic officials, including the athletic director and football coach, had left their posts. The college would only acknowledge that transcripts of high school students might have been altered. Yet the abrupt resignations of Rube McCray, the athletic director and football coach, and Barney Wilson, the basketball coach, suggested that serious problems existed in the athletic department. Immediately, the board planned to call a meeting, and the governor of Virginia, William Battle, expressed confidence that the board members would get to the bottom of what he blamed on "the craze for victory which is well-nigh nationwide." Undoubtedly, Governor Battle had in mind the point-shaving basketball scandals that had come to light earlier in the year and were still under investigation and the cheating scandal at West Point, where an honor code like William and Mary's had been violated by members of the football team.[1]

A Small School and a Big-Time Scandal

As a coeducational school with less than fifteen hundred students, William and Mary had fielded strong football teams since the early 1940s which often defeated Southern Conference institutions such as Duke, North Carolina State, and Wake Forest. From 1940 until 1950 its teams wracked up forty-four consecutive victories against in-state competitors, an achievement in keeping with the board's injunction "to win more games than they lost" against state teams. From 1949 to 1951 the team's schedule included a more formidable group of opponents such as Michigan State and Oklahoma, two of the most powerful teams in the country.

In order to play a major football schedule, the small college needed to recruit big-time players, and to do this the athletic officials engaged in their own admissions scam. Their athletic system began to unravel in the spring of 1949 during the academic counseling that the faculty conducted with its students. The trail of wrongdoing had first appeared when the acting director of admissions, J. Wilfred "Cy" Lambert, learned that a faculty member had discovered a discrepancy in the grade report of a football player. The athlete, who had entered William and Mary with credits in Spanish, insisted that he had never taken language courses in high school. After checking the crude typeovers on the student's transcript, Lambert had traced the typewriter to a Smith Corona with a dirty *e* located in the basement of the gymnasium. Following these revelations, the president of William and Mary, the scholarly John Pomfret, did not seem shocked when Lambert told him that the coaches had hand-carried transcripts of athletes from the high schools and presented them to the admissions office. He was satisfied that Lambert had solved the problem when the dean told him that all potential students would have to submit their records directly to the admissions office, a procedure that would eliminate the role of the athletic department.[2]

The football program benefited from the support of William and Mary's Board of Visitors, which put a far higher premium on football than on academics. The chairman of the board, Judge Oscar Shewmake, had been captain of the football team in the early 1900s, and a majority of the board members were inveterate boosters. The board had consistently exhorted the football coach and athletic director, Rube McCray, and Barney Wilson, the basketball coach, to produce winning teams. The board also rewarded McCray with promotions and salary raises so that he was paid as well as any faculty member on campus. One member later told an interviewer that the board always scheduled their fall meetings on football weekends so that they could adjourn to watch the game.[3]

Unlike the board, many students did not strongly support big-time athletics. Some students chafed at policies that ignored their own interests and concerns, such as eight o'clock classes, which former coach, Frank Voyles, had persuaded the school to introduce in 1944 so that the football team would have more time to practice. Students complained that athletes who worked in the dining room as waiters failed to clear the tables promptly or did not show up for work. While the school provided local reporters and broadcasters first-class transportation and accommodations to out-of-town games, the student sports editor had to pay for trips for road games or rely on secondary accounts of the games.[4]

One William and Mary official, the dean of the college of arts and sciences, Nelson Marshall, would prove to be the figure who relentlessly pursued rumors about the athletic department. Marshall, a marine biologist, had arrived in Williamsburg by way of the college's nearby fisheries laboratory. Named to head the faculty athletic committee, Marshall became disillusioned by the lack of power exercised by the committee. He also observed lapses in athletic administration, which he was determined to pursue in his own investigation. After making a list of spurious practices in athletics, he confronted President John Pomfret in April 1951, threatening to resign unless he were permitted to conduct an investigation.[5]

Observers would later describe Pomfret as dedicated but too scholarly to deal with the nuts and bolts of big-time college sports, a president who preferred to delegate the details of athletic matters to his subordinates. They suggested that, if he had confronted the board with Marshall's suspicions in April, he would have put the board on the defensive. Yet in the spring of 1951 Pomfret seems to have grasped the implications of the athletic misdeeds but preferred to let Marshall pursue an internal investigation. He did not have a strong case against the athletic department, and he undoubtedly knew that the board was head over heels in love with football.

That same month Pomfret had applied for the presidency of the prestigious Huntington Library in San Marino, California. Far from being naive, as some of his colleagues also implied, Pomfret seems to have gauged the implications of the potential athletic scandal correctly. He particularly understood his sensitive relations with the board, whose members had not warmed to the humane scholar-president. So he tried to keep a lid on the scandal until he had enough hard evidence either to root out the problems or to bring them to the attention of the board. In the meantime he prepared a safety net just in case the athletic situation disintegrated.[6]

For the next two months Dean Nelson Marshall put together a report on athletic wrongdoing which demonstrated a pattern of deception and outright cheating. In short, course work and grades were being manipulated so that athletes were able to remain eligible. Two students had received credit for courses when they were actually working in Pittsburgh and New York; one professor had been browbeaten into raising a grade; and the athletic department had blatantly ignored the school's honor code. Marshall would continue his investigation and would soon afterward discover that

students working in the weight room received credits for physical education courses rather than outright pay. Perhaps the worst offense involved a
female student whom McCray had bullied into falsifying the number of
hours that she worked; McCray then took the bogus overtime pay and
bought textbooks for the athletes, thereby violating the Sanity Code, which
had not permitted schools to provide athletes with textbooks.[7]

When Marshall brought his findings to Pomfret in June, the president
had no choice but to act more decisively. He pondered two courses of action. One involved going directly to the board of visitors and divulging the
problem. Instead, Pomfret decided to conduct an internal investigation,
which meant appointing a faculty committee to conduct a probe of athletics. In turn, he had to inform the faculty of the athletic investigation. Pomfret also gave Coaches McCray and Barney Wilson the choice of defending
themselves against Marshall's charges of athletic mismanagement or resigning after their forthcoming seasons ended. This fair but firm approach
meant that McCray would submit a letter of resignation dated February 1,
1952, after he had completed the season's work as football coach. The
coaches opted for the latter approach, which would allow them to finish out
their seasons and quietly depart from William and Mary.[8]

Pomfret also decided to separate the athletic department from physical
education in order to prevent coaches from manipulating grades. The
school had to announce this administrative change, however, and immediately the story of athletic misdeeds that Pomfret had tried to keep under
wraps began to leak out. Al Vanderweghe, a young coach who had been recently fired and who was blamed by McCray for altering transcripts, would
tell his side to local sportswriters. On August 10 McCray and Wilson, who
had already submitted the delayed letters of resignation, journeyed to Cape
May, New Jersey, where Pomfret was vacationing, to submit new, immediate letters of resignation. Already the board of visitors had scheduled special meetings to inquire into the athletic scandal, events that McCray and
Wilson wanted to avoid.[9]

When the board met on August 15 and 18 Pomfret explained the results
of Marshall's investigation and the reason for the faculty committee that
was still investigating the athletic department. The most convenient scapegoat, the nonathletic President John Pomfret, had few supporters among
the board of visitors, a compelling reason not to challenge the board or to
jeopardize the job that awaited him at the Huntington Library. At the meeting on September 8 the board treated Pomfret as if he were a pariah. John
Pollard, a lawyer and former governor's son, described the hostility of the
other members toward the president. They "built up a case" against Pomfret, he recalled, interrogating him as if he were a defendant in a court of
law. Before the meeting ended, the board had raked the president across the
coals for failing to act "with dispatch." In truth Pomfret moved fairly quickly

once he had the results of Marshall's investigation, but he also suffered the fate of presidents who have scandals occur on their watch. The board of visitors, which had declared its support for winning football teams and had treated the college as an adjunct to the football team, needed a scapegoat. Now it expected Pomfret to take responsibility for the policies that it had set in motion. Not surprisingly, Pomfret resigned on September 13, 1951, and soon afterward happily accepted the position as director of the Huntington Library, where, as he put it, he had "no alumni, no football team, and a very small and distinguished board of trustees."[10]

The misdeeds at William and Mary gained more notoriety than they might have at another time because of scandals that had occurred at nearly the same time. In early August the U.S. Military Academy revealed that almost its entire football team, including Coach Red Blaik's son, violated Army's hallowed honor code against cheating and had to leave the academy. Blaik had fielded the nation's best teams from 1943 to 1946 because the Military Academy had cut corners to get big-time football talent. Since Army's Black Knights had captured the imagination of the public in World War II and just after, the incident caused more public attention and outrage. Even President Harry Truman, an "avid football fan," was said to be deeply concerned about the scandal. Because West Point was chiefly a vocational school for future top army brass, the William and Mary episode created more concern among college faculty and presidents, who, after all, were not career army officers.[11]

In the final stage of the William and Mary scandal the board members, who wanted the scandal to disappear as rapidly as possible, clashed with a faculty fed up with athletic excesses. After Pomfret's resignation the visitors briefly turned to the faculty, which had neither participated in the scandal nor divulged its details. The faculty quickly became involved, however, when it drew up a statement declaring in no uncertain terms that the emphasis on athletics had become "detrimental" to academic goals and values. The faculty also repudiated the board's emphasis on winning, which had led to "dishonest athletic programs," turning football from a healthy extracurricular exercise into a commercial enterprise that manufactured winning teams at any cost, including the cost of dishonest academic practices. In their "manifesto" the faculty members called for faculty control of athletics, something that the board totally opposed. While shouldering some of blame for the scandal, the college's faculty unilaterally committed the college to "a sound and healthy program of athletics." They deplored the damage of the fraudulent athletic policies to the college's academic standards as a result of the "dominating position in the College" which college athletics had assumed. In their most memorable statement the faculty members asserted that the idea of honor as represented in honest academics and the cheating of big-time athletics were incompatible. "One set of principles cannot be applied in one relationship and not in another," they insisted. "There is no double standard of honor."[12]

The faculty presented copies of the manifesto to the board of visitors on September 18 and released copies not only to Virginia papers but also to widely read, out-of-state newspapers, including the *New York Times.* The response of the media to this document proved to be immediate and positive, since the statement roundly denounced the evils of college athletics and demonstrated that a group of courageous faculty wanted to make education paramount.

At William and Mary the manifesto reopened the festering wounds recently inflicted by the scandal. Far from applauding the faculty's effort, the board of visitors regarded it as treasonous. The "uppity" faculty, who had placed the college in this embarrassing spotlight, must be put in their place. What the board determined to be necessary was a tough, even dictatorial college president, a sort of czar like the late baseball commissioner Judge Kenesaw Mountain Landis, who would impart square-jawed integrity to the institution while returning the faculty to their unobtrusive role as classroom teachers. Without waiting for faculty recommendations, the board elected as president Vice Admiral Alvin Duke Chandler, son of a former William and Mary president, scuttling the embryonic policy of faculty control. Though the faculty members protested, their complaints fell on deaf ears. The booster board sent a message far different from the faculty manifesto, in effect stating that its public reputation, not the honor and integrity of the college, was at stake. And it was not long until Nelson Marshall and several others followed Pomfret, resigning in protest after the board named Chandler.[13]

Though the board refused to de-emphasize football, William and Mary's gridiron stature would diminish in the next decade. In 1951 the team that McCray had so hurriedly abandoned somehow managed a 7-3 record, including victories over Duke, Penn, Wake Forest, and North Carolina State. Yet the board of visitors was careful not to exhort the team to victories, and the scandal itself forestalled any attempts to revive big-time football. When the big schools formed the Atlantic Coast Conference in 1954, William and Mary gradually found itself relegated to a less prestigious schedule. As the Southern Conference lost ground, William and Mary's football teams became far less capable of winning against the major competitors like Army and Navy, which they still scheduled from time to time.[14]

The failure of the faculty at William and Mary emphasized the stacked deck when presidents or faculty challenged athletic policies supported by boards of trustees. In October 1951 the faculty at the nearby University of Virginia, influenced by the scandal in big-time athletics at William and Mary, appointed a committee chaired by a popular faculty member, Robert Gooch, a former UVa athlete and a Rhodes Scholar, to examine athletic policy. The three-member Gooch committee produced a forty-three-page report calling for faculty control of athletics and a return to amateur, non-subsidized policies toward athletes. Soon after the committee had released its report, an overwhelming number of College of Arts and Sciences faculty upheld it by a 68-9 margin. Most of the alumni and students strongly opposed the policies in the report, as exemplified by a letter from a student leader who said that "when I return here [after graduation], my main interest will be in the football team, my fraternity, and the extra-curricular activities with which I have been associated."[15]

While alumni groups denounced the report, President Colgate Darden and the Virginia board of visitors tried to maintain a neutral stance. Though Darden did not attend faculty meetings, he refused to allow the highly successful team to accept a bowl bid, a reflection in his belief that football could require too much of a student's time. Not unlike the William and Mary Board's reaction to the faculty manifesto, the visitors of UVa showed little sympathy with the Gooch Report. After appointing a committee to consider it, the board gradually allowed it to fade from view. Finally, the board resolved that the faculty should set specific academic standards but should not try to establish athletic policy. The visitors reshaped the athletic committee that controlled athletic matters so that it consisted of four faculty members who could easily be outvoted by the three alumni and two students. Like the William and Mary board of visitors, the UVa board did not trust the faculty, whom, they had good reason to believe, would try again to de-emphasize athletics. Darden, who had learned as a politician to avoid emotional and divisive issues, simply stood above the controversy, even though he was probably more sympathetic with the faculty than the board.[16]

At both William and Mary and at Virginia the influential football alumni emerged as a troublesome factor in the attempts to reassert control of football programs. Since the turn of the century, when Princeton's "oldest living graduate" had embarked on his one-man recruiting junkets, the out-of-control alumni had created problems for major football institutions. At William and Mary the problems had grown from a board of gridiron fanatics who had torn the institution loose from its academic moorings and created the climate in which athletic transgressors could flourish. Virginia's board members had shown more finesse than the visitors at William and Mary but had paid more attention to the alumni chapters than to the faculty.

Because the William and Mary scandal occurred in August 1951, it had more impact than if it had come to light a year earlier or a year later. Indeed, the scandal at William and Mary enjoyed far greater notoriety because of the cheating scandal at West Point. Both scandals, however, flowed into a toxic stream of tawdry revelations from the basketball scandals that had first appeared at Manhattan College in January 1951. Players from five colleges in the New York area, among them the powerful Blackbirds of Long Island University and the City College of New York, the 1950 NIT (National Invitational Tournament) and NCAA champs, were indicted for taking money from gamblers to meet the point spread. The scandals spread to Toledo and Bradley and then to Adolph Rupp's prestigious basketball program at Kentucky. Altogether, nearly forty players and several gamblers faced jail sentences. For the first time college basketball had joined football as a sport in which big-time cheating had become profitable.

Judge Saul Streit, who would preside over the basketball trials in New York, became the moral compass of the 1951 scandals in both big-time sports. In an open-ended sixty-three-page court statement Streit expressed disgust at the reckless disregard of coaches, alumni, townspeople, and "the most flagrant abuse of 'athletic scholarships.'" The court criticized the basketball and football squads at Kentucky as the "acme of commercialism and overemphasis," even though the basketball scandal had taken place on the basketball court. Streit assailed the "athletic scholarship racket" that threatened the amateur code.[17]

The scandals brought the small but persistent reform movement from the prewar era to the forefront; in the 1930s this group of journalists, small-college presidents, and educational reformers had conjured up a vision of amateur athletics without the fanfare of big-time college sports. One of their bête noirs was the postseason game. By the late 1940s opposition to bowl games had become a litmus test of a college football reform, as exemplified in the 1945 Ivy Group agreements, by which the eight schools agreed to reject postseason bids. At the NCAA convention in 1947 the delegate from Virginia Military Institute, Colonel William Couper, introduced a motion to ban all postseason play in football, but the unexpected motion created so much confusion that it was quickly tabled. Nevertheless, the delegates voted to refer the matter to the Constitutional Compliance Committee, and the NCAA became involved.[18]

Put more precisely, many of the bowl organizers had engaged in questionable financial practices, denying the colleges their share of the proceeds. In 1948 the NCAA had appointed its own bowl committee, which sent out questionnaires to fifty bowls but got only seventeen responses. The committee at first called upon its members to avoid playing bowl games but decided, instead, to examine the postseason events, pass rules that limited the members' participation, and then, in 1951, to certify the contests in which its teams could play.

Some of the conferences took a stronger stand than the NCAA, which limited its members to one postseason gridiron appearance. In the fall of 1951 the presidents of the Southern Conference refused to allow its members to appear in postseason play, a sign of alarm over athletic scandals and the big-time football practices of President Curley Byrd's Maryland team.

When Maryland and Clemson received bowl bids in November, the conference presidents rejected the requests to participate, which normally were accepted without debate. With a powerhouse team and needing $125,000 to retire the bonds for newly constructed Byrd Stadium, Maryland disregarded the Southern Conference, as did Clemson; as a result, both schools were placed on probation, which appeared to mean that they could not play conference teams in 1952. As it turned out, Maryland managed to elude the conference penalties and play enough big-time opponents to win the national championship.[19]

The controversy over bowl games signaled that the business-as-usual attitudes toward big-time college football would no longer satisfy the presidents and faculty representatives, many of whom were embarrassed by the scandals and fearful that the NCAA lacked the authority to deal with wrongdoing. Once again, as in the early 1900s, a major scandal enabled reformers who disliked athletic subsidies, aggressive recruiting, bowl games, and out-of-season practice to set the agenda for the ensuing debate. The agenda would spread from specific items such as postseason play and spring practice to a full array of big-time practices.

Scandal and Halting Reforms

Following the William and Mary revelations, almost every conference and educational agency contemplated stricter rules on athletic participation, and faculty members at a few schools, such as Virginia, tried themselves to reform their athletics. Yet the issue of national reforms in big-time athletics had reached an impasse. Because of the failure of the Sanity Code, the NCAA appeared to be incapable of setting standards and regulating the conduct of its members. As a result of the growing uneasiness with scandalous college athletics, several agencies challenged the NCAA as either the accrediting agency for college athletics or as leaders in setting the direction for college athletics.

In the late summer and fall of 1951, however, the NCAA tried to make its presence felt in the debate. Through its council, which met in August, the association proposed a "look-good" twelve-point plan that would restore its credibility without committing it to specific reforms. Because the NCAA was dominated by athletic interests, the council was careful to phrase its points in "either/or" language or to call for adherence to practices already embodied in its bylaws. Still, the twelve points hit many of the hot buttons of reform in a way that would win public approval without offending coaches and athletic directors. The twelve points called for rethinking the length of spring practice, limiting the number of games, reexamining postseason play, reducing the number and amount of grants to athletes, and declaring players who colluded with gamblers ineligible. Because the NCAA had not yet recovered from the Sanity Code debacle, it did not have a concrete policy on subsidies, nor would it even mention the restoration of strictly amateur athletics for fear of hitting the touchy issue of athletic scholarships. The twelve points said nothing about enforcement, an area that had been undermined by the ill-fated attempt to expel the Sinful Seven. The vagueness of its agenda and the apparent weakness of the NCAA invited other groups with more radical goals to try to impose their ideas on the collegiate athletic policy.[20]

In September and October 1951, as the situation at William and Mary dragged its way through the news, the American Council of Education prepared to plunge into the cauldron of athletic reform. As a lobbying and study group that represented colleges and universities, the ACE had college presidents heading its councils, and its highly autocratic director, Arthur Adams, was both a past provost of Cornell and former president of New Hampshire.[21]

The quite obvious fact that the NCAA no longer represented the college presidents could hardly have escaped Adams and the ACE officials. The successes at colleges such as Swarthmore and Chicago, where presidents had reformed football, suggested that college presidents should control college athletics, a position taken by the Ivy League institutions in their 1945 meeting. As a result, the ACE decided that, in order for athletics to play a secondary role to academics, college presidents must provide the vehicle for change.

In November 1951 the ACE announced that a committee of eleven college presidents would undertake a study of college athletics (technically, only ten presidents served because Raymond B. Allen, soon to become president of UCLA, was listed as former president of the University of Washington). The ACE attempted to bring together a cross-section of presidents who headed schools of varying sizes, sources of support, scale of athletic programs, and academic prestige. The presidents came from institutions as geographically diverse as higher education itself, including Yale, Furman, Michigan State, Mississippi, Nebraska, Notre Dame, Southern Methodist, Utah, Washington, and Western Reserve. John Hannah of Michigan State, representing a school that had recently replaced the University of Chicago in the Big Ten, chaired the committee. Because Michigan State did not have the reputation of a Michigan or Notre Dame, the ACE leadership may have thought that Hannah would prove less wedded to the old system of athletic subsidies. In this belief they could not have been more wrong.[22]

As it turned out, Hannah proved an unfortunate choice, a bogus reformer who had engaged in the same practices that the ACE hoped to eliminate. As a graduate of Michigan State and a longtime booster of its football, Hannah knew the dark interior of big-time football. In the 1930s he had joined the faculty of what was then Michigan Agricultural College and later became Michigan State College. While he served in the poultry department, Hannah displayed his booster mentality by consistently attending afternoon football practices. Once he referred to Michigan State as "a diamond in the rough," needing only a victory or preferably two consecutive victories over the University of Michigan to "become a great football institution." If the team won consecutive victories, he reasoned, people would no longer say its success was a fluke.[23]

One of Hannah's friends, a wealthy insurance executive named Fred Jenison, died in the 1930s and left six million dollars to the college for use wherever the "need was the greatest." Hannah knew exactly where to use the money. As executor of Jenison's estate, he applied a portion of the legacy to establish the "Jenison awards," or athletic scholarships. From the Jenison largesse players at Michigan State received scholarships consisting of tuition, room, and board if they maintained a C average. Hannah also volunteered to recruit for football, calling on parents of high school athletes. Finally, after marrying the daughter of Michigan State's president and becoming the college's president himself in 1941, Hannah renewed his efforts to convert the ag school into a major football power, a campaign that resulted in a national championship in 1952 and a national scandal involving illegal recruiting and under-the-table payments a year later.[24]

Though Hannah's actions might not have raised an eyebrow in the Southeast, the blatant subsidies and slush funds brought recriminations from rival University of Michigan, which had dominated football and higher education in the state. After one meeting between the two schools a coach at Michigan State sneered, "They [Michigan] have always been that way; they s—t in the corner, then point the finger at you." In response to Michigan's criticisms, Michigan State charged that Fielding Yost's institution used alumni to recruit and support athletes, charges that grew out of conflicts between two big-time schools crowded into the same state. Reluctantly, Michigan adjusted to the reality of two major college teams in a relatively small area and found that it could enlarge its recruiting territory into much of football-rich Ohio.[25]

Under Hannah, Michigan State shed its "ag school" image, becoming Michigan State University (MSU) and building a school of six thousand students and a four million dollar annual budget into a colossus of forty thousand students and a budget of fifteen million dollars. When Chicago left the Big Ten in 1946, Michigan State lobbied hard for the tenth slot. Despite Michigan's opposition, Hannah won admission for MSU in 1949. While the rapid growth of state universities after World War II provided an essential ingredient for its rise to prominence, MSU's status as a big-time football power helped to demonstrate the school's parity with Michigan and other major midwestern institutions.[26]

When Hannah became chairman of the ACE committee, he had ventured onto the national scene only in 1946, when he addressed the NCAA convention; otherwise, his football activities were not widely known outside the state of Michigan. One would have to conclude that Hannah looked better than anyone else on the panel. Michigan State had recently joined the powerful Big Ten, a conference whose support the panel would need. The president of Notre Dame, Father John Cavanaugh, headed a Roman Catholic institution strongly identified with big-time football, and the public still harbored suspicions about Catholic prelates and presidents. A. Whitney Griswold of Yale, a blue blood from an elite, eastern institution, would have doubtless faced a skeptical reception in the heartland. The presidents of Wesleyan, Furman, Western Reserve, and even Nebraska could scarcely have been expected to make a strong case for national reform. That left Hannah, who had the foresight and guile to see that he could gain prestige for himself and his school by donning the mantle of an athletic reformer.

In November 1951, after the committee was appointed but before the first meeting, Hannah held a press conference in Washington in which he discussed the evils of subsidizing and recruiting. He told the press that the American public had a right to look to the colleges for integrity and high standards. He declared that "most abuses are the result of an excessive desire to win" and that the committee should examine the pressures that made "winning seem too important." Paradoxically, Hannah's involvement with football at Michigan State eloquently spoke to the subject of winning, but his role in building the MSU football program never came up in his three months as head of the committee. Through his attempts to build the reputation of Michigan State, Hannah had made a number of influential friends, including Representative Gerald Ford of Grand Rapids, the future president and a former football player at the University of Michigan in the 1930s.[27]

The ACE Special Committee held two full-dress meetings and a final meeting in January to approve its report. In the first meeting it set as its goal completing its work before the NCAA meeting in January; Hannah said that he hoped the committee's recommendations would provide a basis for the NCAA's discussion of reform. Though the committee set out to study athletics generally, like the Carnegie Report it largely addressed itself to college football. In spite of the basketball scandals, big-time football still remained the rogue elephant of the athletic world. Among other problems the committee had to deliberate on many of the questions that the Sanity Code had raised. Should athletes receive some subsidies as a special class of recipient, and should high school stars be actively recruited? Unfortunately, as some presidents grasped, subsidies had become a fact of athletic life in big-time institutions. The chairman of the committee, John Hannah, probably knew this best of all but was for a time able to play the role of reformer quite effectively.[28]

Despite Hannah's shadowy background, the Special Committee on Athletic Policy of the ACE tried gamely not only to determine the defects in college athletics but also to shape a set of workable proposals—something scores of faculty and presidential committees had thus far failed to accomplish. Even more daunting was their mandate to bring about reform without the backing of the NCAA or any major athletic conference, a lofty ambition only attainable by framing highly regarded reforms that other groups would feel compelled to accept. Given the academic nature of the ACE, the Special Committee, or Hannah Committee, as it was often called, inevitably would take a stronger stand on athletic standards than the NCAA, though the premise of the investigation—that corrupt and bloated athletics endangered education—replayed a shopworn theme.

On every side the presidents saw conflicts and inconsistencies in the athletic system. Since the NCAA had repealed the Sanity Code in January, no effective policy on subsidization existed, and a number of problems cried out for decisive action. Along with the evils of pay-for-play came the problem of recruiting in the high schools, a practice that the NCAA had failed to curtail. Reformers also frowned on spring practice as well as bowl games, both of which seemed to place more emphasis on athletics than on academics. Above all, the purists opposed any form of pay-for-play, which was in their minds a gross commercialization of an extracurricular activity that had infiltrated too many football institutions.

The ACE appointed a number of consultants to meet with the presidents and present their views of the athletic crisis. An underlying, almost muted conflict played out between the realists, usually athletic personnel who favored a controlled system of subsidies, and the purists, who wanted athletes to be treated as other students. The most interesting exchanges involved members of the committee and Lloyd Jordan of Harvard, head of the football coaches association, who represented the interests of big-college coaches, who wanted flexible approaches toward aid, recruiting, and spring practice (though Harvard had itself de-emphasized football).[29]

Jordan opposed blanket regulations such as the Sanity Code, arguing the big-college line that each conference should set its own standards. Unlike Asa Bushnell, the commissioner of the largely small-college Eastern Collegiate Athletic Conference (ECAC), who repudiated pay-for-play, Jordan argued a popular theme with coaches and athletic directors that some form of subsidies were inevitable. He also opposed ending spring practice and favored active recruiting. "Coaches should be permitted to 'sell' their colleges," he argued, "but not necessarily to solicit athletes." In a burst of candor Jordan also accepted and, in fact, approved of the role of college sports in providing entertainment. "We must recognize that colleges are in the entertainment business. The only question is, How far shall we go? But if we do it at all, shouldn't we do it well." This statement resulted in a heated exchange with President John Millis of Western Reserve, who objected to Jordan's frank view of big-time athletics as entertainment; Millis declared that he had never seen a college charter that mentioned entertainment as a legitimate objective.[30]

In its final report the Special Committee disregarded the testimony of the coaches and recommended strictly amateur standards for college athletics. Throughout the report the committee never called for schools to drop football or basketball, though a number of institutions had been forced to abandon football in 1951 because of dwindling revenues and manpower. Nevertheless, it did call for reforms that clashed with big-time football programs.[31]

The presidents' ten proposals had much in common with the reform tradition embodied in the report of the Gates Commission, the Carnegie Report, and even the Angell conferences: The first five recommendations strongly emphasized control of athletics by the institution and, for that matter, by the faculty. The committee recommended that (1) athletics should be controlled by the institution and athletic departments and subjected to the same policies and controls as other departments; coaches should not only be members of the faculty but should not be paid more than other members of the faculty; (2) the same admission standards should apply to both athletes and nonathletes; (3) students should be enrolled in a four-year degree program and be making normal progress toward graduation; (4) no students should play intercollegiate athletics in their freshman year; and (5) seasons for football, basketball, and baseball should not only be clearly defined, but out-of-season practice should also be eliminated except in the weeks before the team began to play its scheduled contests.

The remaining five proposals had to do with recruiting and subsidization as well as athletics for all students. Here the committee decreed that (1) no member of the athletic staff or representative of athletic interests should offer inducements to recruits; similarly, the ACE called for a ban on test camps and all-star games, where players would display their talents, as well as the payment of expenses for recruits to campuses or entertainment of those prospective student-athletes; (2) athletics should be made available to all students (an endorsement of a long-standing belief that colleges should offer intramural athletics to all students); (3) colleges should compete with their "natural rivals—schools that had similar policies and programs"; (4) colleges should provide statistics for opponents, accrediting agencies, and athletic and educational groups on players' grades, class standing, and the numbers receiving financial aid; (5) and scholarships should be based solely on academic need and academic ability rather than on athletic ability.[32]

The section on subsidies was not only the most important but also the longest of the recommendations. While the presidents did not prohibit athletes from receiving financial assistance, they specified that students should receive the aid in order to help them get an education rather than a position on the team. "Athletes holding scholarships or grants-in-aid should be required to meet the same standards of academic performance and economic need as are required of all other recipients," the report declared. There should be no awards based on athletic ability or performance.[33]

Though the ACE standard had much in common with the defunct Sanity Code, it was really a throwback to even stricter standards. Whereas the NCAA had agreed to limited aid to athletes, the ACE repudiated the practice of singling out football players or other athletes for financial aid. There were no expenses to be allowed for transportation to athletic events or meals in season, as permitted by the Sanity Code. In short, the committee's opposition to athletic subsidies would have meant the downfall of big-time football programs, nearly all of which depended on subsidies to athletes; yet committee members of major football institutions such as President Umphrey Lee of Southern Methodist University, John Hannah of Michigan State, Chancellor R. G. Gustavson of Nebraska, and John D. Williams of Mississippi affixed their signatures to the report, betraying either incurable optimism or outright hypocrisy.

As for Father John Cavanaugh's Notre Dame, he had early in 1951 proposed a TV network of big-time football schools which would also institute reforms such as aid to athletes and coaching contracts. This bid to combine reform and revenue failed to interest Notre Dame's gridiron rivals, but it did establish Cavanaugh as a strong-minded president who had broached reform before the scandals reached fever pitch. It is well to keep in mind, however, that Notre Dame's brand of reform did not resemble the Ivy League or small-college versions. Unlike opponents of big-time football, Notre Dame had no quarrel with highly commercialized football, nor did it regard football as outside the university's true mission. In no way did Cavanaugh or his youthful vice president in charge of athletic policy, Theodore Hesburgh, favor downsizing athletics. Quite the opposite, they wanted to continue playing the best teams in the country. More to the point, Notre Dame had less need to promise subsidies because it had an unparalleled recruiting pipeline. And skeptics might still have wondered if some needy Notre Dame athletes did not receive either routine academic aid, income from campus jobs, or support from enthusiastic alumni. In either case the ACE approach would not have blended well with the long-term profit motives of Notre Dame, distinguishing it from schools that wanted de-emphasis of big-time athletic programs.[34]

While the ACE proposals resembled the NCAA twelve points, the two diverged on their approaches to amateur athletics. Like the NCAA, the ACE upheld the principle of institutional control, and both groups opposed attempts to solicit high school athletes with offers of money or "equivalent inducements." They differed radically, however, in the deep chasm between the ACE athletic purists, who adhered to strict amateurism, and the NCAA

realists, who accepted the profit motive in big-time athletics and the need
for subsidies. Unlike the ACE, the NCAA gave a cautious green flag to postseason tournaments or bowl games and allowed twenty-two days of spring
practice. These two points in the 1940s and 1950s represented the litmus test
of athletic ideology. The presidents landed on the traditional, or amateur,
side, while the NCAA would move toward a less restrictive policy more in
line with the practices of big-time football.[35]

The ACE group also called for its standards to be rigorously enforced,
which would begin with strict adherence by the institution itself and would
require the NCAA and the athletic conferences to fall into line. Taking up
an idea that had appeared in the Carnegie Report, the Hannah committee
in the final section of its report called upon the regional accrediting agencies to enforce athletics standards, just as they did with academic standards.
Accrediting teams put together by the agencies regularly evaluated academic
programs, and institutions whose academic programs did not meet this test
seldom were tolerated by the institution. Having been suggested periodically, athletic accrediting had never gotten off the ground, but here was a
weapon that could put teeth into the presidents' recommendations.[36]

Though the agencies were at first willing to cooperate, several of them
would later see the athletic accrediting as a no-win situation. Two of the
smaller agencies—the associations of colleges and secondary schools of New
England and the Middle States—rejected the idea soon after the report was
approved in mid-February. The head of the Middle States group doubted
that his agency wanted to engage in policing. "We do not think it practica-
ble for the association," he declared, "which is a creature of the colleges in
this area, to constitute itself an enforcement agency for any other group."
The New England representative emphasized that responsibility belonged
to the institutions, athletic conferences, and the NCAA, as opposed to academic accreditors. Even the American Council of Education leaders, as opposed to the special committee, did not advocate recruiting the accrediting agencies to police college athletics, and John Hannah did everything that
he could do in subsequent meetings to block the proposal.[37]

One accrediting agency, the North Central Association of Colleges and
Secondary Schools, rallied to the committee's call. Because it was the largest
such group, the North Central had the best chance of controlling athletics
by denying accreditation. In fact, the North Central had long entertained
the notion of accrediting athletics, and the scandals seemed to present the
perfect opportunity.

The North Central had its origins in 1895, when seven school heads, including James Angell of Michigan, Henry Wade Rogers of Northwestern,
and William Harper of Chicago, had organized thirty-six institutions into
an agency to raise academic standards, an effort inspired by the success of
a similar agency in New England. The North Central had expanded its scope

in the intervening years, but its program had barely touched upon athletics. By 1950 the agency had accredited 356 colleges and universities as well as more than three thousand high schools. The North Central leadership believed strongly both in strict academic standards and in methods to safeguard those standards. So pervasive was the influence of the North Central that neither institutions nor their academic programs in the Midwest or the Plains states could be credible without its seal of approval.[38]

In truth the possibility of accrediting athletics had come up in the 1930s, when the North Central had threatened to accredit athletics at Big Ten schools, but the schools angrily objected and the North Central dropped its proposal. Though the North Central manual in 1941 included a section on athletics, it was not until the scandals of 1951 that its long-dormant goal of accrediting athletics sprung back to life. Since the North Central also represented high schools, it had a powerful interest in relieving the teachers and principals of the disturbing presence of athletic recruiters. Articles in North Central publications related how colleges invaded the high schools to visit with top athletes and then showed how colleges like Swarthmore, Johns Hopkins, and Chicago had reformed their athletics. Clearly, the North Central was eager to take on big-time athletics.[39]

In December 1951 the North Central held a meeting in Chicago not only devoted to college athletics but also designed to establish a format for later meetings. The accreditors hoped to work with the NCAA and invited the association's new executive director, Walter Byers, to the meeting. The prevailing wisdom was that, if the colleges wanted to eliminate the abuses, it could be easily done. In the report that was compiled as a result of the meeting, the North Central introduced the idea of "*punitive action as an antidote to that of voluntary conformity* with existing standards and criteria, which has failed to get desired results." To put it bluntly, the discussions with the Hannah committee had virtually guaranteed the North Central a role in the committee's reform plans if the accrediting agency wanted to pursue it.[40]

Speaking from the ACE headquarters in Washington on January 7, one week before the NCAA convention, John Hannah revealed the outline of the committee's proposals. While its plan still had to be ratified by the ACE members, the prestige of the committee and the authority of its executive director, Arthur Adams, ensured that its own convention would give its blessing to athletic accreditation.

Not to be outdone, the NCAA announced on the same day that it would unveil its own plan at its convention the next week in Cincinnati—a sign that the NCAA was vying with the ACE for athletic leadership. On January 8 the NCAA explained that it had devised new powers of enforcement which could be used to crack down on cheating. In place of the defunct compliance committee, the association provided for a membership committee with powers to discipline wrongdoers. It would receive and act on complaints, initiate investigations, make charges, and recommend measures to be taken against the wrongdoers, including expulsion. This proposed change in the bylaws gave the membership committee far more flexibility than the old constitutional compliance committee. It also enabled the association to hand down punishments less drastic than expulsion.[41]

These changes appeared so suddenly as to suggest that the NCAA had bided its time until it saw that the ACE planned to call upon the accrediting agencies. On December 12 Walter Byers, the NCAA's executive director, told the Hannah committee that his organization believed in allowing the conferences to establish their own codes. "Mr. Byers said the purpose was to leave it to institutions and conferences to define in detail what constitutes illegal subsidizing," the minutes read. "He said the NCAA has decided a uniform standard is impractical." Three weeks later the NCAA added a new enforcement clause designed to keep the association from losing control to the ACE and the accrediting agencies. The NCAA leadership knew that it had to move quickly to fill the vacuum that the failure of the Sanity Code had created, or it would cease to be a factor in creating and enforcing athletic standards.[42]

The Triumph of Big-Time Football, 1952

Initial reports left the impression that few differences existed between the ACE and NCAA, but the opposite was closer to reality. It is true that the NCAA had staked out some popular positions, such as normal progress toward degrees and limiting the number of games in each sport. Yet the NCAA's twelve points, passed in August, strongly favored the coaches and athletic directors, who wielded a much larger influence in the NCAA than before World War II. The NCAA's proposals called merely for study of bowl games and spring football drills, both of which had strong support among athletic personnel. As for aid to athletes, the NCAA had no position other than requiring financial aid to come through the institution; the Sanity Code's demise had returned subsidies to the conferences and institutions. Probably the most self-interested proposal called for the NCAA to reconsider unlimited substitution or the two-platoon system, made more costly and less practical by the manpower needs brought about by the Korean War.[43]

The NCAA desperately needed breathing space to work out its own measures and to present its viewpoint on athletic reform to the ACE members, who would consider the special committee's report in February 1952. Just before the NCAA convention met in January, John Hannah conferred with NCAA leaders in Cincinnati and agreed to allow them to represent their proposals as similar to those of the ACE. In so doing, he enabled the NCAA to blunt the sharp focus of the ACE reforms, which, Murray Sperber optimistically believes, could have led college athletics in the direction of the Ivy League's de-emphasis.[44]

The role of John Hannah casts doubt on his commitment to the committee proposals, and, at worst, it leads to speculation that he represented his personal interests and those of Michigan State. In a press conference he denied emphatically that the NCAA and ACE were working at cross-purposes or that the ACE would place the NCAA in its shadow if the code were adopted. Based on the meeting between Hannah and the NCAA, President Hugh Willett of the NCAA claimed his goals mirrored those of the ACE. "The report and the explanation of the report," Willett declared, "showed clearly that the objectives and athletic philosophy of the presidents' committee are the objectives and philosophy of the NCAA." He would concede only that the two groups differed on minor matters and made it appear that the NCAA would support the proposals at its next convention.[45]

While Hannah softened the sharp edge of ACE policies, he did not back down on the crucial measure of enforcement by the accrediting agencies. Though it is doubtful that Hannah wanted to have accrediting teams snooping into athletics at Michigan State, he did make a key distinction between the weakened powers of the NCAA and the apparent clout of the accrediting agencies. He remarked that the agencies were capable of some things that the NCAA could not do as well or could not do at all. So, if he blurred the content, he did hang onto the distinction between the powers of the two groups. If Hannah blunted the ACE's other proposals, the observer is bound to ask, why he did not go all the way? One explanation is that he could not concede this obvious difference without entirely losing the respect of his committee, and he could use his influence in committee to block a clear understanding with the agencies. He could always claim that he made a strong distinction between the ACE's weapon of enforcement and the impotence of the NCAA (as exemplified by its failure to enforce the Sanity Code). Since the new powers of the NCAA were as yet untested, he could not easily have endorsed those powers without publicly betraying both the committee and accrediting agencies.

Yet the NCAA failed soon afterward in a campaign to convince the ACE convention to scale down the provisions of the Special Committee when it met in February. Hoping that they would make their proposals on bowl games and spring practice less uncompromising, President Hugh Willett of the NCAA pleaded with those attending the ACE convention to forgo the accreditors, but to no avail. In the next morning's *New York Times* the headlines read "Group of College Presidents Ignores N.C.A.A. Plea to Soften Rules on Sports." In spite of Willett's plea, the ACE not only refused to back off from its commitment to amateur athletics, but it also persisted in calling for the accrediting agencies to enforce athletic standards.[46]

On February 16, 1952, after the ACE executive committee had approved the proposals, the Special Committee formally released its report. John Hannah held a press conference in Washington, and newspapers dutifully ran stories on the results of the not-quite-three-month study. Because the cheating, transcript, and gambling scandals of 1951 were fresh in the public's mind, the Hannah committee received generally favorable comments from college presidents in the following weeks and months. President Justin Morrill of Minnesota called upon the Big Ten to "set a good example by supporting the ACE code." J. Roscoe Miller, president of Northwestern, was typical of several university heads who endorsed the plan without explaining how their institutions would implement it. Judge Saul Streit, in one of his lengthy judicial sermons at the trial of the basketball fixers, called upon the colleges to follow the recommendations of the ACE, yet Judge Streit's court had no authority over bowl games, spring practice, and player subsidies.[47]

Predictably, the coaches opposed the proposals, which they saw as deemphasizing their sport, a position that eventually was reflected in NCAA policy. Coach Lloyd Jordan of Harvard, the head of the American Football Coaches Association, and Coach Tuss McLaughrey of Dartmouth criticized the ban on spring practice, a change that the Ivy Group had also recently endorsed. Jim Tatum, the coach at Maryland, which gave out eighty-two football scholarships, said that the colleges had not overemphasized football. "We need more emphasis," Tatum declared, "more teams, more pressure to win under the rules of the game." President George Cross of Oklahoma, who was not a coach but presided over the most powerful football program in the nation in the early 1950s, regarded the code as "so restrictive that we may have created another Volstead Act," a reference to the failed Prohibition amendment.[48]

In spite of the brief spate of publicity, the ACE Special Committee and its agenda rapidly failed either to remain in the news or to have much impact. To be sure, many of the ACE proposals had deeply rooted support, but, taken as a whole, the plan flew in the face of so many long-standing practices that it seldom got more than an initial reading. Several conferences talked about passing the ACE code, and many newspaper reports acted as if it the NCAA would automatically adopt it. The influence of the proposals, however, diminished, and the NCAA gradually regrouped. The ACE proposal on banning bowl games had enough support to force the NCAA to appoint a committee and send out a questionnaire. In the end the association, which had already dealt with the worst excesses of fly-by-night bowls, simply let the issue of banning postseason play drop out of sight.

By ignoring ACE proposals and emphasizing its own measures, the NCAA managed to let the ACE proposal for strictly amateur athletics go to the scrapheap of well-intentioned reforms. By its annual convention in January 1953, President Hugh Willett punctured the balloon of NCAA reformism and proclaimed the association's control over college athletics. "A year ago the NCAA stood at the cross roads," he recalled. "It was amply apparent that unless the NCAA and other intercollegiate athletic groups kept their athletic houses in order, other agencies interested in the athletic branch of higher education would do so." The association had adopted measures for enforcing its rules, he insisted, which had shown their determination to enforce athletic good conduct. Now the association had to follow through on that legislation, and the threat from the "other agencies" would vanish. Willett's statement stood as a virtual declaration of victory.[49]

The NCAA had managed to restore order rather than to institute sweeping reforms, an approach quite in keeping with the interests of the coaches, athletic directors, and major conferences. While the ACE proposals won praise, they did not halt the trend toward subsidized athletics, and John Hannah did not make any effort to drum up support for the proposals or even to keep the plan alive. With a few exceptions the ACE initiative would prove to be one of the final attempts to turn the clock back to a misty, golden era of innocence, a fantasy world that existed mainly in the imagination of reformers. Given the reality that subsidies had become a way of life at most big-time football schools, the athletic departments could or would not have changed their policies for the ACE or the NCAA. Big-time football had built a solid foundation of revenues, subsidies, and aggressive alumni support, its modus operandi since the 1890s. The ACE had framed a program that was well tailored for smaller colleges and institutions such as the Ivy League, where de-emphasis had already begun.

In a life span of three months and two working meetings before its proposals were released, the Hannah committee really did not have the time to investigate college athletics or to frame proposals that would command solid support. In their haste to reach the public and the NCAA, the committee members gave up their chance to conduct a more probing study and keep their work before the public. In that sense the committee proved to be a useful public relations tool for reform but ensured that its proposals would fade from view if they were not immediately accepted. Led as it was by John Hannah, the committee stood little chance of mounting a major crusade against big-time athletics. As the clouds of scandal enveloped Michigan State football in 1952 and 1953, Hannah's credibility as a reformer evaporated in the heat of Big Ten investigations.

The ACE Special Committee on Athletic Policy fits the archetype of a group to which society and institutions look for leadership but then fail to heed its recomendations. This is not surprising because the committees often end up too far in front of their constituencies. In November 1951 the ACE leaders had warned the committee of the pitfalls it faced in framing athletic standards: "The dilemma would be, as the NCAA discovered [with the Sanity Code], that standards actually enforceable on a nationwide basis might be so low as to appear to condone abuses, whereas standards high enough to win public acclaim might be unenforceable." History could not have written a more fitting epitaph of the ACE's Special Committee and its work, which won plenty of acclaim but failed to gain a strong foothold among athletic and college officials.[50]

Viewed from a broader perspective, the ACE committee was a product of the "big bang" era in which it was created. The scandals in 1951 would be like the first onslaughts of a new gravitational field that would create wave upon wave of scandal in the years that followed. In time the several crises of 1951, which included finances and television, would change the vocabulary of big-time football. The old words *proselyting, subsidization,* and *honor,* already on the wane, would be replaced by *recruiting* and *scholarships,* and the amateur sportsman would reappear as the scholar-athlete. New standards of semiprofessional athletics would provide a gauge against which to measure and punish wrongdoing.

Whipsawed by successive scandals, the public would lose its sense of outrage as it came to accept the reality of money-driven athletics. Though the old vocabulary and definitions of corrupt football would disappear, it would take several years for the public to assimilate the new gridiron paradigm of scholarships and television. As it had in previous crises, America's premiere college sport would again find a way to elude the wrath of reformers, concentrating on practical profit-oriented competition and demonstrating its remarkable ability to adapt both to old criticisms and new technology.

CHAPTER THIRTEEN

De-emphasis or Demise: Gridiron Decisions of the 1950s

In the postwar era football attendance showed all the signs of repeating its remarkable growth after World War I. In 1946 and 1947 college football soared above record receipts set just before Pearl Harbor, but in the next two years the rate of increase began to slow. In 1949, when college football boasted of its highest attendance figures, cracks in the edifice had begun to appear in the Northeast and Far West, where football attendance dropped precipitously.

The soft underside of college football showed up most dramatically in urban areas, where college football had prospered in the late 1930s. A number of reasons might suffice to explain the weakness in attendance. College enrollments that had burgeoned with the return of veterans with GI benefits now began to return to normal, and fewer students meant declining revenues. The economic boom, which was fueled by pent-up savings after the war, now took a brief vacation before the boom of the mid-1950s. Almost all sports suffered some setbacks in these years.[1]

One exception proved to be professional football. Pro teams attracted far more interest than they had before the war, and they too benefited from the veterans who had played military and postmilitary football at the college level. In 1945 professional football scored a 35 percent gain in attendance, but its record of 1,918,631 easily surpassed figures of 1,300,000 in 1940. In 1946 those gate receipts rocketed to 2,671,696, and some teams even surpassed the top college teams in their weekly attendance figures. In 1950 the pros suffered a slight setback attributed to an experiment by the Los Angeles Rams, which had televised their home games and suffered a severe decrease in attendance, but the next year the NFL showed a 6 percent increase.[2]

Going Out of Business, 1951

As the Los Angeles Rams' decline demonstrated, the most compelling reason for the lack of gate admissions arose from the dramatic growth of television. In 1946 there were only five thousand television sets, but the number mushroomed in the next four years. In 1950, when college football suffered a major decline, the nation had more than seven million sets that could telecast as many games as the market could bear. In small towns and rural areas, however, where television had yet to become a factor, college football attendance actually increased, and the big games continued to draw alumni, students, and townspeople.[3]

The undeclared Korean War, which broke in June 1950, had few of the earmarks of the world wars. Colleges did not dismantle their teams or curtail their schedules, nor did the military invade the campuses to appropriate football for military uses. Because colleges continued to play a peacetime game, they suffered from the manpower shortages but lacked the means to sit out the conflict or add military personnel to their rosters. Ironically, the free-substitution rule, which had been introduced as a wartime measure in 1941 and had evolved into two-platoon football, stretched the manpower needs of college football to its limits. Since the conferences had restored the freshman rule, that extra source of manpower available in World War II remained untapped. Whereas the state colleges and universities had more money and jobs to support athletes, the private colleges in or near urban areas suffered most grievously from the football revenue and manpower crisis. More than fifty colleges, many of them with modest enrollments and fan bases, abandoned football in 1950 and 1951.[4]

In April 1951 Georgetown University shocked the football world when its president, the Reverend Hunter Guthrie, announced that the venerable Jesuit institution would no longer play college football. Being the best-known institution to drop football in 1951, Georgetown had enjoyed a twenty-three game winning streak prior to World War II, but its program never recovered from the wartime lapse of four years. After a series of mediocre seasons in the immediate postwar years, Georgetown had gone to the Sun Bowl in 1949, but it declined the next year to 2-7. In addition, the appearance of a powerful Maryland team on its doorstep, put together by President Curley Byrd and Coach Jim Tatum, reduced the interest in Georgetown football.[5]

Reverend Guthrie tried to cast the decision as an educational reform. In the tradition of Chicago's Robert Hutchins, Guthrie summoned up a litany of anti-football arguments set forth in an article published in the *Saturday Evening Post*. In its seventy-three years, Guthrie declared, Georgetown football contributed little to producing business and political leaders, though he undoubtedly could have found onetime players who had noteworthy careers. He claimed that a recent survey showed that a mere seventy-two out of slightly more than a thousand students entering the institution said that sports had influenced their choice. In a point made by reformers from Charles Eliot to Hutchins, Guthrie insisted that football merely provided entertainment. "It is big business in neon lights," wrote Guthrie, "a spectacle outdated by Hollywood extravaganzas." In a phrase worthy of immortality Guthrie compared funding football to offering P. T. Barnum a chair in educational philosophy.[6]

The Georgetown decision may have been a reform, but Guthrie readily admitted the role of rising football costs and lackluster teams. Gridiron expenses in 1953, Guthrie pointed out, would have amounted to $147,810 out to a total athletic budget of $173,210. Guthrie declared, quite convincingly, that the "invisible deficit" resulting from scholarships to athletes and including lodging, board, books, laundry, and incidental expenses amounted to an even higher figure, which he estimated to be $250,000. Even if his invisible deficit were largely guesswork, the point remained valid. The chronic drain of big-time football on institutional resources presented a compelling argument to leave Hilltop Field to intramural teams.[7]

Many of the best-known colleges that dropped out of football in 1950 and 1951 were, like Georgetown, Roman Catholic institutions that turned out solid or highly ranked teams in the late 1930s, including St. Mary's in Oakland and Duquesne of Pittsburgh. Normally, teams abolished football after compiling poor records, but there were exceptions such as the University of San Francisco, which left the gridiron after going undefeated. Simply stated, the institution could not afford the spiraling costs and dwindling revenues. Some of the schools, such as Marquette and Detroit, suffered through a number of lackluster seasons before succumbing in the 1960s.[8]

The urban teams that dropped football in 1950 and 1951 stood out as the most dramatic examples of change. In most cases financial problems afflicting urban teams were the number one factor leading schools to downscale to less expensive programs, but the changes in the level of competition placed a strong second. Institutions often wrapped these changes in a mantle of reform or, in some cases, used the decline in gridiron fortunes to rid themselves of an unwanted nuisance.

Before World War II college presidents had often used the term *natural rivals* to describe the growing preference of small private colleges to play teams of their own size and strength rather than being mauled by state universities that they had once dominated or resorting to illicit methods to recruit big-time players. The presidents who initiated this downsizing often received praise as reformers, while the athletic finances and failure to compete which set the stage for change were often glossed over. Though the University of Chicago created banner headlines by abolishing football, other college officials at schools like Sewanee, Swarthmore, and Johns Hopkins with less fanfare provided solid models for downsizing or, as it was often called, "de-emphasis."

In the early 1950s *de-emphasis* became the buzzword for reform, connoting not only a disgust with existing gridiron practices but also a practical agenda. Though the movement was a reaction to "overemphasis" in the early 1900s, de-emphasis as a philosophy of reform had emerged in the 1930s when several small colleges adopted strictly amateur reforms. One institution that epitomized the possibilities of de-emphasis, Johns Hopkins of Baltimore, took the radical step in the 1930s of abolishing special admission for athletes and athletic subsidies. Under President Joseph Ames the faculty at Johns Hopkins made a determined effort to place football under its control and to broaden student participation in athletics. Not only did it abolish subsidies, but the school also stripped itself of public relations, scouting, jobs for players, and a school band to entertain spectators at halftime. Moreover, it refused to pay the usual guarantee to visiting teams and abolished gate receipts, making football and other athletics free of admission charges but unable to generate revenues.[9]

In point of fact, many of these reforms had long histories, but Johns Hopkins caught the eye of college football reformers because the new model worked. Reform did not seem to keep Hopkins from fielding winning teams, and in 1948 the school received an invitation to the postseason Tangerine Bowl. To reformers Hopkins served as living proof that reformed football stripped of its commercial trappings could succeed not only on the playing field but also in the classroom. Often overlooked was the fact that the Baltimore institution placed less emphasis on football and directed its big-time aspirations toward lacrosse. Nevertheless, Hopkins, Haverford, and Swarthmore as well as Amherst, Wesleyan, and Williams caught the eye of crusaders like John Tunis, who put them on his A list of clean, amateur schools. In the postwar era the reforms at these schools served as a model for larger private institutions that sought a way out of their gridiron dilemmas.[10]

Barely noticed, a few institutions such as Mercer University in Macon, Georgia, simply dropped football after World War II. Mercer's president, Spright Dowell, who lost his job at Auburn in 1927 because of a losing football team, refused to go along with attempts to revive gridiron subsidies and told the trustees that he would resign if the sport were reinstated. As we have seen, President Compton of Washington University in St. Louis, who attempted to form a strictly amateur conference in 1946, simply withdrew from the Missouri Valley Athletic Conference and eliminated athletic subsidies. Carnegie Tech of Pittsburgh, which turned out giant killers in the 1920s and 1930s, scaled back their football on the eve of World War II and pursued de-emphasis in the postwar era.[11]

In the postwar years the most ambitious attempt to curb big-time football took place in the 1945 agreement between the future Ivy League schools. Since Princeton and Pennsylvania still fielded nationally ranked teams— and several Ivies played major teams such as the Black Knights of Army— it was not clear exactly how many of the schools were ready to move toward a rigorous policy of de-emphasis. All of this changed, however, when in 1951 the scandals in big-time sports sent an urgent message to Harvard and Yale that they needed to separate themselves from the evils of big-time football.

The Ivy League: Safety in Numbers

Since the 1930s, when a sportswriter coined the term *Ivy League,* journalists, coaches, and athletic directors had predicted that the schools would eventually band together in an athletic conference. In 1936 editors of seven student newspapers in what would become the eight-team Ivy League (Brown was yet not included) put out a joint edition calling for "enlightened cooperation." Meeting together in late 1936, the athletic directors of the future Ivy League embraced the idea of an athletic conference.[12]

Why, then, did the Ivy institutions wait so long to formalize a relationship that both the public, students, alumni, and athletic officials had already endorsed? Time after time, the presidents of Harvard, Yale, and Princeton insisted that they were unwilling to give up their traditional independence. Not that the three presidents were opposed to creating a league of their own three institutions. The heads of the Big Three had periodically since 1906 defined eligibility rules, and, much like a diminutive conference, they set requirements for transfer students, requirements for passing grades, condemned subsidies for athletes, and called for a round-robin football contest between their three schools. When President Edmund Day of Cornell proposed an Ivy League agreement in 1940, however, Charles Seymour of Yale squelched the proposal. "I told him," Seymour wrote to Conant, "that I was strongly opposed to anything like an Ivy League with an elaborate code, or any organization that would place the individual institution under the control of a single head and deprive the institution of a free hand in the matter of schedules."[13]

The attitudes of the Big Three changed in World War II, resulting in a new approach best epitomized by President James Conant of Harvard. As a staunch opponent of big-time football, Conant seems to have recognized the need for natural rivals, or, more accurately, allies in his battle against big-time athletics. When A. Whitney Griswold replaced Seymour as president of Yale, Conant found a ready partner who, unlike Charles Seymour, did not oppose more binding and broader pacts. As at other private institutions such as Washington of St. Louis and Western Reserve of Cleveland, the presidents recalling the gaudier excesses looked to the postwar era as an opportunity for reform.

Though the eight institutions had competed athletically since the late 1800s, the incipient Ivy League included gridiron programs that varied considerably in strength and approach. Nowhere did these inconsistencies show up more glaringly than in the case of Pennsylvania, which had established itself in the 1930s as a modern gridiron power. In its first ten years under Coach George Munger, who had take over in 1938, Penn had won thirty-five, lost four, and had five ties against its traditional Ivy rivals. Against the "dismal five" of the Ivies—Yale, Harvard, Dartmouth, Brown, and Columbia—

Penn had not lost in twenty-four games. Not surprisingly, Penn's dominance created hostility because its rivals claimed that its heavily subsidized teams violated the spirit of the Ivy accords.[14]

In the fall of 1948 Harold Stassen took over as Pennsylvania's youngest president ever. Stassen, a former three-term governor of Minnesota, won his first term at the tender age of thirty-one, the youngest governor in the nation's history. In 1944 and 1948 he entered the Republican race for the presidency. After failing to win the nomination at Philadelphia in 1948, Stassen dropped out of political life briefly to take on the job as Pennsylvania's president and big-name fund-raiser. Penn's potential as a big-time football power offered possibilities to the ambitious new president. When Stassen first served as governor in 1939, the University of Minnesota had topped the national rankings; Pennsylvania may have appeared to offer the same big-name potential.[15]

In fairness to Stassen—and neither the media nor the Ivy presidents were particularly fair—Penn suffered in 1949 from the attendance problems that had afflicted many urban institutions, including Ivy League schools. Though Penn's 384,000 paid admissions placed it third in the country behind Michigan and Ohio State, its attendance had skidded in 1949 by nearly 100,000, or, in its seven home games, from an average of 75,000 in 1948 to 59,000 in 1949. When Stassen took office in 1948, Penn finished the season with a near-perfect record. In 1949, when Virginia staged its well-publicized upset, the Quakers won only half their games. Penn still had a large debt to pay on massive Franklin Field and ran an athletic deficit that stood in the way of Stassen's plans to raise money for the school. As a result, Stassen shuffled the longtime athletic director, H. Jamison Swarts, into the purchasing department and hired the dynamic Francis ("Franny") Murray to spearhead a more aggressive policy—at almost twice Swart's salary.[16]

In truth the declining attendance at Penn afflicted eastern football generally, striking the section of the country where television had first sprouted. Among the major conferences or groupings of teams, Ivy League football had declined from an average of 1,498,252 paid admissions in 1947 and 1948 to 1,120,025 in 1949, plummeting by more than 20 percent. The three Ivy teams that suffered most—Penn, Columbia, and Yale—not only had poor seasons but also were located in urban areas. Though the decline stemmed, at least in part, from television, Penn, which had televised its games since 1940, felt that it could tap into a rich vein of TV revenue if it scheduled more big-time games for its normally successful team.[17]

In August 1950 President Stassen held a press conference to introduce Francis Murray, his new director of intercollegiate athletics. Stassen had hired Murray, a former Penn All-American running back, to turn Penn's athletics into a profit center by scheduling big-name teams to play at Franklin Field, or, as Stassen put it, to achieve "victory with honor." In other words, Penn would continue to abide by the principles to which it had subscribed in the Ivy Accords and which the membership in the NCAA required but would also plunge in the waters of big-time football. While continuing to play its "Ivy League" rivals, Stassen declared, Penn would schedule some of the best-known teams from other sections, an approach that put him at odds with his Ivy colleagues. Whereas Stassen seemed to be violating the spirit of the 1945 Ivy agreements, purists sometimes overlooked the fact that General Dwight D. Eisenhower, while president of Columbia in 1949, had also called on his team to win more games than it had previously.[18]

Put simply, Penn's vital edge over its Ivy competitors resulted from its ability to reward student-athletes with state scholarships. Though it had no formal ties with the state of Pennsylvania, Penn had been receiving scholarships for in-state students long before Stassen arrived. While a vast majority of these scholarships went to nonathletes, Penn consistently gave scholarships to a large number of football players drawn from a state rich with gridiron talent. Among Ivy schools only Cornell, a state-supported school, approached Penn's forty scholarships. Stassen insisted that state scholarships "are not connected with athletics at the University of Pennsylvania in any way." Not convincingly, however. The other Ivy institutions correctly believed that the scholarships created a playing field that titled in Penn's favor.[19]

Understandably, Stassen's victory with honor remarks created deep suspicions because they embodied code words signaling a major gridiron offensive. The laconic H. Jamison Swarts, who had to step aside as athletic director, had been extremely popular in eastern athletic circles, where he was known affectionately as the "collegiate Calvin Coolidge." Immediately, after Penn dismissed Swarts, Columbia and Princeton announced that they would drop Penn from their schedules. While Ivy teams might have to fulfill their existing contracts, it appeared that Penn by 1953 would only be playing Cornell.[20]

If Penn had cared only about profits, its change in policy might have set it apart from the other Ivies. But Yale and Harvard also faced financial difficulties that led to a reshuffling of athletic directors. Both schools suffered through the worst records in their histories in the late 1940s and early 1950s. In 1950 Harvard won only a single game, a record nearly matched by Yale in 1951, when it had two victories. Partially as a result of declining football revenues, each school faced serious athletic deficits. Harvard's policy of endowing its athletics may have contributed to its $350,000 deficit in 1950-51, but Yale could trace its difficulties directly to a decline in football revenues. Yale replaced its athletic director in 1950 as an immediate result of athletic shortfalls; in 1951 Harvard fired Bill Bingham, who had been athletic director since 1928 and whose ill-timed remarks had periodically embarrassed James Conant. Though Bingham's athletic policies scarcely differed from

Conant's, he had presided over Harvard's football decline, and some alumni and journalists blamed him for the Crimson's sorry record. The board of overseers, when they relieved Bingham in February 1951, may have been concerned with finances, but they most certainly reacted to alumni and journalists who blamed Harvard's football woes on the longtime athletic director.[21]

Like Swarts, Bingham lost his job following a poor football season, but Harvard's gridiron decline, which had begun in the early 1930s, made Bingham an easy target. One sportswriter for the *Boston Globe* attacked Bingham for scheduling tougher opponents than the team could handle, failing to encourage bright football players to enter Harvard, and ignoring the players once they reached Cambridge. Another columnist for the *Boston American* taunted Harvard in 1950 for hewing to "blue-nose puritanism" and failing to go after big-time football players. "Harvard has steadily lost its customer trade to mail order institutions," he declared, "who fan the schoolboy bushes for big hairy barbarians and sell them back to the public at top prices." The columnist counseled Conant to skim off the top of Harvard's athletic endowment and tell Bingham to buy the "best schoolboy bulls" by ordering the alumni clubs to beat the bushes for football talent.[22]

While Harvard itself did not tie Bingham's demise to the sorry state of its football, his firing strongly suggests that Harvard needed a sacrificial lamb. In the early 1950s the Big Three still had to worry not only about journalists but also about alumni and boosters who wanted to use aggressive recruiting and subsidies to revive Ivy League football. Some of the well-organized alumni of the Big Three institutions recruited and even sponsored informal practice sessions after spring practice had been outlawed. The head of Yale's graduate advisory committee, who carried the same title as Walter Camp, urged Yale alumni to go out and find players—without offering financial inducements. "There is no occasion," Ted Blair contended, "to sing the undertaker's song for Yale football." In 1951 Conant passed along to Griswold a call to arms by alumni who wanted to follow the example of Princeton. The letter had gone out to Harvard alumni asking, "Are we mice or men?" The alumni had a duty, the writer argued, to recruit "the right type of boys for Harvard" and further declared that "there are too many overstimulated introverts and pinkish weaklings and too few good football players and all around he-men." After describing the success of Princeton's alumni in recruiting players, the writer called on alumni and students to seek out "not just athletes but the outstanding boys of the leading schools— or of a community—and build a bond and continuity of strong interest in these schools." Conant and Griswold had fewer worries about aggressive boosters than most other presidents, but they too had to face a football constituency. The Ivy Group agreements proved attractive because it would give the Big Three presidents an upper hand in dealing with football alumni.[23]

To cure Harvard's woes, the alumni made it clear that the Crimson needed to embark on programs to recruit and subsidize its players, a policy that many alumni and varsity athletes favored. The most successful member of the Big Three, Princeton, had used its alumni to initiate an intensive national gridiron recruiting campaign in the late 1930s, and by the end of 1950 the Tigers ranked seventh in the country, having gone undefeated and produced an All-America halfback in Dick Kazmaier. In 1950 Coach Charlie Caldwell lost sixteen of twenty-two starters, but, thanks to the tried-and-true method of spring drills, was able to prepare his young team for another undefeated season. Once again in 1951, Princeton went undefeated, and Kazmaier, though injured in the late-season Dartmouth game, won the Heisman Trophy. Princeton's use of alumni impressed old grads at Harvard as a touchstone for restoring Harvard's gridiron glories. And Princeton had achieved its high gridiron standing, it was said, without resorting to alumni handouts or underhanded recruiting, or, in other words, hewing to the Ivy League agreements of 1945.[24]

Instead of reviving football, Presidents James Conant of Harvard and A. Whitney Griswold of Yale wanted to isolate themselves from the toxins of big-time athletics. With the possible exception of Columbia, the academic standing of Yale and Harvard's professional schools had placed them far above most of the big-time football institutions, thereby making football less essential as a promotional tool. Moreover, the scandals of 1951 coincided with the era of Cold War witch-hunting, and some Ivy Leaguers came under suspicion, most notably Alger Hiss, a graduate of Harvard, and Robert Oppenheimer, a faculty member at Princeton's Institute of Advanced Studies. Harvard's President Conant believed that athletic scandals had the potential to tarnish the image of higher education, and the Big Three already had to cope with the fallout from the anticommunist investigations. Indeed, President Harold Dodds of Princeton, who had more to lose from de-emphasis, seems to have considered the academic reputation of his institution far more sacred than its high standing in the football polls.[25]

In contrast to the Big Three presidents, Harold Stassen, who hoped to develop closer relationships with his Ivy colleagues, found that Penn's football policies merely placed obstacles in his path. In 1951 Penn scheduled with Notre Dame to play a game the next year in Philadelphia against Notre Dame, a possibility that Stassen had first discussed with Father John Cavanaugh in 1949. In Minnesota, when Stassen was governor, a game between the Irish and the Golden Gophers would have created excitement and anticipation. Among the Ivy League officials it was still another sign that Stassen had sold out to big-time football.[26]

In the summer of 1951 Penn's aggressive television policies created still another controversy that jeopardized its relations with the Ivy Group. When the NCAA decided to adopt a game-of-the-week policy in 1951, Penn refused to comply. Instead, it signed a contract with ABC to televise all of its seven home games. Other Ivy institutions, such as Penn and Columbia, which still had games with Penn, threatened to cancel the contest if Stassen and Murray persisted in their policies to defy the NCAA. "We do not believe that any institution should capitalize [on] an opportunity to go it alone during this experimental period," President Grayson Kirk of Columbia declared.[27]

In July 1951, faced with expulsion from the NCAA, Penn backed down from its position and canceled its TV contract, a move that allowed Penn to keep its few remaining Ivy games and remain in the good graces of the NCAA. Nevertheless, Penn's relations with the Ivy League institutions had reached a low point, and the majority of Ivy members would probably have preferred to expel Penn.[28]

In the fall of 1951, following the West Point and William and Mary scandals, Conant and Griswold accelerated their plan for de-emphasis. In fact, the Ivy eight had already come out against a number of big-time practices including postseason play, but Conant strongly wanted the eight to take a stand on spring practice, an institution that went back to the era of Walter Camp and was strongly endorsed by all of the Ivy coaches. The small colleges like Johns Hopkins and Swarthmore which had downsized their football in the 1930s had banned spring drill, and in the 1940s the nearby Little Three—Amherst, Wesleyan, and Williams—had also ended theirs. So convinced were Conant and Griswold of the need to ban spring practice that they were prepared to withdraw from the Ivy Accords if the other schools failed to ban it.[29]

In spite of their institutions' prestige, neither Conant or Griswold were optimistic about getting the Ivy group to support their position on spring practice. Griswold told Conant in November that he would make a wager. "I will lay you two to one that neither Pennsylvania or Cornell will go along with us." Training young players and welding them into the team required the hours of instruction which only out-of-season practice could provide. Without this interlude to train their teams, coaches argued, players faced greater obstacles in learning their gridiron assignments and would be more prone to injuries. "I strongly disagree with anyone who tells me such as elimination is for the good of football," declared Coach Tuss McLaughry of Dartmouth.[30]

Though Conant pushed hardest for the end of spring practice, Yale accidentally fired the first salvo of Conant and Griswold's new campaign. On November 12, just before the meeting of the presidents' committee of the Ivy Group, Yale's decision to end spring practice leaked out to the press; Conant was to present the proposal at a December meeting of the Ivy institutions. Griswold regretted the damage done by the premature publicity, but the news of Yale's decision probably strengthened Conant's position because it forced schools like Pennsylvania to weigh carefully the pitfalls of opposing the influential presidents of Harvard and Yale.[31]

In early December, when the Ivy members met, the question of spring practice came up for a vote. In order to pass, Ivy Group agreements required at least a 6-2 majority, and it appeared, as Griswold noted, that Pennsylvania and Cornell would almost certainly oppose a change that worked so clearly against their gridiron interests. When the presidents voted, however, the ban on spring practice passed by a bare 6-2 majority, the sixth vote coming unexpectedly from Harold Stassen (Cornell and Princeton cast the only two opposing votes). By aligning himself with Harvard and Yale, Stassen became the arbiter of his institution's academic future.[32]

In exchange for this vote Stassen evidently got a key concession from the Ivy presidents, who passed a rule whereby each Ivy institution would play at least one football contest with each of the others in a five-year cycle. In this way Penn would not have to face the boycott and virtual exclusion from the budding Ivy League. By the same token the Big Three, which had opposed an athletic conference, took the first step toward creating a round-robin competition in what would become the Ivy League.[33]

How exactly did Stassen manage to make a deal with a majority of presidents who held Penn in such contempt? One likely explanation lies in the friendship between Harold Stassen and James Conant. Stassen, who knew Conant from his brief stint of navy service in World War II, enjoyed far closer ties with the Harvard president than with other Ivy presidents. In 1949 he had visited Cambridge to confer with his World War II associate, and, almost alone among the Ivy group, Conant agreed with Penn's position that NCAA television policy violated federal antitrust laws. Conant, who had worked in government during the war, had enough political savvy not to break relations with a major political ally in the Republican Party who was expected seek his party's nomination or would certainly receive a major position in the next Republican administration. How Conant and Stassen might have come to an understanding on spring practice is not difficult to imagine. Conant needed all the votes he could get in order to eliminate spring practice, and Stassen, who faced a boycott by the seven Ivy presidents, was prepared to make a deal. In exchange for Stassen's vote against spring practice, Conant would pave the way for Ivy members to play one another at least once in five years, enabling Stassen to wriggle out of the Ivy boycott.

No doubt Stassen realized that his decision would have profound implications for Pennsylvania's future. Because Penn had pursued gridiron policies in scheduling and television so contrary to its Ivy rivals, all of the Ivy League teams on its 1953 schedule, except for Cornell, stood ready to cancel their games with Penn. If its natural rivals no longer scheduled the Quakers in the sport on which the Ivy League was founded, it is hard to imagine how Penn would have kept its standing as an Ivy school. More likely, it would have slipped into the category of schools like Army which had once played Ivy League competitors but were deliberately kept at arm's length, especially in football, because they were big-time football schools whose athletic practices were highly suspect. In contrast, Penn stood to benefit from the prestige of Harvard, Yale, and Princeton if it joined the Ivy League, whereas it would otherwise be known simply as a highly regarded urban school with big-time athletics which had once played Ivy League schools. Stassen, who was hired to raise money for Penn, probably saw the fund-raising potential of the Ivy connection as outweighing the prestige from big-time athletics.

In the December meetings the presidents strengthened the position that they had taken in 1945 against big-time football and then incorporated all of these into a code of reform which the presidents signed on February 18, 1952. In the Ivy Group agreement the eight institutions formalized the essential provisions of what became the Ivy League. Like the report of the American Council on Education Special Committee, the Ivy Accords honed in on big-time athletics. It was doubtful that a team could play big-time football while hewing to the letter of the Ivy League agreements. The 1952 agreement carefully defined eligibility and spelled out amateur practices of Ivy League schools. Beginning in 1954, no student would be allowed to play whose secondary, college, or graduate education was paid for or promised by an individual or individuals not closely related to the family. The language was carefully designed to halt the practice employed by alumni and boosters at big-name schools who adopted a prospect and then subsidized his education from secondary or postgraduate preparatory schools through college and even graduate school. All of the trappings of big-time football, many of which had been dealt with in the 1945 agreement—spring practice, postseason games, athletic subsidies, clinics for high school coaches, and alumni monetary support—became relics of Ivy League, big-time football history. Whereas the presidents had merely gone on record opposing these practices in 1945, they now outlawed them.[34]

Technically, the Ivy League did not yet exist because the schools had not agreed to play a yearly round-robin. To complicate matters, teams like Pennsylvania already had commitments that reached at least two years into the future. Yet the reason that the 1952 agreements incorporated no plan for an athletic league was that the presidents, especially the Big Three presidents, were not ready to commit themselves to formal competition. Undoubtedly, the lingering suspicion of Penn's big-time plans militated against playing a team that would run up big scores against them every year. After all, Penn had completed a fairly successful season, and no one could have precisely foreseen what effect the ban on spring practice and other big-time practices might have on its ability to compete.

Unfortunately for Penn, the transition from Stassen's big-time gridiron program to amateur Ivy competition turned into a painful postscript to "Victory with Honor." Despite the absence of spring practice, the Quakers began the 1952 season on a high note. In a dramatic last-quarter rally Penn tied Notre Dame, 7-7, in its big game in Philadelphia. Penn also broke Princeton's two-year winning streak, a game that would have marked the final encounter between the schools if Stassen had not reached an understanding with the saintly seven. But, because of the Ivy Group agreements, the 1952 season proved to be the last chance for Penn to achieve its grandiose ambitions. The final seasons of 1954 and 1955 before the round-robin began would turn Penn into carrion for the big-time teams that it had scheduled when it had major league ambitions.[35]

Harold Stassen had taken the presidency of Penn as a springboard from which to launch his campaign for the Republican nomination. By the winter of 1952 he was already preparing for the primaries, in which he lost badly to former Columbia president Dwight Eisenhower, doing far worse than Penn's football team. Stassen's ensuing career, in fact, would parallel the decline of athletics at the institution he once headed. After serving as mutual security advisor in Eisenhower's cabinet, Ike dismissed him when he opposed Richard Nixon's renomination as vice president in 1956. And by the late 1960s he would become the reverse image of the "boy wonder," an old war horse making futile, even ritualistic, stabs at the Republican nomination every four years.

The brief but turbulent era of high-profile, intersectional football soon faded into Penn's gridiron history. Soon after President Gaylord Harnwell took office in 1953, he fired Francis Murray, and, in what proved to be Coach Munger's final season, the team suffered through a losing season, though it still had enough material to win three victories. In the next two years the Quakers lost every game they played, and in 1955 suffered through six shutouts and were outscored 270-34.[36]

Penn's collapse occurred just after the Ivy Group agreed in February 1954 to create an athletic conference in which the members would play one another every year. The "once-every-five-years" clause had conditioned the teams to the idea of regular, if infrequent, play, and by 1954 the best teams, such as Penn and Princeton, had declined to the level of their natural rivals. As late as January 1954, Dean McGeorge Bundy, later a major architect of Vietnam War policy under Presidents Kennedy and Johnson, wondered if Harvard really wanted to schedule Pennsylvania, a team it had not defeated since the early 1900s. Nevertheless, the presidents agreed to a round-robin schedule that would begin in 1956, allowing the members two years to fulfill the obligations already in place, a mixed blessing for a team with a fearsome schedule such as Penn. The Ivy League now went into virtual isolation, playing in the equivalent of a small-college conference and avoiding nearly all of the contaminants of big-time football.[37]

Viewed from one perspective, the Ivy League represented the most dramatic example of de-emphasis in college football's history—eight schools that agreed to play by strictly amateur standards and to allow their football to tumble into virtual oblivion. Though the Ivies have excelled in other sports such as hockey, basketball, and lacrosse, they never again fielded more than an occasional gridiron team that could have competed successfully in a mid-level conference. With their big stadiums such as Yale Bowl and Franklin Field, they had the trappings of big-time football but never the substance. Though their movement toward de-emphasis occurred independent of the ACE proposals, they epitomized the spirit of strictly amateur athletics embodied in the ACE Special Committee report released within a few days of the other. Since each of these documents, strictly speaking, came into being immediately after the scandals of 1951, the similarities should come as no surprise.

At another level Harvard and Yale's de-emphasis of football, which led to the Ivy League, reflected a reaction to problems that afflicted other institutions in the era. While economic problems that grew out of athletic shortfalls do not entirely explain the need to de-emphasize, they do provide a piece of the puzzle. Failing football at Yale in 1951 and even at Harvard, where endowed athletics could not support high-priced football, created an urgent need for new policies. Given the paucity of alternatives, the policy of downsizing football seems to have made sense to most of the presidents.

Put simply, the eastern schools could never have justified athletic subsidies either ideologically or financially. Though no one dared to discuss it, the cost of athletic scholarships at private eastern institutions would not only have proved exorbitant but also would have necessitated massive alumni and booster assistance. Instead, the Ivy League institutions ended up providing academic scholarships to promising athletes with solid records and giving a boost to applicants at the low end of the list who happened to play football.

In the 1950s, as Bill Bingham's demise demonstrated, Ivy League presidents still had to worry about journalists, boosters, and alumni who wanted to use aggressive recruiting and subsidies to revive Ivy League football. Yet the Ivy League had always contained an element of make-believe, a league that existed in newspaper standings long before it came into being. Just as Harvard and Yale had previously withdrawn from rowing in the 1870s when they could not longer compete, the Ivy League de-emphasis provided a dignified way to escape the evils and excesses of big-time football. Indeed, the notion of natural rivals who had competed in football since the 1870s and 1880s conjured up football traditions unparalleled at any set of institutions. The Ivies created a league of gridiron has-beens but one that kept alive institutional loyalties and rivalries that would prove useful in enlivening alumni clubs and bringing old grads back to the campuses. On the other hand, de-emphasis enabled them to fend off the worst of the alumni janissaries, such as Princeton's "oldest living graduate" in the early 1900s, by playing a far less serious brand of minor league ball.

Midwestern Ivy: John Millis and the PAC

The Ivy League presidents in 1951 staged the most dramatic example of multiple de-emphasis, but they did not stand alone. In other parts of the country presidents of private institutions wondered how they could reconcile the decline in performance and revenues with the credo of strictly amateur athletics. One of the institutions that played an instrumental role in midwestern de-emphasis proved to be Western Reserve of Cleveland, whose president, John Millis, had served on the ACE Special Committee. Like Harvard and Yale, Western Reserve faced an impasse born of defeat and shortfalls in football revenue and needed a way to ease out of big-time competition. Probably more than any president on the committee, Millis converted his committee service into a solution for his institution's problems.

When Millis returned from his stint on the Special Committee in 1952, his mind was filled with possibilities for reforms at his school and those around it. Western Reserve football had reached its moment of decision, and Millis had come up an alternative. As a former prep school football coach, Millis headed an institution that played in the Mid-American Conference (MAC), created in 1946. The Mid-American had begun as a group of five largely urban and private institutions—Western Reserve, Wayne of Detroit, Cincinnati, Butler of Indianapolis, and Ohio University—all supposedly with the same standards and strengths and all committed to the same ideals.

In the ACE meetings Millis had given a clue to his approach toward athletics when he observed that conditions varied too much from school to school for a comprehensive program like the Sanity Code to work effectively. Not unlike Georgetown, Western Reserve's football had declined so that deficits placed its program in dire straits. It faced a lack of interest in its deteriorating gridiron program, born of defeat as much as of television. And it had to contend with the popularity of professional football after World War II; the Cleveland Browns won the NFL championship in 1950, the team's first year in the league.[38]

Between 1946 and 1953 the character of the Mid-American Conference changed markedly. To be precise, the conference admitted state schools— Kent State, Bowling Green, and Miami of Ohio—which had burgeoning student populations and often fielded teams more powerful than those in the bottom rungs of the Big Ten. Stung by one-sided losses in its own conference and plagued by chronic deficits, Western Reserve once again considered dropping football. Successive committees of alumni, faculty, and trustees concluded that the Cleveland institution had a satisfactory athletic relationship with its Mid-American rivals and should not drop back to a small-college schedule or abandon football altogether. As it struggled to find a financial solution, Western Reserve continued to pay tuition waivers and housing subsidies to as many as seventy-five athletes, but to what end it became harder to say.[39]

Ironically, one of the institutions whose athletic policies led to Western Reserve's pathetic performance in the Mid-American turned out to be Cincinnati, whose president had first proposed an intercity league conference just before the war. Like Western Reserve, Cincinnati suffered from athletic deficits in the early 1950s. Since some Mid-American football teams attracted few spectators, Cincinnati wanted the conference to allow it to play as few as four conference games, which would enable the Bearcats to schedule more big-time, moneymaking games. When the conference refused, Cincinnati withdrew from the Mid-American but for reasons that had all the earmarks of a big-time competitor. Initially seen as natural rivals, the two private urban institutions in Ohio's two largest cities went into entirely different orbits.[40]

In contrast, many Reserve alumni looked back to their small-time past, or, more accurately, to the era of the "Big Four," by which they meant the not-so-big Cleveland area schools—Baldwin Wallace College, Case Institute of Technology, John Carroll University, and Western Reserve. One alumnus scornfully flayed the policy of playing "academic equals" in the Mid-American Conference. "Let's get our head out of the clouds," he wrote President Millis, "and revive the Big Four and this time really promote it."[41]

Arvel Erickson, a former athlete and history professor who headed Western Reserve's athletic committee, made a compelling argument against remaining in the Mid-American Conference. Besides the inequities in size and resources, he pointed out, Western Reserve kept its enrollment at a comparatively low level of nine hundred male students. Western Reserve simply placed more emphasis on academics, beginning with its admission policies, while the state schools could be less selective and attract a far stronger class of athletes.[42]

But Western Reserve was not the only Cleveland team to suffer from the woes that afflicted urban schools. In January 1954 Western Reserve's ancient rival and Cleveland neighbor, Case Tech, quit football. Case faced a lack of interest among the students, athletic deficits, and an absence of clear direction about the future of intercollegiate football. Diehard students at Case held a funeral procession and burial ceremony. The procession was led by a car filled with flowers, followed by a hearse, and capped off by an ROTC honor guard. Football players serving as pallbearers removed the coffin from the hearse. A monument elegantly garlanded with floral wreaths, though weighing more than a ton, was placed in front of the Case campus.

The inscription read, "To the Spirit of Case Football, 1891–1954. A Gift from Those Who Cared."[43]

Unlike the many other schools that quit football in the early 1950s, Case was fortunate to have a traditional rival that had a plan for football de-emphasis. Amid the gloom a shaft of sunlight appeared. Case football only needed a few electric shocks to revive it, and John Millis, playing a benevolent Dr. Frankenstein, helped to accomplish that miracle. His new proposal took advantage of alumni nostalgia for Cleveland's Big Four and the desire to revive a rivalry that had once stirred local interest. Millis's goal was to convert the rivalry into a conference based on the principles of the ACE's Special Committee or, as he staunchly insisted, strict amateurism.

Millis and the president of Case, T. Keith Glennan, sketched out the plan for a conference that would recreate a more old-fashioned, and less expensive, version of regional football. The newly minted conference was dubbed the "Presidents' Athletic Conference" (PAC) reflecting the commitment to presidential control which also characterized the Ivy League. The presidents agreed to meet twice a year to set policy, and, while faculty athletic committees could participate, they would play a strictly advisory role. The policies were to emanate from the presidents.

Like the Ivy Group, the Presidents' Athletic Conference banned recruiting and subsidizing of athletes. Athletes were to be students who happened to play on intercollegiate teams. The athletic departments would no longer ask students to work for their support or force them to practice, work, and then study. The bylaws stated clearly that students, even athletes, came to college primarily for academics. The presidents followed the ACE proposals for eliminating spring practice and postseason games. Coaches became members of the faculty and would qualify for tenure if the institution permitted.[44]

In this way Millis and his three colleagues removed their institutions from big-time athletics, engineering a change of philosophy and practice just as profound as the Ivy League's. Once again, as in the 1920s and early 1930s, Western Reserve had become not only a small-college team but also a school that had a strong commitment to a body of principles. This principled, strictly amateur approach provided a means for Western Reserve and John Millis to abandon a failed, twenty-year experiment at a higher level of athletic competition.

The conference that Millis built in 1954 led to the revival of football in Cleveland (one of the old Big Four, Baldwin Wallace, bowed out and was replaced by Wayne of Detroit). Unlike the Ivy League, however, the Presidents' Athletic Conference would not stand out as a well-known or enduring achievement. The PAC proved harder to solidify than the Ivy League. The conference hoped to strengthen its base by expanding to eight members and instituting a round-robin competition like the Ivy League's. As the

PAC expanded, most of the new members came from the ranks of small, private colleges located in Pennsylvania, West Virginia, or eastern Ohio, including Bethany, Washington and Jefferson, and Allegheny, and the axis of the conference shifted east toward Pittsburgh.

The bedrock of stability which held the Ivy institutions in place—history, longtime competition, relative equality in their undergraduate bodies and, to some extent, the resources to pay for athletic travel—simply did not exist in the PAC. As a result of the lengthy commute between Wayne in Michigan to Allegheny near Pittsburgh, the conference had to drop the round-robin competition in football. The vast difference in enrollments, ranging from fewer than a thousand to more than fifteen thousand, led to a rule allowing the smaller schools to play freshmen, a change at variance with the ACE proposals. President Clarence Hillberry of Wayne State declared that "we cannot live with the great disparity between our size and complexity, the comparative size and character of our small college members, and lack of appropriate satisfaction from athletic contests."[45]

While the tiger of football acrimony never devoured the PAC, Hillberry's complaints highlighted the dissatisfaction felt by one of the charter members. Wayne State of Detroit, a working-class institution in Detroit, should have fit perfectly into John Millis's scheme. Wayne had a strong tradition of amateur athletics instilled by its original athletic director, David Holmes, and was one of the schools praised for its clean athletic policies by no less than the formidable John Tunis. Barely competitive, its teams had now fallen on even harder times, and the small colleges attacked them in a particularly bloodthirsty way. "I at least worry about John Carroll feeling that they must wipe the earth with us," Hillberry complained after the Carroll football coach had run up the score against Wayne. Eventually, Wayne withdrew.[46]

The de-emphasis of football at institutions like Western Reserve saved the sport from the demise that had occurred at Chicago, Georgetown, and very nearly Case Tech. In most of these urban institutions financial shortfalls in football had led to the athletic crossroads at which the schools had to decide whether to de-emphasize or abandon the gridiron. By the same token these same institutions simply could not field big-time, high-profile teams without resorting to strong alumni and booster recruiting or full scholarships that were far more expensive at private than public institutions. As a result, the schools took the high road of reform which enabled them to avoid big-time expenses and play a game in which they did not have to cheat. Though other schools like Johns Hopkins had begun their athletic de-emphasis much earlier, the scandals of 1951 had supplied the catalyst for the Presidents' Athletic Conference.

Because the Ivy League institutions wrapped themselves so completely in the dazzling mantle of strictly amateur athletics, observers have sometimes overlooked the pressures that they faced in 1951, which were similar to those at other private institutions. The Ivy institutions, however, had deeper traditions than other schools and were able to exploit athletic loyalties that simply did not exist in other conferences or regions. Nationally known for academics, they never had to apologize for mediocre football teams. Unlike mid-sized private institutions like Northwestern, Rice, and Vanderbilt, they escaped becoming whipping boys for state institutions in big-time conferences. While alumni continued to play a part in their recruiting, the Ivy League without the pressure cooker of big-time football avoided the booster scandals of higher-profile athletic institutions. Ivy League football proved to be a convenient place to deposit alumni who might otherwise have become a problem for their schools.

Though de-emphasis had its limitations, it nevertheless reflected the changes brought on by the scandals of 1951 and the need to adapt to rapidly changing economic conditions. Demise and de-emphasis were merely one face of the athletic crisis whose effects would be felt throughout the 1950s. While a minority of schools found the solution in downsizing, the bulk of the big-time teams would be committed to the flip side of de-emphasis, or, more precisely, to methods of enlarging their football revenues.

PART THREE

Half-Truths & Halting Reforms

CHAPTER FOURTEEN

The Flight from Disorder: Big-Time Football in Postwar America

In the early 1950s a worst-case scenario might have read like this: the NCAA lacked authority after its failure to enforce the Sanity Code and to enforce standards for college football. Booster clubs flourished whose activities mocked attempts at national reform such as the ACE's special committee report. Television threatened to trigger a decline in college football attendance which would jeopardize the college athletic machine's biggest moneymaker. Put simply, if college football failed, the NCAA would recede into the obscurity that had marked its first forty years. Small college football would soon go out of business, and big-time football would return to its traditional policy of institutional autonomy—that is, if anyone would pay to attend.

The marvel of the 1950s proved to be that television, football, and the NCAA all emerged as winners, a turnabout from the early years of the decade, when television stood poised, it seemed, to ravage college football. More precisely, TV sets, which numbered seven million by 1950 and whose numbers were climbing exponentially, had already cut into all sports. Drastic solutions were called for, but no one knew exactly what to do or if television really would damage football in a way that radio threatened to do in the 1930s.

The TV Threat

Debate over the effects of electronic media had begun with radio in the early years of the Depression. In college football the primary question, aside from the conflict with amateur standards, was whether radio would reduce live attendance. Most colleges were grateful even for the pitifully small revenues from radio broadcasts and pleased when it became clear that radio probably encouraged rather than discouraged attendance.

In contrast, in the years just before World War II the new high-tech phenomenon of television presented little more than an interesting topic for speculation. The earliest prewar telecasts took place in the New York and Philadelphia areas, where the infant television industry emerged. As it turned out, the first full-fledged football game—as opposed to team workouts—was telecast on September 30, 1939, when Fordham defeated Waynesburg of Pennsylvania, 34-7. Given the several thousand televisions in the

New York area, it is likely that few people viewed the game at all, let alone in the privacy of their living rooms. Indeed, the images conveyed on the lone iconoscope camera at the forty-yard line were undoubtedly crude as measured by later standards. Nevertheless, a radio reviewer for the *New York Times* shrewdly discerned that television could offer a distinct advantage because the viewer could see the game more clearly and comfortably. "Television," he declared, "invites audience participation. It is in the living room; the spectator is edged up close; his eye is right in the game." He wondered why spectators would ever want to attend games on rainy or frigid afternoons. Only the black-and-white uniforms, which made the teams virtually indistinguishable on pre-color TV, contrasted unfavorably with the live experience, or so the novelty of the experience led him to write.[1]

The *Times* reviewer wrote that a youthful companion—probably his son—wondered why anyone would pay to see games when they could stay at home and see them for free. In 1949 this prewar prediction returned to haunt college football, as attendance at college football games began to drop off after its dramatic postwar surge. In 1949 the total attendance of 12,398,157 marked a 1.3 percent increase over the bumper crop of the previous year, but the regional declines proved more newsworthy than the record national figure. In the East and Far West, where big-time teams and large urban populations existed, football fell by 2.5 and 2.2 percent, small percentages that raised red flags because attendance had risen so consistently since the mid-1930s.[2]

The NCAA and the Big Ten both saw cause for alarm in the attendance figures, as did professional football. The NCAA appointed a television committee to study the problem and then hired the National Opinion Research Center, or NORC, to conduct a survey of football viewing habits for a robust sum of fifty thousand dollars, a figure that was split with the three major networks. The Big Ten, which had seen a slight increase in attendance, regarded the inroads of television as a major threat and mandated a blackout of all live telecasts in 1950. Probably the most persuasive demonstration of television's power to reshape viewing habits came in 1950, when the NFL's Los Angeles Rams experimented with freely televising their home games. Attendance plummeted from 205,109 to 110,262, a drop of nearly 16,000 for each home game. Delegates to the NCAA convention in January 1951 would have read of these startling figures, even though they refused to dignify pro football by including it in their discussions. What they would not have known but might have intuited was that attendance would rebound, in the case of the Rams to 234,110 in 1951, when the team blacked-out its home games.[3]

By the end of the 1950 season the NORC had completed its first study in time for the NCAA's 1951 season, and the results were alarming enough. In all but the Southwest, Plains, and Rocky Mountains a substantial group of college football fans who could now sit at home and watch games on TV for free had apparently stopped attending games. In New England the drop had amounted to a devastating 28 percent. On the other hand, outside TV areas attendance had actually risen by 13 percent where teams won more than half of their games. Though the total drop amounted to less than one-half of one percent, the trends proved disturbing because of television's rapid growth and the inability of most teams, like Notre Dame, to command large figures to telecast their games.[4]

Television had matured so quickly that the slow growth of radio in the 1920s and 1930s provided little precedent for the new phenomena. Schools such as Notre Dame and Penn which signed contracts to televise their games found that TV could provide a lucrative stream of income. Nevertheless, institutions with large stadiums built in the 1920s had to depend almost entirely on live attendance. In 1950 Notre Dame harvested $160,000 in TV revenue, and Penn had negotiated a $100,000 contract with ABC to televise all of its home games in 1950. Most institutions, however, had to settle for considerably less, since they normally televised only their four or five home games and had a far smaller television audience.[5]

At the annual convention in January 1951 the NCAA devoted much of its time to the threat of televised football. The TV committee had the results of the first NORC study, which pictured television as an invading army. "For all those colleges in areas where 30 percent or more of families own television sets," Tom Hamilton of the television committee reported, "attendance was off 10 percent for all colleges. Outside those areas, either no television at all or less than 30 per cent of set owners, it was up 10.7 per cent." Attendance at small colleges, he declared, had eroded by 7.2 percent, a full three percentage points worse than major colleges in TV areas, and this applied to both TV and non-TV areas.[6]

On the afternoon of January 12, 1951, the business meeting, which was about to bury the Sanity Code once and for all, took up the resolution to ban live telecasts. The only dissent came from Francis Murray of Pennsylvania, who pointed out that Penn had televised its games since 1940 and felt confident that live television could promote college football. Murray insisted that banning live telecasts would not necessarily increase NCAA gate receipts. The Penn athletic director, who probably spoke for Notre Dame as well, argued that it was crucial not to break off its contacts with live television. "If you don't keep abreast and go on when you have your foot in the door," he declared, "you won't have a precedent to form an opinion."[7]

Nevertheless, the motion giving the TV committee almost blank-check powers swept the convention by a 161-7 vote. Given the intense distaste for centralized control embodied in the Sanity Code vote, the support for the iron-clad television resolution raises some puzzling questions. The southern institutions, which had shot the Sanity Code full of holes and would soon dispose of what was left, formed a solid phalanx of support for the ban on telecasts. The South had seen a 5 percent rise in live attendance, but in TV areas this rate of increase amounted to merely half the gain elsewhere. In other words, less populated areas such as the Southwest and the Plains, where television had not yet eaten into live attendance, the solid support was even more remarkable. To put it bluntly, the NORC report had painted such a grim picture that few schools were willing to gamble their gridiron futures on half-measures. As for the large number of small colleges, they faced a bleak TV future and would have suffered as a result of the freely televised big games of their big-time neighbors.[8]

Yet the NCAA did not close the door on media alternatives. Other possibilities did exist at the time, such as pay-for-view and theater television, which the committee resolved to investigate. These innovations would have provided an alternative to the blackout policy, and the NCAA's council discussed them when it met in March 1951. Like cable TV in a later era, phonevision employed telephone lines; telemeter attached a coin deposit meter to the television to unscramble the picture; and Skiatron used plastic tickets to obtain the telecast. All of these measures, which had commercial possibilities, lacked the sophisticated programming to compete with free TV. The NCAA did experiment with paid telecasts in movie theaters beginning in 1951 and later with subscription TV, but none of these media could compete with "free" network television.[9]

Initially, the NCAA's motion had called for a blackout of all live telecasts, but the TV committee used its blank check to fashion a controlled policy. Fearing public reaction and possibly influenced by the networks, the NCAA scaled back its total blackout policy. The NCAA allowed the Westinghouse Corporation to televise games throughout most of the season, permitting a few minutes of free time for the NCAA to publicize its efforts on behalf of amateur athletics. The TV committee still planned to experiment with selective blackouts to determine if no television would lure spectators back to the stadiums. And on November 10 it planned to have a national blackout to determine whether the entire country would return to live football if the televised football disappeared for a week.[10]

In its initial blackout policy the NCAA would find itself edging perilously close to ringing an alarm in the antitrust division of the Justice Department. Already, in a suit initiated by television broadcasters, the NFL faced a challenge to its blackout policies, though that case would not be decided for another year. Two institutions that had much to lose from the TV blackouts, the University of Pennsylvania and Notre Dame, objected in 1951 to the NCAA's TV policy. Both schools had freely televised their games in previous years and had enlarged their lineup of games for the coming season. In addition to its contract with ABC to televise eight home games in 1951, Penn's athletic director, Francis Murray, had negotiated a three-year contract with Du Mont, a smaller network set up by the TV manufacturer Allen Du Mont, for which Penn would receive a total of $850,000 for telecasts of its eight home games. Network contracts, which were in their infancy, promised a windfall for teams that could offer a full schedule or could appeal to a national audience. Located in the section that had by far the most television sets, Penn had a built-in advantage bested only by Notre Dame, which could draw upon a national audience.[11]

In May and June 1951 both Penn president Harold Stassen and athletic director Francis Murray tried to convince the NCAA to change its policy, and Murray appealed to friends in the Justice Department, where he had worked during World War II, to investigate the antitrust implications of the television committee's plans. Stassen went so far as to propose his own plan for local stations rather than the NCAA to negotiate with the schools; he also sugared his plan with a proposal for four blackout Saturdays, two on a local basis and two for the entire nation, which the NCAA rejected. When Murray and Stassen refused to change Penn's plans for full and free TV coverage of all its games, the NCAA declared Penn in violation of its policies and warned the schools that were scheduled to play Penn that they would find themselves, like Penn, "not in good standing."[12]

Notre Dame's Father John Cavanaugh, who charged the NCAA with "dictatorial powers," had much at stake in 1951. Since the 1930s Notre Dame had used its nationwide radio football network to promote the institution as well as to push up gridiron revenues. When television arrived, telecasts of the powerful Irish teams meant larger returns in gridiron dollars and free publicity. Notre Dame, while it would not harvest much more than the $160,000 in 1950, had extracted from its carrier, the Du Mont television network, the right to insert features on Notre Dame's educational programs which would help to lessen its stereotype as a largely football and religious institution.

Regarded with fear and distrust by the Big Ten because of its TV policies, Notre Dame, through President Cavanaugh, received faintly disguised warnings from the powerful Big Ten commissioner, Kenneth "Tug" Wilson. Wilson threatened that the conference would boycott the Fighting Irish if they refused to drop their policy of unrestricted telecasts. Instead of confronting the NCAA directly, Cavanaugh and the vice president in charge of athletics, Theodore Hesburgh, waited to see what would happen to Penn and reluctantly accepted the NCAA decision. The Notre Dame president later calculated that the TV blackout for 1951 cost his school at least a half-million dollars in lost revenues for its three-year contracts and incalculable possibilities to publicize its institution.[13]

In May 1951 President Harold Stassen announced that Penn would abide by the NCAA decisions provided that the Justice Department had declared it consistent with antitrust laws. In fact, he was waiting for a Justice Department opinion that would force the NCAA to step back from its policy of restrictive viewing. To put Penn in the best light he even proposed a plan whereby the institutions would voluntarily refrain from televising twice nationally and twice locally during the season. Unfortunately for Penn, the NCAA's president, Hugh Willett, gave the school until July 19 to drop its opposition or to face expulsion from the NCAA, a deadline that would have precluded any action by the Justice Department even if its antitrust division had decided to investigate. Unlike Virginia and Maryland's opposition to the Sanity Code, Penn had virtually no support from either the Ivy League, the larger Eastern Collegiate Athletic Conference (ECAC), or from fellow NCAA members. When the Justice Department failed to intervene, Murray announced on July 19 that Penn would break its agreement with ABC, return its $80,000 advance on a $100,000 contract, and comply with the NCAA. The NCAA's victory over Penn not only enabled the association to proceed with its TV policies but also allowed it to flex its muscle for the first time since failing to expel the Sinful Seven. For Penn the failure to realize its TV ambitions provided still another reason to align itself with the Ivy League schools in December 1951.[14]

In the fall of 1951 the NCAA's TV policy nearly led to political repercussions and once again brought it to the attention of the Justice Department. College football blackouts became a grassroots issue that resulted in politicians delivering anti-NCAA tirades. On November 10, 1951, Michigan State was scheduled to play Notre Dame in a game that the NCAA had not scheduled for telecast. One week after the NCAA had refused to televise a big game between Michigan and Illinois, Representative Gerald Ford of Michigan, a former University of Michigan star and the future president, announced that he would wire the head of the television committee, Ralph Furey, to protest the NCAA's rejection of a Detroit station's request to televise the game. Since the game was sold out, Furey then reversed his position and announced that the game would be televised. In a blatantly political move the NCAA also announced that it would waive its blackout of football telecasts in Washington on November 10 as a favor to politicians like Ford and football fans among the trustbusters in the Justice Department, a sign that politicians and the media could bully the NCAA. Evidently, the NCAA's TV committee had second thoughts about persisting in an unpopular pigskin blackout in a politically sensitive area like the District of Columbia.[15]

Later in the month the NCAA faced another blizzard of protests when it refused to televise Kentucky and Tennessee, a sold-out game between two top Southeastern Conference teams that were scheduled to play in Knoxville. Matchups involving flagship universities in adjacent states had undeniable appeal, but the blackout did not carry the same weighty implications of withholding a midwestern game in the nation's capital, especially one involving Notre Dame. Nevertheless, a television station, WHAS-TV, together with the *Louisville Courier Journal,* tried to enlist the support of Governor Lawrence Wetherby of Kentucky, who wired the attorney general of the United States, Howard McGrath, to protest what he called a "conspiracy." The governor complained that the NCAA had made a last-minute, arbitrary decision so that viewers could watch Notre Dame and Michigan State. The head of the antitrust division in his reply sounded the death knell for government intervention. While he mentioned the antitrust case against NFL blackouts, he ruled out action against the NCAA until the courts had rendered a decision, an answer that failed to change the status of the Kentucky-Tennessee game.[16]

On the day before, buoyed by a flurry of four hundred irate telegrams, the TV station planned to defy the NCAA ban, but the University of Kentucky refused to go along. Authorities at Kentucky had good reason to refrain from irritating the NCAA; the association was contemplating drastic action against Kentucky's national championship basketball program because its players had cooperated with gamblers in shaving points, one of the most notorious of the point-shaving scandals of 1951.

The NCAA's TV committee had already lost credibility when it did a turnabout on November 17. Viewed in political terms, the states of Kentucky and Tennessee in 1951 simply did not possess the same clout as the highly populated Midwest. As Paul Lawrence has noted, the NCAA used the Kentucky protest to reclaim some credibility for its blackout policies and to wield its authority over a state and institution that had far less influence than Gerald Ford or Notre Dame alumni.[17]

In truth the courts later gave an almost blanket approval to the blackout policy of the NFL in a landmark case that would affect amateur and professional sports. Federal Judge Alan Grim ruled in 1953 that professional football was a "unique type of business" in which unrestrained competition would lead to the strong teams driving the weak out of business, thereby weakening competition. While he limited the commissioner's more arbitrary powers, such as banning radio broadcasts, the thrust of the court's reasoning suggested that college football blackout policy actually promoted competition by protecting the smaller, weaker, and less popular teams.[18]

Viewed broadly, the 1951 TV plan, which sought to erect a wall against the ravages of television, enjoyed mixed success. In spite of the blackouts, total attendance dropped by 6 percent from the previous year, a worse decline than in 1950. The TV committee put the best face on its experiment by observing that colleges in TV-infested areas such as New England enjoyed a less precipitous decline than in 1950. What they glossed over was a far more disturbing and contradictory trend: colleges without TV competition had lower attendance, by two percentage points, which indicated a much broader decline. Moreover, the Southeast and Southwest, which had strongly supported the TV mandate, saw their attendance in both TV and non-TV areas decline at roughly the same rate. If anything, the results suggested that the TV ban had little effect except in those areas such as the Northeast, where television was deeply rooted.[19]

The figures for 1951 proved alarming enough that the TV committee decided to apply stronger medicine. In 1951 NBC had broadcast only three coast-to-coast telecasts; most of the games were local or regional telecasts that seemed to siphon off live attendance. In 1952 the NCAA went to a more draconian policy of scheduling only one national game each week, an attempt to boost attendance and to demonstrate to the Justice Department that the televised games did not compete with local games or at least they did only occasionally. Whereas a Notre Dame–Michigan State game threatened to keep people at home, a contest between Kansas and Texas Christian telecast to all sections of the country would be so far removed from most football fans as to encourage support for local teams—or to divert sports fans to alternate forms of entertainment. While there would be some big games such as Army-Navy, the NCAA would attempt to cover all regions of the country and give no team more than one chance to appear. This policy would reduce the number of games from twenty to twelve, and the number of schools that participated would drop from thirty to twenty-four.[20]

In the meantime the third and most comprehensive NORC report, released in the spring of 1952, seemed to confirm that college football suffered in areas where it competed with television. While television might not hurt the attendance of big-time teams like Ohio State, it appeared to erode the gate receipts of mediocre and poor teams. According to the survey, it had a devastating effect on small-college teams, and, since the small colleges made up the largest single voting block in the NCAA, the association could not easily allow telecasts of big-college games to drive the small-college programs into bankruptcy. Interviews with football viewers also proved to be a cause of alarm. The hands of athletic directors might well have trembled slightly when they read that younger viewers under forty tended to watch football in their living rooms, whereas it was the older football fans who still trudged to the stadiums.[21]

The two areas that suffered least in 1951 were the Midwest and the West Coast. Whereas the Midwest's figures held up remarkably well in both TV and non-TV areas, the West Coast showed a dramatic resurgence in areas where television had eroded attendance. The 1 percent gain in TV areas following a 9 percent drop from the 1947–48 base years, the high tide of college football attendance, seemed to show that football in Los Angeles, San Francisco, and Seattle had prospered. In contrast, teams in non-TV areas, which likely included large areas of the Pacific Northwest, had not done nearly as well, since a 2.5 percent gain had turned into a 10 percent disaster for those unfortunate teams.[22]

These demographics of football in the Big Ten and Pacific Coast Conferences would influence attitudes not only regarding television but also toward the major teams' less prominent competitors. The Big Ten rapidly emerged from its panicky "ban all telecasts" policy and tried to get the NCAA to relax its approach toward regional games. Because of its cohesiveness and the popularity of its football, the Big Ten had a strong influence on athletic politics in the postwar era. In the 1950s the Big Ten, allied with the PCC, had less competition for athletic leadership in the NCAA than it would ever again enjoy. New England football had declined or, in the case of the Ivy League, retreated into an inconspicuous corner of the athletic galaxy; the southern and southwestern schools played strong football but still belonged to the section of the country with less population, wealth, and political power. The Big Seven of the Plains States had not yet come of age, and the other conferences simply could not compete.

The coaches and athletic directors of the Big Ten and Pacific Coast Conferences had concluded by the end of the 1953 season that they had too few telecasts and began to seek a new TV plan that would feature a number of regional games. The national game of the week created not just a monotonously rigid format but also kept big teams from obtaining the revenues and exposure necessary for recruiting. In short the Big Ten advocates of television reform had strong backing from both the public and the institutions. Athletic directors such as Michigan's influential Fritz Crisler appreciated that considerable grassroots demand for regional games existed in the Midwest and chose to exploit it. Already angry legislators had introduced bills in Illinois and Minnesota to allow more frequent telecasts of their favorite big-time schools. Crisler himself would testify before the Ohio and Michigan legislatures to persuade them not to pursue this avenue, but he also used the threat of political intervention at the NCAA convention to lobby for a regional plan.[23]

In 1954 the Big Ten asked to try a regional experiment, but the TV committee refused to jeopardize its defenses against television by permitting this breach in the dike. At the January 1955 convention Crisler employed the canny tactic of wondering aloud how long the Big Ten could hold out against the successful TV policies of the NFL. No doubt Crisler, who had played under Amos Alonzo Stagg at Chicago and coached in the 1930s when pro football still was the poor and maligned stepchild of the college game, had no love for professional football. Ever the realist, however, he correctly observed that professional ratings had been climbing, while college football's had been on the wane.[24]

The determination of Michigan to break through the television barrier did not stop with Crisler. In 1954, before the NCAA conference, the president of Michigan, Harlan Hatcher, hinted that, if the NCAA did not allow regional telecasts, the Big Ten might secede. This threat was echoed by the

Pacific Coast Conference, an odd turnabout from the Sanity Code controversy in 1950, when the southern institutions had threatened to withdraw. In a nutshell, the merest possibility of losing two major conferences that played some of the best football in the country and were located in several highly populated areas had its desired effect. In 1955 the TV committee devised a new plan that kept a national game of the week for eight weeks but singled out five Saturdays in which there would be regional games.[25]

If the college football decline had persisted, the NCAA might have rebelled against the regional scheme. Yet the Big Ten and the NCAA had instituted their restricted TV program when television threatened the worst possible scenario, and their blackout policies seemed to have proved successful. Only a few dissidents, including Francis Murray of Penn and Father Edmund Joyce of Notre Dame, whose interests would be benefited by unrestricted TV, suggested that television might actually increase football attendance as radio had in the 1930s. In truth live telecasts in the early 1950s seemed like a raging bull in a carefully crafted gridiron emporium, and, while football attendance turned up slightly in 1951, supporters of limited access were keenly aware that the figures remained well below the record numbers of 1948 and 1949.

Happily, the revenues from television, which rose from $1,250,000 in 1955 to more than $3 million in 1960, eased some of the pain; both the schools that appeared on TV as well as the nonparticipating schools received a share of the spoils—as did the NCAA. In a truly remarkable turn of events, what was regarded as a scourge of television turned into a nest egg for the NCAA, enabling the association to expand its staff and to create a far more effective law enforcement arm.[26]

The Triumph of the NCAA

To see the turnabout in big-time sports, it might prove helpful to return to 1952, when the American Council of Education had called upon the accrediting agencies to implement its program, and the North Central Association of Colleges and Secondary Schools had sounded its clarion call. To be sure, the ACE had said nothing of television, nor did the North Central care much about a medium that had so far proved more of a danger than a fillip to big-time sports. What the North Central did care about was athletics at big-time institutions in the Midwest, and the players in the accrediting drama turned out to be some of the same institutions that had influenced NCAA television policy.

Beginning in 1953, the North Central sought to restore a model of athletics so excruciatingly strict that the networks would have soon discarded the game of the week. One index of the North Central's attitude toward college sports appeared in an issue of the *North Central Journal* planned in 1953 and published the next year. The North Central devoted space to eight largely small colleges that had de-emphasized athletics in the 1930s and 1940s. The lineup of articles featured the athletic programs at Harvard, Haverford, Swarthmore, MIT, Oberlin, Johns Hopkins, and the University of Chicago. All of those institutions had programs strictly in line with the ACE proposals.[27]

The North Central envisioned athletics in the Midwest and middle states which would have resembled tennis or water polo at a major university rather than big-time football. Using a velvet glove, the North Central adopted a set of rigorous standards and threatened to use its accrediting power to force its members to downsize their football. The association clearly wanted the major football schools to eliminate athletic ability or potential as a factor in awarding scholarships. Because it believed that colleges existed to educate rather than to entertain, the North Central would not allow a student's athletic ability to be a factor in granting financial aid. This stand-ard for admitting students who played sports would have proved more restrictive than the ACE's code for recruiting, which condemned financial inducements but did not rule out athletic potential when combined with academic credentials. Charles Eliot or Frederick Jackson Turner could easily have written the North Central regulation.[28]

At its annual meeting in 1953 the North Central threatened Oklahoma A&M with losing its accreditation if it did not reform its athletics. In the 1950s, as in later decades, the University of Oklahoma and Oklahoma A&M heavily emphasized athletics, and both institutions walked a tightrope with the North Central. The control of athletics at both institutions fell under the jurisdiction of a state agency, an athletic council appointed by the governor, which set Oklahoma apart from many other states whose boards of trustees set gridiron policy. By 1953 the University of Oklahoma had developed the most successful football program in the country under Coach Bud Wilkinson, whose teams had embarked on a winning streak that would eventually reach forty-seven games. Oklahoma A&M (later Oklahoma State), which played in the Missouri Valley Conference, was known as a "jock school" that openly gave subsidies. The North Central placed the Aggies of A&M and Bradley on probation. Sportswriters reported that the Aggies had violated North Central policies by giving subsidies to recruit and support athletes in major sports. Similarly, the NCAA had targeted Bradley because of its booster club, which had illegally given money to athletes, practices that the NCAA forbade in its bylaws.[29]

In all probability, many athletic programs that were up to their ears in illegal subsidies escaped the censure of the North Central. In a phrase Oklahoma A&M provided a particularly convenient target for the accreditors because of the notoriety that it had earned in 1951. In an episode that had nothing to do with subsidies, a lineman for the Aggies had wantonly attacked an African-American running back, Johnny Bright, who played for Drake, breaking his jaw and ending his career, but the school and team had gotten off scot-free. Likewise, Bradley had earned notoriety as one of three midwestern institutions implicated in the sensational point-shaving scandals in 1951 but, unlike Kentucky, had not been disciplined by the NCAA.[30]

The University of Oklahoma figured less prominently in the North Central's offensive, but its high profile in football possibly contributed to the North Central's assault against the state of Oklahoma. President George Lynn Cross of Oklahoma may have attracted the North Central's attention by a remark he had made while testifying before the state legislature in 1950. Cross described the plight of the university and why it needed twice as much as the governor had recommended. After he finished his thirty-minute speech, Cross recalled, "a sleepy-looking senator, just to my right on the front row, raised his hand and said: 'Yes, I'd like to ask the good doctor why he thinks he needs so much money to run the University of Oklahoma.'" Groping for an answer, Cross replied with a flip remark: "I would like to build a university of which the football team could be proud." While this remark got Cross off the hook with the legislator and brought guffaws and applause, the wire services spread the statement nationally, leaving the impression that Cross was using public forums to promote big-time athletics. His remark also reinforced the image of Oklahoma as a state obsessed with big-time college football and willing to go to any lengths to encourage it.[31]

In 1951 the state of Oklahoma had become embroiled in a television controversy, which may have drawn more notoriety because it proved to be the first of the several state protests against the NCAA's restrictive TV policy. In the spring before the annual Oklahoma-Oklahoma A&M gridiron rivalry, college sports enthusiasts became enraged when they learned that the NCAA would only allow one station in Oklahoma City to televise the big game. In March of 1951, months before the game, a legislator introduced a bill into the state legislature to compel TV stations to televise the game. President Cross and Coach Bud Wilkinson, after consulting with the Big Seven Conference, relayed to the lawmakers that the members of the Big Seven would cancel their contests with the Oklahoma Sooners and the NCAA would probably expel Oklahoma. Oklahoma would be free to televise its games but would have no one to play. Instead, the legislature passed a motion urging the NCAA and the Big Seven to lift their virtual blackout.[32]

By placing Oklahoma A&M on probation, however, the North Central found itself caught up in a tangled web of contradictions. If it had been a national agency, its authority would have blanketed all parts of the country, but it was not. While the North Central could discipline Oklahoma institutions, accreditation in Texas fell to the southern accrediting agency, whose standards were less stringent. Whereas Texas institutions of the Southwest Conference could promise athletic scholarships in Oklahoma, schools that belonged to the North Central, such as Oklahoma and Oklahoma A&M, would not be able legitimately to make the same offers to athletes in either Oklahoma or Texas. The schools of the Big Seven and Missouri Valley Conferences correctly believed that their football would deteriorate if the North Central tried to enforce its policies. Only the nine institutions of the Rocky Mountain Conference, which played less competitive football and might benefit by the absence of subsidy offers by neighboring schools, adopted the association's new set of regulations.[33]

Put simply, the major conferences that would have been affected by the North Central's academic fiats refused to allow the accreditors the blanket authority that they demanded. Insisting that the North Central abandon its attempt to eliminate athletic subsidies altogether, the conferences proposed instead that the agency adopt the slightly less strict ACE position on subsidies. Actually, the ACE was trying to impose standards that would have been far more severe than most big-time institutions were willing to meet, and one wonders if the major football schools would have willingly complied—and the North Central's were even more severe. "To proclaim that financial aid to athletes will not be forthcoming from some source or other," Oklahoma's president, George Cross, observed of the North Central's campaign, "is, therefore, not only hypocritical, but tends to promote the very moral evils which the several regulatory agencies are most anxious to approach." Cross, who later headed the NCAA, evidently spoke for many college presidents who regarded the North Central's approach as utterly unrealistic for major gridiron institutions.[34]

Being a formidable opponent at first glance, the North Central rapidly lost its nerve. Several major institutions spread the word that they would pull out if the North Central pursued its quest for athletic hegemony. On June 12, 1953, the twenty-seven schools on the advisory council met with the board of review of the Commission on Colleges and Universities. Much as they had done in the regional TV controversy, the Big Ten presidents stubbornly refused to abandon their big-time policies, and, despite the complaints of smaller, more distant schools, the major colleges won the day. The North Central agreed to modify its policies and to give up pressing for a return to strictly amateur policies. Soon afterward the North Central removed Oklahoma A&M from probation, an obvious concession to the threats of big-time schools and athletic conferences. While the major midwestern athletic conferences did not endorse the athletic "free ride," they made it clear that they would not abandon the central features of big-time football. The effort of the North Central to convert football into a facsimile of small-time sports like tennis or cross-country or to force the major schools to model their athletics after Johns Hopkins and Swarthmore never had a ghost of a chance.[35]

The failure of the North Central proved to be virtually the end of the effort to downsize big-time college sports. The scandals of 1951 had created an illusion that big-time football schools were willing to change, but big-time football had burrowed even deeper into the schools, athletic departments, and college communities. With a few exceptions, such as the Ivy League schools with their highly veneered images and declining gridiron interests, big-time college football had once again shown its remarkable ability to outduel and outwit its critics. Only the NCAA's movement to standardize big-time athletics, which had begun on the eve of World War II, would shift into higher gear. The NCAA, which had failed abysmally with the Sanity Code, became the beneficiary of this accelerated trend.

After the pressures for reform had receded, the NCAA between 1954 and 1957 gradually tightened its grip on college football. To be sure, the NCAA strongly reflected the policies and the agenda of the Big Ten working in tandem with the increasingly scandal-stricken Pacific Coast Conference. The new measures for enforcement, passed by the NCAA Council, showed up frequently in the actions of the association's Infractions Committee. In 1953 the NCAA put Arizona State on two-year probation for the activities of its booster group, the Sun Angels Foundation, which had paid nearly eighty thousand dollars to football players at the school; if it had violated its parole, Arizona State would have been subject to expulsion from the NCAA. In the same year, Notre Dame was censured for providing tryouts for football players in violation of the NCAA bylaws; the association also censured Michigan State, where the Spartan Foundation boosters had made fifty-five thousand dollars in illegal payments to players between 1949 and 1952, enabling it to build a national championship team.[36]

In 1956 the NCAA made its most powerful statement since banning Kentucky from participating in the 1952–53 basketball season. In the wake of bitter and tawdry scandals in the Pacific Coast Conference, the NCAA imposed tough sanctions on four PCC schools, the University of Washington, UCLA, California-Berkeley, and Southern California. UCLA's penalties proved to be particularly harsh; it received a three-year probation, during its probationary status it could not appear on television, and the NCAA censured its chancellor, Raymond Allen; to show its extreme disapproval the NCAA's Infraction Committee prohibited the institution from participating in any NCAA-sponsored event. The other PCC schools received less severe sentences, though Southern California could not appear on television or participate in the Rose Bowl.

The NCAA penalties showed that the association had reached a new base camp on its climb to athletic dominance. Ironically, the booster scandals that destroyed the PCC would play a strong role in the rise of the NCAA and lead to the capstone of its athletic standards, the full ride, or athletic scholarship. Thus, it might be well to examine those scandals and see why they demonstrated so clearly that institutional and conference autonomy would become a relic of the past and why athletic officials, boards of trustees, and college presidents were ready to cede to the NCAA the right of enforcement only eight years after the Sanity Code controversy. It should come as no surprise that the lawless underside of football boosterism paved the way for this remarkable turnaround.

Unnatural Rivalries: The Death of the PCC

In 1952 the NCAA had taken up out-of-season practice, one of the measures that the ACE proposals had sought to eliminate and the Ivy League, as we have seen, actually succeeded in doing. At the annual NCAA convention Victor O. Schmidt, commissioner of the Pacific Coast Conference, acting on behalf of the PCC faculty representatives, moved to outlaw out-of-season practice except for postseason games to be held no later than January 2 (to allow for the Rose Bowl) and continuing until September 1, when fall practice would begin. After strong opposition by Fritz Crisler of Michigan, a former coach at Princeton and Michigan, the convention decisively defeated Schmidt's motion, though it then proposed and passed a measure allowing twenty days of football practice in the time span of thirty days.[37]

For the purposes of this discussion the Pacific Coast Conference's attempt to persuade the NCAA to eliminate spring practice may be more noteworthy than its failed result. The PCC initiative seemed to demonstrate that eight larger conference schools were working in tandem to balance athletics and academics. Moreover, the PCC faculty representatives, in the wake of 1951 scandals, adopted the NCAA's twelve principles, which called for normal progress toward degrees, attention to athletes' curriculum, admission under regularly published athletic standards, and a ceiling on the number and amount of financial grants. PCC institutions evidently wanted their athletes to measure up to the academic requirements of their nonathletic students.[38]

The actions of the PCC institutions might have led one to believe that they scrupulously followed the same rigorous policies toward big-time athletics required by conference rules. Each of the California universities—California-Berkeley, Stanford, UCLA, and Southern California—claimed that the only athletically gifted students they accepted were academically qualified. At UCLA and the University of California at Berkeley all entering students were required to have a B average and to come from the top 25 percent of their high school classes. Though Southern California's admission standards were slightly lower, students there were still expected to be in the top 50 percent of their high school classes. UCLA proudly boasted that fourteen of its big-time athletes had grades averaging about a B level. "We want students playing at athletics rather athletes playing at their studies," proclaimed Robert Sproul, who presided over both campuses.[39]

Likewise, the three schools claimed to avoid favoritism in giving scholarships and other forms of aid. UCLA boasted that it refused to employ athletes, though it paid for tutoring athletes who needed an academic jumpstart. Southern California insisted that it rejected gifts from alumni and boosters specifically earmarked for athletes. And neither institution would countenance aid that was not channeled through the institutions. "The old graduate is often overenthusiastic when he sees a good football or basketball prospect," an unidentified faculty member observed in a 1951 *New York Times* article, "and that seems to be the trouble all over the country."[40]

In truth the PCC's code did not represent the opinions of the coaches, athletic directors, or even some of the presidents. The PCC's code had been passed by the faculty athletic representatives, who served their institutions athletically in much the same way as state and national legislators did in political bodies. Of the faculty reps who served in the 1950s, almost every one had some claim to distinction, the best known being Glenn Seaborg of Berkeley, who had not only won the Nobel Prize for physics but also would later head the Atomic Energy Commission. In addition, Joseph Kaplan of UCLA had a distinguished career as a physicist, and Southern California's Hugh Willett had served as president of the NCAA. Orlando John Hollis of Oregon's law school had served as his institution's acting president, and Donald Wollett of Washington was one of the foremost labor lawyers in the country. In the late 1930s, when an earlier scandal had erupted, the faculty representatives had hired Edwin Atherton, a former FBI official, to root out corruption, and, when Atherton died, his aide, Victor O. Schmidt, had taken over as commissioner. It was the vigorous and well-spoken Schmidt, known for his integrity, who had carried the spring practice mandate of the faculty representatives to the 1952 NCAA convention.[41]

Once a conference of state universities and private colleges, the PCC by the postwar era had reshaped itself into two distinct groups of schools, which included the northern members in Oregon and Washington versus the four institutions in California. Within California strong rivalries existed between Stanford and California-Berkeley, which had dominated college athletics in the early 1900s, and the two major Los Angeles institutions, UCLA and Southern California. The sole remaining small and distant member from the 1920s, the University of Idaho, refused to make the long and costly trip to California to be mauled by the gridiron powers of the conference.

The changes in the PCC athletic power structure reflected the migration of dust bowl workers to southern California in the 1930s, followed by industrial workers and sun seekers to the Los Angeles area in the 1940s. Beginning with the revival of the Rose Bowl in 1916 and the intersectional rivalry between Southern California and Notre Dame, the West Coast's isolation, so evident in the early 1900s, began to disappear. It would be a mistake, however, to conclude that the vast distances no longer played a role in regional gridiron politics. Football teams had to travel a thousand miles, from Los Angeles in the south to Seattle in the north and still farther to Pullman, Washington, where Washington State was located. The alumni of Southern California and UCLA felt that they had less in common with the four schools in Oregon and Washington—Oregon, Oregon State, Washington, and Washington State—than they did with many institutions in the Southwest and in the Midwest, which were, in some cases, no farther than Pullman, Washington.

To put it bluntly, rivalries between flagship institutions in the PCC resembled grudge matches more than traditional rivalries. As an upstart football power in the 1920s, Southern California had also sought to become the academic and athletic leader of the South in the 1920s, but it enjoyed more success in athletics than academics. UCLA's meteoric growth since it moved to its Westwood campus in 1929 had eclipsed USC's dream of academic grandeur. In turn, UCLA still felt the stigma of its origins as a storefront, satellite campus of Cal-Berkeley and chafed at what it regarded as the straitjacket imposed by the older and more prestigious campus. Though each school had a chancellor, President Robert Sproul, who headed the entire institution, favored a unified system. Local and regional jealousies would create something more potent than the traditional football rivalries—a brew of politics, football, and regional jealousies.[42]

One PCC school where cheating first came to light was the University of Oregon, whose football coach had engaged in illegal recruiting practices such as offering one hundred dollars per month as well as a clothing allowance to a promising recruit. When this scandal erupted, in 1951, Victor O. Schmidt, the PCC commissioner, acted decisively by threatening the institution with expulsion and insisting that the school fire its football coach. In turn, Oregon began to suggest that other schools, such as UCLA, were just as guilty of PCC code violations. Orlando John Hollis, the Oregon faculty representative, would come down particularly hard on the California schools, acting as the prosecutor in the later conference tribunals judging the scandal-ridden institutions.[43]

The first big-time slush fund scandal erupted at the University of California in 1954, after Ronnie Knox, a highly sought-after halfback from the Los Angeles area, revealed the existence of recruiting violations upon quitting Cal-Berkeley to transfer to UCLA. To get Knox, Cal boosters, known as the Southern Seas, had promised a job to Knox's stepfather, Harvey Knox, a former Hollywood haberdasher who was hired to recruit Ronnie's former teammates at several high schools that he had attended; Ronnie or Harvey also wangled a job for his son's former high school coach on Cal's football staff.

Ronnie Knox symbolized the mercenary, "hired-gun" character of some big-time football players. This blue-chip recruit emerged as extraordinary not only in his athletic talents but also in the Svengalian influence of his stepfather, who managed Ronnie's sports career. Even before he entered college Knox had led a peripatetic life. Constantly moving, he played at three schools, completing a record number of passes in his senior year and attracting recruiters from across the country. Knox chose California because the athletic program promised a job for his stepfather, Harvey, as well as five hundred dollars a year from the sale of his complimentary tickets, five hundred dollars for pocket money, and funds for his family to travel from Los Angeles to watch him play. As an aspiring writer, Knox was to have a job on a local newspaper while he attended California. While Ronnie languished in freshman football, Harvey traded on his connections, making lavish promises to Ronnie's former high school teammates and leaving a trail for PCC officials to investigate.[44]

Feeling homesick for Los Angeles and convinced that he was being neglected by the coaches at Cal, Ronnie decided to transfer to UCLA. No doubt prompted by Harvey, he revealed the existence of the Southern Seas and their recruiting operations, and, as a result, Victor O. Schmidt levied sanctions on Cal which would keep it from going to the Rose Bowl. Lying about his illegal benefits bothered Ronnie, or so he later claimed. On a visit to Berkeley, Schmidt sought out Knox for questioning. According to Knox, the coaching staff carefully prepared him to cope with the commissioner's interrogation. "If the commissioner asked if I were getting help from alumni," the player claimed, "I was to reply, no. Any inducements to come to Cal? No. Above all, I was not to volunteer any information unnecessarily." Whether he felt remorse or regret, Knox wrote that he had felt "trapped in the mess for keeps."[45]

After leaving Cal-Berkeley and blowing the whistle on the Southern Seas boosters club, Knox transferred to UCLA, where he received seventy-five dollars for a nonexistent college job and twenty-five dollars a week in the film-cutting department of a movie studio. Because he was a transfer student, the PCC freshman rule kept him from competing, but in his junior year he averaged four yards a carry and completed thirty-six passes. Though injured part of the year, he also played in the Rose Bowl on January 1, 1956, against Michigan State. This proved to be his final year of college football; he quit UCLA after his junior year to play professional football in Canada.[46]

In an article written for *Collier's* in 1956, Knox recalled that he had felt alienated from his fellow students at both schools. He revealed that players at UCLA seldom attended pep rallies, even when—as an alumnus once exulted to him—"the big game is in the air." Knox recounted a memorable encounter as a freshman at Cal-Berkeley when he had ducked out on a pep rally, something that players often did. When he went downtown, he happened to see one of the halfbacks and asked him why he was not at the rally. Knox described the encounter: "He smiled and answered sardonically, 'that stuff is for students.'" In other words, members of the football team did not consider themselves students.[47]

In big-time football, Knox declared, you did not simply *play* the game: "You eat it, drink it, and inhale it." He scoffed at the old-fashioned bromide that football built character. Knox reflected that character meant that you had something to believe in, but big-time college players operated like "machinery on the field." Occasionally, a player displayed emotion, even wept if the team lost, but still he operated as a cog in the system. "He is simply an individual with a peculiar talent," Knox insisted, "who is brought in by the colleges at a very nominal fee to furnish entertainment for the masses." Contrary to a common belief, he observed, boosters did not pay for a player's education; education had little meaning for most players (except for the few brilliant students who happened to play football).[48]

Knox credited UCLA with taking care of its players. It provided its players with "enough money for room and board, even though the rules of the conference forbade it." With a rhetorical shrug Knox acknowledged that the conflict between the rules and practice meant that UCLA would get caught; after all, the football staff and its minions ran a successful, businesslike operation. "I guess that it was inevitable that my school should get in trouble," Knox mused, "and it did last summer along with USC, Washington, and California." Faced with the prospect of five games at the most in his senior year, Knox did what the "migratory Knoxes" had done since he began high school; he moved to a better-paying job as an outright professional.[49]

In the fall of 1955 the scandal virus struck at Washington, where the faculty athletic committee had fired coach Johnny Cherberg after the players had complained of his ineptness in handling the team. Cherberg immediately revealed the existence of a booster fund, the Greater Washington Advertising Club, which recruited players by making illegal promises of cash payments and then paying the players. The head of the organization, Ralph "Torchy" Torrance, a former player at Washington, not only headed the operation but also ran concessions for the games and sold printing to the school. Dismissing the fund as a "peanut operation," Torrance refused to name names, but the PCC put the Huskies on probation for two years, banning the team from appearing in the Rose Bowl.[50]

In March 1956 charges of slush funds cropped up at UCLA when a former player who had moved to Cal-Berkeley revealed the existence of the Westwood Club and the Bruin Bench, booster operations that supplied players with a forty dollar monthly stipend—and had been helping players since the 1930s. As a former member of the Hannah committee, UCLA chancellor Raymond Allen refused to allow Commissioner Schmidt to interview the athletes for ten weeks, while Allen claimed to be making his own investigation. As a result, the commissioner assessed the chancellor with a fine of ninety-five thousand dollars. The PCC also docked the whole football team a year of eligibility, a factor that led Ronnie Knox to forgo his senior year and join the pros. A few days after the PCC penalties UCLA students hanged the commissioner in effigy, a tactic of choice for students in venting their frustration against unpopular athletic decisions.[51]

Then the spinning wheel stopped at Southern Cal's doorstep in July 1956. Miller Leavy, a UCLA alumnus who served as deputy district attorney, sent Schmidt documents on the activities of the Southern California Educational Foundation, which had given more than seventy thousand dollars to athletes on the USC team, sums to individuals reaching as high as nine hundred dollars a year. The conference banned the Trojans from the Rose Bowl and exacted a fine of ten thousand dollars for Southern Cal's failure to cooperate with Schmidt's investigation. As at UCLA, forty-two members of the team would have to sit out a year of competition or, in the case of seniors, sit out permanently.[52]

In Los Angeles politicians and boosters in the Los Angeles area poured out vitriol on the conference authorities, the northern California schools, and the institutions of the Northwest which had, they believed, been responsible for the severe sanctions. Governor Goodwin Knight, a native of southern California, found it hard to believe that "California is so different from other members of the conference," by which he presumably meant the schools in Los Angeles. Soon afterward, however, the ubiquitous Miller Leavy turned his heavy artillery to the north, sending evidence to Schmidt that booster clubs at Cal-Berkeley gave money to football players for nonexistent jobs. In response, Chancellor Clark Kerr conducted his own investigation and publicly reprimanded Coach Lynn "Pappy" Waldorf. The PCC levied a fine of twenty-five thousand dollars against California-Berkeley, a penalty well noted by southern Californian schools as far less than those imposed on the Los Angeles schools.[53]

Given the acrimony and the opposition to playing the schools in the Northwest, the California schools, except for Stanford, embarked on a course designed to break up the conference. Indeed, soon after the commissioner handed down the penalties against the Los Angeles schools, the alumni of the two institutions began to talk seriously of seceding from the PCC, both because they regarded its policies as unfair and because they felt the schools of the Northwest offered little competition. A third reason to separate grew out of deep-seated, long-standing resentments toward what Los Angeles considered the snobbish and arrogant "old money" attitudes of San Francisco elites, who disapproved, or so it was thought, of the more casual style prevalent in the South. Melvin Durslag, a Los Angeles sportswriter, dared the faculty reps of the schools to the North—"the sociable seven," as he called them—to turn the offenders out of the PCC. "Confidentially, fellas, you have too much class for these Los Angeles characters," he wrote. "They go around in polo shirts down here and don't even play polo." The schools north of Los Angeles, Durslag declared, should have their own round-robin. While Berkeley played Idaho and Stanford met Washington State, "these poor saps in Los Angeles" would have to watch USC and UCLA play Oklahoma and Michigan State, which were already on their schedules. While Durslag's column probably had his readers snickering at the "poor saps"—by which he really meant the fans of the Bay area schools who would have to watch comparatively dull fare—many alumni of USC and UCLA agreed that intersectional and local rivalries would prove more exciting than games with teams from the drab Northwest.[54]

In 1957 the PCC tried to overcome what the *New York Times* called "a ground swell of disapproval" leading to cries for secession. The faculty representatives changed the financial rules so that players could receive aid if they could not make ends meet. While they refused to eliminate the probationary status for UCLA, USC, and Cal-Berkeley, the faculty reps did scale back the full year's disqualification for the UCLA athletes, changing it to a two- and three-year probation. This meant that the seniors could play but could not qualify for the conference championship or a trip to the Rose Bowl, the only postseason competition that the conference allowed.[55]

Putting aside its resentments, Cal-Berkeley joined the two indignant Los Angeles schools in plotting their withdrawal from the PCC. Probably the state institutions would have remained in the conference if they could have repealed the round-robin provision and scheduled games freely. Not surprisingly, the three California schools demanded to be allowed to pick and choose their opponents, which would have given them veto power over games with the northwestern schools and would have ended the system of conference championships. The state legislature fell into step by holding hearings to set up a state athletic commission, which could also have set schedules, or at least vetoed games with undesirable opponents.[56]

In late 1957, when the PCC held their annual meeting, the schools forced Commissioner Victor O. Schmidt to resign, and then a week later California, UCLA, and USC voted to leave the conference. As a major football power, Washington would no longer have games with the powerful California teams except for Stanford; it might also have trouble recruiting in pigskin-fertile California. Therefore, Washington submitted its resignation in June 1958. The five schools that remained—Stanford, Oregon, Oregon State, Washington State, and Idaho—dissolved the "strife-weary loop" in August 1958. It was doubtful that they could have attracted much attendance without the big California schools, and it was unlikely that Stanford would remain in a conference that included only institutions in small towns of the Northwest. To honor their contracts, however, the teams continued to play through 1959 and sent Washington to the Rose Bowl on January 1, 1960.[57]

When the West Coast teams reorganized in 1960, they created a new conference, the Athletic Association of Western Universities (AAWU), or

PAC-8 and later the PAC-10, including all of the same teams except Idaho. Its makeup hinted that the flagship California universities had decided, upon sober second thought, that three state universities would prove inadequate for a big-time conference; to admit other California universities or state institutions would deplete the pool of major recruits. The only difference initially was that the "poor saps" did not initially have to play one another, since in the first years the California schools got their wish to play largely intrastate and intersectional competition.

The NCAA then followed the PCC in placing the schools that had broken the rules on its own probation and imposing penalties that denied three of the schools gridiron access to television. In 1956 the NCAA Council placed the University of Washington on two-year probation, ruling it ineligible to appear on NCAA football telecasts. The NCAA severely spanked UCLA, placing it on three-year probation and banning it from TV appearances. It also censured UCLA's football coaches as well as Chancellor Raymond Allen and the athletic departments. To show its extreme disapproval, the NCAA Infractions Committee prohibited the Bruins from participating in NCAA-sponsored events in any sport. Southern California received a two-year probation that kept it from appearing on television or participating in the Rose Bowl, while California-Berkeley received a one-year probation plus censure for its football coach, Lynn Waldorf, and a former assistant coach. All of these penalties arose from the operations of booster groups usually in cahoots with the coaches and, in the case of UCLA, with the stonewalling tactics of Chancellor Raymond Allen, who had stood in the way of Schmidt's investigation.[58]

To say that these scandals only hurt football and the PCC would be untrue, for they badly tarnished the reputations of the West Coast institutions, suggesting that the schools cared mostly for the reputation of their football teams. Moreover, the scandals highlighted a persistent, deeply rooted problem of booster organizations working hand-in-glove with the coaches and athletic departments. Presidents such as Raymond Allen of UCLA and Fred Fagg of USC, who had blocked PCC investigations, seemed to be held hostage by boosters and athletic directors.

Once again, it is well to keep in mind that the fallout from the PCC scandals showed the growing muscle of the NCAA and the decline of enforcement by regional conferences. Whereas the PCC foundered on the rocks of West Coast animosities, the NCAA demonstrated that it stood above local animosities. By handing down stiff penalties to schools across the country, the NCAA could appear as the knight in shining armor, acting for the good of college athletics and solving problems in the troubled province of college football. The NCAA television contract had become important enough that penalties involving loss of TV appearances worked a hardship on the guilty institutions. What had begun as a flight from the invading legions of Saturday afternoon telecasts had turned into a convenient tool for bludgeoning the wrongdoers into submission. In this way the epidemic of football scandals on the West Coast had actually strengthened the NCAA and, presumably, the firmament of big-time college football.

In 1957, following the chain of cheating scandals on the West Coast, the NCAA felt strong enough to fill in the gaps on recruiting and scholarships left by the Sanity Code controversy and to insert a clause in its bylaws banning the activities of booster groups. The centerpiece of the new NCAA standards proved to be the full ride, or athletic scholarship. Whereas earlier conventions had failed to overcome institutional and conference autonomy, the unprecedented epidemic of scandals on the West Coast provided the impetus for codifying standards for subsidies and recruiting.

At its convention in January 1957 the NCAA approved the practice of giving athletic scholarships not based on need or the expectation of jobs. To be sure, many conferences, such as the Southeastern and Big Seven (now the Big Eight since Oklahoma A&M had recently joined), had permitted athletic scholarships since the 1930s and 1940s, and the Big Ten had recently adopted the full ride for its athletes. In the end the NCAA did not place a cap on "unearned aid," an excruciatingly neutral phrasing, but instead it merely specified that "scholarships and grants-in-aid should not exceed commonly accepted educational expenses."[59]

To round out the NCAA's new set of standards the association standardized the laws on recruiting as formulated by a special committee appointed in 1956: (1) member institutions could finance only one visit per recruit for a maximum of two days and two nights; (2) groups such as the Spartan Foundation or the Sun Angels were prohibited from pooling money to pay for recruiting activities; (3) college recruiters such as coaches had to obtain the permission of the high school principal before they could contact a potential recruit; (4) athletes would be required to sign letters of intent to enroll at specific institutions; (5) no institution could solicit athletes with offers of financial aid not permitted by the NCAA, an old provision that gained more credibility because of the new rules on athletic scholarships.[60]

All of these changes had grown out of the bonanza that the TV football contractors had provided and from the enforcement powers of the NCAA. In 1953, when the NCAA attempted to prevent the public from access to football telecasts, the NCAA had suffered from recurring bouts of unpopularity and threats of retribution from state legislatures. The TV revenues had helped the NCAA buy public acceptance in the 1950s, and college football attendance by 1957 finally shot above the levels that it had achieved in 1949 but had failed to equal since then.

The demise of the PCC and the rise of the NCAA proved to be still another sign that big-time college football had emerged from the welter of confusion that had dogged it since the end of World War II. Though it had lost valuable ground to pro football, it had eluded the scourge of reformers and television. Scandals always stood ready to be uncovered, but the NCAA had finally established national standards for college football and mechanisms for dealing with them. The hastily drawn defense strategy of NCAA-TV had become a big business rather than merely a castle moat that protected the treasury from invading hordes of football telecasts. Only the still growing presence of professional football firmly hooked to television still loomed ominously on the horizon. By dint of longer seasons and national championships, the professional juggernaut might well break through the inner line of NCAA defenses, a mercenary kingdom of Goths and Vandals threatening to plunder the once mighty and unchallenged domain of big-time college football.

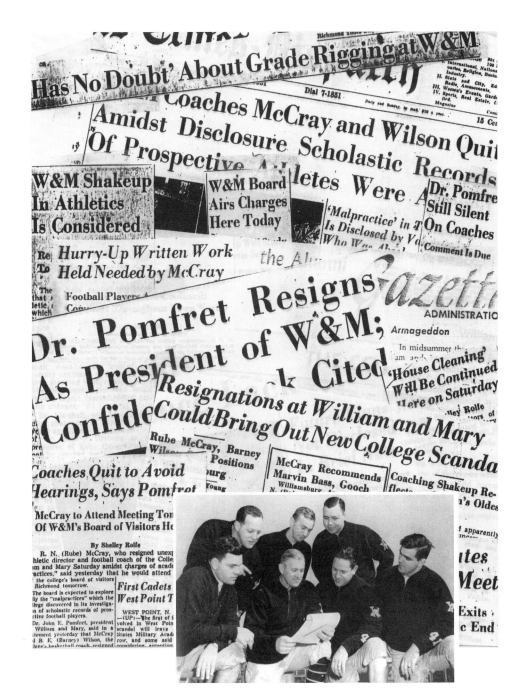

A montage of articles and headlines relating to the William and Mary football scandal in 1951. Still attempting to play big-time football, coaches at William and Mary in Williamsburg, Virginia, altered the transcripts of incoming athletes and engaged in other scams to keep their athletes eligible. President John Pomfret resigned in 1951, and the scandals helped to trigger the second great upheaval in college football. Football coach Rube McCray is shown in front row *second from left.* COURTESY OF WILFORD KALE, CO-AUTHOR OF *GOAL TO GOAL: 100 YEARS OF WILLIAM AND MARY FOOTBALL.*

In November 1955 students at Georgia Tech in Atlanta rioted when Governor Marvin Griffin objected to the Yellow Jackets' Sugar Bowl contest with Pittsburgh. Pitt happened to have a single African-American player, Bobby Grier; Griffin threatened to block the team's trip to the game because it would register a breach of racial segregation, which students clearly believed less important than a bowl appearance. Griffin failed to keep Tech from the game, and, as luck would have it, Georgia Tech won a narrow decision on a pass interference call against Grier. COURTESY OF WIDE WORLD PHOTOS.

The University of Oregon "Ducks" line up in the 1950s, with linemen in the modern three-point stances and, for most schools after World War II, the familiar phenomenon of a racially integrated backfield. COURTESY OF UNIVERSITY OF OREGON ARCHIVES.

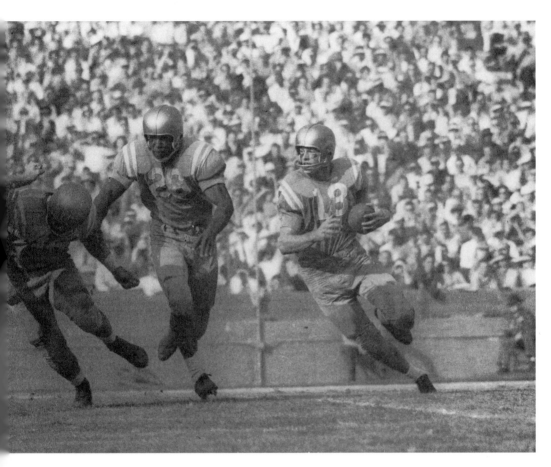

Blue-chip recruit Ronnie Knox, wearing an early face guard and in 1955 playing in one of his few games for UCLA. At the University of California at Berkeley Knox blew the whistle on the booster organization, the South Seas, after his freshman year, setting off a series of slush fund scandals there. Transferring to UCLA, Knox became embroiled in another payments scandal that led to penalties against the team and the end of Knox's college career. COURTESY OF UCLA ASSOCIATED STUDENT SERVICES.

One of the best-known coaches in the country, Paul "Bear" Bryant of flagship state university, Alabama, with his star player, Pat Trammell, in 1962, a year after winning the national championship. In 1963 the *Saturday Evening Post* accused him and Wally Butts of "fixing" the opening game of the 1962 season so that Alabama would be certain to win. Alabama politicians, regents, and newspapers rallied to the popular coach's defense. UNIVERSITY OF ALABAMA YEARBOOK, *COROLLA*, 1963. COURTESY OF SPECIAL COLLECTIONS, UNIVERSITY OF ALABAMA.

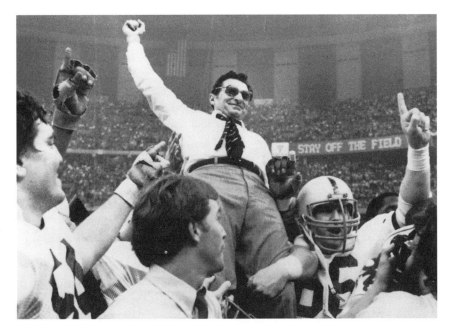

Penn State coach Joe Paterno rides out of the Superdome at New Orleans on the shoulders of his players after the Nittany Lions defeated Georgia 28-23 on January 1, 1983, in the Sugar Bowl, for their first national championship. As a Brown University graduate (and highly regarded college quarterback), Paterno headed one of the most successful and most profitable big-time football programs. COURTESY OF PENNSYLVANIA STATE UNIVERSITY ATHLETICS.

In 1987 Southern Methodist University received the NCAA's "death penalty," a two-year ban on varsity football competition. Boosters had violated regulations by paying members of the football team. Soon afterward Texas governor Bill Clements, former head of the board of governors, admitted that he had approved the payments. COURTESY OF SOUTHERN METHODIST UNIVERSITY *DAILY CAMPUS*.

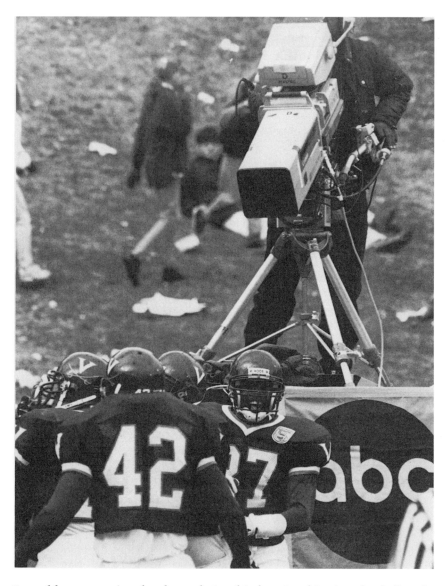

In a tableau capturing the close relationship between big-time football and television coverage, Virginia players in 1994 celebrate a favorable turn of events under the watchful eye of ABC Sports. In the 1970s and 1980s, ABC network sports under the direction of Roone Arledge did more than any other sports medium to revolutionize football telecasts, making Saturday afternoons a shared national experience. COURTESY OF KEITH DONNELLY AND UNIVERSITY OF VIRGINIA MEDIA RELATIONS.

CHAPTER FIFTEEN

The Professional Paradigm, 1956 to 1974

In the 1960s college football entered into a period of unprecedented prosperity. The live attendance went from just under fifteen million in 1956 to more than thirty million in 1971. NCAA-TV revenues, which had broken the two million dollar mark in 1959, reached twelve million dollars by 1970, a testament to both the popularity of college football and the negotiating abilities of NCAA executive director Walter Byers.

Compared to college football, the professional game grew much faster and dramatically. It skyrocketed from two million spectators in 1950 to more than three million in 1960 before reaching almost ten million in 1971. By the mid-1960s members for the New York Giants and Jets made slightly more than the average salaries of Major League baseball players. The growth of franchises, front offices, and coaching staffs provided a bonanza for enterprising college coaches. After being fired from his job as coach of Boston College in 1959, Mike Holovak joined the coaching staff of the Boston Patriots in the new American Football League (AFL). As head coach and general manager of the Boston Patriots (New England Patriots) in the mid-1960s, Hovolak made more than $300,000 on his five-year contract.[1]

In the prosperous 1960s the growth and advances in TV buoyed all sports. The advent of color television in the early 1960s made the picture far more distinct and lifelike than it had been in the early days of television. Roone Arledge of ABC, the guru of sports programming, invented and adapted techniques that made televised football far more compelling than it had been in the post-radio days of bland announcers who merely kept the viewers abreast of what had already happened. Seeking to create a sense of excitement, Arledge employed a panoply of visual and audio devices such as hidden microphones near the field, shots of scantily clad cheerleaders, and instant replays to bring the game into the living room. Arledge demonstrated that televised football did not have to detract from live attendance. While ABC carried NCAA telecasts during the 1960s, Arledge would pioneer the most successful gridiron football innovation of all time, "Monday Night Football," which premiered in September 1970 with the Cleveland Browns playing the New York Jets and enjoyed sensationally high ratings.

The Pro Juggernaut

Before World War II, when college football had a virtual monopoly on spectator interest and no one took the NFL too seriously, college coaches like Amos Alonzo Stagg never tired of declaring that football mercenaries would never play with the spirit of "I'd die for dear old Rutgers," a folksy witticism of the early 1900s. In their view professionals put in their three hours on work on Sunday afternoon for fifty dollars and, like factory workers, put out only enough for what they earned.

While college football reaped the glory and headlines, however, the NFL methodically laid the foundation for a profitable industry, adopting a divisional structure, restricting one team to each city, and initiating a sudden-death championship. With the advent of television after World War II, the NFL used the new medium to allow enough exposure to whet appetites and increase profits. In 1955 Fritz Crisler, who sought to expand the regional games, made it clear that pro football had TV momentum on its side. "It is interesting to observe," Crisler declared, "how their ratings have increased on Sunday, and how ours have declined." He was right. By the mid-1960s seventeen million sports fans watched professional football on an average Sunday, which presented far more numerous games and interesting matchups than the NCAA normally featured.[2]

More precisely, the colleges had already become, as some had once feared, the minor league training ground for skilled pro players. While colleges had always turned out some celebrated, well-paid pros like Red Grange, the average player's pay had soared to nearly sixteen thousand dollars for five months' work, the equivalent of a mid-level manager's annual salary. Unlike the 1930s, when great players such as the University of Chicago's Jay Berwanger spurned the NFL, postwar professional football attracted many stars of the college football firmament.

Professional football had challenged college football for the simple reason that it had become more entertaining than the televised college game of the week. While college football tried to return to single-platoon football in the 1950s, the pros continued to play the more complex two-platoon game. In an era when freshmen did not yet play and redshirting had just begun, pro football players could play longer than simply the three seasons that the NCAA permitted its member institutions, and the pros, if they survived the injuries and perfected their abilities, might play until they were in their early or mid-thirties. According to Green Bay Packers' coach Vince Lombardi, the professional linemen, who weighed in at 235—more than 20 pounds heavier than the collegians—played tougher because they were not only larger but also just as fast and agile. Professional football as a full-time business, he declared, enabled the players to be fully dedicated, whereas student-athletes had to worry about their classes or, at least, about staying eligible. Lombardi's description of dedicated players stood in stark contrast to the outdated premise that collegians played with more spirit than the pros, who supposedly cared only about collecting their paycheck.[3]

Since college teams did not play against professionals, it is hard to determine exactly when pro football became discernibly superior to college football. The only comparison of recent college stars and the top professionals would have been the College "All-Star" benefit game for Chicago Tribune Charities played every year since 1935 at Soldier Field in Chicago, a contest in which the best-known draft choices tested their mettle against the NFL champs. In the early years the All-Stars periodically upset the previous year's champions. Between 1945 and 1950 the former college standouts won three out of the six games, but the badly outclassed All-Stars won only two games in the next decade and probably should have been matched up against the worst rather than the best team from the previous year. After the All-Stars achieved one of their rare defeats over the Green Bay Packers in 1963, subsequent teams never again defeated the pros. In 1976, after a distasteful display by youthful fans during a rain delay, the Tribune Charities mercifully axed the once popular and exciting contest.[4]

In 1958 the NFL proved that it could stage a nationally televised sports event when the New York Giants and Baltimore Colts went into sudden death overtime and quarterback Johnny Unitas deftly guided the Colts to the winning touchdown. Only a year later two Texas billionaires, Lamar Hunt and Bud Adams, frustrated in their attempts to get NFL franchises by a tight-knit group of NFL owners, decided to launch their own American Football League, or AFL. Financially brittle in their first years, the eight franchises survived by securing a thirty-six million dollar contract from NBC, which allowed them to advance money to club owners, who then engaged in a bidding war with the NFL for blue-chip players like Alabama quarterback Joe Namath. Since the NFL had expanded to fifteen teams, the new twenty-six team league after 1966 would blanket the largest cities in the most populous sections of the country. The financial potential of a college football championship game to supplement the bowl games became more compelling after the hugely popular Super Bowl between the two leagues began in January 1967.[5]

While college television moved toward the two million dollar contract, the NFL got nearly twenty million dollars per year from CBS, and the AFL had a contract with NBC which paid out about seven million dollars. In addition, the fifteen-team NFL had received more than three million dollars for its postseason games in 1965, including its popular championship game, which would be superseded by the TV contract for the Super Bowl. It was true that the NCAA-TV had expanded its number of games to twenty-nine telecasts, which was far fewer than the full NFL format, but the participating teams as well as the conference members, the NCAA schools, and the

NCAA all got a piece of the action. As long as college football's profits increased, the major football institutions did not complain.[6]

College football still differed from the pros because the students who played football were, in theory, purely amateurs whose primary goal was to obtain an education. The college athletic departments, which wanted to emulate the professional model, had to pretend that their players came to college to secure a degree, when some of them actually saw college football as merely a prep course for the pros. The oft-used term *student-athlete* conjured up images of college boys who just happened to play football, whereas the pre-professional or quasi-professional took his cues from NFL football. Actually, he was a skilled entertainer who perfected his training by performing before large audiences. Unlike college players, however, the pros did not have to pretend not to play for profit. For that matter, no claims were made that pro football built character or that the NFL had educational benefits. Professionals could devote all of their energies to winning.

Some college athletic officials strained to view college football as different than professional football, invoking the old chestnuts of *amateur* versus *professional.* As late as 1955, a delegate to the annual NCAA convention claimed that amateurs played the game with more enthusiasm. While the pros played only to earn their paychecks, he insisted, college boys played because they had the will to win. The speaker noted that the Chicago Cardinals had established an incentive system for its players so that those who did a little more got extra money. He regarded the will to win as its own reward, a philosophy that ran directly contrary to the show-biz credo of the pros. "The idea that an athlete should run faster or throw farther for a few extra dollars in his pay envelope is so foreign to the true concept of competitive athletics," he declared, "that I shudder to see this type of thinking accepted on the nation's sports scenes, even in the professional sports." The purpose of athletics, he implied, was still to build character as well as to teach self-discipline and self-control.[7]

In the Big Ten a group of older coaches and athletic figures, including Michigan athletic director Fritz Crisler and veteran Big Ten commissioner Kenneth "Tug" Wilson, cranked up the alarm bells. In a report designed to scare the daylights out of their colleagues they attempted to show how the trends in college football, if not abated, would destroy the college game or hand it over to the pros. Entitled "Projection of Findings," the two-page section of a broader report on Big Ten athletics had an eerie resemblance to gloomy, futuristic novels of the 1940s, such as George Orwell's *1984* and *Animal Farm,* in which totalitarian societies moved in lock-step and the old traditions dissolved into oblivion. A new breed of athletes, sports agents, and recruiter coaches, the committee seemed to be saying, would either bankrupt the conference or convert it into a professional minor league.[8]

According to these projections, a series of disastrous events might well overtake college football if it persisted in violating the rules and spirit of the intercollegiate game. It is not necessary to go into all of these twelve scenarios, but some of them had already occurred, and others would actually creep into big-time college sports in the next decades. Seven of the predictions had a close connection with what was happening in the 1950s and 1960s, and not just in the Big Ten. The committee predicted that if current trends persisted: (1) complete financial subsidies would soon be provided; (2) many players would engage in college competition simply as a prelude to entering professional sports; (3) athletic departments would arrange special methods of admission, tutoring, and academic counseling; (4) coaches would be chosen for their expertise in recruiting rather than in teaching the fundamentals of the game; (5) the athletes would become mere gladiators segregated from all campus activities (a scenario that the article by Ronnie Knox would see as already occurring); (6) the Big Ten, because of its superior resources, would become a closed corporation intent on displaying a near-professional level for professional sports; and (7) the differences between college and professional sports would become almost indistinguishable. Other predictions, though uncannily prescient, would not come into full play until the 1970s or later.[9]

As for the seven of its twelve projections listed here, the committee might have looked in the mirror. Most of the seven described big-time football as it existed in the 1940s and 1950s in the Big Ten and elsewhere. In 1951, for example, a recently graduated Michigan player, Allen Jackson, published a highly critical piece in the October issue of the *Atlantic Monthly* on his experiences as an athlete and student. Though he played first-string on Michigan's 1948 Rose Bowl victors, Jackson had been unable to reconcile the conflicting roles of student and athlete. "I can see the benefits of big-time football are either grossly exaggerated or completely imaginary," he declared, "and it seems to me the enormous amount of time I spent on the gridiron was wasted." At Michigan, he insisted, practice sessions and games on Saturday took enormous amounts of his time, as did workouts in the spring. Not only did he spend hours on the practice field, but he also had to watch movies of the next week's opponents in the evening, and, he observed, traveling to other schools and sessions devoted to indoor training wasted even more of his time. In addition, Jackson had to spend three extra weeks in practice for the Rose Bowl, an event that he described as an artificial high. Though he majored in history, his history classes required "about half the time I spent on the gridiron," a conflict in time and energy which would have proved difficult for most players. Unlike the Big Ten committee, Jackson recognized that a big-time football player resembled a professional athlete. "In professional athletics," he wrote, "the individual player is expected to devote his whole person to the game because his livelihood depends on consistent 'professional' performance." College football in the Big Ten required the same.[10]

If college football had become so large and quasi-professional, why did it not self-destruct as the committee had predicted? For reasons seldom stated by school athletic officials, college football had a unique ability to hold onto certain constituencies that were emotionally wedded to big-time college football and, if anything, demanded bigger and better teams. In some regions college football served the loyalties of sports fans who had allegiances to state, community, and their alma mater. Just as it had in the 1920s and 1930s, college football at many flagship state universities provided the same sense of identity which the flag and pledge of allegiance did for patriotic Americans. In truth, its capacity to inspire devotion transcended the appeal of many professional teams that also mixed fan loyalty with entertainment. College football still created believers, fanatics who intermixed football with devotion to their state. To watch one's team take on the flagship university of a neighboring state or to play a high-profile instate rival conjured up visions of warriors for Greek city-states marching off to battle.

Football as Identity: The Dark Side of State U Myths

The trend of mixing state identity with football was nothing new. The near fanatical support of major football teams by legislators, businessmen, and alumni went back to the 1920s, when states that had enjoyed more ridicule than recognition began to sprout big-time teams. On January 1, 1926, when Alabama won a close victory over Washington in the Rose Bowl, it represented a triumph for all the former states of the Confederacy. At each town in which the train bearing the victors stopped in Alabama, cheering throngs presented them with gifts, and fifteen thousand people met the team in Tuscaloosa when it had reached home from the West Coast. Likewise, the state of Georgia rejoiced when their own Georgia Bulldogs traveled north to defeat the once-great Bulldogs of New Haven in 1927, and, when Yale traveled to Atlanta in 1929 and Georgia shut out the Eli's in the heartland of the Confederacy, their emotions knew no bounds. Similarly, after World War II Oklahoma built a pigskin powerhouse that helped to erase the Okie stigma, immortalized by the migrants who had hobbled west from the Sooner state in the 1930s. The coaches who created the big-time teams enjoyed a heroic status attained only by the founding fathers and, in the South, the near mythic figures of the Confederacy.[11]

College football proved that it could still play a role that professional teams had come to play in great cities, and the southern states in the 1950s and 1960s were perhaps the best example. To put it more precisely, white pride in southern football waxed so intense because it was firmly rooted in the history and values of the South. The fanatical devotion to state football had grown from the fertile soil of the nineteenth-century southern code of honor. As Bertram Wyatt-Brown and Elliott Gorn have described it, this code of honor found expression in dueling among the gentry and in the rough-and-tumble wrestling and eye gouging among the poor folk of the southern backcountry. On the one hand, the violent, chauvinistic nature of the southern culture readily translated into loyalty to a game in which violence, ruggedness, and the ability to fight ferociously for inspiring coaches were trademarks of winning teams. Just as the South supplied disproportionate shares of combatants and noncombatants to the American military, its universities turned out hard-nosed gridiron heroes and football boosters who had scores to settle. Moreover, because the South had no pro football until the mid-1960s, college football at flagship universities enjoyed a stature far greater than the less accessible NFL. In short, it expressed a tribal loyalty buttressed by a tradition of fighting for one's honor. In a section that wore its badge of states' rights with pride, state football had a special, nearly mythical status. Football placed the honor and name of the state on a media-magnified pedestal for all the nation to see.[12]

Therefore, it came as a shock in 1963 when the *Saturday Evening Post* ran a story, "The Story of a Football Fix," which alleged that two well-known southern football figures, former coach Wally Butts of the University of Georgia and Paul "Bear" Bryant of Alabama, had conspired to fix their season's opener in September 1962. According to the *Post*'s story, an insurance salesman in Atlanta, George Burnett, dialing into the headquarters of his insurance company, suddenly found himself switched to a telephone conversation between two football coaches. Burnett, a graduate of Texas A&M who had played high school football, realized that, when he heard "Hello Wally" and "Hello Bear," he was listening to a conversation between Wally Butts, Georgia's athletic director, and Coach Paul "Bear" Bryant; the two were discussing details of the opening game between the two schools just over a week away. "Do you have anything for me?" Burnett recalled Bryant asking. Transfixed, Burnett listened as Butts appeared to be giving out inside information on the Bulldogs' football strategy to the leader of the Alabama Crimson Tide. Burnett made notes of the fifteen-minute conversation and then simply folded them in his pocket. One week later the Crimson Tide crushed Georgia, 35-0, in Birmingham; Burnett then thought back to what he had heard but did not divulge his secret until the end of the season, when he told a friend of Coach Johnny Griffiths of Georgia what he had heard. This revelation led to a meeting between Burnett and Johnny Griffiths. The Georgia coach took the notes from Burnett and, according to Burnett, declared: "This looks like our game plan. I figured someone had given the information to Alabama." It had been, after all, the first game of the season, when the Crimson Tide would have had no game films or scouting reports from which to prepare.[13]

George Burnett's whistle-blowing led to further meetings with Georgia officials, who not only questioned his veracity but also cast doubts on his character; they confronted the unsuspecting insurance salesman with several episodes in which he had been caught passing bad checks. Although he passed a lie detector test, Burnett learned the lesson that college football had its own gang of enforcers at the highest levels. After being browbeaten by the head of the Georgia board of regents, Burnett stumbled out of a meeting with athletic and university officials in a state of shock. When a reporter for the *Saturday Evening Post* appeared, Burnett took the advice of his lawyer and sold his story for five thousand dollars, in hopes that it would verify the facts and help him support his seven children. The venerable *Post,* which had seen its revenues plummet in the past several years, had recently adopted a new, aggressive muckraking stance, and the new editor, Clay Blair, saw the opportunity to show his advertisers that the *Post* could break the big story while rendering a *coup de grace* to Bryant, who had sued the magazine over a previous story. Unfortunately, the *Post* reporter relied solely on information from Atlanta sportswriter Furman Bisher, never having seen an actual copy of Burnett's notes and never checking the story's facts before it appeared. Though the article exploded with the impact that Blair had intended, it also created two new lawsuits, one from Butts and still another from Bryant.[14]

Butts still had powerful friends and supporters, including the head of Georgia's board of regents, but Burnett's story aroused enough suspicion that Governor Carl Sanders of Georgia ordered Georgia attorney general, Eugene Cook, to conduct an investigation. The attorney general's probe left no doubt that a telephone conversation had taken place between Butts and Bryant and that Burnett had surely not concocted his evidence. Bryant maintained that the conversation had consisted mainly of friendly banter between two coaches, but Cook's report concluded that "the giving of such information prior to the opening of the football game conveyed vital and important information that could have affected the outcome of the game played." Moreover, it came out that Butts and Bryant had had several other conversations the week of the game, including a sixty-seven-minute phone call on September 16.[15]

Both Bryant and Butts had distinguished careers as football coaches, but Butts's career as a coach had ended two years before. In his final years as coach Butts had lost not only his old coaching magic but also his personal moorings. Frequently drunk in public, Butts had engaged in an affair with a much younger woman, whom he actually took on football trips at the university's expense. In addition, he had engaged in moneymaking ventures, including orange groves, a loan company, and a restaurant, all of which had lost money. His business ventures plunged him into debt, a problem compounded by the expensive trysts with his woman friend in Atlanta, Florida, and the Bahamas. He and Bryant had both invested money in a company owned by a Georgia alumnus and notorious corporate raider of the 1950s and 1960s, Louis Wolfson, whose stock had plunged, leaving Butts with steep losses, far in excess of Bryant's. In 1960 Butts had been forced out as coach but, as a consolation, retained his other position as athletic director.[16]

Bryant, whose Alabama team had won the national championship in 1961, came from a hardscrabble background in rural Alabama to play football for the Crimson Tide and prospered as a coach at Kentucky and Texas A&M. Unlike the old-time coaches, whose salaries remained no higher than senior faculty, Bryant had a combined income as coach and athletic director at a starting salary of fifty-seven thousand dollars and one that quickly rose to a figure that, according to state policy, initially remained just under the salary of Alabama's president, Frank Rose. On top of this, alumni had provided him with a house, car, and country club membership, and, since he coached at Texas A&M, his connections had enabled him to invest (except for Wolfson's corporation) in lucrative business propositions.[17]

Being a harsh taskmaster, Bryant worked his team so hard in preseason practice that he often lost the weaker and less committed scholarship players, leaving a tough gridiron cadre and scholarship slots that he could fill with new talent. In fact, a number of coaches such as Darrell Royal at Texas and Frank Kush at Arizona State would become far more notorious for their grinding workouts and pitiless retribution against players who displeased them. Like Roman legionnaires, the hard-core products of these grim training regimens took no prisoners, and in 1961 one of them inflicted an injury in a game with Georgia Tech which was to lead to Bryant's first round of controversy with the *Saturday Evening Post*. With Alabama leading 10-0 in the final quarter, Chick Graning, a blocker, administered a forearm blow to the face of a Georgia Tech player, Darwin Holt, as he was racing full-tilt toward the Tech punt receiver. Hit just below the face mask, Graning dropped to the turf unconscious, having suffered a concussion and fractures of facial bones as well as of his nose and the bone beneath his eye. In addition, most of his teeth were either knocked out or broken. The official, who had had his back to the play, did not call a penalty.[18]

The violent incident led to an article in October 1962 by Atlanta sportswriter Furman Bisher in the *Saturday Evening Post* entitled "College Football Is Going Berserk," in which Bryant's style of coaching was portrayed as intentionally violent. Bryant, in return, proceeded to sue the *Post*. By 1962, when the Georgia-Alabama game took place, Bryant was trying to put his reputation for violence behind him and, in spite of the incident, had become even more revered in Alabama after his 1961 team won the national championship.[19]

In May 1963 Butts filed a suit for ten million dollars against Curtis Publishing, the parent company of the *Post*, and the jury trial for libel took place in August 1963. Much of the testimony centered not only on whether the notes on plays and formations could possibly have affected the outcome of the game but also on the motives of the former Georgia coach. Butts quit under pressure as athletic director after Burnett's story had become known (he was already scheduled to resign at the end of the school year). In addition to his notorious personal affair, athletic and school officials objected to Butts's transparent jealousy of his successor, Johnny Griffiths, and how in public statements he sought to undermine the young coach. Because the *Post* had done such a slipshod job of preparing the story and checking its facts, the attorneys for Curtis Publishing faced an uphill struggle and, in truth, failed to do an effective job in bringing out the facts. Even if Butts had provided inside information, the number of variables would have made it difficult to "fix" the game in the traditional sense. The information might have enabled Bryant to approach the game with a strong certainty of victory, which could have changed the margin of victory for the Crimson Tide.[20]

Though neither Butts nor Bryant bet on the game, the *Post* and the Curtis Publishing attorneys had to reach further for a monetary motive. Butts did not have the money to bet on games, but it turned out that he knew someone who did. A close associate, Frank Scoby, a Chicago beer dealer, proved to be a big-time gambler who had once helped Butts to get a loan from a Chicago bank and had advised him on his ailing business affairs. Butts made fourteen calls to Scoby in September 1962, calls that were never properly explained. Later, it was speculated that Butts might have disclosed information about Georgia because Scoby wanted to be sure of the outcome or to play the point spread. Butts had two other gambling contacts, but the *Post* attorneys did not try to explore the connections, and they remained a subject of mystery. If Butts did give out useful information, he may have done so because he believed that the outcome of the game was a foregone conclusion and that he was not really harming his institution or its football team, acts that he insisted in court he would never do.[21]

The jury had no trouble deciding that the *Post* had libeled Butts, rendering an astounding award of $3 million to Butts less than a week after its deliberations began, a figure later reduced by the courts to $400,000. Bryant, who already had a pending lawsuit of $250,000 against the *Post* for the brutality issue, filed a separate $10 million lawsuit in Birmingham. Bryant had indignantly denied in his testimony at the Butts trial that he and Butts had tried to fix the game. "Absolutely not," he roared, "If we did, we ought to go to jail." He left no doubt in the jury's mind who was at fault. "Anyone who had anything to do with this [the *Post* article] ought to go to jail," he righteously thundered. "Taking their money is not good enough."[22]

Nevertheless, Bryant settled both lawsuits with Curtis Publishing in February 1963, not long before his $4 million lawsuit was to go to court, for a mere $320,000. James Kirby, a law professor at Tennessee, who was hired by the Southeastern Conference to attend the Butts trial and later wrote a study of the episode, believes that enough evidence was available to threaten Bryant's suit and his reputation if it were properly brought out. As a result of a new judicial ruling (the *New York Times* rule), the burden had in the months following the Butts case fallen on the alleged victim of libel to prove malicious intent.[23]

The facts that came out of the "fix" controversy revealed interesting details about big-time college football at state universities. Butts had wracked up several thousand of dollars in calls at the university's expense not only to Bryant but also to his mistress and to his business contacts. Bryant had profited from the financial help of alumni and boosters at both Texas A&M and at Alabama, including businessmen who steered him into lucrative business deals and virtually took care of his major living costs. His double salary as coach and athletic director eventually made him the highest-paid figure in an extremely poor state in which the average income amounted to less than five thousand dollars and senior college professors were lucky to earn ten thousand dollars.[24]

Because Bryant was an immensely revered figure, the state of Alabama built virtually unassailable defenses around him, and the students, faculty, and trustees of the University of Alabama refused to entertain doubts, at least publicly, about his innocence. One of the most controversial and potentially damaging pieces of evidence against Bryant was a letter written by President Frank Rose of Alabama referring to a phone conversation with Bryant. Rose, a former clergyman and religion professor, informed President O. C. Aderholt, the Georgia president, to whom Bryant had referred a phone conversation in which he casually discussed football plays with Butts. In the trial, however, Bryant denied that he and Butts discussed football plays, and Rose upheld Bryant's testimony by conveniently overlooking three meetings with Bryant after he had learned of Burnett's revelations. Rose explained that he had jotted down a few thoughts regarding his talk with Bryant and let his secretary mail what he called an "interpretation" of what Bryant had said in their phone conversation. He insisted that his secretary did not clear the letter with Bryant.[25]

In truth the alleged conspiracy between Bryant and Butts said something more about college football than the possibility of an athletic director betraying his team. Since the story had appeared on March 23, 1963, newspapers had trumpeted the story across the sports pages. Sportswriters had blared out the charges and tawdry details of the alleged scandal on nearly a daily basis from March through August 1963, when the jury handed down its decision. But then the story almost entirely disappeared from the newspapers and athletic proceedings, springing to life only briefly when Bryant settled his case in 1964 and when the Supreme Court handed down its decision on the appeal in 1967. While the NCAA did take notice of gridiron violence in 1962, it never issued a statement one way or the other regarding the case. Twenty-three years later, when Walter Byers published his autobiography, he never mentioned the fix controversy, though he recounted his and the NCAA's encounters with Bryant. This lapse is perhaps explained by Bear Bryant's later career, when he went on to win more national championships in 1964, 1965, and 1973 and wound up his career breaking Amos Alonzo Stagg's record for total victories before retiring after the 1982 season (since broken by Eddie Robinson of Grambling). When he died in 1983, the story of the alleged fix had nearly vanished from the public memory.[26]

Once again, college football had shown a remarkable ability for surviving scandals intact. The *Post* had predicted that the scandal would permanently damage the sport, but neither institution, let alone college football, suffered serious injury, and, for that matter, Butts and Bryant themselves emerged from the trial relatively unscathed. One could say that Butts and Bryant were lucky that they did not have to prove that the defendants had acted maliciously, which the courts would have required if the case had gone to court six months later. Or that the *Post* rushed into print with a story that was poorly researched or that the lie detector tests showed that Burnett, Butts, and Bryant were all telling the truth, tests that fell below, James Kirby believes, the existing polygraph technology and standards of the testing profession. Or, for that matter, that Bear Bryant had just won the national championship and was far better known than Alabama's president, Frank Rose.[27]

The football controversies and scandals of the 1960s stand out because they appeared to rise above colleges and college athletics into the world of quasi-professional sports. In Alabama, where college football loomed far larger than the distant world of professional football, the state's and university's honor were at stake. The Alabama board of trustees issued a strong statement supporting Bryant and criticizing the *Post*'s "scurrilous attacks on the university." Resolutions introduced into the Alabama state legislature defended Bryant, the state, football players, and the university. And yet would professional football have rushed so confidently into a controversy headed for a highly publicized lawsuit? It is more likely that the NFL, faced with the prospect of a football fix tied to gambling, would have taken drastic steps to ensure that its credibility remained intact. At a flagship state university in a poor state like Alabama, reviled in many quarters for its racial policies, the successful football coach had a reputation second only to the governor. And his "second-to-the-governor" was only because the governor of Alabama happened to be George Wallace, who was busy trying to fend off attempts to desegregate the University of Alabama and who himself had issued a statement calling the *Saturday Evening Post* "the sorriest authority on the truth."[28]

To put Alabama's reaction in perspective, however, it might be well to compare the Butts-Bryant uproar to the intense passions at the University of Illinois in the Big Ten, where a scandal erupted in 1966. In its "secret report" the Big Ten committee in 1956 had projected that the most profitable football programs, such as Michigan's, would have the money to obtain blue-chip talent, and the want-to-be's would have to resort to underhanded methods. The Illinois scandal resulted because of disclosures by a disgruntled candidate for the job of athletic director who accused football coach and athletic director, Pete Elliott, of running a slush fund. Elliott, a former Michigan star, who had taken the Illini to the Rose Bowl in 1964, had also gotten the athletic director's job. Determined to crack down hard on slush funds, the Big Ten not only put Illinois on two-year probation but also required Illinois to fire Elliott and two other coaches. President David Dodds Henry of Illinois engaged in a desperate, eleventh-hour campaign to save Elliot, basketball coach Harry Combes, and an assistant coach, but to no avail. In this instance the faculty reps of a conference founded on faculty control made their judgment stick. In responding to pleas by the Illinois president, Northwestern's president, J. Roscoe Miller, indicated that he was sympathetic but could do nothing to help. "Under this arrangement," Miller lamented, "the Faculty Committee literally has final administrative authority over athletics."[29]

Not only did it reject the pleas of the president, but the Big Ten faculty representatives also threatened to expel Illinois if it did not fire the coaches. Reluctantly, Illinois complied, but the state legislature exploded with resentment. In an action similar to the California state legislature's at the time of the PCC scandals, the Illinois lawmakers voted for a probe of Big Ten practices. The bill's sponsor, state senator Joseph Peterson, labeled as "atrocious" the actions of the Big Ten, presumably because of the tough, no-nonsense stance. "We should stand behind our university," he declared, "and find out what is involved in its relationship with the Big Ten." In a word the Big Ten had made Illinois the scapegoats for what Peterson took to be ill will against the state of Illinois.[30]

The state of Illinois differed from Alabama because it had a big-city professional team, the Chicago Bears, as well as a private university, Northwestern, which also belonged to the Big Ten. Even though he had taken the Fighting Illini to the Rose Bowl, the fleeting success of Pete Elliott in the Rose Bowl year of 1964 hardly compared to the larger-than-life stature of Bear Bryant in Alabama. In the state of Illinois the Fighting Illini football team, like the Crimson Tide, conferred status on the state and served as a symbol for the alumni and the college community. Even in two dissimilar states like Alabama and Illinois, each had flagship universities located in smaller communities that had much in common with mid-sized cities across the country, where college football dominated the sports scene.

Since the faculty representatives played a vital role in the Illinois scandal, they and their fellow faculty deserve some comment. Though only in a matter of degree, the Big Ten differed from other conferences because the faculty representatives had always played a key role in athletic control and could hold their own against presidents and athletic directors. Often appointed by the presidents, the faculty representatives did not necessarily oppose the excesses of big-time athletics, and some of them enjoyed a cozy relationship with the athletic departments. Frequently, they represented professional divisions like the law school rather than the arts and sciences faculty. By the post–World War II era the faculty no longer had the control over student affairs which they enjoyed in the early 1900s, and much of that control had passed to college administrators. There were many reasons for this change. For one thing the state universities such as the Big Ten's had mushroomed to the size of the small cities, becoming so large that it took high-powered binoculars to see from one end of the institution to the other. Ohio State expanded from 31,535 in 1960 to 46,000 in 1964 and by 1968 to 55,000. Equally dramatic growth was registered by the University of Wisconsin at Madison, which grew from 18,811 in 1960 to 34,670 in 1968. The faculty at these "binocular universities" often had closer ties with their professions than with their students, and many of them lacked the interest in big-time athletics which had characterized their predecessors.[31]

This is not to say that faculty and faculty representatives did not occasionally resist this trend. At Ohio State in 1961, when the Buckeyes stood poised to participate in the Rose Bowl, the faculty refused to rescind a resolution against bowl games which had grown out of the intense opposition to postseason contests in the early 1950s. Anguished Buckeye supporters had to accept that their team would not go to the Rose Bowl. This stand, which caused much resentment among the students and in the larger university community, proved to be one of the last successful attempts by faculty to exercise control at a big-time university. In 1974, when George Hanford compiled a study of college athletics, he concluded that most faculty had no interest in athletics. "It would appear," Hanford declared "that *most faculty members, unless forced do so, do not think about intercollegiate athletics at all.*" They were aware of athletics, he believed, but did not regard them worth more than a casual nod.[32]

In spite of the Butts-Bryant episode and the endless parade of pigskin lawbreakers, college football was better off in the mid-1960s than at any time since the immediate postwar period. It had survived nearly all of the crises and had danced into a new era of TV profits which rendered it invulnerable to all but the most severe controls usually imposed by the NCAA. In 1966 college football boasted its version of professional football's 1958 "sudden-death" contest a decade earlier between Baltimore and New York, a show-down between Notre Dame and Michigan State, then ranked one and two in the national polls. The NCAA had initially scheduled the game as a regional telecast, but the game loomed as a showdown for the mythical national title. Since Notre Dame had its vaunted national following, letters poured into the network, ABC, requesting a national telecast, and the NCAA relented, fortuitously as it turned out because "the game of the century," as *Newsweek* called it, attracted thirty-three million viewers. Like the NFL championship game in 1958, this nationally televised game proved to be a nail biter when the two teams reached the final minute deadlocked in a 10-10 tie. The game ended on a note of controversy when Notre Dame coach Ara Parasegian chose to run out the clock to preserve a 10-10 tie in a decision that cemented the national championship for Notre Dame.[33]

The 1967 season turned out to be the end of a brief halcyon era for big-time college football. Beginning in 1968, the growing struggles between black players and coaches kicked off three years of serious disputes reflected in the breakdown of racial relations on college campuses. In addition, the undeclared war in Vietnam would not only strengthen student rebelliousness but would also fuel growing inflation, which drove up costs of big-time football and provided an outlet for divisions between large and small schools. The Periclean golden age of college football prosperity and unity in the 1960s now drifted into a period more like the dark and destructive Peloponnesian Wars.

The Costs of Winning

The major football institutions had been able to shrug off scandals and excesses in the 1960s because the NCAA was finally in a position to punish wrongdoers, and most teams seemed to benefit from the growing affluence and interest in sports. The University of Indiana, which had always lagged behind the rest of the conference, had revenue of $309,516 in 1959, but by 1968 that figure had swelled to $635,941. The gridiron income from college athletics had grown by 160 percent during that period, though expenses had gone up dramatically as well. The Maryland Terrapins, who played in the lower-profile ACC, generated only $25,268 in income, but by 1969 that number had reached $54,415, a gain of 55 percent.[34]

In the early 1970s college football began to suffer from eroding football profits. To begin with, enrollments abruptly began to drop as baby boomers completed college, a trend that reduced income from student athletic fees. In addition, students of that era showed less enthusiasm for big-time sports than their predecessors. A survey by the Gallup Poll reported that 43 percent of 1,061 students queried at sixty colleges admitted that their interest in collegiate sports had declined while they were in school. At California-Berkeley students voted to recommend that the $310,000 used to pay for the athletic deficit should be "reallocated in a manner more broadly representative of all students." Students at Texas protested the $13 million plan to enlarge the stadium, arguing that the funds should be used for the $8 million humanities center. While these protests rarely succeeded, athletic directors worried that they reflected a trend away from support of big-time college sports.[35]

Youthful critics who targeted the Pentagon, corporate giants, and university officials were also suspicious of big-time sports. The accounts of two former football players at top college teams, Dave Meggyesy and Gary Shaw, who published unflattering accounts in 1970 and 1971 of their experiences at Syracuse and Texas, showed that these heresies could reach into the locker rooms. Meggyesy who also played for the St. Louis Cardinals, described the violence, cheating, illegal cash payments, and physical damage of a college program that treated scholarship players as mere pawns. Meggyesy wrote of Coach Ben Schwartzwalder's disgust at his association with "beatniks," in reality graduate and drama students who regarded football with frank cynicism. Eventually, Meggyesy had to cut off contact with them because of the doubts that they raised about football. Shaw, who played under Coach Darrell Royal, described the brutality to which football recruits were subjected and how Royal merely wanted the unfit or less talented to quit school, thereby freeing up scholarships, a charge that had been hurled at Royal's friend Paul "Bear" Bryant. The trainer kept seriously injured players from visiting doctors because they were expected to "tough it out"; one player whose cleat wound would require one hundred stitches had coaches screaming at him to play until one of the coaches nearly retched when he saw the bloody wound. Top players were channeled into easy courses, while "the brain coach" forced the less talented players to take the most difficult ones, hoping that they would flunk out. While these counterparts of Allen Jackson's tell-all may not have themselves harmed attendance, they were symptoms of the opposition to football which had emerged in the era of student protest. The word *dehumanizing,* used to describe racial policies and the war in Vietnam, came naturally when applied to big-time college football.[36]

By the late 1960s and early 1970s the Vietnam War and huge government deficits had revved up the engine of inflation so much that President Richard Nixon, a Republican, tried unsuccessfully to fix wages and prices. The expenses of college football cut into the amount of money that athletic departments had available. Tuitions that had grown slowly in the 1960s increased by 30 percent between 1968 and 1972, creating additional expenses for some football teams which gave up to two hundred gridiron scholarships. In addition, the coaching staffs, which often numbered as many as seven, and the promotions and public relations had grown rapidly. In 1962 the college football rules committee shed the remnant of limited substitution and returned to two-platoon football. Traveling squads of players, which had numbered less than thirty, now soared to nearly fifty. Teams whose stadiums did not measure up to big-time standards had to reach into reserve funds to build new structures.[37]

During the early 1970s the financial crunch in college athletic departments suddenly became a critical issue for some athletic departments and for the NCAA. Syracuse University announced in 1972 that it would terminate its baseball and spring track programs, and the University of Miami (Florida) dropped basketball. The Big Ten decided to cut scholarships for minor sports from thirty-four to fifteen at each member school. At larger institutions football managed to sidestep the requirements of Title IX, an amendment to the 1964 Civil Rights Act which required college athletic departments to introduce a full array of intercollegiate programs for women. Nevertheless, schools would find in the 1970s that their athletic costs would increase as they grudgingly set aside money and scholarships for women's programs. With its insatiable need for scholarship, staff, promotion, and players' dormitories, football stood out as the last bastion of big-time male athletics, requiring far more scholarships than any other sports. Because it returned more revenue than any other sport, football remained dominant but not untouchable. The schools in the middle or at the bottom of the NCAA pack began to demand cost-cutting measures, and football scholarships headed the list.[38]

In 1971 Walter Byers, the powerful executive director of the NCAA, called for changes in the scholarship formula in order to take financial need into account. He also proposed limits on the number of coaches and of scholarships. Football scholarships cut to the core of his argument because in the first decade of these athletic awards the NCAA placed no limits on the numbers of scholarships which schools or conferences could allow. Something like an arms race took place among big-time conferences in attempting to give more scholarships than their competitors. The major southern conferences had practically no limits; the Southeastern permitted each member to give forty football grants to entering freshmen, while the Big Eight and Southwest permitted forty-five and fifty. Texas and SMU, in effect, could have fielded two hundred scholarship players in football, a total that would have smothered opponents in other conferences. Smaller or private colleges hit hard by rising costs and generating less revenue faced nearly insuperable odds. By the 1970s the major colleges had exempted themselves from giving four-year grants but, instead, gave scholarships on a year-to-year basis. As a result, football staffs could drop injured or unpromising drones in favor of more talented players. College players had become, in the unforgettable title of the book by the disgruntled Texan Gary Shaw, on Longhorn football, "meat on the hoof.[39]

When the NCAA took up the issue of cost cutting in 1971, the coaches in major conferences reacted angrily to the NCAA Council's proposal to limit its scholarships to thirty per year. Darrell Royal, Gary Shaw's coach at Texas, warned that, if the big powers could not have their way, they would secede from the association. Instead of cutting the number of scholarships, the schools in 1972 repealed the freshman rule, which in many conferences had kept freshmen from competing in varsity athletics. The NCAA had already allowed small colleges to play freshmen in what many saw as an entering wedge against the freshman rule at big-time institutions. Coaches at large schools would gladly use the talented freshmen who could make the starting lineup or give them a head start by scrimmaging with the varsity. Some schools with smaller gridiron programs such as the Ivy League institutions objected to a measure that neglected freshmen, who might need a year free of big-time athletics to become acclimated to academic life. "There is not a case at all," fumed the *New York Times,* "for subjecting immature freshmen to the demands and pressures and lures of varsity football at major universities."[40]

The financial issue had raised a more fundamental problem of large versus medium and small football institutions in framing athletic policy. In spite of inflation, the big schools that made good money in the early 1970s began to fear that cost-cutting measures would reduce the size and scale of their programs. While few athletic officials talked in terms of dropping out of the NCAA, the cost-cutting initiatives sowed the seeds of discontent and spawned talk of secession. For the time, the big schools demanded that the NCAA subdivide into categories that would more clearly reflect the size and scale of their football programs. Essentially, the NCAA operated on the basis of one vote for each school, but it treated the small colleges as a separate category by holding college basketball tournaments in the 1950s. Though small colleges also held their own roundtable discussion at the NCAA conventions, the association had never tried to create two formal divisions. In 1972, when the NCAA leaders did try to separate the NCAA into two divisions, many of the two hundred small schools of the ECAC (Eastern Collegiate Athletic Conference) voted down the measure by a narrow 218-224 margin because they felt that the broad, two-tiered divisional structure would prove ill suited to their needs.[41]

In August 1973 the membership voted to create a three-tiered structure known simply as Divisions I, II, and III, offering the two lower divisions playoffs in a variety of sports including football. Out of 667 NCAA schools 126 colleges would belong to Division I, but schools could also join the Division I in sports in which they played major competitors. The University of North Dakota, which played Division II football, for example, would join the Division I in hockey. Or Marquette University, which had dropped its football program in the early 1960s, would qualify for membership in Division I on the basis of its big-time basketball.

What appeared at first to settle the nettlesome problem of big and small colleges raised an outcry among big-time football coaches, who would now demand their own division. On top of this, some coaches and athletic directors wanted a division that would encompass only the top forty or fifty football schools, much like the NFL, which by 1970 had twenty-six teams. The major college teams in the early 1970s wanted more TV appearances, and, above all, they wanted a method to create a national championship like the Super Bowl. Put bluntly, the large number of schools in Division I struck them as unworkable. And the basketball powers that did not play football defeated their objective of an elite gridiron grouping. If the smaller schools in Division I limited football scholarships or staffs, the major football conferences hinted that they would drop out of the NCAA.

While the NCAA did not go to need-based scholarships, it agreed in 1974 to limit its gridiron scholarships at 105; the conferences could permit a maximum of thirty new scholarship players each year which would allow for an attrition of fifteen over a four-year period. At the same convention, however, the delegates eliminated the basic 1.6 rule for athletic admissions used to predict whether high school athletes would make a 1.6 out of 4 points as college students, which was only the equivalent of a D+ average. Schools that awarded scholarships essentially had to gamble that football players, the largest single group of recipients, would become eligible or remain eligible to keep their athletic scholarships.

In 1973 the NCAA dropped its standards even further, repealing the 1.6 rule and going, instead, to a 2.0 high school minimum. In effect, this provision opened the floodgates to admitting students from poor high schools, where athletes often gravitated into easy courses. This would open the gates to many nonwhite players who had been segregated in poverty-stricken, academically inferior high schools. By the same token it would create temptations to alter college transcripts or give automatic credit to players regarded as essential to gridiron success. In short, it was an invitation to cheat by the big-time football schools and a way that major colleges could expand their outreach for academically impoverished but athletically talented players. While the 2.0 rule would not save much money, it would definitely strengthen the major football teams.[42]

In the early 1970s ABC-TV had laid the foundation for institutional discontent with the introduction of its hugely popular "Monday Night Football." Roone Arledge had defied conventional wisdom in the TV and football worlds by creating a football spectacle in the time slot reserved for family entertainment. Moreover, he had put together a broadcast team of

Frank Gifford, Don Meredith, and Howard Cosell, who resembled sitcom characters more than a group of professional sportscasters; in addition, Arledge used all the bells and whistles he employed in college football. Walter Byers, who negotiated the contracts with ABC-TV, objected to Arledge's venture into NFL telecasts because the NCAA wanted to keep televised pro football sealed off from college football, a policy that the NCAA had pursued since the 1950s and a carryover from the era in which amateur and professional inhabited two different provinces. The college football audience, however, had fallen far below pro football's, and, beginning in 1972, college gridiron ratings dropped for most of the decade.

To put it bluntly, big-time college football now faced a combustible situation born of lowered academic standards, rising costs, and high expectations, not to mention the NCAA divisional structure, which needed only a few sparks to create an explosion. One prediction of the 1956 Big Ten committee seemed to crystallize in the 1970s. The committee had warned that financial pressures would set off a struggle for TV appearances and lock the major teams' hold on the media. It also projected that the distinction between college and professional sports would become virtually indistinguishable. It was still distinguishable but barely so.[43]

In 1974 George Hanford of the Educational Testing Service did a pilot study of college athletics, the most probing and perceptive study of college athletics since the Carnegie Report. More precisely, the American Council on Education, which sponsored the study, had intended Hanford's work as a pilot study for a new Carnegie-style investigation of college athletics, a project that unfortunately never materialized. Among Hanford's many ideas he adapted the metaphor of an academic procession (originated much earlier by Harvard sociologist David Reisman) to suggest that the once-mighty Ivy League would lead a procession of athletic reform that gradually would transform other institutions into Ivy League models. For those who could not recall it or had never participated in an academic procession, Hanford had to explain how the metaphor applied to colleges and universities. "Higher education proceeds to move forward like a snake," he wrote, "with the leadership at the head going through phases of development at one point that those successively further back in the procession will encounter successively later in time under somewhat altered circumstances." He declared that Harvard and Yale had introduced "all of the evils that are at the root of today's ills, overemphasis, alumni pressure, paid admissions, salaried coaches, recruiting and subsidy of athletes." The other institutions farther back in line would catch up with the procession of reform just as they had come to imitate Harvard and Yale's flawed system of big-time athletics.[44]

Provocative as it was, Hanford's metaphoric procession would go in almost the opposite direction. Sixty of the top hybrid pigskin powers would lead an athletic rather than an academic procession followed by the lesser schools that wanted to raise their gate receipts and football renown. This procession of the 1970s, which was really a struggle for supremacy, would prove to be a movement toward winnowing the athletic tree so that the few could profit from the virtually unpaid labor of student-athletes. It evolved into a movement to create a football meritocracy of the few; only the institutions that could provide the excitement and glamour of the college version of pro football needed to apply.

CHAPTER SIXTEEN

The Accidental Reform: African Americans at Predominantly White Schools

From the 1890s college football has proved to be a powerful agency for catapulting athletes from recent immigrant backgrounds into the front ranks of American college sports. Precisely because it refused to follow the spirit of amateur athletics, football's boosters paid subsidies to talented youth who had the size and agility to make their mark in the gridiron sweepstakes. Beginning with poor Irish boys like Cooney and Hogan, who went from the Pennsylvania coal fields to Andover and Exeter and then starred at Princeton and Yale, the roster of big-time football stars at some schools reads like an ethnic procession. Once the Irish, Slavic, Jewish, or Italian sons of immigrants crossed the threshold into college football, they had made the ritual passage into American life and embraced a facet of American culture highly valued by millions of their countrymen.

Simultaneously, football also reflected the traditional beliefs, values, and conventions within the community; it celebrated primal loyalties to race, economic class, and social caste. Because colleges served the sons and daughters of middle- and upper-class parents, college football was also expected to maintain the stark racial boundaries of the early 1900s, and, as a result, African Americans were barred not only from many predominantly white colleges but also from their athletic teams. Put simply and bluntly, from about 1900 to 1930 few black football players competed for flagship state universities, private colleges, or large private universities. In the South and in the adjacent border states none competed at all or, for that matter, attended the all-white colleges and universities. In the North and West, where fewer obstacles existed, whites frequently refused to acknowledge the athletic ability of African Americans, and in the South and border areas an African-American athlete who outshone a white boy would have challenged the so-called separate but equal caste system. Therefore, the most remarkable story of twentieth-century football history would prove to be the way in which football undid these policies and introduced to black athletes both the vices and virtues of big-time college football.

To be sure, college football never capitulated entirely to the racial exclusion that swept through most big-time sports, though only a few African Americans competed before the 1950s. In the World War I era Fritz Pollard and Paul Robeson became All-Americas at Brown and Rutgers simply because they possessed a talent so boundless that football and, more precisely, their institutions needed them to win. In the East and Midwest black football players appeared one or two at a time at a few schools, but on and off the field they led a marginal existence, suffering from racial slurs, brutality, and segregation. Theirs was a solitary and hazardous world populated by opponents and teammates, both of whom sought to disable them, as well as college administrators who refused to lend them support. The big-time football of black colleges such as Hampton, Howard, Grambling, and Florida A&M would have seemed far more preferable to black players, but a few outstanding athletes took up a challenge that could prove both disabling and even lethal.

The Half-Lives of Black Players, 1923 to 1967

The African Americans who played for predominantly white institutions faced extraordinary hazards and abuse, and occasionally their own ambition to excel created tragic consequences. In 1923 a 6′2″, 235-pound African-American, Jack Trice, playing at tackle in his first game for Iowa State, suffered a broken collarbone early in the first quarter, but he insisted on staying in the game. In the third quarter, seeing that he could not stop the big Minnesota linemen, he attempted a roll block to stop three Gopher blockers in front of the ball carrier. Thrown to his back, he was battered into the turf by the players leading the offensive surge. Carried from the field, he was taken to a Minneapolis hospital, where, on the advice of Minnesota physicians, he was discharged and placed in the back of a Pullman passenger car, lying on a makeshift bed of straw for the return trip to Iowa. A day after the team arrived Trice died in a hospital at Ames of hemorrhaging lungs and general internal bleeding.

Trice, who was the first African American to play for the Cyclones, had written a note to himself the night before the game: "The honor of my race, family and self are at stake," he began. "Everyone is expecting me to do big things. I will!" He went on to describe how he would throw his "whole body and soul . . . recklessly about on the field tomorrow." And, he prepared himself to play with near suicidal abandon, considering how black players were targeted by opponents in that era. In the 1980s Iowa State made restitution to its first African-American player by naming its new football facility Jack Trice Stadium.[1]

While Jack Trice gave his life to play college football, most African Americans at predominantly white schools had to confront a contrary facet of racism—the humiliating prospect of sitting out contests played against southern and border state teams. When a team with black players scheduled a southern opponent, the southerners almost always demanded that the black player be held out of the game, and, as a matter of courtesy, the northern team almost always complied. In 1934 Michigan agreed not to play its

African-American star Willis Ward against Georgia Tech, not in Atlanta but in its hometown of Ann Arbor. Fielding Yost, then the athletic director at Michigan, fearing the possibility of a student and faculty demonstration during the game, hired a Pinkerton detective to identify potential protesters and posted brawny students to break them up—though a demonstration never took place. Denied permission to view the contest from the Michigan bench or from the press box, Ward sat out the game in a fraternity.[2]

On Saturday, November 4, 1940, in a similar situation, an African-American football player, Leonard Bates, who competed for New York University, had to stay behind in New York as the NYU Violets lost 33-0 to the Tigers of the University of Missouri in Columbia. Missouri demanded that Bates not make the trip, and the president of NYU as well as the school's officials and coaches agreed to honor this gentleman's agreement. Unlike other instances, when predominantly white institutions gave into the demands of southern or border state institutions, Bates had become the center of a campus clash in mid-October, when it was announced that he would not play in the Missouri game. The university declared that Bates had been told when he entered NYU that he could not play against Missouri, out of courtesy to the border state team's lily-white policies. And activist students at NYU refused to accept the school's policy.[3]

Why did Missouri insist that Bates not compete—and why did NYU give in so readily? In every state where slavery had existed at the time of the Civil War and in newer, adjacent states like Oklahoma, where southerners had migrated, segregation replaced slavery after the Civil War, and in the early 1900s those states placed Jim Crow laws on the books. Sandwiched between Illinois and Kansas, the urban areas of Missouri, like Kansas City, had more in common with the Midwest in the twentieth century than with the Old South, but southern racial segregationist policies still held sway through much of the state. Beginning in the 1890s, Missouri refused to play against teams from neighboring Iowa if they attempted to place a black player on the field. Why southern and border state universities teams displayed such fear and loathing is deeply layered in southern history and lies beyond the scope of this book. To play teams that had black players would have violated the covenant of white supremacy which underlay both work and play in much of the country during the interwar period. Neither university officials, boards of trustees, state politicians, or, for that matter, coaches and players would have risked their careers by speaking out in favor of an interracial game.

Two weeks before the Missouri game at NYU's Ohio Field the largely white student organizers of the "Bates Must Play" movement circulated petitions among spectators when NYU played the nationally ranked Holy Cross Crusaders. In a sparsely attended game the pro-Bates activists held up signs and even managed to get the signatures of several Holy Cross players. The All-University Group, a coalition of social activists, called upon school officials to compel Missouri to let Bates play or to cancel the game. In response President Harold Chase of NYU insisted that not to respect deeply held beliefs of southerners would injure what was, he believed, slow but steady progress in race relations. "That would not be an act of tolerance," he declared defiantly, "it would be an act of sectionalism, and NYU is not a sectional institution."[4]

President Chase of NYU, a former president of the University of North Carolina, upheld the values of moderate southerners on racial matters. Chase believed that the South was making slow progress in working out its racial problems, but he also joined with southerners who insisted that if northerners tried to impose their policies the South would slide backward, as it had after Reconstruction. One might have wondered if the number of lynchings in the South truly represented racial progress, but moderate southerners pointed to the decline of race-baiting politicians and violent race riots as signs of progress. Chase no doubt believed in 1937 that he had achieved a breakthrough in racial relations when the North Carolina gridders agreed to travel to New York to play an NYU squad that had a single African American, Ed Williams, at tailback. While playing a standout game, Williams had been badly beaten up by the Tar Heel defense, suffering injuries that ended his career.[5]

Bates's attitude toward the game seems to have changed with the emergence of the Bates Must Play movement. According to the university, he had been told when he entered NYU that the Violets would play against Missouri and that he would not be making the trip. Apparently, he had agreed to NYU's terms and at the university's bidding had written a letter to the All-Negro group in October explaining that he had no reservations about following the university's policy. As it turned out, Bates really did not want to sit home, and, when the Bates Must Play movement gathered steam, he told a reporter for a student newspaper that he desired to make the trip and that the NYU officials had distorted the meaning of the letter that he had written to the African-American group. "By playing up one part of this letter," he said, "the press succeeded in creating the impression that I do not wish to play. This, however, is false. I would like to play."[6]

A few forlorn, rain-soaked protesters gathered on the steps of the Main Building at NYU on Thursday evening before the team left, but school officials refused to back down. Nevertheless, student groups remained active after the football season ended and continued to protest racial exclusion in basketball and track—until seven protesters handing out leaflets in the Student Union were summarily kicked out of school in February on the grounds that they had violated university regulations. While Leonard Bates played football the next season, NYU scheduled no less than four big-time southern or near southern teams like Missouri, games in which Bates did not play. That year the Bates Must Play movement vanished, to be replaced by player, student, and alumni protests over the anemic performance of the once powerful NYU team. The attack on Pearl Harbor following the 1941 season put an end to all protests and to the semblance of big-time football at NYU.[7]

Undoubtedly, Bates would have put his physical well-being in jeopardy if he had traveled to Columbia to play against Missouri. A more realistic and humane approach, proposed by one of the NYU student newspapers, was to have NYU establish a policy, as Harvard did in 1940, prohibiting the institution from playing teams that practiced racial segregation. Bates, who never had the chance to realize his gridiron potential, played his most important role in his brief football career as a symbol of opposition to NYU's gentlemen's agreements. Unfortunately, neither the highly confrontational students nor the segregationist NYU administration acted in the best interests of Leonard Bates, who merely wanted to compete on a level playing field.[8]

The Bates episode occurred on the cusp of World War II, and therefore it stands as a harbinger of racial reforms that emerged after the war. While the war uprooted life across the planet, it proved to be a turning point for college football. Some of the subtly shifting views occurred on the playing fields and others in the offices of the Pentagon. Still others took place in the attitudes of the soldiers and in the collective opinion of the American public. In a war that was fought against Aryan racial supremacy, the country inevitably had to face some of the deeply rooted problems in its own society.

The changes in American life during and immediately after the war proved to be the catalyst for profound realignments in sports as well. The opposition to Nazi ideals of racial supremacy took hold, and, as African Americans moved from the South to northern cities, many opportunities presented themselves to sports entrepreneurs. For the first time baseball promoters weighed the possibility of introducing players from the Negro leagues into the all-white major leagues, a break with tradition which culminated in the appearance of Jackie Robinson as a Brooklyn Dodger in 1947. In addition, by 1946 and 1947 a new consensus had emerged among college officials outside the South who refused to concede to southern racial demands.

In 1947 Harvard insisted on playing its 240-pound African-American tackle, Chester Pierce, when the Crimson traveled to Charlottesville to play Virginia. Though Virginia athletic officials were opposed to the move, they put the question to the team. The team of armed forces veterans voted to play Harvard, and the game, which Virginia won 46-0, was played without incident. The atmosphere in the stands and in the town proved to be another matter. Pierce not only faced taunts and slurs hurled at him from the stands, but he was also told that he had to stay in segregated quarters at a nearby hotel and to enter the dining room by a separate entrance. To a man the Harvard team insisted on staying in the same segregated annex and entering by the same Jim Crow entrances which the laws of the Old Dominion demanded of Pierce.[9]

Not surprisingly, the shifting attitudes in college football had their counterparts in the professional ranks. Two pro football teams introduced African-American players immediately after the war. One of the teams, the freshly minted Cleveland Browns, belonged to the new All-America Football Conference, which would challenge the NFL's monopoly for four years (in 1950 three of the teams, including the Browns, would enter the NFL, while the rest collapsed). Marian Motley, a 6'2" hard-driving fullback who had played for Brown's founder, Paul Brown, at Great Lakes Naval Base, and Bill Willis, whom Brown had coached at Ohio State, started for the Browns in 1946. In the same year the Los Angeles Rams of the NFL signed running backs Woody Strode and Kenny Washington, who had played in 1939 on the same UCLA team with baseball pioneer Jackie Robinson. That three great players originated in California was hardly an accident, because these players faced fewer obstacles and less outright prejudice in the less caste-ridden environment of southern California.[10]

The appearance of African Americans in pro football at the same time as Robinson began his new baseball career with the Montreal Royals in 1946 would leave the impression that the two sports had crossed the color line simultaneously, but this was hardly the case. Like college football, the NFL had a history of black players, such as Brown's Fritz Pollard and Paul Robeson, who played professionally while attending law school at Columbia. One African American, Duke Slater, an All-America from Iowa, played professionally from 1922 to 1931, spending his final five seasons with the Chicago Cardinals. In 1934 the NFL, which had cut back on teams and players because of the Depression, imposed a tacit hiring freeze on black players, a variation of the "last hired and first fired" complaint that became a rallying cry in the 1960s. When black players showed up again in token numbers, pro football could hardly boast that it had pioneered gridiron integration.[11]

Nevertheless, the influx of a few African Americans into professional football paralleled the intersectional contests between northern and southern teams in which black athletes were given the chance to compete. In addition to Harvard's Chester Pierce playing at Virginia, the racial firsts included teams with black players such as Pittsburgh traveling to Durham, North Carolina, to play Duke in 1950, a game in which Flint Greene, a tackle for Pitt, became the first African American to participate in a Southern Conference game held in North Carolina. An integrated Nevada squad helped to swamp Tulsa, 65-15, in the first interracial football game played in Oklahoma.[12]

In spite of these few breakthroughs, the games that failed to materialize because of racial deadlocks stand out as much as the few that actually took place. In 1946 Penn State called off a game with Miami because of a law in Florida against black and white athletes playing on the same field; while the coaches wanted to go south as planned, the Nittany Lions, with a squad made up of many war veterans, refused to play without the team's halfback, Wally Triplett. Similarly, Nevada canceled its game with Mississippi State when the Bulldogs objected to its two black players. In 1947 Branch Rickey, general manager of the Brooklyn Dodgers, who had just brought Jackie Robinson into the major leagues, was unable to persuade Rollins College of Winter Park, Florida, to keep its engagement with his alma mater, Ohio Wesleyan, which insisted on bringing an African-American player. Two years later Florida State, an upstart university with an ambitious new football program, called off a home-and-home series with Bradley of Peoria, Illinois, because the school insisted on fielding an integrated team. The faculty of Lafayette College of Easton, Pennsylvania, even rejected a bid to the Sun Bowl in El Paso for January 1, 1948, because the team's single African-American player would have had to stay behind due to the customary southern ban against black players.[13]

In 1951 the apparent progress in the upper South and border states suffered a setback when Johnny Bright, an African-American running back for Drake, was severely injured in what was most certainly a racial episode. Bright had amassed more yards in his three-year career than any other player in college football history, piling up nearly six thousand yards rushing and nearly three thousand passing. Despite his statistics, however, he hardly got the bumper crop of publicity accorded to All-America Dick Kazmaier of Princeton, who won the Heisman Trophy in 1951. Unlike Kazmaier, Bright not only played for a relatively obscure team in the Missouri Valley Conference, but he simply did not catch the attention of sportswriters—that is, until a game played between Drake and Oklahoma A&M on October 20, 1951.[14]

The midwestern and southwestern states on the fringes of the South had always been the scene of explosive race relations since the era of partisan warfare in "bleeding Kansas" just before the Civil War, and these combustibles still existed on the gridiron battlefields of this section. After World War II, when Oklahoma A&M applied for membership in the Big Seven, students at Nebraska and Kansas resisted it because of A&M's segregationist policies. The Aggies played largely a regional schedule, and, whereas their players might have learned more about race relations if they had played Michigan or Michigan State, the A&M players had little opportunity to broaden their outlook. This racial intolerance translated into hostility toward the few African-American players, such as Johnny Bright, whom they happened to encounter in the Missouri Valley Conference. In much the same way that players of the 1890s used to put their opponents "out of business," players for A&M apparently decided that they would go all out to disable Bright, who, besides being nonwhite, was the key to Drake's offense.[15]

It did not take them long. On the first play from scrimmage Bright was gravely injured in an act of wanton violence. As Bright stood on the playing field at least five yards behind and to the side of the ball carrier, a tackle for the Aggies turned and ran at him, delivering a crushing forearm to the jaw. Bright continued to play for seven minutes and gained seventy yards rushing before leaving the game in acute pain and, as it turned out, with a broken jaw. "I remember getting fists in the first two plays we had the ball," Bright declared afterward. The A&M players, he strongly believed, were out to get him. Drake lost the game, 27-14, and the Drake coach vigorously protested. At first the Aggie coach denied that his players had intentionally set out to injure Bright, but, when movies and photos later showed that the A&M player had gone out of his way to deliver the blow, the Aggie coach publicly apologized.[16]

Two weeks later, his jaw wired and face protected, Johnny Bright returned to action against Great Lakes Naval Station, gaining 204 yards in a Drake victory. Reinjuring his jaw, Bright took the advice of an oral surgeon in Des Moines and announced that he would quit college football. The incident did not end, however, with Bright's retirement or with the end of the Drake Bulldogs' season. The school would not let the matter rest and complained formally to conference authorities. When the officials refused to discipline Oklahoma A&M, Drake resigned from the Missouri Valley Conference.[17]

Bright, who made third-team All-America following the season, became a soon-forgotten victim of the racial antagonism that existed along the western borderland of the South. While Bright never won the top gridiron honors that he undoubtedly deserved, his injury highlighted a racial problem that the NCAA had never taken notice of. Since its inception football remained a violent game in which players could be "put out of business" at any time. Injuries to black players in interracial games, however, had another dimension, which teams had heretofore accepted without comment or had gone out of their way to avoid by not allowing their black players to participate. The death of Jack Trice in 1923 and the disabling injury of NYU's Ed Williams fall into that category of the pre–World War II "that's too bad, but it's the way things happen" mentality.

But the postwar era brought efforts to breach gridiron racial taboos interspersed with sporadic examples of racism. The career-ending injury to Johnny Bright might have passed without comment before World War II, but Drake might also have held out its star player. To put it more bluntly, the attitudes of northern schools had changed, but the southern and border state institutions had made glacial progress. Most of the southern institutions, even those in the upper South, such as Virginia and North Carolina, remained almost entirely segregated in the 1940s and 1950s. Though an African-American player tried out for Virginia's team in 1956, he had practically no chance of making the varsity. Farther south, in Alabama and Mississippi, to name two states with the most rigidly segregationist state universities, schools simply did not schedule northern teams if that meant playing against integrated squads. Since the southern teams normally stayed in their region, playing against segregated teams, interracial football never became an issue, since these schools did not schedule desegregated northern teams.

For the southern teams that competed in their own backyard, the problems of integrated play only arose if they were invited to a bowl game. Bowl games, which often took place in the former states of the Confederacy, at first failed to overcome the barrier of segregation but later turned a liability into a temporary showcase for interracial play. Before World War II a northern team invited to a southern bowl, such as Boston College in 1940 and 1941, left its solitary black player at home, but after World War II the policies of northern institutions toward integrated postseason contests changed in the same way as they had during the regular season. For a time the major bowls managed to resolve racial issues, as in 1947, when the Cotton Bowl invited an integrated Penn State squad to Dallas to play Southern Methodist, a Dallas institution whose coach and team were eager to play the Nittany Lions. The bowl officials were able to satisfy Penn State by obtaining special housing for the entire team and scaling down the level of social activities. After a thrilling 13-13 tie on January 1, 1948, the Cotton Bowl invited another integrated team, Oregon, to play the following year. In 1952 an integrated College of the Pacific team played at a previously segregated Sun Bowl, and after the 1954 season the Nebraska Cornhuskers, who had two black players, competed. In spite of the regular season setbacks, the postwar trend that had reversed the Bates scenario seemed to have embraced some major southern teams, college authorities, and bowl promoters.[18]

This trend came to a wrenching halt in 1955, after the Supreme Court's *Brown v. Board of Education* desegregation decision in May 1954. More precisely, the decision whipped up a frenzy of agitation among southern politicians bent on exploiting the dreaded specter of interracial athletics. In November 1955, when the Sugar Bowl invited Georgia Tech to play the University of Pittsburgh in New Orleans, a group of segregationists with ties to recently formed racist groups set off a protest. A member of the segregationist States' Rights Council, who also served on the board of regents, asked Coach Bobby Dodd of Georgia Tech to cancel the bowl invitation.[19]

Once Pandora's box of rabid racism had opened, the segregationist politicians began to buzz. Governor Marvin Griffin, an arch segregationist, who had previously evinced no objection to the invitation, insisted that the board of regents keep the Yellow Jackets from competing. In florid rhetoric Griffin telegraphed the regents: "The South stands at Armageddon. The battle is joined. We cannot make the slightest concession to the enemy in this dark and lamentable hour of struggle." He found no difference, Griffin contended, between "compromising the integrity of race on the playing field than doing so in the classrooms. One break in the dike and the relentless seas will rush in and destroy us." The reason for this florid rhetoric was an African-American halfback, Bobby Grier, who played for Pitt.[20]

At this moment of intense white opposition to integration only the single fanatical regent embraced Griffin's position, which would mean keeping Georgia Tech at home (one regent even branded the governor's position as "asinine"). The president of Georgia Tech, Blake Van Leer, responded that Griffin had not asked him or Georgia Tech to reject the Sugar Bowl invitation. "I have never had any communication from the governor on the Sugar Bowl bid," the president declared, "or on his proposal that Georgia teams not be allowed to play against Negroes." Van Leer added that Georgia Tech always honored its commitments.[21]

In a turn of events which resembled the scenario of "Bates Must Play," the students at Georgia Tech ignored the alarms of the extremist politicians and, if anything, turned their wrath on the chameleon-like Griffin. Realizing that the Yellow Jackets' chances for national recognition would vanish if the team did not go to New Orleans, they demanded that their team be allowed to play. Carrying placards with slogans such as "To Hell with Griffin," two thousand students marched through downtown Atlanta, overturned several cars, and hanged effigies of the governor in front of the governor's mansion. Joined by a small contingent from the University of Georgia, the Tech students demonstrated against Griffin and then, in 1950s style, conducted a panty raid on the women's dormitories. The riot led the governor's office to call out the state police, and, once the mob was dispersed, Griffin promptly criticized President Van Leer for letting the Georgia Tech students get out of hand.

President Van Leer apologized, but, as Griffin learned, football rankings in the 1950s carried more political clout than erecting an impenetrable wall of athletic apartheid. Like their cohorts in the North, those in the postwar college generation at southern universities had subtly shifted their attitudes toward race. While college students at Georgia Tech would have opposed integration in 1955, they could not view a single nonwhite player with the same concern as an arch segregationist like Governor Griffin did. Big-time football again had demonstrated its raw power to undermine traditional mores and cultural values, or, put simply, to force the authorities to allow a highly touted, local team to compete in an interracial game.[22]

Walking their own political tightrope, the regents gave permission (subject to the coach's discretion) for Tech to go to New Orleans. By passing a regulation banning interracial competition within Georgia, however, the board also demonstrated its commitment to segregation. President Van Leer dutifully promised to take action against the Georgia Tech students who had caused the recent mayhem. The students, however, had succeeded in heaping ridicule on Griffin's metaphor of "Armageddon," showing their contempt for a metaphor that conjured up scenes of the northern siege of Atlanta a century before.[23]

On New Year's Day Grier played most of the game, while Georgia Tech eked out a 7-0 victory on a disputed call against Grier for pass interference, a close call that, in itself, caused controversy. Those who had witnessed or read about the angry prelude in Atlanta wondered if Bobby Grier's presence off the field would create problems for the lone "Negro," but Grier went out of his way to accommodate southern race etiquette. He attended the awards banquet, but, instead of trying to integrate an evening dance, which might well have caused an uproar in lily-white circles, he attended a social event at Dillard College, a traditionally black school. Much as they had done with Jesse Owens at the 1936 Olympics, both the *Atlanta Constitution* and *New Orleans Picayune* excluded from their pages the controversies and circumstances surrounding Grier's presence in New Orleans and his role in a tight game.[24]

As Charles Martin has pointed out, the racist seating policies at the Sugar Bowl also initially posed a problem. The seats at Tulane Stadium, where the game was traditionally held, had been reserved for only white spectators, but in preparation for the 1955 match the bowl committee altered its seating policies so that there would be no restrictions in the visitors' section yet kept the Jim Crow policies elsewhere, allowing black spectators in only one of the distant "end zone" sections. Here, too, the intersectional bowl game, with its potential for recognition and profits, had made a small dent in the wall of segregation.[25]

As it turned out, the dent in segregation proved maddeningly meager. Following the game the Louisiana legislature passed a ban against holding interracial games anywhere in the state, and nearby Mississippi did the same. Not to be outdone, the administration at Pittsburgh announced that it would not return to Louisiana because the legislature had banned interracial play. The Georgia legislature tried to pass a bill against all athletic competition between blacks and whites in 1956 and again in 1957. Eight years after the Pitt-Georgia Tech contest an integrated squad from Syracuse University finally reappeared at the Sugar Bowl, an event that caused far less controversy in 1964 than it had in 1956. In one small way Governor Griffin had been right, because the interracial bowl games paved the way for integrated college football and even for integrated colleges. Institutions competing against schools with integrated teams and white players mixing with a black player, as the Georgia Tech players did at the awards banquet following the game, would not likely view integrated football or, for that matter, some form of integrated college life as an apocalyptic threat.[26]

Still, the low-level crisis of interracial football lingered into the early

1960s, when major football schools in the Southwest began to integrate their programs. In 1963 the University of Texas announced that it would drop its bars to athletic integration, and four other Southwest Conference teams also announced an end to segregation. The schools did not immediately integrate their football teams, but the gradual integration of high schools quickly led to interracial high school football, a short step from integrated college teams. At first the big-time coaches at Houston, SMU, and Texas experimented by recruiting a single outstanding player or, conversely, in the case of Texas A&M, carried two black players who rarely participated. The first black scholarship player in the SWC, Jerry Levias of SMU, who signed with Southern Methodist in 1965, had to endure racial abuse on and off the field, including racial taunts, spitting in his face, and unnecessary roughness that referees seldom bothered to penalize. In an incident at a game with Texas A&M members of the A&M cadet corps even released black cats onto the field. Off the field, as Richard Pennington has recounted, Levias had to endure hate mail, insulting telephone calls, and a death threat even while he performed heroics on the playing field and led SMU to a rare conference title. As late as 1969, Texas and Arkansas had no African-American scholarship players on their rosters.[27]

Institutions in the most rigidly segregated states of the Southeastern Conference lagged even farther behind. Given the fact that Governor George Wallace refused to admit black students to Alabama in 1963, it was hardly likely that Alabama—or, for that matter, Auburn, Mississippi, or Mississippi State—would integrate its football teams. In 1963, however, the University of Kentucky made an attempt to moderate the policies of its fellow Southeastern Conference teams. Being the most northern of SEC institutions, Kentucky sent a questionnaire to other conference schools asking if they would be willing to compete against "Negro" players. As a border state across the river from Big Ten powers in the Midwest, Kentucky could ill afford to let the rich African-American talent in northern Indiana and Chicago, let alone in its own state, slip through its hands. Because high schools in Kentucky had rapidly integrated after the *Brown* decision in 1954, the players on their teams and the university itself proved less squeamish about playing integrated athletic teams. Two of the SEC teams, Georgia Tech and Tulane, replied to the Kentucky query that they would play integrated teams at home and away, and the responses of Georgia and Florida indicated that they would probably play. Yet five conference teams—Alabama, Auburn, Louisiana State, Mississippi, and Tennessee—failed to reply. And, though Mississippi State had played a nearly all-black Loyola of Chicago team in basketball, the segregationist governor Ross Barnett opposed this experiment in interracial athletic competition.[28]

In 1967 the U.S. Justice Department warned the holdout teams of the Southeastern Conference to dismantle their racial ramparts or to face the withdrawal of federal funds. Throughout the South the threat of federal intervention drove the diehards to end segregation of their football teams and to discontinue Jim Crow seating at football games. As other southern teams and conferences recruited African Americans, the last-ditchers realized that their football would decline if they did not aggressively pursue talented black players. Already Kentucky and several other schools had desegregated their football teams, and in 1969 a junior linebacker at Kentucky, Wilbur Hackett, became the first African-American co-captain of an SEC team.[29]

Student Rebellion and Black Athletic Power, 1967 to 1970

As it turned out, the end of segregated football in the South occurred on the cusp of more militant racial rebellions. In the late 1960s demonstrations and demands erupted on campuses across the country, with students demanding an end to war in Vietnam, more power to establish their rules and curriculums, and an end to discrimination against African Americans. While these issues blanketed the front pages of newspapers, the sports sections carried stories on the rebellion of black student athletes. African-American players, whose numbers had grown significantly in the 1960s, summoned up grievances that, in turn, led to confrontations with coaches and school authorities.

Not that all gridiron rebels were black. While playing football at Northwestern, as Rick Telander relates in *The Hundred Yard Lie,* he and teammate Mike Adamle went to their coach, Alex Agase, immediately following the shooting deaths of four Kent State students in 1970 to ask if some team members could wear armbands. Agase, who had fought with the Marines at Okinawa, refused to allow the two to wear armbands during games, and Adamle and Telander continued to play. In contrast to the restiveness of these athletes, who echoed a broader student protest, outright rebellions among football players almost invariably involved African Americans, who normally made up a minority of the team members. The grievances varied widely, but the small numbers of black athletes on campus placed them in a more insecure footing than their white counterparts. Still, the numbers of black athletes, not to mention black students, were small enough that solidarity often existed between African-American members of various athletic squads and black student groups that encompassed students elsewhere on campus.[30]

In 1967 Harry Edwards, an instructor at San Jose State who had competed in track and basketball as an undergraduate and then earned a master's degree in sociology, presented a list of grievances to the school president on behalf of fifty-nine black students. Many of the complaints reflected racial slights that students had suffered on and around campus. But the 6'8" bearded former athlete also included a number of "indignities" affecting black student athletes, chiefly arbitrary treatment and decisions by white coaches. He threatened that, if the conditions were not immediately remedied, his group would stage a stadium sit-in during the home opener between San Jose and Texas-El Paso. The president of San Jose State, Robert Clark, immediately canceled the game, and California authorities, in turn, denounced Clark for giving in to the agitators. Governor Ronald Reagan called Clark's decision "appeasement of the lawbreakers" and described Edwards as unfit to teach. In turn, Edwards, who taught at San Jose, dismissed Reagan as a "petrified pig unfit to govern."[31]

From the fall of 1967 to the summer of 1968 Edwards attempted to organize black athletes from across the country in a movement to boycott the Mexico City Olympics in October. Though the boycott failed, the black Olympians became embroiled in controversy in Mexico City when they wore black armbands to protest racial conditions in the United States. Most notorious of all proved to be two medal winners, John Carlos and Tommie Smith of San Jose State, who outraged Olympic authorities by giving the black power salute in the form of an outstretched clenched fist during the playing of the "Star Spangled Banner." Dismissed from the U.S. Olympic squad, they returned to a San Jose campus that seethed with racial and political unrest. Though Edwards had departed to pursue his doctorate at Cornell, the athletes at San Jose persisted in their protests. On November 31, 1968, seven players chose to boycott the game against Brigham Young University, a target of black protesters because it was owned by the Mormon Church, which did not allow African Americans to become members of its priesthood. As a result of this protest, the seven players were dropped from the San Jose football team.[32]

In 1968 a host of black rebellions broke out on various campuses, many of them involving athletes in football. At California fourteen African-American players refused to turn out for spring practice, demanding the right to say which positions they would play, an outgrowth of "stacking" of black players such as pass receivers and defensive backs. At Kansas fifteen players boycotted practice because there were no "Negro" girls leading the "pom-pom" cheers. The university promptly appointed a black woman to the team, and the players returned to practice. And at Michigan State thirty-eight of the school's black athletes threatened to boycott all sports if their demands were not met. They called for the hiring of an African-American football coach and demanded that the university provide counseling to help keep them academically eligible, presumably by directing them into the appropriate courses and majors. After a year of threats and boycotts by African-American players, the NCAA approved a resolution at its convention in January 1969, allowing its coaches and athletic directors to cancel the athletic scholarships of players who refused to obey rules and regulations set by the athletic department.[33]

Nevertheless, the protests grew more frequent and the resulting stand-offs more unsettling. Periodic rebellions flared when a group of black players ran headlong into authoritarian white coaches who were strict disciplinarians and regarded black protests as disruptive to team solidarity. African-American players possessed the numbers and the talent to create problems for their teams if they chose to go on strike. Often infused with political awareness by black student organizers on campus, the athletes perceived some of the coaches' acts such as criticizing their Afro hairstyles or goatees as racial slights. Reinforced by student protests on campus against the Vietnam War, African Americans found more and more telltale signs that they lived in a racist society reaching from the pinnacles of power to the locker rooms and coaches' offices.

One episode that epitomized the black athletic protests and the white reaction occurred in an unlikely location, the University of Wyoming at Laramie, a flagship state institution that enrolled a mere handful of African Americans in a state that had practically none. Among the few black students at Wyoming the African-American members of the football team played a crucial role in the team's success. As an up-and-coming football program, Wyoming had gone to the Sugar Bowl in January 1969, giving rise to a groundswell of enthusiasm and resulting in proposals to expand the football stadium. Cowboy coach Lloyd Eaton was expected to field an even stronger team in the fall of 1969, which drew far more attention than the disturbing events in Vietnam and divisive national politics in the distant urban centers.[34]

Compared to larger schools in more populated areas, the University of Wyoming had remained fairly quiet in the face of the explosive face-offs at the national level and on other campuses. Yet reminders of protests on other campuses periodically flared, as in 1968, when demonstrators surrounded the courthouse in Laramie to protest the Vietnam War and the lack of ideological choice among the presidential contenders. The war itself created sporadic but small protests in Laramie, such as a march in the fall of 1969 in support of an antiwar moratorium, which attracted less than seven hundred marchers (the student population at Wyoming numbered roughly seventy-five hundred). In that same fall semester, inspired by the actions of students on other campuses, the small number of African Americans at Wyoming formed the Black Student Alliance, whose influence soon spread to black members of the Wyoming football team.[35]

By mid-October the Cowboys were undefeated and scheduled to play Brigham Young University on October 19, 1969. On Thursday evening after practice Coach Lloyd Eaton summoned Joe Williams, an African American and one of the team captains. Eaton had just heard from the Black Student Alliance of a demonstration planned for the BYU game. A letter from the alliance stated that the players would wear black armbands, but Eaton warned Williams that if any players wore black armbands on the field on Saturday they would be dropped from the team.

At 9:30 the next morning the fourteen black players appeared in Eaton's office wearing the controversial black armbands. When Joe Williams asked if Eaton would talk with them, Eaton led the players to the cement rows of bleacher seats in the fieldhouse and then delivered a fifteen-minute lecture. The coach began by telling the players, "I can save you fellows a lot of time and a lot of words. You are all through." When the players tried to give their views, he told them to "shut up." He also told them to go back to Morgan State or Grambling—or, better yet, to return to picking cotton. He also told them to go back home and get on welfare.[36]

Later in the day the state authorities reacted as if their university, the state's flagship university, had come under siege. The board of trustees rushed to Laramie, where they held a special session with Governor Stanley Hathaway, university president William Carlson, and the dissident players. The meetings, which extended well into the night, failed to achieve a settlement that would allow the black players to be reinstated in time for the game. When the "Black Fourteen" refused to back down on wearing armbands, the trustees and governors voted to uphold Coach Eaton's decision.

That Saturday a Cowboy team, their adrenalin flowing, routed Brigham Young, 40-7. Signs, hats, and banners, including a Confederate flag flown for three quarters, demonstrated the spectators' overwhelming support for a coach who had recently received an award for outstanding achievement from the alumni association. While the Black Fourteen sat in the stands, the loudspeaker announcer asked for a standing ovation for Eaton. Only a small group of forlorn protesters refused to stand, while the stadium resounded with cheers for the coach. In the meantime a contingent of National Guardsmen waited under the stands in case the rumored busloads of paramilitary Black Panthers from Denver showed up. They failed to appear.[37]

Most of the Black Fourteen never played college football again for the Cowboys. Wyoming won its next game against San Jose State but, after losing several games, fell from the polls. Following the incident, three black track athletes quit the school, and, after a losing season in 1970, Lloyd Eaton also quit. The Wyoming team, which had shown so much promise, now became an "also-ran" in the Western Athletic Conference.[38]

In Wyoming the climate of opinion had remained more conservative than in other parts of the country. Before the Black Fourteen incident Lloyd Eaton warned some of his black players about growing beards or lengthy sideburns, which, in truth, coaches did also with white players. Coaches like Lloyd Eaton, however, frequently treated their nonwhite athletes as if they merely had the good fortune to be playing football for a major team. Placed on the defensive by the sudden student activism, coaches often acted as if the racial situation had barely changed since their days as students. When one of the black players told Lloyd Eaton that he had come to Wyoming to get an education, Eaton corrected him. "Son, you're wrong," he said, "you came here to play Cowboy football."[39]

After the incident of the Black Fourteen, the vigilante justice displayed by the athletic department caused a brief but intense protest. One hundred graduate students, teaching assistants, and instructors met to discuss methods of protesting the dismissal. The Student Senate voted 17-1 to support the football players, and the faculty senate voted 37-1 for a resolution in favor of reinstating the black players to the team. Before an overflow crowd of 750 at the open meeting, 7 faculty members threatened to resign their positions if the athletic department did not change its position, which it refused to do. The Black Fourteen sought a symbolic victory of reinstatement by taking their case to court, but they failed to win the preliminary decisions or the later appeals. A few of the players went on to careers in the NFL, but most of them never played another quarter.[40]

The Black Fourteen not only shook the Wyoming campus but also spoke eloquently of the changes in the racial makeup of big-time college football. No longer one or two players on a team, African-American players had become an essential component of major football (and other athletic) teams. At Wyoming the hard-nosed reaction of the coach, athletic department, and trustees doomed attempts at compromise. At other schools, however, the confrontations wound up in committees and before school officials who attempted to mediate the differences. In truth black athletes at many institutions had achieved the critical mass to make their voices heard, and even at Wyoming the fourteen players' seemingly innocuous protest created an overnight statewide crisis. Unlike his isolated predecessors, the African-American athlete of the late 1960s demanded respect and recognition and had black student groups to which he could turn.

At Oregon State the actions of an arbitrary coach initially created the same deadlock that had occurred at Wyoming. After meeting one of his players while crossing the campus, Coach Dee Andros ordered the player to shave off his goatee by the beginning of the next week. When the player refused, he was dismissed from the team. Like Lloyd Eaton, Coach Andros enjoyed great prestige and popularity, his style reflecting the highly regimented approach of many post–World War II head coaches. Like Eaton, he expected unswerving loyalty from his players. What happened at Oregon State, however, proved to have few similarities to the "cowboy justice" at Wyoming. The episode at Oregon State led to the appointment of a Commission on Human Rights and Responsibilities, which handed down a split decision supporting both parties. Even so, Oregon State, like Wyoming, acquired a reputation as an institution hostile to African Americans. As at Wyoming, that image would have a devastating effect on Oregon State football—and basketball—as the institutions found it hard to recruit African Americans in the 1970s and 1980s.[41]

In 1969 and 1970 a number of racial episodes took place at larger institutions which led to far more protracted disputes. At Syracuse University longtime coach Ben Schwarzwalder suspended seven of nine black players who had taken part in a boycott of spring practice. Racial tensions at Syracuse were running high, and the black players were demanding that the institution hire a black assistant coach. The racial problems swirling about Schwarzwalder, who had coached Jim Brown, Ernie Davis, and Floyd Little, soon landed in the offices of the university chancellor, and a special committee examining the matter pronounced the university guilty of "institutional racism." Because of Schwarzwalder's past successes and alumni pressure, he managed to keep his job and eked out a winning season in 1970, but he eventually had to quit coaching at Syracuse because of his inability to deal with fractious black players.[42]

Even Princeton, an institution that had de-emphasized its football program when it entered the Ivy League, suffered a small rebellion of five black athletes who in 1969 accused the varsity and freshman coaches of racism. They complained that the coaches refused to allow them to become starters, especially in backfield positions. In contrast, the future Dallas Cowboy Calvin Hill, who had won an academic scholarship to Yale, recalled that his classes and athletics only expanded his outlook. Unlike big-time athletic institutions, Yale provided Hill not only with an education but also with a campus at which he was well-known rather than separated into an athletic or racial caste. While Hill participated in the Black Student Alliance, he and other African Americans also belonged to white fraternities and societies. He felt no hostility toward his coaches or toward the university. "We [the African-American students] didn't feel a sense of alienation from the Administration," he declared. "They were there, they listened, and while they didn't always agree, the lines of communication were open."[43]

Not every incident occurred at a major football institution, nor did every explosive episode in football reflect discontent on the football team or a standoff between coach and players. At one small college, Wesleyan University in Middletown, Connecticut, racial protest rose to a fever pitch in November 1969, when a black student was suspended and a black group, the Ujamaa Society, pressed demands on the college administration. Buttressed by a court injunction prohibiting disruptions and protected by twelve police on the sidelines, Wesleyan came into the game with its longtime rival, Williams College, with an undefeated record and sat near the top of the small-college ratings. Political tensions began to rise at halftime, when an African-American spokesman made a statement over the public address system and got into a shouting match with spectators. Despite the threat of off-field violence, the game went to the wire, with Wesleyan winning a nail-biting, 19-17, victory, only assured when Williams missed a last-second forty-seven-yard field goal. Immediately afterward, there was a mad rush from the press box as a result of a bomb threat received during the last play of the game. In point of fact the dispute had no connection with the football team, and some African-American players chose to cross the picket lines. Yet the events surrounding the game and the accompanying racial tension demonstrated that in late 1960s racial protests could overtake athletic events simply because they took place on campus. Wesleyan posed a perfect 8-0 record and won the coveted Little Three championship over its arch rivals, Amherst and Williams, and wound up rated first among small-college teams in the country, an achievement that nearly overshadowed the racial protest.[44]

While grievances lingered at many schools, the organized protests in and around athletics proved to be temporary. By the early 1970s campus rebellions had waned, and the revolt of the black athletes had also virtually disappeared. In the years that followed, the presence of black gridders in far greater numbers took care of many complaints; players could no longer be stacked at a few positions, and their presence required African-American assistant coaches, who were necessary to scour the country for black recruits.

In the 1970s the African-American player would find himself set down in a big-time football system that had a history of violating the rules. He often lived within a collegiate halfway house that provided few incentives for making normal progress toward a degree. The rapid influx of black players would not only change the game as played on the field but would also create even greater competition for big-time talent. Inevitably, this change would sow the seeds of scandal.

Inside the System: The Corruption of the Black Athlete

In the 1960s the success of black players such as Gale Sayers of Kansas, Leroy Keyes of Purdue, Mike Garrett of Ohio State, and O. J. Simpson of Southern Cal had undermined the vestiges of opposition, at institutions outside the South, to integrated college football. Garrett and Simpson became the first black Heisman Trophy winners, and Simpson was voted the outstanding college athlete of the 1960s. By the late 1970s the numbers of African-American football players increased rapidly in major college and professional ranks.

In the 1970s black players enabled college football to field exciting teams that employed daring option and pitchout plays such as the "I" and the "veer" which often depended on the physical skills of African-American athletes. The best runners and defensive backs in the NFL were almost invariably African Americans, and gradually they began to fill the positions on the defensive and offensive sides of the line as well. The freer and spontaneous celebration of black players after they scored provided almost as much entertainment as the scores themselves. The "Hi Mom" and high-fives soon embedded themselves into American culture.

The African-American football player had apparently succeeded beyond the wildest dreams of the black gridiron pioneers of the 1930s and 1940s. Yet colleges that welcomed the talented black athlete with open arms often had difficulty reconciling his athletic skills with normal academic expectations. Because many of the new athletic elite came from poverty-stricken or culturally deprived backgrounds, they encountered far more difficulties in the classroom than on the football field. Athletic departments at big-time schools had to invent ways to lower the admissions standards for black athletes and to find ways to keep the players eligible. As we have seen, football had always had its share of indifferent or poor students, such as Chicago's Walter Eckersall in the early 1900s or Tiny Lewis, the Northwestern halfback, who was given special dispensation to play by university president Walter Scott in 1926.

The sudden influx of so many athletes from disadvantaged backgrounds created the most serious conflict in football's history between the win-at-all costs mentality of athletic departments and the academic goals of major institutions. At Arizona State University in 1979 an investigation of athletic practices revealed that players had received credit for summer classes offered by fly-by-night correspondence schools. The revelations grew out of a much larger scandal involving longtime coach, Frank Kush, who physically abused his players, and a virulent booster group, the Sun Angels, who gave cash and other benefits to football recruits. In an article entitled "Stung by Swarm of Bs," *Sports Illustrated* reported that players had received phony transfer credits for courses supposedly taken at Rocky Mountain College, a school in Billings, Montana, which offered extension courses in the Los Angeles area. The athletic advisor in the ASU athletic office declared that Kush had told him, "My job was to get our players eligible or I would be fired."[45]

The old methods of fudging fraudulent grades flourished on other major football campuses such as Southern California, where the president himself collaborated in a scheme to bring talented but academically unqualified athletes onto campus and to keep them eligible. In October 1980 President James Zumberge, who had recently arrived on campus from his former post at Southern Methodist, revealed that the university had admitted 350 unqualified athletes during the 1970s, most of them football players, a practice condoned by his predecessor, John Hubbard. Hubbard, who had returned to his position in the history department, defended the practice as a primitive form of affirmative action for athletes who would never have attended USC if they had had to meet its admission standards.[46]

The revelations then spread to phony courses for which players had received credit. A former graduate student in history, Jeff Birren, who ran the counseling and tutoring program designed to keep the players eligible, was forced to resign when the USC academics-for-athletes shell game was exposed. Hired with football funds, Birren had depended on tutors to find easy courses such as Speech 380, taught by John DeBoss, coach of the championship debate team. Though the course was not phony, it was found that the instructor inflated the athletes' grades. In December 1979, when some key players lost their eligibility just before Southern Cal's Rose Bowl appearance, Birren tried to set up a special crash course to make the athletes eligible. When a speech instructor failed to cooperate, however, Birren's resignation was demanded. "They tried to make me the villain but I was just working with what I had," Birren declared when the scandal broke. "I knew the situation was soft. I encouraged them to take [Speech] 380, but it got out of hand. I knew the players were not going to class, but what adviser will turn in a teacher? That was my biggest fault. I wasn't self-policing."[47]

Who was policing? Those who should have known or could have uncovered the scam sooner took some belated responsibility. Dr. John Larson, the unpaid faculty representative, said that he should have gone over the class lists more carefully. Coach John Robinson said that he had not done enough to keep on top of the situation. Faculty said, in effect, "Oh yes, we know, football players take junior college courses in water safety, healthy education, acting, and possibly Introductory Russian I [to prepare for the Moscow Olympics scheduled for 1984]."

Some faculty felt that USC exploited the athletes by denying them an education. Nathaniel Hickerson, a professor of education, claimed that only 29 percent of African-American players had obtained a degree, as opposed to an overall average of 51 percent of the football team. "My anger is over the black athletes at USC," he fumed. "There is a philosophy that there is a lessening in the eyes of the alumni if black players are permitted to graduate." In other words, if the athletes graduated, they lacked the motivation to play football or were forced to spend their time preparing for classes rather than games. After examining players' transcripts, Hickerson found that "pre-pro" classes had predominated in the past decade. He referred to a course entitled "Special Problems in Speech Communication," which he called an "invented class," expandable into whatever number of credits the athlete needed. I'll stake my reputation," he continued, "that at least 100 black football players in the past ten years have that to show for their time at USC."[48]

John Robinson, the football coach, who chose Jeff Birren to tutor his players, claimed that "there was a kind of rule of thumb that if a guy met the NCAA requirements, we could tell him he could come to USC." When asked if the special admissions and gut course policies should be changed, he cast his answer in racial terms. "If I were suddenly to say, 'we close the doors [to unqualified athletes],' that's almost a racial move. Our team turns white. That's one thing that happens."[49]

From the president to the tutors the USC campus seemed to accept that Southern California could be described as a jock school of star athletes with low academic potential grafted onto a "rich kids' school" that lacked a demanding undergraduate curriculum. The school's reputation grew out of its film school and the persistent strength of its athletic programs, and scandal appeared to be the price that the school had to pay. Dick Vermeil, a former UCLA coach who led the NFL Philadelphia Eagles, regarded the situation as blown out of proportion. "It's a bunch of baloney. There's a lot worse things than fixing a kid's grades. They hire and fire football coaches on the basis of wins and losses. They don't give tenure like with a chemistry teacher. If the chemistry teacher were evaluated on 12 weekends, on the basis of wins and losses, he'd probably find a way to make sure the students got a little better grades too." In other words, football should have not only its own curriculum but also its own set of ethics.[50]

In 1980 the O. J. Simpson legend pervaded the USC football program. Players and recruits could see his picture in the larger-than-life image on the locker room wall. He had shown up in the press areas at the Rose Bowl in January 1980, "a superstar in rent-a-car," an allusion to his popular Hertz rental ads in which he sprinted and hurdled through airports. "He is on the lips of administrators, in the pitches of recruiters and in the dreams of high school stars," the *New York Times* observed. Simpson, who had quit school before graduating to play with the Buffalo Bills, had not required a degree to race through airports. "I don't remember hearing O. J. Simpson complain about not getting a degree from U.S.C.," athletic director Richard Perry declared. "It may have been the best thing that every happened to him." For O. J. Simpson perhaps, but not for many other African-American athletes.[51]

In a revolutionary change from early 1900s football, black players on predominantly white football teams made the African-American athlete the key figure in the football equation. The athlete had become an actor in a rags-to-riches drama wherein schools like USC encouraged their players to think of the institution as a way-station on their trip to the NFL. Unfortunately, a relatively few—more at USC than at most schools—made the transition, and those who did not often faced a bleak future if they did not have a college degree or had not used their opportunity to study. In Southern California's case the football establishment had rigged an academic scenario that was unfair to all except those who had successful careers in the NFL.

Southern California hardly stood alone in pigskin prostitution. Barely three years after the USC scandal, the University of Georgia became embroiled in nasty litigation that once again raised serious questions of the role of minorities. Jan Kemp, a tutor in remedial English at Georgia, charged that the athletic department had altered the failing grades of nine athletes so that they could play in the Orange Bowl in 1982 against Pittsburgh. Following her revelations, Kemp lost her job, the apparent result of her failure to play ball by big-time athletic rules. In her lawsuit she sued for back pay, reinstatement, and damages. Kemp also said that she had brought suit "to get the university's attention and to get them to clean up the academic corruption that pervades the campus." Georgia unconvincingly claimed that it had dismissed Kemp for being "disruptive." The university also insisted that she had failed to publish—an argument that hardly seemed consistent with her duties as a remedial tutor.

From the beginning the trial proved embarrassing for Georgia athletics, and at times it deteriorated into racial stereotyping. In characterizing the football player who needed tutoring, which appeared to mean the typical black player, the defense attorney contended, "We may not be able to make a university student out of him, but if we can teach him to read and write, maybe he can work at the post office rather than as a garbage man when he gets through with his athletic career." All candor aside, the statement alerted the jurors to the likelihood that Georgia had no interest in providing a college education for its minority athletes.[52]

The trial also had further racial overtones, since the defense implied that Georgia athletics merely served as a vocational program for disadvantaged minorities. Leroy Ervin, assistant vice president in charge of the developmental program and an African American, called Kemp a "bigot," presumably because she had refused to pass black students. As at Southern California, the authorities defended their actions by insisting that athletes not only contributed more but also benefited from attending Georgia because they might learn to read and write adequately enough to obtain a job that would take them off the streets.

In other testimony Coach Vince Dooley acknowledged that some athletes who failed to meet the requirements still managed to win admission. In attempting to explain his institution's policies, President Fred Davison insisted that the institution "would not unilaterally disarm" by requiring higher academic standards than other schools did. He also conceded that Georgia had admitted some unqualified students, defending their utility as revenue producers for the university. In other words, Davison had declared some minority football players qualified for admission only because they earned money and glory for the University of Georgia.[53]

In the end Jan Kemp won her case against Georgia when the jury not only decided in her favor but also made her a large award. The court calculated her lost wages at $79,680 and then awarded her $200,000 for mental anguish. To top it off, a total of $1.5 million in punitive damages was assessed against the assistant vice president, Leroy Ervin, who had to pay $800,000. "It's a victory for academic integrity," Kemp said. "I was interested in widespread therapeutic reform, and I think it can be brought about now."[54]

Yet the double standard that emerged in the testimony hardly boded well for gridiron academics. African Americans embraced both the traditional virtues of big-time football as well as its vices. Whereas the colleges portrayed their athletic policies as affirmative action for minorities, those policies benefited the football programs more than their star athletes. The profits from the players' low-cost labor demonstrated the athletic directors' need to stretch football revenues to the maximum. While the revelations of academic cheating were becoming public, the big-time football institutions would show that win-at-all-cost was not merely a metaphor. As never before in the history of college football, "gate receipts and glory" would become paramount in the policies of the big-time football schools.

CHAPTER SEVENTEEN

The Revolt of the Pigskin Elect, 1975 to 1984

In November 1974 the little-known president of California State University at Long Beach, Stephen Horn, half-jokingly told a convention of the Association of State Colleges that soon only a handful of football teams would remain. The reason: the rising costs of football, which Division I football schools had been struggling to control since the late 1960s.

Academic and athletic officials knew more about Long Beach basketball and its controversial coach, Jerry Tarkanian, and most probably had not heard of Stephen Horn. When he came to Long Beach, Horn had fired Tarkanian, whose fast and loose recruiting had resulted in numerous violations. Earlier in 1974 the NCAA had required Long Beach State to return $94,261 to the association, the share that it had received from Division I tournaments while playing ineligible players. In addition, Long Beach State had been penalized for football violations, and its unprofitable football program could scarcely make up the shortfalls in basketball. Horn needed a quick infusion of funds to resuscitate Long Beach athletics.[1]

The CFA Revolt

In the summer of 1975 the NCAA was still trying to get through the cost-cutting initiatives that it had proposed at its annual meeting in January 1970. The costs of college football had continued to grow, and many mid-sized colleges like Long Beach with low-profile football programs saw their budgets spinning out of control.

Walter Byers and the NCAA Council had tried to find a formula that would satisfy the diverse athletic constituencies. Over the next nine years, however, the NCAA would struggle through one of the most difficult periods in its history. The obsession with maximizing TV profits mixed with a deep distrust of "football freeloaders" who wanted to tap into their revenues as well as cost cutting proved a flash point for divisiveness.

Long Beach State attracted less than four thousand spectators for each home game and had annual revenues of less than $20,000; the University of Michigan received $450,000 for a nationally televised game. Though Long Beach had made money from basketball, the school had to pay back the revenues from tournaments during the Tarkanian regime. Even with its paltry revenues Long Beach State boasted a larger football budget than a number of other Division I schools. Any reduction in costs would prove helpful to its undernourished programs.[2]

The members of the NCAA had made some stabs at cost cutting, but many of those changes made it easier for the big schools to recruit and to field large squads. The NCAA members had repealed the freshman rule, one of the most effective reforms that had from the early 1900s kept freshmen from competing in varsity athletics. The rule not only rid the major schools of expensive freshmen teams but also enabled big-time football to work the talented freshmen into regular season games. In a change that lowered its academic requirements, the NCAA also repealed the 1.6 rule for college entrance and eligibility. The 1.6 rule had consisted of sliding scales that took into account high school grade averages, SAT scores, and the degree of difficulty of athletes' course work. Instead, the so-called cost cutters substituted a 2.0, or C, high school average, which allowed more at-risk student athletes to enter the institution. Once registered for classes, the students might be maneuvered into courses that would keep them eligible. In 1978 the NCAA had placed a ceiling on the number of football scholarships at 105 (30 new scholarships per year, but a total that would take into account players who dropped out of school).

The NCAA had also tried to create separate divisions that would reflect the size of athletic programs, a change that ended up exacerbating tensions. Having swelled to more than six hundred schools, the NCAA could no longer satisfy the needs of the schools of vastly differing sizes. In 1973 the association reorganized itself into three divisions and agreed that a committee would assign the institutions accordingly.[3]

The problems with the divisional structure occurred in Division I, where the big-time football institutions ended up. The demands of big-time football schools had led to the new divisional makeup, but the major institutions recoiled at allowing more than a hundred nonfootball schools to join the division, nearly a majority of the 237 Division I members. Of the 126 football-playing institutions, only about eighty belonged to conferences that played big-time football, and a far smaller number of schools could actually reap lucrative gridiron revenues. On top of this the costs and profits of the major institutions dwarfed those of the smaller institutions and conferences in Division I which also played football. Divisional makeup among the imperial gridiron powers and conferences still loomed as a problem.[4]

Since football at major institutions was the major source of athletic revenue, the big-time schools felt that they belonged to an exclusive club. In spite of concerns about costs, many football institutions had fattened their revenues in the 1970s, and television profits from the NCAA-TV contract with ABC reached sixteen million dollars in 1974, a nice chunk of revenue for teams that managed to enter the charmed circle. While the best-known football schools such as Notre Dame and Michigan reaped large profits, their football monies still had to support a costly array of athletic programs. One of those, women's athletics, mandated by the federal government since 1972, threatened to submerge smaller Division I athletic departments in a sea of red ink. In an era of chronic inflation big-time and near big-time schools saw no prospect of relief from the demands for scholarships, coaches, trainers, equipment, and other costs. The anger that had boiled to the surface in initial attempts to reduce football scholarships and coaching staffs was still simmering. And by 1975, after five years of stubbornly opposing cost-cutting measures, the major schools stood at a crossroads.[5]

In a round-robin letter in 1974 to college presidents before the NCAA's newest round of cost-cutting conventions, President Stephen Horn proposed a number of radical changes designed to create a more level playing field for his institution. He called upon the members to slash the total football scholarships from 105 to 55, a reduction that would save money for Long Beach and allow its team to compete more evenly with larger institutions; it would also compensate for the NCAA penalties, which had reduced the number of Long Beach's scholarships. From the standpoint of the large institutions Horn's scholarship program would virtually dictate a much more modest style of football because the teams would not be able to afford three or four players for each position.[6]

Cost cutting provided a forum for far more subversive plans. Horn stirred up a nest of angry hornets by proposing that the NCAA share its television wealth. Under Horn's plan the NCAA would divide the revenues from football telecasts. After the relatively small 5.5 percent NCAA assessment and a mere 15 percent allotted to the participating schools, the remainder would be divided as follows. Fifty percent could go to Division I schools, regardless of their size, and the remaining half would be divided up between Division II and III schools. The profits would compensate the many schools like Long Beach State which rarely appeared on television or got the big payoffs enjoyed by big-time schools. "As far as I am concerned," Horn declared, "Notre Dame and Ohio State can be on every weekend. If that were so, I think we might get a $30 million contract for the season and it would help everybody."[7]

Horn objected to the existing system because, out of more than 450 football-playing institutions in the NCAA, only 54 teams managed to appear on television, and only 113 teams belonging to the participants' conferences stood to profit. He estimated that the division of spoils under his proposals would amount to forty-nine thousand dollars for its portion of the revenues. As for Long Beach State, Horn masked the revenue-famished condition of athletics at his institution. "We are not going broke," Horn declared, though it appeared that Long Beach State was awash in red ink. "Now, on the other hand, there are Division II and Division III institutions, and some Division I institutions, that are going rapidly broke," he persisted.

"I think the adoption of this proposal would give greater freedom of choice to the American television viewer."[8]

Like a homegrown Karl Marx, Horn also proposed dividing up proceeds of the bowl games. After the bowl teams and bowl committees had skimmed off 50 percent of the profits, he proposed taking the remaining half and splitting it among the three divisions. Division I would receive 25 percent, while the other two would each get 12.5 percent. The president of the NCAA, John Fuzak, would later rule this motion out of order, however, because the bowl participants had freedom to contract with the bowl committees.[9]

To bring the issue back to its originator, Stephen Horn's plan served his own interests far more tangibly than those of the NCAA. "The passionate desire to be associated in the press with the big-name universities," Walter Byers has written, "is best illustrated by California State University at Long Beach and its president, Steven Horn." Noting the troubled finances of Long Beach's athletic program, Byers believed that Horn sought a way to bail out his own program by siphoning off the profits of more profitable schools. While Horn undoubtedly had his own school's financial interests in mind, he also had a golden opportunity to generate free publicity for himself. The former political science professor achieved a reputation as a fiery populist college president but later resigned his position to run for Congress, and the "Robin Hood president" became a Republican congressman from California's thirty-eighth district.[10]

The reaction of the major football powers and conferences to Horn's initiative might be likened to that when a nearby artillery shell explodes. Horn's proposals evoked bitter and fearful reactions and for good reason. Under the existing plan televised schools might expect to receive more than $450,000 for a national game and more than $350,000 for a regional game. The return for the participating schools would far exceed the $95,000 proposed by Horn. The big losers would also have been members of major conferences, like Northwestern or Rice, which rarely appeared on TV because they had perennially losing teams—and would not have shared conference profits. As a result, competition in the major conferences would have grown more one-sided than it had already become.

Don Canham, the athletic director at Michigan, flew into a rage when he heard that the athletic director at Western Michigan University had commented that "the plans have some merit and stand a very good chance of passing." Canham himself described the Horn share-the-wealth plans as subversive. "Hell, that's socialism," he sneered, "and we're not in a socialist state. Why should Michigan play for $40,000 rather than $450,000?" Such a motion would surely have resulted in the big schools withdrawing from the NCAA.[11]

The Robin Hood proposals immediately prompted contacts among the

major football-playing athletic departments and between the major conferences about what could be done to combat the assault of the freeloaders.
In December 1975, before the NCAA convention, when Horn's proposals
were scheduled to come before the delegates, the commissioners of the
major football conferences held a meeting, out of which emerged a steering
commission to establish an organization of big-time gridiron conferences
and schools. The meeting not only discussed the Horn proposals but also
other problems affecting their football interests. One of the problems that
loomed as large as the immediate situation would be the delegates' dissatisfaction with Division I and the need to pare down its membership.

Though the Horn "share the TV wealth" proposal fell far short of gaining even a majority of members, the alarm bells that it set off did not stop
ringing. The major schools had no way of knowing whether the Horn TV
proposal would resurface at the next convention, and many expected that
it would. Nevertheless, the larger problems of big-time football schools,
such as the size of Division I, the problems of cutting the number of coaches
and scholarships, and the need to maximize TV revenues, helped to bring
about a new football-oriented organization. This gridiron caucus would
serve as a lobbying group for big-time members. For the time being the organizers disclaimed any desire to secede from the parent group, though that
possibility loomed in the background.[12]

The earlier contacts crystallized in April in a larger meeting of what
would become the College Football Association, or CFA. The schools
drafted what amounted to a manifesto calling for reorganization of Division I so that major football-playing schools would have their own division.
Most of the five points drawn up by the steering committee were based on
several fundamental grievances. These grievances had to do with the size of
Division I and how the "majors" found themselves outvoted by smaller,
non-big-time, sometimes nonfootball institutions. The NCAA, they declared, had grown too large to deal with the problems of big-time football
institutions and conferences. The size and diversity of the association made
it difficult to generate positive attitudes toward big-time football, or, they
might have said, the number of highly visible scandals had made it difficult to create more football-friendly attitudes.[13]

While the CFA is remembered as the TV monopoly buster, the organization did not start out that way. In its official statements the group did not
offer revenue-producing alternatives but merely sought to separate the
major football conferences into a fourth elite division. One problem vexed
the CFA from the beginning: the absence of two major football conferences,
the Big Ten and PAC-10. Because the Rose Bowl created a special relationship between those two conferences, the presidents met once each year, and
the two groups tended to act in unison. While the athletic directors and
some presidents favored the CFA agenda, the conference presidents voting

as a single group rejected it. They believed that the association created the impression that too much emphasis was placed on big-time athletics and not enough on academics. While many presidents might have agreed with this outlook, it is just as likely that the two conferences refused to join because of their strong position in NCAA policy-making and number of TV appearances under the Byers regime.[14]

In spite of the CFA's numerical strength, it faced a formidable adversary in Walter Byers, the NCAA executive director, who had run the day-to-day business of the association for a quarter-century. Byers struck some as the most inscrutable of people, an executive who had the tusks and hide of a small rhinoceros. Tough and intelligent, Byers had proved himself a skilled negotiator who went head to head with Roone Arledge of ABC and emerged with lush TV contracts. Through the growing football revenues he was able to fund a number of auxiliary groups and events such as Division II and III football scholarships as well as travel money for coaches and athletes. Above all, he kept enough of the 5.5 percent football assessment so that the NCAA had adequate reserves and increased staff, including an investigative unit for tracking down wrongdoers.

Dominating and perfectionistic, Byers insisted that the employees wear coats and ties to work and that they never take their beverages to their desks. Through his influence with the NCAA executive committee he played a powerful role in appointments to NCAA committees and in the policies that emerged from these committees. This influence may have bred opposition among schools that suffered as a result of these policies. In an era when the number of schools on probation increased markedly, Byers's determination to punish lawbreakers and cut costs may have sown the seeds of rebellion among many of the big-time schools in the Southeastern, Southwestern, and Big Eight Conferences, several of the major conferences that founded the CFA.[15]

In 1977 Walter Byers negotiated a highly lucrative TV contract with ABC sports and its programming genius and chief negotiator, Roone Arledge. Knowing that Byers could easily line up CBS or NBC, Arledge agreed to pay twenty-nine million dollars in 1978 and 1979 for exclusive rights to NCAA games, a figure that would rise to thirty million dollars for the next two years. Arledge also agreed to fund a divisional playoff for the lesser institutions if Division I members agree to subdivide. "In the overall deal, it was a small item," Byers casually noted. The small sum, however, helped to solve the NCAA's most vexing problem—its big-time members' discontent with Division I.[16]

In its first legislative effort to subdivide NCAA's Division I, in January 1978, the CFA lost by three votes, 77-74. That opposition would evaporate in less in a year. Threatened by gridiron discontent among the major schools and conferences which could lead to secession, the less prominent Division

I members agreed in the summer of 1978 to go into a separate division known as Division IAA. In return the new division would get to play a televised national championship game funded by ABC, an event that the major football schools, now known as Division IA, had not yet been able to agree upon. As a result of subdividing Division I into IA and IAA, the NCAA would reduce the number of elite teams in Division IA, its major college division, from nearly 250 to a more manageable 105.[17]

The decision to subdivide the NCAA proved to be the turning point for the CFA. Initially, the association served as a lobbying group of major powers within the NCAA, but their actions in the aftermath of the new divisional structure demonstrated that the CFA would not fade into the woodwork. By 1979 the NCAA was not simply facing a group of pouting big-time football schools and conferences but also an organization that reflected the anti-NCAA and anti-Walter Byers sentiment among a majority of big-time powers. Except for the Big Ten and PAC-10, the CFA included all of the remaining seven major conferences such as the Southeastern, Southwest, and Big Eight as well as major independents such as Notre Dame, Penn State, and Florida State. Among the organizers was Notre Dame's Father Edmund Joyce, the vice president in charge of athletics, a close associate of President Theodore Hesburgh and, together with Hesburgh, the brains behind Notre Dame athletics for a quarter-century. In addition, Earl Ramer of Tennessee, a former NCAA president, became the group's temporary president when the CFA held its first full-dress conference in December 1976. Another influential member of the board was Chuck Neinas, the Big Eight commissioner, who had formerly worked in NCAA-TV and who would become the CFA's first executive director. Shortly afterward, the CFA elected an academically prominent figure, President Fred Davison of the University of Georgia, as its permanent head.[18]

The stature of these individuals and institutions points to the CFA's potential for moving beyond the Robin Hood scare of 1976. What had begun as a lobbying group within the NCAA had a number of possibilities beyond divisional reorganization which could make it a competitor to the NCAA. Once again big-time football had demonstrated the challenge of containing it in the traditional, amateur, student-athlete structure that it purported to occupy.

The CFA Challenge

Walter Byers and the NCAA Council had made a step toward preempting the CFA's chief issue, which in 1977 and 1978 had been reorganization. But the CFA leadership still worried about new share-the-wealth proposals as well as the decline of interest in big-time college football—and how to counter it. "We must never forget that we are in competition with the pros for the entertainment dollar," Father Edmund Joyce of Notre Dame concluded in a report for the CFA on the future of football. The three goals of the CFA, according to Father Joyce, should be: (1) maintaining football at a high performance level; (2) assuring "equality of competitive opportunity"; and (3) achieving "total academic integrity."[19]

Not surprisingly, the CFA agitated for a return to a full slate of full-time coaches who had been cut back in the mid-1970s, a move that would restore football's "high performance level." Likewise, it wanted to maximize profits for big-time schools by assuring them of as many appearances on television as possible. Though costs and profits were paramount, the CFA leaders such as Joyce were concerned with the public image of football which had suffered as a result of scandals in the late 1970s. In a speech to the NCAA Joyce referred to John Underwood, a writer for *Sports Illustrated,* who had published three articles in which he was highly critical of football at all levels. Enlarged into a book, Underwood's *Death of an American Game* created enough stir that the CFA and Father Joyce felt compelled to acknowledge the scandals and blame them on selfish interests that, he contended, had proved too difficult for the NCAA to resolve.[20]

That the CFA and its leaders paid some attention to academic standards should not come as a complete surprise. Notre Dame, which had long sought to shed its reputation as a football school and share the academic prestige of the elite institutions, could afford to call for higher academic standards. Its vast recruiting network could supply sound academic recruits to go with the inevitable scholastic failures. The southern and southwestern institutions, however, faced a more complex problem since they had begun in the late 1970s to recruit larger numbers of disadvantaged African-American athletes from scandalously poor school systems. Viewed narrowly, these institutions had to find ways to keep their players eligible, which led to a number of scandals in the late 1970s and 1980s. Yet they also had to find ways to separate student-athletes who would receive four- or five-year scholarships from the merely athletically promising athletes. Some of the recruits with great athletic talent lacked the skills to pass college courses.[21]

The bottom line for the CFA schools, however, proved to be gridiron costs and profits. One of the most controversial and complex issues of the 1970s was Title IX, which required near equality in men and women's intercollegiate sports and threatened to cause financial problems for athletic departments. Both the NCAA and the CFA were extremely wary of the women's sports issue. Since Walter Byers had not yet come up with a plan of action, some CFA leaders feared that Byers meant to spend NCAA football profits to sponsor women's athletic championships. Of all sports football had the clearest-cut gender biases, since women neither played nor coached football and the gridiron sport siphoned off many athletic scholarships. Fred Davison, the president of the CFA and of the University of

Georgia, later declared that the costs of Title IX had been one reason why the CFA came into being and wrote an op-ed piece for the *New York Times* opposing its costly approach to gender equality.[22]

In the beginning the CFA wanted to avoid the rising costs, to limit the numbers in Division I, and to protect existing revenues from share-the-wealth proposals. As time passed, it also looked for new sources of gridiron revenue as well as a more attractive agenda. In 1979 the group established a TV study committee to probe the potential of a broader television program for college football and to explain why TV ratings had slid from 14 to 11 between 1976 and 1979, when the NFL's stood at 30. Since ratings determined profits, the CFA sought to make a strong argument that the NCAA was pursuing an ineffective approach toward television.[23]

The CFA-TV report in 1980 set the stage for a new assault on the NCAA. The report criticized restrictions on the number of telecasts and the practice of negotiating a contract with a single network. It also called upon the NCAA to investigate the potential of cable television, which was just beginning to come into its own. The committee members proposed working within the NCAA to improve its TV ratings but also called on the CFA to come up with its own TV plan. They did not call upon the CFA to negotiate its own contract, but their proposals stopped just short of that point.[24]

One of the authors of the TV report, Chuck Neinas, the recently appointed CFA executive director, had begun his career in athletic administration working in NCAA television under Walter Byers. As a protégé of the powerful athletic director at Michigan, Don Canham, Neinas applied for the vacancy as Big Ten commissioner when it came open in 1971 and appeared to have the inside track. One of the other applicants, Big Eight commissioner Wayne Duke, who had also worked under Byers at the NCAA, ended up with the job. Neinas, who gravitated to Wayne Duke's old job, Big Eight commissioner, felt shortchanged. "Still, Chuck carried the scars from his loss of the more prestigious position," Byers wrote, "and later told Wayne [Duke] that he would show those Big-Ten people." Gregarious and intelligent, Neinas may have wanted to "show" his old boss, Walter Byers; certainly, Byers would leave the impression that Neinas, in his role as CFA executive director, had betrayed him.[25]

In 1979 and 1980 the CFA policy was changing from its earlier objectives to attacking the NCAA football contract. Neinas would later be portrayed as responsible for this major change in policy, especially since he had worked in television at the NCAA. To be precise, Byers portrayed Neinas as a hired gun who shaped the CFA television issue for his own purposes. In this duel of personalities one should not forget that Notre Dame and the southern institutions played a key role in bringing about the changes in the CFA's policies. If Neinas had scars in his past, the athletic leaders at Notre Dame had deep wounds first inflicted when Neinas was still in school. Edmund

Joyce, executive vice president for athletics at Notre Dame and a member of the CFA board, had been a close associate of Father Theodore Hesburgh, the future head of Notre Dame, in the struggles of the early 1950s, when the NCAA had forced Penn and Notre Dame to bury their visions of highly profitable televised football. With both the rebirth of pay for television in the form of cable TV and the discontent of the football elite, Father Joyce may have found that what goes around eventually comes around—and to Notre Dame's benefit.

One might also speculate about the role of NCAA disciplinary measures, which in extreme cases forced the offending schools to forgo TV appearances. One of the institutions on probation in the late 1970s turned out to be Michigan State University; as Walter Byers has pointed out, the penalties against MSU effectively spanked Notre Dame by denying the school the TV revenues from its highly profitable Michigan State game. In addition, Notre Dame had suffered its own less serious but irksome NCAA censure in 1971, when a football coach rather than the institution offered financial aid. While these problems with the NCAA may have contributed to Notre Dame's opposition, Joyce's experience and ability undoubtedly enabled him to think beyond individual games and penalties to the potential of more frequent and profitable TV appearances and possibly to the eventuality of a Notre Dame football network. As its leaders had been careful to do in the 1950s, Notre Dame acted discreetly in promoting wider TV opportunities, and, as it had allowed Penn to run interference in the early 1950s, the institution let the southern and southwestern schools take center stage in the television controversy.[26]

Indeed, the southern and southwestern coaches, athletic directors, and college presidents played a major role in organizing the CFA and served in highly visible, highly confrontational positions when push came to shove. Byers has suggested that southern college and athletic personnel such as coach Vince Dooley and president Fred Davison at Georgia wanted to wriggle out from under the threat of penalties involving TV blackouts. Yet it is also true that the southern athletic directors and college presidents suspected that the Big Ten, the PAC-10, and many of the small colleges had worked hand in glove with Byers in setting NCAA policy. As a result, Georgia, Oklahoma, Tennessee, and Texas all played key roles in the formation of the CFA and in its later confrontation with the NCAA.[27]

Beyond the personal and institutional antagonisms the CFA challenge of the NCAA-TV policies would reflect a strong belief on the part of many athletic directors, faculty reps, and college presidents that Walter Byers had lost touch with big-time football. Though the NCAA-TV contract had increased the pot for conferences and schools, it still had as a primary goal protecting major conferences from overexposure. Some of those conferences, such as the Atlantic Coast Conference (ACC), wondered why they could not have more regional football telecasts, especially when they succeeded so well in basketball. The colleges no longer suffered from the threat of television; indeed, telecasts of regional football had provided a means of encouraging interest in big-time football.

In truth the NCAA-TV contract generated enough revenue that it could be looked upon as a for-profit cartel posing as an arm of a nonprofit educational association. In the 1970s new businesses seeking access to highly regulated markets had used antitrust laws to challenge their competitors' control of the market. By the same token there was a growing conviction that the regulated industries no longer served the needs of consumers. Viewed from this perspective, the restriction of football telecasts denied college football fans access to their favorite games. Though NCAA football was not, strictly speaking, a business corporation like AT&T or IBM, it had gravitated into a big-time moneymaking operation, which made it more vulnerable to antitrust laws than it had been in the 1950s.

While the NCAA had seven major regional conferences, the top independents, and a total of more than sixty football powers in league against it, neither divisional reorganization or even television had proved adequate to draw the Big Ten and PAC-10 into the CFA ranks. These two conferences had fewer reasons to favor a radically new approach to television. Not only did they enjoy good live attendance, but they also appeared frequently on NCAA telecasts and for good reason. As Walter Byers has pointed out, they had nearly 40 percent of the nation's TV audience. In spite of periodic probes, most of the Big Ten and PAC-10 schools had managed to avoid the most severe NCAA penalties, and, except for Illinois, Southern California, and Oregon, who had recently run afoul of the NCAA, most of the members had not suffered repeated sanctions in the 1970s and early 1980s.[28]

By 1981 the conflict between the CFA and the NCAA had entered a new phase in which the group of football powers began to see itself as a smaller, more select version of the NCAA. The CFA would soon challenge the NCAA on the issue of TV profits, one of the association's most vulnerable points, which, like the heart and lungs, produced the life blood for many NCAA operations. If the CFA succeeded, the possibility existed that it would replace the NCAA. It could become a super-conference, an elite group of conferences and institutions that played big-time sports and imposed regulations that would prove more indulgent toward highly visible, profit-oriented football and basketball programs.

Big-Time Football Makes Its Comeback

The desire to increase their already sizable athletic revenues reflected the fact that universities of the 1980s had become far more highly commercialized than in past decades. While the early 1900s presidents had gone out of their way to deplore commercialism, the more than sixty members of the CFA virtually declared that big-time football should earn big bucks. The cant of football serving student-athletes barely existed at institutions so clearly favoring teams that could harvest lush gate receipts. Two of the major institutions in the CFA, Georgia and Oklahoma, showed monetary gains that demonstrated that some major college gridiron programs, far from suffering dwindling profit margins, were undergoing a period of unprecedented growth. In 1974 football at Georgia generated $1,613,000 in revenues and $1,072,000 in expenses. By 1978 the profit figure had soared from $550,000 to $960,000, and, when the stadium was expanded in 1981, the profit would rise to $1.1 million. As for television, Oklahoma saw its TV revenues mushroom from an average of $176,698 in the 1975 to 1978 period to more than $250,000 for each of the years from 1978 to 1981. Far from suffering from runaway costs, these big-time football programs displayed voracious appetites for profits and publicity.[29]

In spite of their often sizable profits, the major CFA football schools agreed with Chuck Neinas that they should be able to profit from more TV appearances. A generation after the first failed attempts at pay television, the emergence of cable TV threatened the network monopoly on sports programming. In the 1970s cable companies began to pirate some of the football games that the networks had contracted to televise. After a quarter-century of contracts with the major networks, the NCAA leaders were ready to experiment with pay television. In Columbus, Ohio, Warner Communications in 1977 convinced the NCAA to allow its cable subsidiary, QUBE, to telecast Ohio State home games, even though it would compete with ABC, the network carrier for NCAA games. While the NCAA regarded the contract as experimental, it ended up in court facing, and winning, a court case against ABC. While the NCAA ended its brief partnership with Warner, big-time gridiron powers such as Notre Dame and Michigan were approached by cable companies that wanted to televise their contests. With cable TV increasingly in a position to challenge the three networks, the CFA leaders felt that they could do even better in negotiations with competing networks.[30]

Over the summer of 1981 Neinas, supported by the board, negotiated a TV contract with NBC and, indeed, Neinas must have believed that he had finally trumped the NCAA. Put simply, the potential for big profits to member schools stood out in clear relief. The network agreed to pay $180 million for the telecasts over a three-year period beginning in the fall of 1982. Each institution would have to appear at least once in a two-year period and not more than seven times. Above all, the CFA schools would not pay any assessment to the NCAA, and independents like Notre Dame, Penn State, and Florida State could keep virtually the entire proceeds from what would likely be close to the maximum number of appearances.[31]

The CFA had declared that its members owned their television rights and could deny the NCAA the power to exercise them. One might compare this property right to states' rights in the United States in the nineteenth century. If CFA members did not admit it openly, the NCAA clearly saw the threat implicit in this interpretation. In June 1981, while the CFA was negotiating its contract with NBC, the NCAA warned its members that the association controlled all televising of college football games. If they wanted to televise a football game, they had to abide by the terms of the NCAA-TV plan. That, in itself, meant that the members would be challenging the NCAA's authority if they chose to cast their lot with the CFA. President James Frank of Lincoln University of Missouri, the elected president of the NCAA in 1980–81 and its first African-American head, made this clear to his members. The NCAA set September 10, 1981, as the date for the schools to conform to NCAA policy, a deadline that recalled the association's ultimatum to the Sinful Seven in 1949. Any school that refused to conform, Franks declared, would become ineligible for NCAA championships. CFA President Fred Davison denied that his members wanted to undermine the authority of the parent organization and accused the NCAA leaders of "sabre rattling."[32]

Two months before the deadline Walter Byers artfully undermined the CFA plan by negotiating an alternate package that achieved the goals of the dissidents. In July 1981 the NCAA negotiators signed a contract with three networks, CBS, ABC, and TBS, or Turner Broadcast Sports. The NCAA contract rights would return $285 million for four years. Ted Turner alone agreed to pay $17.7 million for a mere sixteen games. Teams would receive a half-million dollars for nationally televised games, a figure that would rise to $82.5 million in 1985. From $30 million in its last contract with ABC, Byers and company had vaulted to $285 million, which proved competitive, and in some ways superior, to the CFA contract with a single network. The NCAA had triumphantly responded to the CFA complaint that Byers refused to negotiate with more than one network.[33]

Of course, the CFA contract would return more money to a smaller number of institutions that would not, in turn, worry about low-profile teams appearing on a regular basis. An Oklahoma faculty rep calculated that the CFA contract would permit schools to earn nearly $4 million, whereas the highest amount that a Big Eight school like Oklahoma could get under the NCAA deal would be half of that. Looking back, however, one might wonder if the pigskin powers should have questioned whether the CFA-NBC contract would inevitably lead to juicier future contracts. Though greatly expanded, the NCAA's package still kept a lid on the telecasts of big games and thereby ensured larger profits for the networks from their commercials, the index of a network's success. How football fans and sports buffs would react to a larger number of major college games remained to be seen. That, in turn, would determine the price per minute charged by the networks and the amount that they would guarantee to the gridiron institutions in future contracts. The CFA leaders watched with dismay as the support for their contract with NBC dwindled.[34]

Because it could not count on its members to ratify its contract, the CFA leaders resorted to a more desperate, and ultimately successful, strategy. Georgia and Oklahoma filed a lawsuit in federal district court and Texas another, all of them challenging the NCAA's right to negotiate for its members. Immediately after the lawsuit was filed, a federal judge had then issued a stay order prohibiting the NCAA from coercing its members or, in other words, enforcing its ultimatum. Forced to abandon their hard line, Byers and James Frank adopted the strategy of luring the CFA schools back to their side, or, as Chuck Neinas called it, employing the traditional NCAA approach of divide and conquer. Relying on their newly negotiated contract, the NCAA instead called a special TV conference to meet in December before the general membership convened in January.[35]

As it turned out, the CFA's position in the battle of the TV contracts deteriorated in the fall of 1981. Contrary to what Neinas and Davison hoped, a large number of CFA schools proved reluctant to ratify the CFA contract and thereby precipitate a break with the NCAA. Viewed from the standpoint of their previous objections, many of the big-time football schools decided that the NCAA had met their complaints. The parent association had again reduced the number of NCAA Division IA members, this time from 137 to 92, and negotiated a contract that met the CFA criteria. Faced with the prospect of dividing and dismembering the NCAA, these schools refused to sign the CFA contract, and the CFA's direct challenge to the NCAA-TV contract fell flat on its face.[36]

Nevertheless, the court challenges by Georgia, Oklahoma, and Texas remained. The three plaintiffs charged the NCAA with restraint of trade and called the NCAA a classic cartel. The case had begun as a class-action suit by the CFA members, but the CFA had to drop out because of the heavy legal expenses. Nevertheless, CFA stalwarts with deep pockets, such as Penn State and Notre Dame, not to mention member conferences, responded to pleas by Neinas to contribute financially to Oklahoma and Georgia. Given several smaller antitrust cases in the 1970s, the plaintiffs stood a good chance of winning if the CFA could persuade its members with deeper pockets to help meet the costs.[37]

The University of Oklahoma, which had already tested the legal waters in previous lawsuits against the NCAA, felt confident of its position. In 1974 Oklahoma had gone to court to try to overturn NCAA sanctions that included a two-year TV ban. Oklahoma had tried to argue that the penalties violated the Sherman Antitrust Act, but the court had obligingly agreed with the NCAA's position that it represented educational interests. Shortly afterward Oklahoma tried to reverse a NCAA decision limiting the number of coaches. Teaming up with two of Paul "Bear" Bryant's assistants, Coach Barry Switzer argued that the NCAA as a voluntary association had no right to regulate contracts between employer and employee. Again Oklahoma and Alabama failed to persuade the court that the NCAA, like the American Bar Association and American Medical Association, was exempt from antitrust laws. As the judicial climate changed and the number of suits increased, the NCAA's position began to erode.[38]

President Fred Davison of Georgia, who with William Banowsky of Oklahoma had launched the suit in September, held that Georgia had property rights in its athletic programs and could thereby televise its games at will. Davison had been head of the University of Georgia since 1967, when he became one of the youngest college presidents in the country. As a graduate of Emory University who received a Ph.D. degree in veterinary medicine and doctorates from Iowa State in pathology and biochemistry, Davison's rise from head of the veterinary school at Georgia to its presidency had been little short of meteoric. Since 1967 he had presided over extraordinary growth in enrollment, academic programs, and athletics. Under Davison the institution had weathered the difficulties of racial integration and student turbulence in the Vietnam War era. His institution was probably best known though for its football team and Heisman Trophy winner, Herschel Walker, who led the Bulldogs to a national championship in 1980.

Unlike his predecessor, O. C. Alderholt, who had tried unsuccessfully to de-emphasize football at Georgia in 1951, Davison was an out-and-out supporter of Bulldog football. In a court statement he gave a ringing endorsement of college football as a rallying point for flagship state universities. "Athletics and primarily football at the University is the one focal point that gives cohesion to all of our members, both students and alumni; it brings them back home; it's a kind of celebration in which we all have a common cause. So psychologically it has great impact, and it's not just on the alums; it creates a sense of pride on the part of the people of the state of Georgia."[39]

Georgia, Oklahoma, and the CFA had to wait a year for the courts to reach a decision, but in September 1982 a federal judge in Oklahoma ruled in favor of Georgia and Oklahoma (the courts had dismissed the Texas lawsuit). After the failure in the battle of the TV contracts, the CFA suddenly found itself thrust into the victor's circle. Judge Juan Burciaga held that the two schools could do with their property rights—in this case football telecasts—however they saw fit. For a few days it appeared as if, after thirty-one years of NCAA-TV contracts and failed attempts by Penn and Notre Dame to derail the contract, two prominent CFA members had brought the mighty NCAA and Walter Byers to their knees.[40]

Just as Chuck Neinas was dusting off the 1981 CFA-TV contract, however, the NCAA appealed the decision. In the meantime the courts ruled that the CFA schools had to abide by the NCAA contract until the decision moved through the courts. Oklahoma which had planned to kick off the new era by selling the rights to its first game with Southern California to an Oklahoma City TV station, had to cancel its plans when the federal appeals court issued a stay order keeping the existing contract in effect. This worked to the NCAA's advantage because it continued to operate under its TV contract.[41]

The final decision did not come until two more seasons had passed under the NCAA contract. After a federal appeals court upheld the lower court decision, the case moved to the U.S. Supreme Court, and in July 1984 Walter Byers finally met an unmovable obstacle. By a 7-2 majority the court ruled that the NCAA-TV plan constituted a "classic cartel," in which a group of businesses or organizations tries to fix trade by limiting output. The NCAA had relied on its traditional argument that restrictions on TV appearances promoted attendance and preserved balance among its members. The association also contended that it lacked the economic reach to restrain trade and portrayed itself as far removed from the long-distance cartel of ATT or the old Standard Oil monopoly. The high court held, however, that the NCAA had in effect fixed the price for "particular telecasts" by forcing its members to abide by its television contract. The NCAA boycotted other potential broadcasters such as NBC, the court declared, which could not televise the games. In probably the most telling point for the average consumer, the court insisted that the NCAA artificially limited the output of games available for sale. Justice John Stevens, who wrote the majority opinion, made a market-oriented argument when he observed: "The NCAA creates a price structure that is unresponsive to viewer demand and unrelated to the price that would prevail in a competitive market." The court did not buy into the NCAA argument that it was merely trying to protect the colleges from losing live attendance. The majority on the court saw the NCAA and its football-playing members as pursuing their own commercial interest.[42]

Two of the justices, Byron "Whizzer" White and William Rehnquist (later chief justice), viewed the issue quite differently. White, an All-American running back from Colorado in the 1930s and a onetime NFL player for Pittsburgh and Detroit, argued that the NCAA athletic policy served educational purposes and that the money involved in athletics merely reflected the costs of higher education. He agreed that the NCAA had to impose controls because colleges would compromise amateur athletics by pursuing win-at-any-cost practices. The NCAA controls kept the big-time football powers from "professionalizing" college athletics, he declared, and prevented profits from undermining educational goals. Unfortunately for the NCAA, while this argument might have applied in the 1930s when White played, it had become less compelling in the late-twentieth-century atmosphere of high-profit athletics.[43]

White also raised the point that the NCAA was not the same as a business operation. NCAA limits were initiated to keep wrongdoers at bay and impose some form of control on a game that threatened to spiral out of control. What would happen, after all, if the NCAA could no longer keep its members off television? White implied that the biggest and greediest would undermine the entire football structure. It still remained to be seen, however, whether the NCAA could continue to impose some limits or if a laissez-faire CFA would wrest the contract from the parent organization—or, for that matter, whether the CFA would be able to hold its group of major conferences together.[44]

The Supreme Court decision in 1984 did not rule out a voluntarily agreed upon NCAA-TV contract. Soon after the Supreme Court decision the NCAA presented a new television proposal, but the members of Division IA rejected it. No longer did they risk penalties by ignoring the NCAA-TV provisions, nor did their rejection automatically threaten to destroy the NCAA's authority in matters other than television. It appears, however, that most CFA schools felt that they could increase their TV appearances and profits by negotiating a contract without the NCAA.[45]

The results of the seasons following the decision would prove disappointing because supply would rapidly exceed demand. Compared to the eighty-nine games telecast in 1983, the networks would feed almost two hundred games to the public in the season after the Supreme Court decision, and this meant that a big-time institution would have to appear twice as often to make as much money. The contract that the CFA signed in the summer of 1984 for a twenty-game, thirteen-week package and a smaller contract with the ESPN cable network provided far less revenue than anticipated. The gaping hole in the CFA continued to be the absence of Big Ten and PAC-10; Chuck Neinas, who had failed to become Big Ten commissioner in 1971, never succeeded in luring the Big Ten and PAC-10 into the CFA. The absence of these key players doomed the prospects of a super TV contract. Once they were free to negotiate their own TV package, these two powerful holdouts undercut the CFA by signing their own four-year, ten million-dollar contract with CBS. Even the Ivy League signed a million-dollar contract with public television to televise the games of the saintly eight.[46]

Before the Supreme Court handed down its decision, Chuck Neinas envisioned a highly profitable super-conference within the CFA of forty to fifty institutions. Understandably, he realized that the CFA needed a firm commitment from the major football powers such as Oklahoma, Georgia, Texas, Notre Dame, Penn State, Alabama, and Nebraska, to name the best known. In a confidential letter to CFA president Fred Davison in 1983, Neinas set the stage for what he hoped would be a reorganization within the CFA. He proposed a meeting of representatives from the major institutions to lay the groundwork for an elite grouping. "Oklahoma and Georgia have already carried a heavy burden," he apologized to Davison, "but it is obvious that these universities are in the best position to assemble a group of prestigious CFA members." If they had their way, the really big-time schools would create an even more elite counterpart of Division IA football powers within the CFA and would free themselves from the NCAA's irksome regulations on scholarships and coaches and its objectionable sanctions.[47]

For Neinas and the CFA to put together such a major undertaking would have required schools to redefine their long-standing relationships with other members of their conferences. As a result of these and other difficulties, the super-conference died still-born, and the CFA ran out of steam. More precisely, the same forces that had led to the rebellion against the NCAA ended up undermining the CFA. Soon after the disappointing TV contract for 1984 and the failure of the Big Ten and PAC-10 to reconsider joining, the Atlantic Coast Conference signed its own deal with CBS, and the CFA solidarity showed signs of fraying. Greed, it seems, had created a far more chaotic situation than had ever existed under the NCAA-TV umbrella. While the larger conferences enjoyed media coverage, the smaller Division IA institutions, which had occasionally appeared on network TV, were resentful that the big-time schools soaked up all the TV time and still wanted more.[48]

One rich vein of profit, a playoff system, remained unmined and seemed to offer still another alluring goal for the CFA. Since the 1960s, when the NFL initiated the Super Bowl, the possibility of a national championship for college football had periodically reared its head. If Divisions IAA, II, and III could stage such events, surely the big-time schools could do the same. Some sportswriters who disliked the traditional system of voting proposed playoff plans that would culminate in a series of contests following the bowl games. Playoff proposals like far-off siren songs lured the leaders of big-time football with their bewitching tones. In the summer of 1984 Chuck Neinas outlined the possibility of a $55 million playoff that would use the bowls for semifinal and final games. The advertising rates, he declared, would bring $225,000 for a thirty-second commercial, half the rate for Super Bowl ads but comparable to the World Series and the pro football divisional playoffs. The new cartel would enrich its members, especially those teams that qualified for the eight-team playoff. As in the past, the football playoffs required a series of agreements among college heads, athletic directors, coaches, as well as the bowl committees. If Neinas had presided over a single unified football network, he might have made some headway. As it was, he exercised far less authority than Walter Byers in his prime, and Byers had hardly gone past the first tentative step of proposing an NCAA-sponsored football playoff.[49]

These dreams of riches yielded to the nagging problems of making the new gridiron order work as smoothly as it had in the past. In fact, the loss of unity provided by NCAA-TV proved costly in goodwill and in lost revenues. Under the NCAA-TV contract, for example, all of the schools had played under the umbrella of a single television network. Now "crossover games" between schools allied with the CFA and the Big Ten–PAC-10—or, more precisely, with different networks—posed a thorny problem. In 1984 UCLA and Southern California, whose games were televised by NBC, joined in a suit against Notre Dame and Nebraska (as well as ABC Sports and the CFA), claiming that the defendants had blocked intersectional games between the West Coast teams and their midwestern foes; each side was affiliated with a different network. The Notre Dame athletic director, Gene Corrigan, estimated that his institution had forfeited a million dollars in lost TV revenue as a result of canceled TV contracts. "Everyone is going around shooting each other in the foot," he declared. "It's a mess."[50]

Between 1985 and 1990 the CFA barely managed to retain its key members but just barely. In 1987 SEC commissioner Harvey Schiller negotiated a contract with ABC, a four-year package that totaled twenty-five million dollars for four years to ABC, which also carried Big Ten and PAC-10 games. When the SEC members voted to endorse the contract, the CFA recognized that its survival hung in the balance. After intense lobbying by Chuck Neinas and CFA officials, the SEC voted by a bare one-vote margin to return to the SEC. Nevertheless, the SEC managed to extract concessions from the CFA that made it virtually a separate entity within the CFA. The ambition of challenging the NCAA for athletic hegemony was rapidly fading.[51]

Of all the institutions in the CFA, however, Notre Dame remained essential to the organization's survival. For six years after the Supreme Court decision, Notre Dame bided its time, but in 1990 the Fighting Irish finally bailed out and then opened their golden parachute. In one of his final moves before he retired, Father Edmund Joyce negotiated a contract whereby NBC would pay Notre Dame $35 million over five years to televise every one of its games, leaving a huge gap in the CFA contract. Immediately, ABC complained that Notre Dame's departure had devalued its five-year $210 million dollar contract and called for the CFA to renegotiate. With the defection of the only college team with built-in national appeal, the CFA struggled to keep its members together. In 1994 the Southeastern Conference signed a highly lucrative contract with CBS, and in 1996 the CFA announced that it would fold up its operations the next year. In twenty years it had gone from a lobbying group within the NCAA to an authentic competitor for the parent group's power and then had succumbed to its own success.[52]

By that time Walter Byers had retired from thirty-eight years as executive director of the NCAA, possibly because of the college football wars but just as likely as a result of age and longevity. While he had shepherded the NCAA through the enforcement wars and the CFA rebellion, those struggles had left scars. Though he had led an organization with *amateur* in its name, Byers had presided over an inexorable march toward quasi-professional athletics.

In his autobiography, *Unsportsmanlike Conduct: Exploiting College Athletes,* Byers hinted at a link between the revolt of the football powers and the numerous scandals that began in the late 1970s. With more than sixty well-known members, the CFA hardly qualified as a gang of thieves; in the CFA era a number of Big Ten and PAC-10 schools that never joined the CFA would in fact wind up in trouble with the NCAA. Nevertheless, the rising costs as well as unparalleled appetite for gate receipts and TV revenue, let alone the hunger for recognition, all of which accompanied the emergence of the CFA, made it appear that the scandals and the TV controversy might share some common ground.

One of the trends that Byers singled out in the early 1990s, escalating salaries, actually began in the CFA era. In January 1982 Texas A&M, of the Southwest Conference, raised eyebrows by hiring Jackie Sherrill of Pittsburgh for the largest salary in history. Sherrill, who had won a national championship while at Pittsburgh, would over six years receive $1,722,000, funded by booster groups, plus extensive benefits. This would make him not only the highest-paid coach but also the highest-paid university employee in the country. President Frank Vandiver defended his institution's decision: "An athletic department of the first class at A&M is essential," he declared. "and I don't think that anything of the first class comes cheap."[53]

Constantly pushing at existing boundaries, football had established a new high-water mark for salaries, but the situation was new only in scale. One had only to return to the turn-of-the-century coaches, Foster Sanford at Columbia and Bill Reid at Harvard, who had also earned more than most of the faculty. Nevertheless, as the assistant dean of the A&M Architecture School, who had been a starting tackle there in the 1960s, observed, "It is hard to relate to that kind of money living here in academia." He thought that the salary seemed out of proportion, especially when salaries of top scholars, not to mention college presidents, came nowhere close to that figure. As a result of Sherrill's hiring, boosters at Nebraska opened a fund drive to raise $100,000 for Coach Tom Osborne and his staff. "When you look around the country," one of the organizers observed, "you realize our coaches are not as well as paid as some."[54]

The spiraling salaries reflected not only the hunger for profits but also the win-at-all-costs mentality of many boosters. High salaries placed intense pressure on coaches to produce winners, a state of mind that would lead some coaches to evade NCAA regulations. Such a willingness to pay stratospheric salaries also indicated that boosters might also resort to buying talent or payment schemes to players who performed well. The salaries of coaches and athletic officials would continue to soar, and the number of major scandals would reach epidemic proportions.

One casualty of the football wars proved to be Fred Davison, the president of the CFA. In 1985, a month after the jury awarded Jan Kemp, the former tutor for Georgia athletes, nearly $2 million in damages, reports circulated that irregularities in the remedial program could cost Georgia its accreditation, forcing Fred Davison to resign as president of Georgia. As one of the CFA founders, who had presided over a remarkable growth in the size and sophistication of his institution, Davison had become so involved in big-time football politics that he failed to prevent his own athletic program from spiraling out of control. Davison's resignation provided not only a bitter end for the longtime Georgia president but also a biting commentary on the CFA's rhetoric about improving academic standards for athletes. The scandals associated with academic scams in big-time football had cost him his job. Davison, of course, was neither the first nor last college president to lose his job because of what writer and football critic John Tunis called "the Great God Football."[55]

CHAPTER EIGHTEEN

Sudden Death at SMU: Football Scandals in the 1980s

In August 1984 Sean Stopperich, a former football player and student at Southern Methodist University in Dallas, declared that an SMU booster had induced him to enroll at SMU by making cash payments totaling five thousand dollars to him and his family. The 6′4″, 272-pound offensive lineman, who had quit football because of a knee injury and returned home to Pennsylvania, also claimed that the booster had moved his father to Dallas and found him a job.

Shortly afterward, when an NCAA investigator met with the booster, Sherwood Blount, a former football player and a millionaire real estate investor, he ran up against a stone wall. Instead of even pretending to cooperate as most board members and university officials ultimately did, Blount proved immediately abusive and uncooperative. "With much profanity he dismissed the NCAA and its investigators as a 'bunch of Communists,'" a report in 1987 by a committee of Methodist bishops recounted.[1]

What the NCAA investigator failed to discover was that Blount's activities in the Stopperich case represented merely the tip of the iceberg. The payments to SMU players turned out to be far more extensive and embraced not only the athletic officials but also the president of the university and the board of governors, one of whom was the former governor of Texas, William Clements. When the NCAA talked to Blount in January 1985, the board members were trying to "wind down," or phase out, the payments scheme that had begun in the late 1970s. The wind-down was necessary because the boosters and board members had involved the university in a tangled web of lies and deceit which soon would place their entire football program in jeopardy.

The Biggest Scandal of a Scandalous Decade

In the late 1970s and 1980s a series of multifaceted scandals had come to light or were rumbling just below the surface. Already the episodes at Arizona State, Southern California, Clemson, Florida, and Georgia suggested that athletic corruption had become far more serious than the public would find tolerable. In the early 1980s several major scandals erupted at big-time institutions, leading even the normally quiescent college presidents to draw up plans for an NCAA presidents' commission. By one estimate half of the

106 big-time football teams suffered sanctions from 1980 to 1989. Some of these scandals had ended with the resignation not only of the coaches but of presidents as well.

The University of Florida, which had won the SEC title for the first time in 1980, was charged by the NCAA with 107 infractions, ranging from illegal recruiting to payment of athletes. The most embarrassing charge against the coach, Charlie Pell, involved spying on his conference rivals. The president of the university, Robert Marston, called upon the faculty to conduct an investigation, while Pell asked for a blue ribbon commission. Pell then displayed a pattern of evasion typically exhibited by coaches charged with infractions—initial denials of guilt followed by partial acknowledgments, and ultimately resignation when the results of the NCAA investigation became public or sanctions resulted. By the beginning of the 1982 season Pell not only admitted his guilt but also submitted his resignation at the beginning of the 1984 season.[2]

Ironically, or perhaps not surprisingly, Pell had coached at Clemson before going to Florida, where he left a trail of violations in his wake. Named national champions in January 1982 under Coach Danny Ford, Clemson received two-year penalties from the NCAA, and Ford eventually had to step down. The team could not participate in bowl games, the Tigers could not appear on television, and Clemson had to give up twenty scholarships for two years.

"I think we were very sloppy," President William Atchley declared. "I think we did things very carelessly without thinking what they meant." He vowed that he would take disciplinary action and reorganize the athletic department, and, in the months that followed, Atchley maintained a high-profile stance, publishing op-ed articles in the *New York Times,* even proposing an accreditation system for athletics, and establishing ID cards for recruiters, including alumni.

Unfortunately for Atchley, he failed in his attempts to reorganize the athletic department. In 1985 a second scandal erupted at Clemson; football coaches had obtained anabolic steroids from a trainer at Vanderbilt and distributed them to the athletes. Atchley demanded the resignation of the athletic director, and, when the board refused to back the president, Atchley resigned.[3]

Though many scandals occurred in the South and Southwest, pigskin powers in the Midwest also attempted to challenge the NCAA's and the conferences' authority. As a flagship state school with large ambitions, the University of Illinois used every means in its power to break the Ohio State-Michigan stranglehold on the Big Ten title, even hiring a coach, Mike White, who had been dismissed from Cal-Berkeley because of questionable practices. In 1981 the Illini received a three-year probation for permitting a quarterback transfer student, Dave Wilson, to play, even though his grades at

Fullerton Junior College averaged less than C–. Nevertheless, Coach White, backed by the Illinois authorities, went all out to keep him eligible, even producing the transcript of another player at Fullerton with the same first and last name. When the Big Ten ruled him ineligible, Wilson sued the conference to let him play. He managed to participate in the fall of 1980, during which he set school and conference records. Because of Illinois' continued defiance of the conference, the Big Ten threatened to expel the institution from the conference. When the Big Ten penalized the Illini, the Illinois state legislature denounced the Big Ten, and Wayne Duke, the Big Ten commissioner, had his garage door spray-painted green and yellow. Two years later the NCAA also placed Illinois on probation.[4]

The failure of college authorities to prevent scandals or to root out the athletic culture that served as their breeding ground demonstrated that stronger measures were needed. In January 1984 a resolute group of college presidents, led by Derek Bok of Harvard and Father Timothy Healy of Georgetown, spearheaded a drive to establish an NCAA presidents' commission with veto power over the NCAA legislation involving scholastic standards and financial measures. Proposition 35, as it was known, came as a result of a study by the American Council on Education, the lobbying group for college presidents which had tried to establish the ACE code in 1952. In spite of numerous scandals in the late 1970s and early 1980s, delegations at NCAA conventions failed to give a two-thirds majority to the proposal. Instead of relinquishing power to the presidents, the NCAA passed a watered-down version that established a presidents' commission but gave it largely advisory powers. The only real power given to the commission was to call a special convention to propose measures that could be ratified by the NCAA at its regular convention.[5]

When the presidents' commission of the NCAA failed to get the powers that it wanted, its initiative appeared to have shipwrecked on the rocky shoals of big-time athletics. In fact, the power to call special conventions proved to be a remarkably potent weapon, a penalty branded with SMU's initials. From the beginning it would threaten the survival of Southern Methodist as a gridiron power.

Unlike the other offenders, SMU was not a flagship state institution, but it was closely identified with the proud image of Dallas and of its business elite. In the early 1980s SMU had achieved the top-winning percentage of any team in the country, but the NCAA placed it on probation, and reports of payments to recruits and players led to further NCAA investigations. Southern Methodist had a reputation not only as big-time football power but also as a repeat offender that persistently was being investigated by the NCAA—and this reputation grew worse after sanctions in 1984 and another probe in 1985. When newscaster Tom Brokaw addressed the NCAA at the end of the year, he began by saying: "I was especially flattered when I was asked to be here and do this today, especially when I realized that for $10,000 and a new convertible you could have had the top running back prospect from SMU for this luncheon."[6]

The history of SMU's love affair with football—and its tendency to evade the rules—went back to its earliest days. Begun in 1911, SMU's founders intended the new institution to fill the void in Methodist education in the South left when Vanderbilt severed its ties with the church. Lacking the resources of other freshly minted institutions, SMU devoted itself to football, an activity that would attract attention and please its backers, and in the meantime let its campus development languish. In 1922 the Southwest Conference, which SMU had recently joined, temporarily suspended the school for illegal subsidies. SMU's executive committee had given special "student activity" scholarships to football players and charged the books to the athletic business manager, who was then reimbursed by the university; players received almost twice as much as Methodist theology students, whom the institution had a mission to train. In addition, gridders received under-the-table loans from alumni and held bogus jobs that required no work.[7]

Because of these infractions, Southern Methodist barely escaped being expelled from the conference, saved by a single vote cast in its favor by its own representative. In its internal investigation the SMU faculty report read like a statement from the acerbic pen of Harvard's Charles Eliot. Amateurism had become an endangered species, the faculty warned. Certainly, football had the potential for advertising a school, they declared, but in a statement pregnant with meaning for the future, "it should never take precedence over physical, moral, and intellectual needs of the student body."[8]

When the executive committee of SMU's board reluctantly agreed to the principle of faculty control of athletics imposed by the conference, one member of the committee, Dallas jeweler R. H. Shuttles, resigned. Shuttles believed that the executive committee should run the school just as if it were a business. According to SMU historian Mary Martha Thomas, Shuttles felt that the members of the faculty athletic committee were wrong and even disloyal to criticize university athletics. Apparently, other members of the board agreed, even though they temporarily capitulated. The chairman of the executive committee denied that faculty members should have control of athletics any more than they should run the university. "If this were the case," he insisted, "we would soon have no university."[9]

In spite of the faculty's brief triumph, SMU made rapid progress in football and won SWC titles in 1923 and 1926 under Coach Ray Morrison. In 1935 the team went to the Rose Bowl. In those years, if SMU was known outside Texas, it was for football. As a result of Morrison's success, SMU had mortgaged itself to the hilt to build Ownby Stadium early in the Depression but waited until 1939 to complete its library. Located in Highland Park, a new and affluent section of Dallas, SMU eventually completed its traditional red-brick campus and by 1940 had assembled a reasonably large student body of nearly four thousand undergraduates.

Though it added professional schools in the 1940s, SMU was best remembered in these years for Heisman Trophy winner Doak Walker and for its dramatic intersectional battles with Notre Dame. As its football prowess grew, SMU abandoned Ownby Field less than two decades after it was opened in order to play in the sixty thousand-seat Cotton Bowl. Even when their teams did not win championships after the 1940s, SMU produced blue-chip players such as Kyle Rote, Raymond Berry, Forrest Gregg, and the Dallas Cowboys star and "Monday Night Football" commentator Don Meredith. Even if SMU were not a flagship state university, it still represented the identity and ambitions of Dallas.

Yet SMU was not immune from economic and social forces affecting private institutions in urban areas. As football attendance in urban areas dropped off drastically in the late 1940s and early 1950s, Southern Methodist's performance went rapidly downhill, and the team struggled for two decades with an overall losing record. With the number of big-city attractions and the growth of TV, SMU alumni and gridiron sports enthusiasts would not turn out in large numbers to watch a team that did not have championship quality. From 1951 to 1976 SMU won only a single SWC title, and that title, thanks to Jerry Levias, the first African-American football scholarship holder in the conference. When the Dallas Cowboys were founded in 1960, another competitor vied with SMU for the Dallas sports dollars, and, when the Cowboys began to win championships, Southern Methodist football suffered by comparison.[10]

The decline of SMU football would coincide with a reorganization of the school's board in the early 1960s, a change that would lead downward to the scandals of the 1980s. The SMU board of trustees had changed from a body with a large contingent of powerful Methodist bishops to one in which the Methodist bishops played a negligible role. Though the full board numbered seventy-five, crucial decisions were made by an inner group of twenty-one known as the board of governors. As a result of these decisions, the Methodist bishops disappeared from the governing board, and a new generation of businessmen took their places. In twenty years, from 1967 to 1987, there were only three chairmen of the board of governors: Edwin Cox, Robert Stewart, and Bill Clements (who would serve two terms as governor of Texas), all of them powerful Dallas businessmen. The board of governors was not simply a booster board but also controlled some of the biggest money in a city whose ambition knew no bounds and whose lust for winning was legendary. As the president of the faculty senate at SMU later put it, "If you weren't winning, you were losing." The triad of board chairmen would have grand designs for SMU. "We are on the plateau just below the final step of achievement at S.M.U.," Clements would boast in the early

1980s. "We are now talking in terms of S.M.U. in the future being at the same level as Duke or Stanford." Rather than emulate those two benchmark institutions, the board leaders would act as if winning football were more urgent than building a strong educational base for their proud institution.[11]

Eventually, these men, who were used to winning in business, grew impatient with SMU's inability to field big-time winners in football. As one observer in the 1980s mused, the big-time SMU alumni were tired of the constant ribbing at local country clubs from business associates who were alumni of such winning schools as Texas, Texas A&M, Texas Tech, Oklahoma, and Arkansas. Instead of playing by the rules, they set out to buy a winner.

In 1967 Bill Clements, then a young businessman, took over as president of the inner board of governors, the first of three that would hold power for twenty years. In the 1970s gridiron interests, which had always cast a long shadow, began to intrude on academic decision making. Responding to a demand by a faculty committee in 1972, the newly arrived president, Paul Hardin, relieved Coach Hayden Fry. In December 1973, after firing Fry, Hardin informed the NCAA that his institution's football coaches were paying players from university funds for outstanding performances. Hardin also made a full report on the same subject to the Southwest Conference which resulted in a one-year probation, a mild penalty from a group of schools which had plenty of its own baggage to hide. After the NCAA conducted its own investigation, however, SMU suffered far more severe penalties—a two-year TV blackout with no bowl games. In 1974, a year after the NCAA had meted out its penalties, the board of trustees fired Hardin. He was succeeded temporarily by Willis Tate, a longtime president of SMU (1955–72) and a former Mustang football player.[12]

In truth Hardin also had other ideological conflicts with the board. Cox and other key board members supported the professional schools, and Hardin, the liberal arts. But if, as he believed, athletics led to his firing, the episode went to a more essential problem of presidential authority over athletics. The Carnegie Report in 1929, the ACE Special Committee in 1952, and the Hanford Report all cited the role of the college president as crucial to controlling big-time sports. Yet Hardin's experience seemed to indicate that this was not enough. The president needed the active support of members of the faculty and the board in order to root out big-time corruption. In particular, he needed a board that was not self-perpetuating, as the SMU board had become in the 1960s. As long as an athletic culture held sway at an institution, the president acting alone would find it almost impossible to uproot.

Anatomy of a Scandal, 1978 to 1985

In the late 1970s, after its probation, SMU began to win again. *Sports Illustrated,* in "It's Ninety-Five [Scholarships] and Look Who's Alive," attributed SMU's revival to the NCAA's new limitation on scholarships that enabled teams with fewer players to compete with big teams like Texas. Actually, the new coach, Ron Meyer, who came to SMU in 1976 after stints as head coach at Nevada-Las Vegas and as a scout for the Dallas Cowboys, regarded big-time college football as a commercial and professional activity. He wore his 1981 Dallas Cowboys Super Bowl ring and always made certain that he flashed a hundred dollar bill whenever he removed his billfold. According to players who signed with SMU, the Mustangs actually had far less in illicit money to offer the Houston high school players than other schools, which plopped down five thousand dollars in hundreds and sent the recruits to the local Ford dealer to pick up their new cars. Yet Meyer made up for it in panache, always dressing in flashy clothes and, instead of putting just his card on the high school bulletin board, tacked up his trademark hundred dollar bill with his card, removing it when he left.[13]

Like other successful coaches, Ron Meyer embodied many of the most admired qualities in American society. An extraordinarily hard worker, he put in sixteen-hour days and began his staff meetings at 6 A.M. Being extremely ambitious, he willingly gave all of himself to his job. Unlike Darrell Royal at Texas and Frank Kush at Arizona, no one accused him of abusing his players. In a society that valued salesmanship Meyer had a flair for presenting and promoting himself and an ability to use the then relatively small amount of money at his disposal to impress his potential recruits. In short he would have also succeeded selling oil machinery, real estate, or investments. Unhappily for SMU, he had nothing in common with the academic sector of the institution and operated in a wholly different sphere. Much of what later happened at SMU can be laid at his doorstep.

Meyer forged an alliance with aggressive boosters who made their own recruiting visits and delivered cash payments to players. The youthful boosters at SMU in the front line of the pay-for-play operation contributed money and made preliminary contacts with high school students. They were alumni of the institution, often former football players or athletes, who could not have operated without the tacit knowledge and consent of the board leaders. Brash and confident and fanatically loyal to SMU, they evidently cared a great deal about Southern Methodist. One booster later recalled that his family had attended SMU for three generations. "We were kind of indoctrinated as little kids with S.M.U., S.M.U.," he told the *New York Times*. "S.M.U. could do no wrong." In the 1960s, when this booster was a student, he recalled, it did not require an "Einstein" to deduce what was happening—white Thunderbirds in the parking lot of the athletic department and poor players awash with money. After he graduated, he was recruited by a classmate, a young businessman, to take part in recruiting players. His job was to contact and meet local athletes in his area of Texas, and he contributed thousands of dollars to the Mustang Club. It seemed natural to do this, he declared, almost an act of patriotism, an extension of his loyalty to SMU.[14]

Viewed more broadly, these SMU alumni belonged to a generation of aggressive and hostile boosters who operated as a paramilitary arm of athletic departments and reacted violently when they failed to get their way. The most conspicuous practitioner proved to be Sherwood Blount, the SMU booster, who ended up bankrolling the payments operation single-handedly for nearly a year and who tried to get Donald Shields fired as president when he dared to blame the boosters. Later, after the sordid facts had become public, Blount wrote angry and threatening letters to NCAA officials. As a power center operating independently within the illegal football operation, Blount became a threat to SMU's institutional reputation and, more immediately, to the board members' conspiracy. In addition, he used his ties with SMU football players to launch a new career as a sports agent, representing them in their negotiations with NFL clubs. In his renegade stance toward academic authority and his willingness to plunk down tens of thousands for illegal football operations, Blount was a "take-no-prisoners" threat to the institution itself.[15]

Meyer set up a system whereby players could sell complimentary tickets at a premium, a scam that violated NCAA rules and not long afterward would land Southern California on probation. The coach also flew their parents to games and subsidized flights home for the players whenever they wanted, a form of assistance that violated the athletic scholarship rules of the NCAA and the conference. Meyer cleverly avoided direct payments to players, however, and left a near invisible paper trail. "Nowhere in any of the publicly released documents, nor in the NCAA's own confidential report," David Whitford has written, "is any mention made of slush funds, or payments to players and their families, or motor-home excursions between Houston and Dallas, or any other of the other serious violations that were later found to have been committed."[16]

From 1979 to 1981 the NCAA investigated a charge that the board of governors chairman had offered illicit inducements to recruits. That, in itself, would have created sensational revelations and would have overshadowed infractions at other schools. While the NCAA did not find evidence to support these charges, investigators did uncover enough violations, including the illicit sale of tickets and money for parents to attend games, that they placed SMU on two years probation, prohibiting the institution from TV and bowl appearances. At the end of the 1981 season, as the NCAA investigators began to uncover his illegal acts, Meyer left SMU to become coach of the New England Patriots.[17]

In the fall of 1980, as the NCAA proceeded with its investigation, President James Zumberge resigned to become president at Southern California. Though Zumberge would later have to clean up an athletic scandal left by his predecessor at USC, he may have left because he knew that he would have to face probing questions about possible NCAA violations at SMU. In his place came L. Donald Shields from California-Fullerton, where he had once been the youngest college president in the country. At the start of his presidency Shields got a briefing from the SMU faculty rep, Mike Harvey, who profiled SMU's aggressive boosters and filled in the details of the NCAA investigation. He also appealed to Shields to help in cleaning up the athletic situation at SMU.

Harvey named several notorious boosters and warned Shields to stay away from a particularly aggressive, youthful alumnus and former football player, Sherwood Blount, who had made a quick two million in real estate, drove a white Cadillac, and proved as adept at closing on football recruits as he was in making land deals. Harvey also told Shields that the members of the football team were receiving illegal payments. Shields assured Harvey, however, that he was already familiar with the problem; he even knew the names of boosters from his first day on campus.[18]

As for helping Harvey to clean up the problem, Shields never responded to the faculty rep's plea. And that raises the question of whether he was prepared to take his athletic responsibilities as seriously as the rest of his job. Shields, who would have little rapport with his faculty, may have been reluctant to move against a football program that enjoyed strong support from the leaders of the board. Since he had not come from SMU faculty ranks, Shields lacked a network of friends among the faculty or administrators and showed no inclination to establish one. He preferred to hobnob with the Dallas businessmen and board elite rather than kowtow to the less prestigious members of the SMU faculty.

Shields was also reluctant to jeopardize the success of the football team because the highly ranked Mustangs appealed to his athletic Walter Mitty complex. The booster president attended all the games, rubbed elbows with players and coaches in the locker room, and stationed himself on the sidelines during the game. He appeared to agree with SMU supporters that the charges were merely a result of attempts by its rivals to sabotage the football program. While he pursued a cursory investigation of boosterism, he merely recommended that the board ban one of the boosters, a proposal that the board ignored.

The new SMU president thrived on the success of the football team and for good reason. In the Ron Meyer era the team had become one of the powers in the Southwest Conference as well as in the nation. From 1980 to 1984 the team would have the best winning percentage in the country, and in 1982 it would be the only major team to go undefeated. In his naive enthusiasm Shields was a throwback to the booster presidents of the 1890s, who believed in football and who lent their support and presence to the team. The president's enthusiasm knew no bounds; he even took the unusual step of appointing the new athletic director, Bob Hitch, to the president's executive council, and he always asked at the start of each meeting on the progress in recruiting. In the words of SMU historian Marshall Terry, he was "less than moderate in his love for sport and in his sense of its contribution to making SMU really big time."[19]

The era of cost-effective cheating at SMU proved short-lived. After Ron Meyer left in January 1982, the boosters, who had worked closely and quietly with the coach, became less secretive and more exuberant. Both athletic director Bob Hitch and his new coach Bobby Collins, who had come from Southern Mississippi, did not have the close ties with the boosters which Meyer had forged. As a result, Hitch and Collins paid far less attention to the boosters and refused to support them. Frustrated by attempts to isolate them, the boosters built their own power center within the football program by bankrolling the players and using assistant coaches to make their payments. In spite of the athletic leaders' desire to keep them in the background, the boosters played a far more visible role, not unlike part-owners of a professional football team.

Though SMU was still on NCAA probation from the earlier sanctions, Shields received a letter in 1983 from the NCAA announcing that it would conduct another inquiry. In a list of eighty allegations the NCAA charged that the Mustangs offered automobiles and cash to prospective players. Some of the players named in the allegations ended up at SMU, and others did not. Because of the charges by players on other teams, Shields and many other Mustang supporters believed that its gridiron opponents had ganged up on SMU because its team had become too successful.[20]

That the NCAA charges came, at least in part, from players attending other schools raised in Shields's mind the specter of conspiracies against SMU designed to discredit his institution and its highly successful team. Assuming that other SWC schools had fabricated the charges, Shields engaged attorneys to represent the university in its showdown with the NCAA and used them to begin his own investigation. The booster president assumed that the players would offer testimony that would exonerate Southern Methodist.

When Shields asked the attorneys to interview his own players, he encountered an unpleasant surprise. Instead of telling Shields that the charges from outsiders were pure moonshine, the attorneys reported that two Mustang players admitted that they and others did, in fact, receive monthly payments—as faculty rep Mike Harvey had tried to tell him when he first arrived. Even worse, it appeared that members of the coaching staff were delivering the payments, while boosters met the expenses. The payments were increased as the players matured and their role on the team grew more important.

Once he learned from his attorneys of the payments, Shields hurried over to tell Edwin Cox and the chairman of the board of governors, Bill

Clements. Clements, a Dallas businessman, who had first served as chairman in the 1960s, was better known as governor of Texas from 1977 to 1981. Unhappily for Donald Shields, he ran up against a formidable adversary in Clements, a figure whose power in SMU policymaking, let alone Texas politics, far exceeded his own. When Shields became indignant and said that the payments had to stop, Clements ordered him to "stay out" of the investigation and "go run the university"—the former governor and Edwin Cox would tend to gridiron policy. Clements later met with Shields and related that the boosters had established a $400,000 slush fund for payments and gifts to players. Shields was astonished when Clements told him that the athletic director, Bob Hitch, who had met with his executive council, knew of the payments: "Hitch is a professional," Clements declared, "and it's his job to know."[21]

This meeting with Clements proved to be a turning point, a downward turn for Shields, because it caught him in the spider web of conspiracy. As an NCAA president, Shields had to sign statements that he and the athletic director had complied with NCAA bylaws. Shields now knew from Clements that SMU stood outside of NCAA regulations. By failing to act, Shields joined the circles of conspirators who knew about and sanctioned the payments. Though Shields made a plea to end the payments, he joined the conspiracy by helping the board in its attempts to deceive the NCAA investigators and elude the threat of further penalties.

For Clements, Shields, and athletic director Hitch their immediate task was how to squirm out of the NCAA's grasp. One expedient was to send the boosters into hiding and to scale down the activities of Sherwood Blount, George Owen, and several others. The boosters had access to the locker rooms and sidelines, sometimes even flying with the team on its chartered plane. Hitch met with the boosters and asked them to stop their recruiting, promising that he would not divulge their names during the NCAA investigation.[22]

The public activities of the boosters were only part of the problem. Members of the athletic department continued to pay the players from illicit money that the boosters supplied. When Shields himself interviewed a former player, he learned in detail how payments were made. He also learned from Bob Hitch that Robert Stewart, who had preceded Clements as head of the board, played a key role in funneling money from the boosters to the athletic department. By late 1983 Shields had accumulated enough information that he might have sounded an alarm bell; by dabbling in the scandal, Shields would invite the hostility of Clements. Unlike Hardin, Shields showed no inclination to go public but attempted to convince the board leaders to cut off payments and banish the boosters. Shields's failure to act decisively in the face of a massive scandal shows the dilemma of a weak president whose only option is to come clean and lose his job. If

Shields had acted in late 1983, he might have been able to save himself, as Hardin did, from an even worse fate—the loss of integrity and self-respect. Instead, he became enmeshed in attempts to resolve the problem by warding off the boosters, making himself a part of the problem as opposed to the solution.

In August 1984 SMU's problems deepened, as the NCAA initiated still another investigation, an extension of its earlier preliminary probe—this, in response, to the revelation of Sean Stopperich's admission that Sherwood Blount had promised him five thousand dollars and a free meal ticket for his family if they came to Dallas. Evidently, the payments that SMU promised would be stopped had persisted. When Shields again asked the board if the payments had stopped, he was again told "to go run the university." Since the NCAA tended to go easier on institutions that came clean, SMU and its officials would have done better to cut their losses.[23]

Both Clements and Shields tried to preempt the NCAA investigators by appearing before the infractions committee. Shields promised that he would faithfully observe the bylaws of the association. This appeal, however, was flatly rejected. Also appearing before the committee, Clements tried to convince the members that SMU was simply experiencing the aftereffects of the Ron Meyer era. Clements gave a wholly fabricated account of his attempts to put SMU's house in order and to bring Sherwood Blount to heel. "I've had some very heart-to-heart talks with this young man, again in my office. Mr. Sherwood Blount is listening to me," he insisted. He also asserted that he had made the board's position clear to Hitch and Collins. "We will not tolerate any misbehavior," he declared, "by any of the people in the administration, in the athletic department, the coaching staff, or any of these alums, to the degree that we can."[24]

What Clements left unsaid was that he had merely promised a phasing out of the payments, or a wind-down. The players had to be paid to keep them from leaking the story to the media or coming clean with the NCAA; the team's paymaster, Henry Parker, had given out forty-seven thousand dollars to thirteen players during the 1985–86 school year and lesser amounts to others during the football season. While Shields did not, like Hardin, divulge the continuing payments, he did plead with Clements, Cox, and Stewart to go "cold turkey" and to terminate those payments at once. But Clements was determined to have his way.[25]

Despite Shields's pleas and Clements's lies, the NCAA in June 1985 imposed a three-year probation for SMU on the basis of thirty-eight violations of its bylaws. SMU would be prohibited from giving football scholarships in 1986–87 and was limited to fifteen scholarships for the following year. In addition, SMU could not appear on TV for the first year of its probation nor go to bowl games for two years. Never in its history had the NCAA imposed such a severe penalty, but SMU had failed to convince the Compliance Committee that it had seriously tried to clean up its act. Unlike Clemson and Florida, SMU had received penalties four times in eleven years and had been under investigation much of that time, a compelling reason to hand out tough penalties.

In the summer of 1985, after the NCAA investigation of SMU had ended, the presidents' commission established in 1984 called its first special convention. Meeting at New Orleans, more than two hundred college presidents passed a number of measures which showed their determination to strike at the worst play-for-pay and recruiting abuses. They required each institution to conduct an independent audit of their department, highlighting donations from booster clubs and explaining how the funds were used. Coaches whose programs were guilty of wrongdoing would carry the record with them to their next job. No longer could coaches shift the blame to assistant coaches, as the football and basketball coach at William and Mary had tried to do with a young assistant in 1951.[26]

Most unnerving for Southern Methodist football, the convention passed a regulation that provided for a two-year suspension of a sport in which infractions took place, and, not surprisingly, SMU was one of the few institutions to oppose it. To qualify for the "death penalty," the institution had to be a repeat offender, one that had incurred two major violations in five years. Previously, SMU had merely faced more penalties that would stretch into the late 1980s. Now the scenario had become far more serious. Because it had a history of five major infractions in twenty-five years—1958, 1964, 1974, 1975, and 1981—Southern Methodist would emerge as the prime candidate for the new penalty.[27]

Though SMU planned to wind down its payments, it was still paying its players and, therefore, laid itself open to still another NCAA investigation and further penalties. The compliance committee needed a clear case of flagrant disregard for NCAA regulations in order to deploy the death penalty. If SMU erred again, it could be the end for SMU football in the foreseeable future. Bill Clements may have intended to wind down the payments, but payments to the senior players would persist after the latest penalties handed down in 1985 had taken effect. Clements found himself in a catch-22 situation in which he could only avoid the NCAA penalties if he stayed clean, but, if he stopped the payments, SMU's payments after the last NCAA investigation would most likely be revealed.

Using the hackneyed, Vietnam-era phrase, Clements insisted that he could see "the light at the end of the tunnel"—if the wind-down of payments brought an end in a year or two to the slush fund era. Even Clements had to admit that their stonewalling was risky; too many people already knew the details of the operation. If the school cut out the payments, as Shields advocated, or if disgruntled players or coaches talked to the press, all the world would know that SMU had continued to break the rules. It is also questionable whether SMU was committed to stopping the payments. At the end of the 1985 season the payments to a senior player who had signed a pro contract had been switched to an outstanding junior with a remaining year of eligibility, an indication that the athletic department and possibly the board members had never intended to phase out the payments altogether.[28]

During the fall of 1986 SMU football and the coverup threatened to break down. On the field the performance of the football team deteriorated during a nightmarish season marked by a 69-7 defeat by Notre Dame, the worst in SMU's history, and a 40-0 defeat in the team's final game against conference rival Arkansas. Foreshadowing the NCAA's final blow, two players near the end of the season broke into the locker of Henry Parker, an athletic official and paymaster for the team, and stole the team's entire monthly bankroll. The coaches had no trouble locating the perpetrators, but, when confronted, they refused to return the money. Instead of suspending the players, the coaches had to back off or risk disclosure. In an atmosphere of lawlessness the coaches, in effect, said "What the hell?" and played them in the game the following Saturday. Another well-heeled booster replaced the money.[29]

The Deconstruction of Football at SMU

In the fall of 1986 Bill Clements resigned as chairman and ran again for governor. Because so many people knew some of the details, the payments scheme also created a potential "smoking gun" for the Clements campaign. In particular, Sherwood Blount threatened "to take matters into his own hands"—or, to put it bluntly, wreck Clements's campaign—by divulging the details of the operation. Up to this point Clements's role in the athletics at SMU was not widely known, and the Texas electorate did not associate the NCAA penalties or the payments with the man who was running for the state's highest office. To keep Blount off his back, Clements told the abrasive booster that he would resume his position as board chairman no matter what happened in the election; he also promised that his first task would be to fire President Shields, who had antagonized Blount by publicly blaming the boosters. Blount, who had singlehandedly met "the payroll," as he put it, had nothing but contempt for Shields.[30]

For three tense months Clements managed to keep the football scandal from becoming public, just long enough to be reelected. Soon after his reelection, however, his campaign of manipulating the media and controlling the network of participants fell apart. On November 12, 1986, Channel 8 in Dallas broadcast a documentary on former SMU player David Stanley, who claimed that he had received cash payments before he quit SMU the previous January. In addition, Stanley, once a prime recruit, said that he had de-

veloped a serious drug problem and that SMU had paid for his treatment—
an apparently humane gesture but one that violated NCAA rules. Stanley
and his mother had already talked to the NCAA. On the TV program athletic director Bob Hitch tried unconvincingly to answer the allegations.[31]
Not to be outdone, the *Dallas Morning News* carried a story on November
14 that SMU tight end Albert Reese lived in a rent-free apartment. One of
the boosters whom Cox and Clements had asked to desist had made the
payments.[32]

Abruptly, the scandal that had lain low during the election campaign
had become a factor for the college officials and the board. Donald Shields,
who had recently returned from medical leave related to adult-onset diabetes, invited Cox, the faculty representative Lonnie Kliever, and other
board members to watch a tape of the Channel 8 program on Stanley.
Shields was emotional and weepy, a sickly version of the hearty football buff
who had cheered from the sidelines in 1982. A few days later, Shields told
Kliever and two others that he was considering early retirement for medical
reasons, and he was thinking of suspending SMU football for two years.

When the board members rejected the two-year moratorium and ordered him to halt his own investigation, Shields began to veer toward near
emotional and physical collapse. He first tried to resign, but the board,
which had planned to fire him at the end of the school year, started to put
him off, but on November 21 the university announced his resignation.
William Stallcup, an interim provost and professor of biology, became acting president. Stallcup, at sixty-six, had first joined the faculty in 1945 and
had already postponed his retirement for a year to fill the vacant post of
provost. He would get more than a veteran administrator and faculty member bargained for, and he too would have his reputation compromised by
the unfolding scandal.[33]

Without knowing the depths of the scandal, editorials in the Dallas
newspapers welcomed the change in administration. The press saw Shields,
beset by diabetes and near a breakdown, as hardly the leader to rein in a herd
of out-of-control Mustangs. Throughout this period the press assumed that
SMU's president or college presidents not only could control college football
but also held the key to honest programs. "Shields Should Bear the Brunt
if SMU Erred," a column harangued immediately after the Stanley revelations. Somehow, the fact that the president was hired—and treated like a
high-salaried factotum—by the board of the governors, or in this case by a
cabal within it, was not yet understood. A hopeful sign, according to one article in the *Dallas Morning News,* was that other scandal-marred schools had
managed to refurbish their images. So, there seemed to be hope for SMU.[34]

Indeed, the scandal was just beginning to surface. Because SMU needed
more scapegoats to appease the NCAA, the board decided that athletic director Bob Hitch (who, contrary to his public statements, was fully familiar

with the payments) and football coach Bobby Collins (just as familiar but the most successful coach in SMU history) had to go. The two at length agreed to resign but asked for confidentiality and the rest of their compensation. Should the school honor their contracts, which amounted to $800,000 and involved housing, Cadillacs, and country club memberships? If SMU fired the two, they might go public or, worse, file a lawsuit against the school. So, the decision was made by Cox and the new chairman of the governors, William Hutchison, to honor their contracts.[35]

With its other hand the board leaders designated the faculty representative Lonnie Kliever, a bearded theology professor, to lead an internal investigation—and mislead the NCAA. The board insisted that Kliever himself conduct the probe. If Kliever represented the board, perhaps they could avoid the death penalty and also keep their own role—particularly the activities of Governor-Elect Bill Clements—from becoming public. Even the acting president, William Stallcup, who knew of Clements's role, intentionally kept this information from Kliever, who reluctantly agreed to lead the probe. Assisted by an attorney subject to his orders, Kliever would conduct what the leaders termed "a cooperative investigation" with the NCAA. As part of his agreement with the board, Bob Hitch agreed to help Kliever and fully inform him of the names of boosters, coaches, and players. Because the board would continue to pay him, Hitch would not reveal the activities of board members, with the exception of Robert Stewart, who had resigned because of his direct and more easily identified role in contributing to the slush fund and supporting the cash payments while chairman. Hitch would give the names of the boosters, especially Sherwood Blount, who had bankrolled the payments from the summer of 1986.[36]

In Kliever's investigation he learned from former athletic director Hitch that he and former coach Bobby Collins were involved in payments to the players. For the NCAA's investigator, David Bierst, the news hardly bolstered SMU's credibility, but it seemed to indicate that Kliever and the board members were earnest in their desire to cooperate. Ironically, because the board had agreed to keep the role of Hitch and Collins confidential, SMU officially denied that the two were guilty of making payments.

What about Clements's tracks, which had been so carefully covered during the election campaign? Already in January and February rumors had circulated that Clements was involved. After all, the governor somehow fit the Nixonian role in what was labeled by the *Dallas Times-Herald* as "Ponygate." Even Lonnie Kliever had heard such a rumor from an assistant coach in December, though he had confidently dismissed it. Instead of delving into the rumor, Kliever, like the board, focused on the goal of NCAA leniency.[37]

Naturally, Clements himself had denied any complicity in the payments scheme. When asked on February 25, 1986, just after he resigned from the board after becoming governor, he had responded, "Hell no. Absolutely not." Kliever and Stallcup vigorously denied any knowledge of Clements's involvement in a televised press conference in late February. No one from the administration, Kliever insisted, had any knowledge of the governor's guilt. Yet Stallcup had been present at a meeting in December when Hitch gave an account of a meeting with Clements in the parking lot. In that meeting Clements asked if payments could be continued, and Hitch said they could. "Then do it," he ordered.[38]

Members of the SMU community still had reason to hope that the infractions committee would believe the acting president, the governor, and especially Kliever, who appeared before the committee. If not, they would move a long step closer to the NCAA death penalty. And for a school that thrived on football the demise of the entire gridiron program had all the implications of a death sentence. A number of jobs in the athletic department and in football-related occupations depended on its outcome, as did the financial well-being of teams relying on football revenue. Even for faculty and students who might have been otherwise indifferent to athletics or athletic skullduggery, the notoriety threatened to place a permanent blemish on their academic credentials. And no one could predict how the adverse publicity might affect enrollments and alumni contributions.

In January 1987 Kliever came clean with Bierst, or as clean as he could have, naming a list of boosters and coaches; he was still unable to divulge the identity of insiders, whose role in ordering the payments he did not officially know. In fact, Kliever had spent time with Bob Hitch, someone who could have divulged the inner workings of the payments scheme, but Hitch did not violate his agreement with the board. In a final desperate effort at good faith Kliever gave the NCAA a list of violations (all that he knew about) and proposed sanctions (the latter extracted from the board of trustees with great difficulty), in hopes of avoiding the feared death penalty.

Based on Kliever's investigation, Bierst, an NCAA investigator, recommended clemency to the NCAA infractions committee; indeed, SMU's revelations had helped the committee to build its case. Instead, the infractions committee delivered the dreaded blow—the death penalty—on February 24. Out of respect for SMU's apparent candor the NCAA technically limited the suspension to a single year. But, since the association took away all the Mustang scholarships for the following year and decreed that the team would play no home games, SMU had little choice but to cancel its 1988 season as well. The extent of SMU's repeated violations, the committee believed, forced it to deliver what amounted to a two-year suspension. In spite of Kliever's attempt to come clean, the committee was suspicious of the evasion that had characterized the SMU staff during the investigation. Had they only known that the iceberg went still deeper, they would surely have delivered the most severe punishment possible.[39]

After suffering the death penalty, the skeletons in SMU's football closet began to appear. On March 1, 1987, less than a week after the sentence, the public learned of Bob Hitch's role, hardly a surprise, given his proximity to the payments scandal. The persistent rumors of Governor Bill Clements's involvement, however, created a far larger stir. On the day after the Hitch revelations, Cathy Costello, an SMU vice president, told acting president William Stallcup that she had learned that Channel 8 was working on a story about Clements and the football payments. The media had already learned it from Sherwood Blount, who, enraged by the damage to his reputation after SMU released the boosters' names to the NCAA and then to the public, sought his revenge by revealing that Clements had participated in the payments. So, Clements had no choice but to give a public version of his role in the imbroglio. On March 3 the governor held a press conference in which he acknowledged that the board had made payments to "honor obligations and to wind down and eventually eliminate the obligations."[40]

The news that the inner cabal of the board had authorized the payments shook the SMU campus. At 9 A.M. on the morning of March 4 a teach-in began in front of Dallas Hall, only a few hours before the board of governors was scheduled to meet in a nearby building. Students, faculty, alumni, and the newly appointed chairman of the board of governors, William Hutchison, spoke to the gathering. The event recalled the student-faculty activism of the anti-Vietnam War movement. Calling the scandal "something immoral and unethical in our university," Professor Marshall Terry, an English professor and longtime faculty member at SMU, urged the students to "display themselves" to the board. After speeches in front of Dallas Hall, the crowd responded to an emotional plea from a member of the history department. Someone called for a march across campus to confront the board of governors, which was then deliberating. The moderator of the meeting pleaded with the crowd not to invade the governors' meeting; the sponsors of the teach-in, he declared, would not condone violence or active confrontations. For a brief moment overtones of confrontations at Columbia and Berkeley during the Vietnam era reappeared like the ghosts of protests past.[41]

Instead, the crowd stayed at Dallas Hall, where the new chairman of the board, William Hutchison, was to read a statement. Before he began, people in the crowd loudly complained that the media had placed so much equipment in front of them that they could not see what was happening. "This protest is for us, not the press," one student yelled. The nervous media moved their equipment, and the crowd listened to Hutchison recite the board's resolution. "I am committed, and this board is committed to making sure that this never happens again," Hutchison declared. "Today we unanimously passed a resolution if implemented by the board of trustees (the larger board), will set in motion sweeping reforms to streamline the way SMU is governed."[42]

At that meeting the board resolved to appoint a committee of Methodist bishops to sift through the evidence. Intended to be an impartial body, the bishops would determine the chronology of events and who had known what and when they had known it. In an interview with Channel 8 which was broadcast on March 30, Clements repeated the statements that he had made earlier in the month. Though he may have known more than he divulged, Clements denied any knowledge of what had happened before 1983. Ron Meyer, he said, had recruited the boosters. The committee of four bishops, aided by four attorneys, took sworn depositions from all the board members, who would cooperate and interviewed everyone who might have knowledge of the payments or the events surrounding the resignation of Hitch, Collins, and paymasters Bootsie Larsen and Henry Parker. The committee itself met sixteen days in just over three months, and its attorneys worked continuously from March 12, 1987, until the report was issued on June 19, 1987. While the bishops could not turn back the clock, they did make a belated effort to get at the truth. In addition to their determining the facts, the committee made five recommendations for restructuring the board and strengthening the ties with the church; among their recommendations was reorganizing the board of governors and term limits for all members.[43]

Yet the question remained: how badly had the scandal damaged SMU? Under Donald Shields Southern Methodist had lofty ambitions, as reflected in Clements's rather inflated projection of the school's future. Despite the oil crash in Texas in the early 1980s, SMU made progress under the morally erratic booster president. Annual gifts increased from eighteen million to thirty million dollars in four years, and the endowment nearly doubled. The SAT level rose to 1100, still far below Duke and Stanford, but slightly less than a hundred points below Vanderbilt. By 1986 SMU's endowment was twenty-eighth in the country, though only one-third that of Northwestern, a private institution of Methodist antecedents with about the same number of resident undergraduates. The professional schools prospered, especially the business school, which had benefited from Edwin Cox's continued largesse.[44]

On May 8, 1987, sixteen trustees met, most of them for the last time. The board had reorganized itself, and the older members—some of them tarnished by their inaction—vanished from SMU boards. "This is the first day of the life of the university," Edwin Cox bubbled, "it's going to be super." Hardly super, but perhaps enough to deflect the negative publicity and chart a new course for the gridiron *Titanic*.[45]

In the reorganization the twenty-one-member board of governors, whose leaders had caused most of the damage, was eliminated and the board of trustees reduced in number. In the meantime the chairman of the board for the interim proved to be a businessman, Ray Hunt, the most responsible and least well-known son of oil magnate H. L. Hunt (not one of the sons who had engaged in the notorious and disastrous raid on silver in 1980). Hunt had attended SMU and had served on the board since 1970, though not as part of the inner cabal. After a careful search he made the phone call to A. Kenneth Pye, a law professor and former chancellor of Duke, who became the first nonfootball president since Paul Hardin in the early 1970s. Presumably, SMU would become a stronger institution without the albatross of big-time, corrupt football hung around its academic neck.[46]

Still another group from the bad old days, the football players, rapidly departed from campus. As soon as news of the death penalty hit the wires, recruiters from major universities, their bags already packed, headed like vultures for the airport to scoop up the remnants of SMU's football team. The *New York Times* reported that 130 coaches from 80 colleges arrived at Dallas within two days of the decision. "This is a football area," one coach was quoted as saying. "If you wanted to buy grapefruits, you wouldn't go shopping in Hawaii." Many schools sent teams of recruiters; Alabama, for example, sent six. Some had the job of collaring the players, and others engaged them in casual conversation, softening them up for the hard sell. What would have been regarded as crass commercialism fifty or seventy-five years before was simply looked upon as good business. A fire sale was in progress, and no one cared if the goods happened to have a peculiar odor.[47]

While SMU received the death sentence, other schools in the Southwest Conference were in trouble with the NCAA. Texas Christian (TCU) in Fort Worth was placed on three-year probation in 1986, Texas Tech on one-year, and Baylor on two-year. Texas and Texas A&M were conducting internal investigations, much as SMU had tried to do, and the NCAA would impose a two-year probation on Texas that summer. Though Texas could not appear on television or go to bowl games, its punishment left its football program intact. TCU, which had engaged in a similar payments scheme, had furnished facts and figures to the NCAA and, in return for cooperating fully, was given a less severe punishment. Only Arkansas and Rice had no investigations pending, but neither team competed seriously for the SWC title. Understandably, the SWC members had no stomach for severely punishing their Dallas neighbor.[48]

Like the Pacific Coast Conference, the SWC would soon dissolve, partly because of the large number of scandals and NCAA penalties interfered with TV profits and also because attendance dropped off in the 1980s. In 1995 the SWC teams played their last games, some schools going to the Big Eight and others, like SMU and Rice, headed to the less competitive Rocky Mountain Conference. With a 2-9 record in 1989 and losing records thereafter, SMU no longer fielded a big-time team, and it would not have another winning season until 1997.[49]

Few of the old guard would ever again play a significant role at SMU or in college athletics. Bob Hitch ended up in the dry cleaning business, in which he would not be forced to launder illicit money. Bobby Collins returned to Southern Mississippi, where he served as the head of the Eagle Club, the institution's athletic fund-raising booster arm. Ron Meyer, who coached professionally for the New England Patriots and Indianapolis Colts, would end up back in Nevada coaching the Canadian Football League's Las Vegas Posse and doing sports commentary for a cable TV network. Bill Clements retired after his term as governor of Texas, and Edwin Cox remained in business full-time. Donald Shields left for California, where he gravitated into private industry. His successor, Kenneth Pye, resigned in 1993 because of illness, after his whirlwind reform of SMU, and died in 1994. William Stallcup retired from academic life after an eventful final year, and Lonnie Kliever resigned as athletic representative, returning full-time to a quieter life in the Department of Religion at SMU.

Southern Methodist itself had some problems stemming either wholly or in part from the death penalty. Enrollments declined for two years after the scandal, before the numbers rose again to 9,464 by 1997. Athletics suffered the most damage from the football scandal. Because of the scandals and death penalty, the donations to the Mustang Club dropped from $1.8 million in 1985 to $400,000 in 1987, affecting the entire athletic program. Other sports such as basketball and nonrevenue teams had to struggle even after the resumption of football not only because of booster disinterest but also because gridiron television, attendance, and concessions no longer generated the same levels of athletic revenue. It was difficult to measure the effect of the scandal on the school's reputation, but many people outside Dallas still thought of SMU mainly in the context of football scandals and the death sentence. In a 1997 *USA Today* article, commemorating the tenth-anniversary article on the death penalty, President Gerald Turner, who succeeded Kenneth Pye, admitted that, "As I travel around, as I meet someone, they will say, 'Oh yes, that's the school that got the death penalty.'"[50]

Resuming play in 1989, a much-weakened Mustang team had difficulty competing with big-time teams in the Southwest Conference, and after the SWC's collapse, with competitors in the Rocky Mountain Conference. Because of its poor record and the lack of fan interest, SMU in 1992 debated dropping to Division IAA in order to play a less demanding schedule, but decided, instead, to stick with big-time football and make an effort to field winning teams. In the fall of 1997 SMU managed to eke out a 6-5 record, its first winning season since 1984. Inspired by its return to gridiron respectability, SMU decided to terminate its contract with the Cotton Bowl and build a new stadium on campus to replace Ownby.

The reforms at SMU appeared to have taken hold. SMU pointed with pride to the graduation rate of its football team, which had soared from 30 percent to over 70 percent and paraded a former player, Reggie Pardee, who had been an All-American running back from 1982 until 1985 and had played in the NFL from 1986 to 1990. Pardee, who had done little academic work as a player, returned to Southern Methodist as a student in 1996 and completed his degree in 1999. Instead of playing for pay, as he had in the bad old days, he now got paid for community outreach, serving as a role model and proud trophy of SMU's new regime. College officials, who were seeking high-caliber recruits, insisted that the institution would never return to the corrupt football practices that had nearly destroyed football and seriously tainted the school. (As one of his reforms, President A. Kenneth Pye had initiated a mandatory course in ethics for athletes.) Whether the institution had shed its big-time football culture or at least erected adequate safeguards to prevent a return to the bad old days remained to be seen.[51]

In a different era Southern Methodist might have stood as the road marker leading to a public outcry and a major movement for reform, but big-time football would have required a massive shock treatment to relinquish its preeminent role at major gridiron institutions. In spite of the statements of dismay, the muckraking articles, and the work of the Knight commission from 1989 to 1991, the public and even the academic community failed to muster up the outrage that they had displayed in earlier situations. Perhaps they had seen the scandals caused by the lawless gridiron underside so many times that it had lost its ability to create intense public outcries. Only the pervasive threat posed by scandal to the reputation of higher education, the persistent reports of wrongdoing, and the possibility of outside intervention had brought about the few effective reforms in 1985 and several additional measures in the early 1990s.

The SMU Example and Football Reform

In spite of the absence of a shrill public outcry, the wrongdoing at SMU and other big-time football schools merely created a sense of college athletics in chaos. According to a Lou Harris survey, 78 percent of those polled agreed that big-time athletics had spun out of control. Not surprisingly, the number of articles and even books on the problems in college athletics continued to proliferate in the 1980s, in the past a sign of public concern and impending reforms. After the Georgia, SMU, and Oklahoma scandals, as well as the death of basketball star Len Bias at Maryland from a drug overdose in 1986, big-time college sports appeared to be ready for a forced cleansing. Some critics suggested that Congress might act if the colleges did not. After a decade of scandal which dwarfed the 1890s, early 1900s, and the postwar years, it appeared that an apocalypse had arrived.[52]

In the summer of 1987 the Presidents' Commission of the NCAA called a special convention to consider reforms in college athletics. Those reforms included reductions in the number of scholarships and the number of coaches in major sports. The presidents also wanted to restrict the length of spring (and out-of-season) practice as well as the length of the regular season. Because of opposition by athletic interests, the presidents not only failed to achieve their objectives but actually lost ground. Some of the earlier measures passed or considered by the NCAA in January 1987, such as restrictions on coaches and scholarships as well as shortened playing seasons and out-of-season practice, were rescinded, amended, or defeated. Though it had brought about key reforms in 1985, the monumental scandal at SMU had not created sufficient pressure to reduce the scale of Division IA football.[53]

In fact, the SMU football imbroglio and the death penalty proved to be the prelude to another round of scandals at other institutions. At Oklahoma, the other litigant in the CFA lawsuit against the NCAA-TV monopoly, a serious scandal erupted a year after the SMU death penalty. In 1988 a former big-time linebacker, Brian Bosworth, charged that Coach Barry Switzer rented a five hundred dollar per month apartment with a big-screen TV and cars for players' use parked outside. He recalled that some players, apparently with Switzer's knowledge, went there regularly to use cocaine, even on the day of the game. "If you were a star on the University of Oklahoma team," he wrote, "you could do just about anything you wanted. You had no rules." Switzer roundly denied the story of the flashy, talented, but mercurial lineman who had quit Oklahoma before graduating to play in the NFL. As it turned out, these charges became merely the tip of ongoing revelations and damaging events.[54]

In February 1989 the NCAA placed Oklahoma on probation for illegal recruiting and other violations, but the worst was yet to come. A new chapter in lawless behavior would come to the forefront at Oklahoma, a lawless underside to college football which had begun to afflict other programs at roughly the same time. Whereas violence on the field had marked the first football upheaval of the 1890s and early 1900s, violent and criminal activity would besmirch the gridiron banners in the athletic crisis of the 1980s. The litany of crimes would read like the entries on the pages of a police blotter.

In a *Sports Illustrated* article a writer described how Coach Switzer's players "terrorized" the campus, a word that only slightly exaggerated the reign of lawlessness. To start with, a cornerback for the Sooners shot and wounded a teammate after a quarrel. The most shocking episode involved three players who had reportedly gang-raped two women in the football dormitory. On top of this, a quarterback on the team was arrested for selling cocaine to an undercover agent. The governor of Oklahoma, Henry Bellmon, announced that he was "disgusted" and that the acting president should make "fundamental changes"—though he shortly afterward declared that he had confidence in Coach Switzer, a concession to the diehard Sooner and Switzer supporters. A reunion of the 1949 football team coached by Bud Wilkinson was canceled by a co-captain of that team after he had contacted a number of his teammates; the president of the O Club of Oklahoma City said that the 1949 team wanted "some sort of action, I suppose to relieve people of their jobs."[55]

The criminal acts of the Oklahoma players indicated that Coach Barry Switzer could not, or did not care to, control the behavior of his players. On June 19 the headlines in the *New York Times* read, "Beleaguered Switzer Resigns at Oklahoma." A tearful Switzer, who undoubtedly felt the stress from his players' lawlessness, vowed: "I will never coach at another institution. I can promise you that." He kept his promise. Instead of seeking a job at the college level, he moved to the professionals, coaching the Dallas Cowboys, where his success in producing a Super Bowl team was matched by behavior problems of his players—and by one bizarre episode in which Switzer himself was caught at the airport carrying a loaded weapon in his suitcase, itself an illegal act. The continuing problems made national headlines and contributed to Switzer's demise at Dallas.[56]

In truth lawless behavior among big-time football players had not merely occurred at Oklahoma or, for that matter, in 1989. At Colorado, which had become a football power under Coach Bill McCartney, two dozen football players were arrested between 1986 and 1989. Police charged a second-string linebacker with the rape of one woman and the attempted rape of another. According to *Sports Illustrated,* police suspected the player of being the Duct Tape Rapist, who had raped eight women in 1986, covering their eyes with duct tape before assaulting them. Others were charged with break-ins, stabbings, assault and battery, and various sexual assaults.

Ironically, McCartney, who later quit football to become a born-again evangelist, ran a highly disciplined football program in which players attended class and were firmly discouraged from using drugs. Off the field and beyond the campus, however, McCartney's authority stopped, and he evidently had not screened his recruits for problems with the law. Some observers believed that the criminal and violent tendencies of the gridiron miscreants grew out of the violence and intent to injure which some coaches encouraged and even taught; others saw it as the result of recruiting players who came from severely disadvantaged backgrounds and had been given free rein in earlier years because of their athletic prowess.[57]

Just as other periods of athletic excess had resulted in committees of college presidents, the upheavals of the 1980s produced its own panel of experts. In response to a decade of turmoil, the trustees of the Knight Foundation (then known by the names of its founders, John S. and James L. Knight) of Charlotte, North Carolina, provided two million dollars in 1989 for a commission to study college athletics and devise new approaches. Chaired by Notre Dame's former president, Father Theodore Hesburgh, and William Friday, a former president of North Carolina, the commission consisted largely of college presidents plus a scattering of other standouts such as former Princeton All-American halfback Dick Kazmaier, Donald Keough, who headed Coca Cola, and Congressman Tom McMillen, a former Maryland and NBA basketball star. Compared to previous panels, the Knight commission assembled a far more formidable array of advisor-experts and practitioners from all over the country and from numerous sports. Unlike earlier study groups, the members and participants cut across racial, ethnic, gender, and age barriers. Based on the credentials of its members and advisors, the Knight commission seemed to hold out far more promise than its predecessors.

While the foundation did not attempt an in-depth study like the Carnegie Report, it released a report in 1991 featuring a formula of "One-Plus-Three." The "one," or the cornerstone, proved to be an old standby: presidential control. The report concluded that presidents should not only have the backing of their boards but also should exercise control over athletic conferences and over the NCAA. In addition, presidents needed three supports: academic integrity, financial integrity, and a system of certification. Inspired by the Knight commission, certification of athletic programs and financial audits were passed by the NCAA in the early 1990s. While the Knight commission helped to bring about long-overdue reforms, it remained to be seen if the reforms would solve the most serious problems or would simply be cosmetic changes that eventually would be discarded or subjected to evasion.[58]

Not only did the problems with player behavior persist, but coaches also found ways to persuade college authorities to reinstate gridiron lawbreakers who were essential to their teams' success. At Nebraska in the fall of 1995 a blue-chip running back, Lawrence Phillips, assaulted his girlfriend, a player on the women's basketball team, by knocking her to the floor of the bathroom of a team quarterback's apartment, dragging her down three flights of stairs, and then smashing her head against a wall. Touted as a Heisman candidate earlier that fall, Phillips found himself temporarily dismissed from the team. The formal hearing on the charges against Phillips was conveniently postponed until after the football season.

To demonstrate its concern, the university sentenced Phillips to counseling, community service, and attending class, though the Nebraska authorities and the NCAA allowed the coach to reinstate him for the Iowa State game on November 4. "I was a little surprised how long it took," Coach Tom Osborne declared, referring to the college's decision. To put it bluntly, Nebraska needed Phillips for its campaign to win the national championship. For that reason some observers on campus questioned the severity of the university's sentence against Phillips. "Since when is going to class at a university a punishment?" asked Judith Kriss, the head of the women's center at Nebraska. She and others doubted Osborne's sincerity when he implied that he was concerned with Phillips' welfare and the games with

Iowa State and Kansas. "I don't think it has anything to do with Kansas or Iowa State," she insisted. With Phillips in the lineup Nebraska rolled over Florida, 62-24, in the Fiesta Bowl on January 1, 1996, to wind up atop the polls and harvest eight million dollars for the institution and the conference. Phillips departed for the greener pastures of the NFL, but two of his teammates faced charges of second-degree murder and use of a weapon to commit a felony.[59]

In addition, old problems reappeared in new, disturbing guises. In the early 1900s college athletes such as Knute Rockne bet casually on college contests. In the 1950s basketball point-shaving scandals dominated the headlines, but in the 1990s gambling appeared on the college gridiron. In 1998 a running back for Northwestern, Dennis Lundy, was charged with lying to a grand jury when he denied intentionally fumbling the ball in a play that may have determined the outcome of a close game with Iowa in 1994. Lundy and three other players, it turned out, were placing bets through a former Northwestern player, who had become a gridiron bookie. In 1996 two players for Boston College were accused of betting against their team. Even more disturbing, twenty-five to thirty team members at the institution admitted wagering during the football season, though not necessarily against their own team.[60]

In retrospect the lawlessness of football players reflected many of the changes that football had undergone in the 1970s and 1980s. The interplay of costs and revenues drove the big-time gridiron powers to go all out to create powerful and profitable teams. When the major football powers decided that the NCAA provided too few TV opportunities, they challenged the NCAA as a way to maximize profits. Because of the need to win, teams also admitted players with serious academic and character flaws, often from the disadvantaged groups that they had previously excluded. The fierce competition for players led to the payola and academic credit scandals of the late 1970s and early 1980s. That lawlessness persisted into the 1990s.

Because of the need to restore at least a facade of order, the college presidents were able to pass some reforms such as the death penalty, measures that eventually appeared to bring about gradual improvement, at least by the mid-1990s. The wave of criminality, however, appeared to grow worse. All of these evils, in truth, had one common thread. The colleges and college presidents had not come to grips with the gridiron creed of "bigger is better," a mind-set that had almost from the beginning of college football led to flagrant abuses and periodic upheavals.

Epilogue:
"The Great God Football"

At the end of the first crisis in college football (1905–12), reformers seemed to have solved the most vexing problems of college football. With the introduction of the forward pass and elimination of mass play, football had grown even more entertaining and less prone to injuries and brutality at the line of scrimmage. Stricter rules on the eligibility of players and the status of coaches as well as the number and location of games had evidently rid football of its worst potential for scandal.

Despite this apparent success, the calm was short-lived. The gridiron culture of violence, illicit recruiting and subsidies, academic shortcuts, and big-time profits repeatedly clashed with the values of higher education, and in the 1920s the pigskin paradoxes reappeared. Ironically, the new rules of play contributed to a surge in the game's popularity and led to violations of ethics standards. Many of the abuses that first appeared in the 1890s have repeatedly resurfaced at schools obsessed with playing big-time football.

One of those institutions has been Auburn University in Auburn, Alabama, a campus of twenty-two thousand students where Jordan-Hare Stadium is easily the most visible edifice on campus. Like SMU, Auburn—the land-grant state institution in Alabama—possesses a big-time football culture that extends back to the turn of the century. Coach Mike Donahue, who played quarterback at Walter Camp's Yale, introduced big-time football at Auburn. In his nineteen years as coach at Auburn, Donahue lost only seventeen games. By the 1920s Auburn was clearly a major southern football power, using easy jobs and scholarships to subsidize its players. Though Donahue quit in 1925 to go to Louisiana State, the alumni and boosters at Auburn still expected the institution to play major college football.

In the mid-1920s, after Donahue had left, President Spright Dowell, whose institution was strapped for funds, reduced the player subsidies and the high coach's salary. In 1927 Auburn began the season with a humiliating shutout by a small-time team, Stetson, followed by a loss to then unheralded Clemson. President Dowell, who had attended Columbia briefly after President Nicholas Murray Butler abolished football, regarded the gridiron fetish as economically wasteful and inimical to educational values. As a result of a student riot preceding the third loss to Florida, the trustees held a special meeting at which student witnesses condemned Dowell for ignoring and shortchanging the team. More than a month into a winless season

Dowell submitted his resignation, a sacrifice to Auburn's obsession with winning football. In the oft-repeated struggle between educational values and big-time football, the hunger for football victories had won out.[1]

In the nearly seventy years that followed, big-time football at Auburn not only grew in popularity but also became much more entrenched. In 1989, in a game against Alabama, more than 82,518—the stadium's capacity—crowded into Jordan-Hare to see Auburn defeat Alabama in the first game between the two teams played outside of Birmingham. Auburn, however, was still struggling with problems growing out of its obsession with winning football. In 1991 Eric Ramsey, a defensive end and an African American, revealed that he had recorded a hundred hours of taped conversations that clearly revealed improper promises and payments made by the coaching staff. Coach Pat Dye, who at first denied any knowledge of the details, at length reluctantly conceded, "I may have been lax." More than that, Ramsey's tapes showed that Coach Dye used his connections as a bank director to arrange a loan so that Ramsey could acquire a car. After receiving a reported settlement of $1.1 million, a payoff on his contract, a tearful Dye announced that he was resigning. In 1993 the NCAA put Auburn on two-year probation, banning Dye as well as other former coaches and boosters from any contact with the school.[2]

The scandal at Auburn demonstrated the failure of reform at big-time football institutions like Auburn. Dye's departure and the NCAA's stiff penalties should have led to an examination of football's role in Auburn's hierarchy of values. Instead, it resulted in resentment at Dye's departure and hatred of the whistle blower. When Eric Ramsey returned for his degree in December 1992, he had already received death threats and was under armed guard. Jeers and catcalls greeted him and his wife as they walked across the stage to receive their degrees. In 1992, as in 1927, students and boosters did not forgive the gridiron turncoats who, for whatever reason, harmed their football programs.[3]

In the fall of 1998 Auburn once again began its season with two straight losses, as it had in 1927. This time the coach who had replaced Dye, Terry Bowden, became the sacrificial goat. Bowden had not only been named coach of the year at Auburn in 1992, but he had also compiled the best record of any coach since Mike Donahue. In 1997 Auburn had given him a seven-year contract extension and a raise of twenty thousand dollars on his annual salary. Even before the next season began, however, the NCAA declared eight Auburn players academically ineligible. Then Auburn began with a 19-0 loss to Virginia on national TV and struggled to a record of 1-5 at mid-season. Very quickly Bowden learned that football renown is short-lived at major gridiron institutions. Faced with the opposition of a prominent trustee in Montgomery, Bowden resigned after reportedly being told he would be fired at the end of the season. His downfall was remarkably similar to the demise of President Spright Dowell more than seventy years before.[4]

As Auburn shows us, where the culture of big-time football has become entrenched, reform becomes nearly impossible. The chronic problems at Auburn again underscored the failure of attempts to reform football at schools that measure themselves by their pigskin reputations. The gridiron culture of violence, illicit recruiting and subsidies, academic shortcuts, and big-time profits have repeatedly clashed with the values of higher education. Institutions, conferences, and the NCAA have either found big-time football difficult to change or have not wanted change at all.

The patterns so evident in Auburn's story began in the 1890s and 1900s, when reformers and college officials first came to distrust football because they believed that it compromised academic life or physically harmed the students. Critics launched their most devastating attacks on the game in 1905 because they believed that it brutalized players, compromised academic standards, and caused serious injuries on the fields of play. In spite of vivid images of football's killing fields, the absence of a massive body count in college football suggests that the protests originated from critics who had other agendas: Harvard wanted to seize control of rules reform to implant its own game and replace the version that Yale's Walter Camp had fashioned; educators such as Henry MacCracken of NYU and Frederick Jackson Turner of Wisconsin used the outrage with deaths and injuries in their campaigns to root out football. The most enduring legacy of the Progressive era protest against football proved to be a radical reform in the rules of play, which produced a more attractive but ultimately a more scandalous game.

After World War II the cheating and transcript scandals in football provided another opportunity for change. Committees of college presidents and athletic officials again served up large portions of outrage and drew up lists of reforms to put a halt to subsidies for athletics and runaway recruiting practices. Instead of cooperating to bring about realistic standards, the American Council on Education, the North Central Association, and the National Collegiate Athletic Association competed for control of the direction of big-time football. For all of its idealistic rhetoric college football grew larger and more profit-oriented in the 1950s. A number of booster scandals on the West Coast and in the Midwest left a trail of failed hopes. The elimination of subsidies, spring practice, and postseason play which succeeded in the Ivy League and at strictly amateur small colleges frequently grew out of financial problems that made de-emphasis seem more rational.

Since then, particularly in the 1980s, an epidemic of major slush fund and academic transcript scandals have occurred, and college football has put on its worst performance ever. In spite of NCAA standards and penalties, nearly half of the Division IA football schools had some sort of penalties from 1980 to 1989. One institution, SMU, experienced a scandal that reached from the locker room to the governor's mansion. Athletic departments, boosters, boards, and college presidents have all played a part in breaking the rules. By the end of the decade a number of big-time institutions had players who had committed violent or criminal acts, beginning an epidemic of shootings, rapes, thefts, and drugs.

Corrupt Football and Cultural Trends

One obvious reason for the worsening gridiron scandals has been the decline of the faculty as a controlling factor in college life. In the 1890s faculty and presidents broke up student riots and administered discipline, but by the 1950s at major institutions they were far removed from students' daily lives. Much of the reform energy in the 1890s and 1900s came from the faculty, who still had a large voice in campus life. While that role failed to halt the worst practices in college football, the faculty at least forced some grudging reforms in college football in the early 1900s. That the reforms have failed to endure—and pigskin practices have grown worse—has its roots in the growing indifference of faculty members and their powerlessness in setting college policy.

This change in the faculty's role highlights another irony of the 1990s university—that it has to come to look more and more like the football team. One does not have to hunt far for reminders. Senior faculty members who supposedly came to academic life to teach spend inordinate amounts of time engaging in professional activities that advance their careers and do little for their students, just as the head football coach, who might have worked hands-on with players as a young assistant, now uses the players to promote himself. Big-time grants seekers may spend far more time trying to obtain revenue for themselves and their institutions than they do instructing and interacting with the students. Some of the grant-seeking faculty and institutions have engaged in scams with their monies which resemble the cheating of football coaches and boosters. Similarly, students in journalism, the arts, and music at many institutions, caught up in a system that mimics athletic scholarships, expect substantial scholarships for their talents or even pay. All of these practices might be necessary to the functioning of today's big-time academic institution, but they also create a university in which deans and professors come to bear an uncanny resemblance to football coaches and athletic directors. How can we thus expect football programs to strive toward higher levels when, in fact, institutions seem to be stooping to their levels?

One must also keep in mind that, while football recruiting has created the ingredients for many scandals, schemes by colleges to attract gifted students at cut-rate prices have recently brought academic proselytizing perilously close to the bastardized athletic version. In 1989 a Wesleyan University student charged that Wesleyan and ten other schools exchanged information on students to limit what they might have to give to individuals if they had to compete with other institutions to make the most attractive awards. Outwardly an academic issue, the admissions policies were not much different from the tactics pursued by big-time football powers in awarding the grants-in-aid permitted by the NCAA. If the NCAA exploited its athletes—or, more accurately, allowed its Division IA members to exploit them—the twenty-seven institutions singled out by the Justice Department in its subsequent probe had done the same to their academic recruits. And, just as the courts struck down the television monopoly of the NCAA, the Justice Department forced the eastern institutions to desist in what was an apparent violation of the Sherman and Clayton Antitrust Acts.[5]

This does not mean that football became more sanitized. Indeed, many of the worst recent gridiron scandals have had to do with the blatant attempts to make student-athletes less students and more athletes. Just beneath the scandals lies the colleges' love-hate relationship with professional football. Although pro football leapfrogged over college football in the 1950s and forged far into the lead during the 1960s, the college game did not sit on the sidelines. Instead, it attempted to maximize its profits and build its profile by imitating the National Football League's television and business practices. The so-called student-athletes became highly recruited semiprofessionals and quasi-professionals whose academic needs were left to special tutors and note takers and who were expected to devote more time to football during the academic year than to their course work. Just as a racing stable might care for its prize horses, the athletic departments provided for the food and upkeep of players, whose primary task was to perform on the gridiron. To facilitate their total dedication to the football cause and generate profits for their teams, some schools admitted athletes who fell beneath the cutoff point, created bogus academic curriculums, and gave credit for courses that their players had failed to pass. Others illicitly paid the athletes in much the same way as businesses might give monthly salaries to their employees.

Just as television propelled the NFL into Sunday and Monday Night madness, TV has made colleges into football profit machines. In an age of televised football it takes large expenditures to build a top-twenty team. In fact, illicit booster contributions, TV profits, and unscrupulous coaches have appeared so frequently at some major institutions that the combination has virtually become the formula for winning football.

One explanation for gridiron scandals of the 1970s to the early 1990s has been the obsession with victory—or "victory culture," as Tom Englehardt has described our pre-1970s foreign policy—characterized by the inherent obliviousness to the fact that, for each winner, there must be a loser. Like World War I and World War II, the Vietnam War aided and abetted the cul-

ture of big-time athletics and accelerated the trend toward highly subsidized
football. Indeed, the loosening of restraints in American society in the late
1960s and early 1970s carried over to sports as well as into other avenues of
college life. The aggressive, free-spending, even vicious breed of booster may
have evolved out of the gridiron version of the film hero Rambo, who operated in the fantasy world of soldiering and paramilitary operations which
flourished within a decade after our withdrawal from Vietnam.[6]

Nevertheless, it should be kept in mind that the "take-no-prisoners"
coaches of the 1960s and 1970s, such as Paul "Bear" Bryant, Woody Hayes,
and Frank Kush, grew to maturity during the Depression and another war.
Even in the era of the youthful Foster Sanford, football coaches, managers,
and alumni had learned to evade the rules by operating behind the scenes.
Critics have always focused on the "win-at-any-cost" character of football,
and winning coaches from Amos Alonzo Stagg to Knute Rockne and beyond
have always captured the imagination of the American sporting public.

The Vietnam War, however, coincided with a second surge of popularity in professional football kicked off by the merger of the AFL and NFL and
reaching its apex in the early years of "Monday Night Football." The Ram-
bos of football already existed in the NFL in the form of Vince Lombardi
and George Allen, who emphasized that victory on the gridiron wasn't just
important; to paraphrase Lombardi, it was the only thing. Professional football on television choreographed violence in a way that created beauty out
of broken limbs and torn torsos. Teams in the NFL won championships by
buying talented coaches and scouts who could find single-minded players
who cared about nothing but winning. A professional team did not have
to worry about players getting degrees or controlling runaway boosters. The
point of an NFL franchise was to earn money, and television served as its
most potent weapon. The intersectional showdown between the most popular teams in professional football proved seductive to college teams that
could easily fly within hours to any part of the country where other high-
profile teams happened to play. Because college athletic personnel stood in
awe and envy of the NFL, they also tried to emulate its grouping of elite
players and coaches and to televise as much as the market would bear. The
victory and profit culture of the 1970s and 1980s became a studied imitation
of the NFL and its exclusively business structure.

In addition, football from its beginnings has stood out as one of the few
sports played, coached, and directed almost exclusively by males, a disturbing singularity that has led to much of the excessive violence and unethical
practices by boosters. Admittedly, women have played an auxiliary role as
cheerleaders and, very occasionally, as in the case of Alice Sumner Camp,
have served as quasi-coaches. But the booster mentality that has characterized college football and contributed to so many scandals arises from the
hard outer shell of masculinity. Not surprisingly, nearly all of the partici-

pants in the scandals of the 1970s and 1980s proved to be males, and the most baldly aggressive of the boosters and coaches turned out to be youthful, ambitious, entrepreneurial males such as Sherwood Blount at SMU. In truth men's basketball has shown the same tendencies at the college level, but football easily wins the prize as the most male-dominated sport. Put simply, a winning football team requires large numbers of athletic scholarships, all of them for males, as well as a constant stream of male coaches. In its male exclusivity college football represents a throwback to the colleges and universities of the 1890s and early 1900s, which were made up almost entirely of male students and led by male college presidents. While the male character of football makes it more susceptible to the kinds of scandals that we have seen, it does not preclude reform. Most of the prominent reformers from Theodore Roosevelt to Robert Hutchins have been males, and some of them men who played football or, in Roosevelt's case, boxed.

Until recently, the coaches and boosters who have run big-time football have been almost entirely white. For most of the century the Achilles' heel of big-time college football teams in most parts of the country, and especially in the South, has been the absence of African-American players. The vast majority of African Americans were kept outside the empire of big-time football for more than half the century. In the 1970s and 1980s the number of African Americans playing for big-time state universities grew enormously. Not surprisingly, this new wave of players faced complex pressures and temptations.

Once predominantly white institutions changed their stripes, in the 1950s and 1960s, they began to draw upon the vast resources of African-American players, although many of these players as a group had long suffered from segregated education and have had difficulty negotiating the rocky road of academic requirements. The rapid influx of black athletes contributed to recruiting, payment, and eligibility scandals, which, though nothing new, intensified in the late 1970s and early 1980s. Not unlike their predecessors from the steel and coal mining towns of the Northeast and Midwest, the African Americans came into a system obsessed with winning at any cost, and the recruiters lured them by holding out the prospect of pro careers or by faking academic requirements. Scandals at Georgia, Arizona State, Southern California, and Oklahoma brought home this point with a vengeance.

This further suggests why in recent years the South and Southwest have stood in the forefront of scandal. Certainly, football has always drawn a strong and belligerent following in an area that until recently had no large cities with professional teams. Indeed, flagship state institutions, players, and coaches attracted, and still do attract, intense loyalties and support often identified with professional teams. More recently, as large numbers of Americans and American businesses have moved to the new, air-conditioned South, the southern states have developed freewheeling, fast-grow-ing, often loosely regulated economies.

Whereas the South and Southwest once had few resources with which to buy big-time talent, the spectacular growth of those economies has cre-ated an atmosphere in which anything goes—in politics, business, and foot-ball. The influence of professional sports grafted onto the New South men-tality also forged a militancy and aggressiveness that turned college football into a quasi-religious crusade. Located in a traditionally military-oriented culture, football boosters of the South and Southwest have adopted a take-no-prisoners approach toward supporting their teams and defeating their in-state rivals or flagship institutions in the next state. The casual attitude toward the rules may also reflect a carryover from a period when the South carried a chip on its shoulder and when football was regarded as a way to boost its economy and collective ego.

While southern schools have recently had a disproportionate number of major scandals, it is important to recall the serious scandals that occurred outside the South, such as at Illinois, Southern California, Michigan State, Oregon, and even at Army, and that runaway booster operations thrived at northern and western schools long before the southern institutions per-fected their techniques. In truth some of these scandal-tarred schools sought to raise their institution's profile or recapture the glories of the past by re-sorting to illicit practices to obtain football talent. That trend persists with institutions that have built large football stadiums so that they can win membership in Division IA conferences or have records that qualify them for prestigious and often profitable bowl appearances. In the South, as else-where, new institutions or schools with low-profile programs have latched onto big-time football as a means to gain recognition. Sometimes the ob-session with building a football program too quickly or overtaking an in-state rival results in gridiron wrongdoing.

The apparent migration of scandal southward demonstrates that ram-pant sports boosterism and profit-hungry football programs thrive where businesses seeking a friendlier environment have found new homes. Put an-other way, where the market projects an entrepreneurial version of win-at-any-cost into college sports, payola scandals inevitably occur. The ambitious businessmen turn to the market model of supply and demand to pay sup-posedly amateur football players as they might buy and sell credit services or oil machinery. Similarly, the old guard clings to football at Auburn or Southern Methodist as proud symbols of the way things used to be.

Proposed Solutions

For all its faults and difficulties football on or near big-time campuses will not likely decline or disappear in the next few decades. Through a century of scandals and upheavals the sport has shown an uncanny knack for adapting to new media and enrolling new fans; its remarkable record of emerging from crises and scandals even sturdier and more intractable makes it the sports version of a lush and hardy weed. While college football may place a poor second to the NFL, it still creates loyalties that span the campus constituencies and bind the past to the present. Unfortunately, football also has created situations in which college athletics debase educational standards and tarnish institutional reputations. In a number of well-documented cases it has answered to a handful of football boosters and has mocked the academic standards imposed by faculty and demanded of other students. It still has the capacity to destroy the careers of college presidents and to turn others into collaborators in corruptness. Moreover, the enthusiasm of football boosters and ambitious coaches often translates into chronic cheating or shortchanging athletes.

In at least three periods in the past century, during episodes of gridiron trauma and upheaval, major efforts to clean up and bring academic order out of chaos in college football have claimed center stage. Numerous proposals to curb big-time football have poured forth from critics and reformers, including ideas that have resurfaced in each of the crises.

Let us look at four of the most popular and common remedies for reform of college football.

Make college football more like other academic programs on campus and less like a highly commercialized, quasi-professional form of mass entertainment. In each of the cycles of reform academic critics have pleaded with the colleges to return football to a more healthy version of body, spirit, and mind. Repeatedly, faculty and college presidents such as the ACE Special Committee of 1951–52 have recommended that colleges ban spring practice, postseason games, and outright subsidies to football players. Reformers have deplored high-profile intersectional games, massive stadiums, and sports promotion; they have urged that coaches become tenured members of the faculty and that athletes make normal, four-year progress toward degrees. The attempts to de-emphasize football in the 1940s and 1950s reflected the most coherent statements of this reform philosophy. But in their efforts to reform athletics in the late 1980s and early 1990s many presidents continued to call for downsizing football.

How seriously should we regard the periodic efforts to de-emphasize big-time football? Based on the failed attempts, we would do well to avoid extreme solutions that seek to return football to an era before spring practice, postseason games, athletic scholarships, and systematic recruiting became the norm. Advocates of downsizing point out that smaller colleges such as Swarthmore, Johns Hopkins, Williams, Amherst, and Wesleyan, as well as the Ivy League institutions, successfully reformed their gridiron programs. They forget that most of them did so because they could no longer compete with their big-time rivals or because the costs of playing big-time football no longer matched their resources and needs. At major colleges, however, the attempts to de-emphasize football not only failed but also often created irreconcilable differences between rhetoric and reality, codes of conduct and actual practices. The well-intentioned reforms of the faculty representatives in the old Pacific Coast Conference, it might be argued, contributed to a climate in which booster operations flourished and eventually led to the PCC's demise.

Put simply, the deeply entrenched gridiron constituencies reflect the hard fact that big-time football has come to stay—and that it will inevitably grow larger rather than smaller. Unless football threatens to wreck a school's reputation or simply has shown an inability to compete in the big-time, it makes little sense to stir up a hornet's nest of opposition by setting out to remake football in the image of a purely academic institution. In summary, reforms based on small-college or minor-sport models will not work at big-time institutions.

Eliminate the hypocrisy by paying big-time football player salaries commensurate with the revenues that they earn. Set forth most recently by Rick Telander in *The Hundred Yard Lie* and by former NCAA executive director, Walter Byers, in his autobiographical work *Unsportsmanlike Conduct,* this proposition has probably gained the most articulate following. Byers and Telander focus on the large amounts of money harvested by athletic departments compared to the insignificant amounts paid to the players who entertain the crowds. They also criticize the charade of representing quasi-professional players often majoring in pre-NFL studies as student-athletes who also happen to play big-time football. The payola scandals of the 1970s and 1980s in which players received cars and cash seemed to mock the notion that college athletes were students because they had signed a letter of intent and the institution had promised to pay for their education. College football appears to be helpless in the face of a market economy that rewards gridiron heroes in the same way it does well-known entertainment figures.[7]

This intercollegiate pay-for-play solution, however, has as many pitfalls as does the pretense of amateur athletes. If an institution pays players on the basis of athletic potential and performance, it immediately sets up a monetary hierarchy that leads to salary disputes and brings about situations in which players quit the team to play elsewhere. We are not talking about purely sports enterprises in which athletes might compete for as long as ten years or gravitate toward other organizations that offer to pay them more. Would student-athletes have the right to become free agents after they had played out a year or two-year contract? Would student players who failed to realize their potential be "let go" after one or two years? Would it require unions, sports agents, and elaborate negotiations to carry on what used to be known as a collegiate sport?

One might also legitimately ask if athletes who hold track, soccer, or lacrosse scholarships would also be paid. If eighty male gridiron athletes rate salaries, why wouldn't the women's basketball or field hockey team have a cause for complaint—or even for lawsuits? Why couldn't they justly argue that the university was only rewarding male players in a violent, aggressive, male-bonding sport but failed to give the same benefits to female athletes who worked just as hard at perfecting their skills? Does any institution or group of institutions really want to open this Pandora's box of legal and communal disputes?

The NCAA should give college presidents more authority and responsibility to prevent cheating in college sports and, in turn, presidents should become more proactive in preventing the situations that lead to scandals. No one could quarrel with the notion that college presidents should display more vigilance and do everything in their power to nip athletic wrongdoing in the bud or, for that matter, have more power to set academic standards for athletes. The idea that the college president could serve as the policeman or woman on the athletic beat goes back to the early 1900s, when some strong presidents like Nicholas Murray Butler of Columbia as well as David Starr Jordan of Stanford and Benjamin Ide Wheeler of California abolished or altered the gridiron game on their campuses. The antidote of presidential control appeared in the Carnegie Report in 1929 and in the numerous commission and committee reports, most recently, in the Knight Commission's "Three-Plus-One" formula.

As historical researchers understand, inside information on athletics usually reaches the college president's desk in one form or another. The president knows, or at least should know, more about athletic activities and how they affect the institution than anyone on campus. That said, presidents still cannot always act decisively because they do not make policy and are, all too often, at the mercy of hell-bent booster boards. If Charles Eliot had had his way, the Harvard board of overseers would have abolished football in the 1890s, but it did not. The history of college football abounds with examples of presidents who have lost their jobs because they treated football in a way that boards found unacceptable or irritating.

In big-time football presidents of major athletic institutions face a catch-22 situation. The trustees set policy for athletics, and that policy determines whether a team will enjoy success in football. If the board takes a hard line on football, the team will probably decline in stature and will no longer be known as a big-time competitor. Few board members have the internal fortitude to resist the displeasure of alumni or face the ridicule of sports fans angered by gridiron ineptness. Is it likely that capable academics can hope to obtain the president's job if they have not demonstrated to the board and the alumni that they support big-time college sports? If the president violates board policy, the board will most likely reprimand or fire the president. Though college presidents sign statements pledging that they will follow NCAA standards, they often feel an obligation to pursue the spirit and policy of the board. If their institution wants highly commercialized athletics, the college president must take the lead. This divided allegiance has often led the presidents to overlook or turn their attention from burgeoning athletic scandals and focus on fund-raising and glad-handing. It also prevents them from pursuing the academic interests of the institution in a way that will benefit all the students.

Collectively, college presidents have recently displayed far more determination to rid college football of abuses and raise academic standards. To be as fair as possible, the NCAA College Presidents' Commission enjoyed some success in the 1980s, notably with the death penalty legislation but also in measures that attached a red flag to lawless coaches. In addition, it established the floor of SAT scores, later struck down by a federal judge, Ronald Buckwalter. Unfortunately, it failed to achieve its objective of establishing a veto power for the presidential commission in 1985. The athletic directors and faculty representatives (many of the latter appointed by the presidents) responded by repealing their measures. In the 1980s, faced with the threat of athletics' lawless underside, the reform-minded presidents had their best opportunity to reshape big-time college football. They will not likely have the same opening until big-time college athletics again displays such a wanton and notorious disregard for standards and regulations. Sadly, history demonstrates that presidents will return to "business as usual" once the athletic upheaval resides and the media turn their attention to other matters. One can only hope that the new millennium proves an exception to this twentieth-century malady.

Big-time athletic programs should raise academic standards. No one publicly quarrels with the need for higher academic standards, though many quarrel over the best way to obtain them. College and athletic authorities realize that the institution needs to impose some form of academic standards on big-time athletes. In order to maintain the myth of the student-athlete, major athletic programs boast of team members who maintain high averages in tough majors like nuclear engineering or biology while playing four years of football, though they are relatively few. Most college and athletic authorities would like to see their players receive a degree, and many coaches take pride in the incremental strides of athletes from disadvantaged backgrounds. Nevertheless, the coaches and players know that the primary task of students with football scholarships is to play football.

In the 1990s a new version of accrediting known as certification has become the silver bullet for improving academic standards. Despite the failure of the North Central Association of Colleges and Secondary Schools' initiative in 1953, most faculty representatives and athletic authorities believe in applying accrediting standards to athletics. Champions of the certification system devised in the early 1990s claim that it exacts stricter standards and requires more of coaches than the traditional academic peer review. Still, athletic certification is only as good as the peers who set the standards and the scope of their authority. Certification cannot establish the rules for admitting and educating of college athletes, nor does it change the truth that football players have to spend more time on football than on their studies. In the early 1990s the presidents' commission tried to impose higher standards for admission in the form of minimum SAT scores, and the athletic departments devised new remedial programs to break down the resistance to learning. In this way they tried to ensure that big-time athletes might at least become marginally respectable students and occasionally solid academic specimens.

Judge Buckwalter may have thrown a wrench into the movement to improve academic standards when he struck down the standards for admission imposed by the presidents' commission. If the higher courts do not overturn this decision, the NCAA will have to find some compromise that satisfies the judges. Yet it is clear that the organization and its members face a daunting task in setting realistic standards. By changing the rules in the 1970s and rushing to grab talented athletes from disadvantaged backgrounds, they created precedents for lower admission standards and lower performance by athletes. In fact, the athletes at big-time institutions already spend more time in practice and in games than they do on their course work, and, because of conditioning and spring practice, their season never really ends. Should educational agencies and college presidents expect the standards for big-time athletes to improve when they cannot raise the standards of admission or devote the time necessary for academic training?

And how can big-time football institutions raise their standards if the athletes do not remain there long enough to graduate? Thanks to the efforts of former athletes turned politicians Bill Bradley and Tom McMillan, the federal government began to nose into the athletic cesspool of the late 1980s and early 1990s. As a result, the NCAA passed legislation forcing the colleges to divulge statistics on the graduation rates of athletes and to break down the figures by race. Though the overall percentages of those who receive their degrees have improved slightly, the rate of graduation for major sports at big-time institutions still hovers under 60 percent and is far lower for black athletes than for white. At the best-known football institutions the biggest-name athletes occasionally quit school in order to enter the draft a year or two before their scholarships end, since an injury may eliminate the possibility of getting a lucrative signing bonus.

Raising academic standards for football players remains a noble ambition, but the potential for improvement will be limited by the demands of football and by the players' backgrounds. Unfortunately, the talented athletes who play football or basketball at academically prestigious flagship state institutions or at the few well-known, athletically powerful private institutions often feel like fish out of water, or they have been so flattered and cajoled before arriving on campus as to be impervious to academic and institutional realities. The institutions cater to well-educated, middle-class white or black students who often come from wholly different backgrounds than most of the athletes. Many athletes, both white and black, would do better if they spent their first year or two at community colleges (as do some of those who have failed to achieve the required SAT scores) before playing at major four-year institutions. If big-time athletics allowed players an automatic year or perhaps two years to prepare academically, student-athletes would surely stand a better chance of completing their degree programs. It is doubtful, however, that either coaches, fans, or sympathetic faculty reps would substitute a radically improved academic system for a top-notch athletic program. Even if football programs succeed in graduating more players or raising their grade-point averages, they would not eliminate the fundamental problems.

Gridiron Visions

If these reforms prove unacceptable, what sort of an athletic structure would best serve the athletes, the institutions, and the sporting public? Is there any way to restore the spirit within the college community which football once generated while eliminating the chronic violation of academic, athletic, and behavioral standards? Some cynics argue that college football has long since passed the point at which the colleges can apply the same standards to athletics and athletes which they would to the rest of the college community. As long as we call it college football, however, the colleges must take responsibility for their gridiron programs, including the players and coaches, and the athletic standards.

The gridiron culture has brought name recognition to institutions, but it has placed heavy burdens on their administrators as well as their academic credibility. Obsession with football has created a false sense of values by forming a vast gulf between the athletic meritocracy and the academic drones. At a number of institutions the football coach is not only better paid than the president but also more powerful. As Charles Eliot and James Angell complained, the institutions have become better known for their football teams than for their core academic programs.

Who, then, should determine the length and contours of athletics at academic institutions? The failed or tentative reforms in the three major football upheavals of the twentieth century demonstrate that the faculties need a freer hand in athletics, including big-time sports. Viewed broadly, the century-long effort to cleanse athletics has been a struggle to reclaim the soul of the university, a movement in which the faculty has had the largest stake.

College coaches have been fond of saying that they would not presume to teach French or physics and that, in turn, the faculty should not interfere with athletics. Yet the institution's mission is to teach courses in areas such as French, physics, history, law, business, and medicine—not to produce sporting events for TV. As too often has been the case, football and other big-time sports have created alien and phony curricula that have little to do with higher education. In some instances the athletic interests intimidate faculty members who try to speak out against gridiron practices and, more often, draw unsuspecting faculty sympathizers into their web with free tickets and other athletic perks. Too often these silent minions of the athletic complex help out by giving easy grades to athletes or looking aside when scams occur. Reforms such as certification may prevent the worst payola scandals, but will they make silk purses out of pigskin hide? Not as long as big-time athletics control the presidents and the boards of trustees, who, in turn, either ignore faculty concerns with athletics or have veto power over their decisions.

To prevent these gridiron abuses, the faculty needs to be drawn back into athletic affairs and to exercise a much larger measure of athletic control. One sometimes forgets that the goals of the NCAA's founders in 1905 included restoring faculty control, and at the first meeting in New York anyone such as coaches and physical directors who made their living from athletics was banned from attending. Since then, the NCAA has become a clearinghouse and lobby for athletics, and faculties at most big-time schools have lost control of football. More precisely, they have allowed the athletic curriculum to slip through their fingers. Though athletes may progress toward graduation, they too often end up taking courses lacking academic content. This is not surprising when at most Division IA institutions faculty lack the power to choose the faculty athletic representatives who serve as liaisons with the athletic department and represent the institution at conference meetings. How can we expect our schools to act honestly when they fail to let their faculty govern such a vital province—or when the faculty members allow that control to slip through their fingers? And how will that province maintain its academic reputation if it is subject to the whim of athletic interests? Sadly, the ideal of mind, body, and spirit in big-time athletics has become a charade or, at many institutions, has ceased to exist. And college football, as we know it, no more resembles the ideal of college students competing at the amateur level than do the minor league franchises of Major League Baseball.

For this debacle college administrations bear much of the responsibility. If college authorities and boards truly want to produce student athletes, they need to treat all of their athletes as students. In a world of quasi-professional football players, it is sometimes hard to regard these wards of the athletic department as students. If the institutions still regard the athletes as students, they should require them to meet the standards that they demand of other students.

While administrations have abandoned *in loco parentis* at all but a handful of institutions, we retain it, at least in several ways, for big-time football players. Athletic departments provide remedial classes, tutors, and even note takers. When a football player gets in trouble, the athletic department closes ranks to protect him. Social workers and psychiatrists appear to deal with his personal problems. As James Angell said in 1906, he is treated as if he were "a king in his court."[8]

With all of the attention that players receive, big-time institutions have done a poor job of preparing them for college courses. Most football players spend five years on athletic scholarships because colleges use red-shirted players, who normally train with the team their first year. If colleges were truly earnest about educating their athletes, they would use that first year and perhaps a second year to acclimate the student to college life. One of the most successful reforms in the early 1900s proved to be the gridiron freshman rule. Repealed in the 1970s, the freshman rule gave athletes a year to ground themselves academically, followed by three years to make their contribution on the gridiron as well as in the classroom. If administrations and faculty were serious about giving the gridiron elite a college education, they would first give these often marginalized students a chance to get their feet on the ground. At the end of the first year college and athletic authorities would be better able to predict if the athlete could succeed as a student—and the student would stand a better chance of success. Unfortunately, the NCAA has rejected that option for Division IA athletes, who founder in academic depths or who end up in cushy, custom-tailored classes.

If colleges were serious about athletes' performance in the classroom, they would also do more than push for college degrees. College athletic departments would not only improve the academic performance of football players, but they would also encourage them to excel. Among eighty-five scholarship holders some athletic students have the potential to become strong performers in the classroom, and a few may soar beyond their peers. In truth all big-time student-athletes have opportunities for education which many students would envy. They have a five-year academic scholarship that can be converted into in-depth preparation for graduate school or serve as a stepping stone to a well-paying and prestigious career. With five-year scholarships they even have a rare chance to obtain a four-year degree and then launch themselves into a master's program. Others have the opportunity to use that first year to propel themselves toward success in their final four years and to secure that necessary college degree.

The need for higher standards does not stop with the curriculum. If colleges were serious about making athletes into student-athletes, they would crack down on the misbehavior of athletes. Perhaps because we place such a premium on gridiron performance, we also send signals to athletes that they do not have to abide by the same standards of conduct as others. As a result, football players, not to mention other big-time athletes, have engaged in an orgy of violent and criminal activity off the field, suggesting that the colleges have recruited indiscriminately. This new lawless underside of college sports disrupts the university, undermines its standards, and threatens the community. Coaches, athletic departments, and college presidents need to apply a single standard for all students. If they care about athletes as students, they should declare ineligible the delinquents who are accused of crimes and misdemeanors. Once convicted, these individuals should be dropped from the teams altogether. When the out-of-control athlete commits rape or violently assaults a fellow student, he should not be allowed to play on a team sponsored by an academic institution, let alone remain at the institution. Football players who have worked toward a career in sports surely should know about discipline because most have had to show more discipline than their peers to succeed in big-time sports. Surely, they have the capacity to discipline themselves, and athletic personnel who teach discipline on the gridiron have the credentials to instill personal discipline as well.

One might hope that the recent reforms would at least result in lasting changes in gridiron practices, but history shows that the underlying problems of big-time athletics run far deeper than the patchwork of current reforms. In the late 1990s changes in the governing structure of the NCAA have given the athletic conferences a weightier role in big-time athletics. Too often conferences such as the Southwest have disregarded gridiron excesses and allowed the institutions to persist in wrongdoing. Instead of keeping their own houses in order, the major conferences frantically compete to extend their economic reach by creating ever larger networks of major athletic institutions. How can we expect the dominant schools in these monster conferences to reform big-time football? Given the failure of past reforms, one is tempted to view these changes in athletic governance as marking the end of the reforms following the scandals of the 1980s—another example of the excess that seems to follow every attempt at reform.

Even more ominous, the change in governance suggests a new era of commercialization in college football, a trend that does not bode well. A century of gridiron scandal demonstrates that blatant commercialism and cheating go hand in hand. One movement in college football which smacks of big business is the current building spree, an attempt to imitate professional sports by enlarging stadiums and creating expensive, and profitable, luxury boxes and suites. At the end of the twentieth century Penn State, which has ninety-three thousand seats in Beaver Stadium, plans to add ten thousand additional seats and luxury suites. At such stadiums wealthy backers purchase the right to lease the seats. At Virginia, Scott Stadium will be enlarged from forty-five thousand to sixty thousand seating capacity at a cost of seventy-nine million dollars. After completion forty-four luxury suites will have three-year rental price tags of fifty thousand dollars. If students happen to enter these gridiron palaces, it will be as guests of wealthy parents or patrons. In an age of highly commercial multi-versities college football has carved out its own franchises.[9]

Huge expenditures on facilities, as in the booming gridiron economy of the 1920s, inevitably create strong pressures to pay higher or illegal subsidies to blue-chip players. The same thing may well happen when the next economic downturn occurs and the bidding for suites in these luxurious hippodromes abates. If the biggest football schools fail to produce teams to fill these athletic palaces, incentives to gridiron wrongdoing will zoom upward. In spite of recent safeguards, coaches whose careers depend on a single season or going to a prestigious bowl will likely find shortcuts to cheat. Once more we will see a replay of the cycle of crisis, hand-wringing, halfhearted reforms, and more serious scandals.

To pay for the costly new facilities, the college football franchises will need to attract the most talented players and to train them year round. Much as they did in the stadium building spree of the 1920s, the major teams have declared the gridiron version of an armaments race. Sooner or later, it appears, they may decide on the college football version of salary caps, not merely on coaches' salaries but also on the race to outbuild and outreign one another. Otherwise, the race to erect bigger and more impressive stadiums, weight facilities, and indoor practice arenas may bring about the disastrous, highly professional outcome that the colleges say they want to avoid. As the colleges mortgage themselves to professional athletic practices, the institutions will be held captive by big-time sports and television revenues, and, no matter how successfully they clean up their programs, the fact will remain that they compromise their roles as academic institutions.

The current football building spree as well as the expansion of conferences seems once again to pose the prospect of a league of big-time schools modeled on the NFL. Such a super-conference, however, would enshrine rather than eliminate the problem. There would be little interest in improving the academic performance of athletes and of instituting tighter eligibility standards. College football has become so incompatible with the traditional role of the university that the reforms will only make quasi-professional football harder to uproot.

Even if colleges succeed in cleaning up their athletics, they will still face the fact that their big-time football programs contribute little to the institution's academic life. In truth, if big-time athletes come to colleges for pre-NFL training, they should not have to go through the charade of attending classes and obtaining degrees unless they choose to embrace the standards and courses imposed on other students. Athletic departments and booster clubs who emulate professional sports by installing luxury suites and preferred seating should not pretend to promote amateur athletics. As desirable as reforms might appear, they will never change the fact that big-time football must rely on myth and sleight of hand to justify its presence on campuses designed to serve a university function.

How should universities treat a sport that has grown so far removed from educating students? How can the universities preserve the excitement of big-time football while ridding themselves of its evils? The solutions are not simple, but one can find them. Colleges have themselves provided a prototype in franchising or outsourcing many of their functions to corporations—nonacademic support services as diverse as restaurants, golf courses, rock concerts, and pest control. Viewing college football programs, one cannot avoid the conclusion that they closely resemble professional sports franchises. Since players attend colleges to prepare for pro careers, college football programs should be spun off into university athletic franchises or minor league football teams that play on the university campuses. Football stands out as a likely candidate for big-time franchising by spinning off a moneymaking activity that could still supply glory to the school and players to the professionals. No one would require these players to complete courses or to obtain degrees. Highly motivated players could and should attend classes and obtain degrees. In cooperation with the institution the franchise should subsidize the players' educations—as the institutions have always claimed to do. In the meantime the major franchises could work out details of a conference made up of the top-forty or top-fifty college franchises in competition for the national championship. Once the teams and their players were severed from the universities, football would no longer be the dry rot eating at the foundation of the academic edifices. College football would not have to go through the pretense of posing as an amateur activity associated with an academic institution. The lawless, and dishonest, underside of football which has existed for a more than a century could become lawful, but only if the college presidents and boards end the practice of staging gladiatorial combats.

As we enter the new millennium, the contradictions between the academy and football have become less reconcilable. Player behavior off the field, the potential for slush fund scandals, recruiting violations, the discrepancy between the salaries of coaches and the compensation of players, the intrusion of boosters into football administration, and the inability of many athletes to complete four years of college—all of these problems continue to bedevil big-time, quasi-professional college football. These problems will not change until the institutions, conferences, NCAA, and schools themselves take drastic steps or some other public agency steps in. In 1936 John

Tunis, a onetime admirer of football who later became one of its most trenchant critics, labeled football "a tremendous business with tentacles over the educational world." He issued an eloquent plea for an end to football corruption, one that rings as true today as it did then. "In brief," Tunis declared, "what I'm trying to say is: for God's sake, a little logic! Or is that asking too much?"[10]

APPENDIXES

Casualties in College Football

Deaths and Serious Injuries, 1905 to 1916

Year	Deaths		Injuries	
	At All Levels	Only in College Play	At All Levels	Only in College play
1905	18	3	159	88[a]
1906	11	3	104	54
1907	11	2	98	51
1908	13	6	84	33
1909	26	10	69	38[b]
1910	14	5	40	17
1911	14	3	56	36
1912	10 (11)[c]	0(1)[c]	26	17
1913	14	3	56	36
1914	12	2	NA	
1915	NA		NA	
1916	16	3	NA	

Note: Total number of players unavailable. NA = not available.
[a]Led to 1905–6 crisis in college football.
[b]Cause of the 1909–10 crisis in college football.
[c]Parentheses show revised statistics in which injuries resulted in death.
Source: New York Times and *Chicago Tribune,* various years.

Newspaper Reports on Causes of Death in College Football, Direct and Indirect, 1905 to 1909

Causes of death	1905	1906	1907	1908	1909	Total No.	%
Body blows	4	3	3	3	5	18	22.5
Injuries to spine	4	0	2	3	5	14	17.5
Concussion of brain	6	3	2	3	6	20	25
Blood poisoning	2	2	0	1	2	7	9
Other causes	2	3	5	3	8	21	26
All	18	11	12	13	26	80	100

Note: Figures based on deaths at all levels of play.
Source: New York Times and *Chicago Tribune,* various years.

Head and Cervical Spine Fatalities as Number and Percentage of All Deaths in Football, 1945 to 1994

Year	Head Injuries		Cervical Spine Injuries	
	No.	%	No.	%
1945–54	87	18.7	32	27.6
1955–64	115	24.7	23	19.8
1965–74	162	34.9	42	36.2
1975–84	69	14	14	12.1
1985–94	32	6.9	5	4.3

Source: Figures courtesy of Frederick O. Mueller, University of North Carolina, Chapel Hill.

Reported Casualties in Football in the 1930s Compared with Those in the 1920s

Year	All Levels of Play	Direct Result of Contact during Play	Among College Players
1931	31[a]	13	8
1932	24	11	2
1933	24	5	2
1934	23	10	3
1935	28	9	3
1936	26	8	1
1937	20	9	0
1938	16	3	2
1939	11	5	3
1940	11	7	1
1941	14	10	0

Note: Casualties from all levels of play include professional, college, high school, and sandlot football players.
[a]Initially reported as 40.
Source: Figures courtesy of Frederick O. Mueller, University of North Carolina, Chapel Hill.

Subsidies

Schools That Did Not Give Subsidies, 1929

Bates	Laval	Ottawa	Tulane
Bowdoin	Marquette	Queens	U.S. Military
Carleton	McGill	Reed	Academy
Chicago	MIT	Rochester	Virginia
Cornell	Massachusetts	Saskatchewan	Wesleyan
Dalhousie	Agricultural	Toronto	Williams
Emory	College	Trinity (CN)	Wooster
Illinois	(U. Mass.)	Tufts	Yale

Source: Howard J. Savage et al., *American College Athletics, Bulletin Number Twenty-Three* (New York: Carnegie Foundation for the Advancement of Teaching, 1929), 242.

Subsidization, 1939: John Tunis's Rating of College Football Teams, with Commentary

Group 1
"The terms 'amateur' and 'professional' mean nothing in intercollegiate football today. But there is one group of colleges chiefly interested in the main purposes of education."

Alfred	Colby	Loyola (Chicago)	Stevens Tech
Allegheny	Colorado College	Lynchburg	Swarthmore
Antioch	Dennison	Middlebury	Trinity
Beloit	DePaul	MIT	Tufts
Berea	Emory	Newark	Union
Bowdoin	Gettysburg	Occidental	Ursinus
Bridgewater	Hamilton	Olivet	Wayne
Brown	Haverford	Pomona	Wesleyan (CN)
California Tech	Hobart	Reed	Wesleyan (KY)
Carleton	Johns Hopkins	Renssalear Tech	Westminster
Chicago	Knox	Rochester	Williams
Clark (MS)	Lehigh	St. John's (MD)	

Group 2

"A majority of the eleven are not paid either openly or covertly, but where one or two key men are helped through, often—often not invariably—by the alumni. The president usually knows this, but the chief business of college presidents is not to allow the right hand to know what the graduates are doing."

Boston University	Harvard	NYU	Stanford
Columbia	Indiana	Minnesota	Yale
Colorado	Kansas	Pennsylvania	
Cornell	Nebraska	Princeton	

Group 3

"Many squad members are assisted in one way or another. Few of those named below operate athletic farms, but if a boy is good football material and not up to the entrance exams, a year is usually managed for him at some preparatory school like Dean Academy, Black Foxe, or Kiski. (We have proof that players have been helped through all of these by various college athletic authorities or graduates)."

Arizona	Georgetown	Ohio State	Southern
Boston College	Holy Cross	Oregon	California
Carnegie Tech	Idaho	Oklahoma	Texas Mines
California	Marquette	Pittsburgh	UCLA
Colgate	Manhattan	Purdue	Villanova
Dartmouth	Michigan	St. Mary's	Washington
Detroit	Michigan State	San Francisco	West Virginia
Duquesne	Northwestern	Santa Clara	Wisconsin
Fordham	Notre Dame		

Group 4

"Here are the colleges where the profit motive is important, sometimes decisive. Their teams usually admit it, instead of pretending, as others do, that Money Is Not All. Most of them have 'athletic scholarships,' a formula covering financial assistance to football stars. The Southwest Conference limits payment to $50 a month, but the limit is highly elastic and there is no evidence that the colleges named keep to the rules—any rules. The other conferences listed apparently set no limit to the ante, and the boys shop around. The physical director of a Western woman's college has received letters from boys asking what her school does for athletes."

SOUTHEASTERN CONFERENCE

Alabama	Georgia	Louisiana State	Tennessee
Alabama Tech	Georgia Tech	(LSU)	Tulane
(Auburn)	Kentucky	Mississippi	Sewanee
Florida		Mississippi State	Vanderbilt

SOUTHWEST CONFERENCE

Arkansas	Rice	Texas	Texas Christian
Baylor	SMU	Texas A&M	

SOUTHERN CONFERENCE

The Citadel	North Carolina	Virginia Military	Washington
Clemson	North Carolina	Institute	and Lee
Davidson	State	Virginia	
Duke	Richmond	Polytechnic	
Furman	South Carolina	Institute (VPI)	
Maryland	Virginia[a]	Wake Forest	

SOUTHERN INTERCOLLEGIATE ATHLETIC ASSOCIATION

Center	Mercer	Rollins
Howard	Miami	

[a]Virginia had withdrawn from the Southern Conference.

Source: John Tunis, "What Price College Football?" *American Mercury* (Oct. 1939).

Attendance at College Football Games and the Influence of Television Coverage

Attendance Figures, 1948 to 1950

	Percentage Change from 1947–48 Average	1949–50	
		1949	1950
All colleges	+3.3	−0.3	−3.5
Colleges in TV areas	+1.9	−4.2	−6.0
Colleges outside TV areas	+6.6	+9.3	+2.5
District 1. New England	+2.6	−24.4	−26.3
In TV areas	+0.7	−28.2	−28.7
Outside TV areas	+12.1	+1.1	−9.8
District 2. East	−5.8	−19.5	−15.5
In TV areas	−8.1	−23.0	−16.2
Outside TV areas	+21.3	+33.3	+9.9
District 3. Southeast	+4.7	+4.6	−0.6
In TV areas	+2.5	+1.6	−0.9
Outside TV areas	+7.4	+7.9	+0.5
District 4. Midwest	+0.6	+1.0	+0.4
In TV areas	+0.2	−0.1	−0.3
Outside TV areas	+1.7	+4.1	+2.1
District 5. West Central	+12.2	+11.4	−0.7
In TV areas	+11.1	+11.6	+0.5
Outside TV areas	+13.8	+11.1	−2.4
District 6. Southwest	+16.0	+34.0	+15.5
In TV Areas	+26.0	+49.7	+18.0
Outside TV areas	+4.9	+20.5	+14.9
District 7. Mountain	+13.4	−10.2	−20.8
In TV areas	+14.5	−18.7	−29.0
Outside TV areas	+12.8	−6.1	−16.8
District 8. Pacific	+0.3	−3.4	−3.7
In TV areas	+0.6	−5.8	−6.4
Outside TV areas	−1.5	+8.5	+11.0

Source: NCAA TV Survey, NCAA Yearbook 1950-51, 147–49.

CHAPTER ONE The Origins of
Big-Time Football

1. *New York Tribune,* Dec. 1, 1893; Richard
   Harding Davis, "The Thanksgiving Day
   Game," *Harper's Illustrated Weekly,* Dec.
   9, 1893, 1170–71; Parke H. Davis, *Football: The American Intercollegiate Game*
   (New York: Charles Scribner's Sons,
   1911), 272–81.
2. *Boston Globe,* Nov. 24, 1894; *New York
   Herald,* Nov. 25, 1894.
3. *Boston Globe,* Nov. 24, 1894.
4. Ibid.; *New York Herald,* Nov. 24, 1894.
5. Ibid.
6. Guy M. Lewis, "The American Intercollegiate Football Spectacle, 1869–1917"
   (Ph.D. diss., University of Maryland,
   1964), 110.
7. *New York Tribune,* Nov. 25, 1894.
8. *New York Times,* Nov. 25, 1894.
9. Ibid.
10. *New York Herald,* Dec. 1, 1894.
11. Walter Camp, ed., *Spalding's Official
    Foot-Ball Guide* (New York: A. G. Spald-
    ing, 1891); *New York Times,* Nov. 26, 1893.
12. David Nelson, *Anatomy of a Game:
    Football, the Rules, and the Men Who
    Made the Game* (Newark: University of
    Delaware Press, 1994), 63–74.
13. *New York Tribune,* Nov. 20, 1892.
14. Davis, *Football,* 97.
15. Nelson, *Anatomy of a Game,* 70–74;
    Boston Globe, Nov. 24, 1894.
16. *Boston Globe,* Nov. 25, 1894; *New York
    Herald,* Nov. 25, 1894.
17. *New York Herald,* Nov. 25, 1894.
18. Ibid.
19. *Boston Globe,* Nov. 25, 1894.

20. *New York Times,* Nov. 25, 1894.
21. *Boston Globe,* Nov. 25, 1894; *New York
    Times,* Nov. 25, 1894.
22. *New York Times,* Nov. 25, 1894; *New
    York Herald,* Nov. 25, 1894.
23. *New York Times,* Nov. 25, 1894.
24. *Boston Globe,* Nov. 25, 1894.
25. *New York Times,* Nov. 27, 1894.
26. Ibid.
27. *Boston Globe,* Nov. 26, 1894.
28. Ibid., Nov. 30, Dec. 2, 1894.
29. Richard Borkowski, "Life and Contri-
    butions of Walter Camp to Intercolle-
    giate Football" (Ed.D. diss., Temple
    University, 1979), 165–67.
30. Ronald A. Smith, *Sports and Freedom:
    The Rise of Big-Time College Athletics*
    (New York: Oxford University Press,
    1988), 69–72; Davis, *Football,* 44–50.
31. Davis, *Football,* 62–65; Smith, *Sports
    and Freedom,* 77–78. Alexander M.
    Weyand, *The Saga of American Football*
    (New York: Macmillan, 1955), 11–12.
32. Lewis, "American Intercollegiate Foot-
    ball Spectacle," 23–24.
33. Ibid., 60; Borkowski, "Life and Contri-
    butions," 39–44.
34. Borkowski, "Life and Contributions,"
    56–60; David M. Nelson, *Anatomy of a
    Game: Football and the Men Who Made
    the Game* (Newark: University of
    Delaware Press, 1994), 4 9–50.
35. *New York Herald,* Nov. 28, 1881; Henry
    Twombley, *Personal Reminiscences of a
    Yale Football Player of the Eighties* (New
    Haven, CT: Yale University Press, 1940),
    14–15; Nelson, *Anatomy of a Game,*
    48–49.
36. Borkowski, " Life and Contributions,"

64; Nelson, *Anatomy of a Game,* 48–50, 61–65.

37. Borkowski, "Life and Contributions," 69–80; Nelson, *Anatomy of a Game,* 50–53, 60–63; J. Nadine Goldberg, "The Plastic Football Helmet: History of a Failed Technological Fix" (Master's thesis, Pennsylvania State University, 1994), 31. The eastern colleges also limited eligibility to five years.

38. Borkowski, "Life and Contributions," 102–5; Amos Alonzo Stagg and Wesley Stout, *Touchdown* (New York: Longman's, Green, 1927), 111.

39. Borkowski, "Life and Contributions," 58–59; William Hopher to Camp, Nov. 22, 1889, Walter Camp Papers, Yale University Archives (YUA), New Haven, CT.

40. *Daily Crimson* (Harvard), Dec. 4, 1884; Minutes, Harvard Athletic Committee, 1882–1908, Harvard University Archives (HUA), Cambridge, MA.

41. Ibid.; Smith, *Sports and Freedom,* 88–89.

42. Davis, *Football,* 88–90; Minutes, Harvard Athletic Committee, 1882–1908, HUA.

43. *New York Herald,* Nov. 24, 1889.

44. Andrew D. White, *The Diaries of Andrew White* (Ithaca, NY: Cornell University Library, 1959), 294, entry for Nov. 9, 1889; Lewis, "American Intercollegiate Football Spectacle," 34.

45. Stagg and Stout, *Touchdown,* 93–95.

46. Luther E. Price, "Spoiling a Great Game," *Harper's Illustrated Weekly* 55 (Dec. 11, 1911), 12; reply by Knowlton L. Ames, *Harper's Weekly* 56 (Jan. 27, 1912), 6.

CHAPTER TWO The First Football Controversy

1. W. Bruce Leslie, *Gentlemen and Scholars: College and Community in the "Age of the University"* (University Park: Pennsylvania State University Press, 1992), 109.

2. Ellen Axson Wilson to Anna Harris, Nov. 22, 1892, in *The Papers of Woodrow Wilson,* ed. Arthur Link, 69 vols.; (Princeton, NJ: Princeton University Press, 1966–94), 8:47–48.

3. *New York Times,* Feb. 18, 1894.

4. Henry James, *Charles W. Eliot: President of Harvard University,* 3 vols. (New York: Houghton Mifflin, 1930), 1:68.

5. "President Eliot's Annual Report, 1892–93," *Harvard Graduates' Magazine* 2 (Mar. 1894): 376–83. The report was released in February 1894.

6. Ibid.

7. Ibid.

8. Ibid.

9. James, *Charles W. Eliot,* 1:81–84.

10. *Daily Crimson* (Harvard), June 2, 1886.

11. *Boston Globe,* Feb. 22, 1894. Most eastern newspapers carried front-page stories of the Cornell incident.

12. Ibid.

13. *New York Evening Post,* Feb. 22, 1894; newspaper's italics.

14. *New York Daily Tribune,* Nov. 13, 1894.

15. "College Athletics," *Popular Science Monthly* 23 (Feb. 1884): 496.

16. Ibid.

17. *Yale Daily News,* Dec.18, 1895.

18. *New York Tribune,* Nov. 20, 1892.

19. Seward V. Coffin to Walter Camp, Dec. 1, 1889, Walter Camp Papers, Yale University Archives (YUA), New Haven, CT; Alexander M. Weyand, *The Saga of American Football* (New York: Macmillan, 1955), 68–69.

20. Walter Camp, ed., *Football Facts and Figures* (New York: Harper and Brothers, 1894), v–viii.

21. Ronald A. Smith, *Sports and Freedom: The Rise of Big-Time College Athletics* (New York: Oxford University Press, 1988), 94–95.

22. Camp, *Football Facts and Figures,* 194–95.

23. Ibid., 90, 96.

24. Ibid., 176–77, 209–11.

25. Ibid., 180.

26. Ibid., 161, 181, 189.

27. Ibid., 192, 223.

28. Charles Eliot, "President Eliot's Report," *Harvard Graduates' Magazine* 3 (Mar. 1895): 368–70.

29. *New York Times,* Nov. 30, 1894.

30. Ibid., Nov. 12, 17, Dec. 14, 1897; John F. Stegeman, *The Ghosts of Herty Field: Early Years on the Southern Gridiron* (Athens: University of Georgia Press, 1966), 37–44.

31. *New York Times,* Nov. 27, 1897.

CHAPTER THREE Spreading Scandal

1. S. Dan Brodie, *66 Years on the California Gridiron* (Oakland, CA: Olympic Publishing, 1949), 14; Herbert Hoover, *Memoirs of Herbert Hoover: Years of Adventure, 1874-1929* (New York: Macmillan, 1951), 21–22; *Daily Palo Alto* (Stanford University), Dec. 1, 1892.

2. James H. Kilvran to Walter Camp, Sept. 20, 1892, Walter Camp Papers, Yale University Archives (YUA), New Haven, CT.

3. Richard M. Borkowski, "The Life and Contributions of Walter Camp to American Football" (Ed.D. diss., Temple University, 1979), 155–56; Walter Camp, ed., *Football Facts and Figures* (New York: Harper and Brothers, 1884), 39.

4. Amos Alonzo Stagg and Wesley Winans Stout, *Touchdown* (New York: Longman's, Green, 1927), 102–22; Robin Lester, *Stagg's University: The Rise, Decline, and Fall of Football at Chicago* (Urbana: University of Illinois Press, 1995), 12–13; Erin A. McCarthy, "Making Men: The Life and Career of Amos Alonzo Stagg, 1862-1933," 2 vols. (Ph.D. diss., Loyola University of Chicago, 1994), 1:44–56, 81–84.

5. Stagg and Stout, *Touchdown,* 45–52; McCarthy, "Making Men," 1:26–33, 59, 73, 98–108. According to McCarthy, Stagg played summer baseball briefly in Bergen, N.J.

6. McCarthy, "Making Men," 1:132–35; Lester, *Stagg's University,* 46–47; Stagg and Stout, *Touchdown,* 143–44.

7. Lester, *Stagg's University,* 17.

8. Ibid., 26–31; Stagg and Stout, *Touchdown,* 189–200.

9. Lester, *Stagg's University,* 25–26.

10. *University of Chicago Weekly,* Jan. 3, 1895, 141.

11. Lester, *Stagg's University,* 41–42, 87–88.

12. Frank F. Stephens, *A History of the University of Missouri* (Columbia: University of Missouri Press, 1962), 362–63.

13. Harold Keith, *Oklahoma Kickoff* (Norman, OK: privately published, 1948), 53–54.

14. William Tucker, *My Generation: An Autobiographical Interpretation* (New York: Houghton Mifflin), 334; Walter Camp, ed., *Football Facts and Figures* (New York: Harper and Brothers, 1894), 104–5.

15. "Definition of a University by an Alumnus," *Graduate Magazine* (University of Kansas), 10 (Feb. 1912).

16. *Lantern* (Ohio State University), Dec. 5, 1894.

17. Joseph F. A. Pyre, "Student Life Seen by a Professor," *Daily Cardinal* (University of Wisconsin), Dec. 20, 1899.

18. *Weekly University Courier* (University of Kansas), Jan. 17, 1891; *Lantern* (Ohio State University), Jan. 15, 1895. Students at Ohio State made the same argument.

19. C. R. Griffin, *The University of Kansas* (Lawrence: University Press of Kansas, 1974), 647; C. R. Griffin, Notes, University of Kansas Archives (UKA), Lawrence, KS; Dale Somers, *The Rise of Sports in New Orleans, 1850-1900* (Baton Rouge: Louisiana State University Press, 1972), 259–61; Conference on Intercollegiate Football at Brown University, Brown University Archives (BUA), Providence, RI; Arthur E. Cobb, *Go Gators: Official History, University of Florida Football, 1888-1966* (Pensacola, FL: Sunshine Publishing, 1966), 9; C.H. Cramer, *Case Western Reserve University, 1826-1876* (Boston: Little, Brown, 1976), 163–64.

20. "Faculty Control in Athletics," *Michigan Alumnus* 3 (Jan. 1897): 84–86. "Alumni vs. Purity in Athletics," *Michigan Alumnus* 4 (Jan. 1898): 3; Frederick Rudolph, *American College and University: A History* (New York: Random House, 1962), 374–75.

21. Harold Evans, "College Football in Kansas," *Kansas Historical Quarterly* (1940): 290–91. The player, later a mining engineer in West Virginia, revealed his identity more than thirty years after the game.

22. John F. Stegeman, *The Ghosts of Herty Field: Early Years on the Southern Gridiron* (Athens: University of Georgia Press, 1966), 14–20; Patrick B. Miller, "Athletes in Academe: College Sports and American Culture, 1850–1920" (Ph.D. diss., University of California, Berkeley, 1987).

23. Merle E. Curti and Vernon Carstenson, *The University of Wisconsin, 1848-1925*, 2 vols. (Madison: University of Wisconsin Press, 1949), 2:533; *New York Times*, Nov. 26, 1897.

24. Paul F. Conklin, *Gone with the Ivy: A Biography of Vanderbilt University* (Knoxville: University of Tennessee Press, 1987), 139–40.

25. Daniel W. Hollis, *The University of South Carolina: College to University* (Columbia: University of South Carolina Press, 1956), 227–28.

26. Richard Harding Davis, "The Thanksgiving Day Game," *Harper's Illustrated Weekly*, Dec. 9, 1893, 1170–71; *New York Times*, Dec. 1, 1893, Dec. 1, 1894, Nov. 7, 28, 1897.

27. James H. Smart to Henry W. Rogers, Dec. 5, 1894, Henry Wade Rogers Papers, Connecticut State Library, Hartford; William Harper to Rogers, Dec. 10, 1894, Wade Papers; Charles W. Eliot to Rogers, Dec. 8, 1894, Wade Papers. (Photocopies of all the letters and replies may be found in the Henry Wade Rogers Papers, Northwestern University Archives, Evanston, IL.)

28. James H. Smart to Andrew S. Draper, Nov. 19, 1894, James H. Smart Papers, Special Collections, Purdue University, West Lafayette, IN.

29. Ibid.; Carl D. Voltmer, *A Brief History of the Intercollegiate Conference with Special Consideration of Athletic Problems* (Menasha, WI: George Banta Publishing, 1935), 2–5.

30. Conference on Intercollegiate Football at Brown University, Brown University Archives (BUA), Providence, RI; Walter Camp to Anson Stokes, Dec. 10, 1892, Camp Papers, YUA, New Haven, CT; Ronald A. Smith, *Sports and Freedom: The Rise of Big-Time College Athletics* (New York: Oxford University Press, 1988), 140.

31. *New York Times*, Nov. 14, 1897.

32. Conference on Intercollegiate Football at Brown University, BUA.

33. Smith, *Sports and Freedom*, 140.

34. *Morning Times* (New York), May 24, 1938; *Evening Public Ledger* (Philadelphia), May 24, 1938; Jack N. Wallace, "Foster Sanford Dies," *Rutgers Alumni Monthly* 11 (June 1938).

35. Faculty Committee on Athletics to Seth Low, Mar. 6, 1900, Faculty Athletic Papers, Columbiana, Columbia University, New York.

36. *New York Evening Telegram*, Oct. 28, 1899; Henry Beach Needham, "The College Athlete," pt. 1: "How Commercialism Is Making Him Professional," *McClure's Magazine* 25 (1905): 118.

37. Faculty Athletic Committee to Seth Low, Dec. 8, 1899, Faculty Athletic Papers, Columbiana, Columbia University, New York.

38. *New York Times*, Mar. 17, Apr. 22, 1900; *New York Sun*, Mar. 24, 1900.

39. *New York Morning News*, Mar. 24, 1900; Francis S. Bangs to Nicholas Murray Butler, Feb. 28, 1902, Nicholas Murray Butler Papers, Columbiana; Needham, "The College Athlete," pt. 1: "How Commercialism Is Making Him Professional," *McClure's Magazine* 25 (1905): 118.

40. William T. Reid, "Football," *Educational Review* 31 (May 1906): 451–61; Griffin, *University of Kansas,* 655; "Faculty Asks Coach Woodruff to Resign," *Kansas University Weekly,* Oct. 22, 1898.

41. *Morning Times* (New York), May 24, 1938; *Evening Public Ledger* (Philadelphia), May 24, 1938; Wallace, "Foster Sanford Dies," *Rutgers Alumni Monthly* 11.

42. Needham, "College Athlete," pt. 1: "How Commercialism Is Making Him Professional," 123–25.

43. Ibid., 124

44. Ibid., 122, 125–26.

45. Ibid., 125–26.

46. Ibid., 122–23.

47. Edwin Dexter, "Accidents from Football," *Educational Review* (Apr. 1903): 415–28. That figure, if anywhere near accurate, is less than the percentages in the 1960s and comparable to those for some years in the 1990s.

48. Francis H. Snow to Caspar Whitney, Dec. 4, 1896, C. R. Griffin Notes, University of Kansas Archives (UKA).

49. Walter Camp, ed., *Spalding's Official Football Guide, 1891* (New York: American Sports Publishing, 1891).

50. Burr Chamberlain to Walter Camp, Sept. 24, 1902, Camp Papers, Yale University Archives, New Haven, CT; E. G. Ryder to Camp, Jan. 23, 1906, Camp Papers, YUA; Stagg and Stout, *Touchdown* (New York: Longman's, Scott, 1927), 247–48.

51. David Nelson, *Anatomy of a Game: Football, the Rules and the Men Who Made the Game* (Newark: University of Delaware Press, 1994), 79; *Chicago Record,* Jan. 19, 1898; *Chicago Tribune,* Jan. 29, 1898; *Chicago Tribune,* Sept. 5, 1898.

52. Nelson, *Anatomy of Game,* 91–93.

53. Letter to the Editor, *New York Times,* Nov. 30, 1894; *Volante* (University of South Dakota), Oct. 23, 1901.

54. *Daily Maroon* (University of Chicago), Mar. 1, 1905.

CHAPTER FOUR Football's Longest Season

1. Theodore Roosevelt to Henry Beach Needham, July 19, 1905, Elting Morison, ed., *The Letters of Theodore Roosevelt,* 8 vols. (Cambridge, MA: Harvard University Press, 1951), 4:1280–82.

2. Theodore Roosevelt to Walter Camp, Mar. 11, 1895, Walter Camp Papers, Yale University Archives (YUA), New Haven.

3. Ibid.

4. Ibid.; Theodore Roosevelt, *The Strenuous Life: Essays and Addresses by Theodore Roosevelt* (New York: Century, 1900).

5. *Washington Post,* Oct. 8, 1905; *Boston Globe,* Oct. 8, 1905. The *Post* carried an account of a fracas at Columbia, while the *Globe* mentioned that Maxwell and Stevenson of Penn had been bloodied. Frank Menke, *Encyclopedia of Sports* (New York: A. S. Barnes, 1944), 414; Roosevelt to William T. Reid Jr., Oct. 2, 1905, Theodore Roosevelt Papers, Library of Congress, Washington, DC. The other letters went out on the same day. The story of Roosevelt seeing the photo of Maxwell and threatening to ban football seems to have originated with the article on football in the second edition of Menke's encyclopedia.

6. Henry Beach Needham, "The College Athlete," pt. 1: "How Commercialism is Making Him Professional" (June 1905): 115–28; pt. 2: "His Amateur Code: Its Evasion and Administration" (July 1905): 260–73, *McClure's Magazine.*

7. Anson Phelps Stokes to Editorial Department, *McClure's Magazine,* Mar. 16, 1905, Camp Papers, YUA.

8. Needham, "College Athlete," 118.

9. Ibid., 160–73.

10. Needham, "The College Athlete," pt. 2: "His Amateur Code," 271–72.

11. Ibid.

12. Ibid., June 28, 1905; "The Function of a Great University," *The Works of*

Theodore Roosevelt, 20 vols. (New York: Charles Scribner's Sons, 1926), 16:324–25.

13. Endicott Peabody to Theodore Roosevelt, Sept. 16, 1905, Theodore Roosevelt Papers, Library of Congress, Washington, DC; Roosevelt to Camp, Nov. 24, 1905, in Morison, *Letters*, 5:94.

14. Roosevelt to Theodore Roosevelt Jr., Nov. 19, 1905, in Morison, *Letters*, 5:76.

15. Diary, Bill Reid, entry for Oct. 9, 1905, Harvard University Archives (HUA), Cambridge, MA. See also Ronald Smith, ed., *Big Time Football at Harvard, 1905: The Diary of Coach Bill Reid* (Urbana: University of Illinois Press, 1994), 193–94.

16. *New York Times*, Oct. 10, 1905; Smith, *Big-Time Football at Harvard*, 194–95.

17. *New York Times*, Oct. 10, 1905.

18. *New York Times*, Oct. 8, 1905; Ronald A. Smith, *Sports and Freedom: The Rise of Big-Time College Athletics* (New York: Oxford University Press, 1988), 196–200; Smith, *Big-Time Football*, 276–82.

19. *Boston Sunday Globe*, Nov. 26, 1905; *New York Herald*, Nov. 26, 1905; Smith, *Sports and Freedom*, 197–98; Smith, *Big-Time Football*, 26, 300, 303–4, 316–18.

20. *Boston Globe*, Nov. 26, 1905; Theodore Roosevelt to Paul Dashiell, Dec. 5, 1905, Theodore Roosevelt Papers, Library of Congress; Smith, *Big-Time Football*, 316–18; Charles Eliot to Theodore Roosevelt, Dec. 12, 1905, Charles Eliot Papers, HUA. Roosevelt knew Dashiell from the late 1890s.

21. *Boston Globe*, Nov. 19, 1905; Roosevelt to Theodore Roosevelt Jr., Nov. 19, 1905, *Letters*, 5:82; Roosevelt to Walter Camp, Nov. 24, 1905, Morison, *Letters*, 5:93–94.

22. *Boston Globe*, Nov. 26, 1905; *New York Times*, Dec. 5, 1905; Roosevelt to Dashiell, Dec. 5, 9, 1905; Roosevelt to Charles Eliot, Dec. 9, 1905, Roosevelt Papers, LC.

23. Theodore Roosevelt to Charles Eliot, Dec. 9, 1905, Roosevelt Papers, LC. "Don't you think there is a certain amount of hysteria in the present [word indecipherable] about football," Roosevelt wrote out longhand at the end of his letter.

24. *Triangle* (New York University), Nov. 28, 1905.

25. *New York Times*, Nov. 26, 1905; *Triangle* (New York University), Nov. 28, Dec. 5, 1905, Jan. 16, 1906.

26. *The Triangle* (New York University), Nov. 28, 1905, Dec. 5, 1905, Jan. 16, 1906; Eliot to MacCracken, Dec. 15, 1905, Eliot Papers, HUA.

27. Harold M. Frindell, "The Origin and Development of the National Collegiate Athletic Association" (Master's thesis, New York University, 1938), 10–13; *Triangle* (New York University), Dec.5, 1905, Jan. 16, 1905.

28. *New York Telegram*, Nov. 29, 1905; Smith, *Sports and Freedom*, 199–200.

29. National Football Conference of Universities and Colleges, Dec. 8, 1905, University of California Archives, Berkeley; *Chicago Record-Herald*, Dec. 9, 1905; *New York Times*, Dec. 9, 1905; Smith, *Sports and Freedom*, 199–200.

30. *New York Times*, Dec. 10, 1905.

31. Richard Borkowski, "Life and Contributions of Walter Camp to Intercollegiate Football" (Ed.D. diss., Temple University, 1979), 201–3.

32. Smith, ed., *Big Time Football at Harvard*, 265–66.

33. Ibid.

34. *New York Times*, Dec. 12, 1905.

35. *New York Telegram*, Dec. 22, 1905; *New York Press*, Dec. 22, 1905; *Brooklyn Eagle*, Dec. 23, 1905, Football Scrapbook, Columbiana, Columbia University.

36. *New York Times*, Dec. 11, 1905; Eliot to Theodore Roosevelt, Dec. 11, 1905, Eliot Papers, HUA; Smith, *Big-Time Football*, 300–301. Charles Eliot was delighted by Brill's defection, though Bill Reid regarded him as mercurial and undependable.

37. "From a Graduate's Window," *Harvard Graduates' Magazine* 14 (Dec. 1905):

216–23. Excerpts appeared in the *Boston Transcript.*

38. Ibid.

39. Ibid.

40. *New York Times,* Dec. 29, 1905. The *Times* listed fifty-eight schools, while Palmer Pierce, who became president, later cited sixty-eight schools attending the first convention.

41. *New York Times,* Dec. 29, 1905; Cedric Cummins, *The University of South Dakota, 1862-1966* (Vermillion, SD: Dakota Press, 1975), 89.

42. *New York Times,* Dec. 29, 1905.

43. Ibid. 24. Proceedings of the Second Annual Convention of the Intercollegiate Athletic Association (ICAA), New York, Dec. 28, 1907, 24.

44. Ibid.; Frindell, "Origin and Development," 27–31.

CHAPTER FIVE Football in Crisis

1. *Chicago Tribune,* Dec. 1, 1905; *Chicago Record-Herald,* Dec. 1, 1905.

2. Ronald A. Smith, *Sports and Freedom: The Rise of Big-Time College Athletics* (New York: Oxford University Press, 1988), 203–4; *New York Times,* Jan. 16, 1906.

3. Smith, *Sports and Freedom,* 203; *New York Times,* Jan. 9, 1906.

4. *New York Times,* Jan. 13, 1905.

5. Arthur Hadley to Camp, Feb. 2, 1906, Walter Camp Papers, Yale University Archives (YUA), New Haven, CT; *Chicago Tribune,* Jan. 13, 1905.

6. *New York Times,* Jan. 16, 1906.

7. Edward S. Jordan, "Buying Football Victories," *Collier's Weekly,* Nov. 11, 1905, 19–20, 23.

8. Ibid.

9. Ibid.

10. *Chicago Record-Herald,* Nov. 18, 1905.

11. Edward Jordan, "Buying Football Victories," *Collier's Weekly,* Nov. 28, 1905, 22–23.

12. Ibid.

13. *Chicago Tribune,* Dec. 2, 1905; Ray Allen Billington, *Frederick Jackson Turner: Historian, Teacher, Scholar* (New York: Oxford University Press, 1973), 264–67.

14. Billington, *Frederick Jackson Turner,* 264–67.

15. *Chicago Tribune,* Dec. 3, 1905; Robin Lester, *Stagg's University: The Rise, Decline, and Fall of Football at Chicago* (Urbana: University of Illinois Press, 1995), 83–84.

16. *Chicago Tribune,* Nov. 27, Dec. 16, 1905; Lester, *Stagg's University,* 84.

17. Letter of James Angell, Minutes of the First Chicago Conference, Jan. 19, 1906, Michigan Historical Collections, Ann Arbor.

18. Minutes of the First Chicago Conference, Jan. 19, 1906, Michigan Historical Collections, Ann Arbor.

19. Ibid.

20. Ibid.

21. *Chicago Tribune,* Jan. 22, 25, 1906.

22. Merle Curti and Vernon Carstenson, *University of Wisconsin, 1848-1925,* 2 vols. (Madison: University of Wisconsin Press, 1949), 2:538; Billington, *Frederick Jackson Turner,* 264–67.

23. *Chicago Tribune,* Jan. 22, 25, 1905.

24. *Chicago Record-Herald,* Mar. 10, 1906; *Chicago Tribune,* Mar. 10, 1906. The *Tribune* called it a Michigan victory from beginning to end.

25. Ibid.

26. Ibid.

27. Ibid.

28. *Chicago Tribune,* Mar. 24, 1906; Harold Williamson and Payson S. Wild, *Northwestern University: A History, 1850-1975* (Evanston, IL: Northwestern University, 1976), 127.

29. Billington, *Frederick Jackson Turner,* 270–73.

30. Ibid.

31. Roberta J. Park, "From Football to Rugby—and Back, 1906–1919: The University of California Response to the 'Football Crisis of 1905,'" *Journal of Sport History* 11, no. 3 (Winter 1984): 5–40.

32. Brick Morse, *California Football History* (Berkeley, CA: Gillick Press, 1937), 38; *Daily Palo Alto* (Stanford University), Dec. 1, 1892; *Daily Californian* (University of California), Dec. 7, 1899, Sept. 27, 1900, Jan. 14, 1901.

33. David Starr Jordan to Benjamin Ide Wheeler, Nov. 30, 1905, Benjamin Ide Wheeler Papers, University of California Archives (UCA); Wheeler to Walter Camp, Wheeler Papers, UCA; Camp to Wheeler, Dec. 26, 1905, Camp Papers, YUA.

34. Wheeler to Jordan, Nov. 28, 1905, Wheeler Papers, UCA; *Daily Californian* (University of California), Nov. 8, 1901, Sept. 8, 1904; Morse, *California Football*, 38, 47; Park, "From Football to Rugby," 8–9. Since the peanut vendors at Berkeley were needy students, it was decided to permit selling before the cheer practice began.

35. Wheeler to Jordan, Nov. 28, 1905, Wheeler Papers, UCA.

36. Wheeler to Camp, Dec. 19, 1905, UCA; Wheeler to Camp, Feb. 15, 1906, Wheeler Papers, UCA; W. T. Reid to Wheeler, Mar. 9, 1906, Wheeler Papers, UCA; Park, "From Football to Rugby," 17–18.

37. Wheeler to Nicholas Murray Butler, Dec. 19, 1905, Wheeler Papers, UCA, David Starr Jordan to Henry Mac-Cracken, Jan. 8, 1906, Jordan Letterbooks, Stanford University Archives, Palo Alto, CA.

38. *Daily Californian*, Dec. 4, 1905; Park, "From Football to Rugby," 17–18.

39. *New York Times*, Nov. 27, 1905; Charles Eliot to Benjamin Ide Wheeler, Dec. 5, 1905, Wheeler Papers, YUA; Park, "From Football to Rugby," 39.

40. Wheeler to Camp, Feb. 15, 1906, Wheeler Papers, UCA; Park, "From Football to Rugby," 17–22.

41. Park, "From Football to Rugby," 22–24, 30–33.

42. Elliott, *Stanford University*, 232–38; Park, "From Football to Rugby," 33–40.

CHAPTER SIX The Game in Flux

1. Daniel B. Potts, *Wesleyan University, 1831-1910: Collegiate Enterprise in New England* (New Haven, CT: Yale University Press, 1992), 212–20.

2. *Daily Cardinal* (University of Wisconsin), Oct. 21, 1903; *Daily Maroon* (University of Chicago), Nov. 14, 1902, Oct. 16, 1915; *Harvard Crimson*, Oct. 10, 1905; *Daily Bruin* (University of California), Dec. 7, 1939; *New York Times*, May 8, 1947.

3. Bernard DeVoto, "Football: A Game?" *Chicago Journal*, Oct. 9, 1926.

4. *New York Times*, Feb. 15, Mar. 31, Apr. 15, 1906; David Nelson, *Anatomy of a Game: Football, the Rules, and the Men Who Made The Game* (Newark: University of Delaware Press, 1994), 121; Alexander Weyand, *The Saga of American Football* (New York: Macmillan, 1955), 84.

5. Nelson, *Anatomy of a Game*, 125; *Harvard Bulletin*, Jan. 10, 1906; *Yale Alumni Weekly*, 14, 10 (Dec. 7, 1904), 187–88. In an exchange with a former Harvard player in 1904, Matt Hallowell, Camp first proposed the ten-yard rule.

6. Nelson, *Anatomy of a Game*, 125.

7. Ibid., 124.

8. Ibid., 92–93. The rules also allowed the quarterback, after receiving the ball, to run across the scrimmage line but only five yards beyond where the ball was put in play. This applied only to the area between the two twenty-five-yard lines but later included the whole field.

9. Ibid., 125.

10. Ibid., 115–20, 123–24.

11. Ibid., 122.

12. Ibid., 135–38.

13. *New York Times*, Nov. 26, 1906.

14. Nelson, *Anatomy of a Game*, 113–14.

15. *New York Times*, Sept. 29–30, 1906.

16. *Chicago Tribune*, Oct. 14, 21, Nov. 18, 1906. David Potts, *Wesleyan University, 1831-1910* (New Haven, CT: Yale University Press, 1992), 330; *Hartford Daily*

Courant, Oct. 4, 1906; Allison Danzig, ed., *Oh, How They Played the Game: The Early Days of Football and the Heroes Who Made It Great* (New York: Macmillan, 1971), 178–88.

17. Danzig, *Oh, How They Played the Game,* 178–88.

18. *New York Times,* Nov. 4, 11, 18, 1906; Parke H. Davis, *Football: The American Intercollegiate Game* (New York: Charles Scribner's Sons, 1911), 140–42, 305–7.

19. *New York Times,* Nov. 25, 1906.

20. *New York Times,* Dec. 2, 1906.

21. *New York Times,* Nov. 26, 1906.

22. *New York Times,* Nov. 14, 1909.

23. *New York Times,* Nov. 21, 1906. Some newspapers listed figures that went above thirty.

24. Edward K. Hall to Herbert Reed, Oct. 30, 1931, E. K. Hall Football Collection, New York Public Library.

25. *New York Times,* Oct. 17, 31, 1909. Unlike Army, Harvard completed its season.

26. *Washington Post,* Nov. 14, 1909; *Richmond Times-Dispatch,* Nov. 14, 1909. The author's interviews with nieces of Archer Christian who had known his mother—their grandmother—agreed with these accounts.

27. Ibid.

28. *New York Times,* Nov. 14, 16, 1909. The editorial appeared on Nov. 16, 1909.

29. *New York Times,* Nov. 14, 1909; *Baltimore Sun,* Nov. 14, 1909; *College Topics* (University of Virginia), Nov. 20, 1909; Morris A. Bealle, *The Georgetown Hoyas: The Story of a Rambunctious Football Team* (Washington, DC: Columbia Publishing, 1947), 78–80.

30. John H. Neff to Edwin Alderman, Dec. 4, 1909, Edwin Alderman Papers, University of Virginia Archives (U Va Arch), Charlottesville, VA.

31. *Richmond Times-Dispatch,* Nov. 15, Dec. 12, 1909; Georgetown University, Football, 1910, Georgetown University Archives, Washington, DC. Meeting in December, the fifteeen Jesuit schools led by the presidents of Georgetown, Fordham, and Holy Cross went beyond the injury problem, addressing many of the evils singled out by the Big Nine, including recruiting, football's effects on academic work, the exaggerated role of athletic heroes, and the baneful role of coaches. They also cited football's perversion of moral values and called for faculty control of what should be healthy physical exercise.

32. Charles Eliot to Edwin Alderman, Nov. 14, 1909, Alderman Papers, U Va Arch.

33. Ibid.

34. Edwin Alderman to Charles Eliot, Nov. 18, 1909, Alderman Papers, U Va Arch.

35. *Richmond Times-Dispatch,* Nov. 17, 1909.

36. Ibid.

37. *Richmond Times-Dispatch,* Dec. 12, 1909; Edwin Alderman to Robert B. Tunstall, Nov. 30, 1909, Alderman Papers, U Va Arch; John S. Mosby to Eppa Hunton Jr., Nov. 19, 1909, Alderman Papers, U Va Arch; Alderman to W. H. White, Nov. 30, 1909, Alderman Papers, U Va Arch; Kevin H. Siepel, *Rebel: The Life and Times of John Singleton Mosby* (New York: St. Martin's Press, 1983), 25–29.

38. *New York Tribune,* Dec. 28, 1909.

39. *New York Tribune,* Dec. 29, 1909

40. ICAA, Proceedings of the Fourth Annual Convention, Dec. 28, 1909, 20–22.

41. Ibid., 25.

42. *New York Tribune,* Dec. 29, 1909.

43. Ibid.

CHAPTER SEVEN The Invention of Modern Football

1. Amos Alonzo Stagg to Walter Camp, Nov. 20, 1909, Walter Camp Papers, Yale University Archives (YUA), New Haven, CT.

2. A. Lawrence Lowell to George Harris, Dec. 21, 1909, A. Lawrence Lowell Papers, Harvard University Archives (HUA), Cambridge, MA; Arthur T. Hadley to A. Lawrence Lowell, Nov. 30,

1909, Dec. 1, 1909, Lowell Papers, HUA; Hadley to Lowell, Dec. 23, 1909, Arthur Hadley Papers, Yale University Archives (YUA), New Haven, CT; Woodrow Wilson to Hadley, Jan. 1, 1910, in *The Papers of Woodrow Wilson,* ed. Arthur Link, 69 vols. (Princeton, NJ: Princeton University Press, 1969–94), 19:699.

3. Howard Houston Henry to Wilson, July 5, 1910, in Link, *Papers of Woodrow Wilson,* 20:547.

4. Records of the Football Rules Committee, Feb. 5–6, 1910, 1, Camp Papers, YUA.

5. Ibid.

6. Ibid., 5–8.

7. Ibid., 10.

8. Ibid., 13.

9. Ibid., 16.

10. *New York Times,* Mar. 6, 8, 26, 1910.

11. *New York Times,* Apr. 4, 10, 28, 1910.

12. Records of the Football Rules Committee, Mar. 25–26, 1910, 27, Camp Papers, YUA. Camp presented this along with H. B. Hackett, who represented West Point.

13. Walter Camp to Benjamin Ide Wheeler, n.d., Camp Papers, YUA.

14. Records of the Football Rules Committee, Apr. 19–20, 1910, 32–34, Camp Papers, YUA.

15. Ibid.

16. Ibid.

17. Ibid., 37–43.

18. Ibid., 43–44.

19. Records of the Football Rules Committee, May 13, 1910, 46–53, Camp Papers, YUA. The subcommittee had met on May 9 to work on the pass behind the line; its proposals also allowed players in the center of the line to interchange positions with those in the backfield.

20. Ibid., 54–55.

21. Ibid., 55–57.

22. Ibid., 57–59.

23. Richard Borkowski, "Walter Camp's Life and Contributions to American Football" (Ed.D. diss., Temple University, 1979), 226–28.

24. "Talk to the Football Team," Nov. 10, 1910, in Link, *Papers of Woodrow Wilson,* 22:4–5.

25. Parke H. Davis, untitled tribute to Edward Kimball Hall, 1933, E. K. Hall Football Collection, New York Public Library.

26. Meeting of the Football Rules Committee, Feb. 22, 1912, 3, Camp Papers, YUA.

27. David M. Nelson, *Anatomy of a Game* (Newark: University of Delaware Press, 1994), 156–58.

28. William Johnson, *William Allen White* (New York: Henry Holt, 1947), 216; C. R. Griffin Notes, University of Kansas Archives (UKA), Lawrence, KS.

29. E. Jay Jernigan, *William Allen White* (Boston: Twayne Publishers, 1983), 12–15, 19–20.

30. *The Kansan* (University of Kansas), Apr. 5, 8, 9, 10, 19, 1910; Clifford S. Griffin, *The University of Kansas: A History* (Lawrence: University Press of Kansas, 1974), 657 . Students at Kansas met to protest plans to introduce rugby.

31. "Minutes of the Meeting of the Athletic Board," Feb. 6, 1906, Griffin Notes, UKA.

32. William Allen White to Frank H. Strong, Apr. 14, 1910, in *Selected Letters of William Allen White, 1899–1943,* ed. Walter Johnson (New York: Henry Holt, 1943), 109.

33. George Ehler, "Report on Football Fatalities among College Men, Season of 1912," *NCAA, Proceedings of the Seventh Annual Convention, Dec. 27, 1912,* 25; *Chicago Tribune,* Nov. 23, 1912.

34. Henry Williams, *NCAA, Proceedings of the Tenth Annual Convention, Dec. 29, 1915,* 24; Robin Lester, *Stagg's University: The Rise, Decline, and Fall of Football at the University of Chicago* (Urbana: University of Illinois Press, 1995), 205; Murray Sperber, *Shake Down the Thunder: The Creation of Notre Dame Football* (New York: Henry Holt, 1993), 30–31; *Chicago Tribune,* Sept. 30, 1909.

35. Sperber, *Shake Down the Thunder,* 34–42; Allison Danzig, ed., *Oh, How*

They Played the Game: The Early Days of Football and the Heroes Who Made It Great (New York: Macmillan, 1971), 189–99.

36. Ibid.; Alexander Weyand, *The Saga of American Football* (New York: Macmillan, 1955), 105–6.

37. Weyand, *Saga of American Football*, 106; *New York Times*, Nov. 2, 1913.

38. *New York Times*, Nov. 2, 1913; Sperber, *Shake Down the Thunder*, 46–47.

39. *New York Times*, Oct. 10, Nov. 26, 1913.

40. George Ehler, "Fatalities among Football Players," *NCAA, Proceedings of the Ninth Annual Convention, Dec. 29, 1914,* 28–29, 36; Ehler, "Fatalities among Football Players," *NCAA, Proceedings of the Tenth Annual Convention, December 28, 1915,* 24–25. In his brief 1915 report Ehler declared that serious injuries were the result of improper conditioning.

41. *Chicago Tribune*, Nov. 28, 1915, Dec. 3, 1916. By comparison, the highest death rate in the past forty years was thirty-six fatalities in 1968, out of which seven occurred at the college level and only five resulted from accidents sustained on the gridiron. From 1987 to 1992 there were no direct casualties in college football even though roughly seventy-five thousand athletes participated each year. In 1916 the toll was three in college play and sixteen overall. Frederick O. Mueller and Robert C. Cantu, "National Center for Catastrophic Sports Injury Research: Fourteenth Annual Report, Fall 1982 to Spring 1996," privately issued, 13; Frederick O. Mueller and Jerry Diehl, *Annual Survey of Football Injury Research, 1931–1997*, American Football Coaches Association (1997).

42. Nelson, *Anatomy of a Game*, 165.

43. Ibid.

44. Howard J. Savage et al., *American College Athletics* (New York: Carnegie Foundation for the Advancement of Teaching, 1929), 134. The report was also known as *Bulletin Number Twenty-Three*.

45. Merle Curti and Vernon Carstenson, *The University of Wisconsin, 1848-1925*, 2 ⌄ls. (Madison: University of Wisconsin Press, 1949), 2:545.

46. Charles Savage, "The Professional versus the Educational in College Athletics," *NCAA, Proceedings of the Ninth Annual Convention, Dec. 29, 1914,* 52–57.

47. Horace Coon, *Columbia: Colossus on the Hudson* (New York: E. P. Dutton, 1947), 308–10; Sperber, *Shake Down the Thunder*, 203–6.

48. *New York Times*, Nov. 21, 1914.

49. "Report of the Districts," *NCAA, Proceedings of the Twelfth Annual Convention, Dec. 28, 1917,* 18–19.

50. James Mennell, "The Service Program in World War I: Its Impact on the Popularity of the Game," *Journal of Sport History* 16, no. 3 (Winter 1989): 248–60.

51. Joseph E. Raycroft, "Mass Athletics," *NCAA, Proceedings of the Twelfth Annual Convention, Dec. 28, 1917,* 62–63.

CHAPTER EIGHT Playing and Coaching for Pay in the 1920s

1. Howard Savage et al., *American College Athletics, with a Preface by Henry S. Pritchett, President of the Foundation, Bulletin Number Twenty-Three* (New York: Carnegie Foundation for the Advancement of Teaching, 1929), 283–89.

2. "The Rush to Colleges," *Nation*, Nov. 10, 1920, 521.

3. Manuel P. Servin and Iris Higbie Wilson, *Southern California and Its University: A History of USC, 1880-1964* (Los Angeles: War Ritchie Press, 1969), 166–77; James Whalen Sr., *Gridiron Greats Now Gone: The Heyday of 19 Former Top-20 Football Programs* (Jefferson, NC: McFarland, 1991), 62.

4. Savage et al., *American College Athletics*, 161–68.

5. "Sandy as They See Him," *The Scarlet Letter, 1918* (Rutgers yearbook), George Foster Sanford Collection, courtesy of George Foster Sanford III; *Philadelphia*

Evening Ledger, May 24, 1938, G. Foster
Sanford Collection, Rutgers University
Archives, New Brunswick, NJ.

6. Ibid.; Martin B. Duberman, *Paul Robe-
son* (New York: Alfred A. Knopf, 1988),
19–23; Esland Good Robeson, *Paul
Robeson: Negro* (New York: Harper and
Brothers, 1920), 29–34; *Daily Targum*
(Rutgers University), Apr. 10, 1973.

7. Savage et al., *American College Athletics,*
180–82.

8. Ibid.; Murray Sperber, *Shake Down the
Thunder: The Creation of Notre Dame
Football* (New York: Henry Holt, 1993),
89–90, 194–96, 237–38, 232–34.

9. Sperber, *Shake Down the Thunder,*
164–65, 273–74, 292–93.

10. Savage et al., *American College Athletics,*
164–65; Sperber, *Shake Down the Thunder* 73–74, 292–93.

11. Charles W. Akers and John W. Carter,
Bo McMillin: Man and Legend
(Louisville: Sulgrave Press, 1989), 14–17.

12. Ibid., 19–53.

13. Ibid.; Centre College, Football Clipping
File, Centre College Archives, Danville,
KY. "Centre College Football Record,
1880–," Centre College Archives, (CCA),
Danville, KY.

14. Akers and Carter, *Bo McMillin,* 65–69.

15. Ibid.

16. Ibid.

17. Ibid.; President's Statement to the Board
of Trustees, Jan. 7, 1924, 1–10, CCA.

18. President's Statement to the Board of
Trustees, Feb. 5, 1924, 1–5, CCA. In 1926
nearby West Virginia Wesleyan was
challenged by the North Central Association. The president admitted that
athletes had received the equivalent of
five hundred dollars, in the form of tuition, fees, books, room and board. See
New York Times, Dec. 28, 1926.

19. Akers and Carter, *Bo McMillin,* 75–83.

20. *NCAA, Proceedings of the Sixteenth Annual Convention, Dec. 29, 1921,* 89.

21. George Halas, *Halas: An Autobiography*
(Chicago: Bonus Books, 1986), 66–67.

22. *New York Times,* Nov. 1, 6, 10, 11, 1915;

address, David Eisenhower, Apr. 28,
1995, Conference on the 100th Anniversary of Babe Ruth's Birth, Hofstra University, Hempstead, N.Y.

23. John M. Carroll, *Fritz Pollard: Pioneer
in Racial Advancement* (Urbana: University of Illinois Press, 1992), 44–45;
Sperber, *Shake Down the Thunder,* 57–59.

24. *Chicago Tribune,* Jan. 31, 1922.

25. *New York Times,* Jan. 29, 1922; Sperber,
Shake Down the Thunder, 120–21.

26. "Football History Made by the Illinois
Iceman," *Literary Digest* 87 (Dec. 26,
1925): 29.

27. *New York Times,* Nov. 6, 12, 18, 19, 25,
1925. Grange's coach, Bob Zuppke,
snapped, "Red owes the sports world
nothing." He later changed his mind.

28. Red Grange and Ira Morton, *The Red
Grange Story: An Autobiography Told to
Ira Morton* (Urbana: University of Illi-
nois Press, 1993), 49–59; *New York
Times,* Nov. 23, 25, 1925.

29. Grange and Morton, *Red Grange Story,*
94–95; *New York Times,* Nov. 21, 1925.

30. *New York Times,* Nov. 22, 1925.

31. John B. Kennedy, "The Saddest Young
Man in America," *Collier's* 77, Jan. 16,
1926, 15; Benjamin G. Rader, *American
Sports from the Age of Folk Games to the
Age of Televised Sports* (Englewood
Cliffs, NJ: Prentice Hall, 1990), 137–41;
Grange and Morton, *Red Grange Story,*
90–94.

32. *New York Times,* Nov. 23, 25, 1925;
Grange and Morton, *Red Grange Story,*
101–2.

33. *New York Times,* Nov. 30, 1925.

34. Charles W. Kennedy, report from District II, *Proceedings of the Twentieth Annual Convention of the NCAA, Dec. 30,
1925,* 18–20.

35. Thomas Bergen, *The Game: The Harvard-Yale Rivalry, 1875-1983* (New Haven,
CT: Yale University Press, 1984), 113.

36. Savage et al., *American College
Athletics,* 92.

37. *New York Times,* Apr. 26, 1926.

38. *New York Times,* Apr. 26, May 10, 1926.

CHAPTER NINE The Growth of Subsidized Football

1. *Washington Star,* Nov. 16, 1923; James J. Carlan to Father Donlon, Dec. 7, 1913, Georgetown University Archives, Washington, DC; *Daily Northwestern,* Nov. 7, 1929; Paula A. Fass, *The Damned and the Beautiful: American Youth in the 1920s* (New York: Oxford University Press, 1977), 274–79.

2. *Daily Northwestern* (Northwestern University), Nov. 7, 1929; Percy Marks, *The Plastic Age* (New York: Century, 1924), 78–79, 254.

3. Ellen Condliffe Lagemann, *Public Power for the Private Good: A History of the Carnegie Foundation for the Advancement of Teaching* (Middletown, Conn.: Wesleyan University Press, 1983), 37–44.

4. Ibid., 32–36; John R. Thelin, *The Games Colleges Play: Scandal and Reform in Intercollegiate Athletics* (Baltimore: Johns Hopkins University Press, 1994), 22–23.

5. Howard J. Savage et al., *American College Athletics, with a Preface by Henry S. Pritchett, Bulletin Number Twenty-Three* (New York: Carnegie Foundation for the Advancement of Teaching, 1929), xvii.

6. Howard J. Savage, *Fruit of a Impulse: Forty-Five Years of the Carnegie Foundation, 1905-1950* (New York: Harcourt, Brace, 1953), 157.

7. Ibid.; Thelin, *Games Colleges Play,* 22–23.

8. "The Story of a Graduate Manager [Aug. 1925]," North American Newspaper Alliance. The syndicated articles and follow-ups appeared on different dates in various newspapers.

9. Ibid.

10. *Chicago Tribune,* Sept. 9, 10, 11, 1925.

11. Harold F. Williamson and Payton S. Wild, *Northwestern University: A History, 1850-1975* (Evanston, IL: Northwestern University Press, 1975), 171–72.

12. Ibid., 143–70.

13. Robin Lester, *Stagg's University: The Rise, Decline, and Fall of Football at the University of Chicago* (Urbana: University of Illinois Press, 1995), 136–37; *Chicago Tribune,* Nov. 8, 1925.

14. Walter Dill Scott to Leland "Tiny" Lewis, Oct. 1, 1926, Walter Dill Scott Papers, Northwestern University Archives, Evanston, IL.

15. Amos Alonzo Stagg to Fielding T. Yost, Jan. 22, 1927, Amos Alonzo Stagg Papers, University of Chicago Special Collections, University of Chicago Library; Walter Paulison, *Tale of the Wildcats* (Evanston, IL: Northwestern University Club of Chicago, 1951), 37–42.

16. Stagg to Yost, Jan. 22, 1927, Chicago.

17. Savage, *Fruit of an Impulse,* 138.

18. Savage et al., *American College Athletics,* 242.

19. Ibid.

20. Ibid., 258–59.

21. Ibid., 250–52.

22. Ibid., 256–57.

23. Ibid., 258–59.

24. Ibid., 261.

25. Ibid., 263–64.

26. Ibid., 228–29.

27. Ibid., 230–31.

28. Ibid., 231–32.

29. Ibid., 231–36.

30. Ibid., 244–50.

31. Ibid., 246.

32. Ibid., 146.

33. Ibid., 145; *Washington Post,* Oct. 25, 1929.

34. Savage et al., *American College Athletics,* 140–42.

35. *New York Times,* Oct. 24, 1929; *Washington Post,* Oct. 24, 1929; Savage, *Fruit of an Impulse,* 158.

36. *Washington Post,* Oct. 25, 1929.

37. *New York Times,* Oct. 25, 1929; *Washington Post,* Oct. 24, 1929.

38. *Chicago Tribune,* Oct. 24, 1929.

39. *New York Times,* Oct. 24, 1929.

40. *Daily Northwestern* (Northwestern University), Oct. 30, 1929; *New York Times,* Oct. 26, 1929.

41. *Chicago Tribune,* Oct. 24, 1929.

42. Savage, *Fruit of an Impulse,* 158.

43. *New York Times,* Oct. 24, 1929; Thelin, *Games Colleges Play,* 28–29.

44. Savage, *Fruit of an Impulse,* 158; Savage et al., *American College Athletics,* 265.

45. Savage, *Fruit of an Impulse,* 158.

46. *Chicago Tribune,* Oct. 25, 26, 1929.

CHAPTER TEN   Overcoming Hard Times

1. Annual Report of the Graduate Manager, Jan. 23, 1933, H. Diederich Papers, Cornell University Archives, Ithaca, NY. For the Ohio State and Iowa cutbacks, see *Chicago Tribune,* Jan. 31, 1932, Nov. 29, 1932.

2. Howard J. Savage, *Current Developments in American College Athletics, with a Preface by Henry Suzallo, President of the Foundation, Bulletin Number 26* (New York: Carnegie Foundation for the Advancement of Teaching, 1931), 5–17.

3. *NCAA, Proceedings, of the Twenty-Sixth Annual Convention,* December 31, 1931, 47–48; *New York Herald-Tribune,* Jan. 1, 1931; *Literary Digest,* Dec. 12, 1931.

4. *New York Times,* Dec. 27, 1933, Dec. 29, 1934, Nov. 21, 1935. Professor Floyd Eastwood of NYU began an annual series of reports on deaths and injuries, the first attempt to analyze the injury problem.

5. *New York Times,* Oct. 25, 26, 1931; E. K. Hall to Herbert Reed, E. K. Hall Football Collection, Oct. 30, 1931, New York Public Library.

6. "Preliminary Report on the Commission on College Athletics of the Association of American Colleges," Jan. 21, 1932, President's Papers, Athletics, 1932, University Archives, University of Virginia, Charlottesville. Other presidents were William Mather Lewis of Lafayette, Daniel L. Marsh of Boston University, John L. Newcomb of Virginia, and Ernest H. Wilkins of Oberlin.

7. Francis Wallace, "Test Case at Pitt—The Facts about College Football Play for Pay," *Saturday Evening Post,* Oct. 28, 1939, 14 ff.; Robert C. Alberts, *The Story of the University of Pittsburgh, 1787-1987* (Pittsburgh: University of Pittsburgh Press, 1986), 158–68; Weekly Earnings in Manufacturing Industries: Indexes for Specific States, 1924–39, *Statistical Abstracts of the United States* (Washington, D.C.: Government Printing Office, 1940), 339.

8. Wallace, "Test Case at Pitt," 47.

9. Ibid., 49.

10. *New York Times,* Oct. 12, Dec. 7, 1933, Jan. 3, 1934, Dec. 29, 1935.

11. Donald Parent, "A History of Television and Sports" (Ph.D. diss., University of Illinois, 1974), 40; Radio Football, 1934–50, Comptroller's Papers, University of Minnesota Archives, St. Paul: "Budget of Athletic Association, 1939–40, University of Illinois Archives, Urbana; Eastern Collegiate Athletic Conference (ECAC), Minutes, Dec. 17, 1947, 71, ECAC, Centerville, MA.

12. *Washington Post,* Oct. 25, 1929; Proceedings, NCAA, Jan. 1, 1930, 35.

13. *New York Times,* Jan. 2, 1926; *Atlanta Constitution,* Oct. 14, 1927.

14. T. Harry Williams, *Huey Long* (New York: Vintage Books, 1981), 504–12.

15. Russ Crane to Bob Zuppke, Nov. 30, 1938, Robert Zuppke Papers, University of Illinois Archives, Champaign.

16. *NCAA, Proceedings of the Twenty-Ninth Annual Convention, Dec. 27-28, 1935,* 19, 23, 28; John Griffiths to A. A. Stagg, Feb. 5, 1936, Stagg Papers, Special Collections, University of Chicago.

17. Jester Pierce, "History of the Southern Conference" (Ph.D. diss., University of North Carolina, 1954), 86–96.

18. "Recognized or Not," *Daily Tar Heel* (University of North Carolina), n.d., Presidential Papers, Athletics, 1935–36, U Va Ar.14. *Corks and Curls* (U Va Yearbook), 1936–37 (for Virginia scores and commentary), University of Virginia Special Collections, Charlottesville.

19. "The Time Has Come," Nov. 9, 1936, *College Topics* (U Va); Pierce, "History of the Southern Conference," 98–101; Barron E. Segar to John L. Newcomb, Dec. 2, 1936, Presidential Papers, 1935–36, U Va Arch. Virginia may have left the Southern Conference because of financial aid questions or prospective changes by the conference, but disgust with the practices of other schools was the ostensible reason.

20. Author's interview with Robert Voights, October 1980, Evanston, IL.

21. House of Representatives, Oct. 4, 1935, Athletics, George W. Rightmire Papers, 1936–37, Ohio State University Archives, Columbus, OH; *New York Times,* Oct. 12, 20, 1935, Jan. 28, 1936.

22. Interview with Robert and Blanche Campbell, 1980, Oral History Program, UCLA Archives, University of California at Los Angeles, 66–77. *New York Times,* Jan. 4, 1940.

23. Francis Wallace, "Football's Black Market," *Saturday Evening Post,* Nov. 9, 1946, 20–21, 145.

24. Wallace, "Test Case at Pitt," 51–52.

25. Ibid.

26. Francis Wallace, "I Was a Football Fixer," *Saturday Evening Post,* Oct. 31, 1936, 16–17, 54.

27. Ibid., 54.

28. John R. Tunis, "What Price College Football? The Facts and Figures on Professionalism," *American Mercury* 48 (Oct. 1939): 129–42. See also Tunis, "More Pay for College Football Stars," *American Mercury* 39 (Nov. 1936): 267–72. Tunis gave "semiprofessional" ratings to six of the eight future Ivy League schools and a "professional" rating to Dartmouth.

29. Tunis, "What Price College Football?" 131. See also Tunis, "More Pay for College Football Stars," 268.

30. Robin Lester, *Stagg's University: The Rise, Decline, and Fall of Football at Chicago* (Urbana: University of Illinois Press, 1995), 1:50–52; Hal A. Lawson and Alan G. Ingham, "Conflicting Ideologies Concerning the University and Intercollegiate Athletics: Harper and Hutchins at Chicago, 1892–1940," *Journal of Sport History* 7, no. 3 (Winter 1980): 48–55.

31. Lester, *Stagg's University,* 157–58; Lawson and Ingham, "Conflicting Ideologies," 53.

32. Lester, *Stagg's University,* 148–50; Lawson and Ingham, "Conflicting Ideologies," 53.

33. Lester, *Stagg's University,* 154–55, 159; Howard Roberts, *The Big Nine: The Story of Football in the Western Conference* (New York: Putnam, 1948), 36–37; James Whalen Sr., *Gridiron Greats Now Gone: The Heyday of 19 Former Consensus Top-20 Football Programs* (Jefferson, NC: McFarland, 1991), 62; author's interview with John Jay Berwanger, May 1984, Chicago.

34. Lester, *Stagg's University,* 173–76.

35. Ibid., 172–73, 210.

36. "Alternatives Regarding Football," Presidents' Papers, Special Collections, University of Chicago Library (Sp Col, UCL), Chicago.

37. Ibid., 183.

38. Lester, *Stagg's University,* 151, 212–15; Robert M. Hutchins, "Gate Receipts and Glory," *Saturday Evening Post,* Dec. 3, 1938, 25 ff.

39. Robert M. Hutchins, "Notes on Football," Nov. 8, 1939, Presidents' Papers, Sp Col, UCL; Lester, *Stagg's University,* 178–79, 185.

40. Lester *Stagg's University.,* 177–78; John Nuveen to Walter Ames, Dec. 12, 1939, John Nuveen Papers, Sp Col, UCL; "Alternatives Regarding Football," Presidents' Papers; John Nuveen to Hutchins, Dec. 23, 1939, Presidents' Papers, Sp Col, UCL.

41. Lester, *Stagg's University,* 167–72; John Nuveen to Harold H. Swift, Presidents' Papers, n.d., Sp Col, UCL.

42. Lester, *Stagg's University*, 185, 212; "Football, Conclusions and Recommendations," Dec. 21, 1939, President's Papers, Sp Col, UCL; *Chicago Tribune*, Dec. 22, 1939.

43. Jasper King to Hutchins, Dec. 23, 1939, Presidents' Papers, Sp Col, UCL.

44. *Chicago Tribune*, Jan. 13, 17, 1940.

45. *Daily Maroon* (University of Chicago), Jan. 3, 1940.

46. William A. Comford to Hutchins, Jan. 12, 1940, Presidents' Papers, Sp Col, UCL.

47. Arch Ward, "In the Wake of the News," *Chicago Tribune*, Jan. 15, 1940; Lester, *Stagg's University*, 212 (app. 2). Lester's figures on tuition indicated that Chicago's costs might have been a deterrent to poorer students, though they were no higher than Northwestern's.

48. *NCAA, Proceedings of the Thirty-Fourth Annual Convention, December 29-30, 1939*, 103-4.

49. Address by Palmer Pierce, *Proceedings of Third Annual Convention of the ICAA*, Jan. 2, 1909, 28; John Austin Matzko, "The Early Years of the American Bar Association, 1878-1928" (Ph.D. diss., University of Virginia, 1984), 368-74.

50. *NCAA, Proceedings of the Thirty-Fourth Annual Convention, December 29-30, 1939*, 22, 119-21.

51. Ibid., 99-100.

52. *NCAA, Proceedings of the Thirty-Fifth Annual Convention, December 29-31, 1940*, 158-67.

53. Ibid., 129.

54. *NCAA, Proceedings of the Thirty-Fourth Annual Convention, December 29-30, 1939*, 103.

CHAPTER ELEVEN Saints and Sinners

1. *New York Times*, Dec. 14, 15, 16, 19, 1941, Jan. 2, 1942; *The Volunteer* (University of Tennessee yearbook), 1939; *Tennessee Farmer* (November 1939): 9; Milton Klein, *Volunteer Moments: Vignettes of the History of the University of Ten-*

nessee, 1794-1994 (Knoxville: University of Tennessee, 1994), 95–96; *Orange and White* (University of Tennessee), Nov. 30, 1938; *Corolla* (University of Alabama yearbook), 1937.

2. Donald W. Rominger Jr., "From Playing Field to Battleground: The United States Navy V-5 Preflight Program in World War II," *Journal of Sport History* 12, no. 3 (Winter 1985): 252–64.

3. *Stockton (California) Chronicle*, Sept. 15, 1943; *San Francisco Examiner*, Oct. 24, 1943. Stagg was named "Coach of the Year" in 1943; *NCAA Yearbook, 1943*, 52.

4. Arthur Compton, "The Goal of Collegiate Athletics," Proceedings of the Fortieth Annual Convention, Jan. 9-10, 1946, *NCAA Yearbook, 1945*, 104-5.

5. *New York Times*, Nov. 21, 1945.

6. Arthur H. Compton to James B. Conant, Dec. 20, 1945, Arthur H. Compton Papers, Washington University Archives (WUA), St. Louis, MO.

7. William J. Bingham to Compton, Jan. 3, 1946, Compton Papers, WUA.

8. [Account of Conference, Jan. 10, 1946], "Some Personal Opinions of W. G. B. [Dean W. G. Bowling], n.d., Compton Papers, WUA.

9. *New York Times*, Dec. 2, 1940, Dec. 4, 1941, Dec. 18, 1947.

10. Address by A. W. Hobbs, *NCAA, 1944 Yearbook*, Proceedings of the Thirty-Ninth Annual Convention, Jan. 12-13, 1945, 139-44.

11. Francis Wallace, "Football's Black Market," *Saturday Evening Post*, Nov. 9, 1946, 20–21, 145; *New York Times*, Sept. 12, 1946.

13. *New York Times*, Oct. 2, 1946.

14. *New York Times*, Aug. 28, 1946; Wallace, "Football's Black Market," 20–21. *New York Times*, Aug. 28, 1946.

15. *New York Times*, Aug. 28, 29, 1946.

16. Courtesy of Archives, Mississippi State University.

17. *New York Times*, July 11, Sept. 11, 18, 19, 1946.

18. Report by George Rider, *NCAA, 1943*

Yearbook, Proceedings of the Annual Convention, Jan. 5–6, 1944, 47.

19. *NCAA,* Proceedings of the Annual Convention, Dec. 29–31, 1940, 120, 128–29; *NCAA, 1943 Yearbook,* Proceedings of the Annual Convention, Jan. 5–6, 1944, 47–48.

20. *NCAA, The 1946 Yearbook,* proceedings of 1947 convention, Jan. 7–8, 1947, 71, 78–79, 108; *New York Times,* July 25, 1946.

21. Ibid., 169.

22. *New York Times,* Jan. 15, 1950 (history of Sanity Code); *NCAA, Yearbook, 1947-1948,* proceedings of the 1948 convention, 185–94.

23. *NCAA, The 1946 Yearbook,* proceedings of 1947 convention, Jan. 7–8, 1947, 82–86; Ibid., 35–36; Otto Hughes, "The Recruitment of Athletes," *North Central Association Quarterly* 28, no. 2 (October 1953): 227.

24. *New York Times,* Jan. 5, 1949.

25. *New York Times,* Jan. 11, 1949.

26. *New York Times,* Jan. 4, 1940; Nov. 21, 1946. Other protests came from Southern California, which had wanted to play Army in the Rose Bowl.

27. Joint meeting of the Southern, Southeastern, and Southwest Conferences, May 28, 1949, Records of Office of President, 1946–66, Georgia Tech Archives, Atlanta; *NCAA, 1949 Yearbook,* Proceedings of the Forty-Fourth Annual Convention, Jan. 13–14, 1950, 173–75.

28. Colgate W. Darden to George M. Modlin, June 27, 1949, Presidential Papers, NCAA, 1949, University of Virginia Archives, Charlottesville; memo, John Pomfret, College of William and Mary, Apr. 25, 1949, U Va Arch; Minutes, Board of Visitors, University of Virginia, July 21, 1949, U Va Arch; *New York Times,* Nov. 28, 1949.

29. Francis Stann, "Win, Lose, or Draw," *Washington Star,* Dec. 1, 1949. Board of Visitors, University of Virginia, May 13, Sept. 1, 1949, U Va Arch.

30. William Stewart to John L. Newcomb, Jan. 7, 1938; Beverly D. Tucker to Newcomb, Jan.14, 1937; Newcomb to Tucker, Jan. 7, 1938, Presidential Papers, 1937–38, Uva Arch. Tucker was an Episcopal minister at St. Paul's in Richmond (Jefferson Davis's church) and a former Rhodes Scholar. Statement of Richmond Alumni, Feb. 22, 1937. The Virginia grants at first resembled Rhodes scholarships.

31. Kemper W. Yancey to Colgate W. Darden, June 18, 1949, Presidential Papers, NCAA, 1949, U Va Arch; University of Virginia budgets for 1949–50, U Va Arch; *New York Times,* Oct. 19, 1950.

32. Arthur Gueppe as told to Harry L. Paxton, "Here's How an Upset Happens," *Saturday Evening Post,* Sept. 30, 1950, 22–23; *New York Times,* Nov. 6, 1949.

33. George H. Callcott, *A History of the University of Maryland* (Baltimore: Maryland Historical Society, 1966), 320–59.

34. Draft, H. C. Byrd to Clarence Houston, Sept. 22, 1949; telegram, H. C. "Curley" Byrd to Athletic Directors of Schools in Southwest Conference, Dec. 31, 1949, University of Maryland Archives.

35. *New York Times,* Jan. 13, 1950.

36. *New York Times,* Jan. 15, 1950: *NCAA, 1949-1950 Yearbook,* Proceedings of the 4036. Annual Convention, Jan. 12–14, 1950, 173–75.

37. Ibid.; *New York Herald-Tribune,* Jan. 15, 1950.

38. Byers, *Unsportsmanlike Conduct, Exploiting College Athletes* (Ann Arbor: University of Michigan Press, 1995), 54; Walter Byers, letter to the author, Mar. 15, 1996.

39. *New York Times,* Jan. 15, May 24, Sept. 1, Dec. 18, 29, 1950, Jan. 9, 11, 12, 13, 1951; *NCAA, 1949-1950 Yearbook,* Jan. 14, 1950, 206–7.

CHAPTER TWELVE Crisis and Reform

1. *Norfolk Virginian-Pilot,* Aug. 12, 1951; *Richmond Times-Dispatch,* Aug. 15, 1951; *New York Times,* August 12, 16, 1951.

2. Joan Gosnell, "Kickoffs and Kickbacks: The 1951 Football Scandal at William and Mary" (Master's thesis, College of William and Mary, 1990), 10–12; Transcript of interview with J. Wilfred Lambert, Jan. 8, 1975; College of William and Mary Archives (CWMA), Williamsburg, VA. Lambert gives the date that he learned of the alterations as 1948, and Hocutt gives no date. Gosnell's date of 1949 fits better with the facts.

3. Interview, J. Wilfred Lambert, Jan. 8, 1975, 78–79, CWMA.

4. Minutes, CWM Board of Visitors, Feb. 14, 1948, CWMA; transcript, interview, R. Wayne Kernodle, Nov. 6, 1975, 70, CWMA; transcript, interview, John Pollard, Apr. 30, 1975, 3–4, CWMA; interview, Charles P. McCurdy, Apr. 2, 1975, CWMA, 16–17; interview with John Hocutt, Aug. 6, 1976, 17–18.

5. Gosnell, "Kickoffs and Kickbacks," 17–24.

6. Ibid., 6–8, 11, 15–16; Minutes, WM Board of Visitors, Feb. 14, 1948; transcript of interview, R. Wayne Kernodle, Nov. 6, 1975, 70, Harold Fowler, Nov. 4, 1974, 25–27, and Nelson Marshall, Apr. 14, 1975, 6, CWMA.

7. Gosnell, "Kickoffs and Kickbacks," 25–30; Wilford Kale, Bob Moskowitz, and Charles M. Holloway, Goal to Goal: 100 Seasons of Football at William and Mary (Williamsburg, Va.: Botecourt Press, 1997), 138.

8. Kale, Moskowitz, and Holloway, Goal to Goal, 139–40; report of President Pomfret, minutes, Board of Visitors, Aug. 15, 1951.

9. Gosnell, "Kickoffs and Kickbacks," 38–43; account of Nelson Marshall, exhibit D, 8, CWMA; interview, Nelson Marshall, 9, CWMA; testimony of Al Vanderweghe, minutes, Board of Visitors, CWMA.

10. Transcripts of interviews with John E. Hocutt, Aug. 6, 1976, 17, CWMA; interview with John Pollard, 8–9, CWMA.

11. Richmond Times-Dispatch, Aug. 10, 12, 15, 1951; New York Times, Aug. 8–13, 1951; Gosnell, "Kickoffs and Kickbacks," 61–68.

12. Manifesto, College of William and Mary faculty, CWMA; interview, R. Wayne Kernodle, 59–61; New York Times, Sept. 20, 1951.

13. Gosnell, "Kickoffs and Kickbacks," 73–78; interviews, Harold Fowler, 33; John Hocutt, 22; Charles F. Marsh, Nov. 13, 1974, 42–43.

14. Kale, Moskowitz, and Holloway, Goal to Goal, 146–47, 298–302; interview, David Holmes, Department of Religion, College of William and Mary, Dec. 15, 1996. In the late 1970s a coalition of faculty, students, and alumni successfully protested the governor's attempts to restore big-time football by enlarging the stadium.

15. Charlottesville Daily Progress, Oct. 18, 1951; Cavalier Daily (University of Virginia), Oct. 12, 1951; Charlottesville Daily Progress, Oct. 26, Nov. 17, 21, 1951.

16. Minutes of the Board of Visitors, University of Virginia, 1947–56, 11, Nov. 14, 1952, Feb. 13, 1953, University of Virginia Archives (U Va Arch), Charlottesville.

17. Charles Rosen, Scandals of '51: How Gamblers Almost Killed College Basketball (New York: Holt, Rinehart and Winston, 1978); Randy Roberts and James Olson, Winning Is the Only Thing (Baltimore: Johns Hopkins University Press, 1989), 80–88; Murray Sperber, Onward to Victory: The Crises That Shaped College Sports (New York: Henry Holt, 1998) 294–357; New York Times, Nov. 10, 1951, Apr. 30, 1952.

18. NCAA, 1946 Yearbook, Proceedings of the Forty-First Convention, Jan. 7–8, 1947, 88–89.

19. Jester Pierce, "The Southern Conference" (Ph.D. diss., University of North Carolina, 1954), 122–28, 165; New York Times, Dec. 15, 1951; Paul Lawrence, Unsportsmanlike Conduct: The National Collegiate Athletic Association and the Business of College Football (New York: Praeger, 1987), 89–91.

20. *New York Times,* August 31, 1951; Work Papers for the Special Committee on Athletic Policy of the American Council on Education, Nov. 19–20, 1951, John Hannah Papers, Michigan State University Archives and Historical Collections, East Lansing.

21. Donald M. Stewart, "The Politics of Higher Education and Public Policy: A Study of the American Council on Education" (Ph.D. diss., Harvard University, 1975), 36–37.

22. *New York Times,* Nov. 16, 1951; First Meeting, Special Committee on Athletic Policy of the American Council of Education, Nov. 19, 20, 1951, John Hannah Papers, Archives and Historical Collections, Michigan State University (MSUAHC), East Lansing; Second Meeting of the Special Committee, Dec. 12, 13, 1951, Hannah Papers, MSUAHC.

23. Charles W. Bachman, "The Athletic Side of John Hannah," C. W. Bachman Papers, MSUAHC; Beth J. Shapiro, "John Hannah and the Growth of Big-Time Athletics at Michigan State University," *Journal of Sport History* 10, no. 3 (Winter 1983): 26–40.

24. Bachman, "Athletic Side of John Hannah," 1–3.

25. Ibid., 4.

26. Ibid., 7–8; Shapiro, "John Hannah," 26–40, 36.

27. *New York Times,* Nov. 10, 11, 1951; First Meeting, Special Committee, Nov. 19–20, 1951, Hannah Papers, MSUAHC; Shapiro, "John Hannah," 33.

28. Work Papers for the Special Committee, Nov. 19–20, 1951, John Hannah Papers, MSUAHC.

29. Second Meeting, Special Committee on Athletic Policy of the American Council on Education, Dec. 12–13, 1951, John Hannah Papers, MSUAHC.

30. Ibid.

31. Ibid.

32. *New York Times,* Feb. 17, 1951; Report, Special Committee on Athletic Policy of the American Council on Education,

Feb. 16, 1952, John Hannah Papers, MSUAHC.

33. Ibid.

34. NCAA, "Comparison [between ACE Special Committee and the NCAA Regulations]," A. Whitney Griswold Papers, Yale University Archives (YUA), New Haven, CT; Sperber, *Onward to Victory,* 360–62; Ronald A. Smith, "Notre Dame Chooses Commercial TV," MS, 7.

35. Report, Special Committee, Hannah Papers, MSUAHC; *New York Times,* Jan. 7, 1951; NCAA, "Comparison," [between ACE Special Committee and the NCAA Regulations], Griswold Papers, YUA.

36. Report, Special Committee, Hannah Papers, MSUAHC; *New York Times,* Jan. 7, 1951.

37. *New York Times,* Feb. 28 1952; Plans of the North Central Association, memo to Members of the Special Committee on Athletic Policy of the American Council on Education, Griswold Papers, YUA.

38. Louis G. Geiger, *Voluntary Accreditation: A History of the North Central Association, 1945-1970* (Chicago: North Central Association, 1970), vii–viii, 189.

39. Ibid., 35–36; Otto Hughes, "The Recruitment of Athletes," *North Central Association Quarterly* 28, no. 2 (October 1953): 227.

40. Ibid., 298; Plans of the North Central Association, Memo, ACE Special Committee, Griswold Papers, YUA; Final Report of the Committee on Intercollegiate and Interscholastic Athletics of the North Central Association of Colleges and Secondary Schools, Feb. 1, 1952, Hannah Papers, MSUAHC.

41. *New York Times,* Jan. 8, 11, 1952; NCAA, "Comparison [between ACE Special Committee and the NCAA Regulations]," Griswold Papers, YUA; *NCAA, 1952-1953 Yearbook.*

42. Sperber, *Onward to Victory,* 373–76; ACE, Work Papers for Nov. 19–20, 1951 meeting, Hannah Papers, MSUAHC; Minutes, Second Meeting, Special

Committee, Dec. 12–13, 1951, Hannah Papers, MSUAHC; *New York Times,* Jan. 8, 1952.

43. *New York Times,* Aug. 31, 1951; NCAA, "Comparison," Griswold Papers, YUA.

44. Sperber, *Onward to Victory,* 373–76; Minutes of the First Meeting, Special Committee, Nov. 19–20, 1951, Hannah Papers, MSUAHC.

45. *New York Times,* Jan. 11, 1952.

46. *New York Times,* Feb. 17, 1952.

47. *New York Times,* Jan. 11, Feb. 20, Mar. 5, 1952.

48. *New York Times,* Mar. 23, Apr. 6, 1952.

49. Business Session, Jan. 9, 1953, *NCAA, 1952-1953 Yearbook,* 246.

50. ACE, Work Papers for Nov. 19–20, 1951, meeting, Hannah Papers, MSUAHC.

CHAPTER THIRTEEN
De-emphasis or Demise

1. *New York Times,* Dec. 18, 1947, Dec. 10, 1948, Dec. 17, 1949.

2. *New York Times,* Dec. 9, 1940, Dec. 30, 1945, Dec. 30, 1946, Nov. 3, 1949, Dec. 24, 1950.

3. Donald Edward Parente, "A History of Television and Sports" (Ph.D. diss., University of Illinois, 1974), 56.

4. *New York Times,* Aug. 31, 1951, Feb. 2, 1952.

5. *New York Times,* Mar. 23, 1951; James Whalen Sr., *Gridiron Greats Now Gone: The Heyday of 19 Former Consensus Top-20 Programs* (Jefferson, NC: McFarland, 1991), 181–206.

6. Hunter Guthrie, "No More Football for Us," *Saturday Evening Post,* Oct. 13, 1951, 117 ff.

7. Ibid.

8. Whalen, *Gridiron Greats,* 114, 131, 238, 284, 310–11.

9. G. F. Wilson Shaffer, *Recreation and Athletics at Johns Hopkins: A One-Hundred Year History* (Baltimore, MD: Johns Hopkins University Press, 1977), 33–47.

10. Ibid.; Alexander Guerry, *Sewanee's Fu-*
ture Football Policy: A Statement before the Students of the University of the South, Apr. 8, 1938, Archives, University of the South at Sewanee, "A Sports History of the University of the South, 1875-1948," *Sewanee Alumni News* 15 (Feb. 1949); *Sewanee Purple* (University of the South at Sewanee), Dec. 5, 1940; John Tunis, "What Price Football?" *American Mercury,* October 1939, 2–4; John S. Watterson, "The Occidental Traveler: Frank Aydelotte and the Threat to Football Reform at Swarthmore" (paper delivered at North American Society of Sport History [NASSH], Pennsylvania State University, May 23, 1999).

11. Spright Dowell, *A History of Mercer University, 1883-1953,* (Macon, GA: Mercer University Press, 1958), 299–300, 311, 343–44; Whalen, *Gridiron Greats,* 22; *New York Times,* Oct. 25, 26, 29, 1949.

12. John R. Thelin, *The Cultivation of Ivy: A Saga of College in America* (Cambridge, MA: Shenkman Publishing), 1976), 27–32; *New York Times,* Dec. 3, 4, 5, 15, 16, 1936.

13. James B. Conant to William Bingham, Jan. 17, 1939, James B. Conant Papers, Harvard University Archives (HUA), Cambridge, MA; Charles Seymour to Harold Dodds, Jan. 10, 1941, Charles Seymour Papers, Yale University Archives (YUA), New Haven, CT.

14. Charles Grutzner, "Pennsylvania Ban Seen by the Ivy League," *New York Times,* Mar. 22, 1951; David Goldberg, "What Price Victory? What Price Honor? Pennsylvania and the Formation of the Ivy League, 1950–1952" (Honor's thesis, University of Pennsylvania, 1986), 10–12.

15. Cabell Phillips, "With Stassen on the Hustings," *New York Times Magazine,* Apr. 9, 1948, 12 ff.; Leo Riordan, "Football Blues Hit Penn," *Saturday Evening Post,* Nov. 2, 1953, 25, 95–98.

16. Riordan, "Football Blues Hit Penn," 25, 95–98.

17. Papers of the Office of the President, 1950–55, University of Pennsylvania Archives, Philadelphia; *New York Times,* Dec. 17, 1949; *Newsweek,* Aug. 21, 1950, 82; *New York Times,* Aug. 8, 1950.

18. David Goldberg, "What Price Victory?" 1–4; *Boston Daily Globe,* Nov. 30, 1949; Ivy Group Agreements, Feb.19, 1952, Griswold Papers, YUA, 1986, 10–12.

19. Charles Kutzner, "Pennsylvania Ban Seen by Ivy League," *New York Times,* Dec. 2, 4, 1949, Mar. 22, 1951.

20. Riordan, "Football Blues Hit Penn," 25, 95–98.

21. James B. Herstberg, *James B. Conant: Harvard to Hiroshima and the Making of the Nuclear Age* (New York: Alfred A. Knopf, 1993), 638–39; Diaries, James Conant, Feb. 8, 9, 10, 15, 19, 24, 1951; Griswold to Robert Hall, Griswold Papers, YUA; *New York Times,* Dec. 3, 1950, Dec.4, 1951. The reports of Bingham's firing leaked to the press before he was told, creating an embarrassing situation for Conant.

22. Harold Knaese, "What's the Matter with Harvard Football?" ca. 1950; Austin Lake, "Harvard Is the Victim of Its Own Football Ethics," *Boston American,* ca. 1950, James B. Conant Papers, Harvard University Archives (HUA), Cambridge, MA.

23. To Active and Inactive Members of the Varsity Club, June 6, 1951, A. Whitney Griswold Papers, Yale University Archives, New Haven, CT; *New York Times,* Mar. 14, 1950.

24. To Active and Inactive Members of the Varsity Club, June 6, 1951, A. Whitney Griswold Papers, YUA.

25. Herstberg, *James B. Conant,* 606–37.

26. Goldberg, "What Price Victory?" 23.

27. *New York Times,* June 20, 1951; Grayson Kirk to Harold Stassen, Oct. 10, 1952, University of Pennsylvania Archives (U Pa Arch), Philadelphia, PA. Columbia did play Penn in 1952, while Stassen and Murray persisted in opposing the NCAA television ban.

28. *New York Times,* July 20, 1951; Riordan, "Football Blues Hit Penn," 25, 95–98.

29. Conant to Griswold, Sept. 27, 1951, Conant Papers, HUA, Cambridge, MA.

30. Griswold to Conant, Nov. 14, 1951, Griswold Papers, YUA; *New York Times,* Feb. 19, 1952; Arthur Daly, "Sports in the Times," July 11, 1952; *Daily Pennsylva-nian* (University of Pennsylvania), Mar. 12, 1953. Only Princeton and Cornell reportedly supported spring practice.

31. *New York Times,* Nov. 12, 13, 1951; Griswold to Conant, Nov. 14, 1951, Griswold Papers, YUA; Ivy Group Agreement, Feb. 19, 1952, Griswold Papers, YUA.

32. Goldberg, "What Price Victory?" 57–58; Riordan, "Football Blues Hit Penn," 98; *New York Times,* Feb. 19, 1952. The Ivy Group agreements in February were voted on as a single package.

33. Riordan, "Football Blues Hit Penn," 96.

34. *New York Times,* Feb. 19, 1952; Ivy Group Agreements, Feb. 19, 1952, Griswold Papers, YUA.

35. Riordan, "Football Blues Hit Penn," 98.

36. Ibid.; Goldberg, "What Price Victory?" 60.

37. McGeorge Bundy to Nathan Pusey, Jan. 14, 1954, Pusey Papers, HUA; *New York Times,* Feb. 17, 1954; Ivy Group Agreements, Feb. 16, 1954, Pusey Papers, HUA.

38. First Meeting, Special Committee on Athletic Policy of the American Council of Education, Nov. 19, 20, 1951, John Hannah Papers, Archives and Historical Collections, Michigan State University, East Lansing.

39. Norris J. Coy to Millis, Dec. 20, 1949, Student Affairs, Athletics, Case Western Reserve University Archives (SA, Ath, CWRU Arch), Cleveland, OH; Elmer Hutchisson (acting president, Case Institute of Technology) to Millis, Nov. 14, 1950, SA, Ath, CWRU Arch.

40. Raymond Walters to John S. Millis, Jan. 7, 1953; Millis to Walters, Feb. 24, 1953, SA, Ath, CWRU Arch.

41. Norris J. Coy to Millis, Dec. 20, 1949, SA, Ath, CWRU Arch; Elmer Hutchisson (Acting President, Case Institute of Technology) to Millis, Nov. 14, 1950, SA, Ath, CWRU Arch.

42. Arvel Erickson, Memorandum and Recommendations, Dec. 14, 1953, SA, Ath, CWRU Arch.

43. C. H. Cramer, *Case Western Reserve: A History of the University, 1826-1976* (Boston: Little, Brown, 1976), 175; *Reserve Tribune* (Western Reserve University), Jan. 14, 1954.

44. Questions Most Often Asked Concerning the PAC, Nov. 18, 1963, SA, Ath, CWRU Arch; "New Presidents' Conference Tries Something Old: Simon Pure Athletics," *Toledo Blade,* Jan. 23, 1955; Presidents' Athletic Conference [amended version], Dec. 17, 1954, SA, Ath, CWRU Arch.

45. Memorandum for the file, Presidents' Athletic Conference, Sept. 17, 1956, CWRU Archives; Eastern Michigan University, Questions Most Often Asked Concerning the PAC, Nov. 18, 1963, SA, Ath, CWRU Arch; Clarence B. Hilberry, A Report on the Progress of Intercollegiate Athletics and Introduction to Sports at Wayne University, Jan. 8, 1954, SA, Ath, CWRU Arch; [Clarence B. Hilberry] Memorandum, Wayne State University to the Four Presidents, Mar. 11, 1963, SA, Ath, CWRU Arch.

46. [Clarence B. Hilberry], memo, Wayne State University to the Four Presidents, Mar. 11, 1963, SA, Ath, CWRU Arch.

CHAPTER FOURTEEN The Flight from Disorder

1. *New York Times,* Oct. 1, 15, 1939; Ronald A. Smith, "Sports and the New Medium of Football," MS, 5.

2. *New York Times,* Dec. 17, 1949; Attendance figures, 1949-50, TV II, Office of the President, 1950-55, University of Pennsylvania Archives, Philadelphia; *NCAA, The Nineteen-Fifty Yearbook,* NORC Statistical Summary, 147-49.

3. Benjamin Rader, *In its Own Image: How Television Transformed Sports* (New York: Free Press, 1984), 86; *New York Times,* Apr. 17, 1950.

4. *NCAA, 1950-1951 Yearbook,* Proceedings of the Forty-Fifth Annual Convention, Jan. 11-13, 1951, 147-49.

5. Murray Sperber, *Onward to Victory: The Crises That Shaped College Sports* (New York: Henry Holt, 1998), 384; Ronald A. Smith, "Penn Challenges the NCAA and Ivy League," MS, 9.

6. *NCAA, the 1950-1951 Yearbook,* 147-49.

7. Ibid., 205.

8. Ibid., 203-7.

9. Council at Chicago, Mar. 1-2, 1951, *NCAA, 1951-1952 Yearbook;* Sperber, *Onward to Victory,* 404-6. Sperber has by far the best description of subscription and theater TV.

10. *NCAA, 1951-1952 Yearbook,* Proceedings of the Forty-Sixth Annual Convention, Jan. 10-12, 1952, 163-69.

11. Ronald A. Smith, "Penn Challenges the NCAA and Ivy League," MS, 2-3, 9.

12. Ibid., 4; *New York Times,* June 12, 1951.

13. *New York Times,* June 7, 8, 9, 10, 11, 12, 13, 1951; "Sports vs. TV," *Newsweek,* June 25, 1951, 52; Sperber, *Onward to Victory,* 384; Smith, "Penn Challenges the NCAA and the Ivy League," 5.

14. *New York Times,* July 20, 1951; David L. Goldberg, "What Price Victory? What Price Honor? Pennsylvania and the Formation of the Ivy League, 1950-1952" (Honor's thesis, University of Pennsylvania, 1986), 51-52.

15. *New York Times,* Nov. 7, 9, 10, 1951.

16. *New York Times,* Nov. 22, 23, 1951; *Louisville Courier-Journal,* Nov. 22, 23, 24, 1951.

17. Paul R. Lawrence, *Unsportsmanlike Conduct: The National Collegiate Athletic Association and the Business of College Athletics* (New York: Praeger, 1987), 82.

18. Donald Edward Parente, "A History of Television and Sports" (Ph.D. diss., University of Illinois, 1974), 58-62.

19. *NCAA, 1951-1952 Yearbook,* 162–70.

20. *NCAA, 1952-1953 Yearbook,* Proceedings of the Forty-Eighth Annual Convention, Jan. 9–11, 1953, 167–74; Ronald A. Smith, "Regional Conferences Challenge a National Policy," MS, 3.

21. *New York Times,* May 9, 1952.

22. *NCAA, 1951-1952 Yearbook,* 167–68.

23. *NCAA, 1954-1955 Yearbook,* Proceedings of the Fiftieth Annual Convention, Jan. 7–9 1955, 207–12; *New York Times,* Jan. 19, 1953, Mar. 15, 1953.

24. *NCAA, 1954-1955 Yearbook,* 201–9.

25. *New York Times,* Mar. 6, 7, Apr. 16, 22, 24, 1954, Jan. 28, Mar. 3, 1955; *NCAA, Yearbook 1954-1955,* 189–212, 287–98; Smith, "Regional Conferences Challenge a National Policy," MS, 9.

26. NCAA Television Program Financial Report, Nov. 6, 1974; Walter Byers Papers, NCAA Headquarters, Mission, KS.

27. Manning H. Patillo, "Athletics in Some of the Better Colleges and Universities," *North Central* 27, no. 4 (Apr. 1952): 332–33.

28. Louis G. Geiger, *Voluntary Accreditation: A History of the North Central Association, 1945-1970* (Chicago: North Central Association, 1970), 35–36; James Edmonson, "New Athletic Perspectives," *North Central* 27, no. 3 (January 1952): 297–302.

29. *New York Times,* Mar. 26, 27, Apr. 5, 7, 1953; Geiger, Voluntary Accreditation, 36–38; *NCAA Yearbook, 1953-1954,*123; George Lynn Cross, *Presidents Can't Punt: The OU Football Tradition* (Norman: University of Oklahoma Press, 1968), 173–76.

30. Cross, *Presidents Can't Punt,* 197–201.

31. Ibid., 145–46.

32. Ibid., 154–58; *New York Times,* Mar. 20, 1951.

33. Cross, *Presidents Can't Punt,* 197–201.

34. Ibid., 200.

35. *New York Times,* Apr. 25, 28, June 13, 28, 1953; Geiger, *Voluntary Accreditation,* 37–38.

36. *NCAA, 1953-1954 Yearbook,* 124–25.

37. *NCAA, 1955-1956 Yearbook,* Proceedings of Fifty-First Annual Convention, Jan. 10–12, 1956, 223–27.

38. Charles Grutzner, "Colleges Vary Widely on Methods to Stop Admitted Athletic Evils," *New York Times,* Mar. 23, 1951.

39. Ibid.

40. Ibid.

41. John Thelin, *Games Colleges Play: Scandal and Reform in Intercollegiate Athletics* (Baltimore: Johns Hopkins University Press, 1995), 150–51.

42. Manuel P. Servin and Iris H. Wilson, *Southern California and Its University: A History of USC, 1880-1964* (Los Angeles: Ward-Ritchie Press, 1969), 97–118, 166–83; Thelin, *Games Colleges Play,* 83–87, 142–45.

43. Thelin, *Games Colleges Play,* 130–33; Walter Byers, *Unsportsmanlike Conduct: Exploiting College Athletes* (Ann Arbor: University of Michigan Press, 1995), 112–17.

44. Ronnie Knox with Melvin Durslag, "College Football Is Pro Football," *Collier's,* Oct. 12, 1956, 34–37; Tim Cohane, "College Football's Greatest Folly: The Curious Case of Ronnie Knox, UCLA Halfback," *Look,* Nov. 15, 1955, 141–47; Harvey Knox, "Why Ronnie Knox Quit California," *Sports Illustrated,* Sept. 6, 1954, 33–35; Victor O. Schmidt to all members of the conference, June 21, 1956, 12–18, Pacific Coast Intercollegiate Athletic Conference, Special Collections, University of Oregon Libraries, Eugene, OR (PCIAC, SC, UOL); Victor Schmidt, interview with Lynn Waldorf (U Cal coach), June 16, 1956, Conference Letters, Pacific Coast Intercollegiate Athletic Conference, Manuscripts and Archives, University of Washington Libraries (PCIAC, M&A, UWL), Seattle.

45. Knox with Durslag, "College Football," 36.

46. Ibid.

47. Ibid.

48. Ibid.

49. Ibid., 37. Ronnie Knox, after being de-

clared ineligible and going to Canada to play, got into a dispute with his professional career and left football in late September 1956.

50. Report of Faculty Athletic Committee to Executive Committee, Jan. 1956, University of Washington Presidents, PCIAC, M&A, UWL; memo, Henry Schmitz (president of Washington), July 20, 1956, M&A, UWL; Cohane, "Inside the West Coast Scandal," 72; *New York Times,* May 7, 1956.

51. Donald Wollett to Henry Schmitz, June 16, 1956, 16–17, M&A, UW; Byers, *Unsportsmanlike Conduct,* 111–16; *New York Times,* Dec. 6, 14, June 4, 1957; *New York Times,* Aug. 9, 1958.

52. *New York Times,* July 2, 9, 1956; Cohane, "Inside the West Coast Scandal," 72; Thelin, *Games Colleges Play,* 136–37.

53. *New York Times,* May 20, 22, 23, July 9, 10, 18, Aug. 22, 1956; Cohane, "Inside the West Coast Scandal," 72; Thelin, *Games Colleges Play,* 136–37; Tobin, "The Pacific Coast Conference Scandal and the Los Angeles Press" (Master's thesis, UCLA, 1959), 55–76.

54. Melvin Durslag, "Throw Them Out Please," n.d. [1956], *Los Angeles Examiner,* PCIAC, M&A, UWL; Tobin, "Pacific Coast Scandal," 98–102.

55. *New York Times,* Aug. 1, Dec. 5, 1956, Nov. 10, Dec. 6, 7, 1957.

56. Government Efficiency and Economy Subcommittee, Hearing on Proposed California Intercollegiate Athletic Commission Special Collections, University of Oregon Library (SC, UOL), Eugene, OR. Sept. 24, 1957; *New York Times,* Sept. 25, Dec. 11, 1957.

57. *New York Times,* Dec. 14, 18, 20, 1957, Aug. 9, 1958.

58. *NCAA, 1956-1957 Yearbook,* 281–85, *New York Times,* Aug. 22, 29, 1956.

59. *NCAA, 1957-1958 Yearbook,* 200–210.

60. Ibid.

CHAPTER FIFTEEN The Professional Paradigm

1. E. Selby, "Big Dollar in Pro Football," *Readers Digest,* November 1966, 111–15; *New York Times,* June 10, 1966.

2. *NCAA, 1954-55 Yearbook,* Proceedings of the Fiftieth Annual Convention, Jan. 7–9, 1955, 202.

3. Vince Lombardi with Tim Cohane, "Why the Pros Play Better Football," *Look,* Oct. 24, 1961, 107–10.

4. *New York Times,* Aug. 3, 1963; July 24, Dec. 22, 1976.

5. Ibid., Dec. 30, 1965, June 7, 1966.

6. Ibid.

7. *NCAA, 1954-1955 Yearbook,* Jan. 5, 1955, 159.

8. Jack Star and Clark Mollenhoff, "Exclusive: The Big Ten's Secret Report," *Look,* Oct. 30, 1956, 34–38; Report of a Special Committee, 20–22, Athletics, J. Roscoe Miller Papers, Northwestern University Archives (NUA), Evanston, IL.

9. Ibid. The numbering of the committee's points differs from those used by the authors in the report.

10. Allen Jackson, "Too Much Football," *Atlantic,* September 1951, 27–38.

11. *New York Times,* Jan. 2, 6, 1926, Oct. 10, 1927; John R. Thelin, *Games Colleges Play: Scandal and Reform in Intercollegiate Athletics* (Baltimore: Johns Hopkins University Press, 1994), 77–78.

12. Bertram Wyatt-Brown, *Southern Honor: Ethics and Behavior in the Old South* (New York: Oxford University Press, 1982); Elliott J. Gorn, "'Gouge and Bite, Pull Hair and Scratch': The Social Significance of Fighting in the Southern Backcountry," *American Historical Review* 90 (Feb. 1985): 18–43.

13. Frank Graham Jr., "The Story of a College Football Fix: A Shocking Report of How Wally Butts and 'Bear' Bryant Rigged a Game," *Saturday Evening Post,* Mar. 23, 1963, 80–83; Mickey Herskowitz, *Bear: The Hard Life and Good*

Times of Alabama's Coach Bear Bryant (Boston: Little, Brown, 1974), 217–26.

14. James Kirby, *Fumble: Bear Bryant, Wally Butts, and the Great College Football Scandal* (New York: Harcourt Brace Jovanovich, 1986), 50–53, 55–56.

15. *New York Times,* Jan. 15, Apr. 2, 3, 8, 1964; Kirby, *Fumble,* 26–30, 52.

16. Kirby, *Fumble,* 19–33; Graham, "Story of a Football Fix," 83.

17. Kirby, *Fumble,* 12–13.

18. Ibid., 1–3, 8–10.

19. Furman Bisher, "College Football Is Going Berserk," *Saturday Evening Post,* Oct. 20, 1962, 20–21; Paul W. Bryant and John Underwood, *Bear, The Hard Life of Alabama's Coach Bryant* (Boston: Little, Brown, 1974), 208–16.

20. *New York Times,* Mar. 30, 1963; Kirby, *Fumble,* 26–28, 40, 49.

21. Kirby, *Fumble,* 31, 34, 125, 139–41.

22. *New York Times,* Aug. 9, 10, 11, 13, 1963, Jan. 15, 16, 21, 1964; Kirby, *Fumble,* 117–19; Herskowitz, *Legend of Bear Bryant,* 129–42. Herskowitz, who doubts the veracity of the fix story, relates that Bryant met with Attorney General Robert Kennedy immediately after the *Post* story appeared, and Kennedy's belief in Bryant's innocence might explain his aggressive, even belligerent, testimony at the Butts's trial.

23. Kirby, *Fumble,* 149–88; Bryant, *Bear,* 219–36; *New York Times,* Feb. 5, 1964.

24. Kirby, *Fumble,* 12, 32, 140, 208, 322.

25. Ibid., 141–43, 150–64; *New York Times,* Mar. 21, 1963.

26. *New York Times,* June 13, 1967.

27. Kirby, *Fumble,* 74–75, 198, 226–27; *New York Times,* Mar. 21, 1963.

28. Kirby, *Fumble,* 72; *New York Times,* Apr. 6, 1963.

29. *New York Times,* Feb. 23, Mar. 19, 20, 22, 23, 1967; Thelin, *Games Colleges Play,* 161–62; memo, David D. Henry to Intercollegiate Conference presidents, Mar. 7, 1967, Miller Papers, NUA; J. Roscoe Miller to Ward L. Quaal, Mar. 24, 1967,

Miller Papers, NUA; Dan Jenkins, "Fighting Illini: Slush Fun for Football and Basketball Players at the University of Illinois," *Sports Illustrated,* Mar. 6, 1967, 16–19.

30. *New York Times,* Mar. 22, 23, 1967; Thelin, *Games Colleges Play,* 161–62.

31. Annual Report of the Registrar, 1968–69, Ohio State University Archives, Columbus, OH, and University of Wisconsin Archives, Madison, WI.

32. *New York Times,* Nov. 29, 1961; Oct. 10, 1962; George R. Hanford, *An Inquiry into the Need for and Feasibility of a National Study of Intercollegiate Athletics* (Washington, DC: American Council on Education, 1974), 32–34.

33. Ronald A. Smith, "Roone Arledge and the Influence of ABC-TV," MS, 9–10; *New York Times,* Nov. 20, 21, 22, 1966; "Game of to the Century," *Newsweek,* Nov. 28, 1963, 68.

34. Department of Intercollegiate Athletics, Income and Expenditures, University of Maryland Archives, College Park; courtesy of the University of Indiana Archives, Bloomington.

35. *New York Times,* Jan. 3, 1971.

36. Ibid., Jan. 14, 1973; Gary Shaw, *Meat on the Hoof* (New York: St. Martin's Press, 1971); Dave Meggyesy, *Out of Their League* (Berkeley, CA: Ramparts Press, 1970), 61–95; Byers, *Unsportsmanlike Conduct,* 161–63; "'Meat on the Hoof,'" *Newsweek,* Jan. 8, 1972, 32.

37. David M. Nelson, *The Anatomy of the Game: Football, the Rules, and the Men Who Made the Game* (Newark: University of Delaware Press, 1994), 308–23; Walter Byers, *Unsportsmanlike Conduct: Exploiting College Athletes* (Ann Arbor: University of Michigan Press, 1995), 219–21.

38. *New York Times,* May 28, 1971, Feb. 23, 1972, Sept. 1, 1973.

39. *New York Times,* Jan. 11, 12, 14, 1971.

40. *New York Times,* Jan. 9, 1972.

41. Jack Falla, *NCAA: The Voice of College*

Sports (Mission, KS: NCAA, 1981), 229–30; *New York Times,* Feb. 20, 1972.

42. Falla, *NCAA,* 231–34; *New York Times,* Jan. 14, Aug. 7, 1973.

43. Report of a Special Committee, 20–22, Athletics, J. Roscoe Miller Papers, NUA.

44. Hanford, *An Inquiry,* 21–23.

CHAPTER SIXTEEN The Accidental Reform

1. *Newsweek,* Sept. 17, 1984, 11; Donald Spivey, "'End Jim Crow in Sports': The Protest at New York University, 1940–1941," *Journal of Sport History* 15, no. 3 (Winter 1988): 290–91; *Pittsburgh Courier,* Oct. 13, 27, 1923; *Minnesota Alumni Weekly,* Oct. 18, 1923; *Minnesota Daily,* Oct. 9, 1923. Spivey says that Trice was denied admittance to a St. Paul hospital.

2. John Behee, *Hail to the Victors! Black Athletes at the University of Michigan* (Ann Arbor, MI: privately printed, 1974), 24–29.

3. *New York Times,* Oct. 19, 1940; Donald Spivey, "'End Jim Crow in Sports,'" 282–303.

4. *Heights Daily News* (New York University), Oct. 11, 21, 1940. Despite his pro-southern attitudes, Chase hailed from Massachusetts.

5. *Heights Daily News* (New York University), Oct. 11, 21, 1940; Thomas J. Frasciano and Marilyn H. Pettit, *New York University and the City: An Illustrated History* (New York: Rutgers University Press, 1997), 178. Chase had been president of North Carolina from 1919 to 1930; *New York Times,* Oct. 10, 1937.

6. *Heights Daily News* (New York University), Oct. 21, 31, 1940.

7. *New York Times,* Oct. 19, 1940.

8. *Heights Daily News,* Oct. 21, 1940.

9. *New York Times,* Oct. 12, 1947, Oct. 5, 1997; *Charlottesville Daily Progress,* Oct. 22, 1951.

10. Robert W. Peterson, *Pigskin: The Early Years of Pro Football* (New York: Oxford University Press, 1997), 169–86.

11. Ibid.

12. *New York Times,* Oct. 24, 1948, Oct. 1, 1950.

13. Ibid., Nov. 6, 1946, Nov. 25, 1947, Nov. 24, 1948, Oct. 18, 1951; Peterson, *Pigskin,* 187–88.

14. *New York Times,* Oct. 22, 1951.

15. *New York Times,* Mar. 30, 1947

16. *Pittsburgh Courier,* Oct. 27, Nov. 3, 1951; *New York Times,* Oct. 23, 1951. The *Courier* had the three frames of the film on its sports page clearly showing the wanton assault.

17. *New York Times,* Nov. 22, 24, 28, 1951.

18. Charles H. Martin, "Integrating New Year's Day: The Racial Politics of College Bowl Games in the American South," *Journal of Sport History* 24, no. 3 (Fall 1997): 358–77.

19. *New York Times,* Dec. 1, 3, 1955; *Atlanta Constitution,* Dec. 3, 1955.

20. *Atlanta Constitution,* Dec. 3, 5, 1955; Martin, "Integrating New Year's Day," 370–71.

21. *Atlanta Constitution,* Dec. 4, 6, 7, 1955; *New York Times,* Dec. 4, 6, 7, 1955. Emory College students also burned the governor in effigy.

22. *New York Times,* Dec. 6, 11, 1955. The Student Council agreed to pay for the riot damages.

23. Ibid., Dec. 6, 1955.

24. *New York Times,* Jan. 2, 3, 1956; *Atlanta Constitution,* Jan. 1, 2, 1956; *New Orleans Picayune,* Jan. 2, 3, 1956; Martin, "Integrating New Year's Day," 370–72.

25. Martin, "Integrating New Year's Day," 371.

26. Ibid., 372; *New York Times,* July 3, 16, Oct. 16, 1955, May 26, 1959. The Supreme Court struck down the Louisiana law in 1958.

27. Richard Pennington, *Breaking the Ice: The Racial Integration of Southwest Conference Football* (Jefferson, NC: McFarland, 1952), 78–113. Two other pioneer black players in the SWC were Warren McVea of Houston and John Westbrook of Baylor.

28. *New York Times,* Apr. 13, 1963.

29. Ibid., Mar. 24, 1967, Aug. 29, 1969.

30. Rick Telander, *The Hundred Yard Lie: The Corruption of College Football and What We Can Do to Stop It* (New York: Fireside, 1989), 81–85; *New York Times,* May 7, 1970.

31. Arnold Hano, "The Black Rebel Who Whitelists the Olympics," *New York Times Magazine,* May 12, 1968, 26.

32. *New York Times,* May 10, 12, 19, 1968.

33. David Wiggins, "'The Future of College Athletics Is at Stake': Black Athletes and Racial Turmoil on Three Predominantly White University Campuses, 1968–1972," *Journal of Sport History* 15, no. 3 (Winter 1988): 305; *Spartan Daily* (San Jose State College), Nov. 13, 19, 22, Dec. 16, 1968; *New York Times,* Jan. 9, 1969; *NCAA, Convention Proceedings, 1969,* Proceedings, 99–105.

34. *The Black Fourteen,* videotape, Wyoming Public Television, Laramie, WY, 1989.

35. *Branding Iron* (University of Wyoming), Nov. 8, 1968, Oct. 3, 1969.

36. Ibid., Oct. 23, 1969; *Laramie Daily Boomerang,* Oct. 19, 1969.

37. *Black Fourteen* (videotape).

38. Ibid.

39. Ibid.

40. *Branding Iron* (University of Wyoming), Oct. 31, Nov. 7, 1969.

41. *New York Times,* Nov. 16, 1969; Wiggins, "Future of College Athletics Is at Stake," 316–33.

42. Wiggins, "Future of College Athletics Is at Stake," 311–16; *New York Times,* Aug. 25, 26, Sept. 20, 22, 23, 24, 27, 28, 30, 1970; Feb. 27, Mar. 6, 1969.

43. *New York Times,* Jan. 5, 29, 1969 (no evidence of racism was found); David Zang, "Personal Interview, Calvin Hill," *Journal of Sport History* 15, no. 3 (Winter 1988): 344–46.

44. *Wesleyan University Alumni News,* Nov. 1969, 2–4; *Wesleyan Argus,* Nov. 12, 1969; Wesleyan University, Office of Chancellor, Nov. 11, 1969, Wesleyan University

Archives; Alphonsus J. Mitchell, *The Harmony of Athletics: Sports at Wesleyan,* in Sequicentennial Papers, no. 6 (Middletown, CT: Wesleyan University, 1981), 5–7; interview with Peter Kosacopoulos, Feb. 8, 1996.

45. "Stung by a Swarm of Bs," *Sports Illustrated,* Nov. 26, 1979, 25; *New York Times,* Oct. 14, 15, 16, 18, Nov. 4, 1979.

46. *New York Times,* Oct. 15, 1980.

47. Ibid.

48. Ibid. At one point in the early 1980s five PAC-10 schools were on probation because of grade-altering violations.

49. Ibid. Southern California players became involved in a ticket-scalping scam, which led to more NCAA sanctions.

50. Ibid., Oct. 26, 1980.

51. Ibid.

52. *New York Times,* Feb. 7, 13, 1986; *Atlanta Constitution,* Feb. 13, 1986.

53. *New York Times,* Feb. 7, 13, 1986.

54. Ibid., Feb. 11, 13, 1986; *Atlanta Constitution,* Feb. 13, 1986.

CHAPTER SEVENTEEN The Revolt of the Pigskin Elect

1. *New York Times,* Jan. 7, 8, Nov. 16, 1974; *NCAA Annual Report, 1973-1974,* 58–59, 73, 115.

2. Walter Byers, *Unsportsmanlike Conduct: Exploiting College Athletes* (Ann Arbor: University of Michigan Press, 1995), 248–49.

3. *New York Times,* Jan. 9, 13, Feb. 13, 1972, Jan. 14, 16, Aug. 8, 1973, Jan. 9, 10, 1974.

4. *New York Times,* Aug. 8, 1973; Jack Falla, *NCAA: The Voice of College Sports* (Mission, KS: NCAA, 1981), 233–34; Mitchell Raiborn, *Revenues and Expenses of Intercollegiate Athletic Programs: Analysis of Financial Trends and Relationships* (Mission, KS: NCAA, 1974), 7–9.

5. "Saturday's Hard-Pressed Heroes," *Forbes,* Nov. 15, 1976, 77–80; *New York Times,* Jan. 19, 1974, Jan. 17, 1976, Feb. 24, 1976, May 26, 1976; Benjamin Rader, *American Sports: From the Age of Folk*

Games to the Age of Televised Sports
(Englewood Cliffs, NJ: Prentice-Hall,
1999), 313–14. The number of scholarships was reduced to ninety-five in 1978
and later to eighty-five.

6. Stephen Horn to Harold L. Enarson,
Feb. 22, 1974, Harold Enarson Papers,
Ohio State University Archives (OSU
Arch), Columbus.

7. *NCAA, Proceedings of the Third Special
Convention,* Jan. 14, 1976, 45.

8. Ibid.; Paul Lawrence, *Unsportsmanlike
Conduct: The National College Athletic
Association and the Business of College
Football* (New York: Praeger, 1987),
98–99.

9. Ibid.

10. Byers, *Unsportsmanlike Conduct,* 146.

11. Newspaper clippings, August 1975, Walter Byers Papers, NCAA Headquarters,
Indianapolis, IN.

12. History of the College Football Association, June 11, 1980, William S.
Banowsky Papers, University of Oklahoma Archives (U Ok Arch), Norman.

13. Ibid.

14. Minutes, Council of Ten, May 8, 1978,
Harold L. Enarson Papers, OSU Arch,
Columbus.

15. Background information comes from
various sources, some of whom have
known Byers, and also from Byers's
1995 autobiography, *Unsportsmanlike
Conduct.*

16. Ibid., 146.

17. *New York Times,* Jan. 13, 1978.

18. History of the CFA, June 11, 1980,
Banowsky Papers, U Ok Arch; *New York
Times,* May 26, 1976. Southeastern Con-
ference athletic directors opposed
NCAA limits on coaching staffs and
need-based scholarships.

19. Rev. Edmund P. Joyce, Speech at the
CFA, May 30, 1980, Banowsky Papers, U
Ok Arch.

20. Ibid.; *New York Times,* Jan. 4, 1978; John
Underwood, *The Death of an American
Game: Crisis in Football* (Boston: Little,
Brown, 1979).

21. Interview with Alan Williams, former
Virginia NCAA and CFA faculty representative, Apr. 11, 1999.

22. *New York Times,* Dec. 3, 1978; statement
by CFA on Title IX, Edmund Joyce Papers, Banowsky Papers, U Ok Arch;
Charles Neinas to Edmund Joyce, Apr.
2, 1981, Fred C. Davison Papers, University of Georgia Archives, Athens; Fred
C. Davison, Preliminary Hearing, Universities of Oklahoma and Georgia v.
NCAA, Ralph Beaird Papers, University
of Georgia Archives (U Ga Arch).

23. Charles M. Neinas, memo to CFA TV
Study Committee, Apr. 30, 1980,
Banowsky Papers, U Ok Arch; Report
of the CFA TV Committee, May 22,
1980, Banowsky Papers, U Ok Arch.

24. Report of CFA TV Committee, May 22,
1980, Banowsky Papers, U Ok Arch.

25. Byers, *Unsportsmanlike Conduct,* 255–57.

26. Ibid., 254–56; *NCAA, Annual Report,
1970–71,* 78.

27. Ibid.

28. Byers, *Unsportsmanlike Conduct,* 257,
265.

29. Profit figures courtesy of Georgia Athletic Association and Department of
Athletics, University of Oklahoma.

30. Ronald A. Smith, "The Cable Television
Dilemma—More May Be Less," MS,
8–12, University Park, PA.

31. Charles M. Neinas to CFA members,
Aug. 13, 1981, Central Administration,
President's Office, University of Colorado Archives, Boulder, CO; television
agreement between CFA and NBC,
Aug. 8, 1981, President's Office, University of Colorado Archives, Boulder, CO.

32. Questions and Answers on the National
Football Television Plan, July 9, 1984,
Chancellor's Central Files, University of
Nebraska Archives, Lincoln, NE; P.
Verveer to T. Hansen, Dec. 30, 1981,
Byers Papers, NCAA; Charles M.
Neinas to Fred Davison, July 1, 1981,
Davison Papers, U Ga Arch; Fred Davi-
son, memo, July 7, 1981, Banowsky Pa-
pers, U Ok Arch; Byers, *Unsportsman-*

like Conduct, 267–71; *New York Times,*
July 16, 21, 31, 1981.

33. Byers, *Unsportsmanlike Conduct,* 267–71;
New York Times, July 16, 21, 31, 1981.

34. Carl C. James to Big Eight Members,
Aug. 13, 1981, Banowsky Papers, U Ok
Arch; Dan Gibbens, memo to Big Eight
Commissioner and Faculty Representa-
tives, Aug. 30, 1981, Banowsky Papers, U
Ok Arch; *New York Times,* Aug. 22, 1981.

35. *New York Times,* Sept. 9, 19, 1981. A stay
order prevented the NCAA from retali-
ating against Oklahoma and Georgia.

36. Fred Davison to CEOs and Confer-
ences, July 7, 1981, Banowsky Papers;
Charles M. Neinas, memo, July 6, 1981,
Banowsky Papers, U Ok Arch; *New York
Times,* July 18, Sept. 9, 24, 1981.

37. *New York Times,* Sept. 9, 1981; "June
Trial Probable in Football Television
Litigation," Mar. 15, 1982; Daniel G.
Gibbens to William S. Banowsky, Sept.
10, 1981, Banowsky Papers, U Ok Arch;
Chuck Neinas to CFA members, Sept.
10, 1981, Banowsky Papers, U OK Arch.

38. Ronald A. Smith, "TV Property Rights
and a CFA Challenge to the NCAA,"
MS, chap. 22, University Park, PA.

39. Fred C. Davison, Preliminary Hearing,
University of Georgia and University of
Oklahoma versus NCAA, 1981, Beaird
Papers, U Ga Arch; Thomas G. Dyer,
*The University of Georgia: A Bicenten-
nial History, 1785-1985* (Athens: Univer-
sity of Georgia Press, 1985), 343–45.

40. Chuck Neinas to CFA, Sept. 16, 1982,
Banowsky Papers, U Ok Arch; Judge-
ment and Injunction, Sept. 14, 1982,
Byers Papers, NCAA; "Judge Burciaga
Gets Down to Business with College
Football," *Sports Illustrated,* Sept. 27,
1982.

41. *New York Times,* Sept. 17, 19, 23, 24, 1982.

42. *New York Times,* June 28, 1984.

43. *New York Times,* July 15, 1984; W. Taaffe,
"The Supreme Court's TV Ruling: Will
the Viewer Benefit Most?" *Sports Illustrated,* July 9, 1984, 9.

44. *New York Times,* June 28, July 15, 1984.

45. *New York Times,* July 4, 5, 6, 8, 11, 1984;
W. Taafe, "A Supremely Unsettling
Smorgasbord," *Sports Illustrated,* Sept.
5, 1984, 150–51.

46. *New York Times,* July 20, Aug. 26, 1984;
Don Canham to selected athletic direc-
tors, Nov. 29, 1984, Chancellor's Central
Files, University of Nebraska Archives
(U Neb Arch), Lincoln.

47. "Confidential" Charles M. Neinas to
Fred C. Davison, Feb. 21, 1983, Davison
Papers, U Ga Arch.

48. *New York Times,* Jan. 15, 1985.

49. Charles M. Neinas to CFA Television
Committee, Dec. 5, 1984, Chancellor's
Central Files, University of Nebraska
Archives, Lincoln; Bob Devaney to M.
Massengale, Dec. 14, 1984, U Neb Arch.
Neinas calculated the advertising rate
per minute at $225,000, the same as an
NFL playoff game and half of a Super
Bowl ad minute.

50. *New York Times,* Aug. 26, 1984; Don
Canham to selected athletic directors,
Nov. 29, 1984, Chancellor's Central
Files, U Neb Arch.

51. Byers, *Unsportsmanlike Conduct,*
287–88.

52. *New York Times,* Feb. 15, 16, 1990, Feb.
12, 1994, June 1, 1996.

53. Byers, *Unsportsmanlike Conduct,* 121,
254–58; *New York Times,* Jan. 20, 21, July
27, Aug. 16, 1982, Nov. 4, 1984; D. S.
Looney, "Jackie Hits the Jackpot," *Sports
Illustrated,* Feb. 1, 1982, 26–29.

54. *New York Times,* Jan. 21, 28, 1982; Apr. 6,
Dec. 13, 14, 1988; Sherrill resigned in
1988 over charges of illegal payments to
players.

55. *New York Times,* Mar. 14, 1986; *Atlanta
Constitution,* Mar. 14, 1986.

CHAPTER EIGHTEEN Sudden
Death at SMU

1. *The Bishops' Committee Report on
SMU—Report to Board of Trustees of
Southern Methodist University from the
Special Committee of Bishops of the*

South Central Jurisdiction of the United Methodist Church, Friday, June 19, 1987 (Dallas: United Methodist Church, 1987) (hereafter referred to as *Bishops' Report*), 18–20.

2. *New York Times*, Oct. 14, 1980, Apr. 24, Dec. 14, 1982; *New York Times*, Aug. 26, 31, Sept. 12, Nov. 27, 1984.

3. *New York Times*, Aug. 22, Nov. 23, 25, 27, 1982; Dec. 20, 22, 1982, Aug. 26, 1984, Feb. 16, Mar. 7, 1985.

4. *New York Times*, Sept. 8, 19, 20, 1980, May 2, 3, 7, 13, 14, 1987; Douglas Looney, "The Big Mess in the Big Ten," *Sports Illustrated*, May 22, 1981, 79–85.; Walter Byers, *Unsportsmanlike Conduct: Exploiting College Athletes* (Ann Arbor: University of Michigan Press, 1995), 186–90.

5. *New York Times*, Jan. 9, 10, 1984.

6. *Proceedings of the 80th Annual Convention*, Jan. 13–15, 1986, 131.

7. Marshall Terry, *"From High on the Hilltop . . .": A Brief History of SMU* (Dallas: Southern Methodist University, 1995), 1–12, 22; Mary Martha Hosford Thomas, *Southern Methodist University: Founding and Early Years* (Dallas: SMU Press, 1974), 85–87.

8. Thomas, *Southern Methodist University*, 85–89.

9. Ibid., 89–90.

10. David Whitford, *A Payroll to Meet: A Story of Greed, Corruption, and Football at SMU* (New York: Macmillan, 1989), 13–18.

11. *Bishops' Report*, 18–21; Whitford, *Payroll to Meet*, 43–44, 83–84. Edwin Cox was chairman of the trustees from 1976 to 1987.

12. Terry, *"From High on the Hilltop,"* 61–62; Whitford, *Payroll to Meet*, 77–80; *Bishops' Report*, 14; NCAA, *Annual Report, 1973-1974*, 140.

13. "It's Ninety-Five and Look Who's Alive," *Sports Illustrated*, Oct. 30, 1978, 32–34, 49.

14. *New York Times*, Mar. 9, 1987.

15. Byers, *Unsportsmanlike Conduct*, 35; Whitford, *Payroll to Meet*, 158–59; *Bishop's Report*, 20.

16. Whitford, *Payroll to Meet*, 92.

17. *Bishops' Report*, 15.

18. Byers, *Unsportsmanlike Conduct*, 35; Whitford, *Payroll to Meet*, 158–59; *Bishops' Report*, 20.

19. Whitford, *Payroll to Meet*, 60, 95–96, 100–103, 131–37; Terry, *"From High on the Hilltop,"* 62.

20. *Bishops' Report*, 18; Whitford, *Payroll to Meet*, 130.

21. Ibid.

22. *New York Times*, Mar. 9, 1987; Whitford, *Payroll to Meet*, 109, 126; *Bishops' Report*, 19.

23. *Bishops' Report*, 19–20; Whitford, *Payroll to Meet*, 136–37.

24. *Bishops' Report*, 21.

25. Ibid.; Whitford, *Payroll to Meet*, 157.

26. *New York Times*, June 23, 25, 1985; *Bishops' Report*, 26.

27. *Bishops' Report*, 14.

28. Ibid., 26.

29. Ibid., 27; *Daily Campus* (Southern Methodist University), Nov. 11, 1986.

30. *Bishops' Report*, 27; Whitford, *Payroll to Meet*, 159.

31. *Bishops' Report*, 27; Whitford, *Payroll to Meet*, 159–65; *Dallas Morning News*, Nov. 13, 1986.

32. *Dallas Morning News*, Nov. 14, 1986.

33. Whitford, *Payroll to Meet,*, 159–65; *Dallas Morning News*, Nov. 13, 1986.

34. *Dallas Morning News*, Nov. 22, 1986; Whitford, *Payroll to Meet*, 169–75.

35. *Bishops' Report*, 30, 33; Whitford, *Payroll to Meet*, 180–82; *Dallas Morning News*, Mar. 25, 1987.

36. *Bishops' Report*, 32–33; Whitford, *Payroll to Meet*, 176–89; *Dallas Morning News*, Dec. 5, 1986.

37. *Dallas Times-Herald*, Mar. 8, 15, 17, 1987 (see references to "Ponygate"); *Bishops' Report*, 36–37; Whitford, *Payroll to Meet*, 179–83; *Dallas Morning News*, Nov. 26, 1987.

38. *Dallas Morning News,* Feb. 26, 1987; Whitford, *Payroll to Meet,* 207–8.

39. *Bishops' Report,* 37–38; Whitford, *Payroll to Meet,* 190–96; *Dallas Morning News,* Feb. 25, 1987; *Dallas Times-Herald,* Feb. 25 1987.

40. *Bishops' Report,*11, 39; *Dallas Morning News,* Mar. 4, 1987, June 20, 1987. Clements refused to name names but claimed that at least half the board of governors knew what was happening. See *New York Times,* Mar. 4, 1987, on "Clement Responds."

41. *Daily Campus* (Southern Methodist University), Mar. 4, 5, 1987.

42. Ibid., Mar. 5, 1987.

43. *Bishops' Report,* 4–11, 39–40.

44. "Scandal Stalls SMU's Climb to the Top," *Dallas Morning News,* Apr. 12, 1987; Applebone, "Is There Life after Football?" 73, 76, 78.

45. *New York Times,* Mar. 9, 1987.

46. Applebone, "Is There Life after Football?" 76, 88.

47. *New York Times,* Mar. 7, 1987.

48. *Bishops' Report,* 26; *Dallas Morning News,* Mar. 9, 15, 1987; Mar. 4, Apr. 20, June 18, 1987. The latter article lauded the "Rice Way," which "had made people sit up and take notice of the Owls."

49. G. Cartwright, "0.00 to Go," *Sports Illustrated,* Oct. 30, 1995, 72–78.

50. *USA Today,* Feb. 25, 1987; *Dallas Morning News,* Feb. 25, 1987.

51. Ibid.; courtesy of Southern Methodist University Sports Information.

52. Intro., *Reports of the Knight Foundation, Commission on Intercollegiate Athletics, March 1991-March 1993* (Charlotte, NC: Knight Foundation, 1993), viii–xi, 11.

53. *New York Times,* June 1, 2, 1987.

54. *New York Times,* Aug. 7, 11. 12, 1988.

55. *New York Times,* Feb. 14–18, 26, Apr. 14, June 10, 20, 21, 23, 26, Dec. 9, 10, 1989; Rick Telander and R. Sullivan, "You Reap What You Sow," *Sports Illustrated,* Feb. 27, 1989, 20–26.

56. *New York Times,* June 19, 1989, Aug. 5, Dec. 3, 1997.

57. Rick Reilly, "What Price Glory?" *Sports Illustrated,* Feb. 27, 1989, 32–34.

58. Intro., *Reports of the Knight Foundation, Commission on Intercollegiate Athletics, March 1991-March 1993* (Charlotte, NC: Knight Foundation, 1993), viii–xi, 11.

59. *New York Times,* Sept. 19, Oct. 17, Oct. 25, Dec. 28, 1995, Jan. 3, 4, 1996; Michael Farber, "Coach and Jury," *Sports Illustrated,* Sept. 25, 1995, 31–32; Jeff Benedict and Don Yager, *Pros and Cons: The Criminals Who Play in the NFL* (New York: Time Warner, 1998), 84–86, 100–102.

60. *Chronicle of Higher Education,* Dec. 18, 1998, Apr. 19, 1999; Gerry Callahan, "Dark Days at BC," *Sports Illustrated,* Nov. 18, 1996, 52–55; Murray Sperber, *Shake Down the Thunder: The Creation of Notre Dame Football* (New York: Henry Holt, 1993).

EPILOGUE   "The Great God Football"

1. Andrew Doyle, "'The Public Is All but Intoxicated on Football': Spright Dowell and the Politics of Football at Auburn, 1920–27" (paper presented at the North American Society for Sport History, Auburn, AL, May 25, 1996), 4–5, 12; Guy M. Lewis, "The American Intercollegiate Football Spectacle, 1869–1917" (Ph.D. diss., University of Maryland, 1964), 213.

2. *Montgomery Advertiser,* Oct. 13, 1927; Open Meeting of the Trustees, Oct. 14, 1927, 27, Dowell Papers, Auburn University Archives (AUA), Auburn, AL; *Montgomery Advertiser,* Oct.15, 1927; President's Report to the Board of Trustees, Nov. 5, 1927, 25–26, 32, Dowell Papers, AUA; [News] Release, Nov. 5, 1927, Dowell Papers, AUA.

3. *New York Times,* Oct. 7, 28, 30, 31, Nov. 3, 4, 15, Dec. 22, 23, 1991, Aug. 19, 1993;

Atlanta Constitution, Nov. 20, 1991;
Birmingham News, Oct. 3, 1991.

4. *New York Times,* Dec. 16, 18, 1992.

5. *New York Times,* Sept. 20, 1989, May 22, 1991.

6. Tom Englehardt, *The End of the Victory Culture: Cold War America and the Disillusioning of a Generation* (Amherst: University of Massachusetts Press, 1995).

7. Rick Telander, *The Hundred Yard Lie: The Corruption of College Football and What We Can Do to Stop It* (New York: Simon and Schuster, 1989); Walter Byers, *Unsportsmanlike Conduct: Exploiting College Athletes* (Ann Arbor: University of Michigan Press, 1995).

8. Letter of James Angell, minutes of the First Chicago Conference, Jan. 19, 1906, Michigan Historical Collections, Ann Arbor.

9. Courtesy of Nittany Lion Club, Pennsylvania State University and Athletic Public Relations; University of Virginia; courtesy of Mark Fletcher, Stadium Expansion Project, University of Virginia.

10. John R. Tunis, "More Pay for College Football Stars," *American Mercury* (Oct. 1936): 272.

Bibliographical Essay

The study of college football has many sources and few authorities. While people have written histories of great teams and players, few have asked why football has gained a prominent place within the colleges and how it has affected American society. Many historical studies have been laudatory and, while failing to look for the lawless underside of football, still contain a wealth of useful information. Those authors who have written careful studies of college athletics, however, have framed a picture not only of football's place in the broad evolution of college athletics and academic life but also of the problems that it has created for the institutions and the half-truths that it has perpetuated.

The serious researcher on early American football and athletics might easily begin by diving into the papers of Walter Camp, "the father of American football," which are located at Yale University Archives but are also available on microfilm. Fortunately for football researchers, Camp saved most of the letters written to him, much of his own correspondence, as well as maxims, newspaper columns, and drafts of football histories. Camp's remarkable career as a football rules maker and organizer emerge from this carefully indexed collection. In addition, the material creates a picture of football's early decades and the controversies that surrounded its development.

Collections on early athletics also exist at Harvard and other eastern institutions, often in the papers of athletic committees or in the papers of presidents such as Charles Eliot and his successors, A. Lawrence Lowell and James B. Conant. The minutes of the faculty athletic committee also shed light on the skeptical attitude of the Harvard faculty toward football. For the late 1890s the researcher should also look at the minutes of the faculty athletic committee at Columbia, where the faculty did play a role in reforming athletics following the experiment in big-time athletics in the late 1890s.

For other gridiron collections from the early period, the Amos Alonzo Stagg papers at the University of Chicago Special Collections have material paralleling the importance of the Camp papers and continuing long after the Camp era. Stagg saved almost everything, incoming and outgoing, including diagrams of his plays. In addition, his wife, Stella Stagg, compiled scrapbooks of newspaper articles beginning in the early 1890s, when she married the young coach, to the end of his full-time career at the College of the Pacific in the 1940s. Most of the articles for forty years came from the numerous Chicago papers, but not all concerned Stagg or athletic events. When controversies erupted, Stella Stagg included those articles as well, since her husband was often involved. The letters also build a profile of Stagg's relations with William Harper, Walter Camp, and other figures who played a role in big-time football.

None of the archives in the Big Ten or, more accurately, the historical Big Twelve, if one includes Chicago and Penn State, lack material on football and conference relations. Since the Big Ten dominated college football for several decades, the records past and near present deserve attention. One of the largest caches of correspondence and athletic documents is deposited in the Michigan Historical Collections at Ann Arbor; the James Angell papers provide a view of the reform movement of 1906. The James Smart Papers at Purdue provide a bird's-eye view of the future Big Ten's formation. Among the collections in the Big Ten, the Robert Hutchins papers at the University of Chicago have particular utility because they tell the story of the decline and fall of Chicago football, or, more precisely, of its final year. They allow the historian to decide if Hutchins was a true gridiron reformer or a short-term opportunist.

The NCAA's attempt to set standards and punish athletic offenders occurred nearly a half-century after it began; even so, the published proceedings from its earliest years provide a valuable source of information and perspectives. Following the first New York Conference in 1905, the organization held its annual meeting before the New Year. Even though the NCAA had little power, the discussions of the delegates provide helpful insights into the athletic concerns of the institutions, and their utility persists into the decades after the association became the cop on the athletic block. In the 1960s the NCAA divided the proceedings and the annual reports into separate publications. Taken together, the proceedings and yearbooks contain the raw materials of attempted football reforms as well as attempts to enlarge and preserve the scale of big-time football. More precisely, these NCAA publications provide insights into the problems in college football and into the attitudes of coaches, athletic directors, faculty athletic representatives, conference commissioners, presidents, and NCAA officials. Beginning in the 1950s, for example, the annual publications also catalogue the numerous penalties visited upon various institutions. In addition, at the new NCAA headquarters in Indianapolis the Walter Byers papers are a rich mine of information on matters such as television and investigations pertaining to college football from 1951 to 1987.

In the Far West football was for many years isolated from the mainstream. This isolation is documented in Roberta Park's "From Rugby to Football—and Back, 1906–1919: The University of California–Stanford University Response to the 'Football Crisis of 1905'" (*Journal of Sport History* [winter 1984]). Much material on West Coast college football in the following decades, however, lies fallow in the archives of the defunct Pacific Coast Intercollegiate Athletic Association (PCIAA), also known as the Pacific Coast Conference (PCC), which are housed in the University of Oregon Special Collections. The PCIAA collection contains much detailed information on the politics, scandals, and demise of the Pacific Coast Conference in the 1950s. The materials also provide a detailed history of Commissioner Victor Schmidt's valiant efforts to uphold the high conference standards in the face of growing scandals and venomous rivalries.

Almost everyone who has written about football has had to go to newspapers on microfilm, and for the 1890s and early 1900s they remain essential. Researchers who look for the story of football crises and reforms will find the New York, Boston, Philadelphia, and Chicago newspapers the most fecund source of information on games, injuries, reform, and public opinion. While the New York newspapers give the best picture of football in its early era, the *New York Times* stands out because it not only developed into a national newspaper but also has an index that reaches back into the 1800s. Similarly, college newspapers present an even closer look at events and attitudes on campus rivaling big-city dailies for news and views. Magazines such as the *Saturday Evening Post* and *Collier's* once functioned as sources of football opinion and information much as *Sports Illustrated* has done since the 1950s.

Many collections of writings and correspondence give intimate details about early football. Occasionally, published volumes of writings and correspondence have yielded up valuable material on football, especially if the subject happened to be a president of the United States. Arthur Link's sixty-nine-volume *Papers of Woodrow Wilson* (Princeton, NJ: Princeton University Press, 1966-94) contains valuable material on Wilson's role in football from his years as a young professor to the brink of his entry into national politics in 1910. A less extensive collection, the eight-volume *Letters of Theodore Roosevelt* (Cambridge: Harvard University Press, 1951), contains a number of letters from 1905, the year that Roosevelt became involved in football reform. Much of the nonpresidential material may also be found in the Theodore Roosevelt Collection in the Widener Library at Harvard University. A far more extensive collection, the Theodore Roosevelt Papers, in the Library of Congress and on microfilm, has more detailed material from November and December 1905.

The task of the serious gridiron researcher requires piercing the athletic veil that cloaks the activities of coaches, athletic directors, and alumni. One of the most valuable sources of information on athletic practices between the wars gathers dust on the shelves of countless libraries. The Carnegie Report of 1929, or, more precisely, *American College Athletics* by Howard Savage et al., contains a wealth of information on how colleges recruited and subsidized their athletes in an era in which the NCAA had no rules and in which the concept of strictly amateur athletics was challenged by varieties of subsidies. Except for George R. Hanford's report, *An Inquiry into the Need for and Feasibility of a National Study of Intercollegiate Athletics,* (Washington, DC: American Council on Education, 1974), most of the committee and commission reports contain little background material, nor do they come up with innovative conclusions or penetrating insights.

The best monograph on early college athletics—and, by definition, college football—remains Ronald A. Smith's *Sports and Freedom: The Rise of Big-Time College Athletics* (New York: Oxford University Press, 1988). Smith, who will soon publish a volume on TV and college sports, has spent much of his career tracking down the story of early college athletics, burrowing into college archives and immersing himself in college officials and athletic committee papers. His study ends at the football crisis of 1905. It demonstrates that big-time athletics, or college athletics, almost from the beginning, operated as a highly organized activity that caused scandals, transgressed the moral boundaries, and had as its guiding principle the maximizing of power and profit. One may disagree with parts of Smith's interpretation, but his thorough research poses a challenge for any historian of early American college athletics.

Much of Smith's work pertains to college football, including his editing of *Big-Time Football at Harvard, 1905: The Rise of Big-Time College Athletics* (Urbana: University of Illinois Press, 1994), Harvard coach Bill Reid's diary, written in the fall of 1905. Smith's edited volume not only shows how a major football coach prepared his team for the big games but also gives valuable insights into the Harvard-dominated reform movement that began in the fall of 1905 and in which Reid played a starring role.

The most valuable history of football's impact on a single institution, *Stagg's University: The Rise, Decline, and Fall of Football at the University of Chicago* (Urbana: University of Illinois Press, 1995), by Robin Lester, using the rich collections at the University of Chicago, presents a more human, sometimes unflattering portrait of the great coach Amos Alonzo Stagg. In addition to the collections at Chicago, Lester draws on a remarkable array of materials to present a carefully drawn picture of how an early coach and full-time athletic director manipulated the university to get his way and cut corners in order to make football a center of power on the Midway. Because Lester deals with so many topics, including the demise of football at Chicago after Stagg's departure, he has had to move out of a strictly chronological presentation. Together with the notes and appendices, *Stagg's University* presents a view of the rise of college football and its growing role in the university that should become a model for future historians and biographers if they are fortunate to have the wealth of material at their fingertips. This study drastically changes the heroic view of Stagg's life and role, which he embellished in his entertaining and informative but highly self-serving memoir, *Football* (New York: Longman's Green, 1927). Written with Wesley Winans Stout, Stagg's book became the archetype for many lesser sports autobiographies in later years.

Relatively few histories of athletics since the 1920s can claim to cover the full expanse of institutions and regions. Yet John R. Thelin's *Games Colleges Play: Scandal and Reform in College Athletics* (Baltimore: Johns Hopkins University Press, 1994), a remorselessly probing and critical study, covers much of this territory, and his bibliography remains a valuable guide to anyone studying big-time athletics since 1929. The theme of cheating by athletic departments and college administrations permeates this study—not just cheating in practice but cheating also in the ways colleges have represented college sports to the public. Thelin largely ignores issues outside of academia such as television or professional football, and he spends little time on the scandals of the 1980s, though he shows that he is aware of them. The book's primary strength derives not only from the relatively short time focus of his narrative (which extends largely from the 1950s to the 1980s) but also from its ability to penetrate the cant of big-time athletics. A narrower study by Paul R. Lawrence, *Unsportsmanlike Conduct: The National Collegiate Athletic Association and the Business of College Football* (New York: Praeger Publishers, 1987), portrays the NCAA as an economic cartel but also incorporates much valuable material on issues relating to college football, especially television. Jack Falla's official history of the NCAA sets forth the basic facts of the association's growth and change but takes a wholly uncritical position.

Many historians have treated the athletic history of one institution. Few have done it better than Murray Sperber, who has written using the Rockne Papers and presidential papers at Notre Dame. His book *Shake Down the Thunder: The Creation of Notre Dame Football* (New York: Henry Holt, 1993) does just that with the Rockne myth. This voluminous study presents the organizational genius as well as the half-truths behind Notre Dame football; it also shows Rockne's opportunism as well as the periodic opposition by Notre Dame presidents and faculty to his regime. In his study of the 1951 athletic upheaval, *Onward to Victory: The Crises That Shaped College Sports* (New York: Henry Holt, 1998), Sperber leans heavily on the official papers at Notre Dame as well as numerous public relations sources to paint a duplicitous picture of athletic politics, especially the NCAA and its allies. Historians might differ with Sperber about whether big-time sports might have gone toward a less subsidized, Ivy League model in 1952 and whether the NCAA misrepresented the threat of TV in the early 1950s. These athletic exposés extend the knowledge of what happened beneath the glitter and glamorous facade of big-time college sports but with a distinctly Notre Dame flavor.

One little-noticed volume that fills a major gap in the history of college football and also draws upon personal experience is *Anatomy of a Game: Football, the Rules, and the Men Who Made the Game* (Newark: University of Delaware Press, 1994), by David M. Nelson. As a member of the football rules committee for thirty-three years and twenty-nine as its secretary-editor, he rates in longevity of service as the Walter Camp of the modern era. Nelson played football at Michigan, coached at Delaware, and served as Delaware's athletic director. He clearly lays out the complex changes in the rules and has elaborate 150-page appendices that show the changes year by year. Unfortunately, Nelson died in 1991, before his book was completed; as a result, some of his documentation for the early period remains incomplete.

A more frankly personal memoir, by Walter Byers (with Charles Hamner), *Unsportsmanlike Conduct: The Exploitation of College Athletes* (Ann Arbor: University of Michigan Press, 1995), is full of history from his forty-five years as executive director of the NCAA. Like his papers at the NCAA, Byers's account of his athletic battles contains a great deal of useful information that points the researcher toward important events and issues. Like other memoirs, this highly readable, often opinionated book is colored by the personalities of his friends and adversaries, but the researcher on modern college athletics should read it carefully. The title, *Unsportsmanlike Conduct* (not to be confused with Paul Lawrence's study of the NCAA), has more to do with Byers's battles and the institutions that broke the rules or threatened NCAA policy, as opposed to exploiting college athletes, the subject of the final chapter.

One of the first historians to treat football as an activity of the colleges and their students, Frederick Rudolph, included a lively chapter on college football in his book *American College and University: A History* (New York: Random House, 1962). Rudolph based some of his material on scanty materials. As a result, the apocryphal story of Teddy Roosevelt's threat to ban football (because he saw Swarthmore's Bob Maxwell's bloody face after the Penn game) found its way into the study. Probably Rudolph picked up this story from David Reisman and Reuel Denny, who wrote a brief article, "Football: A Study in Cultural Diffusion" (*American Quarterly* 3 [1951]: 309–25), on the spread of football and incorporated this story in their narrative. Like Rudolph, they mainly had encyclopedias of sport and college histories as their sources, some of which proved misleading and erroneous.

In his Ph.D. dissertation "The American College Football Spectacle, 1869–1917" (University of Maryland, 1964) Guy M. Lewis put together the first history of college football which tried to show how colleges, athletics, newspapers, and gridiron crises fit together. Though his research has seldom appeared in published form, Lewis demonstrates a remarkable breadth of research from American football's origins in the 1870s to the end of the first reform era in 1917; it draws from a vast array of resources, but lack of organization makes it difficult to follow. Another dissertation that has received insufficient attention, Richard Borkowski's biography of Walter Camp, "Walter Camp's Life and Contributions to American Football" (Ed.D. diss., Temple University, 1979), contains a reservoir of valuable information on Camp's pivotal role in organizing football both at Yale and elsewhere, some of the material drawn from interviews with former associates of Camp. The title of Borkowski's work, Camp's "contributions," gives a clue to both the strengths and weaknesses of this work that provide extremely valuable details about Camp's remarkably prolific career as athlete, rules maker, virtual team advisor, athletic director, publicist, and much more but fails to examine critically enough the major character traits and controversies identified with Camp's career.

John Hammond Moore, in the 1960s, wrote the first article on the injury crisis of the 1890s and early 1900s for the short-lived *Smithsonian Magazine of History* in its fall 1967 issue. "Football's Ugly Decades, 1893–1913" remains eminently readable, a source of visual and periodical information, though it does not delve into the reform of football culture or explain the background of the movement for abolition which accompanied this flood of criticism. Unfortunately, neither Moore nor other historians of early football paid much attention to the second crisis of 1909, which proved to be far more than a footnote to what happened in 1905 and 1906. Guy Lewis, however, in one of his rare published works, wrote a useful if less colorful account, "Theodore Roosevelt's Role in the Football Crisis of 1905" (*Research Quarterly* [1969]).

To be sure, historians outside of academic life have written studies of football which told a story of its early development. One of the first authors, Parke H. Davis (*Football: The American Intercollegiate Game* (New York: Charles Scribner's, 1911), played football in the 1890s at Princeton, coached at Wisconsin, and belonged to the football rules committee in the reform period. Alexander M. Weyand, a former captain of the Army football team, wrote *The Saga of American Football* (New York: Macmillan, 1955), which takes football from the 1869 contest between Rutgers and Princeton to the 1950s. Succinct and fast-paced, Weyand's history masterfully depicts the game's origins, its early stars and teams, the geographic expansion of football, and the changes in its rules. Twenty years later Allison Danzig, a sportswriter for the *New York Times,* chronicled the games and players in *The History of Amer-*

ican Football (Englewood Cliffs, NJ: Prentice-Hall, 1955) and in an anthology, *Oh, How They Played the Game* (New York: Macmillan, 1971). Both of his books are useful and exhaustive in showing how teams and strategies developed as well as describing football's sensational high points. Danzig wrote for a popular audience; he rarely divulged that football had a shadowy, less palatable side and made no effort to show how football fit into college life.

Two forms of literature deserve special mention because they have nuggets of invaluable material on the growth of football. Some of the finest literature produced by outstanding historians have been college histories. The two-volume history of the University of Wisconsin by Merle Curti and Vernon Carstenson stands out because of its detail and attention to athletics—and its ability to weave athletics into the life of the university. C. R. Griffin's book *The University of Kansas* (Lawrence: University Press of Kansas, 1974) provides a lot of material on college football, and Griffin's notes on his football research may be found at the University of Kansas Archives. Anyone who wants to understand early student athletics should examine W. Bruce Leslie's *Gentlemen and Scholars: College and Community in the "Age of the University"* (University Park: Pennsylvania State University Press, 1992), which compares the changing role of students and faculty at four institutions—Princeton, Swarthmore, Bucknell, and Franklin and Marshall—in the late nineteenth and early twentieth centuries. Probably the best volume for putting together all of these trends is Laurence R. Veysey's *Emergence of the American University* (Chicago: University of Chicago Press, 1975), which places football in the tradition of changing student culture.

A second source—in-house histories of football at various universities—runs the gamut from booster chronicles of games and players to careful histories of gridiron seasons, eras, and formative influences. Despite their shallow commercial base, some of the "great players and great games" genre contain interesting material on the early history of such gridiron zealots as the president of Florida who scrimmaged with his team. In *Goal to Goal: 100 Seasons of Football at William and Mary* (Williamsburg, VA: Botetourt Press, 1997), a model for gridiron histories of a single institution, Wilford Kale, Bob Moskowitz, and Charles M. Holloway have put together a beautifully illustrated and carefully researched volume that not only serves up interesting football lore but also describes the William and Mary football scandal in 1951 as objectively as possible as well as the changes that accompanied it. Using a different approach, Thomas G. Bergin's study *The Game: The Harvard-Yale Rivalry, 1875-1983* (New Haven: Yale University Press, 1984) provides countless details about Harvard-Yale football, such as the building of the Yale Bowl. For a uniquely interesting and useful source of information on the rapid decline of some largely urban institutions, anyone with an interest in college football should browse James Whalen Sr., *Gridiron Greats Now Gone: The Heyday of 19 Former Top-20 Football Programs* (Jefferson, NC: McFarland, 1991).

Undoubtedly, much of the history of college football will emerge in the form of regional and institutional studies of athletics. One literary scholar, Michael Oriard, has demonstrated the importance of newsprint by building his *Reading Football: How the Popular Press Created an American Spectacle* (Chapel Hill: University of North Carolina Press, 1993) largely around newspaper and magazine accounts of games in the 1890s and early 1900s. In a single issue of the *Journal of Sport History* (Fall 1997) Andrew Doyle ("Foolish and Useless Sport: The Southern Evangelical Crusade against Intercollegiate Football") and Patrick Miller ("The Manly, the Moral, and the Proficient: College Sport in the New South") show the intricate texture of ideas and attitudes that underlay the foundation of early southern college football.

Viewed broadly, the study of college football—like much in athletic history— has merely reached a point at which historians and observers can see more clearly the social and economic factors that influenced the game. As layer upon layer are peeled away, more sophisticated and elaborate histories will emerge. They will delve with more precision into social attitudes, educational and academic theory, and the psychology of business and professional elites that have so heavily influenced the growth of this remarkable phenomenon of American college life.

Index

Library of Congress Cataloging-in-Publication Data

Watterson, John Sayle.
    College football : history, spectacle, controversy / John Sayle Watterson.
        p.   cm.
    Includes bibliographical references and index.
        ISBN 0-8018-6428-3 (hardcover : alk. paper)
        1. Football—United States—History.   2. Football—Social aspects—United States—
    History.   I. Title.
GV950 .W28 2000
796.332′63′0973—dc21
                                                        00-008247